Major Recessions

Major Recessions

Britain and the World, 1920–1995

Christopher Dow

OXFORD UNIVERSITY PRESS
1998

Oxford University Press, Great Clarendon Street, Oxford OX2 6DP
Oxford New York
Athens Auckland Bangkok Bogotá Buenos Aires Calcutta
Cape Town Chennai Dar es Salaam Delhi Florence Hong Kong Istanbul
Karachi Kuala Lumpur Madrid Melbourne Mexico City Mumbai
Nairobi Paris São Paulo Singapore Taipei Tokyo Toronto Warsaw
and associated companies in Berlin Ibadan

Oxford is a registered trade mark of Oxford University Press

Published in the United States
by Oxford University Press Inc., New York

British Library Cataloguing in Publication Data
Data available

Library of Congress Cataloging in Publication Data

Dow, J. C. R. (J. Christopher R.)
    Major recessions: Britain and the world, 1920–1995/Christopher
Dow.
        p.   cm.
    Includes bibliographical references (p.).
    1. Recessions.   2. Economic history—20th century.   3. Recessions—
    Great Britain.   I. Title.
    HB3716.D68   1998
    338.5'42—dc21   98-36848

ISBN 0–19–828858–1

1 2 3 4 5 6 7 8 9 10

Typeset in 10/12 pt Times
by Newgen Imaging Systems (P) Ltd, Chennai, India.

Printed in Great Britain
on acid-free paper by Bookcraft (Bath) Ltd,
Midsomer Norton, Somerset

Preface

This preface is intended mainly to express thanks for the many acts of assistance I have received while writing this book. Its production has occupied most of the ten years from 1988 to 1997. Together with *A Critique of Monetary Policy*— written jointly with Iain Saville and planned as part of the same project—it has occupied the thirteen years since I retired from the Bank of England in 1984.

My debts are of four chief sorts.

I must thank first those who over the years read successive drafts of the book, so providing ears for words otherwise long unread: more especially Bryan Hopkin for repeated astringent criticism; also Andrew Britton, formerly Director of the National Institute. I similarly thank those who read individual chapters: Ian Little (Chapter 4), David Worswick (Chapter 6), Mervyn King (Chapters 6, 9 and 12), Alan Budd (Chapters 9 and 12), Douglas Wass (Chapter 12), William Keegan (Chapter 12), and Robert Neild (Chapter 12). I must equally thank those who undertook to read the book in draft: Robin Matthews (who read all), and Mike Artis and Frank Hahn (who read large parts). Despite their assistance, I am sure there remain many faults big and small.

In the United States a work of this sort would probably have been funded on a scale many times larger. That might not have made the book many times better. But the increasing difficulty in raising money for research in the United Kingdom, and the necessity to search for ever smaller bites of support, must surely put this country at a disadvantage and undermine the quality of the work we can do. Things being what they are, long-continued work such as this would hardly have been possible but for the facts, first, that I was in receipt of a pension and retained an appetite for research; and second, that the National Institute of Economic and Social Research, by making me a Visiting Fellow, provided me with a base over this long period.

I thus owe a deep debt to the National Institute: to Andrew Britton and Martin Weale, successively its directors; and to Kit Jones, Hilary Steedman, and John Kirkland, in turn secretaries of the Institute. I have to thank Fran Robinson for her brick-like support; also Rita Charlton for repeated retyping, Claire Schofield, the librarian of the Institute, and many others of the support staff for help of many sorts.

Funding was required chiefly to provide statistical assistance on what worked out to be about a half-time basis. The array of charts and tables in the book makes evident what I owe to the three people who laboured in turn over the statistics: Mrs Hilkka Taimio (mostly Chapter 8); Pierre van der Eng (Chapters 3, 4, and 6); and Chao Dong Huang (Chapters 2, 5, and 7–12).

The statistics presented in the study remain I know untidy. Tables and charts illustrating earlier episodes, written up first, use statistics available at the time of writing without updating for later revisions unless there was reason to expect that that would alter the conclusions. But where comparisons over the whole or most of the period are made (Chapters 2, 5, 11 and 12), figures are of recent vintage. Given the slender resources available and the range to be covered, short cuts where available had to be taken. While operating on a shoestring has compensating advantages, I expect that others will do better some of what I have done quickly.

Anything like this study would not have been possible without the prior labours of Charles Feinstein on the national accounts for earlier periods, and for later periods those of the national accounts statisticians of the Central Statistical Office (now Office of National Statistics) who, since the days of Dick Stone, James Meade, and Teddy Jackson, have so greatly extended the data available to us. They seldom get thanked; the rich information to be derived from their work is far from being completely exploited.

Lastly, I am indebted to the following bodies for the provision of a series of fourteen grants of different sizes, some larger, some small, but all exceedingly welcome: the Economic and Social Research Council, the British Academy (four separate grants), the Leverhulme Trust, the Nuffield Foundation (two grants), the Bank of England (three small grants), and Sir Adrian Cadbury, who generously gave repeated support from his private trust. I hope the results, often long deferred, will appear to justify their trust. I have also to thank the Rockefeller Foundation for the privilege of a month's residency with my wife in June 1994 at the Bellagio Study Centre, where the conclusions of the study took shape.

Authors frequently thank their wives for their forbearance. In my case that is not necessary. I did not give her more to bear than from whatever else I would have been working at; and it would in any case be a small part of the whole.

London C.D.
September 1997

Contents

List of Figures   xi
List of Tables   xv

1 Introduction   1
  1.1 The aims and methods of the study   1
  1.2 The plan and character of the book   6

PART I Prior Assumptions and Methodological Preliminaries

2 The Facts to be Explained   13
  2.1 Conspectus of the whole period, 1920–95   13
  2.2 The measurement of trends and fluctuations   18
  2.3 Comparison of the three main phases since 1920
     in the UK and other countries   27
  2.4 Profits, factor shares, and real wages   34
3 The Causal Structure of the Economy   38
  3.1 The main routes of causation in the economy   38
  3.2 How growing supply creates growing demand   41
  3.3 The explanation of unemployment   42
  3.4 Implications for later chapters   49
  Appendix A3.1 The theoretical debate on the features of the
          economic system that allow the possibility of
          unemployment   51
  Appendix A3.2 The High Real Wage theory of unemployment   53
4 Supply and Demand Influences on the Rate of Growth   57
  4.1 Some main facts about rates of growth   57
  4.2 Explanations of variations in the rate of growth   70
  4.3 Conclusions about rates of growth: supply versus demand factors as
     determinents of output growth   77
  Appendix A4.1 Notes on growth accounting, and
          two other studies of growth   81
  Appendix A4.2 Estimates of the growth of six countries' output
          and exports of manufactures, 1870–1970   85
5 Shocks and Responses in Major Fluctuations   88
  5.1 The economy's response to shocks   88
  5.2 Indicators of demand shocks and tests of their ability
     to explain fluctuations   101
  5.3 The causation of fluctuations: a first survey   111
  Appendix A5 New estimates of fiscal policy impact   118

PART II Case Studies of Five Major Recessions

6 The Two Interwar Recessions   133
  6.1 Overview of the interwar period   133
  6.2 The 1920–1 recession and its aftermath   146
  6.3 The Great Depression: the world and the United States, 1929–33   157
  6.4 The world depression and the UK depression   184
  6.5 Economic recovery in Britain, 1932–40   195
  6.6 Theoretical conclusions   209
  Appendix A6.1 A critique of Friedman and Schwartz's
         A Monetary History of the United States   211
  Appendix A6.2 The gold standard as a cause of the Great Depression:
         a critique of Eichengreen's *Golden Fetters*   217
  Appendix A6.3 A model of the international transmission
         of the US Depression   223
  Appendix A6.4 List of statistical sources   230
7 The Long Interval without Major Recession, 1945–73   234
  7.1 Overview of the period   235
  7.2 Reasons for faster growth and high demand   247
  7.3 Minor fluctuations of the period   257
  7.4 Was the Golden Age doomed anyway?   266
  7.5 The behaviour of the economy: conclusions from the 1945–73
    experience   271
8 The Two OPEC Recessions (1973–5 and 1979–82)   273
  8.1 Background issues: political developments and
    the oil price shocks   276
  8.2 A demand-side explanation of the OPEC recessions   291
  8.3 Assessment of the 1970s experience   310
  Appendix A8 The inflationary surges of the 1970s   317
**9 The Credit Expansion of the Late 1980s and the
Recession of the Early 1990s**   321
  9.1 Summary of thesis: the interrelation between real and
    financial disturbances   321
  9.2 Boom and recession in other countries   323
  9.3 Boom and recession in the UK   335
  9.4 What the 1989 recession contributes to our ideas about the
    behaviour of the economy   360
  9.5 Postscript: the resumption of growth, 1992–5   361

PART III Conclusions

10 The Theoretical Model: The Economy's Behaviour in Major Fluctuations   367
  10.1 A picture of an economy lacking some elements of
    self-adjustment   367
  10.2 The nature of major recessions   370
  10.3 The shape of major recessions and the role of expectations
    (or confidence)   374
  Appendix A10 A formal account of interactions during recessions   378

**11 The Causation of Major Recessions: Summary and
Discussion of Empirical Findings** 383
11.1 Estimation of constant-employment growth rates:
the loss resulting from major recessions 383
11.2 Explanation of major recessions in terms of
exogenous demand shocks 385
11.3 Case studies of the major recessions: summary 392
11.4 The long period without major recessions (1945–73):
possible lessons 398
11.5 Concluding remarks on public debt, and
on the predictability of major recessions 401
Appendix A11 The National Debt since World War II 410
12 Are Recurrent Major Recessions Inevitable? 414
12.1 Background issues: theory; politics; inflation 415
12.2 The traditional tools of macroeconomic policy 427
12.3 Possible policies to counter major recessions 437
12.4 The chances of avoiding major recessions in future 443

References 447
General Index 463
Author Index 469

Figures

Figure 2.1   The course of the UK economy, 1914–1995
Figure 2.2   Growth rate in six major countries, 1920–1995
Figure 2.3   Rates of UK inflation, 1900–1995
Figure 2.4   Labour productivity in the UK and USA, 1920–1940
Figure 2.5   Labour productivity in the UK and four other OECD countries, 1960–1990
Figure 2.6   GDP and constant-employment (C/E) GDP, 1920–1993
Figure 2.7   GNP and constant-employment GNP: USA, 1920–1938
Figure 2.8   The share of wages and profits: UK, 1950–1989
Figure 2.9   Prices and profits on different assumptions: UK, 1973–1989
Figure 3.1   Notional causal structure of the economy
Figure A3.1   Real wages and percentage unemployment, 1920–1989
Figure 4.1   Productivity growth, 1870–1979, as a function of 1870 productivity in sixteen OECD countries
Figure 4.2   Cumulative country shares in output of manufactures, 1870–1989
Figure 4.3   GDP and output and exports of manufactures in six countries, 1870–1989
Figure 4.4   UK shares in combined output and exports of manufactures of six countries, 1870–1989
Figure 4.5   Growth rates of output and exports: five main countries, 1920–1992
Figure 5.1   Gross non-residential capital stock, GDP, and gross fixed non-residential investment in the UK, 1920–1939
Figure 5.2   Gross non-residential capital stock, GDP, and gross fixed non-residential investment in the UK, 1960–1989
Figure 5.3   Fluctuations in GDP and indicators of five shocks in the UK, 1920–1993
Figure A5.1   Public expenditure and revenue: UK, 1920–1990
Figure A5.2   Comparison of various estimates of fiscal impact: UK, 1925–1990
Figure 6.1   GDP fluctuations and unemployment in the UK, 1920–1938
Figure 6.2   GNP fluctuations and unemployment in the USA, 1920–1938
Figure 6.3   GDP of industrial countries, 1920–1940
Figure 6.4   Exports of industrial countries, 1910–1940
Figure 6.5   World terms of trade, 1915–1940
Figure 6.6   Price trends in the UK and the USA, 1915–1940
Figure 6.7   Estimates of fiscal impacts: UK, 1920–1939
Figure 6.8   Prices in the USA, 1920–1940

Figure 6.9   Manufacturing and other output in the USA, 1919–1939

Figure 6.10   The balance sheet of the banks and the money stock: USA, 1929–1933

Figure 6.11   Interest rates and bond yields in the USA, 1929–1933

Figure 6.12   International effects of the US depression: trade links between three main blocs, US, primary producers, and Europe

Figure A6.1   International effects of the US depression

Figure A6.2   Secondary effects of induced recession in Europe on US and primary producers, and tertiary effects back on Europe

Figure 7.1   Sixteen countries' growth rates in the three main periods

Figure 7.2   Identification of UK mini-cycles, 1947–1973

Figure 7.3   Comparison of cycles in the UK and other OECD countries, 1947–1973

Figure 7.4   Cycles in the USA, 1947–1973

Figure 7.5   Inflation in the UK and six other OECD countries, 1950–1975

Figure 7.6   Fluctuations in export growth: UK and industrial countries, 1950–1975

Figure 7.7   Terms of trade of the UK and of twenty-one industrial countries, 1950–1975

Figure 7.8   The investment ratio in the UK, by sectors, 1950–1975

Figure 7.9   Explanation of UK fluctuations in terms of exogenous shocks, 1948–1973

Figure 7.10   Degree of innovation in fluctuations of GDP, unemployment, and inflation

Figure 7.11   Indicators of the scale of exogenous shocks in three subperiods, 1921–1992

Figure 8.1   UK output growth 1973–1987 compared with the pre-1973 trend

Figure 8.2   The slowdown in output growth and the associated slowdown in employment and productivity growth, 1973–1987

Figure 8.3   World oil and commodity prices, 1970–1987

Figure 8.4   Comparison of cycles in the UK, EC, and USA, 1970–1983

Figure 8.5   Inflation in the UK, Europe, and the USA, 1970–1982

Figure 8.6   Output fluctuations in the UK, EC, and USA, 1970–1983

Figure 8.7   Sundry UK economic indicators, 1972–1984

Figure 8.8   The course of total expenditure by quarters, 1970–1977

Figure 9.1   Booms and recessions in ten countries, 1980–1993

Figure 9.2   Excess growth of money in ten countries, 1980–1992

Figure 9.3   Households' debt in G7 countries, 1980–1992

Figure 9.4   Corporate debt in nine countries, 1980–1992

Figure 9.5   Household saving in ten countries, 1980–1992

Figure 9.6   Short-term interest rates in ten countries, 1980–1992

Figure 9.7   Share price indices in ten countries, 1980–1992

Figure 9.8   House prices in the UK, 1981–1993

Figure 9.9   Setback to output and productivity in the UK, 1989–1993 recession
Figure 9.10   Debt–GDP ratios in the UK, 1980–1992
Figure 10.1   Conventional model of cycles compared with the present model of major recessions
Figure 11.1   Estimates of downward displacement of path of capacity growth at major UK recessions
Figure 11.2   Stylized picture: the five major UK recessions
Figure 11.3   National debt–GDP ratio in the UK, 1950–1992
Figure 11.4   National debt–GDP ratio in the UK, 1970–1992
Figure 11.5   Investment and saving ratios, 1920–1995
Figure A11.1   Contributions to changes in the UK national debt–GDP ratio, 1950–1975
Figure A11.2   Contributions to changes in the national debt–GDP ratio, 1970–1992

Tables

Table 2.1 Rates of growth of output and output per head and level of unemployment: UK, 1920–1993

Table 2.2 Relation between changes in GDP and unemployment: UK, 1920–1993

Table 2.3 Alternative estimates of constant-employment output growth rates: UK, 1920–1993

Table 2.4 Dating and depth of major recessions and fast-growth phases: UK, 1920–1993

Table 2.5 Recessions and output, 1920–1993

Table 2.6 Rate of growth of expenditure components by periods: UK, 1920–1987 (constant prices)

Table 2.7 Contributions of expenditure components to output growth by period: UK, 1920–1987

Table 2.8 Growth of labour productivity and total factor productivity: UK, 1855–1989 (% annual growth rates)

Table 2.9 Large recessions in UK before 1914

Table 2.10 The pace and steadiness of growth: UK and seven other countries by main sub-periods, 1920–1990

Table 2.11 Unemployment rates: UK and seven other countries by main sub-periods, 1920–1990

Table 3.1 Relations between some main macrovariables

Table A3.1 Major changes in unemployment, 1920–1989

Table A3.2 Simple correlation of percentage unemployment and real wages, 1920–1989

Table 4.1 UK growth rates, 1800–1995

Table 4.2 Country shares in total production and export of manufactures, 1870–1988

Table 4.3 Factor contribution to output growth in five major countries, by sub periods, 1913–1984

Table A4.1 Adjusted estimates of productivity growth: five major countries, 1913–1984

Table A4.2 Relation between increases of output and of exports of manufactures: nine countries by sub-periods, 1973–1988

Table 5.1 Rates of growth of capital and output in interwar and postwar years

Table 5.2 Additional fluctuation resulting from stock changes, by three subperiods, 1920–1990

Table 5.3   Components of shortfall of expenditure in five major recessions, 1920–1993

Table 5.4   Statistical definition of indicators of exogenous shocks

Table 5.5   Explanation of annual changes in GDP: regression results

Table 5.6   Explanation of fluctuations in terms of shocks

Table 5.7   Explanation of fluctuations in terms of shocks: summary

Table 5.8   Characteristics of different types of fluctuations

Table 5.9   Major UK recessions 1920–1993, together with US Great Depression

Table 5.10   First year of resumed growth after major recessions

Table 5.11   Four main phases of above-trend growth

Table A5.1   Estimates of fiscal impact: weights assigned to budget items

Table A5.2   Estimates of impact of fiscal policy in the UK, 1920–1992 (as contribution to % changes in GDP)

Table A5.3   Estimates of fiscal impact in the USA, 1930–1989

Table 6.1   The 1929–32 Great Depression in different countries

Table 6.2   Recessions and partial recoveries, 1920–1937: partial explanations

Table 6.3   Key political events 1919–1930

Table 6.4   Output, unemployment, and the general price level in the UK, 1914–1922

Table 6.5   Impact of fiscal change, 1918–1921

Table 6.6   Components of change in total final expenditure: UK, 1919–1925

Table 6.7   Changes in UK prices and costs, 1917–1923

Table 6.8   Components of change in total final expenditure: USA, 1919–1924

Table 6.9   The Great Depression in industrial countries

Table 6.10   Components of change in total final expenditure: USA, 1924–1929

Table 6.11   Contributions to change in total final expenditure: USA, 1929–1933

Table 6.12   Fiscal policy impact in the USA, 1930–1933

Table 6.13   The Great Depression in Germany

Table 6.14   Banks' assets and liabilities, 1929–1933

Table 6.15   Recovery in the USA, 1934–1939

Table 6.16   Components of change in total final expenditure: France, 1929–1932

Table 6.17   The fall in European GDP, 1929–1932

Table 6.18   The pattern of world trade in 1929

Table 6.19   The fall in world trade in 1929

Table 6.20   International effects of US depression, 1929–1932: illustrative calculation

Table 6.21   Impact of depression abroad on UK, 1929–1932

Table 6.22   Changes in prices, relative prices and real incomes, UK 1929–1932

Table 6.23   The constituents of demand during the Great Depression in the UK, 1929–1932

Table 6.24 The slowdown in growth and the growth in unemployment: UK, 1929–1932

Table 6.25 Change in output and employment: UK, 1929–1932

Table 6.26 The 1930s recovery in Britain: demand-side changes, 1932–1940

Table 6.27 Recovery 1932–1940: alternative presentation

Table 6.28 Supply-side changes, 1932–1941

Table 6.29 Above-trend growth in output and expenditure, 1931–1936

Table 6.30 Rate of growth of the capital stock, 1929–1938

Table 6.31 Exchange rate indicators, 1929–1938

Table 6.32 Output and imports in total and for manufactures, 1929–1935

Table 6.33 Indicators of fiscal policy, 1932–1935

Table 6.34 Four influences treated as exogenous shocks, 1932–1935

Table 6.35 Classification of factors accounting for the first stage recovery, 1932–1935

Table 6.36 Fiscal impact and the increase in defence spending, 1933–1940

Table 6.37 Classification of factors accounting for the second-stage recovery, 1935–1938

Table 6.38 Indicators of structural unemployment

Table A6.1 The pattern of world trade in 1929

Table A6.2 Assumed value for domestic multipliers in Europe and the USA

Table A6.3 International transmission of the Great Depression, 1929–1932

(*a*) Impact of the US depression on Europe and primary producers

(*b*) Terms-of-trade-effects

(*c*) Impact of the depression in Europe on USA and primary producers

(*d*) Summary of five main influences on USA and Europe, 1929–1932

Table A6.4 International transmission: effect of doubling the size of the domestic multipliers

Table 7.1 Key political events, 1945–1973

Table 7.2 Change in capacity working across World War II analysed by expenditure categories and propensities

Table 7.3 Change in rate of output growth across World War II analysed by expenditure categories and propensities

Table 7.4 Expenditure components of growth: fast and slow phases, 1947–1973

Table 7.5 Expenditure components of growth: summary, 1950–1973

Table 7.6 Explanation of mini-cycles 1950–1972: fast phases

Table 7.7 Explanation of mini-cycles 1950–1972: slow phases

Table 7.8 Explanation of inflation, 1950–1973

Table 8.1 Four phases of recession and growth, 1973–1987

Table 8.2 Key political events, 1973–1982

Table 8.3 North Sea output and the balance of payments, 1973–1982

Table 8.4   Current balances of OPEC and the developing countries, and OECD exports, 1973–1987

Table 8.5   Setback to productivity growth in OPEC recessions in five main countries

Table 8.6   Classification of US energy use

Table 8.7   Trend to economy in energy consumption, 1913–1984

Table 8.8   Energy input as a percentage of GDP, 1973, 1983, and 1987

Table 8.9   OECD growth rates, 1967–1973

Table 8.10   OECD inflation rates, 1967–1973

Table 8.11   The boom and two recessions of the 1970s–early 1980s in the UK: partial explanations

Table 8.12   The 1972–3 boom: expenditure composition

Table 8.13   Effects of terms of trade on real income, 1972–1975

Table 8.14   The first OPEC recession: the UK and EC compared

Table 8.15   Fiscal impact of 1979 oil price shock

Table 8.16   Effects of terms of trade on real income, 1977–1981

Table 8.17   Contrasted behaviour in respect of productivity and unemployment growth in the two recessions

Table 8.18   The second OPEC recession: the UK and EC compared

Table A8.1   Correlation analysis of UK inflation, 1970–1982

Table A8.2   Correlation analysis of inflation in other EC countries, 1970–1982

Table 9.1   Boom and recession UK 1985–1993: partial explanations

Table 9.2   Selective calendar of events, 1979–1993

Table 9.3   Chief economic indicators: UK, 1980–1993

Table 9.4   Expenditure composition of expansion and recession: summary, UK, 1982–1993

Table 9.5   Composition of changes in total final expenditure: UK, 1980–1993

Table 9.6   Persons' borrowing, saving, and acquisition of assests: UK, 1982–1992

Table 9.7   Companies' borrowing, saving, and acquisition of assets UK 1982–1992 (% of GDP)

Table 9.8   Forecasts and outturns, 1986–1988

Table 9.9   Estimated effect of exogenous shocks, 1992–1995

Table 10.1   Shock caused by a once–only rise in persons' spending

Table 11.1   Summary: estimated causation of five major UK recessions 1920–1993 (together with US Great Depression)

Table 11.2   Summary: estimated causation of four types of fluctuation, 1920–1993

Table A11.1 Factors responsible for changes in national debt ratio, 1950–1992

Table 12.1   Coincidence of major recessions with periods of high inflation, 1920–1993

Table 12.2   Public debt ratios in OECD countries, 1980–1995

1 Introduction

The main aim of macroeconomics is to explain rates of growth of total output and fluctuations in rates of growth, and associated fluctuations in expenditure and employment.[1] Many books, theoretical and empirical, have addressed themselves to this task. This book concentrates on the most extreme fluctuations, in particular major recessions. These are few in number—too few to make a statistical sample—so that treatment has to be individual, and thus different in style from how most economists look at experience. Attention will focus on the UK, but other countries will be included when required to trace causality or when international comparison is illuminating. The book analyses experience since World War I, a period long enough to contain a number of major recessions and a variety of experience, without going too far back into history.

Though the book contains much detailed history, its purpose is not historical but theoretical—not just to narrate events, but to derive a theory that explains why big recessions happen—and this purpose has determined its structure. This introductory chapter explains the book's aims and structure, and indicates how it differs from other studies and may thus be novel and useful.

1.1. The aims and methods of the study

The recession of 1973 occurred after more than twenty-five years when steady growth had come to seem assured: since then it has no longer seemed assured. There has been much discussion of why this break occurred. The idea of this study was to go back to the prewar period in order to broaden the range of observation.

Looked at in that light, the economic history of the UK since 1920 may be divided into three broad phases, with alternating characteristics, each broadly

---

[1] This formulation echoes Blanchard and Fischer (1989: 1). 'Underlying the existence of macroeconomics as a separate field of study are the phenomena of economy-wide movements in output, unemployment, and inflation. Although developed economies are characterised by growth, this growth is far from steady. Expansions and recessions alternate over time, associated with movements in unemployment. Occasionally, recessions turn into depressions, such as the US depression from 1873 to 1878, the Great Depression of the 1930s, and the long period of high unemployment in Europe in the 1980s. Periods of price deflation, such as the prolonged price level decline in the last two decades of the nineteenth century, the recession of 1920–1, and the Great Depression, appear to be something of the past: most economies now alternate between periods of low and high, sometimes very high, inflation. It is the main purpose of macroeconomics to characterise and explain these movements of output, unemployment and prices.'

coinciding with one of the last three quarters of the twentieth century:

1. the interwar period, with high unemployment and moderately slow growth;
2. from World War II to 1973, with low unemployment and relatively fast growth;
3. the post-1973 period, with slower growth overall and again high unemployment.

This study accordingly set out to seek explanations of a sort that could explain both the first transition (from high to low unemployment and slow to fast growth) and, in reverse, the second (from low back to high unemployment, and fast back to slow growth).

It quickly appeared [ch. 2.2]² that the contrasts between these three phases were due mainly to there having been large recessions in the first and third quarter-century, but none in the second. The aim thus became to explain why these major recessions occurred and why they occurred in those periods and not in the second.

'Major' recessions were defined initially as occasions when GDP showed a clear absolute fall between one calendar year and the next. (On all but one such occasion, the decline in output continued for at least two years.) There were also small recessions (sometimes called growth recessions), when the rate of growth of output fell but remained positive; most of these, as it happens, were in the second main period, the quarter-century after World War II.

Output change and unemployment change are inversely related. The rate of output growth at which unemployment tends to remain constant is here called the capacity rate of growth, estimated [ch. 2.2] at about 2.5–3 per cent a year for the UK. Over a period of years the capacity rate tends to be close to the average rate of growth, but that is not necessarily so and the two concepts are not the same. Recessions are best defined as shortfalls below the capacity growth rate, thus accompanied by growing unemployment. The initial definition of a large recession (that output should fall absolutely) is thus equivalent to a requirement that the rate of output growth should fall below the norm (or capacity rate) by more than the norm itself.

Five periods were identified on these criteria as major recessions: 1920–1, 1929–32, 1973–5, 1979–82, and 1989–93.³ [Ch. 2.2 explains the principles on which starting and end dates were established.] In considerable degree, though with some difference in dating, other industrial countries underwent similar recessions.

To be symmetrical with the definition of a major recession, a major recovery would have to be defined as a case where output grows by more than twice the

---

² Square brackets will be used throughout to indicate references to other sections/chapters.

³ The last three are sometimes grouped as one enormous recession. But there were gaps between them; moreover, reasons can be found for why the next one started. They therefore seem better treated as separate phases.

capacity rate (i.e., on my estimates, by more than 5–6 per cent a year in the UK). Such cases however hardly happen, no doubt because expansion at that rate sets up inflationary strains and proves unsustainable. There were four phases in periods 1 and 3 when output grew at significantly more than the capacity rate and which can rank only as recoveries (i.e. not major recoveries): 1922–5, 1933–7, 1972–3, and 1985–8. The study considers these phases, though less fully than major recessions; and in the relatively stable quarter-century after World War II it also considers the faster-than-normal and slower-than-normal phases of the minor fluctuations then experienced.

If all fluctuations, minor and major, are regarded as part of the same sample, they may appear to have roughly constant periodicity. If one looks only at major recessions, the regularity disappears. The intervals between the starting dates of the five major recessions as here defined were 8, 41, 6, and 10 years. This weakens the hypothesis (usual in the trade cycle literature of the 1940s and 1950s)[4] that fluctuations are produced by a self-generating, self-perpetuating endogenous mechanism, producing fairly regular cycles. It points rather to the hypothesis, subsequently dominant, that major fluctuations are produced by erratic exogenous shocks, acting on a system prone to exaggerate shocks.[5] [See ch. 5.1 for fuller discussion of these contending hypotheses.]

The reason for distinguishing big from small recessions is not only that big ones do more serious harm, but that the economy behaves differently in big ones. The reason why large recessions are large seems to be partly that the initial shock is larger; but also partly because [ch. 5.1] the processes by which an initial shock gets amplified are then more powerful. The effect on consumption is larger because consumers' expectation of future income, and thus also their spending, fall more in response to a large shock. Similarly, the response of investment to an initial shock is larger because firms' expectations of sales and profits are affected proportionately more by a deep and prolonged dip in present income than by a mild one soon reversed.

Another asymmetry is that descent into a major recession is steeper than any recovery from it. This sequence of sharp descent and protracted recovery has long been observed as a feature of major recessions,[6] and the resultant zig-zag pattern of growth appears in many charts in this study. Since large recessions are followed by incomplete reversals—a full downward leg being followed by an amputated upward one—the term *cycle* is inappropriate and *fluctuation* is usually here preferred.

Method of investigation

The type of data with which this study is concerned has dictated the methods of investigation. Two factors limit the use of econometric methods. First, with

---

[4] i.e. the models by Harrod, Kaldor, Kalecki, Hicks, Samuelson, and others.
[5] The line of explanation stemming from Frisch (1933) and Slutsky (1937).
[6] e.g. Marshall and Marshall (1879: 525); Burns and Mitchell (1946).

only five major recessions available for study, the sample is too small. (The last of the five recessions, indeed, occurred only when the study was at the halfway stage.) Second, even if this had not been so, important nonlinearities seem to be present, which appear to preclude statistically rigorous testing of hypotheses.[7] Nevertheless, on subsidiary issues extensive resort is had to econometric methods of a simple sort.

Major conclusions were not based exclusively on this evidence. Large reliance—perhaps prior reliance—was placed on case studies of successive major recessions. The procedure involved in these case studies is essentially commonsensical, and can be divided into two stages. First is close inspection of the data in order to accept or reject potential or likely causes of the effects to be explained (i.e. the shortfall of output at successive phases of each recession below previous trend). The selection of possible causes depends on what theory suggests, and on empirical evidence obtained either from previous studies or on what earlier commentators going over the same ground have supposed. Assessment of possible causes depends in part on the temporal sequence of potential cause and effect. (Tomorrow's shock does not usually cause today's reaction.)

The second stage entails an assessment of how much should be attributed to each of the several factors accepted as potential causes. That depends on what the data show, which may not be easy to assess given the inaccuracies in the basic data and the need to adjust for irrelevant (e.g. seasonal) influences. It depends also on the scale of effect to be *expected* from different causes, these expectations being again derived from previous theoretical and/or empirical studies.

Use of such methods does not permit conclusions that can claim anything close to certainty. They have indeed obvious limitations: examination of 'qualitative evidence' does not in fact settle issues any more than do statistics.[8] In some cases it has been possible to construct what seems a plausible and complete explanation, though one that is still disputable; in others the explanation proposed seems incomplete, or especially speculative and insecure. But there is no reason why one should always be able to say why events occur. The spirit of the study therefore will be not to strain unnaturally at complete answers but to see virtue in remaining sceptical.

In many cases—perhaps most—it may be impossible to be sure why recessions have happened. All one can do may be to construct a picture of how

---

[7] See e.g. discussion of chaos theory in Mullineux *et al*. (1993: 25–6).

[8] The phrase is from Friedman and Schwartz (1963: 686). Commenting on the inability of statistical association to determine causality, they say: 'A great merit of the examination of a wide range of qualitative evidence, so essential to monetary history, is that it provides a basis for discriminating between the possible explanations of the observed statistical covariation. We can go beyond the numbers alone and, on at least some occasions, discern the antecedent circumstances whence arose the particular movements that become so anonymous when we feed the statistics into the computer.' They go on immediately to claim that their narrative makes 'abundantly clear' that changes in monetary aggregates caused changes in business conditions, not the reverse. I find their evidence singularly unconvincing [app. A6.1].

events may *very well* have happened. But even that provides some basis for theorizing about the economy's behaviour, and for thinking about the implications for policy; and it is the aim of this study to show that, despite the dubiety of knowledge, important conclusions can be arrived at.

The methods followed in this study may to some appear unsophisticated, antiquated, and unacceptably imprecise. Since there are so few cases to look at, it is not possible to undertake the rigorous testing of hypotheses to which econometrics aspires, or to summarize evidence in terms of a simple statistic of goodness of fit. Nevertheless, it is not clear how great this loss is. Econometric procedures have proved much less valuable than most of us hoped a generation ago. They have enabled few if any major propositions to be established beyond doubt. Nor have model-based methods done well in predicting recessions, or even at *ex post* explanation [ch. 11.5].

It is evident that case study procedure is judgemental in two other ways— ways, however, that equally apply to econometric procedures. First, the procedure is dependent on which (theoretically derived) assumptions are accepted as priors. Second, it is dependent on the selection of the hypotheses to be tested; that is likely also to depend on what prior theory is accepted. One cannot eradicate this danger of bias, which is inherent in all scientific enquiry. All one can do is to make the assumptions explicit. To meet this need, Part I of the study sets out a rather full justification for the precise questions that the empirical part of the study tries to answer. Conclusions can be finally assessed only on the basis of the overall results.

For some important questions, such as those studied here, the method of case studies appears the only way. Though it is inexact, it has two advantages. First, it permits due attention to detail. Asymmetry and nonlinearity tend to get steamrollered out of sight by standard averaging procedures;[9] and the 'stylized facts' are the nearest to reality that it is now fashionable for most economists to get. The present study, by contrast, rests on a close inspection of the unstylized facts of what happens in individual major recessions.

Second, close confrontation with historical reality may fertilize productive theorizing. Much modern research on fluctuations starts with theoretically inspired hypotheses, and experiments with variants to see which best fits (stylized) reality.[10] The process is guaranteed to produce ingenious results, but it is surely an indirect route to truth. The explanations offered in the present study claim to be generated as a result of a more direct confrontation with facts, and are offered as possible explanations superior to existing theories. That is—perhaps—the classic mode of scientific enquiry. The scientific status of case studies can be defended on these grounds.

---

[9] Blanchard and Fischer remark (1989: 7) on how this kind of feature gets ironed out in more stylized treatments of fluctuations: 'Some of the richness of the Burns–Mitchell analysis, such as its focus on asymmetries between recessions and expansions ... may well have been lost.'

[10] It is fair to apply this description, for instance, to the whole line of research that Blanchard and Fischer present with such *élan* in their *Lectures on Macroeconomics* (1989).

Economics, in its ambition to be scientific, has chosen to become highly deductive in method and largely mathematical in language. That is typical of physics now. But it appears not to have been true of physics in its infancy, nor true of most of the exact sciences now. Thus, advances in chemistry and biology depend on the interplay of experiment and theory, and theories are qualitative rather than highly mathematical; the great scientists, it seems, have mostly been great experimenters.[11]

In economics, where controlled experiments are barely possible, we should not pass over the chance to look at such experiments as history offers. Close inspection of the facts may be the nearest we can get to scientific experimentation; and theorizing provoked by such confrontation[12] may be the nearest equivalent to the interplay of experiment and theory in the exact sciences.

The conclusions of the present study rest only in part on historical case studies. These were accompanied by a statistical analysis [ch. 5.2] which attempts to explain deviations of output from trend in terms of indicators of four or five types of exogenous shock. The case study of each recession provided a first version of the causation of each recession, together with an indication of the relative magnitude of the different causes operative in each; thus, suggested hypotheses were tested by the general statistical analysis outlined above.

The conclusions of the study thus have a twin basis: neither the results of the case studies nor those of the statistical analysis were accepted without reservation, each having been checked against the other.

1.2. The plan and character of the book

The book is in three parts. Part I deals with preliminary theoretical questions; Part II contains the historical case studies (which constitute the bulk of the book); Part III presents conclusions.

Part I covers the theoretical questions that arise in the course of attempts to interpret history, but which are too complicated to consider in the course of historical narrative, and therefore have to be discussed in advance. The following examples indicate the kind of questions taken up.

The *explicanda* in this study, i.e. the phenomena I try to explain, are the deviations of output from trend. Therefore I have first to discuss the best way to calculate trend [ch. 2.2]. But there is then also the (quite complex) theoretical question [ch. 3.2] of what mechanisms must be presumed to operate to keep the economy growing on trend, when not displaced from it by shocks. Chapter 2 contains a short overview of the three-quarters of a century covered by the study; it compares UK experience with that of other industrial countries,

---

[11] Pippard (1989): see also Gooding *et al.* (1989).
[12] What R. R. Nelson (1994: 292) labels 'appreciative theorising'.

and shows what happens to the relation between costs and prices, and hence profits and real wages, in the course of major recessions.

Another question that, though the subject of theoretical discussion for decades, requires discussion here [ch. 3.3] is why unemployment (which for example accompanies a recession) is not quickly corrected by self-adjusting mechanisms, but can persist for lengthy periods. I argue that the economy lacks an automatic ability to self-adjust in this sense. A further question (also subject to dispute) is whether [ch. 2.2] a major recession permanently lowers the growth path of the economy.

Many theorists explain recession as an effect of supply-side disturbances. Chapter 4 is a short review of what we know about the determinants of variation in growth rates—included here to justify the proposition that the abrupt changes in growth rates observed in major recessions originate in shortfalls of demand, not supply.

I present statistical indicators [ch. 5.2] that purport to measure the scale of such demand shocks and seek to justify their use, despite the many theoretical objections that can be made to them; for instance, the shock indicators were presented to help explain deviations of output from trend. (Tests of the effects of shocks so measured comprise the statistical analysis referred to above.)

I started out with a presumption that the causes of changes in real output were to be sought solely in changes in real variables, i.e. magnitude such as figure in the national accounts. Work on this study compelled recognition of the importance of psychological factors. I argue below [ch. 5.1] that the scale of the economy's response to demand shocks is determined by induced changes in consumer and business confidence. On occasion a decline in confidence appears capable on its own of causing a recession, without a preceding shock.

Part II of this study contains the historical case studies. These four long chapters [chs. 6–9] are summarized at the end of the study [ch. 11.3].

Chapter 6 deals with the two major recessions of the interwar years (1920–2 and the Great Depression, 1929–32), along with two phases of above-average growth (1922–5 and 1933–7). This chapter contains a digression on the Great Depression in the United States, held to be the chief source of depression elsewhere in the world—transmitted to other countries (it is argued) via effects on trade volume flows and commodity prices.

Chapter 7 discusses what caused the fast growth, high demand, and low unemployment of the 'golden age' that followed World War II, and lasted until the onset of the first major postwar recession in 1973. The question in reverse is: why were there no major recessions in this period? The minor cycles in this period are also discussed.

Chapter 8 considers the two OPEC recessions of 1973–5 and 1979–82. Both (it is argued) were in part caused by the large rise in the price of oil imposed on the world by oil producers. The first was also in part a reaction to the boom of 1972–3; the second, to restrictive fiscal and monetary policy in the early Thatcher years.

Chapter 9 discusses the 1989–93 recession, which, unlike its predecessors, occurred to all appearance without the provocation of exogenous shocks; it is attributed here to confidence effects generated by the preceding boom. Also covered are the effects of the previous financial deregulation and the previous build-up of private debt.

The causation of the five major recessions appears (it is argued) to have been different in each case: if true, that alone justifies the method of the present study.

Part III sets out conclusions. Its first two chapters provide a summary of the book.

Chapter 10 summarizes the theoretical model that comes out of the study— the elements of which, having been built up piecemeal chapter by chapter, are there put together. Though the study did not start out intending to be theoretically innovative, many elements (as will be evident from this summary) diverge from orthodoxy. It is in this chapter that the present view of the economy is compared most fully with other models. The separate elements of the present model do not stand or fall together; some may appear more acceptable than others.

The character of the book

Although this study is full of historical facts, they are included as a description of what it is that has to be explained; the purpose of the book is not historical, but theoretical or scientific.

Works of economic history often seem to be content with a description of what happens, with attributions of causality thrown in rather lightly; often it seems that there is little recognition of the extreme difficulty of establishing causality. The aim of this study is not to narrate, but to interrogate history so as to understand why things happened as they did. That involves asking large counterfactual questions of a sort that history written by historians shies away from—questions to which there is no easy answer, and which only economists ask. This sort of history is difficult to write since the mass of facts constitutes a heavy weight, and study of them is of value only if it is directed not according to the narrative interest, but so as to bear on the theoretical questions at stake.

History considered as scientific experimentation involves a circular process. One takes previous theory with one to look at the facts; one sees how well it explains them; and finally, one may extend, or revise, previous theory to explain the facts better. At the present time, given the divisions between different schools of economists, one has also to select which existing theories to take as a starting point, and to give reasons for that choice.

The view of the economy with which I started rested not merely on what previous economists had written, but also (as I suppose must generally be true) on what one might call common observation. If one follows events closely,[13]

---

[13] The nature of the work I was doing as an economist in various official organizations, and the kind of research I have done, has meant that for the last 50 years I had to try to keep a rather

one gets an impression about the chief channels of causation from the order in which events occur, and from what participants say about what happens to them. Different observers nevertheless derive very different lessons: common observation is perhaps valuable chiefly in suggesting hypotheses, and in a work of this sort, evidence needs to be produced in support of them.

The present study contains little about the role of money in the system, because that was discussed in the previous book, undertaken as precursor to the present one (Dow and Saville 1988: since the fields to be covered and the methods of argument were very different from the present study of recessions, a separate book seemed needed). Reasons were given there for believing broad money in large part to be heavily determined by the course of the economy, and thus in large part to be endogenous.

The picture of the economy here taken as a working model differs (as will be evident) from that which many theorists assume as a starting point. What is to be explained is taken to be not absolute changes in output, but as divergences of output from the capacity rate of growth. It is assumed that such short-term output fluctuations are caused by fluctuations in demand, not supply; and that in turn they (and not for instance the level of real wages) are the chief cause of fluctuations in employment and unemployment; that changes in the rate of growth of money do not determine the rate of real output growth (which is rather caused as above), or (at least in any one-to-one way) the rate of increase in prices, but rather that money growth is caused by changes in output and prices otherwise determined; that the rate of growth of the *value* of output is composed of these two separately determined price and quantity components and is not itself of great interest (and, incidentally, is not, as it is often taken to be, a serviceable measure of demand pressure).

It is argued that the economy has a very limited power of self-adjustment in respect of total demand, i.e. limited power to regain high employment once lost or to eradicate overfull demand. After a major recession, any tendency for output to recover from recession is (in the absence of further favourable shocks) weak, so that underemployment, once in place, persists. The persistent nature of unemployment [chs. 3.2 and 3.3] springs not from defects in the labour market (e.g. wage stickiness), but from more basic features of the macroeconomy which make not only labour, but also capital, subject to underemployment.

In the present study, then, the assumption of certain kinds of market failure is taken as an acceptable starting point—indeed, as a basic feature of reality, not easily correctable; and there are seen to be powerful reasons, valid at the micro level, for the long-lasting nature of what some may regard as disequilibrium situations. The study is thus typified by a disinclination (which in a general sense may be said to be Keynesian) to idealize the economic system.

close watch over events. Knowledge so gained, as I say above, seems to me valuable but not infallible.

What now seems somewhat clear to me was earlier often not at all clear: on some big questions, for instance, I have changed my mind several times. Though subsequent revision has smoothed out some of the process, I have tried not to make the text too smooth but have let it retain some of the untidiness of experimentation and of 'feeling one's way'.

The proximate aim of the study has been to understand how the economy behaves. The ultimate underlying purpose is to provide a basis for thinking how to better its performance for the sake of society. Though for purposes of policy one would like certain knowledge, in practical affairs that is rarely if ever to be had. The conclusions reached are not presented as certainties, but as a picture of how the economy may very well have behaved (and in my view probably did). I hope that readers may find the results a useful basis for thinking about questions of macroeconomic policy.

Finally, it also seemed helpful and proper to set out my own conclusions on policy [ch. 12]. Though Keynesian in tinge, they will not I think seem over-hopeful, as Keynesian views are often taken to be.

Part I

Prior Assumptions and Methodological Preliminaries

2 The Facts to be Explained

The theoretical propositions set out later in this book are intended to help explain the behaviour of the economy in the course of major recessions. This chapter summarizes the chief relevant facts and gives background information about the UK and the other main economies in the period since 1920.

Section 2.1 gives a first conspectus of the whole period, 1920–95. An analysis of fluctuations must confront the question of how best to separate trend and divergences from trend; this is discussed in section 2.2. Section 2.3 provides a brief account of fluctuations and growth rates in the UK and other main countries. Section 2.4 notes the impact of major recessions of profits and factor income shares.

2.1. Conspectus of the whole period, 1920–1995

The experience of the UK falls into three distinct subperiods [table 2.1]:

1. interwar period;
2. World War II–1973;
3. 1973–present.

In these three subperiods the *rate of growth* was in turn relatively

  slow–fast–slow,

while *unemployment* was successively

  high–low–high.

The objective of this book is to explain why these alternations occured, how they were related to the incidence of major recessions, and why the five major recessions, and also the four main phases of fast growth, occurred. The analysis focuses on real output and expenditure, and brings in price changes and financial developments only as relevant to explaining real output and expenditure.

Figure 2.1 gives a broad picture of fluctuations in the UK. It shows first the course of GDP (top part of chart) and thus the falls in GDP during each of the five major recessions. (Recessions are shown by the shaded bands: how their dating was established is to be explained in the next section.) As will be seen, the major recessions (as here defined) came either in the first twelve years after 1920, or in the last twenty-two years before 1995, at the end of the period—with none in the intervening forty-one years.

Table 2.1   Rates of growth of output and output per head and level of unemployment: UK, 1920–1993

	Inter-war (1920–38)	Post-WWII (1950–73)	Post-1973 (1973–93)	Post-1973 excl. North Sea oil
Growth rates (% p.a.)[a]				
Output	2.0	2.9	2.0	1.8
Output per head	1.3	2.5	1.9	1.6
Unemployment (%)[b]	9.6	1.8	7.6	7.6

The table omits World War II; it also omits as unrepresentative of the post-WWII period the first years after the war.

[a] Fitted log-linear trend.

[b] Earlier figures are adjusted to conform to the coverage of 1973 official figures. Excludes those on official training schemes for unemployed persons which became much more extensive in the late 1980s and by 1987 amounted to 1.1% of labour force.

Source: Feinstein (1972); CSO, *UK National Accounts*; *Economic Trends* (various issues).

This figure also provides a first analysis of what was happening. It shows first, along with the course of actual output, trend lines for output adjusted to a constant-employment basis (top of chart—methods of estimation are to be explained in the next section). As will be seen, output at each major recession fell below what it would have been on a projection of the previous trend; and after each major recession remained below the old trend with relatively little recovery. In the three major recessions after 1973, divergence from trend thus tended to be cumulative.

The divergence of output from previous trend is shown separately (in the middle part of the chart). As will be seen, this deviation broadly mirrors the course of unemployment, which is shown inverted in order to facilitate this comparison (bottom part of chart). This correspondence must suggest that the course of output is determined by the same factors as determine the course of unemployment. It will be noted that, although unemployment tended to mirror the deviations of output from the constant-employment trend, fluctuations in unemployment were about half the scale of deviations of output from trend. The other half of output deviations reflected a shortfall of productivity growth from trend. Productivity growth fell off at each major recession, and by and large failed to recover. One interpretation of that (to be discussed in the following section) is that there was a lasting downward displacement of the path of productivity growth, and hence in the capacity of the economy, during the major recessions.

Other industrial countries experienced a similar alternation of slow–fast–slow growth [fig. 2.2, also table 2.11 below] and high–low–high unemployment [table 2.12]. Figure 2.2 shows that, even in the postwar period, the USA and (still more) the UK maintained only moderately fast growth. This means that

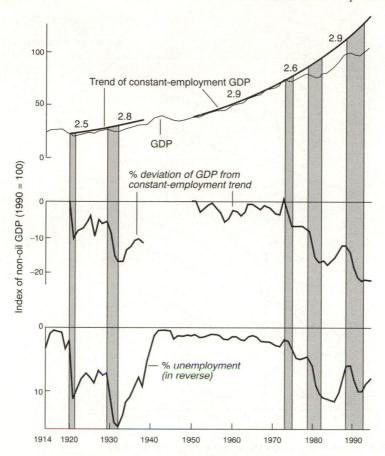

Fig. 2.1 The course of the UK economy, 1914–1995

Trends are fitted to constant-employment GDP estimated as explained in ch. 2.1, with results as shown in table 2.4, method A. Constant-employment GDP = GDP$(1 + U - U^*)$, where U = rate of unemployment and U^* = average of unemployment in each subperiod.

Deviation of GDP from trend is set at zero in 1920 and 1950, with readings for 1920–32 chained to those for 1932–8, and those for 1950–73, 1973–82, and 1982–95 also chained to form a continuous series. The unemployment series is as in table 2.1. Shaded areas highlight the major recessions.

Sources: basic data as for table 2.1.

the fast-growth countries (Japan, and also Germany, Italy, and France) were indeed responsible for the bulk of the increase in world GDP in this period. Figure 2.2 shows how abruptly the first OPEC recession (1973–5) broke this phase of rapid growth.[1]

---

[1] Fig. 2.2 is too compressed to show in detail the impact of major recessions on growth in different countries, for which see tables and charts in Chs. 6–9.

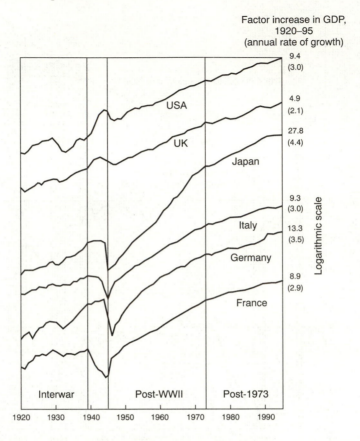

Factor increase in GDP,
1920–95
(annual rate of growth)

Fig. 2.2 Growth rate in six major countries, 1920–1995
For Germany, growth rate for years 1945–91 is West Germany only.
Sources: Maddison (1989) and IMF, *International Financial Statistics.*

This study will not seek to explain countries' growth experiences as a whole: most differences between countries must be due to differences in supply conditions, and investigation of them would require a separate study. But it does seek to explain the impact the major recessions may have had on growth [ch. 4].

Figure 2.3 shows rates of inflation in the UK during the period 1900–95. Inflation is here measured by the rate of change of the deflator of total final expenditure, the most comprehensive measure of changes in final prices. Prices appear to have become less flexible over the century. They rose rapidly during, and just after, World War I, fell steeply in, and just after, the 1921 recession, and fell in most subsequent years up to 1934. But the general price level has

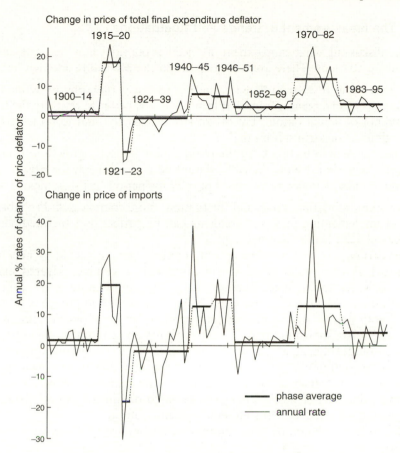

Fig. 2.3 Rates of UK inflation, 1900–1995
Source: as for table 2.1.

hardly ever fallen since then, and has tended only to rise. World War II produced a second large wave of inflation. The third wave resulted from the world boom of the early 1970, and the two OPEC price shocks of 1973 and 1979.

In each wave, as figure 2.3 shows, the faster rise in UK final prices was accompanied by a faster increase in import prices—on a scale sufficient to explain a good share (though not all) of the acceleration in final prices. The course of import prices reflected steep rises in world commodity prices, including, in 1970–82, world oil prices. The acceleration of inflation in each period was thus a worldwide phenomenon as much as a domestic one, and reflected worldwide high demand.

2.2. The measurement of trends and fluctuations

Before discussing what causes them, we need to consider how best to measure output fluctuations. There are two novelties in the procedure adopted here.

1. It is usual to fit a trend to actual output over a period, and to define fluctuations as divergences from that trend; but it is better to estimate the trend rate not of actual output, but of growth of capacity, and to measure fluctuations as departure from that.
2. There appear to be breaks in the trend rate of capacity growth at times of major recession; trends therefore should be estimated not for periods that extend *through* major recessions, but only for periods *between* them.

That makes estimating trends and fluctuations more complicated. Probably no way of implementing these requirements can be perfect, but the methods set out below seem better than nothing.

The existence of severed trends is only recently being accepted.[2] There have been several attempts to devise sensitive methods to estimate severed trends. These however appear unsatisfactory in that they apply more or less complex statistical analysis to the output series only.[3] The present approach is to make use of both output series and unemployment. A fall in output during a recession, as already shown in figure 2.1, accompanies a rise in unemployment, and a rise in output during an unusually fast phase of growth accompanies a fall. Some of the output change in a recession or recovery thus represents a change in the degree to which capacity is employed. The estimates below attempt to eliminate this part of output change in order to obtain the rate of growth of 'fluctuation-adjusted' or 'constant-employment' output.[4]

The evolving relation between output and employment may be written as

$$DGDP = a_t + b\ DEMP - a_r,$$

where

$DGDP$ = change in GDP
$DEMP$ = change in employment
a_t = a constant representing the normal rate of growth of productivity
a_r = a discontinuous and occasional downward displacement of productivity at times of major recession.

---

[2] For instance, the conclusion of a recent study reviewing international productivity experience since about 1960 concludes: 'On balance there is a preponderance of evidence that a widespread slowdown occurred in both labour and total factor productivity after the first energy shock in 1973' (Hickman 1992: 24, summarizing studies by Helliwell and Chung, Santo and Tokutsu, Tange, and Jorgensen and Kuroda).

[3] They also seem to require a large judgemental input: see the review article by Barrell and Sefton (1995). The studies included in that review are R. G. King and Robelo (1989), Blanchard and Quah (1989), Chouraqui *et al*. (1990), R. G. King *et al*. (1991), Harvey and Jaeger (1993), and Evans and Reichlin (1994).

[4] A more usual phrase would be 'cyclically adjusted'. I prefer to avoid the term 'cycle' in favour of 'fluctuation' in view of the connotation of regularity, inevitability, and endogeneity which 'cycle' conveys.

A first rough approach to estimating capacity growth and breaks in trend

There are various approaches to guesing the path of growth of capacity and breaks in the path. One way to try to isolate the growth of capacity is to look simply at the behaviour of labour productivity.[5] Figure 2.4 shows the course of labour productivity in the UK and the USA in the interwar years, and figure 2.5 its course in the UK and four other countries in the years 1960–90. These appear to show distinct breaks in trend at times of major recession—downward displacements of the order of 5 or 6 per cent in the UK, and at times apparently much larger breaks in other countries. In the UK the rate of growth after a recession seems as a rule to have been the same as the rate preceding a recession; elsewhere it has at times been faster (the USA after 1934) or slower (Japan after 1975).

These deductions from the course of labour productivity probably exaggerate how much economic capacity was reduced in major recessions; for the downward displacement of labour productivity during major recessions could in part reflect 'labour hoarding' of a sort that would be reversed after the recession.[6]

The preferred approach to estimating capacity growth and breaks in trend

An alternative approach, here preferred, is to adjust output to a 'constant-employment' basis and to fit trends to that. Two estimates were made, both utilizing the relationship between unemployment change and output change.

1. *Method A* assumes that changes in the percentage of labour unemployment during a major recession measure the degree to which overall economic capacity is unemployed; i.e., the change in the percentage unemployed since some base point is to be added to GDP to give an estimate of the course of potential or capacity output.
2. *Method B* makes use of the short-term relation between output and employment (known as Okun's Law: see Okun 1962), taking big and small fluctuations together. Regression of year-to-year changes produces for the UK a coefficient varying between 0.47 and 0.19 according to period [table 2.2]. To give an estimate of the course of capacity output, an adjustment is thus added to GDP equal to between two and five times the change in the percentage unemployed since some base point.

These two methods provide alternative estimates of constant-employment output. To each series, trends were fitted for years between recessions. If the estimated trend lines before and after a recession lie approximately on a single

[5] The growth of economic capacity includes not only the growth of productivity per head but the growth of the labour force. But the latter grows only slowly, and here we are interested in short-term changes that take place during major recessions. In that context, changes in the available labour force are small.

[6] The figures show little sign of such reversal; but the data on which such a judgement could be based are sparse.

United Kingdom [a]

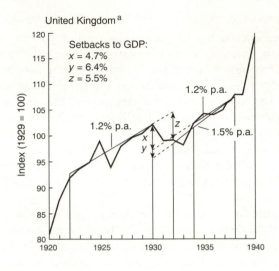

United States [b]

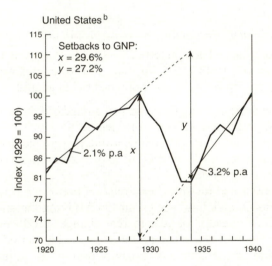

Fig. 2.4 Labour productivity in the UK and USA, 1920–1940

[a] Growth trends fitted for periods 1922–30 (excluding 1926 because of the General Strike) and 1932–8, alternatively 1934–8.

Source: Feinstein (1972).

[b] For the years after 1933, the continuous line shows GNP including government expenditure on work relief schemes divided by numbers in employment including those working on work relief. Growth trends fitted for periods 1920–9 and 1934–40.

Sources: *National Income and Product Accounts of the United States*, 1986; *Historical Statistics of the United States*, 1975; Darby (1976).

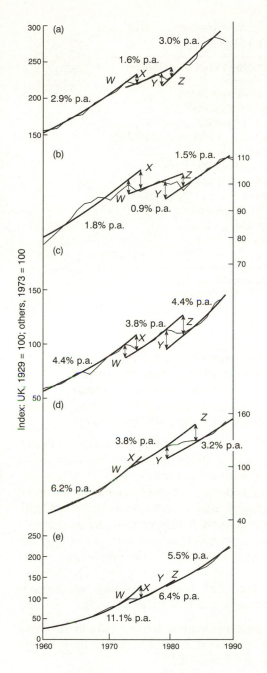

Fig. 2.5 Labour productivity in the UK and four other OECD countries, 1960–1990

(a) United Kingdom

Setbacks to GDP:
W: 4.4%   *Y*: 6.8%
X: 6.5%   *Z*: 5.6%
Growth trends fitted for 1960–73, 1975–9, and 1981–9.

Sources: Feinstein (1972) and CSO, *Economic Indicators*.

(b) United States

Setbacks to GNP:
W: 3.7%   *Y*: 6.3%
X: 7.3%   *Z*: 6.3%
Growth trends fitted for 1960–73, 1975–9, and 1982–90.

Sources: *National Income and Product Accounts of the United States*, 1986; and *Survey of Current Business*.

(c) Germany

Setbacks to GDP:
W: 12.1%   *Y*: 15.9%
X: 13.5%   *Z*: 13.4%
Growth trends fitted for 1960–73, 1975–80, and 1983–9.

Sources: OECD *National Accounts* and *Labour Force Statistics*.

(d) France

Setbacks to GDP:
W: 2.3%   *Y*: 10.8%
X: 5.8%   *Z*: 12.5%
Growth trends fitted for 1960–73, 1975–9, and 1984–9.

Sources: OECD *National Accounts* and *Labour Force Statistics*.

(e) Japan

Setbacks to GDP:
W: 11.3%   *Y*: 2.5%
X: 21.8%   *Z*: 2.3%
Growth trends fitted for 1960–73, 1975–9, and 1981–90.

Sources: OECD *National Accounts* and *Labour Force Statistics*.

Table 2.2   Relation between changes in GDP and unemployment: UK, 1920–1993

Relationship with output growth (OLS estimation)

A	1920–38 (19 observations)
	$\Delta U = 1.0292 - 0.46745 \Delta Y$
	(2.1214) (−4.4037)
	$\bar{R}^2 = 0.50540$; $S.E. = 1.9915$; $DW = 2.3839$
B	1950–73 (24 observations)
	$\Delta U = 0.59671 - 0.18689 \Delta Y$
	(6.7715) (−7.3388)
	$\bar{R}^2 = 0.69680$; $S.E. = 0.21538$; $DW = 1.6480$
C	1973–92 (20 observations)
	$\Delta U = 1.1192 - 0.39247 \Delta Y_{-1}$
	(4.4588) (−5.1184)
	$\bar{R}^2 = 0.57012$; $S.E. = 0.90025$; $DW = 2.0771$

ΔU: change in % unemployment, $\Delta U = U - U_{-1}$.
ΔY: annual % change in GDP excluding oil.
t-ratios in bracket.

Sources: as in table 2.1.

line, this was taken to imply that there was no break in trend; if not, that there had been a displacement. Method A suggests that there were breaks in trend at times of major recession [fig. 2.6]: on method B no breaks appear.

The best estimate of what we are seeking to measure, in my view, lies between methods A and B but closer to A for the following reasons:

- At times of major recession, with which we are chiefly concerned, employment (and unemployment) reacts more fully to output changes than in the average year-to-year fluctuation as reflected in Okun's law.[7]
- The fact that method A produces a downward displacement of the trend implies that potential unused capacity after a recession is much less with method A than method B. Thus, method B implies that the addition to unemployed capacity after a major recession amounts to something like 10 per cent. That seems unrealistic: with method A the addition is a third as large.[8]
- General reasons lead one to expect that major recessions will damage economic capacity—and thus produce a break in trend [ch. 4.2].

Figure 2.7 illustrates the effect of applying method B to US data in the Great Depression. In this case, even with method B, there appears to have been a large downward displacement of the growth path.[9]

---

[7] See table 5.6 below, which relates changes in unemployment *during periods of recession* to change in output: a still higher figure would probably have resulted if lagged changes had been used. An alternative method of adjusting to a constant-employment basis would have been to base

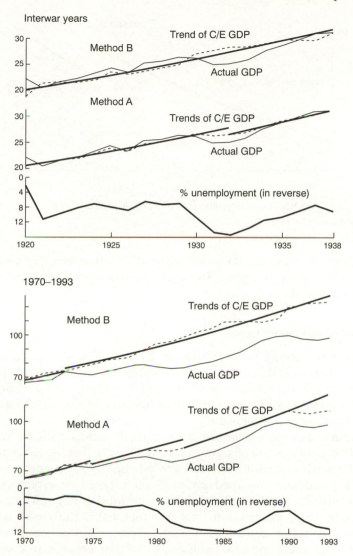

Fig. 2.6   GDP and constant-employment (C/E) GDP, 1920–1993

Method A adjusts output in proportion to $100 - u/100$, where u is the percentage of unemployed. Method B adjusts GDP by use of the coefficient obtained by regressing output change on unemployment change. Log-linear trends are fitted to GDP so adjusted.

Sources: basic data as for table 2.1.

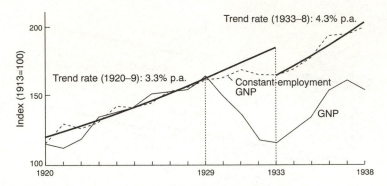

Fig. 2.7   GNP and constant-employment GNP: USA, 1920–1938

Source: basic data as for table 2.1.

Since these estimates are uncertain, alternative estimates using methods A and B are given in later chapters. However, discussion will build mostly on the results of method A.

Legitimacy of estimating trends

The practice of seeking to extract trends from time series has come under attack on the grounds that econometric tests show no evidence that a deviation from estimated 'trend' tends to be followed by a return to 'trend'.[10] Shocks, it is argued, thus have permanent rather than transient effects, which means that the concept of trend is illegitimate.

The hypotheses proposed in this study partially concur with the results, if not the method, of this line of argument. I would argue that the effect of shocks on capacity needs to be distinguished from the effect of shocks on output. The estimation procedures discussed above claim to produce estimates of the growth of capacity; and it is argued that downward (but not upward) demand shocks produce a permanent shift—not in output, but in capacity. I also argue that it is only major downward demand shocks, such as occur in major recessions, that affect capacity significantly, so that between recessions it is legitimate to estimate trend growth rates.

the adjustment not on changes in percentage unemployment but on changes in percentage 'non-employment', i.e. in the percentage of persons of working age not in employment. This too would show a higher response.

[8] Estimates produced by alternative methods (see charts in Barrell and Sefton 1995) also appear to show relatively small 'output gaps' i.e. under 5% not 10% or 20%. That however is a product of the methods used, and I would not count it as good evidence.

[9] Kendrick also (1973: 41–51) claimed evidence for an effect of this sort in the data for US productivity through the Great Depression.

[10] e.g. C. R. Nelson and Plosser (1982), De Long and Summers (1986) and Beaudry and Koop (1993).

I will argue later [ch. 4] that the rate of growth of capacity, and hence also of output, may change greatly over long periods as a result of supply factors. Such changes would make it illegitimate to assume that observations of growth rates over several decades belong to the same universe; and this would also seem to make it invalid to apply to output series over long periods the complex econometric procedures on which the studies under discussion are based.

Methods used to date recessions and to measure the size of fluctuations

In this study estimates of trend growth rates are required chiefly to date recessions and estimate their depth [table 2.3]. But it may be noted that the growth rates shown are higher than many other estimates of trend growth, which include recession periods that the present estimates exclude. Although the present estimates are not presented as the best possible, they suggest that standard methods of calculation may underestimate capacity growth rates during periods between major recessions.

Since modern economies tend normally to grow each year, recession and recovery are best defined in terms of departure from that norm. The start of a recession therefore is taken here not as the date at which output starts to fall absolutely, but at the (earlier) date at which its rate of growth falls below the estimated trend rate of capacity growth, i.e. the date when the degree of utilization of capacity starts to fall. The end of a recession, similarly, is put not at the date when output starts to rise absolutely, but at the (later) date when its rate of growth regains the capacity rate of growth. (The interval between the point when output starts rising absolutely and when it reaches the capacity growth rate is referred to as a 'pick-up' or 'resumption of growth' and is not considered a recovery.)

The term 'recovery' is reserved for periods when growth exceeds the capacity growth rate, and when underemployed capacity accordingly is in process of

Table 2.3   Alternative estimates of constant-employment output growth rates: UK, 1920–1993

Growth rates of output[a]	Interwar		Post-WWII	Post-1973	
	1920–29	1932–38	1950–73	1975–79	1982–93
				(Annual % changes)	
Method A	2.5	2.8	2.9	2.6	2.9
Method B		2.5	3.2	2.6[b]	

[a] Growth rates are estimated by fitted log-linear trends. Method A assumes that in major recessions changes in output and % unemployment are (inversely) proportionate. Method B adjusts output using the relation obtained by regressing annual changes in output on annual changes in unemployment over periods mostly not of major recession.
[b] Including North Sea output, the trend is 2.8.

Sources: as in table 2.1.

being re-employed. Not all phases of above-trend growth come soon after a recession, so that not all can be regarded as recoveries from recession: more isolated phases are referred to as phases of above-trend growth, or fast growth. The start and end of a fast-growth phase are defined as the dates when reabsorption of unemployed capacity starts and stops.

The dates adopted for the start and end of the five major recessions, and of the four main phases of above-trend growth, are listed in table 2.5. Whether method A or B is used to estimate trends makes little difference to the dating of fluctuations and does not affect which calendar years are chosen to represent starting or terminal dates.

The depth of a recession is measured as the gap between the projected previous trend and actual output at the bottom of a recession (or increase in the gap, if the gap was above zero to start with). The scale of a recovery or boom is measured analogously. In this case the choice of method A or B to calculate trend does somewhat affect the results [table 2.4].

The 'depth of recession' so defined is similar to the concept of 'output gap'. That phrase however may be used to mean not the amount by which (as an

Table 2.4   Dating and depth of major recessions and fast-growth phases: UK, 1920–1993 (% divergence from capacity trend)

	Dating of fluctuations		Estimate of depth of recession or scale of fast growth as compared with trend[a]	
	Start	End	Method A	Method B
Recessions				
I	1920	1921	−10.3	−10.3
II	1929	1932	−11.9	−11.9
III	1973	1975	−7.8[b]	−8.3[b]
IV	1979	1982	−10.0	−10.0
V	1989	1993	−11.6[b]	−10.4[b]
Fast-growth phases				
I	1922	1925	4.7	4.7
II	1933	1937	9.5	8.5
III	1972	1973	4.1	4.3
IV	1985	1988	7.4	6.4

Sources: Feinstein (1972); *Economic Trends*. Sefton and Weale (1995) give estimates in which GDP(O) GDP(E) and GDP(I) are differently weighted. Their figures give a larger scale for recession I (of over 13%).
[a] % change in output from start to end of recession or fast-growth phase *less* (years × annual trend % growth rate).
[b] If measured as the fall in output below trend starting from the beginning of the previous boom (i.e. from 1972 or 1985), the depth of recessions would be for 1973–5 3.9% (method A) or 4.4% (method B); and for 1989–93 5.7% (method A) or 4.5% (method B).

observation about the past) output has fallen relative to trend, but the amount by which (as a judgement about the future) output could be raised without encountering physical bottlenecks or provoking an acceleration of inflation. The two concepts are different: if capacity has contracted during a recession, firms will not be able to re-employ immediately all the labour previously discharged, and the risk of inflation will be greater.

The picture of a recession as here envisaged differs more than might appear from the usual view, underlying which is a picture of a sine curve where each downward phase tends automatically to be followed by an equal recovery [see fig. 10.1 below]. Here the picture is of a downturn not automatically followed by recovery: it will be argued more fully later [ch. 3.2] that the economy left to itself tends to resume normal growth—but not to exceed it unless a new favourable shock intervenes. Thus, the cycle is amputated: the economy limps, with a strong downward leg but only a stump for the upward leg.

2.3. Comparison of the three main phases since 1920 in the UK and other countries

As noted in section 2.1, the period 1920–95 falls into three main subperiods. This section compares the three main phases in the UK in greater detail and gives some comparisons with other countries.

The impact of major recessions on growth rates in each subperiod

The major recessions must have considerably reduced the average rate of growth both in the interwar period and since 1973 [see fig. 2.1]. It is interesting to get some idea of how much they may have reduced it.

The two recessions in the *interwar period* may have reduced output by the end of the recession by 10 and 12 per cent respectively [table 2.5], each being followed by a considerable recovery. By 1929 output was probably still (perhaps 3 per cent) below what it would have been if the 1921 recession had not happened. Output fell further as a result of the Great Depression, and even

Table 2.5 Recessions and output, 1920–1993

	Interwar period	Post-WWII period	Post-1973 period
Actual annual growth rate (as in table 2.1)	2.0	2.9	2.0
Rough indication:			
of recession effect	0.5	—	1.0
of hypothetical rate in the absence of major recessions	2.5	2.9	3.0

after the subsequent partial recovery may still by 1939 have been a further 6 per cent below trend. Over the whole period 1920–39, therefore, the average rate of growth may have been reduced by 0.5 per cent a year.

The three recessions of the *post-1973 years* may have reduced output at the time by 8, 10, and 11 per cent respectively, but after the second recession there was a considerable recovery in the years 1985–8 (by 6 or 7 per cent). Output at the end of the period in 1993 may then still have been more than 20 per cent below what it would have been without the recessions, so that the average rate of growth over the period 1973–93 may have been reduced by 1 per cent a year [see table 2.5].

Had the five major recessions not occurred, the average rate of growth in the three main subperiods might then have been more nearly equal. That validates the belief that much of the difference between the three main subperiods was due to the occurrence of major recessions in the first and third, but not the second, of these periods.

Slow–fast–slow growth: the expenditure counterparts

Table 2.6 shows the expenditure counterparts of output growth in the three main subperiods.[11] There are two notable features: first, the acceleration in the postwar growth of investment expenditure compared with that of the interwar period, followed by the much larger decline after 1973; and, second, the rapid growth of exports after World War II, *not* here followed after 1973 by much slowdown. The rise in exports was in part a reflection of the fact that rapid postwar growth in the UK was a worldwide trend. But there was also a similar rapid growth of imports: essentially, industrial countries were trading more with each other, and becoming more closely interrelated. The acceleration of consumer spending was relatively modest in relation to the acceleration of GDP growth [table 2.7, penult. col.]. That may indicate that it was largely a multiplier effect, reflecting rises elsewhere, rather than an independent force. (The consumption ratio changed little [see table 2.6].)

The deceleration in growth after 1973 [table 2.7, last col.] reflected, overwhelmingly, the fall-off in investment. Steady rapid growth in the decades after World War II could have been the cause of the progressive rise in investment then [table 2.6], and interruptions to growth after 1973 could have been the reason for investment rising subsequently only slowly.

The growth of productivity and the growth of capital

Table 2.8 shows the course of labour productivity since 1855.

In the *interwar* period, labour productivity appears to have increased more rapidly than in the decades before 1914. That is not true of total factor productivity (TFP).

---

[11] The table shows growth between single years at the beginning and end of each period: attention should thus be paid only to large changes.

Table 2.6 Rate of growth of expenditure components by periods: UK, 1920–1987 (constant prices)

	Interwar 1920–38	Post-WWII 1950–73	Post-1973 1973–87
		(annual % rates of change[a])	
Consumers' expenditure (C)	1.5	2.7	2.0
Government current spending on goods and services (G)	2.9	2.0	1.4
Investment (I)[b]	4.2	5.0	1.0
of which: Dwellings	8.8	5.5	0.7
Non-residential	3.0	4.8	0.9
(of which			
public sector		(5.1)	(−5.2)
private sector)		(4.6)	(3.3)
Exports of goods and services (X)	−0.4	4.2	3.6
Final expenditure	1.7	3.3	1.9
Imports (M)	1.8	4.8	3.1
GDP (Y)	1.7	3.0	1.7
(Non-oil GDP)			(1.3)
Consumption ratio ($\dot{C}/\dot{Y}$)[c]	0.88	0.90	1.18
Import ratio ($\dot{M}/\dot{Y}$)[c]	1.06	1.60	1.82

[a] 1938 prices for 1920–38, 1980 prices for 1950–73, and 1985 prices for 1973–87.
[b] Excluding investment in stocks.
[c] Calculated as annual growth rate of consumers' expenditure ($\dot{C}$) or of imports ($\dot{M}$) divided by that of GDP ($\dot{Y}$), where the overdot indicates percentage rate of change.

Sources: as in table 2.1.

Table 2.7 Contributions of expenditure components to output growth by period: UK, 1920–1987

	Contributions to annual % rate of growth of output				
	Interwar (1920–38)	Postwar (1950–73)	Post-1973 (1973–87)	Change, interwar to postwar	Change, postwar to post-1973
Consumers' expenditure	1.20	1.65	1.23	0.45	−0.42
Government current spending	0.35	0.45	0.28	0.10	−0.17
Investment	0.55	1.00	0.04	0.45	−0.96
Exports	−0.07	0.85	0.95	0.92	0.10
less Imports	0.32	0.98	0.85	−0.66	−0.13
GDP	1.72	3.00	1.65	1.28	−1.35

Sources: as in table 2.1.

Table 2.8   Growth of labour productivity and total factor productivity: UK, 1855–1989 (% annual growth rates)

	Labour productivity	Total factor productivity (TFP)[a] as estimated from		
		(i) Gross capital/ gross product	(ii) Net capital/ net product	(iii) Latter, adjusted
Pre-WWI				
1855–84	1.3	0.9	0.8	0.9
1884–1903	0.8	0.7	0.7	0.7
1903–13	0.5	0.0	0.1	0.1
Interwar				
1922–9	1.6	1.0	1.1	1.1
1929–38	1.0	0.7	0.8	0.8
Post-WWII				
1950–60	1.9	1.5	1.3	1.5
1960–73	2.9	1.5	1.3	1.7
Post-1973				
1973–82	1.4	−0.4	0.0	−0.2
1982–9	2.3	2.5	3.0	3.1

[a] TFP was estimated on three bases:
 (i) the productivity of employment and gross capital input in producing gross domestic product (statistically the more reliable basis);
 (ii) the productivity of employment and net capital input in producing net domestic product (theoretically preferable);
 (iii) the latter with a lower weight assigned to capital input, on the grounds that the share of non-employment income in total national income (usually taken as the weight) represents, in addition to the services of capital, the reward of entrepreneurship; on this treatment, entrepreneurship, though contributing to TFP, is not treated as labour input.

Sources: as in table 2.1.

After World War II the growth of labour productivity again accelerated (again, more rapidly than TFP). That is probably because of greater investment. Up to World War II the capital stock had increased fairly steadily, broadly in line with employment, whereas after the war it increased considerably more rapidly, and more rapidly than employment. Some of the increase in the growth of labour productivity after the war compared with before must therefore be attributed to the greater input of capital. Table 2.8 shows the course of both labour productivity and total factor productivity; on either measure, the years after World War II remain a period of faster growth than in all previous periods. In the decade after 1973, the growth of labour productivity slowed and TFP showed a cessation of growth. The seven years 1982–9 saw a short-lived recovery in TFP growth—even above those of the Golden Age after World War II.

Estimates of total factor productivity (TFP = output divided by a weighted average of labour and capital inputs) are presented in table 2.8 on three alternative bases. The third version gives capital input a lower weight than usual on the grounds that the share of non-employment income in GDP may in part represent not the reward of capital, but that of entrepreneurship [app. A4.1]. On all versions, the growth of TFP is slower than that of labour productivity. On each version, the differences between the three main subperiods remain pronounced, and go in the same direction as labour productivity. Many later charts and tables in this book will refer to labour productivity rather than TFP: as will be seen, while that misses some significant points, it captures many of the more important ones.

Were there major recessions before the twentieth century?

This study is about the period since 1920. It may be asked: was the economy subject to major recessions before that date, or are they an entirely modern phenomenon? Table 2.9 tabulates facts about recessions between 1855 and 1914. The data are less reliable than for later years (expenditure and output indicators of GDP frequently diverge), and some features of the economy's behaviour seem erratic by modern standards and thus are less easy to interpret.[12] Though much

Table 2.9 Large recessions in UK before 1914[a]

	No. of years in which output fell	% change in				Change in % unemployment[b]
		GDP(A)	GDP(O)	Output per head	Fixed investment	
(1858)	1	0.3	−0.3	2.6	2.7	3.1
1867	1	−1.0	−2.6	1.9	−12.0	3.7
(1869)	1	0.7	−0.7	−0.9	−3.1	−0.8
(1877)	1	1.0	−0.6	1.2	−1.6	1.0[c]
1879	1	−0.4	−3.7	4.6	−14.0	4.5[c]
1883–85	2	−0.3	−2.5	4.7	−15.0	6.7
1891–93	**2**	**−2.4**	**−2.8**	**−0.6**	**3.7**	**4.0**
(1903)	1	−1.1	−1.5	−1.2	2.3	0.7
1908	**1**	**−4.1**	**−3.2**	**−0.6**	**−12.3**	**4.1**

[a] The table shows all years in the period 1855–1913 in which GDP(O) fell. Years in parentheses cannot be classed as major recessions. Of the five remaining, 1891–93 and 1908 (shown in bold) have best claim to be called 'major' recessions.
[b] Years shown are years when output also fell. There were eight other years when unemployment rose but output did not fall.
[c] Unemployment rose continuously, from 4.4% in 1877 to 10.7% in 1879.
Source: Feinstein (1972: tables 6, 20, 40, 57).

has been written about the severity of nineteenth-century recessions, most of the economic historians who did so thought chiefly in terms of price developments, and had no national income estimates to help them.

Major recessions are defined in this study as occasions when there was a sizeable absolute fall in real output. Before 1914 that happened very rarely: there were only two occasions [see table 2.9] when output fell for two years running, and one other year (1908) when the fall in output, though confined to a single year, was unusually steep. On only two of these (1891–3 and 1908) can the setback to productivity growth have amounted to much. Another test is whether investment was affected. There were four occasions when investment fell by over 10 per cent, but only one (1908) when the associated fall in GDP was significant.

My conclusion is that there were only two occasions (and those near the end of the century) that even came near to ranking with the major recessions after World War I; and that major recessions of the kind experienced in the twentieth century are a modern phenomenon.[13]

If this is correct, one possible reason (suggested by the discussion in later chapters) is that the economy was not then subject to such large shocks. Most large shocks have probably originated in acts of government; and government was much smaller before this century. Another possibility is that, since banks were smaller, the extension of credit that they were able to make in a boom, and contract in a recession, was smaller in relation to GDP than now. Fuller research would be needed to speculate confidently.

The UK in comparison with other industrial countries

All main industrial countries shared in the pattern of slow–fast–slow growth as between the three main subperiods [table 2.10, final three cols.]; and also shared in the pattern of high–low–high as regards unemployment [table 2.11]. For almost all countries, too, the postwar period was a period not only of high growth and high employment, but of *steady* growth without major fluctuations; i.e., deviations from average growth rates [table 2.10] were lower in the postwar phase than in the interwar years (which for many countries was a highly disturbed period). In the UK, though not elsewhere, the post-1973 period was also a rather disturbed time in this sense, because the recessions seem to have been deeper. In general, other countries had recessions at about the same time as the UK, though the precise timing differed [see chs. 6–9].

The partial parallelism between different countries' experiences means that to some extent we must seek explanations that could explain developments in industrial countries as a whole. But the divergences between the experience of the UK and that of other countries are wide enough to demand explanations that are partly special to the UK.

---

[13] Robin Matthews has suggested to me that if we had annual data for years before 1855, some earlier phases (e.g. 1841–2 and perhaps 1826) might qualify as major recessions.

Table 2.10 The pace and steadiness of growth: UK and seven other countries by main sub-periods, 1920–1990

	Average growth rates[a]			Average % deviation[b]		
	1920–38	1950–73	1973–90	1920–38	1950–73	1973–90
UK	2.0	2.9	1.9	3.3	1.4	2.6
Other countries						
USA	1.6	3.7	2.6	9.9	2.6	1.6
France	2.2	5.1	2.5	7.2	1.4	1.4
West Germany	4.3	5.9	2.2	8.0	5.2[c]	2.2
Italy	2.2	5.5	2.6	3.3	1.5	1.7
Japan	3.5	9.3	4.0	3.2	2.8	0.9
Canada	2.5	5.1	3.5	6.8	1.7	1.4
Sweden	3.3	4.0	2.0	3.2	2.6	1.4
Aggregation for seven countries[d]	2.2	4.8	2.9	7.5	1.8	1.3

[a] Fitted logarithmic trend of real GDP for each period.
[b] Average % deviation of GDP from the fitted logarithmic trend of GDP for each period.
[c] The deviation is high because the German growth rate in the recovery period after World War II was very high and subsequently declined.
[d] Fitted trend of aggregate real GDP of seven countries combined and average % annual deviation from trend.

Source: Maddison (1989: 120–3); 1987–90: IMF, *International Financial Statistics*, 1990, except for UK which is as in table 2.1.

2.4. Profits, factor shares, and real wages

This section discusses the behaviour of profits and shares of factor incomes. Profits fluctuated inversely with the fluctuations in productivity already discussed. Fluctuations in profit shares are much the same thing in reverse as fluctuations in real product wages.

Consider first the longer-term changes. Broadly, the share of profit incomes rose through the interwar period. It fell from 1950 up to 1981 [fig. 2.8] and then rose again. One can only speculate why these changes in trend occurred. For instance, the interwar trend might have reflected interwar recovery; the post-1950 fall might have reflected increasing openness to international competition; and the years after 1981 might have reflected a belated recovery from the two OPEC recessions.

Short-term movements are more clearly related to movements in economic activity. Thus, the three years of the Great Depression, the couple of years apiece of the two OPEC recessions, and then the late-1980s recession each saw a marked dip in the profits ratio (and, by the same token, a marked rise in the share of labour incomes).

The factor shares shown in figure 2.8 are factor incomes as shares not of GDP, but of total domestic income (gross domestic product at current factor

Table 2.11   Unemployment rates: UK and seven other countries by main sub-periods, 1920–1990[a]

	Average % unemployment in sub-period		
	Interwar (1920–38)	Post-WWII (1950–73)	Post-1973 (1973–89)
UK	9.6	1.8	7.3
Other countries			
USA	11.2	4.6	6.9
France	2.6	2.0	7.1
West Germany	6.2	2.5	4.7
Italy	4.4	5.7	8.3
Japan	n.a.	1.6	2.2
Canada	8.4	4.7	8.3
Sweden	4.3	1.8	2.3
Average for 16 countries[b]	(1921–38) 7.5	(1950–73) 2.6	(1974–89) 5.7

[a] As estimated using official definitions of unemployment, which however are not identical between countries.
[b] The above eight countries plus Australia, Austria, Belgium, Denmark, Finland, Netherlands, Norway, and Switzerland.
Source: Maddison (1991a) except for UK, which is as in table 2.1.

costs *plus* stock appreciation.[14] The chart excludes North Sea profits from the total of profits and GDP on the grounds that they have little connection with the behaviour of the mainland economy.[15]

Over the long term, real wages increase over time as productivity grows. This is because, although there have been short-lived changes, the share of profits in GDP does not rise or fall indefinitely. That implies that firms increase product prices less than the rise in wages and salaries, the difference being equivalent to the rise in labour productivity [see further ch. 3.1]: in that way a share of the benefits of rising productivity are handed on to wage-earners (either as product price decreases, or as nominal wage increases).

During major recessions, productivity growth changed abruptly from steady advance, as in the previous phase, to abnormal absolute decline. Since the transition was sudden, it is likely to have been unexpected; that probably explains why

[14] That definition is chosen because firms have typically based prices on historical (not currently incurred) costs and tend to view profits, as their accountants present them, inclusive of stock appreciation (see Dow 1964). At times when world commodity prices rose steeply (and stock appreciation was therefore high, i.e. in 1947–51), profits as a share of GDP fell more than as a share of TDI (and the share of labour incomes rose more).

[15] Here, and in many later tables and charts, North Sea oil and gas extraction is treated as falling outside the UK, and domestic consumption of North Sea oil is treated as an import. North Sea profits rose from about zero in 1975 to about 3% of GDP in 1980–5, and since then have declined.

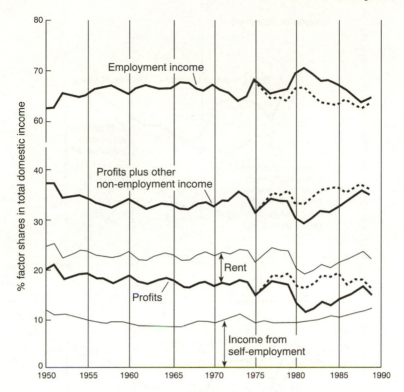

Fig. 2.8   The share of wages and profits: UK, 1950–1989
North Sea oil excluded; broken line shows shares with latter included.
Source: as for table 2.1.

the fall in profit shares at these times was so large. For, if firms following past experience base prices on an expected upward trend of productivity, an unexpected fall in productivity will result in unexpectedly low profits. A test was made of the hypothesis that prices are determined in this way: it showed that such a hypothesis could explain most of the observed variations in profits.[16]

In order to maintain profit shares in spite of the drop in productivity, prices would have had to have been about 5 per cent higher than they were in each OPEC recession phase [fig. 2.9]. Subsequently, after each of these recessionary phases, prices were raised more rapidly than costs, so that profit shares recovered. Following the 1973–4 recession, half the previous dip in shares had been made good by 1977. In the 1978–82 recession profit shares again dipped; this fall was

---

[16] The hypothesis tested was that rises in prices equalled actual wage increases *less* expected productivity increase and that expected productivity growth, as incorporated in price determination, equalled productivity growth over the previous n years. This formula (with $n=5$) was able to explain most of the changes.

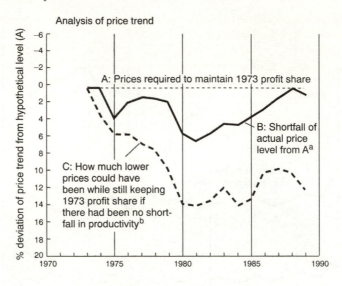

Analysis of price trend

% deviation of price trend from hypothetical level (A)

A: Prices required to maintain 1973 profit share

B: Shortfall of actual price level from A[a]

C: How much lower prices could have been while still keeping 1973 profit share if there had been no short-fall in productivity[b]

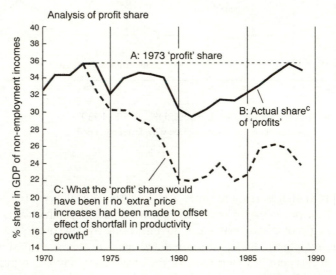

Analysis of profit share

% share in GDP of non-employment incomes

A: 1973 'profit' share

B: Actual share[c] of 'profits'

C: What the 'profit' share would have been if no 'extra' price increases had been made to offset effect of shortfall in productivity growth[d]

Fig. 2.9 Prices and profits on different assumptions: UK, 1973–1989

[a] % deviation of actual GDP deflator (adjusted to include stock appreciation and to exclude North Sea output) from level of GDP deflator required to maintain the 1973 share of non-employment incomes in GDP, given the actual course of output per head.

[b] How much lower the GDP deflator would have been if it had maintained the 1973 share of non-employment income in GDP, and if output per head had grown as fast as in 1960–73.

[c] How far the actual share of non-employment income in GDP fell below the 1973 share.

[d] How much the share of non-employment income would have fallen below the 1973 share if firms had assumed that output per head had continued to grow as fast as before 1973 and had raised prices only enough to maintain the 1973 share.

Sources: CSO, *National Accounts* and *Economic Trends*.

subsequently made good by 1988. On this reasoning, prices were 10 per cent higher in 1990 than if there had been no setback to productivity growth (dotted line in chart).

These fluctuations in real wages and (inversely) in profit shares result from the suddenness of changes in productivity during major recessions, combined with the slowness of the adjustment to such changes of product prices. That has implications, which we will need to consider later, for interpreting the effects of real wage changes [ch. 3.3]. The resulting abrupt fall in profits at such times (amounting to several per cent of GDP) must also have forced sharp contractions in fixed investment and in stocks, and thus must have strongly exacerbated the size of recessions. This has implications (which we will also need to consider later) for the transmission mechanisms that operate during major recessions [ch. 5.1], and must be another reason for the asymmetry between pronounced recessions and the slowness of recoveries.

3 The Causal Structure of the Economy

Any such study as this necessarily makes assumptions about the causal structure of the economy, and about the nature of under- or over-full employment. These involve much-argued theoretical questions.

This chapter discusses three issues. Section 3.1 states assumptions about the basic causal structure of the economy. Section 3.2 considers the continuing shift implicit in steady growth in the price of factor input relative to that of output, and how this mechanism operates. Finally, Section 3.3 discusses the phenomenon of persistent underemployment, which it argues is a stable state: that implies that the economy lacks any general power of self-adjustment of the sort that would restore high employment.

The discussion is more heterodox than novel; defining the assumptions that are made involves taking a view on a number of controversial issues. There are two appendices. Appendix A3.1 is a note on the theoretical discussion about the features of the economic system that allow the possibility of unemployment. Appendix A3.2 summarizes the case against the High Real Wage theory of unemployment.

3.1. The main routes of causation in the economy

Interpretation of events cannot depend only on unstructured observation, but has also to be based on assumptions (derived from prior knowledge or reasoning) about the causal structure of the economy, i.e. what variable determines what. Although this study is not econometric, it conceives the structure of the economy on lines similar to a standard macroeconometric model. Total demand is defined in terms of real final expenditure; its level (in the absence of shocks) is determined by previous income; its result is output, in the course of producing which income is generated; income in turn goes to determine demand in the subsequent period. But the model departs in some respects from what much other macroeconomic discussion assumes.

Figure 3.1 gives a simplified picture of the linkages assumed, i.e. the routes by which short-term changes in the economy come about.

1. The rate of growth of output is seen as a constant (trend), subject to fluctuations about trend in response to exogenous demand shocks and to breaks in trend [ch. 2.2].
2. Fluctuations about trend are viewed as variations in the degree to which economic capacity is employed, and are mirrored by inverse variations in unemployment. Fluctuations in output and employment are seen as caused by fluctuations in demand.

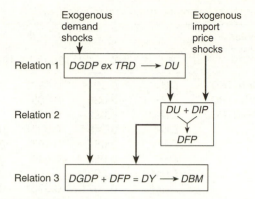

Fig. 3.1 Notional causal structure of the economy

DGDP = rate of growth of output
DGDP ex TRD = *DGDP* less trend *GDP*
DU = change in percentage unemployment
DIP = rate of import price inflation
DFP = rate of change in price of final expenditure
DY = rate of growth of nominal GDP
DFM = rate of change of broad money

3. Final price inflation is determined by the degree of employment of capacity (pressure of demand), along with the rate of change of import prices.
4. Change in nominal GDP equals the sum of change in real GDP plus change in final prices, each separately determined as at paragraphs 1 and 3 above, and can be whatever their separate determinants dictate; i.e., it is *not* here assumed that there is a preordained total for the sum of the two, such that the more there is of the one the less there will be of the other—a belief often held.[1]
5. Change in nominal GDP determines change in broad money. Money is thus not the driving force of the economy, but rather the residuary determinant—a proposition discussed further below.

Table 3.1 shows the correlation between the variables included in figure 3.1. The correlations are given for each of the three main subperiods since 1920. They show that the schema of figure 3.1 is in a broad way consistent with the facts—but not that it is the only schema that could encompass these facts.[2]

[1] The idea is reflected for instance in the title of Okun's *Prices and Quantities* (1981) and remains influential. Blanchard and Fischer (1989: ch. 8) review the discussion; an example of this view appears on p. 375, where the authors, after alluding to 'fluctuations in nominal demand, *which we take to be fluctuations in nominal money*', say: 'when there are changing costs or prices...price-setters may decide not to adjust their prices in response to small shifts in demand, and movements in nominal money may *accordingly* lead to movements in output' (my italics).
[2] Reverse causality is frequently also consistent with the facts, as for instance with the causality of money (compare variants 3 and 3B in table 3.1). Variant 2B indicates that broad money along with import price change (but not on its own) could appear to explain inflation.

Table 3.1   Relations between some main macrovariables[a]

Relation	Variables		$\bar{R}^a$			
	A	*B*	1920–38	1950–73	1973–93	1920–93[b]
1	DGDPexTRD	DU	0.501*	0.697*	0.479*	0.401*
	DGDPexTRD1	DU	−0.036	0.085	0.545*	0.064*
	DGDPexTRD2	DU	0.052	0.058	0.062	0.060*
2	DIP	DFP	0.748*	0.627*	0.494*	0.676*
	DIP1	DFP	0.082	0.167*	0.639*	0.370*
	DIP2	DFP	−0.059	−0.044	0.215*	0.097*
3	DY	DBM	0.293*	0.465*	0.072	0.304*
	DY1	DBM	0.202*	0.375*	0.081	0.345*
	DY2	DBM	0.082	0.235*	0.041	0.304*
Two variants:						
2A	DIP, DBM	DFP	0.833*	0.652	0.465	0.744*
	DIP, DBM1	DFP	0.835*	0.622	0.486	0.735*
	DIP, DBM2	DFP	0.792*	0.612	0.558*	0.738
3A	DBM	DY	0.293*	0.465*	0.072	0.304*
	DBM1	DY	0.029	0.349*	−0.027	0.130*
	DBM2	DY	−0.030	0.141*	0.051	0.039*

[a] Definition of terms as in table 3.1. All changes referred to are changes between calendar years. Final numbers to terms indicate that explanatory variable (*A*) is lagged 1 or 2 years. * indicates that the regression coefficients are significant (t ratio > 1.8). All regressions included a constant term (not shown).
[b] Includes 1939–49.

Sources: as in table 2.1.

The different parts of the economy are interrelated in a complex way, such that sector A affects sector B which affects sector C, which in turn affects sector A, and so on. Since many magnitudes show statistical correlation with many others, any interpretation of observations has to depend on prior suppositions about the dominant channels and direction of causation—these suppositions being derived from prior argument or evidence.

The reasons for denying money a determining role derive from Dow and Saville (1988).[3] The argument is that the central bank can influence money only indirectly. Thus, it can influence interest rates; they influence demand and output; that in turn influences inflation; prices plus output (the value of output) in turn determine bank lending and thus changes in money. Interest rates have little *direct* additional influence on money. Hence money is endogenous; the central bank can control money (and inflation) only by shocking the economy, but here the effect (via interest rates) is powerful [ch. 5.2].

---

[3] The view that money is endogenous, though perhaps heterodox, has distinguished advocates, e.g. Kaldor (1986) and Hicks (1989).

3.2. How growing supply creates growing demand

This section describes the mechanism whereby steady growth of supply tends to be accompanied by steady growth of demand. The argument abstracts from demand shocks.

In a growing economy (in which the productivity of the factors of production increases each year), the unit price of factors rises more (or falls less) than the price of a unit of output by the amount of the rise in output per unit of factor input. Factoral purchasing power thus rises at the same rate as the rise in productivity; this enables factors to buy their own product. These propositions follow from the national income identities. How this is achieved differs according to whether or not there is perfect competition.

To illustrate, make some simplifying assumptions. Suppose that there is one factor only, labour; call the reward of labour, wages. Suppose that all goods are consumer goods, bought out of wages, and that all wages are spent on them, so that demand for consumer goods depends on the purchasing power of labour incomes. Now suppose that the unit wage is constant. In a perfectly competitive economy, firms would be driven to reduce prices by the extent of the productivity gain they could achieve, so that as a result of the competitive process the real purchasing power of incomes would rise by the amount necessary for factors to buy the growing output that is produced.

But as argued below [ch. 4.2], in a growing economy competition is necessarily imperfect; for progress depends on separate firms' success in improving products or processes, and some firms will be ahead of others. Under imperfect competition, firms set prices: what price each sets depends on what prices it expects others to set. That could result in the same outcome as under perfect competition, i.e. with all potential output being bought. Alternatively, it is possible to imagine scenarios in which, out of conservatism, the growth and purchasing power provided are less than enough to take up fully the output that could technically be made available, and in which the slow growth of the effective market discourages efforts to improve productivity; this would tend to validate the initial conservatism. In that case, the pace of growth would depend not only on technical or supply-side factors, but also on the idea firms hold about the normal pace of growth: whichever was lower would set the pace.

The shift in the relative price of factors' input and output, and what this involves for firms' behaviour, underlies the following features here assumed about the working of the macroeconomy.

1. In the absence of disturbances, we may retain the picture of growth proceeding at a steady pace, with prices being reduced in line with productivity and real factoral purchasing power keeping pace with growth. This provides justification for the econometrician's assumption that normal growth can be represented by a trend, from which shocks produce deviations.

2. During a major recession productivity growth is interrupted [ch. 2.2], so that the productivity growth path is displaced downward.
3. After a major recession productivity growth is resumed; the shift in the relative prices of output and factor input thus starts up again, and normal growth of factoral purchasing power is also resumed. Thus, after a major recession there are forces that bring about a resumption of trend growth; i.e., *positive demand shocks are not required to bring a resumption of normal growth.*

These assumptions render more precise the phenomena that this book tries to explain. In both the statistical analysis [ch. 5.2] and the historical analysis [chs. 6–9], the aim is to explain divergences of growth rates, positive or negative, from trend.

3.3. The explanation of unemployment

Discussion of unemployment often starts from the assumption that unemployment arises because the cost of labour is too high relative to that of other factors of production, which equilibrating wage–price adjustments should remove; it explains unemployment as a failure of such adjustments to operate.[4]

In this study, a recession and accompanying unemployment is taken to arise because of downward shocks to demand; unemployment persists because mutual interactions between different sectors ('intersectoral interdependence') lock the economy into any position of demand insufficiency at which the occurrence of shocks leaves it. This means that unemployment is due not, as usually implied, to a deficiency in the working of the labour market, but to a more general feature of the economic system. It should be recognized that capital as well as labour gets unemployed.

The interpretation of unemployment raises basic issues for a study such as this, but has here to be discussed very briefly. I will describe first how the mechanism of sectoral interdependence is held to operate; and will then explain the inadequacies (as I see it) of other, more orthodox, explanations of unemployment. Finally, I will note some qualifications to my main line of explanation.

Sectoral interdependence as an explanation of stable underemployment

The persistence of underemployment is here explained as a result of what is called sectoral interdependence. The idea is illustrated in a phrase by Hahn (1984: 182): 'involuntarily unemployed labour can only signal its willingness to

---

[4] An extreme version of this view (e.g. Lucas 1978) asserts that the equilibrating process works instantly, so that involuntary unemployment is illusory: if people are unemployed, it must be because they prefer it.

work, not, until it is employed, its willingness to buy'. That gives in a nutshell a theory of persisting involuntary unemployment.

The argument starts from the circularity in the determination of income and output. Unemployed labour cannot spend because it is unemployed; but, equally, labour is unemployed because demand for goods and services is inadequate. In order to illustrate the argument, the consequences of the interdependence between sectors may be set out more fully. The argument for simplicity assumes a closed economy.

Consider a society of individuals, each of whom has two aspects: as provider of factor services for which they receive income, totalling Y; and as spenders, with collective expenditure E, which creates the demand for factor services. In any one period, $Y = E$. Assume that this year's expenditure E_1, is determined by, and equal to, this year's expected income, Y_1^e, which equals last year's actual income, Y_0. Such a sequence would be completely historically determined; and if (as above) the system were completely closed, the sequence would iterate endlessly:

$$Y_0 \rightarrow E_1 = Y_1 \rightarrow E_2 \cdots$$

Any initial level of output and employment would persist indefinitely.

Another case which can illustrate the same principle can be constructed by supposing an economy with two sectors, firms and households. Assume no changes in prices: let the output (Q) of firms be entirely of consumer goods sold entirely to households; let all income (Y) be distributed to households; and let their income come entirely from working for firms and be spent entirely on consumer goods (E). Also assume, as before, one lag: this period's income determines next period's expenditure. Then, if some households are initially unemployed and their income is correspondingly restricted, firms can sell only part of full-employment output and will produce only that, and therefore will continue to employ only part of households; so households' incomes will continue to lie below full-employment level. As before, the system will iterate indefinitely:

$$Y_0 \rightarrow E_1 = Q_1 = Y_1 \rightarrow E_2 \cdots$$

Initial unemployment will persist.

If, notwithstanding past history, all firms together agreed to employ all households, they would find that in the event they could sell all they would then produce. But no single firm is in a position in advance to make such an offer. Similarly, if all households together agreed to buy full-employment output, firms would employ them; and in the event households would find that they had sufficient income to spend on this scale. But again, no single household is in a position in advance to make such an offer. Firms or households may be fully aware that full employment is potentially possible; but unemployment is not due merely to incomplete information, nor does knowledge alone cure it.

Apart from lucky chance, only collective action can dramatically break the circle: collective action by all members of one sector, or of the other sector, or by the state acting on behalf of all.

To summarize the argument, it is convenient to refer to the exposition by Barro and Grossman (1971). They note that (1) Keynes's marginal propensity to consume implied (as Clower 1965, claimed) the dependence of expenditure on income; and (2) Patinkin's (1965) exegesis of the *General Theory* (especially chapter 13) treated the demand for labour as a derived demand dependent on the demand for goods (as one may suppose Keynes also saw it). These are the essential constituents of a model of interaction between the business and household sectors. Barro and Grossman set out such a two-sector analysis in terms suggested by these precedents:

In Patinkin's analysis the effective demand for labour was derived for a given level of demand for current output. To close this model, the demand for current output must be explained. In Clower's analysis the effective demand for current output was derived for a given level of demand for labour. To close this model the demand for labour must be explained. Thus the Patinkin and Clower analyses are essential complements. When appropriately joined they form a complete picture of the determinants of output and employment in a depressed economy. (Barro and Grossman 1971: 88)

That picture of mutual sectoral interdependence corresponds precisely with the explanation for stable underemployment here proposed.[5]

Barro and Grossman themselves (I think unfortunately) later took the view that persistent underemployment derives not from this sectoral interdependence but from wage and price stickiness. I will argue (immediately below) that that is not the case.[6]

In a growing economy, the propositions asserted above about a stationary economy require only simple transformation, provided that (as is valid for short periods) the growth of productivity can be assumed to be a steady process. The simple model here outlined of two-sector interdependence is elaborated and made more realistic in the concluding part of this study [app. A11].

---

[5] Chick (1978) gives a similar account of stable underemployment. She ascribes involuntary unemployment to the sequential way in which decisions get taken, as a result of which there is 'a system of interaction between households and firms in which households do not always get exactly what they want because they have no power to effect changes. The result does not rely on monopoly, irrationality or market imperfections. These might compound the problem, but the problem is independent of any of these factors ...'

[6] The view that persistence of underemployment derives from price stickiness appears now to have become the prevailing view, which has thus returned to the 'classical' position that Keynes sought to controvert (viz., that involuntary unemployment derives from wage inflexibility). Analysis of excess supply/demand situations created by wage/price inflexibility is (ironically, I think) therefore usually now called Keynesian. The view here proposed can also claim to be Keynesian; but what Keynes wrote clearly was not clear, and what he must be understood as saying is clearly a secondary question.

The kind of stable reiteration depicted above is similar to the assumptions of a standard macroeconomic forecasting model. In such a model, it is assumed that demand will grow at the capacity rate of growth, unless the course of demand is disturbed by an exogenous shock. This implies that the normal mechanisms of the economy will ensure that in the absence of shocks the economy will continue at its initial degree of underemployment. When examined, that appears to amount to the same as the primordial Keynesian assertion as to the possibility of stable ('equilibrium') underemployment.

Full employment is not here conceived of as an equilibrium to which the economy tends to return, nor is underemployment viewed as a disequilibrium position in that sense. Thus, the present analysis makes no use of the aggregate supply/aggregate demand type of diagram, which depicts the intersection of an aggregate supply schedule with an aggregate demand schedule. That type of diagram, though many writers use it, appears to me an illegitimate construction.[7]

Explanation of unemployment in terms of wage inflexibility

The more usual explanation of unemployment nowadays is that it arises because of wage inflexibility, not demand insufficiency. Unemployment is seen as a disequilibrium situation, i.e. as between the supply and demand for labour. It is generally true that disequilibria can be resolved by price adjustments, and the forte of economics is to analyse how such adjustments work. It is assumed that they would work in this case.

This picture would be true if unemployment arose because the price of labour relative to other factors of production (e.g. capital) was excessive. This is what the High Real Wage (HRW) theory of unemployment asserts. Appendix A3.2, where this theory is discussed more fully, argues, first, that the HRW theory is incomplete and lacks any account of how real product wages are determined; and, second, that the empirical evidence claimed in support of the theory (mostly confined to the 1970s) is based on a misinterpretation of the low profit shares to be expected in major recessions.

---

[7] That sort of diagram makes sense for the supply and demand for a particular product, where the parties supplying and demanding are separate and opposed, and price is measured in terms of a second commodity (or a composite of other commodities, or money). But the case is different when it is total supplies that are set opposite to total demand: here those who demand what is produced are those who produce it, and what they demand is not independent of what they produce; 'price', moreover, is not a price that arbitrates between two separate groups. Some accounts try to give sense to such an aggregate diagram by deriving 'demand' from an independent entity like the money stock (see Blanchard and Fischer 1989: 518–23): that device harks back to primitive Quantity Theory, and is here rejected since money is not seen as an exogenous policy instrument. Nor in my view is the stock of money identifiable with demand. If these criticisms are accepted, the diagram is not the kind of analytic construction that can properly be used to illuminate the effect of the 1973 and 1979 oil price shocks and to explain the simultaneous appearance then of high inflation and low output. That can better be described in other ways [ch. 8.1].

The most telling counter-argument to the HRW theory is that in a recession not only labour but also capital become unemployed: their joint disemployment cannot therefore be due to a high price of labour relative to that of capital.

The High Real Wage theory refers to wages in general. It is not in dispute that high relative wages for particular sorts of labour reduce employment of those sorts of labour.[8] That is, unemployment can arise as a result of an inflexibility of *relative* wages, which permits continuance of a mismatch as between the supply and demand for particular classes of labour in respect of age or skill or geographical location. This is important (and is further discussed below); but it does not undermine the basis of the present study. Such supply/demand mismatches for particular classes of labour (or indeed for particular classes of capital) change relatively slowly (see e.g. Nickell 1985). They do not account for the rise in labour unemployment during recessions.

The relation of one region to a whole country is analogous to the relation of one country to the world. Unemployment in one country may happen because real wages in that country are too high in relation to real wages in the rest of the world—either because money wages in that country have risen, or because productivity has fallen, or because the exchange rate has risen. (In the short run, the cause of a change in relative real wages is most likely to be a change in the exchange rate—which is treated in this study as one sort of shock: see ch. 5.2.) The fact that high real wages relative to those in the rest of the world can cause unemployment lends spurious plausibility to the quite different proposition that high real wages relative to the price of domestic output (i.e. high product wages) can have that effect.[9]

Attribution of unemployment to wage inflexibility is thus based (as Kalecki, 1944, noted) on an illegitimate transposition to the macroeconomic plane of what is true on the microeconomic plane. In the case of partial equilibrium, deficient demand for good A can be expected to cause the price of A in relation to other goods to fall, which will raise the demand and reduce the supply of good A as against other goods—to the point where supply and demand are

---

[8] Too high a price for labour of one grade or in one region will result in too high a price for the product it makes. Assuming that total demand stays unchanged, high relative wages then cause demand to switch to competing products. Labour of that grade (that region) will price itself out of jobs; unemployment will rise for that grade (that region), but will fall elsewhere so that total employment is unchanged.

[9] Another proposition which may seem similar to the HRW proposition needs to be distinguished. It is sometimes said that *aspirations* for high real wages, or attempts to achieve them, may cause unemployment. The argument is that wage pressures, stemming from the *desire* for high real wages, may threaten to increase the rate of inflation; that to counter this the government will adopt deflationary measures; and that these will result in unemployment. The crucial act here however is government *policy* (treated in this study as one sort of shock): that is different from wages being actually excessive, which is alleged to produce unemployment by virtue of *private* economic forces.

equal. If that happened in the general case, unemployment would persist only when prices were inflexible and failed to adjust in that way.[10]

The same adjustment process does not work in the case of total demand because what is being considered is not an adjustment of one part of the economy to another. In the case of the whole economy, a fall in wages would reduce the cost of the goods that labour produces (which on its own would increase demand); but at the same time it would reduce wage incomes (which on its own would reduce demand). The result would be a simultaneous fall of all nominal prices and incomes, but that would leave the relation between real supply and real demand unchanged. Unemployment therefore would also remain unchanged.

There is a second line of argument of a quite different sort which claims that wage flexibility would remedy unemployment. This is the argument from the real balance effect. It is different because it starts by admitting that unemployment is caused by deficiency of demand; but it goes on to claim that wage flexibility opens the way for forces to operate which will progressively restore demand and thus remove the unemployment.

Unemployment is assumed to make wages and prices fall. That (the argument continues) then raises the real value of money balances or, in a credit economy, raises the monetary base, either of which constitutes part of private wealth; and the rise in wealth raises private spending. A broader form of the same argument is that a fall in prices raises the real value of private holdings of national debt, with similar effect. In either case, the effect of the state's countervailing loss of wealth is ignored.

There are three defects to this argument.

1. On any reasonable assumptions, the process would work very slowly; for example, even if it did work it could take twenty years to restore unemployment by means of this mechanism.
2. When the private sector is enriched, the state is impoverished: one should not ignore the effects of that.[11] In general, arbitrarily asymmetric behaviour assumptions, which are the basis of the real balance effect, are not a valid basis for general propositions about the equilibrium of the economy.
3. Third, though underemployment may reduce the pace of inflation, prices nowadays do not fall absolutely [fig. 2.3]. The posited price adjustment—which is the start of the argument—therefore does not occur. Though the status of this objection is merely empirical, it is decisive.

---

[10] Strictly speaking, the argument would have to start by supposing that some shock had produced inadequate demand (which would have to be regarded as the primary cause of unemployment) and that it persisted only because wages were inflexible—which would thus have to be seen as the secondary cause or condition of persistent unemployment.

[11] The state might of course decide not to reduce its own spending in line with its impoverishment. But that should be accounted an act of expansionary fiscal policy—and the whole real balance effect should be seen to come about in that way. That is in fact the most revealing way of presenting the issue.

For these reasons, the real balance effect is not the conclusive argument that it is generally taken to be.[12] I conclude that, if a deficiency demand persists because of the mechanism of sectoral interdependence, that mechanism will continue to operate, and underemployment will remain, whether or not wages and prices fall because of unemployment.

Limitations to some general concepts underlying this interpretation

This study treats unemployment as arising primarily through deficiency of demand. In fact, as already indicated, other factors have also been operative, and thus need to be allowed for in interpreting events. I list below some of the more important factors. These do not greatly affect the interpretation of events during major recessions, which are the chief interest here.

The underemployment ratio is a comparative concept in that it implicitly compares the actual level of output with what the economy is capable of producing. (The phrase 'pressure of demand' is here used as a term to describe the degree to which the demand for output exhausts the quantity potentially available.) The concept of economic potential, or economic capacity, is admittedly rough. Even at high levels of demand, more could usually be produced at the cost of inflationary strain. Moreover, the potential of the economy depends on the pattern of demand; for example, an economy geared to war cannot immediately be converted to produce what people want in peacetime. Capacity is therefore difficult to define for a number of years after each world war, and to a lesser extent after the half-dozen major changes in the exchange rate (which also are likely to have altered the pattern of demand).

These are cases in which there is a mismatch between the pattern of demand and that of potential supply. Such a mismatch could be reduced or eliminated by adjustments to relative wages, i.e. by increases in wages in areas of excess demand and decreases in areas of excess supply. In such cases governments are right to try to bring about increased wage flexibility. But in practice such efforts have had little short-term effect, and mismatches have remained. Two causes of mismatch seem to have grown in importance at the end of the period here under study.

1. Manufacturers have transferred many manufacturing processes from the UK and other older industrial countries to countries with lower labour costs. This 'globalization' of production has left the older countries with an excess of unskilled labour.
2. Service industries have expanded more rapidly than manufacturing, because productivity in these industries (computers; the rising domination of retailing by supermarkets) has increased more rapidly than before. This has

---

[12] 'To an astonishing degree the theoretical fraternity has taken the real balance effects to be a conclusive refutation of Keynes' (Tobin 1992: 21).

increased the demand for women more than men and for part-time rather than full-time employees.

Influences of this sort make it difficult to interpret the post-1993 recovery, and the fall in unemployment in this phase probably reflected not only a rise in total demand but the effect of such influences [app. A9.1].

Nevertheless, despite these qualifications, in most periods these imprecisions can be lived with; and there is sense in comparing actual output with potential output. That is particularly the case when changes over a short period are being considered, as over the course of a recession.

3.4. Implications for later chapters

This chapter has discussed a number of theoretical questions on which opinion is likely to remain divided. Section 3.3 argued that the stability of unemployment as a persistent state was due to interlocking sectoral interdependencies, and suggested that that sort of stability was the same thing as the tendency assumed in most econometric modelling for the balance of demand in the economy to remain stable in the absence of shocks. The role of sectoral interdependence was proposed in opposition to the view that the stability of underemployment was due simply to wage inflexibility.

It is a fact however that wages and prices are inflexible; and it is probably also true that that must favour the kind of macro stability here in question and, together with the effect of sectoral interdependence, must reinforce it. (The system might not behave in such a stable way if prices were perfectly flexible and free to rise or fall violently under the influence of varying expectations.) The two factors probably join together to produce the result; but that does not undermine the theoretical argument that lack of demand is the primary factor.

There are consequences for policy. If one takes the view (contrary to the argument of section 3.3) that unemployment reflecting an apparent lack of demand persists only because wages are inflexible, then steps to increase wage flexibility have to be seen as a route to raise employment. On the present view, greater wage flexibility is useful for diminishing the mismatch between the supply and demand for particular types and locations of labour—or capital. But it does not help with general underemployment of labour and capital, which remains as long as demand stays low.

This does not mean that reinflating demand is an easy option. There is always likely to be considerable difficulty in bringing workers disemployed in a recession back into employment when demand revives—either because the physical or organizational infrastructure has disappeared with its disuse, or because human skills have deteriorated or not been kept normally up to date, or because reabsorption of unemployed resources at any rapid pace would create inflationary pressures.

The main truth is that lack of demand causes unemployment, and revival of demand cures it. The second most important truth is that reabsorption is not smooth and problem-free. The third truth is that, slow though re-employment has to be, it is not impossible, and there are many historical examples of unemployment widely called 'structural' disappearing when demand revived. These questions will resurface in many subsequent chapters including the discussion of policy in chapter 12.

Appendix A3.1 The Theoretical Debate on the Features of The Economic System that Allow the Possibility of Unemployment

The question discussed in section 3.3 is why unemployment is not quickly eliminated. This appendix discusses the prior question of how it is that the unemployment was able to arise in the first place. The question is considered here in order to make clear that it is a separate issue, and that the two should not be confused.

The discussion often takes the form of comparing the real world with an imagined perfect state in which unemployment could not arise, and asking what element is missing in the real world. This is to suppose that there could be, or at one time has been, a Golden Age which was perfect in this respect. That may seem an unreal supposition. But it is reasonable to ask whether one can point to some feature of the existing world which, if changed, would make it impossible for underemployment to arise.

Non-existence of the Great Auctioneer

Leijonhufvud (1968) attributed involuntary unemployment to the lack of the 'Walrasian auctioneer'. The trouble with this is that, even in a fantasy world, it asks so much of the Great Auctioneer. One could perhaps imagine that He would be able to move towards a set of relative prices which, given present incomes, would clear all markets for given stocks of goods, by a process of successive approximation ('tatonnement'). But that would not be enough to ensure high employment—which is not a question of relative prices. The Great Auctioneer would also have to ensure that everyone had the income he or she would have in full employment: this would require that each person believed that other people would act on the belief that each of them also had a full-employment income. To build such a mutually supporting system of interacting confidence would require not powers of rational problem-solving, but irrational powers to inspire faith.

Lack of coordination between savings and investment decisions

To have to search around for an imaginary organizational addition to existing market structures is an indication that market mechanisms are defective. But the nature of that defect is not necessarily revealed by the imaginary construction. Let us then start from another angle.

Changes in the level of underemployment occur because of changes in the level of demand. A change in the level of demand must arise from a change in the desire either to save or to invest (as usual, counting an excess of government revenue over expenditure as public-sector saving, and counting an excess of exports plus income from abroad over imports as investment abroad). If a decision to save more (or less) were always accompanied by a decision also to invest equivalently more (or less), there would never be any change in total demand or in the level of underemployment.

Absence of a barter economy

It can therefore be said that disturbances to the level of activity and employment happen only because decisions not to spend now are not accompanied by definite orders for future deliveries (Keynes 1936: 211). It could be said further that that could not happen in a barter economy, or in an economy with commodity (not credit) money;[13] for in such an economy income has to be disbursed on goods and services; and a decision to spend less on, say, nondurable goods has to result in spending more on durables, or on commodities serving as money. If it is further supposed that in such a primitive economy, from which our present economy may be supposed to have descended, *there was originally no underemployment*, then it can be said that our present underemployment has happened only because credit money has developed.

The interest rate's failure to equilibrate

Even with credit money, one can imagine conditions in which disturbances to stable employment were impossible. If (as the classical theory supposed) the rate of interest equalized *ex ante* savings and investment, then (on the same argument set out above) disturbances to total demand would not arise. It can thus be said that changes to the degree of unemployment would not occur if the rate of interest worked as the classical theory asserts.

The reason why the rate of interest does not perform this function appears to be that, within broad limits, neither decisions about how much to save nor those about how much to invest change much or quickly in response to changes in the rate of interest; the necessary equivalence between them therefore gets brought about by adjustments to income levels (Dow and Saville 1988: 44–7). The reason for the slow response of savings and investment to interest rate changes, in turn, is probably the difficulty/ impossibility of foreseeing with any precision income and claims on income over the long time-horizon that is relevant to savings and investment decisions.

The incompleteness of the existing set of markets

The same point is sometimes stated more generally: unemployment, it is said, is possible only with incomplete markets, i.e. without a complete set of futures markets (though that is a tall order, since the markets would have to operate perfectly over all future time periods to infinity). That seems unnecessarily general. If the rate of interest functioned as the classical theory asserts, nothing more would be needed.

One can say then that what the actual economy crucially lacks is a perfectly functioning mechanism for matching savings and investment, which in a very good sense can be called a perfectly functioning capital market. If that existed, changes in unemployment of the sort that are due to deficiency of demand would not occur because disturbances from the demand side would never arise.[14] It follows that unemployment arises not out of the imperfection of the labour market, but out of this more pervasive imperfection of the system.

This is an imperfection that becomes manifest only when people are given too much choice, and when they are allowed 'not to choose', i.e. are allowed to refrain from fully allocating their income in terms of real expenditure of real goods and services.

---

[13] Banks play a crucial role in, e.g., permitting an investment-led expansion or contraction. For banks [ch. 11.2] can grant credit to borrowers which when spent will be matched by deposits before those who will make the deposits have decided to make the extra savings from which the deposits will be made, or before they have even received the income out of which the saving will come (Dow and Saville 1988: 198–9).

[14] Strictly, that would not suffice to rule out the existence of unemployment: it would rule out only departures from some constant level. But if there had always been a perfectly functioning capital market, then, in the course of transition from the Golden Age (where one must presume there was no unemployment), unemployment could never have grown up along the way.

Appendix A3.2 The High Real Wage Theory of Unemployment

It is often argued that high real wages cause unemployment, and are the chief cause of the rise in unemployment during recessions. This proposition is related to the proposition discussed in the text that, had some other shock caused unemployment, a fall in wages would have made firms re-employ the unemployed; but that wages are slow to adjust. Here the proposition is that the initial cause of the unemployment was precisely a rise in real wages, which made it unprofitable to employ labour—the active version of the sticky-wages story. I dispute this proposition on theoretical and factual grounds.[15]

'Real wages' here means 'real product wages' (nominal wages divided by the price of the product that wage-earners help to produce). To simplify, we may treat factor incomes as consisting of only two types: labour incomes (here called wages), and non-labour incomes (profit and property incomes here called profits).[16] The High Real Wage (HRW) theory thus asserts that low profits ($\equiv$ high wages) cause unemployment.

Factual arguments

One measure of real wages, so defined, is simply the share of wages in national product, shown for the years 1920–89 in figure A3.1 (top curve). A second estimate of real wages is obtained by deflating employment income by the GDP deflator and detrending the resultant series (second curve).[17] Of these two series, the second is probably the less reliable, chiefly because detrending removes much of the relevant variation during recessions, i.e. at the most interesting times: in the years 1973–82 the second series is of dubious if any significance. The course of percentage unemployment since 1920 is also shown on figure A3.1.

The main changes in unemployment are seen to have taken place in a few, relatively large, short jumps—i.e. after recessions, during pre-World War II rearmament and in World War II, and in two smaller recovery phases (table A3.1). If the High Real Wage theory provided the explanation, it would require that real wages, after being very low immediately after World War I, should quickly have become high to cause the leap in unemployment in 1921, and a second leap in 1929 to produce the unemployment of the Great Depression; then to have become very low to produce the minimum unemployment of the war years, and to have stayed that way for twenty-eight years afterwards; then to have had two upward leaps to explain the rises in unemployment after 1974 and after 1980; and finally after 1985 to have fallen a bit.

---

[15] A more extended critique of the HRW theory of unemployment was given in my 1990 Keynes Lecture for the British Academy: see Dow (1990*a*, 1990*b*).

[16] Profit incomes in a narrow sense vary very much in parallel with the wider total. There is no essential difference between wages and salaries.

[17] In these estimates, 'wages' are represented by income from employment and include salaries. Profits (and factor incomes in total) are defined gross of stock appreciation (not as in the standard national accounting convention which excludes it) on the grounds that firms themselves thought (at least until recent years) chiefly in terms of their accountants' definition of trading profits, which includes stock appreciation. Most other studies follow the standard national accounts convention.

Which treatment is adopted makes a considerable difference when world prices are changing a lot: after OPEC I, and again after OPEC II, the usual treatment raises real wages by several percentage points. That matters, because these high real wages are then treated (wrongly in my view) as a cause of the unemployment that followed soon after.

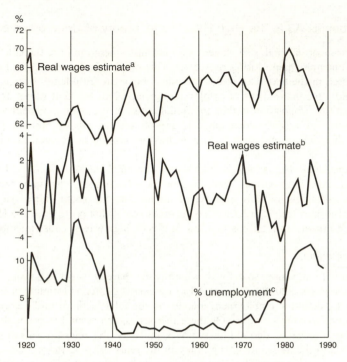

Fig. A3.1   Real wages and percentage unemployment, 1920–1989

[a] Income from employment as a % of total domestic income (including stock appreciation), excluding North Sea income.

[b] % deviation of real income per employee from trend. Average employment income is deflated by the GDP deflator adjusted to include stock appreciation in GDP and to exclude North Sea income. Trend is estimated from trend lines fitted to separate subperiods 1921–39, 1950–73, and 1982–9 (with the years 1974–81 being an interpolation between points shown for the terminal years).

[c] % unemployment, including (after 1982) numbers on government training programmes. This adjustment increases the percentage figure by 1.6 points in 1989.

Source: as for table 2.1.

Figure A3.1 shows few of these associations. Neither the 'wage' share nor detrended real 'wages' was unusually high during the interwar period or low during the war and postwar years up to 1973. It was only in the post-1973 period that the 'wage' share (though not detrended real 'wages') was above average. The impression is confirmed by the correlation results shown table A3.2. The correlation coefficients are generally small and often of the wrong (negative) sign. Only in the post-1973 period were high wages closely correlated with unemployment. (Most of the published econometric studies are about this period.)

Theoretical arguments

High Real Wage theorists usually treat real wages as exogenous, and as determined by what happens in nominal wage bargaining—whose outcome (it is implied) is dictated

Table A3.1 Major changes in unemployment, 1920–1989

Period	Length (years)	Change in % unemployment[a]	
		Increases	decreases
1920–1	2	+9	
1921–3	2		−3
1929–31	2	+8	
1933–7	4		−8
1938–41	3		−8
1974–6	2	+2	
1980–2	2	+6	
1987–9	2		$-3\frac{1}{2}$

[a] Approximate change between averages for calendar years.

Sources: Feinstein (1972) and *Economic Trends*.

Table A3.2 Simple correlation of percentage unemployment and real wages, 1920–1989

Explanatory variables lagged by (no. of years)	Sub-period/ whole period	Detrended real wage		Employment income as % of GDP		Employment income as % of adjusted final ouput[b]
		Standard definitions	Adjusted GDP[a]	Standard definitions	Adjusted GDP[a]	
0	1920–39	0.191	0.381	−0.046	0.027	0.576
	1950–73	0.233	0.188	0.391	0.203	0.157
	1973–89	−0.380	0.549	−0.340	0.226	−0.194
	1920–89	−0.325	−0.259	−0.311	−0.149	0.430
1	1921–39	−0.011	0.355	0.158	0.298	0.291
	1950–73	−0.203	−0.114	0.467	0.478	0.349
	1973–89	−0.409	0.335	0.118	0.514	0.036
	1921–89	−0.327	−0.269	−0.231	−0.014	−0.452
2	1922–39	0.120	0.458	−0.148	0.068	0.121
	1950–73	0.214	0.155	0.710	0.466	0.453
	1973–89	−0.442	0.054	0.275	0.659	0.026
	1922–89	−0.304	−0.285	0.155	0.028	−0.438

[a] Total domestic income including stock appreciation, but excluding income from North Sea oil and gas.
[b] GDP adjusted at (*a*) plus imports of goods and services.

Sources: Feinstein (1972); CSO, *Economic Trends*, 1990, and *UK National Accounts*, 1990.

by the strength of trade unions or is a compromise resulting from union–employer negotiations. But in fact, only *nominal wages* are so determined: *prices* are determined by firms alone, and on principles barely discussed by High Real Wage theorists.

The HRW argument is that, *even though demand is adequate*, labour may be unemployed because it is too expensive. I argue that it is implausible to suppose that firms are driven to sell at prices that are relatively so low that they are forced to contract their operations at a time when, by definition, demand is adequate: in such conditions, firms can and do raise prices. Nor is the argument plausible when applied to falls in unemployment.

High Real Wage theorists often go on to argue that some external event can happen that converts a given level of real wages, initially acceptable, into being 'too high'. Thus, it is argued that the rise in oil prices during OPECs I and II resulted in profits being squeezed ($\equiv$ real wages getting too high). This argument involves the idea of an 'equilibrium' level of real wages at which all labour would be employed. That idea presumably rests on the idea of a production function, and implies that the price of labour has got so high that capital is being substituted. But that kind of adjustment must be a very slow process, and can have no role in determining what happens in a recession extending over one to three years, as in table A3.1. Moreover, it cannot explain why not only labour but also capital becomes unemployed in a recession.

My reading of this evidence is that when demand falls in a recession profits fall disproportionately because productivity falls unexpectedly [s. 2.4]. The squeeze on profits must admittedly make firms all the more anxious to trim employment. But the causal sequence must be seen to start not with high wages but with low demand, as recessions have frequently resulted in a low share of profits in national income (i.e. a high share of labour incomes). They did so more particularly in the 1970s [fig. A3.1]—which was the time when the HRW explanation of unemployment resurfaced.[18]

The High Real Wage theory is perennial, and always seems to come to the fore at times of high unemployment. It was espoused for instance by Hicks (1932) and Robbins (1934); revived after the first oil shock of 1973 by Malinvaud (1977, 1980, 1984), whose work was followed by a spate of econometric studies (Bruno and Sachs 1985 and many others: for references see Dow 1990*b*). People may now have lost interest in the idea, but I suspect it will revive in the future whenever unemployment grows a lot in response to a serious lack of demand.

---

[18] Only in the post-1973 period do high real wages correlate with unemployment. Whether or not wages have a high share of national income depends chiefly on whether employment contracts when output falls [ch. 2.4]. This varies, and employment changed much more in prewar major recessions than after 1973 [table 5.7].

4 Supply and Demand Influences on the Rate of Growth

This book is mostly about demand, and how in the short term fluctuations in demand cause fluctuations in output and productivity growth. Over the longer term, major variations in growth rates have undoubtedly originated from the supply rather than the demand side. The aim of this chapter is to summarize what is known in general about variations in the rate of growth; and to argue that the kind of effects that supply-side factors have is different from what is needed to explain the abrupt short-term falls in output that occur in major recessions.

The discussion thus touches on a large subject of which knowledge is incomplete. But since its relevance is indirect, discussion can be brief and will touch only on what is essential for the present purpose. Section 4.1 summarizes what we know about variations in growth rates. Section 4.2 first gives a general explanation—eclectic but not basically novel—for the process of growth, and then goes on to offer explanations for some particular ways in which growth rates have varied since 1920. Section 4.3 summarizes conclusions.

Terminology used and the logic of the argument

The *degree of capacity working* is held to be determined by the strength of demand. The *strength of demand* is therefore seen as measured by the level of capacity working (proxied by the inverse of labour unemployment). It is thus a relative concept; i.e., it refers to the relation between actual demand and potential supply, or capacity.

In the present context, what we need to explain is not the rate of growth of output, but the rate of growth of productivity. The varying rate of growth of the working population is assumed as an approximation not to be determined by economic forces, and is taken as a datum. Where GDP growth is looked at below, it is for the light it may throw on productivity growth.[1]

4.1. Some main facts about rates of growth

This section reviews some of the main ways in which growth rates have varied.

---

[1] Ideally what we want to measure may be total factor productivity (TFP) growth; but there are problems (discussed later) about measuring that, and changes in the growth of labour productivity serves as a proxy.

4.1.1. Divergence and convergence in historical growth rates

Before the industrial revolution, growth by later standards was extremely slow; Maddison (1982: 6) suggests a growth rate (GDP per head) of 0.1 or 0.2 per cent a year as typical, compared with 1–2 per cent after the industrial revolution. Pre-industrial growth however was not negligible. In settled times and places, such as western Europe in the Middle Ages, there seem to have been long periods of fairly continuous slow growth (Persson 1988; Cipolla 1993). By the fourth quarter of the nineteenth century many countries had gone through the industrial revolution; and from then on the poorest of these (not so poor) countries began to grow more rapidly than the richer and to catch up with them.

The UK growth rate seems to have begun to accelerate rapidly about the middle of the eighteenth century,[2] and then to have grown at a new faster rate which remained fairly stable throughout the nineteenth century [table 4.1]. Output seems to have grown at 2 per cent a year or a bit more and output per head at about 1 per cent. World Wars I and II seem to have more or less

Table 4.1   UK growth rates, 1800–1995

Period	Annual % growth rates	
	GDP	GDP per worker
1800–30	2.4	1.0
1830–60	2.0	0.8
1856–73	1.9	1.0
1873–99	2.1	1.2
1899–1913	1.3	0.4
1913–24[a]	−0.4	0.0
1924–37	1.9	0.8
1937–51	2.0	1.3
1951–60	2.7	2.5
1960–73	3.2	2.9
1973–82[b]	0.1	0.7
1982–95[b]	2.5	1.9

[a] 1913 adjusted to exclude southern Ireland.
[b] Excludes output of North Sea oil and gas.

Sources: GDP: 1800–30 from Maddison (1982: 169); 1830–60 from Mitchell (1988: 837–38); employment growth rates: 1800–60 from Matthews *et al*. (1982: 25); 1856–1960 from Feinstein (1972); and 1960–95 from CSO, *UK National Accounts*, 1996.

---

[2] Matthias (1963/83), Habakkuk and Deane (1963).

stopped growth, and (more surprising) there appears to have been a serious check to growth between the turn of the century and World War I. Growth in the interwar period, while slower than later, compared favourably with this previous peacetime period (1900–14). Indeed, after World War II, despite the Great Depression, there was a resumption of something close to the nineteenth-century pace; in other words, it is 1900–14 that seems an aberration. The transitions between the interwar period and the quarter-century of fast growth after World War II, between that and the slowdown after 1973, and the renewed fast growth after 1982 are the three major variations that call for explanation here.[3]

Convergence

As many studies have shown, many of the *fairly advanced* countries have for many decades been growing faster than the *most advanced* (the leaders) and have thus been 'catching up'. This phenomenon of convergence is however an indication of how far the leaders had previously got ahead, i.e. had achieved *divergence*: convergence is not a general natural law, and the opposite tendency must historically be equally prevalent. The evidence of 'catching up' is not itself an explanation but rather a grouping of factual observations—though such grouping may provide clues as to causality.

The comprehensive survey by Baumol *et al.* (1989) quotes Maddison's figures for sixteen countries [fig. 4.1]. These illustrate the broad pattern of convergence. The data show a clear inverse correlation between (*a*) the annual rate of growth of labour productivity (GDP per man-hour) over the period 1870–1979 and (*b*) the initial (1870) level of labour productivity.

Data relating to many countries and extending over a period of a century cannot be highly reliable, but data inaccuracies can hardly account for this correlation. More important is the criticism (Romer 1986; De Long 1988) that the selection of countries is biased, since the countries were selected as *ex post* success stories.[4] The same picture however emerges from Summers and Heston's (1984) analysis of a much larger group of countries.[5] Analysis of this larger sample also shows important differences between the behaviour of different groups among them. The less developed countries as a group grew, but less rapidly than the industrial countries and thus did not converge towards

---

[3] Some readers have objected to the choice of 1982 as an illustrative year, on the grounds that 1982—unlike other years shown—marked the 'bottom' of a recession. That implies that recessions are followed by an inevitable upturn. The picture of fluctuations presented here [ss. 2.2 and 3.2] is that no upturn automatically follows a major recession (and such a subsequent upturn in fact appears rare). The choice of dates in the table therefore correctly shows that the two recessions of 1973–5 and 1979–82 depressed the rate of growth in the period 1973–82. The next period shown, 1982–95, is a mixed period of resumed growth interrupted by renewed recession.

[4] The countries chosen 'include Japan, which no one would have listed among the industrial nations a century ago, and exclude Argentina, which might well have seemed then to be among the world's most promising economies' (Baumol *et al.* 1989: 94).

[5] Summers and Heston use output growth as a proxy for productivity growth in 72 countries in the period 1950–80.

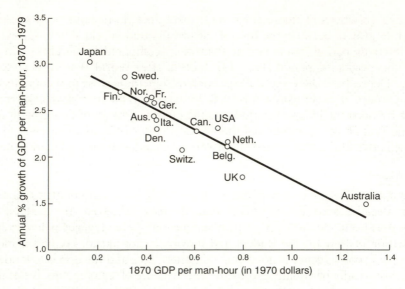

Fig. 4.1 Productivity growth, 1870–1979, as a function of 1870 productivity in sixteen OECD countries

Source: Maddison (1982: 212), used in Baumol *et al.* (1989: fig. 5.3).

them. Like the industrial countries, though not at the same rate, two other groups—the 'centrally planned' and 'intermediate' countries—showed convergence. With the important exception of the less developed countries, most countries (say Baumol *et al.* 1989) during the last century thus seem to have been members of the 'convergence club', though for some it was 'only as second- or third-class members'.[6] Baumol *et al.* sum up as follows:

For perhaps the top 15 countries convergence has been marked and unambiguous between 1950 and 1981, though there has been something of a retreat in the last few years. Taking all non-LDC countries together (48 in all), there has also been some overall convergence. However, the complete sample of 72 countries contains a number of fairly extreme deviants. Some of these are countries like Uganda and Nigeria, desperately poor nations that have fallen far behind the top group. On the other hand, countries like Japan and Taiwan, with relatively low initial economic levels and subsequent outstanding performances, are deviants in the other direction. Thus, the data are not inconsistent with the view that a convergence club of countries does indeed exist, at least in the postwar period. Use of *ex ante* samples does not undermine this conclusion. Besides that, there are some other countries that are knocking insistently at the doors of the club or have even achieved membership. But this movement is still far from universal. (Baumol *et al.* 1989: 99)

[6] The reason why less developed countries did not make the grade was probably their lack of an educated workforce. That certainly helps to explain differences in the performance of different less developed countries compared with each other (Baumol *et al.* 1989: 204–6).

A further study by Dowrick and Nguyen (1989) of OECD countries' experience since World War II adds to this picture. It is in terms of total factor productivity, not labour productivity. This seems to show that (as one might expect) some growth differences which previous studies would have described as productivity growth should be seen as the effect of high or low rates of investment. When adjustment is made for this, it is claimed that 'convergence' (of TFP) has (for this fairly small group of rich countries) proceeded very steadily.

Evidence from cross-section correlations, however, says little about the dynamics of growth or equality.[7] As already emphasized, convergence cannot be the general rule—or countries would never have become so unequally rich as they now are. The correlations in any case are not perfect, for many countries lie well above or well below a fitted regression line.[8] Moreover the most important questions are not answered. Individual countries are put into place within one system of observation; but what determines the rate of advance of the system as a whole is not explained. Why has world labour productivity grown at about 3 per cent a year on average during most of this century,[9] and not for instance at 1 per cent or 10 per cent? Growth, too, has not proceeded at an even pace: the fact that world labour productivity during the quarter-century after World War II grew at roughly double the rate before and immediately after that period is not to be explained by a hypothesis of smooth convergence.

Divergence

It is useful to look at two major cases of divergence in growth rates. The first is the UK industrial revolution, to be dated at around the middle of the eighteenth century. Until it was overtaken by the United States in the mid-nineteenth century, England was for about a century and a half the biggest industrial country [fig. 4.2]. Three groups of reasons have been suggested for why the breakthrough happened there.[10]

1. One condition was a sufficient period of political stability and order. That includes absence of destructive foreign wars, and also internal order (security of person and property, and dependable processes of law). This in turn required strong but not arbitrary central government: both the English and the Dutch (for a time their chief rival) tamed royal power early.

---

[7] As is emphasized by Quah (1993): abandoning cross-section correlations, he concludes that the growth rates of 134 countries show that the disparity between very rich and very poor countries has been widening.

[8] Which countries appear eccentric depends on the choice of countries iucluded, the period examined, the factors chosen as explanatory variables, and the statistical procedures used. On all analyses, UK performance stays poor.

[9] Maddison's (1987) figure for five major industrial countries 1913–84.

[10] See e.g. Landes (1969); Matthias (1963/83).

Figure 4.2   Cumulative country shares in output of manufactures, 1870–1989
Sources: see app. A4.1.

2. Nothing would have happened without a capable and prosperous middle class. The existence of practical-minded landowners (concerned not solely with aristocratic pomp and show but also with projects of 'improvement') and a strong merchant class deserves to rank as a second condition. Historically, a mercantile class got established through foreign trade, success in which at that time demanded naval strength, if not naval supremacy.[11]
3. A long period of prosperity had produced a wide range of manual and mechanical skills, much of it in scattered rural industry.

Other factors often mentioned as important are the existence of water power, coal and iron deposits, and a navigable river system linked by canals. Historians have scanned world history for times and places that became very prosperous and where favourable conditions existed for such an industrial revolution, yet where no take-off happened—and have found a few, such as China under the Sung dynasty (tenth to thirteenth centuries) or Tokugawa Japan (seventeenth to nineteenth centuries).[12] Adam Smith (1776) focused on

[11] Pepys's work at the Admiralty may have had macroeconomic consequences.
[12] See North and Thomas (1973); Boserup (1981); Jones (1988).

what may have been decisive: the organization in factories of hand-manufac-
turing processes, and the striking gains in productivity to be had from
machines devised to replace them.

The developments that followed from these innovations have so changed the
world that it is strange that history had to wait until the eighteenth century for
it to happen in England. It must have been something of an accident that it
did, just as there is always something essentially unexpected about a discovery.
(It perhaps follows that one cannot hope fully to explain the pace of economic
growth.) The attribution of causality in respect of a unique event in any case
can hardly be conclusive. Though it must be consistent with historians' comparative analysis, the story has to depend chiefly on deductive reasoning about
the necessary conditions.

When other countries followed, the causes were probably rather different,
since (as Schumpeter has taught us) imitating is not the same thing as innovating—so that the UK case is not a complete guide. The most striking case of
catch-up was for many decades that of Japan; and some of the reasons for it,
which have been much debated,[13] may be worth listing.

1. Much must have been due to the skills and education possessed by the
   Japanese workforce, and the mutual suitability between these and the
   technical processes available for implantation.
2. Much is usually attributed to the actions taken by Japanese governments,
   from 1850 on, to speed economic development—in the first place, for
   instance, by sending workers for training in the West and establishing
   training establishments at home.[14]
3. Many observers think that Japanese workers have liked to submerge
   themselves in group activities and in devotion to a common cause. This may
   not always help Japan to grow fast, but up to now it may have.
4. Japan's success in foreign trade in recent decades may also have helped its
   economic growth [see further s. 4.2].

The general slowdown of growth after 1973 considerably changed the ranking
of economies with respect to catch-up, including that of both Japan and the
UK [s. 4.1.3].

4.1.2. Growth rates and export performance

For the purposes of this study, an analysis was made of the growth since 1870
of production and exports of manufactures of the six main producing countries.

---

[13] Among others: Storry (1960); Shinohara (1970); Morris–Suzuki (1994).

[14] Most bureaucracies may be conservative and without commercial sense. But if a government
happens to have flair and dedication, that may surely help growth as much as a private
entrepreneur possessing these qualities.

The six were [table 4.2]: France, Germany, the UK and the USA (who were the four major manufacturing countries throughout the period), Belgium (a major manufacturer at the beginning but a minor one by the end), and Japan (which started nowhere but ended as a major producer). In the 1870s and 1880s these six countries must have accounted for most of the world output of manufactures, and even by the 1980s they still accounted for the greater part. The present estimates involved a patchwork of different statistics [app. A4.2], but while not perfectly accurate they probably indicate main trends. All three of the series shown in figure 4.3 rose manifold over these 120 years, and— with the exception of exports in the interwar years—all rose at roughly the same pace.

Figure 4.3 shows the UK's continued loss of share in this century and a quarter, both of production and (even more) of exports. In the early part of the nineteenth century, the UK must have accounted for the greater part of world manufacturing output; but as early as 1870 it accounted for only some 30 per cent of the combined total of the six countries, and by the 1980s for only some 6 per cent.

Table 4.2 Country shares in total production and export of manufactures, 1870–1988

	% of combined output for the six countries					
	Belgium	France	Germany[a]	Japan	UK	USA
Production						
1870	6.7	21.1	24.3	1.3	31.2	15.4
1900	6.0	19.9	26.6	1.7	26.5	19.4
1913	4.1	14.3	30.7	2.5	18.7	29.8
1929	4.0	13.8	26.2	4.4	16.1	35.6
1938	3.5	10.3	33.3	8.2	19.1	25.6
1950	2.9	9.9	14.9	3.3	20.0	49.0
1973	2.1	10.5	18.5	19.9	11.1	37.9
1988	1.9	9.1	16.1	22.4	8.1	42.4
Exports						
1870	9.3	15.5	18.8	0.0	53.7	2.7
1900	7.6	15.3	26.8	1.6	41.7	6.9
1913	7.6	13.3	33.2	1.5	35.4	9.0
1929	4.9	18.1	28.6	2.2	25.0	21.7
1938	4.4	14.0	25.3	8.0	25.0	23.2
1950	4.0	18.5	8.6	2.3	35.1	31.5
1973	8.2	12.2	27.4	14.6	15.5	22.0
1988	7.5	11.4	27.4	21.6	11.5	20.6

[a] West Germany after World War II.

Sources: see app. A4.2.

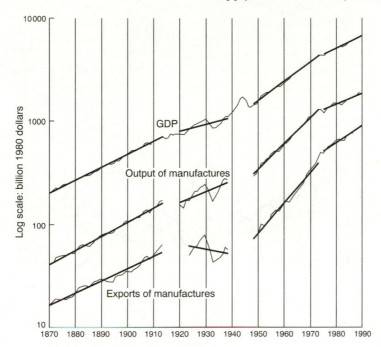

Fig. 4.3 GDP and output and exports of manufactures in six countries,[a] 1870–1989

[a] Belgium, France, Germany, Japan, UK, USA.

Sources: see app. A4.1.

As other countries industrialized in the nineteenth century, they grew more rapidly than the UK—who lost share first (before mid-century) to France and Germany, then to the United States, and, in the interwar period and much more rapidly after World War II, to Japan. Figure 4.4 is a picture of that process of displacement [see also table 4.2].[15] It shows the proportionate distribution between each of the six countries of their (growing) combined output. As will be seen, France and Germany each had 20–25 per cent of the combined total in 1870, compared with the UK's 30 per cent, and the USA's 15 per cent. In the next half-century (up to the early 1920s), the United States was the country that gained share. (World War I helped that country, as later did World War II.) Between the wars, relative positions shifted less, although

---

[15] The process was fairly steady but not quite continuous. As fig. 4.4 shows, the UK temporarily increased its share of manufacturing output through the Great Depression, because the depression in the USA was so much deeper than elsewhere. The UK again temporarily increased its share through World War II, because the war reduced output in Germany and Japan to a fraction of what it had been.

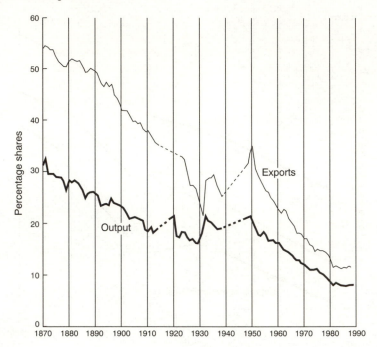

Fig. 4.4 UK shares in combined output and exports of manufactures of six countries,[a] 1870–1989

[a] Belgium, France, Germany, Japan, UK, USA.

Sources: see app. A4.1.

Germany[16] gained a bit and Japan was starting on its rise. After World War II, Japan was the star performer. Up to 1938 France consistently lost share, though more slowly than the UK; and in the great age of world growth after World War II, the United States too lost share rapidly.

What happened to shares in output was paralleled by the evolution of shares in *exports* of manufactures [table 4.2]. This is so even for the USA—where, one could think, since it is large and relatively self-contained, output and exports might well follow a separate course. (The exception is Belgium, which retained its share in export markets despite its growing insignificance as a producer.)

These statistics have a considerable descriptive interest. But any attribution of causality is inevitably speculative, and difficult or impossible to verify. There is a weak statistical relation between countries' shares of world *export* markets in manufactures and their shares of world *output* of manufactures [app. A4.2].

---

[16] The figures for Germany are throughout given a weight appropriate for West Germany, but before World War II the growth rate is for all Germany.

But that might be either because better-than-average growth performance gave a country advantages in exporting; and/or because success in exporting benefited output performance, or because both stemmed from common underlying factors. A case will be made [s. 4.2] for supposing that a country's performance as regards both export markets and shares of output is truly competitive, i.e. depends on the sort of process in which any country's success disadvantages others, and in which past relative success improves a country's chance of success in future.

My tentative belief is that in the early nineteenth century the UK's rate of productivity growth benefited from the UK having been the first to industrialize. As other European countries industrialized, the UK was for a time able to sell manufactures to a third world of countries not yet industrialized, which then industrialized in turn; the loss of privilege was thus long-drawn out. But there is more to explain than that. It is always unlikely that all countries will grow at the same rate, and it hardly requires explanation if one lags for a time. However, the UK grew more slowly than average for a century or more. It seems possible that this was in part the cumulative result of unsuccess breeding unsuccess. (In the period 1982–95, however, the UK grew almost as fast as the OECD average: see next section.)

4.1.3. Variations in growth rates after 1920

After 1920 most countries went through the same succession of growth. Table 4.3 shows the succession for the five major countries.[17] Factor input showed some of the same slow–fast–slow alternation as output, but on smaller scale. Thus, with the exception of the USA, rates of growth of total factor productivity followed the same pattern as GDP and fluctuated about as much. One reason why GDP in France, Germany, and Japan grew faster in the 1950–73 period than before or after was because of structural shifts of various sorts, such as the movement out of agriculture (column (6) in table). In four of the five countries the growth of productivity was also faster then. In the UK this can be explained as resulting from increased underemployment of capacity in the first and last periods, but not the second [ch. 2.3]. But for the three fastest-growing countries the acceleration of growth went well beyond what could be accounted for in this way: the table shows how greatly France, Germany and, even more, Japan outpaced the UK. In the slowdown after 1973, it was the three countries that had earlier accelerated most that now decelerated most.

---

[17] Comparable data for all five countries on factor input are available only for certain benchmark years. Table 4.3 regroups Maddison's categories so as to focus on total factor productivity (TFP) (which Maddison seeks to explain away). There are questions about the conventional method of estimating capital input [app. A4.1].

Table 4.3   Factor contribution to output growth in five major countries, by subperiods, 1913–1984[a]

	Contributions to annual rate of % change in GDP						
	GDP	Quantity of input		Total factor productivity	*of which* to be attributed to		
		Labour	Capital		Quality of input	Various shifts	Residual
	(1)	(2)	(3)	(4)	(5)	(6)	(7)
UK							
1913–50	1.29	−0.20	0.34	1.15	0.25	0.00	0.90
1950–73	3.02	−0.11	0.99	2.15	0.41	0.49	1.25
1973–84	1.06	−0.93	0.77	1.22	0.58	0.12	0.52
France							
1913–50	1.06	−0.67	0.31	1.42	0.81	0.13	0.48
1950–73	5.13	0.01	1.10	4.02	0.91	1.32	1.79
1973–84	2.18	−0.86	1.20	1.84	0.91	0.48	0.45
Germany							
1913–50	1.30	0.18	0.26	0.87	0.67	0.20	0.00
1950–73	5.92	−0.03	1.63	4.32	0.71	1.43	2.18
1973–84	1.68	−0.90	1.03	1.55	0.42	0.56	0.57
USA							
1913–50	2.78	0.25	0.54	1.99	0.70	0.38	0.91
1950–73	3.72	0.85	1.02	1.85	0.80	0.28	0.77
1973–84	2.32	0.95	0.85	0.52	0.79	0.02	−0.29
Japan							
1913–50	2.24	0.36	0.78	1.10	1.06	0.71	−0.67
1950–73	9.37	1.09	2.49	5.79	1.10	1.78	3.91
1973–84	3.78	0.40	2.17	1.21	0.79	0.70	−0.28

[a] In addition to the five countries shown here, Maddison includes also the Netherlands, which is here omitted. He 'explained' GDP change in terms of 17 causal factors, here rearranged. Two factors comprise the quantity of labour and capital, shown separately above; four, the quality of factor input, here shown as one group; four are grouped as 'various shifts' ('catch-up effect', 'structural effect', 'foreign trade effect', and 'economies of scale'). The residual above includes Maddison's remaining effects *plus* his unexplained residual.

Source: Maddison (1987: table 20).

Figure 4.5 roughly eliminates recession effects by simply omitting the fall in output in years of recession when calculating average growth rates.[18] When direct recession effects are eliminated in this way, growth in the UK, as we have

[18] Some readers have queried the validity of this kind of adjustment. The adjustment eliminates the effects of reduction of capacity utilization during recessions. It admittedly does not eliminate effects of above-trend growth which could follow recessions. But, on the analysis of this study, recovery effects of this sort are not automatic, and they were in fact rare.

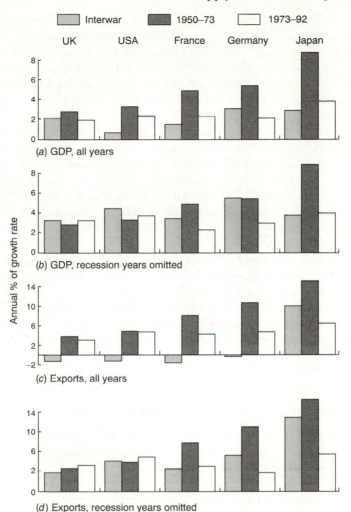

Fig. 4.5 Growth rates of output and exports: five main countries, 1920–1992

Growth rates are annual rate of growth between terminal years. The dates for the three periods varied. For 'all years', the dates for all countries for the three periods were 1920–38, 1950–73, and 1973–92. For 'recession years omitted', the dates were:

	UK	USA	France	Germany	Japan
Interwar	1921–9 &	1921–9 &	1921–9 &	1920–9 &	1920–9 &
	1932–8	1933–40	1932–8	1932–8	1932–8
Post-1973	1975–9 &	1975–9 &	1975–92	1975–9 &	1975–92
	1982–9	1982–9		1983–92	

Sources: Maddison (1991a); OECD, *Economic Outlook*.

already seen [ch. 2.3], was much the same in the Golden Age as in periods before and after. In France and Japan, however (not Germany), it remained considerably faster then. The bottom half of figure 4.5 makes the same adjustment to countries' rates of export growth. In the 1950–73 period it was the countries with fastest output growth that achieved the fastest growth of exports: indeed, the bulk of the absolute increase in world exports was then concentrated on the exports of the fast growers.

The fast output growth of these countries after World War II may have partly reflected favourable underlying supply conditions. New technical opportunities may have accumulated unused in the war years (or even before them), or conditions in these countries could have reached a stage particularly favourable for development. But this would not explain why fast growth ended abruptly, at roughly the same time in all countries. That makes it natural to see its ending as due to recession—and thus the growth before that as due in part to high world demand.

Fast growth in the world as a whole after World War II may then have created a favourable environment and greater confidence that it would continue; and that may have encouraged efforts to improve productivity. The favourable export performance of the fast growers may in turn have resulted from the high productivity increases thus achieved. This line of explanation is consonant with the earlier discussion of the relation of trade to growth [ch. 1.2] and is amplified in the following section.

4.2. Explanations of variations in the rate of growth

This section offers possible explanations for observed variations in the rate of growth, as described in the previous section. The particular features for which explanations are offered here are:

1. secular divergence and convergence as between countries in respect of levels of productivity;
2. the acceleration of growth, and the widening of the spread of national growth rates, in the Golden Age following World War II, and the reverse after it;
3. the sudden falls in output and productivity at times of major recession, and how in major recessions some potential for production appears to get destroyed.

These features tend not to emerge from the usual stylized summary of the facts of behaviour.

Much recent theorizing about the roles of supply- versus demand-side factors—or 'real' versus 'monetary' factors—in determining output growth rates starts from average behaviour over large and small fluctuations. But many of the questions we are trying to explain are about sorts of behaviour that occur only in major recessions.

The explanatory scheme here offered is not an equilibrium model in that it assumes that states of unemployment can be persistent [ch. 3.3]. The present account of the growth process is essentially Schumpeterian. It sees growth as an endogenous process though not a process with the static equilibrium-seeking character of 'endogenous growth' theory.[19] It accepts that many longer-term variations in the rate of growth of capacity originate in changes in knowledge about productive techniques, or in the availability of new techniques. It differs from Real Business Cycle theory in not assuming that such supply-side changes are the only source of variation in the rate of growth; and argues that demand conditions also affect the rate of growth by causing variations in investment. It has similarities with the 'evolutionary' theorizing (of Verspagen 1993), particularly in the attention paid to the relation between countries' output growth and export performance. For various reasons, little use was made of the two very different studies of growth by Olson (1982) and Scott (1989) [see app. A4.1].

The present section is in two parts. The first sets out a general account of the growth process; the second builds extensions to it intended to explain specific aspects (as listed above) of what seems to happen. Since the behaviour of an economy reflects the behaviour of its constituent firms, many questions can be discussed either at the micro or at the macro level; discussion here will veer from one to the other as convenient. The propositions set out below are proposed as hypotheses. There is no claim that at the end of the day we will be able to prove their validity, but only that when seen against the facts as a whole they constitute a consistent and plausible set of explanations.

4.2.1. A general account of the growth process

It is convenient to set out points as a series of numbered propositions.

P1. Growing supply creates growing demand. It has already been argued [ch. 3.2] that in a growing economy, where the productivity of the factors of production increases each year, the unit price of factors rises more (or falls less) than the price of a unit of output by the amount of the rise in output per unit of factor input. Factoral purchasing power thus rises at the same rate as the rise in productivity, which enables factors to buy their own product.

P2. The rate of growth depends on expected growth. Competition, as argued later, is imperfect, so that firms set prices. What prices they set depends on how fast they expect productivity to grow. Since administered prices are altered only at discrete intervals, they have to be fixed in the light of expectations about productivity growth.

---

[19] As in the literature following Romer (1986) and Lucas (1988), surveyed e.g. in Andersen and Moene (1993).

In the absence of disturbances, we may retain the picture of growth proceeding at a steady pace, with prices being reduced in line with productivity and real factoral purchasing power keeping pace with growth. If in a recession productivity growth is interrupted and then resumed, there are then forces that bring about a resumption of real income growth and a resumption of growing demand.

P3. The role of innovation in the process of growth.   The growth accounting approach leaves only an accidental place for innovation. Labour and capital combine in a static production function to produce output. The portion of output attributable to each factor is held to be measured by the shares of wages and profits in national income, on the rationalization that the economy is at or close to equilibrium so that the price of factors equals that of marginal productivity (Solow 1962). On this approach, output should grow in proportion to factor inputs. Growth accounting exercises always in fact show—despite numerous efforts to quantify changes in input quality, etc.—that output increases more than input, so that most growth gets attributed to this unexplained residual. The estimate of total factor productivity so obtained is then regarded as being due to exogenous technical change and represented by a constant time trend. This treatment wrongly suggests that growth just happens without human effort.

P4. Innovation requires effort.   Productivity growth requires continuing effort by management to improve products and production methods. Such improvement may well be conditional on technical discoveries, but the introduction of the resulting new methods and products still requires care and effort.

Consider the characteristics of successful development by a firm, which can take various forms: an improved product, or improved methods of production; exploitation of a new market, or new source of materials or components; or simply a new organization of a firm, or group of firms (Schumpeter 1912/1934: 66).

Development implies departure from an established pattern.[20] Since it is path-breaking, making it happen typically requires unusual qualities of energy or initiative on the part of the entrepreneur. Improvement over time of the quality of the product and of production processes depends on continuous management attention. That is likely to involve continuing installation of improved plant and machinery, and continuing adaptation of working methods (hence the training/retraining of workers, and discussion and negotiation with them), without which new equipment alone would be useless. Thus, the growth of productivity year by year is not just a time trend that goes on regardless, but happens only if managements make it happen. Even though firms typically

---

[20] 'Carrying out a new plan and acting according to a customary one are things as different as making a road and walking along it' (Schumpeter 1912/1934: 85).

implant technology developed elsewhere, transmission of that technology is not costless.[21]

P5. Successful innovation creates entrepreneurial rent. Successful innovation will put a firm ahead of its rivals, and give it a (temporary) monopolistic advantage and for a time exceptional profits (or rent). That will cause competitors to imitate its innovation, eliminating its advantage and eroding its special profitability. The process of growth thus involves a continuous opening and closing of disequilibrium positions, the first phase coinciding with the divergence of the performance from the average by firms that are in the lead, and the second phase with convergence of average performance on that of the leaders. (I discuss later divergence and convergence as between national economies.)

One implication of this analysis is that a growing economy is not an area of perfect competition. Firms are not on a level playing field, but are trying their hardest to create 'slopes' in favour of themselves, and often succeed in doing so for long periods. To stay successful, a firm must try constantly to keep ahead of its competitors and constantly to recreate its monopolistic situation.

Organization for growth requires that the different aspects of a firm's performance—product design, market development, production methods and materials and components sources, plant location and investment decisions, and labour recruitment and training—be coordinated over a horizon stretching many years ahead. In many firms, organization for growth requires management to devote most of its time to planning for the future rather than overseeing current operations.[22] The cost of organizing productivity growth is in many ways similar to investment in physical capital: it has a cost and yields a return, and the same circumstances are likely to encourage or discourage it.

This kind of entrepreneurial input will here be referred to as investment in human or intangible capital. The break-up value of a firm's assets is usually considerably less than the firm's value as a going concern. This is not only, or even mainly, due to the fact that the second-hand market in industrial and commercial equipment and buildings is imperfect; it is because the value of a firm as a going concern depends not only on the value of its physical capital, but in part also on many intangible assets—the training and habits of its workforce, and its network of contacts external to the firm with suppliers of materials and components, and with distributors, agents, or retailers involved in sales of the product and its image with the public. The difference can be regarded as representing the value of the stock of human or intangible capital

---

[21] Firms have to watch for what is suitable; and it can be held that that is an important function of firms' R&D (Cohen and Levinthal 1989).

[22] Freeman (1974: 190) finds an association between innovating firms' success and how high a status inside a firm is given to those responsible for planning.

embodied in the firm. This concept is wider than, but includes, the human capital represented by the education and training of individuals.

4.2.2. Possible explanations for particular features of growth

Set out below are possible explanations for the main ways in which growth rates between countries have varied in the past three-quarters of a century. These build on the analogy with firms' behaviour.

How growth depends on prospects of expanding demand

Under perfect competition, how much a firm invests in improvement would be independent of the level of total demand: if its product were better or cheaper than its rivals, a single firm could sell more whether or not total demand expanded. But in the conditions of imperfect competition in which most firms operate, firms are not faced with flat supply curves for labour or supplies, or with flat demand curves for products.

Innovations that increase a firm's productivity entail either an increase in output and sales, or a fall in employment.

- Under conditions of imperfect competition, firms are likely for well-known reasons to avoid an overt contest for market share, i.e. to avoid an increase in sales which can only be had at the cost of a loss of sales by others.
- If on the other hand a firm seeks to improve productivity without increasing output, it has to reduce employment, which is likely to be resisted by the workforce; this can also be costly.

Fast-growing demand is therefore likely (within a range) to encourage the introduction of innovation, and a lack of growth of demand to its postponement.

Financial link between demand and innovation

Investment in physical assets is one aspect of the general process of improving productivity; and the general reasons why capital-deepening is sensitive to demand have been set out above. In addition, there is a financial reason. In a major recession the shortfall in output is likely to be unexpected. That being so, profits suffer disproportionately [ch. 2.3]. That discourages investment in both tangible and intangible capital, and thus in effect also discourages efforts to improve productivity.

Destruction of economic potential in major recessions

There is reason to think that major recessions destroy some economic potential, and thus lower the path of productivity growth [ch. 2.2]:

- Prolonged underemployment of physical plant is likely to lead to reduced investment and premature scrapping of plant.

- Poor demand prospects will not only lead to less effort to improve products and methods, but will also cause actual deterioration of existing working arrangements. Suppliers or customers may go out of business; working practices may be disrupted, and work teams disbanded. This means that some intangible capital, built up by repeated effort in the past, is in effect destroyed; i.e., the productivity growth path is displaced downward.

A permanent loss of productivity

This loss tends in practice to be more or less permanent, because there is a limit to the scale of efforts that can be made in any period to improve productivity. This is because it requires the efforts of management, whose time and energies are finite; for management cannot be divided among additional people without cost and/or loss, and is a firm's scarcest resource. There is thus a limit to the rate of change that a management team can manage (though in time it may learn to enlarge that limit). A management team produces not a (storable) physical output but a (perishable) service, which, if not utilized in year 1, cannot be put into store and used later. If what could have been done to improve performance in year 1 goes unutilized, it cannot be replaced by greater effort in year 2, because management may then be fully stretched anyhow.

Divergence and convergence between firms

Innovations by a successful firm are imitated by others, who thereby raise themselves to the leader's previous standard. But the leader is one step ahead and can innovate further. The result may then be either convergence or further divergence; and there must be a good chance that the successful firm will at least keep up.

A successful firm enjoys five advantages:

1. Successful innovation produces profits which can be ploughed back into further investment in equipment and management input.
2. The larger scale of output may allow gains in productivity (hence power to compete) not possible without it.
3. The market for the product—especially for a new or advanced product— may be limited, leaving room for only a few firms or only one. Markets for new products of advanced design are particularly likely to be specialized and narrow markets. If a firm establishes a large share in such a market, just by so doing it puts rivals at a disadvantage.
4. Good management practices once established may put a successful firm in a better position to continue to improve its methods.
5. Success also creates a name, which attracts talented recruits and makes it easier for the firm to sell its products.

These advantages could be cumulative, helping a successful firm to keep or extend its lead. But success does not last for ever (perhaps because easy profits erode dedication, and riches soften the sinews: cf. the Yorkshire tag, 'clogs to clogs in three generations').

Divergence and convergence at the country level

Similar processes operate at the level of countries, especially with respect to export markets.[23] The following examples assume (as is realistic) that exchange rates fail to adjust immediately to equalize countries' shifting relative competitiveness.

1. Suppose that country A achieves faster productivity growth than its competitors, which leads to a reduction in the relative price of its product in export markets; or that it improves the quality of its products more rapidly than others. In either case it can increase its market share. That in turn strengthens country A's efforts back at home to improve productivity (by giving its firms greater assurance of an expanding market for their products,[24] and by providing greater profits and hence finance for development). Country A's growth rate therefore rises.
2. For 'advanced' products, world demand is limited (as argued above), perhaps leaving room for only one or few firms. A country that establishes a lead in product design may thus establish a quasi-monopoly hold on the markets for its products. Such 'advanced' products may be particularly important for productivity growth.

In each case success is cumulative; and in each case growth—like exporting—can be seen to be a competitively exclusive game. Country A would in effect be attaching to itself an undue share of the growth of world demand (and in the second case securing a disproportionate grip on the market for key products, i.e. on the sections of demand most favourable for rapid future growth).

Japan may provide an example of fast growth feeding on itself in these ways. Its fast growth went along with rapid product improvement, with cost-cheapening greater than other countries, and with a rapid growth in export sales. It seems also to have led to an increasing dominance by Japan in those product subsections of international markets where income elasticity is high, and perhaps where by now price elasticity is low, i.e. the areas with the best prospects for present profits and future growth. (The process is documented in convincing detail in Petri's (1984) study of Japanese–American trade.)

---

[23] The following arguments differ from those of Kaldor and others in the 1960s who proclaimed the benefits of export-led growth: that argument appealed to the more rapid growth of productivity in manufacturing.

[24] This argument appears in the 1960s discussion of export-led growth: see Batchelor *et al.* (1980: ch. 7).

Acceleration and deceleration most affect the fastest

The particular dependence of the fast-growing countries on international trade could explain why, when the rate of world growth rose after World War II, the growth rate of the fast-growers benefited most, and why the reverse happened after 1973 when world growth slowed.

As must be evident, the explanations offered above for countries' export performance are speculative and tentative.

4.3. Conclusions about rates of growth: supply versus demand factors as determinants of output growth

The purpose of this chapter is to suggest some conclusions about the respective roles of supply and demand factors in determining the pace of output growth. I will discuss separately:

1. causes of differences in rates of (positive) growth over extended periods;
2. causes of falls in output in general;
3. causes of falls in output experienced in particular in major recessions.

4.3.1. Differences in national growth rates

I will first discuss long-term differences as between different periods (e.g. periods of 50 or 100 years and more) in the pace of growth of output in one country, and also differences in the growth rates of different countries at any one time that persist for a decade or more.

Since the eighteenth century, there must have been a great speeding up in the pace of world growth because (*a*) more and more countries have become industrialized, and (*b*) national growth rates in many countries seem to have increased with time. There are a number of reasons why world growth has accelerated.

- The adoption of industrial techniques has made more and more of a difference to how fast industrializing countries grow. (Growth rates of 10 per cent a year or more are now relatively common but were unheard of a century ago.)
- More countries have become eligible for industralization as educational levels have risen.
- The transfer of technology has become faster with better education, greater contact between peoples, and better communications.

These are all supply-side factors, which are likely to be relatively stable, i.e. not to vary abruptly over periods of a year or two.

There are limits to the rate of growth. Countries do not grow at 100 per cent a year, but rather at most, say, 10–12 per cent. This is probably because social factors impose limits:

- Growth implies continual change not only in how workers work, but in how and where they live; there is a limit to how much change any society will tolerate, and thus on how hard people will work to produce change.
- Growth also requires investment, which (as a normal rule) firms will not be able to undertake (or be allowed by the authorities to undertake) without matching saving. That depends on the (not unlimited) willingness of individuals to abstain in the present so as to better themselves in future.

These too in a broad sense are supply factors, and are unlikely to change much over short periods.

The abrupt and widespread acceleration of growth after World War II compared with the interwar period can hardly be explained by sudden and widespread change in such supply-side factors, since these are slow-moving; nor, similarly, can the sudden and widespread deceleration of growth after 1973. These transitions however can be accounted for [ch. 2.3] by the absence of major recessions in the 1945–73 period, and their presence in the preceding and following periods. Thus, if (as here argued) those recessions were caused by lack of demand, the worldwide acceleration/deceleration of national growth rates could also be attributed to demand factors.

One further sort of growth rate variation requires explanation. When world growth accelerated in the transition to the Golden Age (1945–73), some countries accelerated much more than others; and again, when world growth decelerated after 1973, the same countries decelerated much more than others. What was true of countries' growth performance was also true of their performance in export markets.

It is here argued [s. 4.2] that success is self-reinforcing: success in exporting helps growth performance, which in turn helps export performance. The explanation for this disparity of growth performance may then be, not only that (*a*) in the Golden Age after World War II export growth (as usual) accelerated more than output growth, and vice versa in the deceleration after 1973; but also that, (*b*) growth being to some extent 'competitive', the acceleration of international trade was of special benefit to countries that were in any case set to grow fast. This explanation supposes that there are supply-side differences between countries at any time, and that these interact with demand factors.

4.3.2. Cases of falls of output

Amid the general prevalence of rising output, cases of major falls in output are quite rare. It is worth looking at some of these more broadly before looking at falls in output in recessions.

Just as there are innumerable cases where civilization advanced and brought rising output, so there are a number of major cases where the opposite happened and the deterioration in social conditions brought declines in output. Some examples are the probable decline in output in the Roman Empire during its protracted disintegration in the third century AD; the vast economic setback during the time of the Russian revolution and civil war in 1917–22, and during the revolution and political upheaval in China in the decades after 1950; the economic decay of most of sub-Saharan Africa since the 1950s with the rise of corrupt and incompetent military dictatorships; and the vast dislocation after 1989 following the collapse of the communist regimes in the ex-Soviet and satellite countries. These falls in output originated in political conditions which affected the productive capacity of the economy, and thus can be said to have come from the supply side. There have also been many cases of widespread drought. In all such cases, the cause of the fall in output was as obvious as the effect; it was the sort of thing that would get reported as fact, not supposition, in the market-place, or nowadays in newspapers or on television.

Apart from these large-scale events, the history of the UK contains some smaller cases where supplies were interrupted for short periods, resulting in falls in output. Thus, output fell at the end of World Wars I and II, in the transition from war to peacetime conditions [chs. 6.2 and 7.1]. There have also been three cases in the UK [chs. 7.1, 8.1, and 9.3] where for periods of months the supply of energy (coal) was temporarily inadequate to support output, and GDP fell (early 1947, and during the miners' strikes in early 1974 and 1984). These cases, too, can be called supply shocks; and again, it is obvious what the shocks were.

4.3.3. Supply versus demand as a cause of major recessions

The above cases differ from the falls in output experienced during major recessions. At such times all three of the following developments have to be explained:

1. The normal rise in output gives place to a fall (a shortfall typically of, say, 10 per cent).
2. Productivity also falls, but by less (a shortfall typically of, say, 5 per cent).
3. Unemployment, instead of remaining roughly constant, rises (by up to 3 or 4 percentage points).

All these changes take place abruptly, and generally extend over periods of one to three years.

One explanation commonly offered is the Real Business Cycle (RBC) approach, which holds that recessions originate in technological shocks on the supply side. This approach is motivated by a desire to find an explanation of recessions consistent with the supposition that all markets remain in continuous equilibrium (which is necessary, it is held, to provide a satisfactory micro foundation for the macro theory). For reasons already indicated, I find this approach implausible. To ordinary eyes it must surely appear perverse to seek to account for what to most people must seem an obvious market failure (viz. umemployment) by an explanation that denies *ab initio* the possibility of market failures.[25]

Another explanation—which could also be considered a supply-side one—of the rise in unemployment after 1973 is that real wages became unduly high; if this were true, it would presumably also explain (some of) the fall in output in 1973–5 and 1979–82. However, this line of explanation does not explain the coincident fall in productivity. Theoretical and empirical reasons have already been given to reject it [ch. 3.3 and app. A3.2]. No one, it seems, wants to explain the fall in unemployment into and during World War II as due to a fall in real product wages.

4.3.4. Conclusion

The conclusion I come to is that major long-term variations in the rate of growth of productivity—in the same country over time and also between countries—have probably originated (chiefly) on the supply side. On the other hand, the kind of abrupt short-term falls in output, productivity, and employment that occur in major recessions—usually in many countries simultaneously or at nearly the same time—must have originated largely or entirely from the demand side, and must occur essentially through the effect of recession on employment and on (human and physical) investment.[26]

[25] Such verification as there is for the RBC approach rests on a complex interpretation of macroeconomic time series; major recessions are not examined separately, discussion being in terms of the typical cycle. If supply interruptions had in fact been interrupting output so badly, they ought (one would have thought) to have been easily visible; but no one has pointed to any direct evidence of them. Moreover, the RBC approach has (not surprisingly) found it difficult to explain the rise in unemployment during recessions. The evidence for the approach produced to date by numerous studies thus appears to be strikingly unsupportive: see McCallum (1989), and Mullineux *et al.* (1993: ch. 2).

[26] These conclusions are based on the experience of developed countries. The experience of less developed countries also seems to support the view that sustained high demand favours productivity growth and that major recessions reduce it: see Little *et al.* (1993) and Joshi and Little (1994).

Appendix A4.1 Notes on Growth Accounting and Two Other Studies of Growth

This appendix comments on two aspects of the methodology of growth accounting, and on studies of growth by Olsen (1982) and Scott (1989).

The general methodology of growth accounting

The contribution of an increase in the input of any factor to the growth of output is conventionally measured by weighting the proportionate increase in factor input by that factor's share in GDP. That assumption is derived from the theoretical argument (Solow 1957; Denison 1967: ch. 4) that the price of each factor should correspond to its marginal productivity. The assumption is valid only on static equilibrium assumptions, i.e. if there is perfect competition and the system is in equilibrium.

That assumption (as argued in the text of this chapter) can hardly apply to a growing economy. Growth occurs unevenly as between firms; and the more innovative firms are likely (as in Schumpeter 1912) to earn abnormal profits (or rents) in the interval before other firms catch up, a process that is constantly renewed. Firms will also try to differentiate their products in more permanent ways from their rivals' so as to gain normal monopolistic profit. What national accounts record as profits thus contains three elements:

1. the pure return on the services of capital: following Böhm-Bawerk (1889), that can be regarded as the greater productivity of 'roundabout' methods of production; it would be the return to capital under perfect competition;
2. the temporary profits resulting from uneven growth (innovatory rent);
3. the monopoly profit element arising from imperfectly competitive markets.

In growth-accounting exercises the weight used to calculate the contribution of increments in the capital stock thus consists of $a+b+c$; but it should be a alone. The result is to overstate the contribution of investment to growth and to understate the size of the residual (i.e. the increase in total factor productivity) that can be taken to measure technical advance.[27]

One indicator of how greatly the use of the profit share overstates the marginal product of capital is the spread between the realized rate of return on capital and the rate of interest.[28] On that basis, use of the total profit share could possibly overstate even by as much as a factor of four.[29] It is certainly consistent with what one commonly observes, that the more innovative and successful firms do a good deal better than their less successful rivals.

---

[27] This bias is recognized by Denison (1967: 35) in respect of monopoly profits, but is not treated as of much importance. Monopoly profits are however probably less important than innovatory rent. Monopoly profits are to some extent matched by monopoly elements in the wages of some categories of labour.

[28] As Denison (1967: 35n) also notes. The rate of interest on the safest sorts of financial assets must approximate the pure return on the services of capital.

[29] In the UK in the postwar era the real return on capital, though varying considerably, seems to have averaged about 8% (Matthews *et al.* 1982: table 6.1.6; and after 1973 *BEQB* 1988: 381). The return on long-dated government bonds in real terms has also varied greatly, but for the period 1962–92 it averaged under 2%. The *ex post* return on capital indicated above is however gross of depreciation.

To illustrate the possible distortion table A4.1 takes a less extreme assumption, namely that the share of capital in factor rewards overstates its contribution to growth by a factor of 2, and reworks a typical growth-accounting estimation with weights adjusted accordingly. Estimates for five major countries for most of this century are

Table A4.1 Adjusted estimates of productivity growth: five major countries, 1913–1984

	Contributions to annual % output growth				
	Total factor productivity				Labour productivity[c]
	As estimated by Maddison[a]	Adjustments[b]		Adjusted for A and B	
		A	B		
	(1)	(2)	(3)	(4)	(5)
France					
1913–50	1.42	0.30	ng[d]	1.72	2.0
1950–73	4.02	0.55	ng	4.57	5.1
1973–84	1.84	0.78	0.09	2.71	3.4
Germany					
1913–50	0.87	0.08	ng	0.95	1.0
1950–73	4.32	0.91	ng	5.13	6.0
1973–84	1.45	0.71	0.08	2.34	3.0
UK					
1913–50	1.15	0.21	ng	1.36	1.6
1950–73	2.15	0.51	ng	2.66	3.2
1973–84	1.22	0.49	0.12	1.83	2.4
USA					
1913–50	1.99	0.22	ng	2.21	2.4
1950–73	1.85	0.33	ng	2.18	2.25
1973–84	0.52	0.23	0.03	0.78	1.0
Japan					
1913–50	1.00	0.29	ng	1.39	1.7
1950–73	5.79	1.02	ng	6.81	7.7
1973–84	1.11	1.00	0.06	2.27	3.2

[a] From Maddison (1987: table 20): equals growth of output *less* input of labour and capital, *without* Maddison's allowance for quality changes.
[b] Adjustment A gives capital input a weight of 0.15 instead of 0.30, and labour input a weight of 0.85 instead of 0.70. Adjustment B is a rough adjustment for the unemployment of capital, and equals the effect of reducing the PIM estimate of the growth of the capital stock in proportion to the growth in % unemployment of labour, *times* the weight given to capital input in calculating its contribution to output (0.15). This adjustment is shown for the third period only on the grounds that, taking the other periods as a whole, variations in unemployment in earlier periods were less serious.
[c] From Maddison (1987: table 2).
[d] ng = negligible.
Source: Maddison (1987).

conveniently collated in Maddison (1987).[30] They show [table A4.1] the speed-up in the growth of total factor productivity after World War II (1951–73) compared with the interwar period (represented by 1913–50); and the decline after 1973 (1973–84) to something closer to the interwar rate. If the contribution of capital input to growth is overstated by a factor of 2, the implied growth of total factor productivity will have been understated—in most cases by under 1 per cent a year, but in the case of postwar Japan by as much as 2 per cent a year. The effect of the adjustment is to move estimated total productivity growth halfway to the estimate of labour productivity (shown in column (5) of the table). Though the broad ranking of countries, and of the same country in different periods, remains the same, the detail is significantly different. These figures are presented not as better alternative estimates, but to illustrate the possible scale of error. They certainly provide grounds for not treating the results of growth-accounting exercises as completely accurate.

The table also illustrates the effect of another, smaller, source of error. Growth-accounting allows for underemployment of labour but usually not for the capital stock being at times underemployed.[31] In a recession, growth-accounting using unadjusted perpetual inventory method (PIM) estimates therefore overstates the contribution of capital input (and again understates the residual). Table A4.1 assumes as a rough approximation that underemployment of capital equals that of labour,[32] and suggests that the error is negligible.

The significance of the 'residual'

Growth accountants tend to regard the residual in their estimates of sources of growth as a sign of failure of their endeavour. This bias leads them to try to estimate the scale of factor quality enhancements, which can then be treated as an additional input, thus reducing the unexplained residual. It seems often to be assumed that extension of this procedure would eliminate any element of residual and enable output growth to be completely explained.

There are however two arguments against this. First, the estimation of quality change is inexact and incomplete. For instance, labour productivity probably benefits as much from learning at work (where the benefit can hardly be measured) as from learning in formal education (for which years of education is only a very rough measure). Nor are data on the rent of different types and vintages of capital adequate.

Second, and more serious, the residual should not be seen as an error. One should expect innovating entrepreneurs to earn a rent over and above the value of bought inputs; the residual is a measure of the scale of innovation that is taking place—and perhaps the most interesting result of the calculation.

---

[30] Maddison (1987) includes in addition the Netherlands, here omitted. His figures are based (along with other sources listed) on national studies; three for the USA, by Kendrick (1961, 1973), Denison (1962, 1974, 1979, 1985), and Gollop and Jorgenson (1980) respectively; Carré *et al.* (1972) for France; Ohkawa and Rosovsky (1973) for Japan; Matthews *et al.* (1982) for the UK.

[31] Denison (1974: 66–7) however makes broad adjustment for underemployment of capital.

[32] In the UK in the period after 1973 part of the capital stock also was retired prematurely. Thus, part of the capital stock as given by PIM estimates will not only have been put out of use but put out of existence. Estimates of the scale of scrapping vary widely. Smith (1987) estimates that the size of the capital stock, as estimated officially by the PIM procedure in branches other than government, agriculture and housing, was as much as 25% too high in 1983. Wadhwani and Wall (1986) put the error at about 4% in 1982.

In so far as the value of factor quality enhancement is 'embodied' in the factors as bought and sold, a portion of total factor productivity growth will be reflected in an increase in the market price of factors. Estimates of quality enhancement give a rough measure of how much of productivity growth is taking that form. But the degree to which that happens, or to which it can be measured, is fairly arbitrary.[33] Growth-accounting exercises are however probably correct in showing that technical progress (as measured by the residual) rather than investment usually explains most of growth, and also explains most of the variations in growth between countries and over time [as e.g. in table 4.3].

Most economic significance therefore attaches to the rise in total factor productivity as a whole, without subtraction of that portion which can be roughly identified as factor quality enhancement. Though changes in the quality of inputs have some interest, it seems preferable, when presenting the main results, to focus attention on technical progress as a whole, and therefore to measure factor inputs in the first instance without quality adjustment.

Comments on Olson (1982) and Scott (1989)

The present account, for reasons indicated below, draws little on the two (very different) studies of economic growth by Olson (1982) and Scott (1989).

Olson explains variations in the rate of growth as varying inversely with the power of special interest groups, on the grounds that when strong they obstruct the process of growth. I am persuaded that the mediaeval guilds and caste restrictions in India, for instance, must have played an important negative role. Olson, however, treats them as a brake which slows down or releases an unvarying and constant propulsive force; he neglects (in my view unconvincingly) all other factors that have been held to explain why growth rates differ. I have already argued [s. 3.3] that variations in unemployment are not due to rigidities in wage rates—which Olson sees as one effect of the kind of restrictive arrangements he is concerned with, and to which he (naively I think) attributes unemployment.

Scott's study, like the present account, attributes a large role to investment in human capital. But he includes under this heading only investment embodied in personal skills and not, as here, intangible investment by firms in their working arrangements and their relationships with other firms. More generally, his procedures jettison the production function as a basis for estimation of the contributions to growth of different factors of production. That seems to me a major loss, since it deprives estimation of its underlying theoretical rationale. Empirical fitting without this constraint leads him to ascribe all variation on growth rates to variation in investment and 'quality-adjusted' employment, so that nothing is left over for the usual growth-accounting 'residual'; that, and the concept of total factor productivity, Scott rejects as meaningless. On my interpretation (in the previous subsection), the residual is seen as the semi-monopolistic reward for innovation. Scott's account assumes perfect competition, and also is directed to the long-term; i.e., he explicitly abstracts from what happens in large recessions, which is here the main interest.

---

[33] The proportion of growth explained or left unexplained varies from study to study depending on the methods used, and on how much is attributed to improvement in the quality of factors. The very detailed study of the postwar USA by Jorgenson *et al.* (1989) seeks to explain the growth of output gross of intermediate input separately for 51 sectors. Special care was devoted to estimation of the quality change of capital input. Mainly for this reason, the contribution of the latter was increased somewhat as compared with previous studies; as a result, the residual was reduced to 32% of total growth, compared with 42% in Denison (1967).

Appendix A4.2 Estimates of the Growth of Six Countries' Output and Exports of Manufactures, 1870–1970

This appendix details the sources for the estimates in section 4.1 of six countries' GDP, gross value added in manufacturing, and exports of manufactures 1870–1970.

Sources of data

Data for most tables and charts are for Belgium, France, Germany, Japan, the UK, and the USA. For continuity, German series for years before World War II have a weight appropriate to West Germany only.

Indices of GDP in constant prices in figure 4.2 are from Maddison (1982, 1989) and OECD *National Accounts* except for France 1870–1900, which is from Toutain (1987). To obtain values in 1980 international dollars, all series were linked to 1980 values of gross value added in US dollars from Maddison (1989).

Output of manufactures given in table 4.2 and figures 4.2–4.4 is from UN *Yearbook of Industrial Statistics*, the UN *Growth of World Industry*, and the UN *Monthly Bulletin of Statistics*, with the following exceptions: *Belgium*: 1870 and 1880–1900 from Hilgerdt (1945), 1870–80 interpolated, 1900–57 from Carbonelle (1959); *Germany*: 1870–1959 from Hoffmann (1965), pre- and post-World War II series being linked using data for 1936 and 1950 from *Statistisches Jarhbuch für die BRD*, 1932; *France*: 1870–1968 from Toutain (1987); *Japan*: 1874–1938 from Shinohara (1972), 1938–85 from *Historical Statistics of Japan*, 1987; *UK*: 1870–1970 from Feinstein (1972) and CSO *Economic Trends*; *USA*: 1870–1980 from *Historical Statistics of the United States*, 1976. To obtain values at 1980 US dollars, all series were linked to 1980 values in US dollars from *World Tables*, 1990.

The aggregates for exports of manufactures (as shown in the same table and charts) are new estimates compiled from numerous detailed sources by Pierre van der Eng: all are at constant prices. To obtain them, current value series obtained as below were deflated by average value series for the countries concerned or (if that was not available) by a world deflator. For 1870–1913 this deflator was the index of unit values of UK exports of manufactures; for 1913–32, a geometric average of the indices of the unit values of UK and US exports of manufactures; and for 1932–50, the index of unit values of US exports of manufactures. (Estimates of the deflators were obtained from Schlote (1952), and CSO *Statistical Abstract* and *Historical Statistics of the United States*, 1976.)

The current value series were taken from the following sources. *Belgian data* for 1870–1913 were interpolated quinquennial indices from Capelle (1938); for the 1913–27 series in current prices from *Annuaire Statistique de la Belgique*, deflated by the world deflator; for 1927–68 from *Bulletin de l'Institut de Recherches Economique à Louvain*. *German data* for 1870–1960 were from Hoffmann (1965); and for 1961–7 from *Bevölkerung und Wirtschaft*, 1972. For *France*, series in current prices for 1870–1913 were from *Annuaire Statistique de la France*, 1922, deflated by the world deflator; and for 1913 and 1919–68 from *Annuaire Statistique de la France*. For *Japan*, data for 1893–1913 were from *Historical Statistics of Japan*, 1987, deflated by the world deflator; data for 1905–50 were calculated from Ohkawa and Rosovsky (1973); and for 1950–68 were from the *Japan Statistical Yearbook*. For *UK*, data for 1870–1932 were from Schlote (1952); for the 1932–47 series in current prices from Mitchell (1988) deflated by the world deflator; and for 1947–68 also from Mitchell (1988). *US data* for 1873–78 were from Hilgerdt (1945) interpolated; and for 1878–1968 were from *Historical Statistics of the United States*, 1976. To obtain values at 1980 US dollars, all these series were linked to the exports of manufactures for 1968–88 in 1980 US dollars from *World Tables*, 1990.

Additional data on the relation between the growth of output and exports

Table A4.2 reports a test of the relationship between increases in output and exports of manufactures for a wider group of nine countries (the original six plus Italy, Canada, and Sweden). Errors may have arisen because the data for output and exports were derived from different sources, and the methods of deflation were approximate.

Table A4.2   Relation between increases of output and of exports of manufactures: nine countries by subperiods, 1973–1988

Values for R^2

Separate subperiods, all countries	(1)	Individual countries, all subperiods	(2)
1873–83	0.06	UK	0.09
1883–93	0.78	France	0.48
1893–99	0.01	Germany	0.63[a]
1899–1913	0.03	USA	0.47
1913–23	0.05	Japan	0.65
1923–29	0.02	Belgium	0.47
1929–37	0.77	Sweden	0.16
1937–50	0.73[b]	Canada	0.06
1950–55	0.36	Italy	0.32
1955–65	0.57	UK, Germany, USA and	
1965–73	0.01	Japan all periods	
1973–79	0.04	combined:	0.58[c]
1979–83	0.08	All countries,	
1982–88	0.80	all periods	
		combined:	0.40[d]

[a] Excluding 1937–50, $R^2 = 0.57$.
[b] Excluding Germany, $R^2 = 0.63$.
[c] Excluding Germany 1937–50, $R^2 = 0.56$.
[d] Excluding Germany 1937–50, $R^2 = 0.38$.

Sources: For six countries (Belgium, France, Germany, Japan, UK, USA), the sources are as detailed above. For *Sweden*: output is from Hilgerdt (1945) and Mitchell (1975); exports from Hilgerdt (1945) and *Statistisk Arsbok*, linked with Maizels (1963: 481). For *Canada*: output is from Hilgerdt (1945), Mitchell (1983), and UN, *Yearbook of Industrial Statistics*; exports 1870–68 series in current prices from Urquhart and Buckley (1965), *Bank of Canada Statistical Summary Supplement*, 1964, and *Canadian Statistical Review, Historical Summary*, 1970, deflated for 1870–1926 by world deflator and 1926–68 by 30 Industrial Materials Price Index for Canada. For *Italy*: output is from Ercolani (1969), Mitchell (1975), and UN, *Yearbook of Industrial Statistics*; exports from Hilgerdt (1945) and *Annuario Statistico Italiano*.

The correlations were calculated not for annual changes but for changes of output and export volume over fourteen periods of varying length averaging eight years. There is a degree of association between changes in shares in output and exports respectively, but the correlation was often low.

For the whole sample, with all countries and all periods combined, the correlation was only 0.4; but it was higher for some individual countries or some periods. Thus, if one takes only the four countries that were the main actors throughout (UK, USA, Germany, and Japan) the correlation was notably higher (0.6). If one takes all periods combined (column (2)), the correlation was low for some individual countries, but for five of them (and those were the fastest growing) the correlation was near 0.5 or above. Taking all countries combined, and looking at separate subperiods (column (1)), the correlation on average was low, but it was high in five of the fourteen periods (often periods of fast growth). There is thus evidence of some correlation between growth and export performance.

5 Shocks and Responses in Major Fluctuations

This chapter discusses how the economy behaves in the course of major fluctuations. The detailed case studies of individual major recessions in part II [chs. 6–9] have suggested extensions to the standard account of the economy's response to shocks. These are expounded in section 5.1, which thus completes the theoretical introduction to the case studies provided by part I. Section 5.2 is primarily empirical, and tests statistical indicators of some main types of shock. Section 5.3 uses this material to give a summary characterization of big and small fluctuations.

5.1. The economy's response to shocks

Two interpretations have been dominant in the discussion of business cycles— or, as I would say, economic fluctuations—over the past fifty or sixty years. The first (the older view) is of self-driven, self-perpetuating, and thus *endogenous* cycles.[1] The second view (more common at least until the 1980s) is of an economy responding to shocks coming from outside, so that fluctuations are produced by *exogenous* forces.[2] The present account is nearer to the second of these versions, but gives more emphasis to swings of confidence as a mechanism that propagates the impact of shocks (and at times may provide the initial impulse). All these accounts assume that output fluctuations are driven by fluctuations in demand, a view that was justified in chapter 4.

5.1.1. The elements of the model

A model describes the interrelations between different parts of the economy included in the model. Exogenous shocks are unexpected changes affecting elements included in the model but originating from outside it. This study is about the UK economy; thus, exogenous shocks here mean changes coming either from the rest of the world or from alterations in the policy of the UK authorities.

The analysis is directed primarily at explanation of the five major recessions since 1920 [ch. 2.2], and of the four main phases of above-trend growth that

---

[1] This was the view of business cycle theorists of the 1940s and 1950s, e.g. Samuelson (1939), Kalecki (1937*b*), Kaldor (1940), Hicks (1950). In more recent times most economists appear to take the view that 'periodicity does not occur' (Blanchard and Fischer 1989: 277). A case however can be made for a halfway view, as in Britton (1986*a*). Many features of reality could also be explained by nonlinearities, now being given increased emphasis.

[2] See Frisch (1933); Slutsky (1937).

came between major recessions. Comparisons are also made with the minor fluctuations of the period 1945–73. Big recessions have varied greatly, and each has been different. This section looks in turn at (*a*) the reaction to a shock of consumers, (*b*) the reaction of business, and (*c*) the reaction of the whole system.

(a) The reaction of consumers' expenditure to a shock

The standard multiplier analysis makes consumer spending dependent on income, but incorporates psychological factors by making spending depend also on expectations of future income. The aim of this section is to get some idea of how greatly consumer spending is liable to be affected by expectational or confidence factors in the course of a major recession.

Standard multiplier analysis incorporates such factors by making consumers' spending depend not just on past income, but on expectations of future income (such expectations themselves perhaps being held to be dependent on past income). Let

$DGDP_1$ = the initial shock, i.e. change in GDP in period 1
$DGDPE_1$ = the change in expected income induced as a result in period 1
DCE_1 = the change in consumer spending (measured by the domestic factor cost component) induced in period 1 by $DGDPE_1$[3]

A shock will then be followed by the following sequence

$$DGDP_1 \rightarrow DGDPE_1 \rightarrow DCE_1$$

$$\rightarrow DGDP_2 \rightarrow DGDPE_2 \rightarrow DCE_2, \text{ etc.}$$

Let c, the *marginal consumption ratio*, $= DCE_1/DGDP_1$ in period 1, so that

$$1/(1-c) = \text{the multiplier.}$$

Take as a starting point a formulation in which the marginal consumption ratio is determined by a constant marginal propensity to consume out of income, operating with a constant lag; and consider the effect of varying these assumptions in three ways.

1. The extent to which a shock to income will be amplified will vary according to what is expected to follow. If consumers expect that after a fall the initial level of income will be restored quickly, their expenditure will respond little to the fall. If they firmly expect the fall to be permanent, expenditure will fall in proportion to income (i.e., the marginal propensity will equal the average). The UK average propensity in the 1970s and 1980s was of the order of 0.9. On this reasoning then, the marginal propensity can vary between zero (in a recession expected to be very transitory) and close to unity

---

[3] Measurement at domestic factor costs here excludes the tax component and the import content included in consumer spending at market prices. That is convenient in summing the total contribution to domestic product of the amplified sequence.

(e.g. up to 0.9 if the fall in income is expected to be permanent); according to the expected permanence of the shock, the multiplier could thus vary between 0 and 10. Expectations are more likely to be disproportionately affected by a big shock than a small one, which must be one reason why big recessions are big.

2. A large recession may reduce consumers' lifetime income expectations; the change in planned saving will then be more radical. If it lowers the *rate of increase* of expected income over their lifetime, that (as can shown) could increase saving in the early years, i.e. could reduce spending by more than income has fallen.

3. Consumers are likely to reduce spending *in anticipation* of any fall in income; i.e., the lags between the fall in income and the fall in spending may be reduced. Collectively, their lower spending will further reduce the income of each, which also may be anticipated: if many lags are concertina'd, there is no limit to the size and speed of the reaction.

The algebraic sequence set out above suggests an orderly process through time. But *a*, *b*, and *c* between them transform that process into something much less stately. Multiplication no longer proceeds in an orderly manner on a scale dependent on a multiplier that varies somewhat, but not much, in the course of the multiplication—in which case the process might run for some time, e.g. years. Rather, the scale of amplification gathers strength as the process proceeds, and lags are truncated, so that the process may become almost instantaneous. This fact of great volatility is not adequately described by calling the multiplier 'unstable'. To mark this volatility, the multiplier will usually here be referred to instead as the *consumption amplifier* (in parallel with what will later be called the *investment amplifier*).

To describe events in terms of changing income expectations may also over-intellectualize reality. Typically, agents do not have clear expectations about their future income—nor even about their length of life. For this reason, vaguer terms are more appropriate, to indicate that it is more a matter of 'feeling optimistic', or the reverse, than of any quantifiable changes in expectation. Hence I prefer to speak not of changes in income expectations but of changes in *consumer confidence* (similarly, later, *business confidence*).

Autonomous changes in expectations treated as an endogenous disturbance   In the account so far, changes in expectations or in confidence have been treated as a response to present change in real income. But confidence can also develop a life of its own, in which the present state of confidence is a function of how it has changed in the past. In a speculative boom, confidence for a while gets continuously enlarged; then at some point the boom bursts, and confidence gets continuously deflated.

This sequence, once started, follows its internal law of development, and so could be called endogenous. But history suggests that a boom is likely originally to have been started by an exogenous shock, and is not a self-generating train of events following an inevitable course (as in the theoretical concept of an endogenous business cycle). For that reason, it is regarded here as exogenous.

The role of debt in economic fluctuations Debt often has attributed to it a species of disembodied independent power. Thus, it is sometimes argued that high debt acquired in a boom becomes a negative force when the boom is over and is thus a *cause* of subsequent recession—a process that is therefore often described as 'debt deflation'. This idea is largely false; and it is worth a digression to show why.

One needs to look at the sequence as a whole, i.e. at the process of both debt creation (in a boom) and debt repayment (in or after a recession). A pattern of lifetime expenditure in which consumers save in working life to spend in retirement does not require that they borrow; and a change in the lifetime pattern that reduces current spending is clearly possible without resort to borrowing. Nevertheless, many consumers do borrow and save at the same time.[4] The ability to borrow may be essential to a downward adjustment of saving desired as a result of a favourable shift in income expectations; and the scale on which credit is available may constrain the scale of adjustment. If a consumer can borrow, he will then go further than he could without borrowing towards the pattern of lifetime spending that he now (with greater optimism) prefers.[5] *But the greater borrowing is due to the greater optimism*: the ability to borrow only enables the desire to spend more (as the result of greater confidence) to be expressed more fully.

In a recession the reverse adjustment occurs: income falls (or ceases to expand so rapidly), and prospects now appear less favourable. Consumers therefore prefer to spend less than when they were optimistic. If debt was incurred in order to move to the spending pattern appropriate to favourable prospects, the size of the debt will appear a 'burden' when recession comes; and some of it will be repaid. The reason why debt is now perceived as a burden and some is repaid is solely that prospects have worsened: were prospects to revert to appearing as favourable as before, the debt would again cease to seem a burden, and would become what consumers willingly chose as a means to achieve their preferred spending pattern. The greater the increase in debt in the upward direction, the greater also the adjustment that consumers make when prospects worsen: but the change in expectations is the operative force.

---

[4] They do so for two main reasons: (1) to buy a durable good (including a house or flat) which yields services over several years and whose services cannot (advantageously) be hired (e.g. for a rent) as they arise; and (2) to maintain contractual savings arrangements (payments for pensions or life insurance) which they wish to maintain because of tax privileges or other reasons, but which exceed what they wish to save.

[5] That is the general effect of financial deregulation [ch. 9].

(b) *The reactions of investment to a shock*

Accelerator theory builds on the theorem that greater output typically requires greater fixed capital capacity, and its simplest version requires the rates of growth of capital and output to tend to equality. But that relation holds only in equilibrium; and if for any reason (recession, war, other change in the rate of growth) the capital stock is distant from what that relation would posit, it can take many years of adjustment to get near it. Meanwhile, investment reacts to new shocks, so that in the short term it varies with output (i.e. not as under the accelerator, where it is the *level* of capital that varies with output). I discuss fixed investment first and investment in stocks (inventory changes) later.

The statistics indicate little short-term equality between the rates of growth of capital and output: that is so whether attention is concentrated on total fixed investment or (as in the accompanying tables and charts) on non-residential investment (which might be expected to bear a closer relation to output than investment in dwellings). In the interwar period the UK capital stock grew only half as quickly as GDP [table 5.1 and fig. 5.1]. Since World War II capital has grown rather faster than output, both before and after 1973. This presumably was because capital depleted in the war was being replaced (which took a long time), and because the growth of the capital stock was being adjusted to the faster postwar rate of output growth. Had the growth of output continued at 3 per cent a year instead of falling away after 1973, the arrears of adjustment might well in time have been worked through and the growth of the capital stock probably would have slowed down—perhaps to about 3 per cent a year, in line with the growth of output.

In major recessions, the rate of growth of the capital stock falls off, but the response to the fall in output is usually muted. The capital stock as usually

Table 5.1 Rates of growth of capital and output in interwar and postwar years

| | | % annual rates of change | |
		Gross capital stock[a]	GDP
Interwar			
Pre-recession	1923–9	1.2	2.4
Post-recession	1929–38	1.2	1.9
Postwar			
Pre-recession	1960–73	4.2	3.2
Post-recession	1973–88	2.2	1.7

[a] Excludes dwellings.

Source: Feinstein (1972) and CSO, various issues.

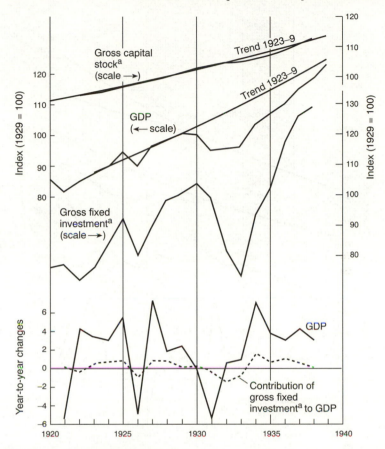

Fig. 5.1 Gross non-residential capital stock, GDP, and gross fixed non-residential investment in the UK, 1920–1939

[a] Excludes dwellings.

Source: Feinstein (1972).

measured[6] continued to grow throughout even the largest of the UK recessions [figs. 5.1 and 5.2], and even if allowance is made for premature scrapping of equipment it can hardly have undergone much decline.[7] Since gross investment is small in relation to gross capital stock (e.g. 1 : 20), even sizeable reductions in investment affect the size of the stock only slowly.

---

[6] I.e. by the perpetual inventory method (PIM): see later discussion [ch. 9] of premature scrapping in the aftermath of the 1979–82 recession.

[7] Only in the extreme case of the Great Depression in the USA do capital and output growth appear to have run parallel. Before the Depression the capital stock had grown strongly; then, over the decade 1929–39, there was no increase at all in the estimated capital stock, or in output, which by 1939 had barely regained its 1929 level.

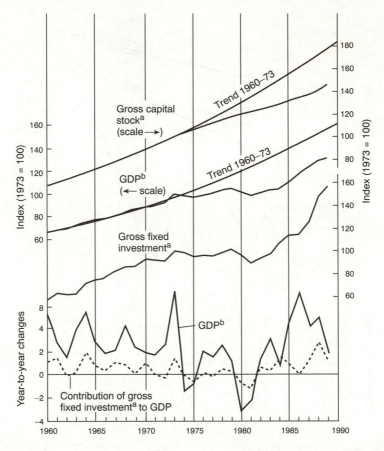

Fig. 5.2 Gross non-residential capital stock, GDP, and gross fixed non-residential investment in the UK, 1960–1989

[a] Excludes dwellings and capital stock of mineral oil and natural gas industry.
[b] Excludes North Sea oil.

Source: CSO, *National Income and Expenditure*, various years; *UK National Accounts*, 1990.

Changes in investment, by contrast, are fairly closely related to changes in output in large fluctuations. In all major recessions but recession I [table 5.9], there was a fall-off in fixed investment below its trend rate; similarly, investment growth was above trend in all four phases of above-trend output growth [table 5.11].

There are two reasons for this short-term relationship.

1. Firms plan to increase capital stock only if they expect that it will be reasonably fully employed, so that, if they start near capacity working, they

will aim to increase capital in line with expected output. What output firms expect is much influenced by current output.

2. Firms' investment is in many cases limited by finance, and both inside finance (profits) and the availability of outside finance (borrowing) vary in the short term with output.

In the aggregate firms' sales vary closely with GDP (even though those of individual firms may not), so that the aggregate of firms' expectations about their sales implies a collective view about GDP here called *business confidence*. When output rises (falls) in relation to trend, confidence is likely to strengthen (weaken). As confidence improves and firms foresee higher demand, some or all firms (depending on how fully employed they are to start with) will raise investment to meet demand. As confidence weakens, firms will reduce investment.

Confidence factors are reinforced by financial factors. Profits suffer in a recession, first because employment is not cut as much as output, so that labour productivity fluctuates procyclically, and second because, since these fluctuations are unexpected, output is underpriced in recessions, which depletes profits [s. 2.4]. Both factors reduce firms' internal finance. Availability of external finance[8] is also reduced: the finance that lenders (either banks, or via the stock exchange) are willing to make available to a firm depends on its expected profits (hence on present profits). The availability of finance thus varies with the rate of growth of output, reinforcing confidence factors.

We may define the *marginal investment ratio* (n) analogously to the marginal consumption ratio. Where

DN_1 = the induced change in investment (again measured at domestic factor cost) in period 1

and, as before,

$DGDP_1$ = the initial shock to GDP and

$DGDPE_1$ = the change induced as a result in expected future GDP,

then $n = DN_1/DGDP_1$ in period 1. There will be a similar sequence as with consumption:

$$DGDP_1 \rightarrow DGDPE_1 \rightarrow DN_1$$

$$\rightarrow DGDP_2 \rightarrow DGDPE_2 \rightarrow DN_2, \text{ etc.}$$

[8] Outside finance consists of equities or debt. Since managements fear takeovers, firms have become reluctant (at least in the UK) to reduce dividends when profits fall. In recent years dividends have thus become more like a fixed charge, so that the distinction between debt and equities has been eroded. For present purposes we may ignore the difference and talk simply of outside finance, referring to all outside finance as debt or borrowing. Borrowing is limited also by what the firm itself judges prudent: that too depends on its profits, since dependency on outside finance increases the risk of insolvency: see Kalecki (1937*a*: 95).

In precise analogy with the multiplier or consumption amplifier we may define the *investment amplifier* as

$$1/(1-n).$$

Since a shock may at times affect confidence little and at other times much, the size of the investment amplifier (like the consumption amplifier) must vary greatly, and at some points in major recessions is likely to be large, i.e. up to several times unity. Consumption and investment amplifiers are likely to operate at the same time and reinforce each other.

An account of fluctuations must clearly take account of the relation between investment and output changes. Most accounts, focusing on the accelerator, do not. Allowing for it does not mean that the accelerator relation is superseded. Investment is a function not only of output change, but of the relation of current plus past investment (=capital) to output. Thus, demand in the post-1945 Golden Age was fed by high investment, resulting both from the low stock of capital after the war, and from the optimism engendered by continuing growth [ch. 7].

The reaction to shocks of investment in stocks   It is unclear on theoretical grounds whether stock changes in general reduce or amplify the amplitude of output fluctuations (see Blanchard and Fischer 1989: s. 6.4). Consider two possibilities:

1. If fluctuations in sales are unexpected, and output can be adjusted only with delay, fluctuations in sales will be met out of stock; i.e., inventory holdings will function like a buffer stock. That seems most likely to be the case when fluctuations are small and frequent, in which case firms are likely to expect a steady underlying trend in sales and plan for it, so that on average output remains close to the trend of sales.
2. Alternatively, stock changes could be perversely timed so that additions to (subtractions from) stocks coincide with high (low) sales. In a large recession, for instance, firms may at first avoid output changes by running up stocks; but then after a while they will be forced to correct the stock build-up and to contract output more than sales, thereby increasing the scale of fluctuation.

Whether stock changes are stabilizing or not may, then, depend on the situation and the period considered.

The facts seem partially to confirm these suppositions. Table 5.2 gives results of a first analysis. It looks at all years in the period 1920–90, and reports the effects of stock change on the steadiness of output. For each of the three main sub-periods since 1920, the standard deviation from trend of total final sales (sales to final purchasers) was compared with the standard deviation from trend of total final expenditure (expenditure inclusive of changes in stocks). The inclusion of stock changes somewhat *increased* the degree of fluctuation in

Table 5.2 Additional fluctuation resulting from stock changes, by three sub-periods, 1920–1990

Sub-period	% of trend value of TFS of TFE		
	Standard deviation from own trend of:		Additional fluctuation due to changes in stocks
	Total final sales (1)	Total final expenditure[a] (2)	(3)=(2)−(1)
1920–39	3.49	3.99	0.50
1950–70	2.49	2.55	0.06
1970–90	4.38	4.68	0.30

[a] Total final sales *plus* changes in stocks *equals* total final expenditure.

Source of basic data: as for table 2.1.

periods 1920–39 and 1970–90, but on this showing left it practically unchanged in the period 1950–70 (when growth was relatively steady).

The effect of stock changes is probably better judged by looking not at single years, but at phases (runs of years) identified as fluctuations. In almost all such phases, the effect was destabilizing. Thus, stock changes contributed to almost all recessions, big or small, and to all cases of above-trend growth [tables 5.3, 5.9, and 5.11; also 7.6 and 7.7].[9] The conclusion is that in fluctuations stock changes have added to output instability. Thus, if stock changes are included along with fixed investment in the investment propensity, the value of *n* is raised somewhat.

The 'burden' of debt   Debt-deflationists (Fisher 1933; Minsky 1982*a*, 1986) argue that firms' debt is a cause of recession. As so phrased, that proposition is not correct. As in the case of consumers, recession is caused by a change in the outlook as perceived by firms, and by their response to the change. But (again as with consumers) the larger the extension of borrowing in the preceding expansionary phase, the larger is the cutback when prospects worsen. Firms however are more exposed to debt problems than consumers, because more of their expenditure is financed by outside finance, and because firms cannot immediately adjust either fixed investment or investment in stocks when recession starts, and have inevitably to continue for a while to borrow. Thus, in a recession, firms that have borrowed are left with high debt-servicing charges.

---

[9] There are some side-effects, not taken account of in the tables, which might partially offset the direct effects; e.g., a stock decline in a recession sets free finance, the lack of which would otherwise have compelled a cut in fixed investment, and a rise in stocks in a recovery diverts finance which would otherwise have been available for fixed investment. But these offsets are likely to be only partial.

Table 5.3 Components of shortfall of expenditure in five major recessions, 1920–1993

Categories of expenditure	Contribution to % change in TFE	Contributions to shortfall of TFE from previous trend during recessions[a]					
	Contributions to annual average % rate of growth 1960–73	I 1920–21	II 1929–32	III 1973–75	IV 1979–82	V 1989–93	Average of 5 recessions
Consumer expenditure	1.4	5.5	2.7	3.8	3.4	5.0	4.1
Government[b]	0.4	0.0	0.0	-0.4	0.0	0.6	0.0
Exports	0.8	3.7	6.4	0.8	3.7	0.5	3.0
Fixed investment	0.7	-0.4	2.7	2.1	3.7	3.1	2.3
Changes in stocks	0.1	0.3	0.8	2.9	4.2	0.7	1.8
Total final expenditure (TFE)	3.5	9.3	13.1	9.6	14.8	9.9	11.3
% shortfall from trend in GDP	3.2	8.2	11.9	8.0	12.6	11.3	10.4

[a] For dating of turning points and estimation methods, see ch. 2.1.
[b] Government current expenditure on goods and services.

That forces them to cut spending (and thus worsen the recession) more than they otherwise would.

Firms differ: while some will have borrowed to invest, others will have met investment from their own resources. Those that borrowed will have increased their gearing and raised the ratio of (fixed) debt servicing charge to (fluctuating) profit, and hence will be more exposed to the risk of further unfavourable events. For these reasons, firms that have borrowed will contract investment more than non-borrowing firms in response to an identical series of demand fluctuations.

We need then to distinguish carefully. Greater access to borrowing is likely to worsen fluctuations. But the role is permissive: debt itself does not cause fluctuations. High debt amplifies the power that a weakening of confidence in any case has to reduce investment and output; but it does not give debt an independent power to depress spending, as some debt-deflationists have claimed.

The behaviour of the system

Consumers' behaviour and firms' investment behaviour together determine the economy's response to shocks, and go far to determine macro fluctuations.

I have defined the consumers' marginal expenditure ratio (c) and marginal investment ratio (n) as the change in consumption and investment respectively induced by a change in GDP. Each implies that a shock to GDP will be amplified. I have defined the *consumption amplifier* as $1/(1-c)$, and the *investment amplifier* as $1/(1-n)$. The *combined amplifier* is $1/(1-c-n)$.

How large might that be? I have argued that, if a reduction of income reduces expected income a lot, then the marginal consumption ratio can for a short while become very high (perhaps even exceeding unity). The investment ratio is also likely to vary in the course of a recession and at some points to become fairly high, especially with investment in stocks included. The combined multiplier could then for short periods become infinite; i.e., a shock could become explosive upward or implosive downward. The impact of any shock depends crucially on how consumers and firms react to it. If they treat a shock as trivial and transitory, its effects will be trivial; if it alters their view of prospects radically, its effects will also be radical.

One cannot, then, adequately analyse fluctuations, and big fluctuations in particular, without bringing into the discussion changes in psychological states (e.g. 'confidence'); nor can one hope to explain them fully by a system of explanation couched solely in terms of measurable magnitudes (e.g. items of national expenditure) and with constant relationships between them.

One implication is that one should not be surprised when [as in s. 5.2] measures of exogenous shocks fail to give a complete explanation of recessions. An unexplained residual may indicate not error in measuring shocks, but the fact that shocks were not the only factors at work and that there had been a change in psychology.

Nor should one expect all fluctuations to be the same. Recessions and recoveries appear to differ. Major recessions are marked by a sudden break in confidence, followed by a slower and more gradual return to greater confidence. This kind of behaviour is perhaps a way of dealing with a world in which future uncertainties are largely unknowable; where action, as Keynes said, is undertaken only under the impulse of animal spirits, not following exact calculation; and where a fright causes a collapse of courage that only time can gradually restore.

It also seems likely that confidence will be affected disproportionately in a large recession compared with a small one. But, just as mini-recessions leave confidence largely intact, so large ones (short of the US mega-recession of 1929) may leave confidence partially intact. On this view, one could see a recession as usually contained within certain limits, i.e. so that it would come to an end of itself. Even at the bottom of a recession, there may be a residual optimism that the recession will not go on for ever, so that at some point hope will prevail over deepening gloom. That alone would explain the fact that recessions occur only within certain limits. It remains possible that fluctuations are also kept within bounds by such limiting factors as the trade-cycle theorists of the 1940s and 1950s thought it necessary to posit (Matthews 1959: 16–18). Following their lead, three reasons for there being a ceiling seem possible:

1. Output reaches the capacity ceiling: output increases cease to be above normal, and optimism ceases to grow.
2. Near the capacity ceiling inflation accelerates, and the authorities intervene to reduce demand.
3. Agents anticipate that one of the above will happen so that near the ceiling fast growth ceases to produce greater optimism and starts to produce greater caution.

Similarly, possible reasons for there being a floor might be that it becomes more difficult at some point to cut spending further, e.g. gross fixed investment reaches zero; or stocks get exiguous; or consumers face increasing hardship. Deepening pessimism may thus at some point begin to fail to produce lower spending.

In this study I am concerned chiefly with the origin of recession or recovery, and do not attempt an integrated theory of growth and fluctuations as a whole. Consequently I do not need to come to a definite view about the possibilities sketched above.

It is interesting to speculate how far the nature of fluctuations may have changed over the last century or so. In the three-quarters of a century covered by this study, there have been enormous changes in the structure and environment of the UK economy. It is a question whether they have made the economy more or less prone to fluctuations. Real income and wealth have both risen fourfold or more; and with this, the share of saving and investment has doubled. The UK no longer trades chiefly with countries dependent on commodities but more with manufacturing Europe. Trade still fluctuates, but perhaps less so. Firms have got larger, probably more oligopolistic, and more prone to setting prices—which (whatever classicists may say) could make for a sort of stability. At the same time, transport and communications have improved vastly, so that a national economy is more of a single entity, and is quicker to react, and thus perhaps more sensitive to shocks. It is hard to say on general grounds which way the balance lies; and there have been too few big recessions to enable us to judge the trend.

5.2. Indicators of demand shocks and tests of their ability to explain fluctuations

This section first discusses the difficulties in the way of measuring shocks; then describes the statistical indicators here used to represent the main types of shock; it goes on to test those indicators' ability to explain fluctuations.

5.2.1. The difficulties of measuring shocks

There are difficulties of many sorts in the way of measuring shocks, and it is ambitious to try to devise statistical measures of them. The claim here is that rough indicators can be constructed that are better than nothing.

The most fundamental difficulties arise from theoretical disagreement about the way the economy works. An extreme classical theoretical view can suggest that an unexpected event sets up offsetting reactions and that these offsets operate quickly, in which case the economy is not disturbed by the event. If that were so, it would be purposeless to try to measure the impact. A case in point is the doctrine of Ricardian equivalence, which denies to fiscal changes the power to disturb demand. There has been much discussion in particular of the admissibility of indicators of the impact of fiscal policy. To some extent, similar questions apply to the other shock indicators shown here. The issues are discussed in the appendix to this chapter.

An idealizing approach to the economy may also suggest that economic agents fully foresee future developments, so that no events are unexpected, and for this reason too the economy is not disturbed. A general answer to extreme idealizing views is that the economy does in fact at times follow an erratic course, and that the most plausible explanation is that unexpected events cause divergence. The present exercise assumes not that events are completely unexpected, but that they are partially unexpected and that the extent to which they are unexpected is fairly constant.

Fundamental theoretical questions aside, there are formidable difficulties in the way of devising statistical measures of shocks as initiating events. Any unforeseen event must be supposed to set off a series of adjustments, and some of these adjustments can be supposed to be relatively rapid, i.e. to be completed within a year or two; these will often have the effect of removing or reducing traces of the original disturbance. One has to measure the force of an unforeseen event by *ex post* measures of magnitudes, e.g. changes in a given expenditure component between two dates which may, as in this study, be two calendar years. Such an indicator is likely to provide only a blurred index of the *ex ante* forces at work.

In addition to these basic underlying points, there were the usual difficulties that dog any empirical exercise.

1. For some kinds of shock it did not seem possible to devise any statistical measure (e.g. measures of 'real' interest rates seem especially difficult: see below).
2. Some relationships assumed to be stable may in fact be erratic, or at least nonlinear (e.g. where trigger-points are involved).
3. In testing the effect of shocks thus crudely measured, lagged relationships have in practice to be represented very crudely.

The present approach has been to test whether the (highly imperfect) indicators here devised have explanatory power. Given the difficulties and crudities involved, it would not be surprising if they did not. But in fact (as will be shown), they appear to be explanatory. Note that all the difficulties listed above apply not only to the above exercise, but to any econometric estimation aimed at explaining events in terms of reactions to shocks, i.e. most econometric models.

5.2.2. Description of indicators of shocks and amplifiers

The indicators of exogenous shocks initially included five sorts of event (of which one, and one variant, were subsequently dropped):

1. changes in *fiscal policy* (*FP*);
2. changes in both nominal and real short-term interest rates representing changes in *monetary policy* (*MP*);
3. changes in *export volume* (*EX*);
4. changes in the *terms of trade* (*TOT*), seen as having a short-term impact on the purchasing power of domestic factor incomes;
5. changes in *stock appreciation* (*SA*) or inventory profits, a variable originally included since it affects the availability of finance for investment.

The statistical definitions of the five shock measures are set out in table 5.4. They purport to measure only 'first-round' effects; i.e., they do not allow for amplifier effects (whose scale is assumed to vary according to circumstances: see s. 5.1). Except for *MP*, the statistical definitions are so chosen that the scale of the effect indicates the expected percentage effect on GDP; e.g., when the indicator reads 0.5 it is expected to add 0.5 per cent to GNP.[10]

---

[10] The correlation exercises (presented below) rarely show exactly this expected effect. In the case of the monetary policy variable (*MP*), the scale represents the cause and not the effect, i.e. the change in percentage interest rates.

Table 5.4 Statistical definition of indicators of exogenous shocks

Contributions to % change in GDP[a]

Dependent variable	
DGDP:	% change in GDP(A) *less* trend growth rate[b] of GDP in subperiod
Explanatory variables (all with expected positive sign)	
EX	Change in export volume *less* trend change in exports in subperiod, all as % of GDP in previous year
FP	Change in fiscal policy (see text); includes effect of all general government expenditure, current and capital, but not investment of public corporations: revenue items weighted to represent effect on private expenditure
MP	Change in short-term interest rates (Bank rate, MLR, and, after 1981, banks' base rates), multiplied by (-1).
TOT	Effects on the purchasing power of domestic factor income over final output, calculated as $TOT=(\dot{P}_{GDP}-\dot{P}_{TFE})$, the difference between inflation rates of GDP deflator and TFE deflator.
SA	Change in scale of stock appreciation: annual change in stock appreciation/GDP at current prices, multiplied by (-1).

[a] All explanatory variables except *MP* are defined in such a way as to provide a measure of their contributions to % change in GDP allowing for import leakage.
[b] As estimated in ch. 2.

Real interest rates were subsequently omitted because of the evident unreliability of the estimates.[11] That seemed to require the omission also of stock appreciation, for the following reason. On the initial treatment price changes were credited with two opposite effects: one working via interest rates as above (where a rise in prices had a positive impact on demand), and the other via stock appreciation (where a rise increased stock appreciation and had a negative impact). Inclusion of only one of these effects would have created a bias. Since the first effect via interest rates was being excluded, it seemed necessary also to drop the second (opposing) effect via stock appreciation.

Notes on individual indicators

1. Fiscal policy effects have been represented in many previous studies by the change in the cyclically adjusted budget balance. The present estimates [app. A5] obviate the need for cyclical adjustment by defining expansionary

[11] Estimates of real interest-rate changes were obtained by deflating nominal rates by lagged and current price changes. The sign, and size, of estimated real interest changes however depended critically on the lags assumed.

(contractionary) tax policy as a fall (rise) in the ratio of tax revenue to GDP,[12] and expansionary (contractionary) expenditure policy as a rise (fall) in the ratio of expenditure to (GDP *less* trend). More precisely, the impact of changes in fiscal policy is measured as:

change in the share in real GDP of general government real expenditure on goods and services

less change in the share of current-price GDP of taxes

plus change in share of current-price GDP of transfers, grants, and subsidies including debt interest.

The estimates are for general government (i.e. central *plus* local) and include all government expenditure (i.e. current *plus* capital).[13] No adjustment is made for inflation [for justification see app. A5]. Different weights were given to different items of the budget according to their assumed impact on private spending.

2. The impact of *monetary policy* was (as noted) measured by changes in short-term nominal interest rates, not by changes in the rate of growth of one or more monetary aggregates [for reasons see s. 3.1].

3. Changes in UK export volume are taken to measure the combined impact on UK GDP of changes in (i) world demand and (ii) UK competitiveness. Competitiveness is assumed to vary in the short term chiefly with the effective nominal exchange rate, here regarded as exogenous.[14]

4. Short-term changes in the *terms of trade* originate chiefly from changes in world commodity prices (which for a single country are exogenous). A rise in commodity prices raises import prices (and hence final prices), while home factor incomes are much affected only later, so that changes in the terms of trade affect domestic real purchasing power, and are here treated as a demand shock. The effect is measured here by the difference between the change in the GDP deflator (which reflects changes in nominal factor incomes) and the final expenditure deflator (which includes the cost of imports).[15] This effect is implicit in most econometric models.

---

[12] When incomes are rising, fixed progressive tax rates raise the ratio of direct tax to income. Failure to reduce tax rates to offset such fiscal drag is here treated as an increase in the rate of tax.

[13] Estimates including current expenditure only were also made [table A5.2]. An additional variant including investment by public corporations is not reported since its inclusion made little difference to the estimate of fiscal impact.

[14] An important omission is that the explanatory scheme does not include the effect of the exchange rate on import volume. Another defect is that the effect attributed to interest rates will include any effect on exports coming from the exchange rate. That is a defect because it results in double-counting, since exports are already included as an exogenous factor.

[15] By the 1980s the UK had become self-sufficient in oil, which altered the content of imports. Adjustments were made here to allow for this. By 1980 much of the oil consumed in Britain came from the North Sea. But the rise in its price (which followed the world price) at the time of OPEC II (1979) continued to have effects similar to those from OPEC I (1973) when the oil still came from OPEC. Most of the profits earned by North Sea companies was appropriated by the UK government as taxes, and, given the prevalent philosophy of fiscal policy, one can assume that there was no consequent increase in government spending. In OPEC II the extra saving was thus done not as in OPEC I by OPEC governments but by the UK government. To put the two cases

Notes on indicators of confidence effects

1. Changes in the *ratio of consumer spending to GDP* were used to measure changes in the consumption multiplier. The ratio will be affected by changes in consumer confidence as one factor among others.[16] Changes in the ratio for whatever reason will change total demand.

   2. Changes in the *ratio of non-residential investment to GDP* were used as a partial measure of changes in business confidence.[17]

   3. Changes in the *ratio of investment in stocks to GDP* were also included as an amplifying factor. The generation of stock changes is complex, but whatever their origin they too influence demand.

Changes in these ratio do not result only from changes in confidence. But changes in confidence must work by changing these ratios; all may represent endogenous mechanisms which amplify the effects of exogenous shocks; and they appear in fact to help to explain fluctuations.

5.2.3. Tests of the explanatory power of the shock indicators

Testing the explanatory power of the shock indicators was carried out in two stages.

1. First, tests were made of the ability of annual changes in the indicators to explain annual changes in GDP. The results [table 5.5] showed that statistically significant correlations could be obtained even on that crude test.
2. These results were used in the second stage, which took changes over the phase (usually of two to three years) of recessions or fast-growth phases, and compared the estimated impact on GDP of the changes in all shock indicators with the actual change in GDP over each phase. An analysis [table 5.6] was made of three types of episode, i.e. the five *major recessions*; the four *periods of above-trend growth*; and the fast and slow phases of the *'mini-cycles'* that occurred in the period of relatively steady growth in 1950–72.

Explanation of annual changes in GDP

Annual changes in each of the shock indicators [fig. 5.3] were correlated with annual changes in GDP. The results showed that GDP changes cannot be explained in terms of any single variable; but, taken together, three variables (*EX, FP,* and *MP*) explained 50–80 per cent of the annual variation in GDP in each subperiod.

---

on an equal footing, North Sea output was excluded from UK mainland output and treated as 'imports from the North Sea'. The rise in world oil prices in OPEC II was thus treated as causing a deterioration in the terms of trade in the same way as in OPEC I.

   [16] The personal saving ratio appears to reflect not only changes in confidence, but also at times the desire to rebuild stocks of financial assets eroded by inflation.

   [17] Changes in the ratio will also be affected by changes in profits and the availability of outside finance, and by tax and interest rate changes.

Table 5.5   Explanation of annual changes in GDP: regression results[a]

Period	$\bar{R}^2$	EX	FP	FP_{-1}	MP_{-1}	TOT	TOT_{-1}	SA
(a) 'Theoretical' values of parameters[b]								
I 1920–41		1.0	0.67	0.33	(1.0)	—	1.0	—
II 1948–73		1.0	—	1.0	(1.0)	—	1.0	—
III 1973–89		1.0	—	1.0	(1.0)	1.0	—	—
(b) Estimated coefficients obtained by correlation								
I 1920–41	0.78	2.11	0.35	0.18	—	—	—	—
II 1948–73	0.51	1.74	—	0.17	0.76	—	0.44	—
III 1973–89	0.59	2.33	—	0.81	0.43	0.90	—	—
All periods								
1920–89	0.66	1.92	0.41	0.09	0.44	—	—	0.36

[a] The equation estimated was of the form $DGDP = a + bEx + cFP + dFP_{-1} + EMP_{-1} + fTOT + gTOT_{-1} + hSA$, with terms defined as in table 5.4.
[b] The value shown for *MP* is a fairly arbitrary assumption.
Source of basic data: as for table 2.1.

Table 5.5 shows (part *b*) the correlations and the values for the parameters as estimated by the preferred equations. The table also shows (part *a*) the values of the parameters theoretically to be expected, given the definition adopted for each indicator [table 5.4]. As will be seen:

- the values of the parameters as estimated vary considerably from subperiod to subperiod, as might be expected, given the paucity of data;[18]
- they also depart considerably from the size of effect that each variable (given the way it is defined) might be expected to have. Thus, the estimated parameter for exports (part (*b*) of the table) is twice what might be expected (part (*a*)), and the other parameters are roughly half. The latter is explicable given that lagged effects (which must be important) must go largely undetected by the necessarily crude methods used. The large parameter for exports must be suspect.[19]

In the case of *MP*, no theoretically expected value is available, since this shock indicator is not (like the others) defined in terms of national accounts magnitudes. The value given in the table is a rough estimate (see note to table), as are the estimated effects of monetary policy in later tables.

---

[18] The three subperiods contained 22, 26, and 17 annual observations. There was high covariance in some subperiods between *EX* and *TOT*, *TOT* and *SA*, and *EX* and *SA*; and at times some explanatory variables showed little variance.

[19] If the parameter is indeed too large, it must be reflecting the effect of some additional variable; e.g., exports might have special effects on confidence. International correlation between fluctuations in different countries would make it likely that exports would vary with GDP, but would not produce a large parameter for the effect that export fluctuations had on GDP.

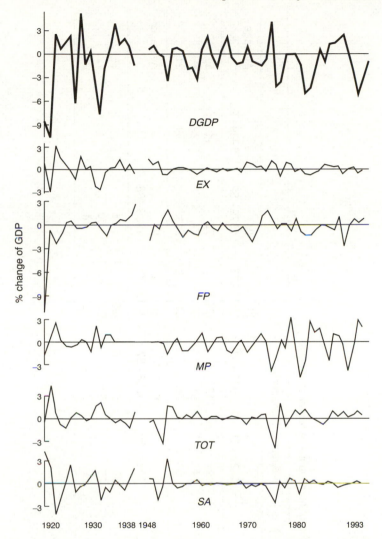

Fig. 5.3 Fluctuations in GDP and indicators of five shocks in the UK, 1920–1993
Except for *MP*, shock indicators show expected contribution to % change in GDP.

The results of this stage are nevertheless relatively encouraging. Most estimated coefficients are right-signed and of the broad order expected. Taken
together, they give surprisingly strong confirmation of the hypothesis that shocks
are a main cause of fluctuations. Particular estimates need to be treated with
caution, but they appear good enough to be used in stage 2 of the tests. Given
the unreliability of the empirically estimated parameters, the 'theoretical' values
of the parameters (here called method AA and shown in part (*a*)) were accepted

Table 5.6 Explanation of fluctuations in terms of shocks

	Measure of accuracy[a]					
5 major recessions	I 1920–21	II 1929–32	III 1973–75	IV 1979–82	V 1989–93	Average
Shocks, method AA[c]	89	12	[96][b]	76	–23	52
Shocks, method BB[d]	84	91	69	74	[–22][b]	59
Change in S/I ratios[e]	5	38	21	21	69	31
4 main phases of above-trend growth	I 1922–25	II 1933–37	III 1972–73	IV 1985–88		Average
Shocks, method AA[c]	36	56	[96][b]	85		68
Shocks, method BB[d]	75	68	63	80		72
Change in S/I ratios[e]	62	37	2	–14		21

Table 5.6 (Continued)

Measure of accuracy[a]

Mini-cycles, 5 slow phases	I 1950–52	II 1955–58	III 1960–62	IV 1964–67	V 1968–72	Average
Shocks, method AA[c]	[40][b]	89	83	[41][b]	33	57
Shocks, method BB[d]	66	63	97	88	–33	56
Change in S/I ratios[e]	6	6	–36	–41	50	–3

Mini-cycles, 4 fast phases	I 1952–55	II 1958–60	III 1962–64	IV 1967–68	Average
Shocks, method AA[c]	[26][b]	46	43	[82][b]	36
Shocks, method BB[d]	55	37	28	30	37
Change in S/I ratios[e]	107	–43	36	–58	11

[a] The measure of accuracy equals $100 \times$ (actual change in GDP *less* error in predicting GDP)/actual change in GDP, where error = |actual *less* prediction|.

[b] Occasions when the accuracy measure differs from the proportion explained (i.e. when the latter exceeds unity).

[c] Method AA is estimated from actual changes in shock indicators *times* 'theoretical' value of shock effect.

[d] Method BB derives scale of effects by use of regression coefficients as estimated in table 5.4.

[e] See fn. *d* to table 5.7.

Source of basic data: as for table 2.1.

as the more reliable and were used in subsequent calculations; but the empirically derived results (method BB) will also be shown.

Tests of ability to explain GDP changes over fluctuation-phases

The shock indicators were next used to explain changes in GDP over the five phases of major recession, for the four chief phases of above-trend growth, and for the 'up' and 'down' phases of the mini-cycles of 1950–73. The explicatory power of changes in the three investment–savings ratios was also tested. Table 5.6 shows the sum of the effects so estimated together with the GDP changes which it is hoped they will explain (i.e. the cumulative deviation, over each slow-growth or fast-growth phase, of GDP from trend).

The summary results [table 5.7] suggest that exogenous shocks explain half of the average major recession, and two-thirds of the average major

Table 5.7   Explanation of fluctuations in terms of shocks: summary

	Measure of accuracy[a]		
	Completeness of explanation[a] provided by shock indicators		Extra explanation from changes in savings/ investment ratios[d]
	Method AA using 'theoretical' value of parameters[b] (1)	Method BB using estimated value of parameters[c] (2)	(3)
5 major recessions	52	59	31
4 chief growth phases	68	70	21
5 mini-recessions[b,c]	57	56	−3
4 mini-recoveries[d,c]	36	37	11

For more detail see table 5.6.

[a] The measure of accuracy equals 100 × (actual change in GDP *less* error in predicting GDP)/actual change in GDP where error = (actual *less* prediction). The measure differs from the proportion explained only when the latter exceeds unity.
[b] Method AA is estimated from actual changes in shock indicators *times* 'theoretical' value of shock effect, expressed as % of (change in GDP excluding North Sea oil *less* GDP trend).
[c] Method BB derives scale of effects as in estimated regression coefficients (table 5.5).
[d] Additional effect of changes in saving/investment ratios, i.e. change in ratio of personal savings to GDP, non-residential investment to GDP, and investment in stocks to GDP. The figure shown represents the degree of explanation additional to that shown in column (1). It is net of the *TOT* effect included in column (1) because changes in *TOT* are likely, *ceteris paribus*, to cause either changes in the ratio of personal savings to GDP, or changes in the ratio of non-residential investment to GDP: inclusion of *TOT* would therefore be likely to result in double counting.

Source of basic data: as for table 2.1.

fast-growth phase.[20] Considering the incomplete nature of the indicators, that is a good deal. If we include also the explanatory power of changes in the three saving–investment ratios, 80–90 per cent of major fluctuations appear, on average, to be explained in these terms. The mini-recessions of 1950–73 were about as well explained as major recessions by the shock indicators (though changes in the saving–investment ratios were of no help). The mini-recoveries of the 1950–72 period were less well explained.

Averages however can mislead: results vary greatly from case to case [table 5.6]. Three of the major recessions appear largely explicable, but one (recession V) cannot be explained in these terms, and the Great Recession (recession II) is not well explained. This patchy performance could provoke the conclusion that this method of explanation is unreliable. An alternative view is that this is not a measurement failure, but the truth—that recessions varied greatly, and that some were caused not by shocks but by changes in consumer and business confidence of a sort that we are unable to measure well. On the latter view (which I prefer), some trust can be placed on the shock indicators.

If this is accepted, the evidence of the shock indicators, as far as it goes, supports the following hypotheses: that shocks occur (i.e. that events are partially unexpected), and can be roughly measured; that fluctuations are to be explained in terms of demand rather than supply factors; and that they are largely due to exogenous shocks and not endogenous self-perpetuating cycles.

5.3. The causation of fluctuations: a first survey

This section provides a first survey of the causation of fluctuations. Table 5.8 compares the average characteristics of major recessions and other types of fluctuations, big and small.[21] Major recessions lasted on average about as long as smaller ones (two to three years); the difference lay only in their amplitude. Major recessions showed an average deviation from trend of over 10 per cent. That is double the scale of the four main phases of fast growth (5.5 per cent), itself almost double that of the average mini-cycle (3 per cent).

1. *Scale of shock*   One reason why big recessions were big may be that (to judge by measures of shocks here used) the exogenous shocks that produced them were rather bigger; but the evidence is not clear-cut since individual cases differ so much.

2. *Types of shock*   In all cases both external shocks and policy changes were important; and the policy changes went in the same direction as external shocks and thus reinforced them. In upward phases (big and small), external shocks outweighed domestic policy effects; but in downward phases policy influences

---

[20] Tables 5.6 and 5.7 employ a 'measure of accuracy' defined in the footnotes to the tables. On this measure, great over-explanation of GDP change is counted not as a very good, but as a very poor, result.

[21] The table includes only those phases where growth is reckoned to be markedly above or below trend. Such phases include two-thirds of all peacetime years in the period 1920–95.

Table 5.8 Characteristics of different types of fluctuations

	Mini-cycles (1950–72)		Maxi-fluctuations (1920–38; 1972–93)	
	4 fast phases	5 slow phases	4 fast phases	5 major recessions
Average duration of phase (years)	2.0	2.8	2.8	2.6
Height/depth of boom or recession (%)[a]	2.4	–3.8	5.6	–10.9
Reflected in change in[b]				
Productivity	2.1	–2.1	1.9	–3.5
% unemployment	–0.3	0.6	–3.1	5.3
Unemployment reaction[c]	(13)	(16)	(55)	(51)
Estimated effect of shocks[d]				
Exports (EX)	0.1	–0.7	1.4	–2.2
Terms of trade (TOT)	1.4	–0.4	1.0	1.2
Monetary policy (MP)	(0.6)	(–1.3)	(0.8)	(–2.6)
Fiscal policy (FP)	0.1	–1.4	0.9	–1.3
Total exogenous shocks[e]	2.2	–3.8	4.1	–3.9
Selected expenditure items[f]				
Consumer spending	1.1	–1.5	1.7	–4.4
Fixed investment	1.3	0.1	1.7	–1.7
Stock change	1.0	0.6	1.9	–1.0
Total final expenditure[g]	3.5	–2.2	6.1	–10.1

Averages for each type of fluctuation. Details for individual recessions and fast growth phases are given in following tables and for mini-cycles in tables 7.6 and 7.7. Starting and end-dates of fluctuations are determined as in ch. 2.2.

[a] % deviation of GDP from constant-employment trend.
[b] There is also a small residual arising from change in working population which tends to vary with pressure of demand.
[c] Change in % unemployment as % of % deviation of GDP from trend.
[d] Effect of shocks as % change in GDP estimated on method AA.
[e] For these case averages, the estimates on method BB are little different (see table 5.6).
[f] % change in each expenditure item *less* % change in GDP trend in each phase expressed as contribution to % change in TFE.
[g] Includes contributions of exports and government spending.
Source of basic data: as for table 2.1.

were dominant. Export change usually went in the same direction as output change, probably because fluctuations tended to be international (as also, perhaps as a consequence, the policy cycle).

3. *Expenditure composition of fluctuations* Big and small fluctuations had a rather different expenditure composition. *Stock changes* contributed to all sorts of fluctuation but were on average of about the same absolute size in all cases, and thus constituted half of mini-fluctuations, but only one-sixth of major recessions. The decline in *fixed investment* was more important than stock

change in big recessions, but negligible in small ones. (Stock cycles are inherently restricted in scope, and likely to be soon reversed; but fixed investment is governed by swings of confidence which are only slowly reversed.) Falls in *consumption* were important in both big and small recessions, but as a proportion of the fall in GDP were more important in small ones.

4. *Unemployment effects* In small fluctuations unemployment changed relatively little so that almost all the fluctuation in output got expressed in productivity change. In major fluctuations, only half as much was reflected in productivity shifts and most was reflected in unemployment change. (This probably indicates that confidence was more greatly affected in big recessions so that firms retained underemployed labour much more in small recessions than big.)

In table 5.9 the five major UK recessions are shown separately (together with estimates for the US Great Depression of 1929–33). As already noted, recession II (1929–32) appears poorly explained in terms of shocks. (Chapter 6 will show that over the first two years of this recession shocks explain most of the output shortfall. Chapter 9 will also confirm the impression given by the table that recession V (1989–93) was caused not by shocks but by confidence factors.) The table suggests that the kind of shock that initiated recessions varied greatly from recession to recession.

In all major recessions, fixed investment was heavily affected and in most cases constituted a fair share of the recession (e.g. a quarter). In two cases (1973 and 1979) this was in part the result of contractionary monetary policy. In all cases it probably reflected also a lessening of confidence induced by the fall in output. Loss of confidence evidently also affected consumer spending in some cases. Thus, changes in mood seem to have been a factor in all major recessions.

Table 5.10 attempts to show what happened in the *first year of resumed growth* after each of the major recessions. The large rebound of growth after the 1920 recession clearly owed much to exogenous factors (in particular, exports). Monetary policy, also, was usually relaxed at the end of a major recession. But otherwise the contribution of exogenous factors seems to have been quite small: this is consistent with what was proposed earlier [ch. 3.2] on theoretical grounds: that when the disturbances causing a recession cease, trend growth resumes.

Table 5.11 shows behaviour in the *four main fast-growth phases*.[22] The first two (both in the interwar period) came a little after a major recession, and can properly be seen as recovery periods. By contrast, the second two (both after 1972) immediately *preceded* major recessions, and helped to cause them. All are discussed at greater length in following chapters.

- *The 1922–5 recovery* [ch. 6.2] reflected fast export growth, rapidly expanding investment, and large replenishment of stocks. All these expenditures can be

---

[22] The 1920–1 recession, like several later, was preceded by a boom which would deserve to rank as a fifth fast-growth phase; but it was a confused time of postwar transition in which it is difficult to interpret the data [see s. 6.2]. The years 1993–5 might also seem to have a claim as a fast-growth phase, but there again there are problems in interpreting the data [see app. A9].

Table 5.9 Major UK recessions 1920–1993, together with US Great Depression

	% change during each recession						
	Interwar			Post-1973			Average of 5 major UK recessions
	I 1920–21	(US) (1929–33)	II 1929–32	III 1973–75	IV 1979–82	V 1989–93	
No. of years of recession	1	(4)	3	2	3	4	2.6
Change in GDP[a]	−10.6	(−46)	−12.6	−8.1	−10.6	−12.4	−10.9
Reflected in unemployment[b]	88	(47)	66	11	49	32	51
% of GDP change explained by separate factors							
Exogenous shocks[c]							
Exports	29	(5)	41	8	18	3	20
Terms of trade	4	(−2)	−33	22	−10	−27	−9
Monetary policy	(15)	(3)	(−3)	(79)	(39)	(14)	(29)
Fiscal policy	40	(2)	7	−4	29	−13	12
Total	89	(8)	12	104	76	−23	52
(Accuracy measure)	89	(8)	12	[96]	76	−23	50
Selected expenditure items[d]							
Consumer spending	63	(−1)	29	47	34	50	43
Fixed investment	−7	(42)	13	17	25	35	17
Stock change	2	(9)	4	33	11	3	10

[a] % deviation of GDP(A) during each recession from constant-employment trend.
[b] The change in % unemployment as % of % deviation of GDP from trend.
[c] Estimated on method AA. Shocks as estimated on method BB explain a larger proportion of recession II but are elsewhere less divergent (see table 5.11).
[d] Shortfall of each expenditure component below its trend as % of shortfall of TFE from trend. For USA, the figures show the *absolute* fall in each expenditure component as % of absolute fall in total.

Source of basic data: as for table 2.1.

Table 5.10 First year of resumed growth after major recessions

	Contributions to change in GDP					
	I 1921–2	II 1932–3	III 1975–6	IV 1981–2	V 1982–93	Average of all episodes
Size of shocks						
Exports	3.4	0.2	0.9	−0.5	−0.4	0.7
Terms of trade	0.6	0.2	−1.2	0.3	−0.8	−0.2
Monetary policy	(2.1)	(0.8)	(0.6)	(1.1)	(0.6)	(0.8)
Fiscal policy	−2.3	0.0	0.2	−0.4	2.5	0.0
Total	3.7	1.1	−0.8	0.4	1.9	1.3
Change in GDP(A)						
Total	5.1	2.9	2.6	1.2	2.1	2.8
due to						
Exports	4.4	0.2	2.2	0.2	0.8	1.6
Government spending	−0.7	0.1	0.3	0.2	−0.1	0.0
Consumer spending	2.9	2.2	0.3	0.6	1.6	1.5
Fixed investment	−0.7	0.3	0.3	0.8	0.1	0.2
Stock change	0.2	−1.6	1.7	0.6	0.4	0.3
less imports	−2.5	0.0	−1.1	−1.2	−1.0	−1.2
(Unaccounted for[a])	(1.6)	(1.8)	(−1.0)	(−0.1)	(−0.2)	(0.4)

Recessions are defined as ending in the year when the rate of growth begins to rise at near the trend rate of growth.

[a] GDP(A) *less* GDP(E).

Source of basic data: as for table 2.1.

attributed to the carryover of high demand from the war. If fiscal policy had not continued to be very restrictive, recovery might have been as rapid as had been the downturn in 1921.

- *The 1933–7 expansion* [ch. 6.4] was the result partly of growing exports (resulting from the 1931 devaluation, not from any great rise in world trade); and partly of expansionary fiscal policy (government spending on rearmament).
- *The 1972–3 expansion* [ch. 8.2] was a one-year affair, brief and furious, fully explicable by exogenous factors. The UK was in phase with a worldwide expansion and had fast export growth; fiscal policy was very expansionary; and bank lending controls had been removed, which allowed a strong expansion of credit.

Table 5.11   Four main phases of above-trend growth

	Interwar		Post-1972		Average of four
	I	II	III	IV	fast
	1922–5	1933–7	1972–3	1985–8	phases
No. of years of					
fast growth	3	4	1	3	2.8
% change in GDP[a]	4.7	7.3	4.7	5.6	5.6
% reflected in					
unemployment[b]	72	86	17	43	55
% of GDP change explained by separate factors[c]					
Exogenous shocks[d]					
Exports	42	25	27	3	24
Terms of trade	−30	−10	30	77	17
Monetary policy	(50)	(12)	(0)	(−1)	(16)
Fiscal policy	−26	29	46	6	14
Total	36	56	104	85	70
(Accuracy measure)	36	56	[96]	85	68
Other explanatory factors					
Change in personal saving ratio	−36	−1	−10	36	−3
Change in non-residential investment	14	20	5	18	14
Change in investment in stocks	54	22	37	9	31
Total	32	41	32	63	42
Total shocks and other factors[e]	98	107	106	71	95
Selected expenditure items					
Consumer spending	2	6	20	67	24
Fixed investment	34	37	11	30	28

[a] % deviation of GDP(A) over each phase from constant-employment trend.
[b] Change in % unemployment as % of % deviation of GDP from trend.
[c] As estimated on method AA. Method BB explains more of phase I and less of phase II (table 5.6).
[d] Contribution to % change in total final expenditure.
[e] Omits terms-of-trade effect to avoid double-counting (see table 5.7, fn. *d*).

- *The Lawson boom of 1985–8* [ch. 9.3] was not due primarily to exogenous factors, though it owed something to the fall in import prices. Rather, it was a speculative boom, permitted by policy, but owing little directly to it. High levels of confidence led to high investment, both business and residential; and the removal (four years earlier) of restrictions on bank lending again allowed free rein to credit expansion.

Half or more of above-trend growth in these phases can be explained directly by exogenous shocks—which, perhaps surprisingly, came quite largely from outside the UK. A further fraction was probably due to induced confidence effects; and, in the three longer expansionary phases, the revival of confidence probably owed something to the continuing character of expansion. That is the only type of endogenous recovery for which this study will find evidence.

The fact that the four phases of above-trend growth were only half the scale of the major recessions is part of the reason why the setback experienced in recessions I and II was made good only by war spending in World War II; and why the new setbacks in recessions III, IV, and V had not been reversed by 1995. The upward shocks responsible for the main fast-growth phases were almost as large as the downward shocks which were responsible for the recessions [table 5.8]. But confidence probably reacted less strongly: it takes longer to restore than to destroy confidence, and once destroyed it may respond less to new positive impulses.

These questions about the general behaviour of the economy will need to be considered more fully in the course of the historical case studies [chs. 6–9] and I will come back to them [chs. 10 and 11]. The minor fluctuations of the years 1950–72 will be discussed in chapter 7.

Appendix A5 New Estimates of Fiscal Policy Impact

Many earlier studies of fiscal policy have used estimates of the cyclically adjusted budget balance (CAB) to measure the impact of fiscal policy on output. That indicator has evoked considerable academic criticism,[23] which is discussed in the following section. The alternative method, used here to measure fiscal impact, is described in section A5.2.

A5.1. *Criticism of the cyclically adjusted budget balance* (CAB) *as an indicator of fiscal impact*

The most basic criticism of the CAB as an indicator of fiscal policy impact attacks the idea that fiscal policy has an impact on demand and output: if that were the case, there would be no point in seeking to measure its impact. The best known of such lines of theorizing is the argument of Ricardian equivalence (Barro 1974: far-sighted consumers see that any fiscal change entails contrary future tax changes, and therefore alter their own consumption now, thereby offsetting the effect of the fiscal change). There are good general arguments and sufficient evidence against this view.[24] The present study can also count as evidence: it suggests that in the UK in the period studied changes in fiscal policy did indeed have an impact, and help to explain fluctuations.

Gramlich (1990) lists three alternative lines of theoretical reasoning which also would deny a fiscal impact. First is the monetarism of Friedman (1962)—that interest rates rise to crowd out the fiscal impulse. Second is the open-economy theory of Mundell (1963) and Fleming (1962)—that expansionary fiscal policy stimulates capital inflows, which raises the exchange rate and reduces net exports so that the fiscal impact is offset by this route. Third is the line of Lucas (1972) and Sargent and Wallace (1975)—that fiscal expansion raises prices and lowers the real quantity of money, which keeps output constant. All three of these arguments assume that the value of the money stock is held constant. That is an arbitrary assumption and probably also an impracticable aim for policy. I would argue too that none of the offsetting effects supposed would operate within the time scale here relevant, *viz.* the two to four years occupied by a major recession.

Other lines of criticism accept that fiscal policy changes do impact on demand but question the use of the CAB as a measure of the impact. I see this criticism of the CAB as valid up to a point, but overstated, for the following reasons.

1. One criticism has been that the CAB does not measure other aspects of fiscal policy in which the critic may properly be interested, e.g. whether a given fiscal policy is sustainable. That is true, but it does not invalidate its use as an indicator of the impact on demand.

2. A related criticism is that fiscal policy may affect the supply side of the economy, which the CAB does not measure. That also is true. But supply-side effects surely operate over periods of many years; i.e., the supply-side impact of a fiscal change over the period of a single recession must be small compared with the impact on demand.

---

[23] See review of the discussion in Blanchard (1990) and Gramlich (1990).

[24] For example Buiter and Tobin (1979), Tobin (1980) and Buiter (1985). The doctrine of Ricardian equivalence is surely one of those clever views which is by no means the whole truth, and if true at all is probably the lesser part of it. The doctrine, as Blanchard says, 'strains credulity ...' and 'has no claim to be an empirical benchmark'. See also Dow and Saville (1988: 102–3).

3. Another line of attack has been that fiscal changes will be foreseen: hence the change in the CAB is not a measure of shock. Here the answer (as with other shock indicators) is that agents' foresight, even if partial, is incomplete. Even in financial markets, where operators try to survive by being a step ahead, corroboration of a widely expected event usually moves the price. Financial markets, moreover, are often quite wrong. This must be even more true of non-financial markets. The evidence in the present study that fiscal policy changes in fact affected output is, again, evidence that foresight was less than perfect.

4. A fourth criticism has been that the CAB as an indicator makes no adjustment for inflation. This seems to me a valid criticism but not a fatal attack. My own view is that, ideally, an inflation adjustment should indeed be made. The loss suffered by owners of government (and some other forms of) debt is likely at times to have had a significant impact on expenditure. That effect however depends not on the shape of fiscal policy, but on the incidence of inflation; and would be better captured by an additional shock indicator (along with the fiscal policy indicator). This has not been done in the present exercise because the effect seemed difficult to estimate. If an estimate had been possible, it might well have improved the explanation of recessions. But omission of this element does not discredit the results presented below, which claim not to be complete but to estab-lish the case that shocks (even as imperfectly measured) appear to affect demand.[25]

5. A final line of criticism is that the concept of the CAB inevitably involves controversial questions about the nature of cycles or fluctuations [ch. 2.2].[26] I am sympathetic to this criticism. The method of calculating fiscal impact used here, and described below, eliminates the need for cyclical adjustment of the budget balance, and evades this line of criticism.

A5.2. *The present estimates of fiscal impact*

The present estimates of budget impact are based on *ex post* figures of changes in the budget balance.[27] Any such indicator has to distinguish between that part of any change in the budget position resulting from changes in the economic environment and that part resulting from changes in policy. Policy may be neutral, expansionary, or contractionary. A neutral (or no-change) policy may be defined as one that brings no change to the degree of capacity working of the economy (or, as a proxy for that, no change in the degree of labour unemployment).

If economic growth is proceeding at a steady pace, neutrality on the expenditure side can, then, be defined as an increase in real expenditure proportionate to the 'normal' or trend or non-cyclical rate of growth of the economy. This approach can be applied

---

[25] The effect of inflation on spending is best regarded as arising because unexpected inflation causes not a loss of income but a loss of capital. The propensity to consume out of wealth must be small (e.g. 0.05) compared with the propensity to consume out of income (e.g. 0.9). But, with national debt of the order of 50% (of GDP, and with inflation in the worst phase (1973–5) accelerating from about 5%) to about 25% in the course of a recession, the acceleration of inflation could well have reduced output significantly (e.g. by something of the order of 0.5%). At other times the effect would have been less or a lot less. Allowance for this factor might at least in some cases have improved the degree of explanation obtained by the present exercise.

[26] The process of cyclical adjustment, as Blanchard (1990; 6) says, '[by] constructing a trend in whatever way ... takes a position on the issues of whether there are cycles around a stable trend, of whether the economy will return to lower unemployment and so on'.

[27] The estimates were largely the work of Pierre van der Eng (van der Eng 1992).

most naturally to expenditure on goods and services; and the calculation is best done (as in the present estimates) in real terms. Expenditure on grants, subsidies, and transfers are treated as reverse (direct or indirect) taxes. (Payments of interest are treated as a transfer, so that an increase in such payments, whether due to a rise in outstanding debt or a rise in rates of interest, is treated as expansionary.)

With a progressive tax system a rise in incomes, whether due to economic growth or to inflation, will raise tax revenue as a proportion of GDP at current prices. A neutral policy on the revenue side is here defined as a policy that leaves *that ratio* unchanged. A contractionary policy thus may result either from an increase in explicit tax rates, or from a failure to correct for fiscal drag (the effect of rising incomes in raising the tax share). This part of the calculation is best done (as here) at current prices.

This procedure eliminates the need for cyclical adjustment. Such adjustment is relatively straightforward in periods when growth is fairly steady, when unemployment is on average low and with little trend, and when fluctuations around the average rate of growth are relatively small. In such circumstances cyclical changes can be satisfactorily defined in terms of such fluctuations.[28] The method becomes dubious in periods when there are major interruptions to growth and when, accordingly, there is doubt as to what the underlying trend was.[29] The procedure employed in the new estimates presented here sidesteps these difficulties as far as the revenue side is concerned. An arbitrary element remains in the treatment of the expenditure side; but what the estimates assert can be given a clear interpretation which makes economic sense.

Weights were allotted to the change in different categories of public expenditure and revenue according to their assumed impact on spending.[30] For expenditure on goods and services the weight was unity; for revenue and transfer expenditures the weights were under unity according to the assumed propensity to spend out of the kind of incomes affected by the change in the rate of tax or transfer [table A5.1].

The present calculation may be summarized as follows. The impact on spending of fiscal policy changes is calculated as the following sum:

(i) [percentage increase in public expenditure on goods and services at constant prices *less* percentage increase in 'trend GDP'[31] at constant prices] *times* the weight of government expenditure in GDP in the previous year

[28]   Studies employing variants of this approach are Hansen (1969); Synder (1970); and Ward and Neild (1978). Some early studies sought to evade the difficulties of cyclical adjustment by making use of contemporary official estimates of the effect of changes in tax rates, which by subtraction from the actual revenue change gave an estimate of the revenue changes caused by economic growth or price changes (see Dow 1964; Musgrave and Musgrave 1968; and Price 1978). This procedure however is tedious, and is only as accurate as the original official forecasts of the effects of tax changes. (It is also a limitation that—in the UK—the latter are available only for central government.)

[29]   This is apparent in studies of the 1970s and 1980s: see Savage (1982), Biswas *et al.* (1985) (who took alternative arbitrary figures to illustrate the possible trend after 1973), and Price and Muller (1984) (who interpolated between peak years of high employment in the early and late 1970s). Similar difficulties arise in the interwar period as a result of the major interruption to growth caused by the Great Depression.

[30]   Only in a few years (1927, 1969, 1972, 1978) did use of weighted estimates greatly alter estimated fiscal impact [table A5.2].

[31]   Since there appear to have been downward steps in the growth path [ch. 2.2] during periods of major recession, trend rates of growth were estimated separately for each of the intervening periods during which the rate of growth was relatively constant.

Table A5.1   Estimates of fiscal impact: weights assigned to budget items

	Weight
Expenditure items	
Goods and services, current and capital	1.00
Subsidies and grants	0.65
Debt interest	0.20
Tax items	
Taxes on income[a]	0.60
Taxes on expenditure	0.80
Taxes on capital	0.20
Other revenue items	
National insurance contributions	0.80
Gross trading surplus of public bodies	0.33
Rent, interest, dividends received by the government	0.20

Overseas grants and imputed charge for consumption of non-trading capital are allotted zero weights and are not shown.

[a] Including taxes on companies' profits.

less

(ii) [percentage increase in weighted aggregation of 'net receipts' (tax and other revenue *less* grants, transfers, and subsidies) *less* percentage increase in actual GDP at current prices] *times* the weight of net taxation in GDP at current prices in the previous year.

The result provides an estimate of the effect of fiscal policy in expanding (or, if negative, contracting) total demand, expressed as a percentage of GDP. Year-to-year changes in the effect thus give an estimate of the contribution of fiscal policy to year-to-year percentage changes in GDP.

The present estimates of fiscal impact seek to measure the first-round effects only, without allowance for subsequent stages of multiplier or amplifier processes. Only the initial impact was estimated, since it is argued [ch. 5.1] that the scale of amplification is not constant, but varies with circumstances.

The estimates are tabulated in table A5.2, and summarized in figure A5.1. Similar estimates for the USA are showing table A5.3. The estimated impact of fiscal policy during major recessions is shown in table 5.9 and the main fast-growth phases in table 5.11.

The present estimates differ from those used in some other studies in three main respects:

1. The estimates cover general government, i.e. are not confined to central government.
2. They follow a different treatment in years where a shift occurs in the growth path: as already argued, the treatment used here produces better estimates.

Table A5.2 Estimates of impact of fiscal policy in the UK, 1920–1992 (as contribution to % changes in GDP)

	Annual change in % share in GDP of:				Net fiscal impact		Including also capital spending weighted[c]
					Including only current spending		
	Current expenditure items[a]	Current and capital spending[a]	Tax receipts	Transfer, grants, etc.	Unweighted[b]	Weighted[c]	
1920	−15.3	−12.7	0.0	−0.5	−11.0	−11.0	−9.2
21	0.4	2.6	3.3	2.9	0.0	−0.3	1.3
22	−1.1	−2.3	2.5	0.6	−2.1	−1.9	−2.7
23	−0.9	−2.1	−0.6	−0.5	−0.6	−0.8	−1.6
24	−0.3	0.0	−1.8	−0.7	0.6	0.5	0.7
1925	0.2	1.1	−1.1	−0.4	0.7	0.6	1.3
26	−0.1	0.4	1.8	1.8	−0.1	−0.4	0.0
27	−0.2	0.0	−0.1	−1.5	−1.1	−0.4	−0.3
28	−0.2	−1.0	0.3	0.3	−0.1	−0.2	−0.7
29	−0.1	−0.3	−0.6	0.1	0.4	0.3	0.1
1930	0.0	0.1	0.1	0.6	0.3	0.4	0.5
31	0.5	0.9	2.4	1.8	−0.1	−0.1	0.2
32	0.1	−0.7	2.5	0.5	−1.3	−1.0	−1.6
33	−0.3	−1.2	−0.6	−1.1	−0.5	0.0	−0.7
34	−0.1	0.0	−1.7	−1.4	0.2	0.2	0.3
1935	0.7	1.2	−0.7	−0.5	0.6	0.7	1.1
36	1.1	1.8	0.0	−0.8	0.2	0.4	0.9
37	1.6	2.4	−0.6	−1.0	0.8	1.1	1.7
38	3.3	3.8	−0.3	0.0	2.5	2.4	2.8
39	11.6	NA	0.6	−0.7	7.2	7.5	NA

1940	45.6	NA	0.4	-1.5	30.6	31.1	NA
41	18.9	NA	6.1	0.0	8.9	10.4	NA
42	3.2	NA	3.1	0.5	0.4	1.1	NA
43	1.7	NA	3.4	0.5	-0.8	-0.1	NA
44	-5.9	NA	1.8	0.9	-4.8	-4.7	NA
1945	-17.9	NA	1.4	2.7	-11.6	-12.2	NA
46	-36.1	NA	-1.2	4.6	-21.2	-23.0	NA
47	-12.9	NA	-1.0	-0.3	-8.6	-9.0	NA
48	-1.6	NA	1.3	-0.8	-2.6	-1.7	NA
49	0.7	0.2	0.6	-1.2	-0.7	0.1	-0.3
1950	-1.0	-1.1	-1.7	-1.1	-0.3	-0.5	-0.5
51	1.3	1.6	-1.4	-1.0	1.2	1.1	1.4
52	2.0	2.6	-1.6	-0.1	2.4	2.0	2.4
53	-0.2	0.2	-1.8	-0.6	0.8	0.5	0.8
54	-1.1	-2.3	-0.4	-0.3	-0.7	-0.6	-1.4
1955	-1.8	-2.4	0.0	-0.4	-1.5	-1.4	-1.9
56	-1.2	-1.7	-0.9	-0.3	-0.4	-0.5	-0.9
57	-1.3	-1.7	0.3	-0.1	-1.2	-1.0	-1.3
58	-1.5	-2.2	1.0	0.9	-1.1	-1.2	-1.6
59	-0.3	-0.5	-0.4	0.0	0.0	0.1	0.0
1960	-0.3	-0.5	-1.3	0.2	0.9	0.5	0.3
61	0.1	0.1	1.3	0.6	-0.4	-0.3	-0.3
62	0.0	0.2	1.9	0.1	-1.2	-0.7	-0.5
63	-0.3	-0.4	-1.6	-0.1	0.7	0.3	-0.3
64	-0.4	0.5	-0.2	-0.6	-0.6	-0.5	0.2

Table A5.2 (Continued)

	Annual change in % share in GDP of:				Net fiscal impact		Including also capital spending weighted[c]
	Current expenditure items[a]	Current and capital spending[a]	Tax receipts	Transfer, grants, etc.	Including only current spending		
					Unweighted[b]	Weighted[c]	
1965	−0.1	−0.3	1.8	0.6	−0.9	−0.7	−0.9
66	−0.1	0.4	0.9	0.2	−0.6	−0.6	−0.3
67	0.8	1.2	2.3	1.3	−0.1	0.1	0.3
68	−0.5	−0.3	2.1	0.9	−1.2	−0.9	−0.8
69	−1.0	−1.4	2.7	−0.2	−2.7	−1.9	−2.1
1970	−0.2	−0.5	0.6	−0.4	−0.8	−0.5	−0.7
71	0.1	−0.4	−2.8	−0.7	1.5	1.3	0.9
72	0.3	0.0	−2.8	0.8	2.7	1.9	1.6
73	0.2	1.3	−1.1	−0.2	0.8	0.6	1.4
74	0.0	−0.3	3.5	2.9	−0.4	−0.3	−0.5
1975	0.9	0.0	0.2	−0.2	0.3	0.3	−0.3
76	−0.3	−0.7	−0.6	0.5	0.6	0.2	−0.2
77	−1.0	−2.0	−0.6	0.0	−0.3	−0.6	−1.4
78	0.0	−0.5	−1.7	0.4	1.5	0.9	0.6
79	−0.1	−0.2	1.4	0.6	−0.6	−0.6	−0.8
1980	0.0	−0.4	2.4	0.9	−1.1	−0.8	−1.1
81	−0.3	−1.0	2.9	1.9	−0.9	−0.8	−1.4
82	−0.1	−0.4	0.8	0.7	−0.2	−0.2	−0.4
83	−0.3	0.1	−1.1	−0.6	0.2	0.0	0.3
84	−0.5	−0.4	−0.2	0.6	0.2	−0.1	0.0

1985	−0.7	−0.8	0.1	0.0	−0.5	−0.4	−0.5
86	−0.3	−0.3	−0.6	−1.0	−0.5	−0.6	−0.5
87	−0.4	−0.6	−3.5	−1.1	1.4	1.1	1.0
88	−0.5	−0.9	2.4	−2.0	−3.4	−2.5	−2.8
89	−0.4	0.0	−1.1	−1.1	−0.3	0.0	0.3
1990	0.9	1.3	−2.2	−0.8	1.6	1.4	1.7
91	0.8	0.6	−0.4	0.4	1.1	0.8	0.7
92	0.2	0.2	−1.3	2.1	2.5	1.6	1.6

[a] Expenditure on goods and services.

[b] All items refer to general government. Unweighted fiscal impact shown equals changes in % share of current spending *less* that of tax receipts *plus* that of transfer, grants, subsidies, and debt interest. Capital spending of public corporations is excluded throughout. Total multiplied by 0.7 to allow for import content.

[c] Main categories of tax receipts and grants, transfers, etc., are given the weights shown in table A5.1. Weight of expenditure on goods and services is 1.0.

Sources: Feinstein (1972); CSO *Economic Trends*, various issues.

Table A5.3 Estimates of fiscal impact in the USA, 1930–1989 (as contribution to % change in GNP)

	Annual change in % shares of:			Net fiscal impact	
	Current expenditure items	Tax receipts	Transfers, grants, etc.	Unweighted	Weighted
1930	1.8	1.0	0.3	1.1	1.0
31	1.1	0.5	2.0	2.6	1.5
32	−0.1	2.8	0.2	−2.7	−2.4
33	0.0	1.4	0.4	−1.0	−0.8
34	2.6	−1.1	−0.5	3.2	3.2
1935	−0.8	−0.5	−0.1	−0.4	−0.3
36	1.7	0.4	0.8	2.1	2.5
37	−1.9	−0.5	−1.4	−2.8	−2.3
38	0.2	0.3	0.8	0.7	0.2
39	−0.4	1.0	−0.1	−1.5	−1.3
1940	−0.4	0.9	−0.1	−1.4	−0.4
41	7.8	2.6	−0.9	4.4	7.4
42	22.7	0.6	−0.4	21.7	22.8
43	17.6	5.0	−0.3	12.3	14.5
44	2.9	−1.5	0.3	4.7	3.4
1945	−11.2	0.7	1.8	−10.2	−11.3
46	−37.1	−0.8	3.9	−32.4	−34.8
47	−4.4	0.6	−0.8	−5.8	−4.7
48	2.0	−1.8	−0.2	3.5	3.1
49	1.6	−1.0	1.0	3.6	2.3
1950	−0.3	2.3	−0.4	−2.9	−1.0
51	6.9	1.8	−2.0	3.2	5.0
52	3.6	0.2	−0.4	2.9	2.7
53	1.1	−0.1	−0.1	1.1	1.1
54	−3.8	−1.3	0.6	−1.9	−3.0
1955	−2.0	0.7	−0.1	−2.9	−2.3
56	−0.7	0.5	0.0	−1.2	−1.3
57	0.3	0.2	0.4	0.5	0.2
58	0.0	−0.7	0.8	1.5	0.7
59	−0.7	1.2	−0.2	−2.0	−1.3
1960	−0.5	1.6	0.9	−1.2	−1.3
61	0.5	−0.1	0.4	1.1	0.8
62	0.4	0.5	−0.3	−0.4	−0.2
63	−0.3	0.3	0.0	−0.6	−0.4
64	−0.3	−1.0	−0.2	0.6	0.2

Table A5.3 (*Continued*)

	Annual change in % shares of:			Net fiscal impact	
	Current expenditure items	Tax receipts	Transfers, grants, etc.	Unweighted	Weighted
1965	−0.5	−0.3	0.0	−0.2	−0.2
66	1.5	0.7	0.1	0.9	1.0
67	1.1	0.9	0.8	1.0	1.0
68	0.1	1.4	0.4	−0.8	−0.4
69	−1.0	1.3	0.2	−2.1	−1.9
1970	−1.5	−0.9	1.2	0.6	−0.6
71	−0.9	−0.5	0.7	0.2	−0.2
72	−0.5	1.2	0.1	−1.6	−1.2
73	−0.9	0.1	0.3	−0.7	−0.8
74	0.0	0.8	1.0	0.1	0.1
1975	0.0	−1.4	1.7	3.1	1.8
76	−0.6	0.8	−0.2	−1.6	−1.0
77	−0.3	0.1	−0.5	−0.9	−0.6
78	−0.1	0.0	−0.4	−0.5	−0.3
79	−0.4	0.5	0.2	−0.6	−0.6
1980	0.1	0.3	1.3	1.1	0.5
81	0.0	0.9	0.7	−0.1	−0.5
82	0.1	−0.2	1.4	1.7	0.7
83	−0.5	−0.5	0.2	0.2	−0.1
84	0.1	0.0	−0.6	−0.5	−0.3
1985	0.4	0.7	0.4	0.1	0.0
86	0.5	0.4	0.1	0.2	0.5
87	−0.3	0.5	−0.4	−1.1	−0.6
88	−0.6	−0.4	−0.2	−0.4	−0.5
89	−0.3	0.5	0.3	−0.5	−0.5

Sources: *National Income and Product Accounts of the United States 1929–1982*; and later official estimates.

3. Tax changes are defined not in terms of changes in administrative tax rates, but as a change in the ratio of tax to GDP (and similarly for changes in rates of transfers, etc.).

A comparison of the present results with other estimates reveals many divergent results [fig. A5.2]. Looking at the crucial episodes, the present estimates show stronger fiscal deflation in the 1929–32 recession than others. But at some other crucial points, such as the size of the fiscal stimulus in 1971–3 and the large deflationary impact in 1979–81, the results are less dissimilar. In the period of relatively steady growth in the quarter-century after World War II, there is the (surprisingly) least convergence between the different estimates.

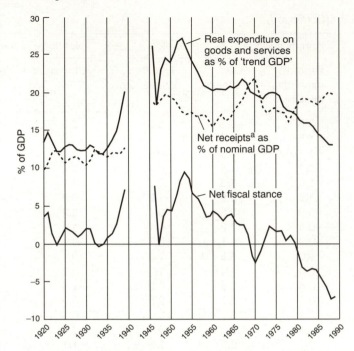

Fig. A5.1   Public expenditure and revenue: UK, 1920–1990

[a] Tax and other receipts, *less grants*, transfers, and subsidies including debt interest.

Sources: Feinstein (1972); CSO, *National Income and Expenditure*.

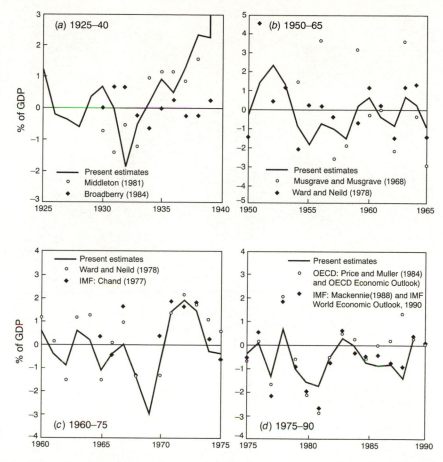

Fig. A5.2 Comparison of various estimates of fiscal impact: UK, 1925–1990

Part II

Case Studies of Five Major Recessions

6 The Two Interwar Recessions

Through most of the interwar period, UK unemployment was high: it was high after the recession of 1921, and higher again during and after the Great Depression of 1929–32. I argued previously [ch. 3.1] that if the economy becomes underemployed it tends to stay underemployed. If that is so, the question is not why unemployment stayed high after 1921 or remained higher after 1929, but what caused the breaks at these two dates, checked output and pushed unemployment higher then, and after 1932 brought unemployment down.

Section 6.1 below gives an overview of the whole interwar period. Section 6.2 looks at the 1921 recession and the following years. Since (it is argued) the depression of 1929–32 was dominated by events in the United States, section 6.3 is a digression on the US Great Depression. Section 6.4 then looks at the international transmission of that Depression and its manifestation in the United Kingdom; and section 6.5 at the UK recovery after 1932. Conclusions of theoretical interest are stated in section 6.6.

Three appendices discuss Friedman and Schwartz's (1963) *Monetary History of the United States*, Eichengreen's (1992) *Golden Fetters*, and the international transmission of the US Depression. There is also a statistical appendix.

6.1. Overview of the interwar period

6.1.1. Economic events

UK developments from 1920 until the outbreak of World War II can be divided into six phases [fig. 6.1]. After the boom of the immediate postwar years came the sharp *recession* of 1921. Then came *partial recovery*, followed by six years of what Pigou called *the doldrums*—moderate growth but not fast enough to make any decisive inroad into unemployment. The *Great Depression* of 1929–32 then took unemployment to over 15 per cent. From there it declined only slowly and gradually to 11 per cent by 1935 (*recovery I*), and under rather different impulses to just under 6 per cent by 1939 (*recovery II*). The continuous high level of unemployment makes the interwar period very different from nineteenth-century fluctuations.

The United States had a considerably different experience from the UK, but with broadly the same timing [fig. 6.2]. It experienced much more expansion and lower unemployment through most of the 1920s; a much deeper depression in 1929–33; then, despite renewed growth, unemployment significantly higher than in the UK throughout the 1930s.

Some other countries underwent the same recessionary phases; others suffered less or escaped wholly [fig. 6.3]. In 1921 output fell in the United States, France,

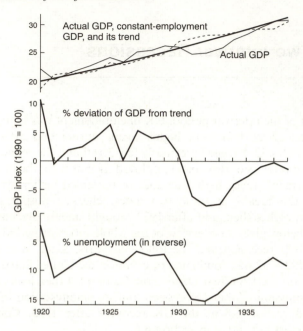

Fig. 6.1 GDP fluctuations and unemployment in the UK, 1920–1938
For the estimation of GDP trend, see table 2.2, method B.
Source: basic data as for table 2.1

and Italy, but much less than in the United Kingdom; in Germany on the other hand and (not shown on chart) Sweden and Japan it continued to rise. Unemployment rose as steeply in the United States (and Sweden and Denmark) as in Britain, but perhaps did not rise elsewhere.[1] British exports fell sharply in 1921 [table 6.1]; other countries had a smaller fall in exports [fig. 6.4].

The Great Depression was more nearly universal but was very uneven, and some countries were unaffected. In the United States output fell by 29 per cent (1929–33) and unemployment rose to 23.5 per cent—probably the largest recession experienced anywhere.[2] The recession in Germany and France was also extremely severe [table 6.1]. In most other countries the fall in output was much less, though still large by normal standards.

Primary product prices fell 10 per cent in the 1921 recession, and fell about as much in the Great Depression [fig. 6.5]; they had started falling in 1925, and by 1929 had already fallen 17 per cent. The price level in industrial countries was still volatile [fig. 6.6]: the UK GDP deflator had fallen 10 per cent in 1921 and fell 6 per cent in 1929–32. The US deflator had fallen 14 per cent in 1921

---

[1] Figures of unemployment in 1920 and 1921 are not available for all countries.
[2] The fall in output in the ex-Soviet countries after the collapse of communism was as severe, but it was due to political chaos not lack of demand.

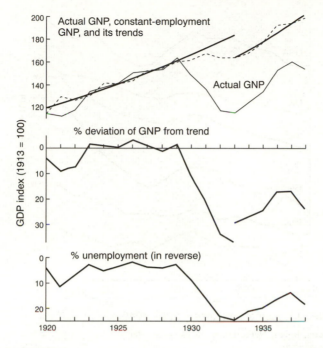

Fig. 6.2   GNP fluctuations and unemployment in the USA, 1920–1938
Estimation of trend by method B (see table 2.2).
Source: Maddison (1991*a*)

and in the Great Depression fell 24 per cent—for one reason because the depression was much worse than in other countries, for another because the United States was still about one-quarter agricultural. It will be argued that the downward volatility of prices in the UK and USA, both in 1921 and again in 1929–32, helps to explain the steepness of the interwar recessions.

A commentator writing now about events between the wars is better placed than someone writing any time before the 1970s; for Feinstein's national accounts data, which appeared in 1972, are much more complete than any previously available. Even so, interpretation is by no means straightforward. Table 6.2 summarizes the provisional conclusions reached earlier [ch. 5.2]— which it will be the business of this chapter to confirm or modify—about the causes of the two recessions in the UK, of the Great Depression in the USA, and of the two phases of partial recovery in the UK.

6.1.2. Political developments and the nature of economic policy in the interwar years

The character of the government was of less economic importance in the interwar period than later, since governments did not then try to play an active

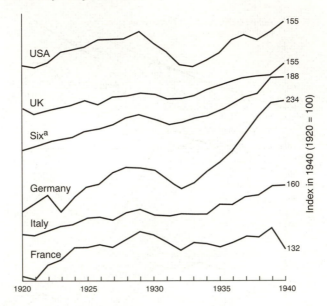

Fig. 6.3   GDP of industrial countries, 1920–1940

ᵃ Belgium, Canada, Japan, Netherlands, Norway, Sweden.
Source: Maddison (1989).

role in steering the economy. The period up to 1931 was in the UK a time of weak and short-lived governments, and a time also of much labour unrest culminating in the short General Strike and the long and bitter Coal Strike of 1926. It was an age of political transition, which saw the death of the once-great Liberal Party and Labour beginning to emerge as the alternative to the Conservatives.

The strong and reforming Liberal Party that had taken Britain into the 1914 War still dominated the Coalition Government at the end of the war, with Lloyd George now its head [table 6.3]. The election of 1922 gave the Conservatives under Baldwin a slender majority. The 1924 election left neither major party with a majority: the Labour Party under MacDonald had a first taste of power as a short-lived minority government. Five years followed with the Conservatives in power, again under Baldwin, until in 1929 they lost their majority in another inconclusive election. The Liberals, rather than take office without a majority, preferred to put Labour back in office, again as a minority government.

Thus, in an age when unemployment meant hunger and destitution, it fell to a weak and inexperienced Labour government to deal with the mounting unemployment of the Great Depression, and finally with the crisis of 1931—on which the party split. Ramsay MacDonald then joined with the Conservatives and a section of the Liberals to form the National Government, and won a

Table 6.1 The 1929–32 Great Depression in different countries

	Fall as % of 1929		% unemployment	
	GDP	Exports	1929	1932
USA[a]	−29.4	−47.8	3.1	23.6
Germany	−15.8	−40.5	5.9	17.2
United Kingdom	−5.2	−37.6	7.2	15.3
France	−14.7	−41.5	1.2	—
Italy	−3.8	−42.1	1.7	5.7
Six other industrial countries[b]	−6.3	−25.7	1.2	4.1

[a]1929–33.
[b]Belgium, Canada, Japan, Netherlands, Norway, and Sweden.
Sources: GDP and export indices from Maddison (1982, 1989). The indices for the six countries were aggregated by linking them to the 1980 values of GDP and exports in international and US dollars respectively. Unemployment in USA, Germany, UK, France, and Italy from Maddison (1982: 206) Belgium and Sweden calculated from *Yearbook of Labour Statistics*, various years; Canada from Urquhart and Buckley (1965: 61); Japan from *Japan Statistical Yearbook*, 1948; Netherlands from *Negenting Jaren Statistiek in Tijdreeksen*, 1989, p. 76; Norway from *Langtidslinjer i Norsk Ikonomi*, 1966, p. 29.

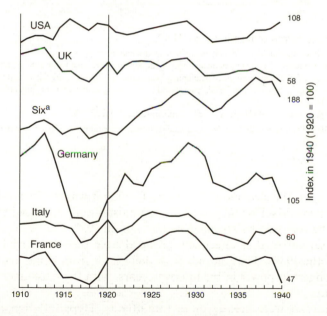

Fig. 6.4 Exports of industrial countries, 1910–1940
[a] Belgium, Canada, Japan, Netherlands, Norway, Sweden.
Sources: For 1919–24 the estimates for Belgium, Canada, Japan, Netherlands, Norway, and Sweden are rough estimates only, arrived at by deflating the current value of exports with the average UK/US unit value of exports of manufacture (see n. *a* to fig. 6.5). For the years 1924–40, Maddison's volume series (1982, 1989) are used.

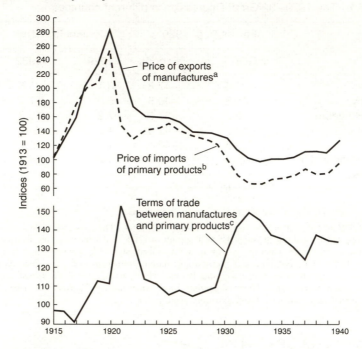

Fig. 6.5　World terms of trade, 1915–1940

[a] Average of unit values of US and UK manufactured exports.
[b] Average of unit values of primary products imported by the UK and the USA. Each series is the weighted average of the unit values of the main components ('food' and 'raw materials' for the UK, 'crude materials', 'crude foodstuffs', 'processed foodstuffs', and 'semi-manufactured products' for the USA).
[c] Ratio of *a* and *b*. Lewis (1952) gives a very similar series for 1921–38.

Sources: Schlote (1952); CSO, *Annual Abstract of Statistics*, various years; *Historical Statistics of the United States*, 1960.

huge majority in the election of that year. Though it was in effect a Conservative government, MacDonald stayed prime minister until displaced by Baldwin in 1935, to be followed by Neville Chamberlain in 1937.

The Conservatives thus effectively presided over the still partial economic recovery of the 1930s. That did not save them later from being associated, as the party longest in power in the interwar years, with the mass unemployment of those years.

Events abroad were greatly more tumultuous. Hyperinflation in France, Germany, and many countries of central Europe in the first years after World War I had left a vivid memory everywhere. The Great Depression in Germany in the early 1920s, also very deep though less so than in the United States, was followed by the triumph of Hitler as leader of Germany. As German

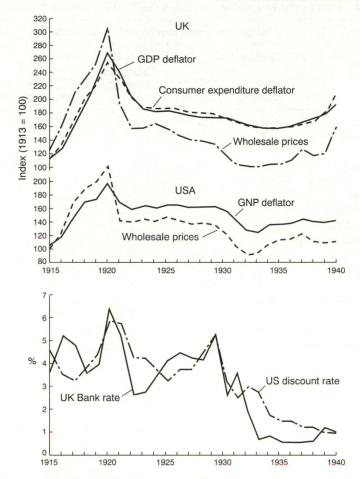

Fig. 6.6 Price trends in the UK and the USA, 1915–1940

Sources: Feinstein (1972); Mitchell (1988); Kendrick (1961); *National Income and Product Accounts of the United States*, 1981; *Historical Statistics of the United States*, 1960.

rearmament became increasingly threatening, Britain belatedly followed suit. In the United States Roosevelt was elected President in 1932. His more interventionist New Deal policies claim some credit for the gradual and still partial US recovery.

6.1.3. Economic policy in the interwar years

Before World War II, people's ideas about economic policy were not what they have since become. Economic fluctuations tended to be viewed more as an act

Table 6.2 Recessions and partial recoveries, 1920–1937: partial explanations

	Change during each recession or recovery				
	1920s in UK		Great US Depression 1929–33	1930s in UK	
	1920–1 recession	1922–5 recovery		1929–32 recession	1933–7 recovery
% change in GDP[a]	−10.6	4.7	46	−12.6	7.3
No. of years of recession or recovery	1	3	4	3	4
% of GDP change less trend explained by separate factors					
Exogenous shocks[b]					
Exports (EX)	29	42	5	41	25
Terms of trade (TOT)	4	−30	−2	−33	−10
Monetary policy (MP)	(12)	(40)	(3)	(−2)	(10)
Fiscal policy (FP)	40	−26	2	7	29
Other explanatory factors					
Change in saving ratio (SR)	1	−35	−16	−4	−1
Change in non-residential investment (NRI)	−3	14	17	6	20
Change in investment in stocks (CS)	2	54	8	4	22
Measure of accuracy[c]					
Total shocks, method AA[b]	86	26	8	15	54
Shocks method BB[d]	84	75	—	91	68
Changes in savings investment ratios[e]	−5	62	9	38	51

For definitions and methods of estimation, see ch. 5.2.

[a] % deviation of GDP(A) over each recession or recovery from constant-employment trend. The figure for the US Great Depression includes a rough estimate for the trend.
[b] As estimated on method AA using the 'theoretical' value of parameters (see ch. 5.2).
[c] Defined as table 5.7, fn. *a*.
[d] Method BB uses values for parameters as estimated in table 5.5.
[e] Degree of explanation additional to the effect of exogenous shocks, i.e. net of terms-of-trade effect (TOT) to avoid double-counting (see table 5.7, fn. *d*).

Source of basic data: as for table 2.1.

Table 6.3 Key political events 1919–1930

Complexion of government[a] / Prime minister	Chancellor of Exchequer	UK key policy events	Political and economic events abroad
1916 *Coalition gov't* Lloyd George	A. Chamberlain till 1919, then Sir R Horne		
1919		Cunliffe Committee recommends early return to gold standard	World War I ends Treaty of Versailles
1920		'Geddes Axe' spending cuts Montague Norman governor, Bank of England Southern Ireland independent	League of Nations instituted
1922 *Conservative gov't* (345) Bonar Law till May 1923, then Baldwin	Baldwin till May 1923, then N. Chamberlain		
1923			Occupation of Ruhr by France and Belgium Hyperinflation in Germany[b]
1924 *Labour gov't* (151) MacDonald	Snowden		Dawes Plan gives loans to Germany

Table 6.3 (Continued)

Complexion of government[a] Prime minister	Chancellor of Exchequer	UK key policy events	Political and economic events abroad
1924 Conservative gov't (419)			
Nov. Baldwin	Churchill		
1925		Return to gold standard at $4.86 to £	
1926		General Strike (one week) Coal Strike (7 months)	
1929 Labour gov't (288)			
MacDonald	Snowden	Macmillan Committee set up (reports June 1931)	
1931		May Committee calls for big cuts in government spending Britain leaves gold standard	
1931 National gov't (521)			
MacDonald	Snowden	Import Duties Act	Roosevelt president of USA
1932			US dollar devalued

Year	Government		
1933			World Economic Conference: nil result Hitler chancellor of Germany
1934		War Loan Conversion (5% to 3.5%)	
1935 *National gov't (432)* Baldwin till May 1937, then N. Chamberlain	N. Chamberlain till May 1937, then Sir J. Simon		Italy invades Abyssinia
1936		Edward VIII abdicates 'Shadow factory' scheme for aircraft production	French franc devalued
1938			Munich: Chamberlain meets Hitler
1939			Sept.: UK declares war on Germany

[a] In brackets, number of government supporters out of a total of 615 MPs.
[b] Price rise 1918–23 = 10^{12}.

of nature than as something which it was the job of government to prevent. Economic policy, of the sort that later came into fashion—and then went out and is now partially back—was hardly a real possibility. Some aspects of the situation did nevertheless arouse concern, and did motivate policy to some degree; and there was a gradual evolution of such concern throughout the period, with 1931 perhaps a watershed. Up to 1931 much of what policy there was came from the Bank of England (throughout the period under Montague Norman, and still privately owned), though *in extremis* recognizing its subordination to the elected government.

Describing the character of ruling ideas means assigning motives to the men who made policy. Different citations from others of those close to power could undoubtedly modify the picture presented here. But however perilous, it is worth singling out some aspects.[3]

1. Britain had been effectively off the gold standard during the war. After the war it was accepted without argument that Britain should return to it, though not immediately: Keynes and some others apart, the prevailing view was that return should be at the previous parity. If there was a clear reason for these views, it probably was that the gold standard was a protection against inflation.

2. Fear of inflation was a powerful concern, especially in the light of the hyperinflation that was occurring in continental countries. The steep rise in prices in the boom of 1919 and 1920 created a familiar dilemma: the traditional response would have been to raise interest rates, but that would be bad for employment. Thus, the Bank rate was raised to 7 per cent only in August 1920.[4]

3. It had generally been expected that the war would be followed by unemployment; and there was a general concern not to add to it. That appears to be why plans for a slow and gradual dismantling of wartime controls were cast aside. Similarly, immediate return to the old parity would have required high interest rates, which were seen—however imprecisely—as discouraging to trade and employment. There was no great pressure even from the Bank for an immediate return to gold in 1919.

4. There was, more than now, lack of a clear and agreed picture of how the macroeconomy worked. The circle of people close to power seems to have accepted some connection between prices, employment, and interest rates; but ideas were far from precisely clear.[5] *Inter alia*, statistical data were far poorer, and serious study of macro behaviour was in its infancy.

---

[3] Of the many studies of the period, I have relied most on Howson (1975) and Moggridge (1972) because of their detailed citation of official sources, and also on Pollard (1962). See also Youngson (1960), Skidelsky (1967), Sayers (1976), P. Clarke (1988) and Williamson (1992).

[4] Not only the Bank of England argued for high rates: Keynes had wanted a rise to 10 per cent (Howson 1975: 20).

[5] Montague Norman's reluctance to admit under cross questioning before the Macmillan Committee that high interest rates damage trade and employment is an illustration: 'The Governor

5. The Budget was not seen as an intrument of economic policy. It was almost unquestioned that the Budget should balance.[6] Keynes and others advocated public works to reduce unemployment, but they were not in power.[7] The orthodox 'Treasury view' (as the Chancellor said in 1929) continued to be: 'whatever ... the political and social advantages, very little additional employment, and no permanent additional employment, can, in fact, and as a general rule, be created by State borrowing and State expenditure'.[8]

6. The exchange rate too was not seen as an instrument of policy. Once the gold standard was restored and the parity fixed, there was no questioning of it. Nor did the Labour Government in the run-up to the crisis of 1931 ever thing of devaluing.[9]

Once Britain's departure from gold had happened, the Treasury appears to have felt a certain relief. Without a high exchange rate which had to be supported, interest rates could be lowered; and it seems that after 1931 the Treasury saw cheap money as desirable, as a way to stimulate industry.[10] Another sign of change was that by 1935 senior Treasury officials could even see a role for public works if private demand failed,[11] and the positive impact of fiscal policy became considerable [fig. 6.7]. When it came to it, increased defence spending (from 1935 on) was, with whatever demurs of conscience, financed by borrowing.

The lack of grip by those in power was never greater than in the crisis of 1931. On financial matters, the government relied on advice from the Bank of England as much as from Treasury officials (who in any case reflected City views as relayed by the Bank). The Labour Government that was in office in 1931 was not at all acquainted with financial matters, and was fairly completely

at first denied that the high bank rate he was forced to impose to maintain the gold standard was responsible for creating unemployment (Questions 3328, 3334–8, 3343–51); he was then driven to concede that it had some such effect (Qs. 3390–2, 3398–9); and finally to admitting that his high bank rate was designed directly to create unemployment (Qs. 3492–3). The burden of his evidence to the Macmillan Committee was that he was under such constant pressure to keep up rates to prevent a drain abroad that he could not, even had he wished, consider the effects on industry, but that until 1930, at least, he had not greatly troubled about them.' (Pollard 1962: 220, quoting from *Report of the Committee on Finance and Industry* (1931, Cmnd. 3897); *Minutes of Evidence*, 18th day). Economists of course had clearer ideas, but not always the same ideas, or necessarily right ones—they are still debated.

[6] Or more than balance: interwar budgets made provision for regular payments to a 'sinking fund' to repay wartime debt.

[7] Public works figured largely in the Liberal Party's programme of 1928, produced by a Committee which included Keynes and Hubert Henderson (Skidelsky 1967: 51–6). But Keynes I think never challenged the orthodox view directly by advocating deficit spending as such.

[8] Winston Churchill's budget speech, April 1929 (cited in Pollard 1962).

[9] As Keynes once said, devaluation was 'a thing that no nation ever in cold blood felt able to do' (Keynes Papers November 1930, quoted by Moggridge 1972: 229). (In the summer of 1931, however, Keynes appears to have contemplated a departure from the gold standard: Howson 1975: 79n.)

[10] Howson (1975: 86): Pollard (1962: 236–7) seems wrong in suggesting that this motivation only came after 1933.

[11] Howson (1975: 118).

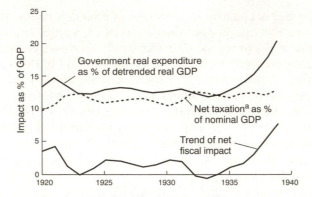

Fig. 6.7   Estimates of fiscal impacts: UK, 1920–1939

[a] Transfers and grants *less* direct and indirect taxation and other revenue, each type of transaction weighted to allow for different propensity to consume.

Sources: Feinstein (1972). For details of methods of estimation, see app. A5.

dependent on the (often unwelcome) advice its advisers gave.[12] After the Labour Government had resigned, when the bill suspending the gold standard was hurriedly passed on 21 September, one of its members could say, 'Nobody told us we could do this.'[13]

Despite some movement towards a more active economic policy, the *Full Employment* White Paper of 1944 would have been unthinkable before the War. Though the ambitious activism of the decades that followed has since faded, governments can no longer stand aside from the performance of the economies over which they preside, and when it is good they now claim credit for it. But it is unhistorical to assume that recent ways of thinking applied before 1939.

6.2. The 1920–1 recession and its aftermath

The 1921 recession emerged out of the blue and departed as quickly, but though brief it went very deep. Although by no means confined to the United Kingdom, it was deeper in the UK than elsewhere. Neither in the United States nor in Britain did anything comparable occur after World War II: that needs to be kept in mind when considering explanations.

---

[12] 'Under a Conservative government [there was] a network of personal relationships ... between the members of the government and the City of London; they had been to the same schools ... had ... hunted and shot and fished and dined together.' Under a Labour Government these relationships were severed. In 1931 there was not a single member of the Labour Cabinet who had any personal or practical experience of the working of the financial world.' (Goronwy Rees 1970: 168.)

[13] A remark variously attributed to Sydney Webb (by Taylor 1965: 297), and to Tom Johnston (by Rees 1970: 189).

6.2.1. A first survey of the recession

In the transition phase after World War I, events moved rapidly and moods could change in a very volatile way. The evidence is not straightforward to interpret. The task of this survey is to identify and explain recessions—in the sense of sudden shortfalls of demand relative to supply, such shortfalls being normally reflected in a growth of unemployment. The transition phase after World War I was a confused time, in which not only demand- but supply-side factors were undergoing rapid evolution, and whose influence on output is difficult to sort out.[14] The basic series that have to be made sense of are those of output, unemployment, and the general price level [table 6.4].

During the war the economy had operated under extreme pressure. Output had been expanded very rapidly in 1915, and more moderately in 1916, not only by absorbing the unemployed (unemployment fell to minimal levels), but by drawing greatly increased numbers of women into the labour force and by means of working long hours of overtime.[15] In the last two years of the war there was little further rise in output, as if the economy were operating at a ceiling. Prices rose briskly despite price controls and rising food subsidies—from 1915 on by around 20 per cent a year.

In the first years after the war, the signs appear contradictory:

- Output fell steeply in 1919, 1920, and again in 1921.
- Unemployment rose fairly sharply in 1919, but fell again next year before its huge rise in 1921.
- Prices continued to rise about as rapidly as in the war till 1921, when they fell sharply (and fell even more sharply in 1922).

One clearly cannot attach the normal significance to these diverse signals: I interpret them as the result of two complicating features:

1. There was a split economy. The war economy was being run down at breakneck speed, and demobilized men could not immediately be put into civilian employment—even though, given the large backlog of demand left unsatisfied during the war, civilian demand was very high.
2. In reaction to the exertions of wartime, there was a sharp supply-side contraction as hours of work fell and women left war work and returned to their homes.

I accordingly do not see the fall in output in 1919 and 1920 as a recession, and read the price rise as signifying overall boom conditions. Only in 1921 do all the signs—output, employment, and prices—point to a major recession.

---

[14] There has been a considerable discussion of whether World War I had permanent effects on the course of output. That is not of direct concern here. The further question of whether what happened during the war partly explains the recession of 1920–1 will be discussed later.

[15] After the war (according to Pigou 1947: 63), hours worked fell 10%. There seems also to have been a fall in output per hour.

Table 6.4　Output, unemployment, and the general price level in the UK, 1914–1922

	GDP[a]: annual % change	Unemployment[b]		Prices[c]: annual % change
		Level %	Annual % change	
1914	1.0	3.3	1.2	0.7
1915	8.0	1.1	−2.2	10.8
1916	2.3	0.4	−0.7	14.3
1917	0.9	0.6	0.2	26.5
1918	0.7	0.8	0.2	18.7
1919	−12.2	3.4	2.6	17.9
1920	−6.0	2.0	−1.4	20.4
1921	−8.8	11.3	9.3	−10.5
1922	5.3	9.8	−1.7	−16.1

[a] GDP at constant factor cost, average of income and expenditure series only till 1921, when output series also becomes available.
[b] % of civilian unemployment: see notes to Feinstein (1972: table 5).
[c] GDP factor cost deflator.

Source: Feinstein (1972).

That is how it appeared at the time. Indeed, unemployment had been expected to emerge immediately the war ended. Government expenditure fell with the cutback in defence spending in 1919 and 1920—but taxes were not cut [table 6.5]. Consumer spending rose in 1919; fixed investment rose most in 1920 [table 6.6]. There was a similar large demand in other countries, which Britain was better placed to satisfy than countries that had suffered more from war and postwar disorganization. UK exports therefore rose rapidly.[16] Apparently there was no build-up of stocks [table 6.6]: during the war stocks had been depleted, but according to Feinstein's estimates there was no very large build-up after the war and a decline in stocks as early as 1920.[17] The inflow into industry of men from the forces seems to have been accompanied by a fall in productivity; certainly there was a wave of strikes and industrial unrest.

Some of the fall in output in 1921—and consequently some of the rise in unemployment—may have been a result of continued supply-side contraction.

---

[16] Exports rose rapidly—as Pigou (1947: 64–5) says—because of the 'enormous needs for rehabilitation in many foreign countries alongside of the virtual disappearance of competition in exports from our prewar rivals'. But the volume of UK exports in 1920 was still below the 1913 level.
[17] In a very sharp short recession like 1921 one would expect inventory fluctuations to play a large role. Though Feinstein's estimates suggest that this was not the case, estimates of stock changes are one of the least reliable parts of the national accounts; and the estimates for the 1920s must be less reliable than for more recent years, particularly in this phase when the rapid change in prices must have bedevilled conversion of value into volume series. In 1921 there was a large residual in the national accounts which might represent unrecorded disinvestment in stocks. If so, disinvestment in stocks would explain a quarter of the fall in output.

Table 6.5 Impact of fiscal change, 1918–1921

	1918	1919	1920[a]	1920[b]	1921
			(£m)		
Current expenditure on goods and services	1840	930	520	490	490
Other current expenditure	440	630	660	640	670
Total expenditure	2,280	1,560	1,180	1,130	1,160
Tax receipts	820	1,050	1,170	1,130	1,080
Other receipts	150	90	70	70	120
Total receipts	970	1,140	1,240	1,200	1,200
Current balance	−1,310	−420	60	80	40
Change	−140	890	480	—	−40
Fiscal impact as % of GDP[c]	(..)	(..)	(..)	−(9.2)	(1.3)

[a] Includes southern Ireland.
[b] Excludes southern Ireland.
[c] From table A5.2: not available before 1920.

Source: Feinstein (1972).

Table 6.6 Components of change in total final expenditure: UK, 1919–1925

Categories of expenditure	Contribution to annual % change in final expenditure						
	1919[a]	1920[a]	1921	1922	1923	1924	1925
Consumer's spending	7.8	0.2	−4.1	2.5	2.0	1.6	1.6
Government	−18.7	−6.7	0.1	−0.6	−0.5	0.1	0.3
Fixed investment	0.5	2.3	0.9	−0.6	0.2	1.0	1.0
Exports	4.1	1.0	−3.4	3.7	1.7	0.6	−0.1
Final sales	−6.3	−3.2	−6.6	5.0	3.3	3.3	2.8
Investment in stocks	0.0	−2.6	−0.2	0.2	0.4	0.8	1.8
Total final expenditure	−6.3	−5.9	−6.8	5.2	3.7	4.1	4.6
less Imports	1.4	−0.1	−1.8	2.2	1.1	1.6	0.4
GDP(E)	−7.7	−5.8	−5.0	3.0	2.6	2.5	4.1
(% change in GDP[b])	(−10.9)	(−6.0)	(−8.1)	(5.1)	(3.2)	(4.2)	(4.9)

[a] Includes southern Ireland.
[b] GDP(A).

Source: Feinstein (1972).

But most must probably have been due to a fall in demand. The uncertain, possibly mixed, origin of the output fall creates a similar ambiguity in interpreting the expenditure figures. Some of the fall in total expenditure (like that in output) could have reflected a supply constraint, e.g. the strikes in the textile industries. But it seems likely that most of the fall in exports, and most of the fall in consumers' expenditure, represented a fall in demand.

In a downturn, employment usually falls (and unemployment usually rises) proportionately much less than output: on this occasion the reverse was true, and unemployment rose as much or more. It rose over 9 percentage points in 1921 and the number of employees fell by 11 per cent, against a fall in output of only somewhat over 8 per cent [table 6.7]. I have not seen an explanation of why this happened. Perhaps there had been an element of speculation in firms' previous recruiting. In the first rush of demobilization in a vigorous boom, firms may have taken on workers in the expectation that they would be needed; and for this reason could have been quick to turn them away when this optimism proved mistaken. It also seems the case that profits declined very markedly as early as 1920; and they declined further in 1921 [table 6.7(*b*)].[18] That must have put great pressure on firms to cut back hard on costs, including employment.

Whatever the reason, the fall in employment helps to explain why consumer expenditure was cut back so abruptly in 1921. Estimates are not available on how real personal incomes fared, but the larger part of total employment income fell over 10 per cent in real terms, chiefly because of the sudden cut in numbers employed.[19] This fall in real employment income occurred despite the fact that the terms of trade, taken on their own, improved domestic purchasing power by 2 per cent in 1921 [table 6.7(*a*)].

Contemporary opinion saw the turning point as coming in 1920, even though the full scale of the recession was not seen till next year. The timing of the recession has some relevance to the question of what caused it. Pigou dates its start as the spring of 1920, but he was looking at prices and bank deposits rather than real indicators. Industrial production, exports, and unemployment all indicate a later turning point, in the last quarter of 1920. (The turn in the United States seems to have been somewhat earlier: industrial production turned down in the spring and wholesale prices in May.) The recession was at first more of a check to output growth and rapid inflation than a recession. But in the autumn prices, output, and confidence took a sudden downturn. We are interested in this recession because it was so deep; and to explain the sudden deepening is as relevant as why it first started.

---

[18] Companies' nominal trading profits fell in 1920 (Feinstein 1972: table 1); in real terms they must have declined much more. That implies that firms' product prices in 1920 lagged behind costs, though it is not clear why they should have done so when both costs and prices were rising steeply.

[19] In effect, the consumption multiplier must have been much larger than in other recessions because employment was cut much more in relation to output than in normal times.

Table 6.7 Changes in UK prices and costs, 1917–1923

	% change in expenditure deflators					
	1918[a]	1919[a]	1920[a]	1921	1922	1923
(a) Changes in final prices						
Government						
expenditure	14.5	15.6	−2.8	−1.1	−5.2	−3.7
Consumers'						
expenditure	22.0	10.1	15.4	−8.6	−14.0	−6.0
Fixed investment	9.5	16.7	29.0	−17.2	−9.6	−14.6
Exports	10.9	6.5	29.9	−31.3	−24.2	−4.9
Total final prices	16.1	17.1	20.0	−15.3	−14.4	−5.9
of which						
Imports	9.0	6.7	18.8	−33.3	−19.9	−1.9
GDP[b]	17.7	16.7	19.5	−8.9	−13.8	−7.1
Change in						
terms of trade[b]	1.9	−0.2	11.1	2.1	−4.3	−2.9
(b) % changes in labour costs and profits						
Average real income						
from employment[c]	2.1	−14.9	−10.6	0.8	−1.3	0.7
Number in						
employment[c]	−0.8	12.1	9.4	−10.9	0.4	1.6
Total real						
employment						
income[c]	1.3	−2.8	−1.2	−10.1	−0.9	2.3
Real unit profits[d]	−5.2	3.4	−20.7	−2.6	28.3	4.1

[a] Includes southern Ireland
[b] Index of export prices divided by index of import prices *less* 100.
[c] Assumes that number of employees changes in proportion to number in civilian employment.
[d] Total non-employment income inclusive of stock appreciation per unit of real GDP deflated by TFE deflator.

Source: Feinstein (1972).

6.2.2. The 1921 recession in the United States

Developments in the United States were in some ways similar to those in Britain. As in Britain, output fell in the first two years after the war [table 6.8]—probably here too for supply-side reasons of a similar sort, for it is clear that in the USA too these were years of high demand. As in Britain, defence spending declined precipitately; by 1921, as in Britain, the rundown was over. Friedman and Schwartz (1963: 232) can remark that, 'although this contraction was relatively brief … it ranks as one of the severest on record'. Even so, the fall in output was much less steep than in Britain. (GNP fell only 2.5 per cent in 1921; indeed,

Table 6.8 Components of change in total final expenditure: USA, 1919–1924

	Contributions to % change in TFE					
	1919	1920	1921	1922	1923	1924
Government expenditure	−8.1	−5.1	1.2	−0.2	−0.0	0.6
Consumers' expenditure	2.5	3.0	4.3	2.7	6.4	5.1
Fixed investment	0.3	−1.3	−1.1	4.0	3.0	0.8
Exports	−1.7	−1.0	−1.6	−0.1	0.2	0.5
Total final sales	−6.9	−4.3	2.9	6.3	9.6	7.0
Stock change	2.8	1.8	−5.6	0.5	3.1	−4.1
Total final expenditure	−4.2	−2.5	−2.7	6.8	12.7	2.9
of which						
Imports	0.6	−0.5	−0.6	1.0	−0.0	0.0
GDP	−4.8	−1.9	−2.1	5.8	12.7	2.9
% change in GDP	−5.0	−2.0	−2.3	6.1	13.3	3.0

Source: Kendrick (1961) and *Historical Statistics of the United States*, 1960.

final sales that year *rose* quite strongly.) Exports certainly declined, as British exports did; but US exports (which had benefited much during the war from the interruption of competing sources of supply) had been declining quite steeply for the previous two years. Consumer expenditure after the war was extremely strong and had been rising massively ever since 1918, as it was to go on doing for the next three years. In the United States, therefore, the recession (unlike what Feinstein's figures show for the UK) seems to have been entirely an inventory recession. (On Kendrick's estimates, the turnround in stockbuilding was enough to cause GNP to fall nearly 6 per cent.)

Against this background, the rise in unemployment in the United States is even more striking than in the United Kingdom; for it was almost as large, and as sudden. (On figures quoted by Maddison, 1982, unemployment rose from 3.9 to 11.4 per cent.) As the fall in output was moderate, the rise in unemployment was proportionately several times the change in output. Why that should have happened is no more clear than for the United Kingdom.

6.2.3. Proposed explanation for the UK recession

Before proposing possible explanations for the UK recession, I first reject one explanation which must, I think, be wrong. Pigou asserts that the underlying reason for the slump was simple: that postwar excess demand left over from the war had been worked off by 1921.[20] But that I think was clearly not the reason. Not much capital had been replaced by 1920: according to Feinstein, the cumulative disinvestment of the war years was not made good till 1926. Gross investment rose in 1921 (in total and most categories) and declined only *after* 1921, i.e. presumably as a result, not an originating cause, of the recession. The high consumer spending after the war was (not surprisingly) reflected in Feinstein's negative figures for personal saving. Unreliable though these figures must be, they form a consistent picture, with negative saving continuing up to 1923 and low saving for a further three years.

My proposed explanation is threefold:

1. Fiscal policy in the first years after the war had a large negative impact.
2. This was superimposed on an economy in which, after a period of high boom, confidence anyhow was ready to collapse.
3. There was a worldwide collapse of demand, causing a big drop in UK exports.

The first and last of these factors is reflected in table 6.2. However, one would not expect a standard table of this sort to do justice to the oddities of a very odd recession. Thus, the table taken at face value leaves little room for expectational effects ('other' factors sum to zero.) The true effect of monetary policy, again, was probably to trigger this collapse in confidence—another effect not well measured in the table.

The impact of Budget changes

In the war years the Budget had been in heavy deficit. In 1918, the peak year of spending, current receipts covered under half the current spending of the public authorities [table 6.5]. In the two following years spending fell rapidly but tax rates did not, and by as early as 1922 the previous very large deficit was eliminated.

The positive fiscal impacts of the war years, when war expenditure was growing, thus gave place to large negative impacts as spending fell off. The postwar surge of private demand must at first have been so great as to offset this extremely large deflationary impact. (The negative fiscal effect would have been more than enough on its own in 1919 and 1920 to account for the recession [table 6.5].)

Getting the budget quickly back into balance clearly seemed the right course to those in charge of policy. There were strong pressures at the time to re-establish conditions of financial orthodoxy. The Cunliffe Committee had been set up during the war to report on future policy towards the 'currency and foreign

---

[20] Pigou (1947: 188) says: 'after the war there was an enormous mass of what we may call once-for-all work to be done. Huge losses of shipping awaited replacement. The capital equipment of railways and many industrial establishments had been allowed to deteriorate and an immense amount of maintenance and repair was called for. The stocks of many things in the hands of dealers and shopkeepers had perforce fallen very low and needed to be built up again. When these various tasks had been carried so far as it was found practicable to carry them, there was nothing obvious to take their place. That was the primary force at work.'

exchanges'. It reported strongly in favour of a return to the gold standard at the prewar parity as soon as possible; an early cessation of government borrowing was among the means seen as necessary to that end, together with high interest rates for some years.[21] To modern eyes this can appear a deliberate strategy of deflating the economy in order to restore a fixed exchange rate at too high a parity;[22] but at the time the ends and means of policy were not so distinct and apparent.

Expectational and confidence factors

The general state of expectations before the recession was probably ambivalent. Accounts of the boom stress the rapid inflation and widespread speculation. There was 'much speculative buying of commodities, securities and real estate', frequently financed by bank loans, accompanied by the 'flotation of new companies, the sale of old ones, and the issue of new shares' (Howson 1975: 10). Speculative excesses were most evident in the older industries (e.g. cotton and shipbuilding), and these found themselves over-indebted when prices and profits fell. But as noted, there had earlier been a general expectation that after the war the economy unsupported by war expenditure would fall into early recession. When this did not occur, many people must have deferred the expected event but gone on expecting it. They may also have expected that the authorities would step in to control excessive speculation. Such speculation was indeed a major concern of the authorities in both the United Kingdom and the United States, and lay behind their eventual decision to raise interest rates. Though many traders continued to act as if rising prices would go on for ever, speculative expectations must always be fragile and conceal a potential readiness to change if the times change.

Once the downturn started, speculative forces must have gone into reverse and accentuated the downward movement (see Pigou 1947: 194–5). The way in which expectational and confidence factors reinforced each other must have been much more powerful in a period when it was as likely that the price level would fall as that it would rise. It is now many decades since such price instability existed, and how the economy operated under such conditions has ceased to be part of our direct experience.

Exports

The fall in exports also made a major contribution to the recession of 1921 [table 6.2]. It is not clear why exports fell off so steeply, but three possible reasons may be indicated. First, as other countries got back into production, and as the immediate postwar shortages of shipping were remedied, supplies became

---

[21] *Interim Report*, August 1918; *Final Report*, December 1919.

[22] E.g., 'The severe deflation of 1920 onwards became the first step in a consistent policy which had one overriding aim: the restoration of the gold standard at the old parity at the earliest possible moment' (Pollard 1962: 216).

available from other sources. (But why then did exports revive in 1922 [table 6.6] by as much as they had fallen in 1921?) Second, it was argued above that there was a large speculative element in home demand. The same may have been true of overseas demand; i.e., stocks of goods in course of transshipment and distribution may have got too high. Third, there were numerous strikes, especially in 1921, in textiles and coal mining, both then heavy exporting industries;[23] that would rank as a supply contraction not a demand recession.

Monetary policy

Bank rate was raised to 7 per cent in April 1920,[24] which except for July and August 1914 was its highest level since the crisis of 1907. April is the date often given for the end of the boom, though (as noted) only at the end of the year did the recession get going in earnest. Hawtrey and others have attributed the recession to the 7 per cent Bank rate; Howson disagrees, on the ground that the rise was too small to have had much effect. It could however have triggered a major change in business confidence, which could have been potent (which is what Hawtrey appears to have meant: see Hawtrey 1933: 414, and Pigou 1947: 190).

There has been the same dispute in the United States about the effect of the rise in interest rates. (They rose a little earlier than in Britain.) After most Federal Reserve banks had raised their discount rates to $4\frac{3}{4}$ per cent in late 1919, rates were raised to a uniform 6 per cent in January/February 1920. This was 'the sharpest single rise in the entire history of the system' say Friedman and Schwartz (1963: 230), who see it as crucially important, and brand it as too much and too late; while Wilson (1942) argues that the rise in rates was too small to have mattered, given the pace at which prices were changing at the time. But again, it could have had a large effect on market psychology.

There is some question whether the 1921 recession may not have originated in the United States. But this was the sort of recession in which expectational factors expressing themselves through price movements were important; and influences were quickly transmitted and quickly became worldwide. That makes it difficult to distinguish how much came from one place rather than another, and less meaningful to try.[25]

It has also been suggested that the fall in output in the recession was somehow due to the shock of World War I. Gregory and Oxley (1996) for instance argue that continuing low employment after the war was due to a rise

---

[23] The UK share in the exports of the main industrial countries seems to have fallen heavily in 1921 and revived in 1922.

[24] Bank rate had been raised from 5% to 6% in November.

[25] Compare Friedman and Schwartz (1963: 236): 'The price and output movements of the post-World War I years in this country were, of course, part of a worldwide movement. Throughout most of the world, for victors, vanquished and neutral alike, prices rose sharply before or into 1920 and fell sharply thereafter. About the only countries that avoided the price decline were those that were to experience hyperinflation.'

in the exchange rate—which (on some estimates) occurred during, not after, the war. That could have been one factor; but it does not help to explain the sudden fall of output in 1921 and partial recovery afterwards.[26]

6.2.4. Aftermath of the recession

Output rose quickly in the years after the recession, making good half its fall in 1921 [table 6.6]; it continued to rise relatively fast for three more years, then fell back to no more than trend growth. Table 6.2 suggests that the recovery of 1922–5 was due to three large favourable factors which more than offset three large unfavourable ones. The favourable ones were:

1. the growth of exports, reflecting worldwide recovery from war scarcities (despite some probable rise in the effective exchange rate in preparation for the return of gold);
2. very high stockbuilding;
3. the (partial) relaxation of monetary policy (an effect which table 6.6 perhaps exaggerates).

The three countervailing unfavourable factors were:

1. the continued deflationary impact of fiscal policy (though now somewhat less extreme);
2. the resumption of positive personal savings after the dissaving of the early postwar years;
3. the restoration of more normal (i.e. less favourable) terms of trade for industrial countries [fig. 6.5].

There was thus no simple single cause of this recovery phase. All the six factors, as they operated at the time, may probably be counted as exogenous. Most may be seen as manifestations in one way or another of worldwide recovery from World War I. Expansion in the UK was somewhat less rapid than in other countries [fig. 6.3]—perhaps because of generally cautious UK policy in the years leading up to the restoration of the gold standard in 1925.[27] The recovery was a new phase, and does not throw much light on the causes of the recession that preceded it.

---

[26] Greasley and Oxley (1996) discuss the considerable literature on the effects of World War I. Their aim is to detect and explain discontinuities in industrial growth in the first 30 or 40 years of the century. In my view, it is a defect of their analysis that they failed to distinguish between discontinuities in the growth of supply potential and discontinuities in the degree of its employment. It does not require elaborate analysis to discover that unemployment became much higher after 1920 than before.

[27] This proposition would however take more detailed analysis to justify reasonably firmly. Figure 6.3 for instance does not show that UK output relative to trend grew less fast than other countries' output relative to their trends—though that was in fact probably the case. Nor has an international analysis of the causes of relative growth rates been attempted.

6.2.5. Summary of conclusions

The explanation that I propose for the 1921 recession is as follows.

1. The major tightening of fiscal stance, as war expenditure fell off, had a major deflationary impact; at first this was offset by a hectic boom in private demand, but it was revealed when the boom collapsed.
2. There were large elements of speculative demand in the postwar boom, based on the expectation of a continuation of high demand and also of rapidly rising prices.
3. That was a bubble situation, the proximate cause of whose collapse might well have been the rise in interest rates in Britain and the United States.
4. The fall in demand was magnified by the downward flexibility of prices that then existed. This collapse of optimism, it is suggested, affected not only stockholding but also exports and employment, and via that consumer expenditure.[28]

To what extent should the causation of this recession be described as exogenous? Changes in fiscal and monetary policy are exogenous events. Their impact, it is suggested, was greatly intensified by the unstable speculative conditions on which they were superimposed. The collapse of a bubble is at some point inevitable and therefore can be regarded as an endogenous event. Behind that, however, the high demand that started the process was itself exogenously caused—as will be the case also in several later recessions.

6.3. The Great Depression: the world and the United States, 1929–1933

The Great Depression of the 1930s in the United States was so large that no explanations carry full conviction and all are controversial. For most of the two-thirds of a century since it happened, economists have seen it as primarily a US phenomenon, and looked to the United States for its causes. More recently some have claimed it as an international phenomenon and have even seen its causes in international financial arrangements. Here it will be argued that the older view was right. This section therefore looks chiefly at the USA, and brings in other countries only inasmuch as their experiences help to explain events in the USA.

What has to be remembered in reading this section is the extreme nature of the Great Depression. GNP fell in real terms by the order of 10 per cent—not just for one year but for three years running. Whatever way one looks at it,

---

[28] Milton Friedman blames the authorities' actions as being too late and too large, and, as on later occasions, thus sees the recession as the fault of the authorities. It might have been better if they had acted earlier to restrain the boom. But the authorities cannot take nicely calculated action when trying to tame a strong speculative boom: they are in the position of St George faced with an untameable monster. Milton Friedman's belief in the omnipotent effect of controlling the growth of the money stock ironically makes him into something of a believer in fine-tuning.

that is enormous: it could mean one firm in ten ceasing production in each of those years, or every firm reducing output by a tenth (and employment as much).[29] One must think of this being done very rapidly: of consumers cutting their spending each year by a tenth, some by less some by much more, without waiting to see what this year's income was going to be: or of firms cutting investment by a third each year, again without waiting to know what profits were. It must, when one thinks of it, have been more panic than orderly process, and it should not be surprising if an orderly explanation fails to fit.

Since the story is so wide-ranging, it seems best to start with a summary of the argument, and to attempt some justification for choosing to take this line in cutting a way through the tangle. I then set out what seem the main causes (and what the minor ones), first for the onset of the recession, and second, and as important, for its huge depth. The section concludes with brief remarks on the US recovery.

6.3.1. Summary of the argument

It has become fashionable to say that the Great Depression of the 1930s was not just a US but a world depression. That is less than half true. Quantitatively much the greater part of the depression was in the United States; and (it will be argued) the causes of both its origin and its amplification lay mostly there also.

Any recession causes a country to import less, and a large one much less. Transmission by international trade spread the recession by direct and indirect routes to most countries, and, it will be argued, was the main route by which the recession was transmitted. The trade transmission mechanism, though obvious enough, has not previously been given much emphasis. (More emphasis has been placed on the reduction of US capital outflows, which it is here argued were not a cause but a consequence of recession.)

Most countries experienced a fall in output over the three years 1929–32; but not all countries did, and the extent of the fall was very uneven. Whereas in the USA the fall was 28 per cent (29 per cent over the four years 1929–32), in France and Germany it was about 15 per cent, and in Europe as a whole (including France and Germany) it was half that again, around 7 per cent.[30] In some industrial countries, output rose significantly through these three years.

The extent of the fall in output during the recession is better measured by the shortfall of output below trend. In the USA (where GNP fell absolutely by 29 per cent) I estimate the shortfall below trend as 46 per cent. The other industrial countries, which were then mainly confined to Europe, had a combined GDP that was about equal to that of the USA; there (on rough

---

[29] Even these figures understate the scale. Compared with what might have been—as indicated by the trend—output fell by nearly a half [see table 6.2].

[30] Detailed figures are in table 6.1.

estimates) the absolute fall in GDP was probably about 5 per cent, and the shortfall below trend maybe 12 per cent. If this is so, 80 per cent of the Great Depression, in so far as it affected industrial countries, was in the United States [table 6.9].

The recession also severely affected the less developed countries who supplied the industrial countries with primary commodities. Total US imports fell in volume by a third, in value by twice that. Imports from the primary producers fell the most; their export earnings probably fell to a third of what they had been. As a consequence they had to cut imports of manufactures, and the larger part of that cut fell on Europe. This indirect effect on Europe via third countries' trade was the chief way in which the US recession reduced demand in Europe. Europe's exports to primary producers had amounted to 5 per cent of its GDP: by 1932 they had fallen to 2 per cent. That was an appreciable slice off total demand in Europe, concentrated on the most industrialized European countries. This immediately provides an explanation for a good part of the recession in countries outside the United States.

As demand fell in these countries, they too reduced imports—including imports from the USA; and that, as the recession deepened, further reduced demand in the United States itself. In so far as the channel was as described above, that should be regarded as a secondary effect of the US recession being re-exported back to the United States, i.e. not a new exogenous factor. However, it is true that in Germany and France, the two European countries with the largest recessions, there must have been independent factors at work. However, compared with the other routes just described, the impact of these two local recessions on the USA (and on the UK) can have been only quite small.

The following analysis will make an heroic attempt to stay with a handful of causes which must have been the major ones. The picture of the trade transmission process described above provides some magnitudes against which to judge the scale of different effects, and to separate out the large from the smaller effects. Since our prime interest here is on the United States, we will need to pursue the smaller trains of causation only a certain way.

Table 6.9 The Great Depression in industrial countries

	Index (100=US GNP)		
	USA	Europe	Total
GNP/GDP	100	100	200
Absolute fall, 1929–32	32	5	37
Fall below trend	46	12	58
Proportion of total (%)	80	20	100

Source: see appendix A6.3.

The depression could have originated, in whole or in part, in events that happened before 1929, perhaps well before 1929. The following paragraphs therefore give a selective account of events both in the rest of the world and in the United States itself, concentrating on those for which a case can be made for thinking that they contributed significantly to the depression.

6.3.2. The antecedents of the Great Depression

A vast amount has been written about the US depression, perhaps more than anyone can now master; and this section is a digression about the USA in one of a set of chapters about the UK. The digression will thus aim to be brief, but even so will have to be detailed and fairly extensive.

I shall begin with the factors that could have got the US Great Depression started—and even in the first year could have produced a large recession. It is another question what made the recession go to the extraordinary depths it did: this will be discussed in section 6.3.3. I start with what I regard as probably the main factor, a *swing from high to low consumer and business confidence.* This is discussed along with

- US monetary policy;
- the stock market boom and crash.

Other factors discussed are:

- the possibility that investment opportunities had been exhausted;
- the rise and fall in demand for housing;
- depression in Germany;
- the instability of trade between industrial and primary-producing countries;
- defects of the gold exchange standard.

The swing in consumer/business confidence

It should be noted that it is difficult to use econometric tests of the contribution of various factors discussed below to the causation of the Great Depression, because all important variables turned down together. Statistically, consumer expenditure accounts for a large part of the fall in output—which must in turn have influenced share prices, and that in turn, consumer expenditure. Given the rapidity of events in 1929, these interrelations cannot be disentangled. Much the same applies to fixed investment, which declined along with output, profits, and share prices: between each pair of these four variables, there must be presumed to be bidirectional causal relations.

In the case of the 1921 UK recession, I argued that the downward flexibility of prices must have been a major factor in promoting the rapid decline in output. In the Great Depression, the US price level did not at first fall much (the final expenditure deflator fell only 4 per cent between 1929 and 1930 [fig. 6.8]), though later it fell more steeply (9 per cent in 1930–1, 11.5 per cent 1931–2).

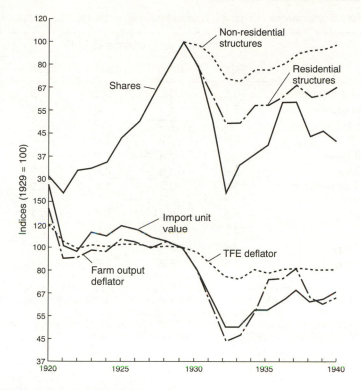

Fig. 6.8   Prices in the USA, 1920–1940

Sources: *National Income and Product Accounts of the United States*, 1986; *Historical Statistics of the United States*, 1975, pp. 891 and 1005.

The depression followed several years of very rapid growth during which there were clear signs of demand having become partly speculative, i.e. inflated by anticipatory buying undertaken in the expectation that prices would continue to rise. That is a bubble situation, familiar from other episodes, in which over-confidence is inherently fragile, and is bound at some stage, as a result of minor events, to give place to a depressed state of confidence and therefore lower spending.[31]

In the United States, unlike the United Kingdom, the period 1922–9 was a period of extremely rapid growth. GNP grew on average by 5.5 per cent a year; and after the high unemployment of 1921 and 1922 (11 and 7 per cent respectively) unemployment came down to a low average of 3.5 per cent. The instability of prices in the immediate postwar years in the USA was succeeded by eight years

---

[31] In the first draft of this chapter I gave little weight to the effect of such swings in confidence and did not include it as one of the main factors. In now giving confidence factors prominence, I have been influenced by their having appeared to be important in two UK recessions (1920–1 and 1973–5), and the main factor in 1989–93.

Table 6.10   Components of change in total final expenditure: USA, 1924–1929

	Contributions to % change in TFE				
	1925	1926	1927	1928	1929
Government expenditure	0.5	0.0	0.3	0.3	0.3
Consumer expenditure	−2.1	5.7	1.6	1.6	4.0
Fixed investment	1.5	1.2	−0.7	0.3	−0.3
Exports[a]	0.4	0.5	0.5	0.2	0.3
Total final sales	0.2	7.4	1.9	1.8	4.2
Stock change	2.8	−0.5	0.8	−0.8	2.0
Total final expenditure *of which*:	3.0	6.9	1.1	1.1	6.2
Imports[a]	0.2	0.4	0.2	0.2	0.7
GNP	2.3	5.6	12.6	2.8	2.3
Residual[b]	0.4	0.4	0.0	−0.3	−0.2
% change in GNP	2.3	6.5	1.0	1.1	6.1

[a] Exports and imports of goods and services at 1929 prices, estimated by deflating the exports and imports of goods and services in current prices with the unit value indices of exports and imports of commodities only, from *Historical Statistics of the United States*, 1960.
[b] The difference between Kendrick's estimate of GNP calculated with net foreign trade and the estimate of GNP obtained with exports and imports estimated as in n. *a*.
Source: Kendrick (1961).

when prices were approximately stable. The rate of growth however saw large fluctuations [tables 6.8 and 6.10]: there was a vast expansion in 1923, a growth of over 5 per cent in three other years (1922, 1926, 1929), and quite slow growth in the years in between (1924, 1925, 1927, 1928). These minor cycles—the National Bureau distinguishes two and a half cycles between the trough of July 1921 and the peak of June 1929—are more easily seen in a chart of the quarterly index of industrial production [fig. 6.9]. Continued rapid expansion generated (so it is reported) a widespread illusion that America had found the secret of continual prosperity. The rapid changes of pace, and the relatively short period of really hectic growth, cannot however have created deep-seated confidence that it would last.

The rapid expansion was bound to be checked some time. It was checked in mid-1929 [fig. 6.9]. There followed in 1930 a big fall in consumption, a very big fall in fixed investment, and a big fall in stocks [table 6.11]. These abrupt falls in demand fully fit the hypothesis that there was a large downward shock to expectations of a sort that is likely to follow an excessive boom; they are indeed difficult to explain on any other hypothesis.[32] There is thus indirect evidence

[32] Part of the fall in consumption must have been the multiplier reaction to the fall in investment, but it was too large to be only that; i.e., the personal savings ratio rose. Similarly, the fall in investment must have been a reaction to the fall in consumption, but, again, was too large

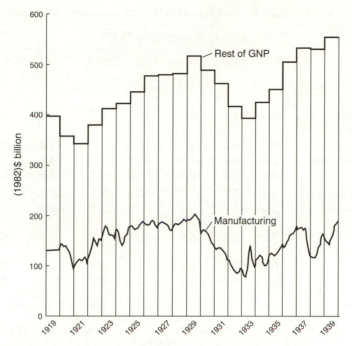

Fig. 6.9 Manufacturing and other output in the USA, 1919–1939

The monthly indices of manufacturing output were linked to a continuous index covering the years 1920–47. The 1947 real value of GNP in manufacturing was extrapolated backwards to 1920 with the annual averages of the monthly series. For 1919 the annual index number of manufacturing output was used for this purpose. GNP in construction was extrapolated backward to 1919 with the annual series of real expenditure on new construction. The annual estimates of GNP in manufacturing and construction thus obtained were deducted from total GNP. The remainder is shown as the top of each bar.

The annual estimates of GNP in manufacturing and construction were transformed into monthly figures, using the monthly indices of manufacturing output.

Sources: *National Income and Product Accounts of the United States*, 1986; *Statistical Abstract of the United States*, various years; *Historical Statistics of the United States*, 1975, p. 623.

that, in effect, the Great Depression was started by the previous boom having been too fast to be sustainable.

Given a potentially unstable situation, the downturn could well have been triggered by monetary policy (the official discount rate was raised to 7 per cent in April 1929); or by the stock exchange crash in November. It has been argued that these two factors acted as more than just triggers and deserve to rank in their own right as causes of the downturn. These contentions do not seem to me convincing.

and too abrupt to be only that; i.e., it must have largely reflected not just a change in firms' real circumstances, but a change in firms' reactions to them.

Table 6.11   Contributions to change in total final expenditure: USA, 1929–1933

	Contributions to % change in TFE						
	1929	1930	1931	1932	1933	Total[a] 1929–33	Indication of error[b]
Government expenditure	(0.3)	1.2	0.5	−0.7	−0.7	0.3	0.1
Consumer expenditure	(4.0)	−4.2	−2.6	−6.0	−1.2	14.0	0.2
Fixed investment	(−0.3)	−4.0	−4.6	−4.6	−1.0	14.2	0.9
Exports	(0.3)	−0.9	−0.9	−1.0	−0.1	−2.9	0.1
Total final sales	(4.2)	−7.9	−7.6	−12.3	−3.0	−30.8	0.7
Stock change	(2.0)	−1.6	−0.9	−1.5	1.1	−2.9	0.5
Total final expenditure	(6.2)	−9.5	−8.5	−13.8	−1.9	−33.8	0.2
of which:							
Imports	(0.7)	−0.5	−0.4	−1.1	0.1	−2.0	0.1
GNP	(5.7)	−8.9	−8.1	−12.7	−2.0	−31.8	0.3

[a] Sum of annual % changes over the four years. Note that total % fall in GNP between 1929 and 1933 is 33.6% as compared with the sum of annual % changes shown above.
[b] Kendrick's estimates for the years 1920–40 differ considerably from the later official estimates, and his estimate of the fall in GDP in 1929–33 is considerably larger than the later estimate shown in table 6.1.
Sources: 1929 from Kendrick (1961); other years from *National Income and Product Accounts of the United States*, 1986.

The influence of monetary policy

The monetary authorities in the period before the Wall Street crash were pre-occupied chiefly by the stock market boom. Faced with that, the Federal Reserve Board was divided in purpose. It wished to restrain speculation, and a rise in interest rates (for instance in the course of 1928) might have done so. On the other hand, it did not want to act in such a way as to halt the economic expansion.[33]

Friedman and Schwartz (1963: 292) claim that this division of purpose worsened the subsequent depression; for 'a vigorous restrictive policy in early 1928 might well have broken the stock market boom without its having to be kept in effect long enough to constitute a serious drag on business in general'. Firm action not having been taken earlier, they claim, monetary policy was kept tighter than it need have been in 1929 in the interests of restraining the stock market; and that exerted 'steady deflationary pressure on the economy'. But the evidence they adduce for the latter assertion is weak.[34]

[33] Official discount rates had been raised to 6% only in August—though before then the official purchasing rate for bills was stepped up several times.
[34] The evidence cited is that high-powered money was constant or fell in 1928 and 1929, that the narrow money stock declined slightly, and that wholesale prices declined slightly from the autumn of 1928.

What was perhaps more important is that the nervousness of the authorities must have been evident to the markets, and itself a major influence overhanging them.[35] European stock markets peaked six to twelve months before Wall Street (Kindleberger 1973: fig. 6). When therefore the discount rate was at length raised in August it must have given a powerful signal. That could have been crucial not only for expectations in the stock market, but for the expectations of business generally.

Friedman and Schwartz (1963) argue that money stock determines real national output. The reasons I find their general argument defective are set out in Appendix A6.1; their view that the trend in money was decisive at the start of the Great Depression also seems to me unconvincing. 'The trend of the money stock', they note, 'changed from horizontal to mildly downward': it declined 2.6 per cent in the year to October 1930, mostly in the second part of that year, by which time the depression was in full swing. They claim that other depressive effects were 'strongly reinforced' by this (rather slight) check to monetary growth. Bank failures, important later, can hardly have been a causal factor at this point, because the first big wave of failures did not come until May 1930 [fig. 6.10]. Fiscal policy (in contrast to monetary policy) is hardly mentioned in most of the discussion. In 1930 and 1931 its impact appears to have been substantially expansionary, and to have become contractionary only in 1932 and 1933 [table 6.12].

The Wall Street crash of October 1929

The preceding boom on Wall Street had been unprecedentedly large. Share prices rose fairly continuously in the three and a half years before the crash in October 1929. Between March 1926 and October 1929 the rise was 2.2 times, somewhat accelerating in 1928 till a pause in early 1929 [fig. 6.8 shows annual figures].

Though there was a strong speculative element in its later stages, the boom had not been due simply to wildly exaggerated speculation. Stock market prices rose in every year between 1921 and 1929 at an average annual rate of 18 per cent. Nevertheless, as Wilson (1942: 144) noted, 'by far the larger part of the increase in [share] prices was the consequence of an enormous rise in the earning power of capital, and was therefore a right and proper occurrence'.

One can say, then, that the boom reflected confidence that growth, and the profits associated with growth, would continue—and that the crash represented a sudden loss of that confidence, by at least the wide segment of the population that owned shares. Share prices fell about 20 per cent between 1929 and 1930; but the real plunge in prices came over the next two years, and by 1932 was to

---

[35] At the end of March 1929—7 mos. before the crash, it became known that the Federal Reserve Board was meeting in daily session (Galbraith 1955: 42–3). The Board however maintained what soon became a 'demoralizing silence'. In Galbraith's words, a 'wave of fear swept the market'—which could have ended the bull market then, not in October, but for the action of the New York Fed (going directly against the line of the Washington Board) in arranging for money to be lent to support the market.

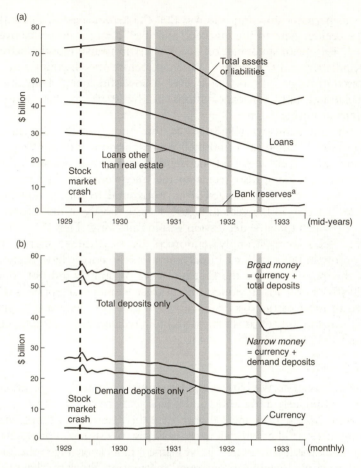

Fig. 6.10 The balance sheet of the banks and the money stock: USA, 1929–1933
(*a*) Assets of the banking system (all banks)
(*b*) The nonbank public's holdings of money

Shaded areas show worst periods of bank closures, i.e. months when deposits of suspended commerical banks exceeded $100 m (from Friedman and Schwartz 1963: chart 30).
[a]Banks' holdings of high-powered money, defined as vault cash plus deposits with the Federal Reserve.

Sources: *Historical Statistics of the United States*, 1960; Friedman and Schwartz (1963: tables A1 and A2).

carry the index down to under 30 per cent of its 1929 peak. (That is relevant to the question, to be looked at later, of why the depression continued for so long and sank to such depths, but not to the present question of why recession started.)

Among central bankers, the end of the stock market boom was greeted with relief, not fear that it would lead to depression. Although the popular view at the time was that the crash caused the depression, which is perhaps itself some

Table 6.12   Fiscal policy impact in the USA, 1930–1933

	Contribution to % change in GNP		
	Effects of change in expenditure on goods and services[a]	Effects of change in ratio of tax and other receipts *less* transfers, etc.[b]	Total fiscal impact[c]
1930	1.8	−0.8	1.0
1931	1.1	0.5	1.6
1932	−0.1	−2.3	−2.4
1933	0.0	−0.8	−0.8
Total 4 years	2.8	−3.4	−0.6

[a]Change in expenditure on goods and services as % of detrended GNP, all at 1982 prices. Trend GNP is the product of the fitted trends of output per worker and total labour force.
[b]Change in tax and other receipts *less* grants, subsidies, and transfers as % of GNP at current prices.
[c]For methods of estimation, see app. A5.
Sources: *National Income and Product Accounts of the United States*, 1986.

evidence that it was an important influence, there is no way of establishing just how important it was. Studies of postwar experience suggest that capital gains/losses affect consumer expenditure. Applied to 1929–33, such econometric studies are open to counter-argument, mainly because (as already noted) all important variables turned down together. Nevertheless, it is reasonable to retain the possibility that the stock market crash could have helped to transform what might have been an erratic movement into a downward spiral.

A temporary exhaustion of investment opportunities

There was a steep fall in investment in 1930, but that does not show that there was an exhaustion of investment opportunities, as some earlier writers have maintained. It is true that new industries were important in the expansion of the 1930s. Especially in the years up to 1926, there was a very rapid expansion of the automobile industry. Investment in producing cars, though rising rapidly, was itself much less important than the investment stimulated by their greater use—in roads, service and supply centres, and oil refining and the new urban and suburban building that occurred as households moved out of cities once they had cars. This was indeed to some large extent a once-for-all stimulus. The same is true of the post-1921 investment boom in electric power, other public utilities, and the telephone system. But this does not mean that investment opportunities were exhausted. Had the depression not intervened, there is no reason to think there would not have been other profitable avenues for investment.

Previous overbuilding of dwellings

The previous course of residential construction seems to explain some part of the fall in output in 1930: but how much? There was a boom in residential construction in 1920–3 which more than accounted for the rise in total fixed investment in this period. Residential construction continued to rise at a slower pace up to 1926, and was accompanied by a boom in commercial construction. After 1926 both declined substantially; and that appears to more than explain the check to total fixed investment in the period 1926–9.

The housing boom was partly the result of an earlier postwar imbalance (1919–22) when housebuilding had been slow though the number of urban families was growing sharply, and when there had been unsatisfied demand left over from the war. Speculation, fed by imprudent lending both by individuals and financial institutions, increased the boom. That contributed to overbuilding, and was followed later by foreclosures and disorganization of the mortgage market. Residential and commercial construction, which had been declining in the years leading up to 1929, declined precipitately in (and partly presumably because of) the depression. But it would probably then have declined a bit anyhow, and thus could well have been part cause of the economic downturn.

Gordon and Wilcox (1981, following Hickman 1973 and Mishkin 1978) have argued that the housing collapse was enough to explain a fall of several per cent in GNP. (This effect, they argue, was delayed until 1929 by the stock exchange boom and its stimulatory effect on consumer spending.) Metzler (1981) objects on two grounds: first, in so far as it depends on population trends, these ought to have been foreseen and therefore they ought not to have shocked the economy (an objection which perhaps reflects his general philosophical position rather than how people actually behaved); and second, that the decline in construction could have been a response to changes generated by the recession itself in the yields of assets other than property. This kind of argument illustrates some of the difficulty of establishing any definite explanation of the depression. It leaves me disposed to retain the housing collapse as a possible contributory cause.

Foreign influences

External factors must partly account for the US Great Depression. For exports turned down in 1930—though only enough to account for a 1 per cent change in total final expenditure (which in total fell nearly 10 per cent [table 6.11]. For this there seem two main reasons: depression in Germany, and in the primary-producing countries.

Depression in Germany   The depression in Germany started before that in the United States. Between 1925 and 1928 Germany had experienced a rapid expansion in which GNP rose nearly 20 per cent [table 6.13]. This had been supported by heavy external borrowing, largely from the United States, much of it short-term. It is often said (e.g. by Arndt 1944) that America abruptly ceased lending to Germany because of the greater attraction of investing in the booming US stock exchange. It would be more correct to say that, because the US authorities raised interest rates in 1928 in order to damp down speculation,

Table 6.13   The Great Depression in Germany

	GNP	Imports[a]	Total final expenditure[a]	of which:	
				Fixed investment	Exports[a]
			(bn (1929) Reichsmarks)		
1925	75.2	11.8	87.0	10.3	9.3
1926	77.3	10.4	87.7	10.5	10.5
1927	85.0	15.0	100.0	12.4	10.8
1928	88.8	14.5	103.3	12.9	12.2
1929	88.4	14.0	102.4	11.2	13.6
1930	87.2	12.5	99.6	10.3	12.9
1931	80.5	10.5	91.0	7.2	11.8
1932	74.5	9.8	84.3	5.6	8.1
1933	79.1	9.6	88.8	6.9	7.6

[a] Visible trade only: international trade in services not included.

Sources: Index of GNP in constant prices from Maddison (1989), linked to 1929 value of GNP in current prices form *Statistisches Bundesamt*, 1972. Shares of fixed investment in GNP in current prices from Keese (1967: 57): these are used to approximate fixed investment in constant prices from GNP in constant prices. Indices of volume of foreign trade from *Review of World Trade*, 1938, linked to 1929 value of exports and imports in current prices from *Statistical Yearbook League of Nations*, 1931/2.

there was strong pressure on Germany's exchange reserves; and that, given the recent history of hyperinflation, the German authorities wished above all to avoid devaluation;[36] they reacted therefore by raising interest rates (the official discount rate rose from 5 per cent in early 1927 to 6 per cent at mid-1928 and to 7 per cent in October) and tax rates. The atmosphere of crisis could also have caused banks to restrict credit (as is suggested in Bernanke and James 1991). Taken together, these influences might have been enough to trigger the fall in investment, which seems to have turned well before exports, and may have been the main expenditure component to fall in the initial stages. (The figures are poor: see table 6.13.) Industrial production seems to have reached a plateau as early as mid-1927, at which date unemployment also seems to have started to rise (see Falkus 1975).

[36] Studies of the impact of the Great Depression on European countries date back to the prewar annual *Economic Surveys* by the League of Nations. These contain estimates of countries' capital accounts, derived essentially as the inverse of their trade or current account positions. Changes in such overall positions must overwhelmingly reflect causation from the side of the real economy, not forces acting on long-term capital flows. Thus, the figures for Germany must chiefly reflect the effect of Germany's depression in reducing its trade deficit. They cannot be taken to represent the impact of US financial or monetary conditions on US capital flows to Germany. Nor are estimates of specific types of short- or long-term capital outflows or inflows to be taken to represent the movements of the total. The story of the US 'withdrawing' capital from, or 'suspending' outflows to, Germany dates back to these prewar studies, and is based on this misinterpretation of balance of payments figures.

It is not necessary, however, to probe this story very fully. For whatever the explanation, the impact on the United States must have been very small. US exports to Germany in 1929 constituted only 0.4 per cent of US GNP; thus, though they fell in volume by 33 per cent between 1928 and 1930, the direct impact on the USA in this phase must have been negligible. The indirect impact via the effect on the commodity-producing countries must also have been small. The German depression can therefore hardly figure as an important originating cause of the depression in the United States.[37]

In the course of the depression output in *France* fell almost as much as in Germany. But unlike Germany the decline started only in 1929, so that it can hardly figure as an initial cause of the US depression, which is our present interest.

Trade with primary-producing countries   Trade with primary-producing countries may have given the US economy a deflationary impulse in 1929–30. The world terms of trade had been shifting in favour of manufactures and against primary products since 1927 [fig. 6.5]. In the two years 1927–9 they moved by about 5 per cent (after which the shift became much larger). That reduced the primary-producing countries' capacity to import. Many of them had borrowed heavily since the war and had large fixed payments of interest to make, and that magnified the impact on their ability to import. These are probably the reasons why the exports of industrial countries (all countries but Germany and the USA) slowed in 1928, and why all countries' exports fell in 1929 [fig. 6.4]. It explains most of the fall in US exports, which reduced total US demand by almost 1 per cent in 1930 [table 6.11].

The shift in the terms of trade, however, increased domestic purchasing power in industrial countries; this will have compensated for much of the effect on total demand of the fall in exports. Between 1929 and 1930, the US import deflator fell by nearly 16 per cent, but the GDP deflator fell by under 3 per cent. Even though imports constitute a relatively small component of final expenditure in the United States, this will have increased purchasing power by about 0.6 per cent, i.e. by two-thirds as much as the effect on demand of the fall in exports. Most of this shift in the US terms of trade will have been due to the shift in the terms of trading with primary-producing countries, and thus indeed acted as a counterpart to the fall in exports. (Primary-producing countries' propensity to cut spending, however, will probably have been larger and prompter than that of US consumers to spend more.)

The net impact of trading with primary producers, therefore, can have reduced US demand in 1929 by only a small amount (e.g. by half a percentage point—the more noteworthy, however, for marking a change in course from

---

[37] The German depression went on to become second in depth only to that of the USA, and must have been driven chiefly by forces internal to Germany. These will have had a somewhat larger impact on the later stages of the US depression; but, as will be shown in s. 6.4.1, even so they would account for only a very small share of the decline experienced in the USA.

growth to decline). From the point of view of the United States, this was an exogenous shock.[38]

Conclusions about the start of the recession

This discussion has identified five factors which probably gave the US economy a perceptible downward exogenous shock in 1929: the end of the housing boom, the rise in interest rates, the Wall Street crash, the beginnings of the slightly earlier and largely independent recession in Germany, and the contraction of the exports of the primary-producing countries. The impact on the United States of these shocks can in each case have been only small. Even in total, they are not enough to explain the plunge in GNP of over 9 per cent in the first year. Nor do they explain why business fixed investment should have fallen so steeply and so promptly, or why consumers' expenditure did likewise. The first stage of recession, therefore, seems inexplicable except as a swing in consumer and business confidence—a swing likely anyhow, in reaction to preceding boom.

6.3.3. Reasons for the depth of the US depression

The previous section sought to explain why, as early as 1930, a major recession should have begun. There remains the even more important question of why depression in the United States then went on to become so extremely deep. In order to deal with so vast a subject, I confine myself to the bare bones of a view which can be summarized in three points.

1. The reasons why the recession quickly became (in its first year) a major affair as serious as that of 1921 have been tentatively suggested in the previous subsection. After that there were a number of additional factors which may, each in a small way, have acted as adverse shocks. But such identifiable factors seem to go only a little way to explain the depression.
2. The only factor that seems capable of explaining its great depth is the effect of bank closures, more particularly via their interruption of accustomed sources of credit. Widespread bankruptcies (so induced) of non-bank firms must have further weakened banks and impeded credit flows. Their joint effects could explain the depression. (One has then to explain also why it was that so much of the banking system collapsed.)
3. The depression was not due to mistakes of policy of the sort to which Milton Friedman attributed it, nor as (still widely held) to resulting inadequate growth of the money stock.

I discuss these three assertions in reverse order. Before doing so it is useful to summarize the chronology of the depression.

---

[38] For the world as a whole, it could be regarded as part of the adjustment of the supply of primary products to industrial countries' demand for them, and thus could be thought to have been endogenous.

After a slow start, the decline in output from end-1929 to early 1933 was fairly steady and continuous [fig. 6.9 shows the monthly course of manufacturing output]. But there were two pauses. Output started to rise for a time in early 1931: Friedman and Schwartz in their *Monetary History* (1963: 313) say 'the first four or five months ... if examined without reference to what actually followed, have many of the earmarks of the bottom of the cycle and the beginning of revival'. The same could be said of the more pronounced revival in the middle of 1932. There seems no compelling explanation for either of these short-lived revivals or of what brought them to an end, though conjectures can be offered. It therefore seems more profitable to concentrate chiefly on the depression as a whole. Figure 6.10 shows the course of the monetary aggregates, and also (shaded areas) the successive waves of bank closures, the heaviest phase running from end-1930 to early 1932.[39]

Gross investment declined to practically zero by 1933, and that decline explains nearly half the decline in final sales over the four years of the depression [table 6.11]. If one could explain that, one would have gone far to explain the depression. The marked acceleration of the output decline in 1932 reflected mostly the very large fall in consumer expenditure in that year. (That was due not to a sudden rise in saving—indeed, the saving ratio rose—but to a steep fall in pre-tax income.) Disinvestment in inventories reduced inventories by perhaps a quarter over the three years 1929–32, i.e. about in proportion to the fall in GDP, so that the fall in inventories (which accounted for one-eighth of the fall in final expenditure) can be regarded as an effect as much as a cause of the depression.

The monetarist interpretation

Monetarists tend to believe that a fall in the stock of money (or a slowdown in its growth) is a measure of a fall (or slowdown) in demand, and so is likely to cause a fall (slowdown) in output; and, having (as they claim) explained the trend in money, they almost assume that that is the same as having explained the trend in output. I treat the course of monetary aggregates only as an alleged cause of real events and not as a causal factor in which I instinctively believe, any more than I discern any close statistical association between real output and money.

So far the course of money has not been included among the factors that could have helped to get the depression going. A number of other events have been isolated (including a rise in interest rates) which may have done so; and later we will consider some further non-monetary events which, after the depression had started, may have given additional downward shocks, or amplified the effect of shocks already imparted. If they indeed had such effects, it follows that by the time the stock of money started to decline (e.g. mid-1930) there were other factors at work that did not stem from the course of the monetary aggregates,

---

[39] The indication of heavy periods of closures differs somewhat from that shown in Friedman and Schwartz's chart 30, where the frequency of closures is not very clear.

which could well explain why activity was already falling. This conclusion has an important bearing on how the monetary aggregates themselves have to be interpreted.

The dominant component in the argument of Friedman and Schwartz (1963) is that the depression was caused by the authorities' failing to ensure that the stock of money did not decline; and that the fact that it did decline is of itself taken as sufficient evidence that this was the cause. (A fuller critique of Friedman and Schwartz (1963) is given in app. A6.1.) The reasons why I find the argument unpersuasive can be put as follows.

Friedman and Schwartz argue that the reason why monetary growth did not continue is that the authorities kept the banks too short of reserves. This implies that banks' customers wished to borrow more than they did, that their credit standing was sufficient to make the banks judge them good risks, and that the banks' capital was adequate to have provided a basis for larger lending, i.e. that a shortage of reserves was the only constraint. These necessary implications of their view are not made clear because Friedman and Schwartz have practically nothing to say about the banks as lending institutions.

If in fact there were non-monetary factors that were at work before the aggregates started to fall, these assumptions cannot be made. Their clients' incomes and profits will already have been falling. Banks will have been seeking to restrict lending for reasons of normal commercial prudence; borrowers too will have felt it unwise to continue borrowing on the earlier scale; and the authorities will not have had it in their power, merely by making reserves more freely available, to prevent a decline in the money stock. Friedman and Schwartz at times pay lip service to the possibility of reverse causality of this sort in which the real economy drives the aggregates; but they never seriously face the problems that arise in interpreting the monetary statistics if two-directional causality is an important reality.

There is a second version of the Friedman–Schwartz hypothesis which did not get great stress in their *Monetary History* itself, but which since appears to have become the accepted reading (see the discussion in Brunner 1981). There are two parts to the thesis: first, that the monetary contraction was caused not by the monetary authorities, but by the closures of banks; and second, that the monetary authorities are still to blame for not ensuring that a *compensatory* monetary expansion took place (which, it is held, the provision of adequate reserves would have ensured). I agree that the effect of bank closures (see below) was highly important—not however for their effect on the monetary aggregates, but for their direct effect on the economy. They thus are to be included as among shocks other than those stemming from the aggregates which depressed the economy. That having happened, the banks would not want to make greater loans, and the authorities would not have been in a position to make them want to do so. Thus, the Friedman–Schwartz case, in my view, is not saved.

It is convenient at this point to note Bernanke's later (1983) explanation for the depression. He accepts Friedman's monetarist story as part explanation, but claims it is insufficient; and adds as supplementary explanations (*a*) the effect of bank failures in disrupting financial flows, and (*b*) the restriction of lending by banks because of increased lending risk as a result of defaults and failures among non-banks. As will be clear, I agree that these were major factors; but in my view Bernanke's attempt at statistical demonstration of the importance of these 'non-monetary financial' factors fails because it rests on the validity of the monetarist explanation—which he seeks to supplement, not replace—that money determines output and not the reverse.[40]

My interpretation seems to agree very well with what happened to the banks' balance sheets during the depression. In 1929 the banks' asset/liabilities stood at about 70 per cent of GNP. Some 58 per cent of their assets consisted of loans, of which 16 percentage points were loans against property. The remaining 42 percentage points were 'other loans' to persons and firms; and it was these that fell heavily in the depression [table 6.14 and fig. 6.11]. The other 42 per cent of the banks' assets apart from loans (i.e. 42 per cent of total assets consisted of investments (which were nearly a quarter of total assets); two-fifths of this was cash (12 per cent) or US government or state or other official obligations).

Over the four years of the depression (end-1929 to end-1933), banks' balance sheets contracted by 29 per cent—a large fall, but much less than the fall in nominal GDP which was some 50 per cent. Nearly half the contraction took place in the course of one year, 1931. By far the greater part of the contraction on the assets side consisted of the fall in the bank loans already noted. Though loans against real estate fell a bit, these 'other' loans fell by 59 per cent—enough to account for nearly 25 percentage points out of the total fall of 29 per cent in banks' balance sheets. By contrast, banks' 'investments' were almost unchanged; and their holding of government stock rose in these three years.

On the liabilities side of the combined balance sheets of the banks, deposits fell by just over 30 per cent. Demand deposits fell rather more (37 per cent)—which is not surprising, since, in reaction to the bank failures, the public switched out of deposits into cash. On a broad definition of money (i.e. including time deposits), the stock of money (deposits plus cash) held by the public fell by 19 per cent; on a narrow definition, it fell by 32 per cent—still small in relation to the fall in nominal GDP. The banks' reserves (on the definition used by Friedman and Schwartz) remained about constant: the ratio of reserves to deposits thus *rose* very considerably.

---

[40] Bernanke's procedure can be summarized as follows. (1) In order to isolate purely 'monetary' influences on the economy he starts with a model (based on Lucas 1972) in which 'monetary' shocks are supposed to affect production decisions by creating price uncertainty. (2) 'Unantici-pated' changes in money are taken (as in Barro 1978) to be given by the residuals from a regression of M1 growth on output growth and price growth. (3) Money shocks so estimated were used to explain detrended output growth (and are said to have explained only half the decline in output shown by monthly data between mid-1930 and March 1933). (4) Two additional explanatory variables were also tested. This is clearly a perilous chain of calculations. But my basic quarrel is that the first step (1), and hence all the rest, can be appropriate only if it is assumed that money determines output.

Table 6.14 Banks' assets and liabilities[a], 1929–1933

	Mid-1929	Mid-1933	Change 1929–33	% change
		($ bn)		
Banks' assets				
Loans, total	41.9	22.3	−19.5	−47
Real estate	11.7	9.9	−1.8	−15
Other	30.1	12.3	17.7	−59
Investments, total	17.3	18.1	0.8	5
of which:				
US government obligations	5.4	8.2	2.7	50
Obligations of states, etc.	2.8	3.1	0.3	11
Total assets or liabilities[b]	72.3	51.3	−20.9	−29
Liabilities				
Deposits, total	58.2	41.6	−16.5	−29
Deposits of non-bank public	53.9	37.3	−16.5	−31
Demand deposits	25.1	16.0	−9.1	−36
Time deposits	28.7	21.3	−7.4	−26

[a] All banks.
[b] No adjustment made to exclude government or interbank deposits.
Source: *Historical Statistics of the United States*, 1960.

In my view, the fall in deposits occurred predominantly because the banks reduced their lending; and that happened because, as the depression progressed, the banks reduced their assessment of their customers' creditworthiness (evidenced in part by the increased likelihood of their customers becoming bankrupt). The banks' desire to contract credit must in turn then have become not merely a passive reaction, but an active force which further accentuated the depression.

The macroeconomic effect of bank closures

The bank failures during the Great Depression were on a scale probably elsewhere unparalleled. Even before the depression, bank suspensions on a smaller scale had been almost continuous. Between 1920 and 1929 they averaged 500 to 600 a year; in 1930 the number doubled; and in 1931 doubled again (*Historical Statistics of the United States*). Over the four years of the depression, the number of suspensions (chiefly of smaller banks) totalled over 9,000; and in this period the number of banks was reduced by 40 per cent, chiefly by suspensions (though some suspended banks later reopened) but also by amalgamations. The deposits of banks suspended in these four years totalled nearly $6.9 billion, or 15 per cent of banks' total deposits at end-1929 (Friedman and Schwartz 1963: 351–3).

The losses incurred by depositors and shareholders were about $2.5 billion, of which shareholders bore rather under and depositors rather over half. This

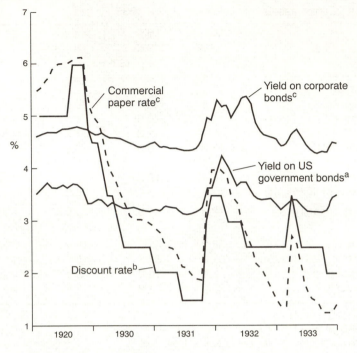

Fig. 6.11   Interest rates and bond yields in the USA, 1929–1933

Sources:
[a]*Federal Reserve Bulletin*, 1938, p. 1045.
[b]*Banking and Monetary Statistics*, 1943, p. 441.
[c]*Historical Statistics of the United States*, 1949, pp. 346–7.

means that about a fifth of the deposits of suspended banks—or about 3 per cent of total deposits, or 2 per cent of GNP—were lost in the course of the depression (and thus a fraction of that in any single year). But the remaining four-fifths was rendered inaccessible for the periods during which banks were suspended while being investigated. Thus, at any one time, perhaps another 5 per cent of total deposits (4 per cent of GNP) may in effect have been blocked. In total, this must have had a significant effect on the expenditure of depositors, especially in 1931 when suspensions were most numerous.

The effect on those who borrowed from the banks must have been as important as the effect on depositors. If a suspended bank was later able to reopen, or amalgamated with another bank, loans outstanding at the date of the closure might be continued. But if a bank had to be closed, loans outstanding would have been called in; and firms or persons who had borrowed from the bank would then have had to dispose of assets in haste and probably at a loss. They themselves may well have been put into bankruptcy; or if not, they would be unlikely to have undertaken as much investment as otherwise.

In principle, customers of suspended banks could go to another bank and get an equivalent loan; but in conditions of severe depression this must usually have been impossible. The curtailment of bank loans may then have been on a scale almost equivalent to the deposits of suspended banks; that would be equivalent to 10 per cent of GNP, and would alone account for two-fifths of the total reduction of bank loans in the course of the depression.

The shock to the economy imparted by bank closures must then have been very large. Private expenditure may not have been reduced fully commensurately with the sums involved when deposits were lost or blocked during the period of investigation, or loans previously granted by suspended banks were called in. But even if the effect was only half as large, that would still have amounted to 10 per cent of GNP, i.e. enough to explain a third of the fall of GNP in the course of the Great Depression.[41]

The cause of bank failures Bank failures occurred, first, because the American banking system was shown to be especially vulnerable; and second; because the situation that confronted it was especially unfavourable. Banks failed in the United States—as in other countries and in the USA in earlier periods—in part because they were small and local and their loan books were therefore not diversified but concentrated on local industries.

Small banks, moreover, were for several reasons at a remove from the authorities. First, the Federal Reserve System had discouraged banks from using the discount window. Second, banks themselves feared to borrow from the Fed, since when it got known that they had done so it further damaged their standing. Third, banks in difficulty were often non-member banks, without direct access to the discount window, for whom the Fed felt little responsibility. There was thus a gap in understanding towards the country banks on the part of the authorities, and also on the part of the town banks, who might have acted as a channel but tended to see closures merely as a sign of improvidence and bad management. Friedman and Schwartz (1963: 395) blame the Federal Reserve System for not lending freely in a crisis, as Bagehot had prescribed. But, given the setup, that would not have been possible. Blame should rather attach to defects of the structure—to the vulnerability of a system of numerous small banks, to scanty banking supervision, and to an absence of effective arrangements for last resort lending.[42]

Massive bank failures occurred in the depression because the financial difficulties of their customers were particularly severe.[43] Failures became massive

---

[41] This is much larger than the effect that Friedman and Schwartz attribute to bank closures. They attach no importance to bank closures unless they led to a reduction in the stock of money in a direct, accounting sense.

[42] Friedman and Schwartz blame the authorities also for not suspending the obligation of banks to repay deposits in cash, as had been done during earlier runs on the banks. That rough-and-ready treatment might indeed have reduced bank suspensions, and thus mitigated the depression.

[43] For evidence that bank failures reflect real shocks, see e.g. Calomiris and Garton (1991).

only at the end of 1930. But by then the fall in real output was probably already greater than had occurred in any previous recession. Many failures were concentrated in the older industrial areas of the United States—areas where recession was especially severe. Many failures also continued to occur in rural areas, where, because of the volatility of agricultural prices, the fall in income must have been at least twice as high as in the rest of the country (see below).

A recession, especially if accompanied by a falling price level, creates pockets where income losses are particularly large.[44] Financial intermediaries act to generalize such losses. The collapse of firms that have borrowed from banks, and the fall in the price of assets taken as collateral by the banks, create losses for the banks. The banks therefore are forced to contract credit, or to suspend operations and call in loans completely. That in turn forces their customers in general—not only those initially in difficulty—to contract investment and curtail or suspend production, which in turn reduces the demand for the products of yet other firms. Bank failures thus provide a mechanism that powerfully amplifies a recession, and by so doing generalizes it.[45]

This process cannot be observed in detail at the aggregate level. The process works at the level of individual firms or quite small sub-aggregates, with adverse shocks being transmitted from one to another quite rapidly. Nor, therefore, is it possible to estimate precisely how much of the recession can be accounted for in this way. But we do know, from the size of the deposits of suspended banks, that the effects must have been very large. That can easily be imagined to have had further large depressive effects via its effect on credit risks and on consumer and business confidence.

There are then qualitative grounds for thinking that the US Depression can be explained in these terms as the effect of bank failures viewed as a strong amplifying mechanism. Partial corroboration of this view is that the depression ended when deposit insurance was introduced and other measures were taken under the New Deal that put a stop to bank failures.

The contribution of possible new shocks

It remains to consider how far new shocks contributed to the continued deepening of the depression in the course of 1930 and after; in particular:

- fiscal policy;
- the Hawley–Smoot tariff;
- the decline in foreign demand;

---

[44] Corporate profits before tax were in aggregate negative in 1931 and 1932; after tax they were negative in all four years 1930, 1931, 1932, and 1933. Though the largest corporations remained in profit throughout, smaller firms incurred losses and many failed (Bernanke 1983). Debt defaults were commonest among homeowners (about half of residences were mortgaged at the beginning of the depression, 40%–50% of which were in default by the end) and farmers (nearly half were in arrears by 1933).

[45] Temin (1989: 53–4) attempts to dispute Bernanke's emphasis on the effects of bank failures by showing that the output of big firms was as much affected as that of small ones. Small firms

- the stock market decline;
- the decline in agricultural prices;
- the decline in the general price level.

The argument will be that in some cases (though not the first two) these could have acted as downward shocks; but that their effect must have been small in comparison with the financial factors discussed above.

1. *Fiscal policy* was significantly expansionary in the first two years of the depression, mainly because government expenditure on goods and services continued to rise [table 6.12]. In the second two years it was contractionary on an almost equal scale, as taxation increased relative in GNP more especially in 1932. Over the whole period it was about neutral.

2. *The Hawley–Smoot tariff* of June 1930 has—erroneously, I think—been held responsible by Metzler (1976: 469) for converting 'a sizeable recession into a severe depression'. (By June 1930, however, the depression was already severe.) Metzler claims that the tariff altered 'the division of nominal income'; i.e., it raised the price of final output so that (he argues) output had to fall more. This reasoning assumes that the value of nominal income in total (price and real components taken together) is fixed and predetermined—a style of logic which I dispute [see ch. 3.1], arguing that output and price are each determined separately. The effect of the tariff was surely the opposite of what Metzler contends. The tariff increased the effective rate of duty paid on imports by almost 50 per cent between 1929 and 1932. By reducing foreign competition, it will have diverted demand from imported to domestic supplies, and raised output.

3. *Equity prices* had by 1932 fallen to about a quarter of their 1929 value [fig. 6.8] or, relative to the price of current goods and services, to about a third. There is some reason to think that the main effect was not via consumers' expenditure but via investment.[46] It must have reduced investment by reducing the market valuation of firms' financial assets (and thus their borrowing power), and also by reducing the market valuation of the future earning power of their real capital. It must be difficult to distinguish the effects these had on investment from that of the general collapse of confidence.

4. *The fall in exports* in 1930 (as we have seen) was one factor explaining the start of the depression. It continued; and over the three years 1929–32 was equivalent to a fall in final sales of 3 per cent—which is small in the present context, though not negligible. But for the most part the fall in exports must be regarded as an indirect effect of the reduction of other countries' incomes caused by the US Depression itself, and not an independent cause [see s. 6.4.1].

were more liable to go bankrupt, but the effects on demand must soon have been spread throughout the economy.

[46] The decline in equity prices must have affected consumer expenditure. But it will have expressed itself by reducing spending relative to income; and in fact, the saving ratio rose little and that only in the first two years. The effect of falling equity prices via consumption may then have reduced output by only a percentage point or two.

As already noted, the associated shift in the terms of trade had counter-effects. The fall in the price of US imports will have increased US domestic purchasing power by as much as it reduced that of the primary-producing countries. The net effect on US demand must have been small—much less than the effect of the fall in exports taken in isolation.

5. *The fall in US farm prices* can be regarded as a domestic counterpart to the fall in world commodity prices. US farm prices fell by 50 per cent between 1929 and 1932, or nearly 20 per cent a year [fig. 6.8]. But what farmers bought also got cheaper, and in real terms farmers' incomes fell only about half as much, i.e. by 10 per cent a year. That represented a transfer of real income from farm to town. Though farmers were worse off, cheaper food increased by as much as the real purchasing power of the urban population. (The fall in farm prices also had further effects, already discussed, by leading to bank failures.)

6. *The fall in the general price level* probably also had a demand deflationary effect. (As I argue, it had in Britain in 1920–1 [s. 6.2].) For the two years 1930–2 when the fall in output was steepest, the US GNP deflator fell by nearly 10 per cent a year. That will have depressed profit expectations. (That may be said to be money illusion; but, especially at the early stages of a depression, firms have no means of knowing that a fall in the price of their products and in their profits will be paralleled by a fall in all other prices.) Second, falling prices will have imposed financial stringency on all firms with fixed commitments as regards interest payments. (The fall in the general price level was itself caused by the depression, and could be regarded not as a shock but as an amplifier of other shock effects.)

6.3.4. Conclusion about the US Depression and comments on the recovery

I shall now summarize conclusions about what caused the US depression, and comment briefly on why it stopped and what brought about the recovery.

The depression: three main causes

Economists have gone on arguing about the Great Depression because it was uniquely large, and in the circumstances there can be no 'normal' ways of explaining it. There seem to have been no identifiable exogenous shocks of the size necessary to account for it; and economies are not normally subject to endogenously generated fluctuations of that sort.

The explanation proposed above is twofold.

1. The US Depression in its early stages was a reaction to the excessive boom conditions of the preceding years. It was probably triggered by the Wall Street crash and by the rise in interest rates, and by other minor causes such as a small fall in exports. But basically, it was a bubble situation, arising from an excess of confidence earlier on the part of both consumers and firms.
2. The depression was then greatly amplified by the fragility of a banking structure organized locally and out of reach of any system of central bank

support. Usually we treat the stability of banks as something to be taken for granted: this was an example of the kind of 'melt-down' that can happen when they do not hold firm.

These explanations of why the Great Depression happened are put forward not as certain or rigorously testable, but merely as possible ways (or even, given the lack of plausible alternatives, the most probable ways) of explaining why it happened and why it went so deep. They are different from those proposed for other recessions; but the depression itself was very different.

What stopped the recession?

I would give pride of place to the institution of deposit insurance, which seems (as already mentioned) to have practically stopped bank closures. That must have brought to an end a powerful force which had previously made the depression so deep.

In addition may be mentioned three factors, which were probably both cause and effect:

1. Exports practically ceased to fall in 1933 [table 6.11]. That could be because the world price of commodities had touched bottom in 1932 [fig. 6.5]. That in turn could be because world supply and demand for commodities had reached a temporary low equilibrium as US contraction slowed. However, the fact that exports ceased to fall will then itself have been one (small) reason why US output ceased to contract.
2. In 1933, the fourth year of depression, stock change became a positive factor [table 6.11]. In a large recession firms' efforts to cut stocks by reducing orders are for a time constantly frustrated by new unexpected falls in sales. By 1933, the rate of decline of final sales had decelerated. Perhaps that enabled firms to begin to catch up with the game, so that, though inventories went on falling, there was no need to *increase the rate* of inventory decline (which is what counts here).
3. Fixed investment, after falling extremely steeply for three years, fell little in 1933 [table 6.11]. That might well have simply reflected the end of bank closures and credit contraction. It could also have been in part for independent reasons: for instance, net investment having been reduced to zero, a point may have been reached where no further reductions could be made; or where people began to think that output would not fall for ever but would revive some time, and ceased to cut investment further.

The recovery 1933–7

I argued earlier [ch. 3.2] that, in the absence of exogenous shocks or disturbances, an economy tends to grow at its trend rate: it is only growth above or below the trend rate that needs to be explained. As and when productivity rises, real factor incomes necessarily (by the national income identities) also grow; and that provides the purchasing power to support rising expenditure. When output growth was resumed in 1934, productivity growth [table 6.15] also revived—as is normal after a recession.

In the four years 1933–7 real GNP grew at not much less than 9 per cent a year [table 6.15]; in the six years 1933–9 GNP grew by just over 6 per cent a year. This growth of 9 per cent a year was split fairly evenly between employment growth (almost 4 per cent a year) and growth of labour productivity (just over 4 per cent a year). The growth of employment was enough to halve unemployment (from 20 per cent in 1933 to 9 per cent in 1937). Output growth was rapid by normal standards in each of these four years, and extraordinarily rapid in 1936 (over 13 per cent).

It was not till 1937 that US output regained the 1929 level. (If the depression had not happened, output would probably by then have been 20–25 per cent higher.) This recovery is usually characterized as slow and partial, and reasons are sought to explain why it should have been so slow. The emphasis is in my view misplaced: GDP rose almost as quickly as it had fallen in the depression years. It takes skill and organization and risk-taking to make economic expansion happen; and, entrepreneurial resources being finite, there is a limit to how quickly output can be organized to grow [ch. 4.2]. This depression having been exceptionally deep, the economy could not have been expected to climb out of it more quickly: contrary to the usual view, what requires explanation is why growth should have been so rapid.

This is not the place to attempt a full account of the recovery; but the pattern of final expenditure [table 6.15] gives some hints. In total, final spending rose 36 per cent over the four years 1933–7, probably over twice the trend rate. To this, government expenditure on goods and services contributed 5 percentage points; rather little (2 percentage points) came from exports; half the rest came from fixed investment plus investment in inventories, the other half from renewed growth in consumer spending.

When the shocks that had depressed output ceased, the economy could be expected (on the assumption of this study) to resume growth at its trend rate. Growth over and above that (say, some 20 per cent over the four years 1933–7) needs to be explained by exogenous shocks, as amplified by multiplier effects. The exogenous stimulus must have come predominantly from the reduction of interest rates, and from fiscal policy [table 6.15, n.]. But in this situation a great deal must have been due to the return of confidence—perhaps inspired to some degree by the plethora of measures under the New Deal.[47]

---

[47] The New Deal consisted of a series of hasty improvizations, and certainly displayed massive intervention on the part of the government (Schlesinger 1960). Many schemes were designed to impose restrictions on industrial and agricultural output: these seem to me more likely to have caused a redistribution of demand than an addition to demand in total. The positive elements were notably the fiscal stimulus, and the measures affecting banking (mentioned above). In general, the manifest efforts by government to promote recovery probably carried some credibility, though in business and financial circles there was certainly much scepticism.

Table 6.15 Recovery in the USA, 1934–1939

	1929–33	1934	1935	1936	1937	1933–7	1938	1939	1933–9
Contribution to % change in TFE									
Government expenditure	1	2	0.5	3	-0.5	5	1.5	1	7.5
Consumer expenditure	-15	2	4	6.5	2	14	-1.5	3.5	16
Fixed investment	-11	2	2	3	2	9	-2.5	2	8.5
Exports	-3	0.5	—	0.5	1	2	—	0.5	2.5
Total final sales	-2.8	7	7	13	4.5	32	-2.5	6.5	36
Stock change	-5	0.5	2.5	0.5	0.5	4	-2.5	1.5	3
Total final expenditure	-33	7.5	9	13.5	5.5	36	-5	8	39
of which:									
Imports	-2	-0.5	1.5	—	0.5	2	-1	0.5	1.5
GNP[a]	-31	7.5	8	13.5	5	34	-4	7.5	37.5
% changes/% of labour force[a]									
Labour productivity	-19	0	4.5	7	2.5	15	-2.5	5	18
Employment	-12.5	6	3	5.5	2	17	-2	2	17
Unemployment level (%)	—	16.1	14.3	9.9	9.1	—	12.4	11.2	—
Change	—	-4.7	-1.8	-4.4	-0.8	—	3.3	-1.2	—
Change in GNP deflator	-23	10	1.5	0	4.5	16.5	-2	-1	13.5

[a] National product includes output attributed to those on work relief; employment includes (unemployment excludes) number on work relief and emergency workers; labour productivity is on this inclusive basis.

Sources: National Income and Product Accounts of the United States, 1968; Historical Statistics of the United States, 1975.

6.4. The world depression and the UK depression

This section seeks to substantiate the view that the 1930s' depression in the United Kingdom was the result of a world depression emanating primarily from the United States. It starts by considering the international transmission process, which is illustrated in terms of a stylized model of the world economy. It will be shown that the most important effects of the depression on Britain, and on other European countries, arrived indirectly via trade with third countries. The effects included not only loss of British and European countries' exports, but also a large improvement in these countries' terms of trade. The latter explains one unexpected feature—that consumer expenditure in the UK rose throughout the depression.

Discussion of the international transmission of the Great Depression has sometimes given an important role to variations in capital flows. Through much of the 1920s, there had been large capital flows from the USA to Germany. These largely ceased from 1928 on. Some assert that this was because of monetary policy (or financial conditions) in the United States and that the ending of this flow precipitated Germany's plunge into recession in 1928. The reasons for rejecting that view have already been set out in section 6.3.2.

Other authors have given a crucial importance to the effects of adhering to the gold standard in constraining countries' monetary and fiscal policies. The main reason for rejecting the idea that the gold standard caused the Great Depression is that the depression was concentrated in the United States, and the United States was plainly not inhibited by staying on the gold standard in the way that some other countries might have been.[48]

The following analysis claims that the Great Depression in the USA explains much of what happened in the UK and in much of the rest of the world. But the analysis is centred on the UK and does not attempt a complete world view. It does not, for instance, explain the large recessions in Germany and France, where additional psychological or institutional factors (perhaps going back to the war, the Versailles settlement, or the postwar hyperinflations) may have been important.

6.4.1. The international transmission of the Great Depression

Outside the United States the depression was deepest in Germany, the small countries neighbouring on Germany, and France [table 6.16]. (Germany and her smaller neighbours comprised nearly a third of Europe defined as in table 6.17.) Among other countries, some suffered and others benefited; and on

---

[48] This factor is not made much of in discussing the UK, because the effects of monetary and fiscal policies followed by the UK can be seen to be small compared with the effects coming from international trade. The effects of leaving the gold standard in 1931 are discussed in s. 6.5 below as part of the post-1931 recovery. See further app. A6.2.

Table 6.16 Components of change in total final expenditure: France, 1929–1932

	Contributions to % change in TFE (at 1929 prices)				
	1929	1930	1931	1932	1930–2
Government expenditure	0.0	3.2	0.0	1.4	4.8
Fixed investment	1.7	1.6	−2.3	−3.1	−3.8
Exports	−0.1	−1.2	−1.7	−2.3	−5.2
Other domestic spending, etc.	(6.3)	(−4.8)	(−1.3)	(−4.5)	(−10.4)
Total final expenditure[b]	7.9	−1.3	−5.2	−8.2	−14.7
of which:					
Imports	1.2	1.7	0.8	−1.8	0.7
GDP	6.7	−2.9	−6.0	−6.5	−15.4

[a] A residual item which includes not only consumer spending and stock change but exports *less* imports of services at constant prices.
[b] Omits exports of services.

Source: These estimates are pieced together from various sources and are therefore poor estimates. GDP is from Toutain (1987); government expenditure and fixed investment are from Cawe *et al.* (1976)—who show investment only as a share of GDP; and exports and imports (commodity trade only) are from *Annuaire Statistique de la France*, 1966.

balance (apart from Britain) there was not a fall, but a pause in growth—though still a significant break in trend.

The international transmission of the depression must have passed largely via trade flows. (There could also have been some psychological link, e.g. news of events in the United States could have lowered confidence in other countries.) The impact on trade can conveniently be analysed in terms of relations between three blocs: (*a*) the United States; (*b*) Europe, the other main area where industrial production was at that time heavily concentrated; and (*c*) the rest of the world, which with some exceptions consisted predominantly of countries that exported primary commodities.

In 1929 the national product of Europe was in total probably about equal to that of the United States. The trade flows between the blocs were relatively small in relation to the GDP of either area [table 6.18]; but the proportionate fall in trade during the depression was large [table 6.19] and thus had a significant impact on activity. Table 6.18 shows the parttern of world trade in 1929. Since it is intended for use in an analysis of the impact on the output of one bloc coming from events outside that bloc, it omits trade within blocs, i.e. *within* Europe, and *between* primary-producing countries.[49]

The estimates shown in table 6.18 are heroic rough estimates. Thus, the basic data on the value of trade between areas, and hence of the changes at current

[49] Such intra-trade was about 10% of Europe's GDP; trade among primary producers was much smaller. The volume of such intra-trade can be taken to be an endogenous effect of the level of activity within each area and not an exogenous factor determining it.

Table 6.17   The fall in European GDP, 1929–1932[a]

	1929 weight	% change in real GDP	Contributions to % change in GDP of Europe
Germany and neighbours	30.8		−4.2
Germany	20.9	−15.8	−3.3
Netherlands	2.6	−7.6	−0.2
Czechoslovakia	2.2	−10.3	−0.2
Switzerland	1.9	−8.0	−0.1
Austria	1.7	−19.8	−0.3
Belgium	1.5	−7.1	−0.1
France and UK	35.2		−3.3
France	14.6	−14.7	−2.1
UK	20.6	−5.1	−1.1
Other countries	34.0		0.4
USSR	10.4	6.9	
Italy	8.5	−2.4	
Spain	4.6	5.0	
Sweden	2.6	−4.3	
Denmark	1.5	−4.3	
Yugoslavia	1.2	−11.9	
Norway	1.1	5.7	
Hungary	1.1	−11.5	
Portugal	0.7	13.3	
Finland	0.6	−2.8	
Greece	0.5	6.7	
Bulgaria	0.4	−5.4	
Total Europe	100.0	−6.9	−6.9

[a] Countries' GDP converted to US dollar at current exchange rates. This certainly is inferior to use of purchasing power parities, had they been available, but perhaps chiefly for the poorer (and less important) countries.

Sources: as listed in app. A6.4.

prices between 1929 and 1932, are themselves not completely accurate [see app. A6.3]. Price data are even more scanty: for lack of anything better, the average value of US and UK exports of manufactures was taken to represent the price of US and European exports to primary producers; the average value of their imports of commodities was taken to measure the price of primary producers' exports; and an average of the two was taken to represent the price of trade in each direction between Europe and the United States. The difference between the first two was used to measure the great deterioration in the primary producers' terms of trade (or the improvement in those of the USA and Europe). The estimates suggest that trade flows fell in volume by 30–50 per cent

Table 6.18 The pattern of world trade in 1929[a]

	US: trade		Europe: trade		Primary producers: trade	
	From EU	to PP	From USA	to PP	From USA	to EU
GDP	100		100			
Imports	1.2	2.7	2.4	5.2	2.6	4.1
Exports	2.4	2.6	1.2	4.1	2.7	5.2

[a] US/GDP = European GDP = 100.
Omits intertrade within Europe and among primary producers. Exports and imports expressed as % of US/Europe's GNP/GDP.

Source: For trade flows see table A6.3(*c*); for GDP see table 6.17.

Table 6.19 The fall in world trade in 1929

	USA: Imports from		Europe: Imports from		Primary producers: Imports from	
	EU	PP	USA	PP ($ bn)	USA	EU
1929 value	1.33	3.0	2.60	6.23	2.82	4.50
1932 value	0.39	0.93	0.85	2.70	0.79	1.66
Prices (1929 = 100)	52.5	44.6	52.5	44.6	60.0	60.0
1932 value at 1929 prices	0.74	2.09	1.52	6.05	1.32	2.77
Fall in volume (%)	44	30	41	3	53	38

[a] Omits intertrade within Europe and among primary producers.

Source: See table A6.3.

between 1929 and 1932—an indication probably broadly correct if not in detail.[50]

A stylized model of the international transmission process

The following model relates to trade between the three blocs: the United States, Europe, and the primary producers (denoted as US, EU, and PP). Industrial countries' imports are treated as a function of income, and primary producers' imports as a function of export earnings. Assumptions are made about (1) the shape of import functions (defined in volume terms); (2) the determinants of primary producers' export prices; and (3) the size of the internal 'multipliers'

[50] As already noted, the fall in output in Germany and France was so much larger than the average that it has to be attributed chiefly to additional forces peculiar to those countries. Europe's imports of commodities probably fell less than other flows but perhaps not by as little as the 3% shown in table 6.19.

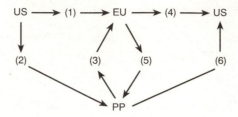

Fig. 6.12   International effects of the US depression: trade links between three main blocs, US, primary producers (PP), and Europe (EU)

in industrial countries which determine how income responds to a change in exports.[51] Given assumptions on these three groups of relationships, it is possible to simulate (*a*) the effects of a change in US output on primary producers' earnings (and, at a further remove, on their imports from the USA and Europe); (*b*) the effects of a change in US output on Europe's exports to the USA; and (*c*), as a feedback, the impact on US output of the induced fall in US exports [fig. 6.12]. The feedback on the United States (legs (4) + (6)) initiates a repetition of the same sequence. But, given that the weights of exports from the relevant areas are small relative to national product, the feedback on the second round on any reasonable assumptions about parameters is small in relation to the initial shock; and the feedback on a third round trivial. The same is true of legs (3) and (5) of the sequence, which also reiterate indefinitely but to relatively small additional effect.

A calculation of the scale of the various effects, obtained by making plausible assumptions about the three relevant parameters, is summarized in table 6.20. With the values assumed, an initial domestically generated fall in US GNP of 26 per cent produces, via the contraction of the *volume* of world trade, a feedback on US GNP of a further 3 per cent. However, the contraction of demand for internationally traded commodities produces a fall in their price relative to that of manufacturers; and that generates an offsetting *increase* in US real domestic demand of nearly 2 per cent. The net feedback on the United States is thus little more than 1 per cent. The impact on Europe is estimated to be of the same order.

The values selected for the relevant parameters entering into the calculation are stated in the note to the table. The size of the internal 'multipliers' in the USA and in Europe is probably the most uncertain assumption. Given the difficulty in explaining the size of the US depression, the size of the internal 'multipliers' in the United States was probably large; and a combined 'multiplier' of 4 was assumed; for Europe a combined 'multiplier' of 2 was assumed. With these values, the US depression would explain a fraction of Europe's 7 per cent

---

[51] In this chapter the term 'multipliers' is used as a commonsense expression that covers the reaction functions which ch. 5 christened 'consumption' and 'investment amplifiers'.

Table 6.20 International effects of US depression, 1929–1932 illustrative calculation[a]

	Assumed domestically generated change in GNP = −26%	
	In USA	In Europe
Effect on output of changes in trade volumes	−3.2%	−2.8%
less effect of induced shift in terms of trade	+1.9%	+1.9%
Total impact on output	−1.3%	−0.9%

[a]For details see app. A6.3. The calculation assumes (i) that for the USA and Europe real imports vary proportionately with real GDP and for primary producers, in proportion to export earnings; (ii) that, because of induced shifts in terms of trade, the change in primary producers' export earnings is 2.5 times the change in the volume of imports from them by USA plus Europe; (iii) that the combined multiplier in the USA was 4 and in Europe, 2.

The fall in US output shown in the table (26% + 1.3%) is less than the actual fall in this period (28%) because some of the latter must be attributed to domestically generated depression in Europe (see app. A6.3).

fall in GDP. (The induced fall in Europe's exports would explain a 3 per cent fall in GDP, but the accompanying gain in the terms of trade would offset two-thirds of this [table 6.20].) Given the importance of confidence effects in the depression, the internal 'multipliers' could well have been larger: if they had been double those assumed, the effects shown in table 6.20 would also be doubled.

The broad conclusions to be derived from the model, then, are that depression in the United States cannot explain all of the depression in Europe: most of the 15–20 per cent fall in output in Germany and France, which is where Europe's depression was concentrated, must have been home-bred. But for the United Kingdom, where output fell only 5 per cent, a considerable share of the fall can well be attributed to US depression (with the fall in demand in Germany and France and neighbouring countries only a small additional influence).

6.4.2. Depression in the UK

I turn now to the effects of the depression on the UK. I look first at the effects of international trade, then at the effects of UK fiscal and monetary policy, and finally at the especially deep recession in the UK's older industries, especially textiles.

The impact of the fall in world trade

Though it is clear that depression in the UK followed on from the depression in world trade, it is not easy to say exactly how large the impact was. There are two approaches. We can show the contribution of the absolute fall in exports to the absolute fall in GDP—which overstates the role of exports—or we can look at *shortfall below trend* of exports as a contribution to the shortfall of

GDP—which is potentially more revealing except that trend is difficult to quantify.

Table 6.21 shows the actual impact on UK GDP of the fall in world trade in the period 1929–32. The fall in exports to the United States was by itself a minor influence (accounting for a 0.5 per cent fall in GDP). The effect of the fall in exports to France and Germany together was of the same order, as was the fall in exports to the rest of Europe; both must reflect not only the effect of recession in those countries but widespread new trade barriers. The fall in exports to primary-producing countries was of greater importance, and was itself enough on this calculation to reduce UK GDP by 4 per cent. As already shown, that reflected the effect of recession on primary producers, initiated chiefly by depression in the United States. The counterpart, which reduced the primary producers' purchasing power, was a rise in the purchasing power of incomes in countries like Britain [see table 6.22]. That offset much of the effect of a fall in the number of persons employed, and supported consumer demand throughout the depression. On this reckoning, taking account of this terms-of-trade effect, the net impact of developments abroad was only 2 per cent [table 6.21].

Table 6.23 shows how different categories of final expenditure behaved. The fall in exports was as big as the total fall in final demand. Consumer spending,

Table 6.21   Impact of depression abroad on UK, 1929–1932

	Weight (% of GDP)	% change in export volume, 1929–32	Contribution to % change in GDP, 1929–32
Impact of volume change in exports to			
USA	1.1	−57.9	−0.6
Germany and France	1.6	−38.9	−0.6
Other Europe	4.4	−17.9	−0.6
Primary producers	10.3	−41.6	−4.3
Total	17.5	−36.3	−6.3
	Imports as % of 1929 GDP	Change in terms of trade[a]	Contribution to % change in GDP
Offsetting effect from change of terms of trade			
Total imports	20.3	21.6	4.4
Imports only from primary producers	(12.9)	(33.3)	(4.3)
Net impact from abroad on UK GDP			−1.9

[a] $(100 + \% \text{ change in export prices})/(100 + \% \text{ change in import prices}) - 100$.

Sources: *Statistical Abstract for UK*; Schlote (1952); Feinstein (1972).

Table 6.22 Changes in prices, relative prices and real incomes, UK 1929–1932

	1929	1930	1931	1932	Total change 1929–32
			(% changes)		
Effect of terms of trade on domestic income					
Import deflator	0.3	−0.6	−2.4	−2.7	−5.6
GDP deflator	−0.9	−0.8	−2.0	−2.2	−4.8
Final expenditure deflator	−1.1	−3.1	−5.1	−3.0	−10.8
Purchasing power of domestic factor income[a]	0.2	2.4	3.3	0.8	6.7
Personal income, nominal and real					
Personal income[b]	1.6	−1.2	−3.8	−2.0	−6.9
Consumers' expenditure deflator	−0.9	−2.8	−4.3	−2.6	−9.3
Consumers' purchasing power[c]	2.5	1.6	0.5	0.6	2.7

[a] Change in index of factor income per unit of output (=GDP deflator) *divided by* final expenditure deflator.
[b] Change in total nominal personal income (in total not income per unit of output as fourth row).
[c] Personal income *divided by* consumers' expenditure deflator.
Source: Feinstein (1972).

far from falling, as one would normally expect, rose. (Without the favourable shift in the terms of trade, it would probably have fallen a lot, e.g. by 5 per cent or more.)

In principle, however, it is more revealing to look at the shortfall below what would have happened if growth had continued at some trend rate. Table 6.2 estimated the contribution of the shortfall of exports below trend to the shortfall of GDP below trend, here measured as a line fitted to all years between 1922 and 1929. On this calculation, exports explained only 40 per cent of the shortfall of GDP. Table 6.23 shows an alternative estimate in which the trend is calculated over the shorter period 1924–9: the shortfall of exports then explains the entire shortfall of GDP. The truth is probably within that range; i.e., one can say that the shortfall in exports must account directly for much of the fall in GDP. Perhaps half must have been offset by the associated favourable shift in the terms of trade.[52] Greater exactitude seems impossible: alternative calculations show the uncertainties of this type of calculation. A look at the year-by-year contribution of exports [table 6.24] makes it probable that the export shortfall was the predominant factor in 1930, and was still important in 1931. In 1932 the proximate cause of the fall in output was the

---

[52] The shift in the world terms of trade means that the worst of the depression was in effect exported to the countries who supplied the UK with food and materials. The depression brought a halving of the real price of their products: what that meant to them, most of which were already poor, one hates to think.

Table 6.23   The constituents of demand during the Great Depression in the UK, 1929–1932

	Contributions to % change in GDP				
	Annual average 1924–9[a] (1)	Change from previous year			Total
		1930 (2)	1931 (3)	1932 (4)	1929–32 (5)
Government expenditure	0.2	0.2	0.2	0.0	0.4
Consumer expenditure	1.5	1.2	0.8	−0.5	1.5
Fixed investment	0.5	0.0	−0.2	−1.2	−1.4
Exports	0.3	−2.8	−3.4	−0.3	−6.5
Total final sales	2.5	−1.4	2.5	−2.1	−6.0
Stock change[b]	0.6	0.3	−1.5	0.2	−1.0
Total final expenditure[b] *of which*:	3.1	−1.0	−4.0	−1.9	−6.9
Imports	0.4	−0.3	0.7	−2.3	−1.9
GDP[b]	2.6	−0.8	−4.7	0.4	−5.1

[a] The change between 1924 and 1929 is taken to represent the previous trend of growth since these are two years in which unemployment was about the same.
[b] Includes residual GDP(A) *less* GDP(E).
Source: Feinstein (1972).

shortfalls in fixed investment and in consumer spending—these can be seen as having been provoked by the earlier fall in exports.

Other deflationary factors

Table 6.2 showed fiscal policy over the whole period of the recession as having been a small deflationary factor. But it did not become so till the last year of the recession: the estimates of fiscal impact shown in table A5.2 indicate that fiscal policy swung from a small expansionary impact in 1929 to a major deflationary one in 1932.[53] That was the predictable result of the financial orthodoxy of the day: Snowden, the Labour chancellor, strove rigidly to keep his budget in balance despite the inroads that depression made into tax revenues (see Pollard 1962: 212–3; U. K. Hicks 1938). This astringent policy expressed itself mainly in increases in taxation and cuts in transfer payments— including the 1931 cut in unemployment benefits, which caused the break-up of the Labour Government.

Table 6.2 also shows monetary policy as having been a small expansionary factor. Bank rate was raised after the New York stock exchange crash in

[53] Measures of fiscal stance that adjust for inflation (i.e. include allowance for the effect of inflation on the real value of government debt) do not show this result (see Broadberry 1986: 157). For a discussion of this question see app. A5.

Table 6.24 The slowdown in growth and the growth in unemployment: UK, 1929–1932

	Contributions to % change in GDP			
	Shortfall below 1924–9 average[a]			Total shortfall 1929–32
	1930 (6)	1931 (7)	1932 (8)	(9)
Government expenditure	0.0	0.0	0.2	0.1
Consumer expenditure	0.4	0.7	2.1	3.2
Fixed investment	0.4	0.7	1.7	2.8
Exports	3.1	3.7	0.6	7.3
Total final sales	3.9	5.0	4.6	13.4
Stock change[b]	0.2	2.1	0.4	2.7
Total final expenditure[b]	4.1	7.1	5.0	16.1
of which:				
Imports	0.7	−0.3	2.7	3.0
GDP[b]	3.4	7.3	2.3	13.0
Unemployment (% of civilian working population)				
Change in % unemployment	+3.9	+3.9	+0.5	+8.3
Level of % unemployment	11.2	15.1	15.6	

[a] Column numbering continues from table 6.23. Column (6)=(1)−(2), column (7)=(1)−(3), etc. Column (9)=(6)+(7)+(8).
[b] Includes residual GDP(A) *less* GDP(E).

Sources: Table 6.23 and Feinstein (1972).

October 1929. Thereafter the general intention of central bank policy (in London and the USA) was to ease policy in order to counter the gathering slump;[54] as a result, interest rates in the depression were kept lower than before it started [fig. 6.6]—despite the uncertainties of the payments position.[55]

Political uncertainty resulting from the nature of the government in power might also be suggested as a contributory cause of the depression. Though Snowden was as orthodox a chancellor as the City could wish, the government of 1929–32 was an inexperienced administration and a minority government. Nowadays that would not attract financial and business confidence, but there was then no widespread assumption that governments could or should manage the economy; and there is no reason to think that the style of the government contributed to the depression.

[54] See Howson (1975: 66–8), relying largely on Sayers (1956) and S. V. O. Clarke (1967).
[55] The fact that the stock of money fell I regard as no evidence that policy in Britain exerted a contractionary effect, any more than in the United States [s. 6.3]: I see it only as a sign that the banks were reducing their lending as the business of their customers contracted.

The fall in prices during the depression I see as having been a contractionary influence, as in 1920–1 [s. 6.2]. But the decline in the price level was mild. (The GDP deflator fell only 6 per cent over the three years.)

The uneven incidence of the depression in the UK

Severe depression in traditional export industries, combined with the maintenance of domestic consumer purchasing power, meant that different industries fared very differently [table 6.25]. Shipbuilding practically ceased, and most metals and engineering output fell (but not electrical engineering, which expanded through the recession years). Textiles and clothing output plunged in 1930—but recovered by 1932, as also did chemicals output. Output of gas, electricity, the food industry, and most service industries also fell. These diversities in output growth were paralleled by employment changes. Since the declining industries were concentrated regionally, most of the growth of unemployment was concentrated in Scotland, Wales, and Northern Ireland, while the south remained relatively more prosperous.

The changes in investment through the Great Depression were similarly diverse: not all were what might have been expected in the worst recession in UK experience. Though fixed investment by manufacturing industries did fall,

Table 6.25   Change in output and employment: UK, 1929–1932

	Annual average, 1924–9	1930	1931	1932	Total, 1929–32
% change from previous year					
GDP	2.4	−0.1	−5.5	0.7	−4.9
Total employment	1.2	−2.5	−2.4	0.5	−3.7
Industrial output	3.2	−4.3	−6.5	−0.4	−10.8
Employment in industry	0.6	−5.1	−6.0	−0.6	−11.3
of which:					
Textile & clothing					
Output	0.1	−8.1	−3.1	5.4	−0.1
Employment	0.1	−18.6	−5.7	−9.3	−16.0
Metals & engineering					
Output	3.5	−6.8	−17.6	−2.9	−25.5
Employment	1.4	−6.5	−12.1	−2.4	−19.8
Change from previous year ('000)					
Total in employment	+220	−364	−450	+88	−726
of which, in					
Textiles & clothing	+1	−242	−61	+93	−210
Metals & engineering	+30	−146	−255	−45	−446
Other industries	+35	−68	−91	+37	−122

Source: Feinstein (1972).

by far the greater part of the fall in investment was in transport and communi-cations—chiefly ships, roads, and road transport vehicles. Investment in social and public services and gas and electricity production rose. Investment in dwellings showed no fall.

Conclusions about the depression in the UK

My conclusions then are as follows. The main cause of the depression in the UK was the loss of exports. That was partly offset by the associated gain from the terms of trade; but, even taking account of that, these two world trade effects could explain, say, half the fall in GDP. The rest may perhaps be accounted for as the result of domestic multipliers (i.e. resulting from induced falls in consumer and business expectations) and thus the indirect consequences of the loss of exports. Some of the loss of exports probably reflected a particularly UK problem in export markets, which might have happened anyway; but the greater part probably stemmed from the US depression. The UK depression is thus fairly fully explicable as the effect of an exogenous shock and the reactions to be expected from such a shock.

A final question is: why did the depression bottom out? Just as world events must have played the dominant role in bringing it on, so they can be seen as bringing it to an end. Exports ceased to fall. That in turn must have been partly because the US depression itself was bottoming out, and partly because that in turn meant that the vast swing in the terms of trade, which had previously depressed the incomes of primary-producing countries—so reducing their purchases of UK and other industrial countries' exports—had run its course. From the point of view of one country like the United Kingdom, it need only be said that an external exogenous shock—the fall in exports—had continued for a time and then stopped, and with it the shift in the terms of trade that had cushioned it. The end of recession does not represent recovery: recovery itself is considered in the next section.

6.5. Economic recovery in Britain, 1932–1940

There has been a long discussion of what caused the recovery after the British depression of 1929–32.[56] The viewpoint has usually been somewhat different from that taken below. The question asked here is not: why did growth resume (since it is taken for granted that a modern economy will reattain its trend rate of growth unless a new shock intervenes: ch. 3.1), but rather: what caused output to grow at a rate high enough gradually to reabsorb the unemployment left by the depression? This difference of approach alters the emphasis, so that evidence cited and reasoning adduced in previous discussion has to be reassessed.

---

[56] Four articles or books that give a general overview of the period, incorporating results of more specialist studies, are drawn on here: Worswick (1984*a,b*) Sedgwick (1984), and, more ambi-tious, Broadberry (1986).

Table 6.26 The 1930s recovery in Britain: demand-side changes, 1932–1940

	Contributions to % change in TFE (1938 market prices)									
	1st phase: investment			3-year change	2nd phase: rearmament			3-year change	Transition to war	
	1933	1934	1935	1932–5	1936	1937	1938	1935–8	1939	1940
Government expenditure	0.1	0.2	0.5	0.8	0.7	1.0	1.8	3.5	5.6	21.4
Consumer expenditure	1.8	2.0	1.9	5.6	1.9	1.1	0.5	3.6	0.4	−5.9
Exports[a]	0.2	0.5	1.5	2.1	−0.4	0.6	−0.8	−0.6	−0.8	−3.1
Fixed investment	0.2	1.6	0.3	2.1	0.7	0.3	0.1	1.2	−0.9	−1.0
Stock change	−1.3	1.9	−0.5	0.1	−0.2	0.9	0.4	1.2	0.2	0.7
Residual	1.7	−0.0	0.1	1.8	1.5	−0.5	−1.4	−0.5	−0.8	−4.9
Total final expenditure[b]	2.6	6.1	3.9	12.6	4.3	3.4	0.6	8.4	3.7	7.2
of which:										
GDP[b]	2.6	5.4	3.2	11.1	4.0	2.9	1.0	7.8	2.4	6.9
Imports[a]	0.0	0.7	0.7	1.4	0.4	0.5	−0.3	0.6	1.3	0.3

[a] Goods and services.
[b] Includes residual GDP(A) *less* GDP(E).

Source: Feinstein (1972).

6.5.1. A first look at the recovery as a whole

Tables 6.26–6.29 provide a general analysis of what happened in the recovery. Table 6.26 shows year-to-year changes in expenditure, on the presentation used in earlier phases. Since the imposition of tariffs in 1931 must have reduced imports, table 6.27 shows an alternative presentation in which changes in imports along with other changes in expenditure contribute to the change in GDP, not, as before, final expenditure.

The fall in unemployment started in 1933, but became rapid only in 1934. The expenditure elements that produced faster growth were chiefly high fixed investment and high stockbuilding (a response, presumably, to moderate growth being resumed in the previous year). The counterparts on the supply side are shown in table 6.28.

We want to know not why output grew, but why it grew fast enough to reduce unemployment. Table 6.29 therefore shows the excess of output growth over trend rate and a rough indication (see note to table) of the expenditure trends that produced it. In 1932 the output increase was well short of what was needed to reduce unemployed capacity; in 1933 it increased more than enough, and in 1934 much more. The pick-up of output in 1932 is shown to have owed much to the fall in imports; the acceleration in 1933 reflected unusually fast growth of consumer expenditure (as well as the absence of growth in imports). In 1934 these two factors were powerfully supplemented by higher fixed investment and investment in stocks. (Government spending will be discussed later with concurrent tax changes.)

Table 6.27 Recovery 1932–1940: alternative presentation

	Contribution to % change in GDP								
	1932	1933	1934	1935	1936	1937	1938	1939	1940
Government expenditure[a]	0.0	0.1	0.2	0.6	0.9	1.2	2.1	6.6	25.3
Consumer expenditure	−0.5	2.1	2.4	2.2	2.3	1.3	0.6	0.4	−7.0
Fixed investment	−1.2	0.3	1.8	0.4	0.9	0.3	0.1	−1.1	−1.2
Stock change[b]	0.2	0.4	2.2	−0.4	1.5	0.5	−1.2	−0.7	−4.9
Exports[a]	−0.3	0.2	0.5	1.8	−0.4	0.7	−0.9	−1.0	−3.7
Imports[a,c]	2.3	0.0	−0.8	−0.9	−0.5	−0.6	0.4	−1.5	−0.3
GDP[b]	0.4	3.1	6.4	3.7	4.7	3.4	1.1	2.8	8.2

[a] Goods and services.
[b] Includes residual GDP(A) *less* GDP(E).
[c] Increase in imports shown as negative contribution to output growth.

Source: Feinstein (1972).

Table 6.28   Supply-side changes, 1932–1941

	1933	1934	1935	1936	1937	1938	1939	1940	1941
				(annual % changes)					
GDP[a]	2.9	6.6	3.8	4.5	3.5	1.2	1.0	10.0	9.1
of which:									
Output per worker	0.9	3.6	2.0	1.3	0.2	0.9	−3.0	6.2	5.0
Employment	2.0	2.9	1.8	3.2	3.4	0.3	4.1	3.6	3.9
Working population	0.3	0.3	0.8	1.3	1.6	1.9	0.1	0.8	1.7
% unemployment[b]									
Change	−1.5	−2.2	−0.9	−1.6	−1.6	+1.5	−3.5	−2.5	−2.1
Level	14.1	11.9	11.0	9.4	7.8	9.3	5.8	3.3	1.2

[a] GDP(A).
[b] % of civilian working population.
Source: Feinstein (1972).

Table 6.29   Above-trend growth in output and expenditure, 1931–1936

	Contributions to % change in GDP				
	1932	1933	1934	1935	1936
Government expenditure	−0.3	−0.6	−0.5	0.0	0.2
Consumer expenditure	−2.6	0.2	0.5	0.3	0.4
Fixed investment	−1.5	0.1	1.7	0.2	0.7
Exports	−0.8	−0.1	0.3	1.5	−0.8
Imports[a]	2.9	0.4	−0.4	−0.5	0.0
GDP(E)	−2.2	−1.7	4.0	1.0	0.3
Change in % unemployment	0.5	−1.5	−2.2	−0.9	−1.6

[a] Decrease in imports shown as positive contribution to growth.
Source: Feinstein (1972).

Investment, however, never became really strong. Throughout the interwar period, growth of the fixed capital stock remained very subdued, well below the rate of growth of output. Over the period 1920–38, while GDP growth averaged 2 per cent a year, the rate of growth of the stock of dwellings fairly consistently exceeded that; but the rest of the capital stock grew markedly less fast. Having grown very slowly in 1933 and 1934, it did then begin to accelerate, but it never became a main source of strong growth [tables 6.29 and 6.30]—as it was to be in the boom of the 1980s.

Table 6.30 Rate of growth of the capital stock, 1929–1938

| | Gross capital stock at 1938 replacement cost | | | | |
| | Gross capital stock (£1938 bn) | | | Annual % rate of growth | |
	Dwellings	Non-dwellings	Total	Dwellings	Non-dwellings
1921	3.42	11.41	14.83	2.4	0.8
1922	3.48	11.51	14.99	11.7	0.9
1923	3.54	11.61	15.15	1.7	0.9
Average for years 1920–3				*1.9*	*0.9*
1924	3.62	11.75	15.37	2.2	1.2
1925	3.73	11.91	15.64	3.0	1.4
1926	3.86	12.03	15.89	3.5	1.0
1927	4.00	12.16	16.16	3.6	1.1
1928	4.11	12.32	16.43	2.7	1.3
1929	4.24	12.48	16.72	3.2	1.3
Average for years 1923–9				*3.0*	*1.2*
1930	4.35	12.67	17.02	2.6	1.5
1931	4.48	12.81	17.29	3.0	1.1
Average for years 1929–31				*2.9*	*1.3*
1932	4.61	12.89	17.50	2.9	0.6
1933	4.77	12.95	17.72	3.5	0.5
1934	4.96	13.08	18.04	4.0	1.0
1935	5.13	13.24	18.37	3.4	1.2
1936	5.29	13.45	18.74	3.1	1.6
1937	5.45	13.68	19.13	3.0	1.7
1938	5.60	13.72	19.52	2.8	0.3
Average for years 1931–8				*3.2*	*1.0*

Source: Feinstein (1972).

A note is needed on two lines of explanation which appear to me wrong. First, just as the depression is sometimes explained as having been due to excessive real wages, so it is alleged that recovery was due to real wages falling.[57] I have earlier set out reasons to reject that interpretation [ch. 3.3].

A second explanation is that recovery was due to a sort of blossoming of innovation: recovery, according to Richardson (1967), was due to a combination of supply and demand factors creating a great expansion in the output of new sorts of durable consumer goods.[58] Reasons against this view are given by Worswick (1984a) and Broadberry (1986). Productivity did not grow more

---

[57] This view was propounded at the time by e.g. Robbins (1934) and in more recent years by Beenstock *et al.* (1984) and Minford (1983). Adverse comment on the latter two is in Dimsdale (1984).
[58] See also Richardson (1962) and Aldcroft (1970).

rapidly in the 1930s than in the 1920s (as Richardson seems to imply); recovery was not due to unusual developments on the side of supply; while there were several identifiable shocks on the side of demand [table 6.2] that could explain it.

From the point of view of this study, most interest attaches to the second phase of recovery, which ranks as a fast-growth phase. But I devote some space to the first phase simply because it has provoked so much—as I think wrongly focused—discussion.

The first phase of recovery, 1932–5

As the influences that had caused the depression fell away, one would anyhow expect positive growth to have resumed. Going beyond that, there were several expansionary changes in UK policy: (1) Britain imposed tariffs in 1931, and abandoned the gold standard, at which point the exchange rate fell; (2) monetary policy aimed at cheap money, and interest rates were reduced; and (3) with growing defence spending, fiscal policy gradually became expansionary. Abroad, however, other countries also imposed tariffs (which hurt UK exports); and at different dates also abandoned gold. Other countries were also recovering from depression (which helped UK exports); but on the other hand the terms of trade started to retreat from the extreme levels of the depression years (which helped UK exports to the third world, but reversed the benefit that consumers had enjoyed during the depression).

The influences at work were thus complex. The evidence suggests that the first phase of recovery can be explained as the combined effect of five major influences:

1. the depreciation of sterling;
2. the imposition of tariffs;
3. changes in the terms of trade;
4. changes in fiscal policy;
5. the effects of the housing boom.

The depreciation of sterling When Britain severed the link with gold in September 1931, sterling fell against the US dollar by over 25 per cent [table 6.31], but by 1934 it had recovered its previous dollar parity. (Note that the £/$ cross-rate does not represent the effective rate.) France, along with Switzerland, Belgium, and Italy, clung to gold longer, but (followed by other countries) eventually devalued in 1936, and again in 1937. Even then, much of the effect of the 1931 devaluation of sterling remained. The effective exchange rate of sterling (here proxied by a simple average) probably fell in 1931 along with the sterling–dollar rate, and thereafter rose gradually; but even by 1938 it probably remained well short of its 1929 level.[59]

---

[59] Neither of the two available measures of the effective rate is adequate. That of Dimsdale (1981) of 11 manufacturing countries' exchange rates is weighted by their share of world trade in manufactures (not, as would be better, according to their importance as competitors to the UK).

Table 6.31 Exchange rate indicators, 1929–1938

	£/$	Average exchange rate[a]	Real exchange rate[b]
		Indices (1929=100)	
1929	100.0	100.0	100.0
1930	100.1	99.6	98.5
1931	93.3	93.7	94.2
1932	72.1	75.2	81.4
1933	86.8	77.2	82.8
1934	103.8	75.4	81.7
1935	100.9	74.5	81.8
1936	102.3	77.7	86.1
1937	101.8	84.7	91.9
1938	100.7	86.9	91.8

[a] Average of 11 industrial countries' exchange rates against £ weighted according to countries' shares in world trade in manufactures.
[b] As *a*, but deflated by relative retail prices.

Source: Dimsdale (1981: 125).

The fall in the exchange rate, taken on its own, must have increased exports and reduced imports in volume terms; and that will have raised output. Probably the best estimate is obtained by applying estimates of the price elasticities of imports and exports (obtained in econometric analyses of other episodes) to the actual changes in relative prices that occurred between 1931 and 1932. Broadberry's estimate, based on stylized assumptions about elasticities, suggests that the devaluation raised output by 2.5 per cent[60]—an outcome that must be presumed to have taken effect gradually over a period of years. This estimate appears high in relation to the actual change in trade volumes (see below). By 1936 the real effective rate appears to have been rising again, so that in the later stages of recovery this stimulus was being reversed.[61]

Redmond (1980) uses as weights the shares of 28 countries in world trade in all commodities, which is not very appropriate for an explanation of UK trade. Table 6.31 shows Dimsdale's index.

[60] Broadberry (1986: 129), based on Moggridge's (1972) equally stylized estimates of the effect of the high exchange rate in the 1920s. The figure of 2.5% is calculated from Broadberry's estimate of 3% for the improvement at *current prices* in the current balance as a percentage of GDP and is here transformed to provide an estimate of the change in the *volume* of net trade as a percentage of GDP.

[61] There are many disputable questions about the determination of the changes in the exchange rate. Mostly they have little relevance to judging their effect; but one question does have relevance. It can be argued that the exchange rate fell because of the deficit in the balance of payments during the depression, and that it rose later because the deficit was reduced. One reason why the deficit was reduced must have been that tariffs were imposed. Hence (it could be argued) it would be double-counting to add the effect on output of exchange rate depreciation to that of tariffs. The counter-argument (which appears to me valid) is that the fall in the exchange rate was due to sterling being released from the straitjacket of the fixed parity which had previously kept it too high; and that later on its rise was due to UK intervention; i.e., all movements reflected exchange rate policy. There is no easy way to settle this kind of dispute, which can stand as an illustration of the difficulty of providing uncontroversial explanations as to why the recovery occurred, and more generally.

The imposition of tariffs, 1931–2   Until 1931 all but some 2 or 3 per cent of imports were duty free. Tariffs were imposed on an emergency basis in the autumn of 1931, and were then regularized by the Act of February 1932. Food and raw materials remained exempt. Manufactures (except for the small quantity of imports that came from the Empire) paid duty: two-thirds at 10–20 per cent, the rest at higher rates.

It would be possible to estimate the effect on UK output of the imposition of tariffs by a calculation similar to that for exchange rate depreciation (which to my knowledge has not been done). The change in the relative price of domestic and foreign manufactured goods caused by the tariff must have been of the same order as that caused by devaluation. But since only imports, not exports, were affected, one would expect the effect on output to have been less. (For example, if depreciation is correctly estimated to have raised output by 2 per cent, tariffs might have raised it by 1 per cent.[62])

The combined effect of devaluation and tariffs   These conclusions seem roughly confirmed by the change over the period 1932–5 in UK imports and exports of goods and services. The rise in the volume of exports plus the fall in the volume of imports was equivalent to nearly 3 per cent of GNP [table 6.27]. The current balance is determined in part by the cyclical position of the UK relative to that of other countries, and in part by factors affecting competitiveness. In this period the UK may have expanded about as rapidly as other industrial countries [fig. 6.3], so that the improvement in the foreign balance probably reflected not changes in the relative cyclical position, but factors affecting competitiveness, which in this phase were chiefly devaluation and the new tariffs. (That conclusion is also corroborated by the course of output and trade in manufactures [table 6.32].)

Changes in the terms of trade   There was an unfavourable counterpart to these favourable volume effects. During the depression [s. 6.4] the shift in the world terms of trade in favour of manufacturing countries and against the primary producers had depressed exports to the latter countries like Britain—but, as we

---

[62] Two attempts illustrate the difficulties of making a more refined estimate. Foreman-Peck (1980) concludes that tariffs raised GDP by 2.3% over the five years 1930–5. But some of the rise in the relative price of imports, e.g., will have reflected not tariffs but the fall in the effective rate (nearly 20% in real terms), and any estimate (like this one) obtained as a residual leaves room for large error. Eichengreen's (1979) attempt is more sophisticated but raises even wider questions. He assumes that the first effect of a tariff on the balance of payments is *adverse*—on the grounds that the proceeds of the tariff can be treated as though they had been distributed by the government. That, he argues, will have raised imports more than their higher price reduced them. In fact, the government did not distribute the proceeds. (Snowden, the chancellor at this juncture, was ultra-conservative, and aimed at a surplus. The central government financial deficit was heavily reduced in 1932, despite the automatic effects of worsening depression.) The further steps in the transmission process that Eichengreen predicates appear over-sophisticated, and statistically his results are poor (see discussion in Broadberry 1986: 135).

Table 6.32 Output and imports in total and for manufactures, 1929–1935

	1929	1930	1931	1932	1933	1934	1935
			(% of 1929 GDP)				
GDP	100	99.1	95.0	95.2	99.2	104.5	109.2
of which:							
Manufacturing							
output	26.6	25.7	23.7	23.8	25.6	27.9	30.5
Imports[a]							
Goods and							
services	22.8	22.3	23.5	20.8	21.5	22.2	23.7
Manufactures	8.5	9.0	8.7	5.4	5.2	5.7	6.0

[a] Import propensities in volume terms applied to index of output and the manufacturing component therefore.

Source: Feinstein (1972); Sedgwick (1984).

have seen, it also cheapened British imports from them, and thus supported domestic purchasing power and consumer demand. By 1934 the terms of trade were swinging back against the manufacturing countries [fig. 6.7], so that these effects were going into reverse. Similarly, the 1930 depreciation of sterling, though it had favourable volume effects on the balance of payments and on output, also worsened the terms of trade, reduced domestic purchasing power, and moderated consumer demand. An estimate of all terms-of-trade effects taken together is included in table 6.34.

Changes in fiscal policy   The impact of fiscal policy was as important as any of the other exogenous changes. Fiscal policy had been greatly tightened in 1932 [table 6.33]: both direct taxation and, even more, indirect taxation had been increased, and (not distinguished in the table) unemployment pay was cut. Fiscal policy was expansionary in 1934 (the burden of tax was reduced) and again in 1935, when government spending increased. In 1932 fiscal policy restraint may have been enough to cancel the expansionary effect of tariffs and devaluation [table 6.33]. By 1935 it had become positive at a time when exports were rising strongly, and joined with it in giving an appreciable boost to expansion.

The housing boom   The housing boom was important—perhaps of predominant importance—in the early years of the recovery.[63] It provided a stimulus directly, by providing employment not only in the building industry but in trades that provided materials and components (a stimulus all the greater since

[63] It has been given great emphasis by many writers, e.g. Bellman (1938), MacDougall (1938/1975), Bowley (1947), Howson (1975), Nevin (1953), Richardson (1967), Worswick (1984a), and Sedgwick (1984).

Table 6.33   Indicators of fiscal policy, 1932–1935

	Contribution to % change in GDP or as noted			
	1932	1933	1934	1935
Effect on output of:				
Change in government expenditure on goods and services	0.0	0.1	0.2	0.6
Change in net indirect taxes[a]	−1.2	0.1	0.2	0.2
Change in direct taxes on personal income[b]	−0.6	0.3	0.4	0.0
Total of above	−1.8	0.5	0.8	0.8
Estimate of total fiscal impact[c]	−2.2	−0.8	0.3	1.3

[a] Change in net indirect taxes as % of GDP at current factor cost.
[b] Change in personal direct tax liabilities, including employee's national insurance contributions, as % of personal income.
[c] From appendix A5. The estimate also differs in concept from previous estimates (e.g. Maddison 1981), notably by a different definition of what constitutes a tax change and by including local as well as central government.

Source: Feinstein (1972).

the import content was very low). The national accounts (used in table 6.34) indicate that investment in dwellings accounted for almost a third of the (slightly above-trend) rise in GDP in 1933, but very little of it in 1934; in 1935 investment in dwellings fell.[64]

There are differences of view as to what caused the housing boom. At the time, the policy of lowering interest rates was seen (not necessarily in a very precise way) as a means to encourage economic recovery.[65] Since recovery did in fact materialize, this explanation of it has persisted, and cheap money has continued to be seen as the main influence. But although it was one reason for the housing boom, there were other reasons also. The boom was probably part of a long swing in housebuilding going back to the 1920s (Matthews *et al*. 1982: 410–13)—amplified no doubt by cheap money, but reflecting also the movement of population to the south, improvements in transport which favoured suburban housing development, and the rise in real personal incomes which (as we have seen) had continued right through the recession. Mortgage rates themselves were not greatly reduced (perhaps not at all in real terms). But lower market rates of interest produced an inflow of funds to the building

---

[64] The employment statistics suggest that the contribution of house building was larger. Worswick estimates that 30% of the rise in employment between 1932 and 1935 was due to employment in building and ancillary trades (Worswick 1984*b*: 86).

[65] Contemporary ideas about economic relationships differed so much from current ones that a simplistic reading of official statements made at the time can be misleading: see the account of Treasury views in Howson (1975: 71).

Table 6.34 Four influences treated as exogenous shocks, 1932–1935[a]

	Contribution to % change in GDP				
	(1932)	1933	1934	1935	Total for 3 years 1932–5
Tariffs and depreciation[b]	(2.0)	0.2	−0.3	0.9	0.8
Terms of trade effect[c]	(0.8)	0.2	−0.6	0.0	−0.4
Fiscal policy impact[d]	(−2.2)	−0.8	0.3	1.3	0.8
Housing boom[e]	(0)	0.9	0.4	−0.2	1.1
Total of above	(0.6)	0.5	−0.2	2.0	2.3

[a] The treatment here differs somewhat from the definition of exogenous shocks used in chapter 5.2.
[b] As proxied by change in volume of exports *less* that of imports (as in table 6.27).
[c] % change in GDP deflator *less* % change in TFE deflator multiplied by 0.7; see table 5.4.
[d] As in figure 6.7: see also appendix A5.
[e] Change in investment in dwellings as contribution to % change in GDP.

Source of basic data: Feinstein (1972).

Table 6.35 Classification of factors accounting for the first stage recovery, 1932–1935

	Contribution to % change in GDP			
	1933	1934	1935	Total 3 years 1932–5
Four exogenous influences[a]	0.5	−0.2	2.0	2.3
Non-residential fixed investment	−0.6	1.4	0.6	1.4
Investment in stocks[b]	0.4	2.2	−0.4	2.2
(Expenditure unaccounted for[c])	(−0.2)	(0.3)	(−0.7)	(−0.6)
Output growth in excess of the capacity rate of growth	0.6	3.9	1.2	5.7

[a] The effect of tariffs and depreciation (as proxied by change in export *less* import volume), terms-of-trade effects, fiscal policy, and housing boom from table 6.34.
[b] Includes National Accounts residual GDP(A) *less* GDP(E).
[c] The residual item in this table = consumer expenditure not accounted for by changes in fiscal policy or terms of trade.

Source of basic data: Feinstein (1972).

societies, and allowed them to ease the severity of their rationing of mortgage lending.[66]

Whatever its precise causation, the housing boom can be regarded as an exogenous event; and, if not the main factor, certainly one of the three main factors [table 6.34] that got recovery going at an above-trend rate.

[66] See Sedgwick (1984: 47) and Bowley (1947).

Table 6.36   Fiscal impact and the increase in defence spending, 1933–1940

	Contribution to % change in GDP							
	1933	1934	1935	1936	1937	1938	1939	1940
Fiscal impact	0.0	0.2	0.8	0.5	1.3	2.8	8.2	33.3
Increase in defence spending	0.1	0.1	0.5	0.9	1.4	2.3	N/A	N/A

Source: Fiscal impact as estimated in app. A5, weighted and with current spending only; and Feinstein (1972).

To conclude, the above five exogenous factors probably account directly for half the above-trend growth on this first stage of recovery [table 6.35], and indirectly via their multiplier effects must account for considerably more. One can conclude that, without them, expansion might well have been not much different from the trend rate: that is, there is no reason to think that endogenous forces alone would have produced a movement back to high employment.

6.5.2.   The second phase of recovery: 1935 into World War II

After 1935, growth (with a significant pause in 1938) continued to be fast up to and into the war years [table 6.26] and (except in 1938) unemployment continued to fall [table 6.28].[67]

In this second phase of recovery, growing defence expenditure was clearly the decisive reason for continued fast growth, and for the rapid reversal of the setback in 1938. In principle, the policy was to finance defence spending out of taxation, but the rule was relaxed. The Budget deficit grew progressively after 1935, as defence spending began to build up. After 1934, my estimate of the expansionary impact of fiscal policy corresponds fairly closely to the growing scale of defence spending [table 6.36].

Other exogenous influences on the rate of growth of output were erratic and generally negative [table 6.37]:

1. Foreign trade was a consistently adverse influence, partly because the 1931 devaluation was in effect being reversed [table 6.31].
2. The world terms of trade were now moving fairly strongly against the United Kingdom: commodity prices (after their trough in the depression) were rising (except in 1938) faster than UK domestic prices and costs. That must have depressed domestic demand.
3. The housing boom was over [table 6.37].

---

[67] Many people think there would have been a serious recession after 1938 if the war had not come. That seems to me very possible.

Table 6.37 Classification of factors accounting for the second-stage recovery, 1935–1938

	Contribution to % change in GDP					
	1936	1937	1938	Total 3 years 1935–8	1939	1940
Four exogenous influences						
Tariffs and depreciation[a]	−0.9	0.1	−0.5	−1.3	−2.5	−4.0
Terms of trade effect[b]	−0.7	−1.6	1.4	−0.9	0.3	−3.5
Fiscal policy impact[c]	0.5	1.3	2.8	4.6	8.2	33.3
Housing boom[d]	0.0	−0.2	−0.0	−0.2	−1.0	−0.8[e]
	−1.1	−0.4	3.7	2.2	5.0	25.1
Non-residential fixed investment	0.9	0.6	0.3	1.7	−0.1	0.3
Investment in stocks[f]	1.5	0.5	−1.2	0.8	−0.7	−4.9
(Expenditure unaccounted for)[g]	(0.9)	(0.2)	(−3.6)	(−2.5)	(1.9)	(−6.0)
GDP[f] less rough estimate of capacity rate of growth = output growth in excess of the capacity rate of growth[h]	2.6	0.9	−1.4	1.7	0.3	5.7

[a] As proxied by change in exports *less* imports.
[b] $100 \times$ (ratio of GDP deflator in year $t-1$ to year t to year $t-1$ ÷ ratio of TFE deflator in year t to year $t-1$)
[c] As in app. A5.
[d] Change in investment in dwellings.
[e] Figure for 1940 is proportionate share in change in investment in new building and works.
[f] Includes national accounts residual GDP(A) − GDP(E).
[g] Residual item in table = consumer expenditure not accounted for by changes in fiscal policy or terms of trade.
[h] As in table 6.29 (capacity growth rate assumed to be 2.5% p.a.).

Source: Feinstein (1972).

The fast rate of growth after 1936, which continued to eat into unemployed capacity, has thus probably to be explained entirely in terms of defence spending.[68]

The short-lived recession of 1938, like the depression of 1929–32, has to be seen as originating abroad, and was probably a result of the fall in output in the United States [fig. 6.3]. Exports, however, fell not only in 1938, but also in 1939 and even more largely in 1940 [table 6.26]—as did fixed investment. These latter declines probably reflected not lack of demand, but supply shortages: capacity formerly available for civilian purposes was being pre-empted by defence production. Even in 1938, some of the expenditure changes may have been due to capacity constraints rather than demand factors.

Other developments on the supply side also deserve comment. The unemployment generated during the 1939 depression had been concentrated [s. 6.4] on certain industries and certain areas; even before the depression, unemployment had been heaviest in the old industrial areas of the North of England and Scotland and Wales. The differential unemployment in these areas (over and above the rate of unemployment in the more prosperous South and Midlands) accounted for 3.5 per cent of the insured population out of total unemployed of 10.5 per cent [table 6.38]. By 1932 this margin had risen to 6.5 per cent out of a total unemployment amounting by then to 22 per cent. By 1937, when the total had come down to 11 per cent, the 'extra' in the North and West, though still considerable, had come down to 5 per cent. This margin is an (imperfect) indication of the extent of 'structural unemployment'. The interesting point is that it varied with the strength of demand. It was to fall further in the early war years as labour was progressively absorbed by the armed forces and the war industries.

6.5.3. Conclusions about the recovery

This section has sought to explain why output after the depression grew more rapidly than the trend rate of growth. That seems explicable in terms of a number of identifiable exogenous factors. The analysis suggests that without exogenous stimuli—devaluation, tariffs, and the housing boom in the first phase, and rearmament in the second—growth might have been at no more than the trend rate; i.e., there would have been no resumption of higher employment. Given the recovery, investment demand revived; but even so, it did not revive very strongly, and was not a main driving force. This recovery will later need to be compared with the fast-growth phases after 1972 [ch. 8].

In the first phase of the recovery most of the important stimuli came from policy actions. But, though in some degree policy was motivated by a desire to encourage expansion, it would be a mistake to regard it as an explicit expansionist policy. The same is true of the second phase of recovery, when the

---

[68] Explanation of output in terms of expenditure is however necessarily imperfect, because in some years there is a very large residual in Feinstein's estimates of the national accounts. Thus, his estimates show GDP(0) falling 1% between 1937 and 1938 but GDP(E) rising 3% [table 6.37].

Table 6.38 Indicators of structural unemployment

	1929	1932	1937
	% of insured population		
South and Midlands regions	7.1	16.2	6.8
North, Scotland and Wales	13.7	28.0	15.0
Great Britain	10.5	22.1	10.8
of which is *due* to:			
Extra in North, Scotland and			
Wales above South and			
Midlands[a]	4.4	7.8	5.2
Remainder	6.1	14.4	5.6

[a] Unemployment in these regions over and above the average % rate in the South/Midlands as % of insured population aged 16–64.

Source: Beveridge (1944: 61).

stimulus came predominantly from government defence expenditure. That was to be carried much further during the war itself. This experience leaves little room to doubt the effectiveness of such spending as a means to increase output and put idle resources to work. To that extent, it would appear validation difficult to controvert of a broadly Keynesian view of the effectiveness, at least in the short term, of fiscal policy.[69]

6.6. Theoretical conclusions

The underlying objective of this study is not an explanation of events (as is the aim of economic history) but an analysis of the way the economy behaves (the proper aim of economic theory). To obtain a basis for conclusions, one has to immerse oneself in history; to draw general conclusions, one then has to stand back. Though full conclusions will have to wait for the end of this study [chs. 10 and 11], it may be useful to try to state some first conclusions at this stage.

Attention has been directed to explaining why the economy behaved in such a way that employment grew or fell, i.e. to explaining why output grew more quickly or more slowly than usual. That involves the idea of a normal growth rate, which is difficult to measure exactly. But the experiment of posing the question this way and trying to explain divergences from trend in terms of demand and shocks seems to show that it can provide a generally plausible account of events.

Three of the four episodes examined—the 1920–1 recession, the UK depression of the 1930s, and the subsequent recovery—appear relatively well explained in terms of identifiable demand shocks. The other main episode—the Great

---

[69] The sustainability of an expansionary fiscal policy will be discussed in ch. 12.

Depression in the United States—proved far less fully explicable in this way. In all cases, more complete explanation seemed to require the supposition that the effect of severe demand shocks was amplified by changes in consumer and business confidence; and, in the case of the USA in 1929–33, by the effects of the collapse of banks under the stress of a very severe demand shock.

In two of the three cases of downward fluctuation, the extent of the fluctuation was large but not extreme; i.e., output went down 10–15 per cent below the high-employment capacity growth path. In the case of the US Great Depression, output fell almost 50 per cent below previous trend. In that case investment fell close to zero—which might have set some sort of lower limit. Reasons need to be found for less extreme stopping points.

All these questions will need to be considered further in the light of the analysis of later fluctuations.

Appendix A6.1 A Critique of Friedman and Schwartz's *A Monetary History of the United States*

Since Friedman and Schwartz's *Monetary History* (1963) has had such a considerable impact on the debate about the causes of the Great Depression, it seems desirable to explain at greater length than possible in the body of the text my reasons for finding their explanation unsatisfactory and implausible.

Interpretation of the theoretical aspects of the book is rendered difficult by its being primarily an historical not a theoretical work. It provides a dense and scholarly account of monetary developments and the evolution of policy in the ninety-three years after 1867. The four depression years take 120 pages of the 700 pages of the book (a fifth of the space being footnotes). Within that, are around 40 passages varying in length from a paragraph to a sentence which state or imply a view about the causality of the depression; in addition, there are about 20 more such passages in the final chapter. These passages are scattered and embedded in not difficult, but dense and demanding, discussions of statistical developments and conflicting views and personalities, themselves requiring attentive reading; they are therefore difficult to do justice to on a first reading or to extract and collate afterwards.

The massive nature of Friedman and Schwartz's history is indicated by the structure of each of its main chapters. Chapter 7 on the Great Depression starts with a general review, covering almost everything discussed later. Section 2 appears to be constructed on the plan of discussing chronologically different monetary aggregates and sub-aggregates and the relations between them (ratios and identities); but much else is included within that framework. Section 3 is about bank failures, already discussed once; and section 4 about financial events abroad. Then come two sections discussing, first, monetary policy and contemporary discussions of it and, second, Friedman's comments thereon. Repetition in analytical narrative is impossible to avoid, but Friedman and Schwartz have allowed many layers of it to remain.

The steady thoroughness of their prose acts to induce acceptance of preannounced propositions long before evidence in support of them comes into sight. Chapter 7 for instance is entitled 'The Great Contraction'; and since that phrase is used in a dual sense, it functions as a suggestion of causal connection. The 'Great Contraction' can apply on the one hand to the great decline in real output; but it can apply also (and more aptly) to the contraction of the money stock. The impression given is thus that the two were inextricably intertwined and that the monetary contraction was the essence of it. That is indeed what Friedman and Schwartz believe, and say on the third page; but to which they never later give precision, or even by the end, much evidential support.

The title of the final section of Chapter 7 is equally indicative. One might have expected here a connected discussion of whether monetary contraction might have been not cause but the effect of the real contraction, a question of which the authors are aware: had that been the case, it could have been difficult for the authorities to stop money contracting. Instead, the question is begged. The title of the final section is: 'Why was Monetary Policy So Inept?'—as if by this time the authors had earned their licence to drop the appearance of scholarly caution and objectivity—and we are given an explanation (of something that has never been shown to require explanation) in terms of a 'shift in power' within the Federal Reserve System (p. 411).

In the following paragraphs I try to analyse Friedman and Schwartz's argument by collating statements made at different places. I will discuss it under four heads:

1. why the real depression occurred;
2. why the monetary contraction occurred;
3. the effects of bank failures, capital inadequacy, and the flight to cash;
4. the authors' identification of three occasions on which in their view the Federal Reserve system acted in a sharply restrictive fashion.

Underlying everything that Friedman and Schwartz say on the causation of the Depression is the assumption that (in the short term as well as the long) the 'velocity' of money 'reflects the money-holding propensities of the community' (p. 679). Under the normal *certeris paribus* procedure, tastes can be taken to be unchanged. By this logic, the authors are enabled to write as though a movement of the monetary aggregate itself *implied* a simple and direct sympathetic influence on real output.

To one of another way of thinking, this line of argument appears tendentious. In my view, clarity of thought requires recognition of the fact that the money supplied by the banking system is not necessarily in equilibrium with the stock the public want to hold, and that in the short term velocity is therefore no more than a ratio between two magnitudes determined in partial independence. Friedman and Schwartz's view is connected with the fact, discussed further below, that they give little or no weight to the role of banks as lending institutions.

1. Though the general tone of what Friedman and Schwartz say about the depression clearly implies that it was caused by the monetary contraction,[70] their statements are often hedged and unclear, and appear at times contradictory. One statement is:

prevention or moderation of the decline in the stock of money, let alone the substitution of monetary expansion, would have reduced the contraction's severity and almost as certainly its duration. The contraction might still have been relatively severe. But it is hardly conceivable that money income could have declined [as much as it did]. (p. 301)

This statement however comes just after one that seems to run in the other sense:

True, as events unfolded, the decline in the stock of money and the near collapse of the banking system can be regarded as a consequence of non-monetary forces in the United States and monetary and non-monetary forces in the rest of the world. (p. 300)

But by the end of the book they appear quite clear:

there is ... only one sense in which a case can be made for the proposition that the monetary decline was a consequence of the economic decline. (p. 691; see also p. 694)

This is a view which they say is possible only if the Federal Reserve System is held to have been a prisoner of contemporary opinion. That, as they say, is not a matter of economic interrelations, and is not what we are concerned with.

---

[70] For instance, in the opening to the chapter on 'The Great Contraction', after discussing the changes in attitude to the question whether 'money matters', they remark that 'the contraction is in fact a tragic testimonial to the importance of monetary forces' (p. 300). It is tragic presumably because of the poverty and unemployment it caused, and the implication clearly is that that was due or largely due to 'monetary forces'.

There are thus some difficulties of interpretation which basically arise because *A Monetary History* does not provide a connected account of why in the authors' view the depression happened.

2. Friedman and Schwartz for the most part take a simple and extreme view of the cause of the monetary contraction:

the monetary authorities could have prevented the decline in the stock of money— indeed, could have produced almost any desired increase in the money stock. [p. 301; note the 'almost'] The monetary collapse from 1929 to 1933 was not an inevitable consequence of what had gone before. It was the result of the policies followed during those years. (p. 699)

On the question of how the authorities could have controlled the money stock, they answer: 'by extensive open market purchases' as a means to increase bank reserves. What they say of the first year of the depression seems to express their general view:

It has been contended with respect to later years (particularly during the period after 1934 ...) that increases in high-powered money, through expansion of Federal Reserve credit or other means, would simply have added to bank reserves and would not have been used to increase the money stock. ... We shall argue later the contention is invalid even for the later period. It is clearly not relevant to the period from August 1929 to October 1930. During that period, additional reserves would almost certainly have been put to use promptly. Hence the decline in the stock of money is not only arithmetically attributable to the decline in Federal Reserve credit outstanding: it is economically a direct result of that decline. (pp. 341–2)

Friedman and Schwartz however never seriously consider the possibility that the banks were held back by factors other than their reserve position. That is because they take practically no note of the asset side of banks' balance sheets. It is striking that, though the book contains many charts and tables of bank *liabilities*, it has only one table of bank *assets* (and then for selected years only). Their conceptual picture allows little place for the role of banks as financial intermediaries who live by striking a balance between the needs of two types of client: depositors (the public as asset owners) and borrowers (the public as investors and debtors). Nor does it allow for the fact that banks as intermediaries operate in a world of uncertainty, that banks' assessment of their clients' creditworthiness varies, and that in the short term their lending determines the size of the money stock.

If these effects are accepted as important, the stock of money has to be seen as determined at least in large part by the business situation.[71] On my view, the scale of bank lending in the Great Depression must have been greatly restrained by banks' bad debts, by banks' increased caution in lending to customers whose profit expectations had deteriorated drastically, and by capital inadequacy.[72] It must have been these

---

[71] For the general argument see Dow and Saville (1988: esp. ch. 3).

[72] Friedman and Schwartz admit that capital inadequacy was a serious problem (p. 330) but argue that the authorities could and should have remedied this by buying securities (to raise their price, hence increasing banks' capital) and lending to banks after August 1932 through the Reconstruction Finance Corporation. But the former would have been only partial indirect help, and the latter would have augmented banks' capital only if the authorities had taken bad assets in exchange for good.

considerations, not the size of bank reserves, that imposed a limit to the size of the money stock.

On this interpretation, the fact that the banks' reserves even by the end of the depression had fallen little though banks' total assets/liabilities fell by about a third is presumptive evidence that reserves remained on the whole ample. (I admit that there may have been particular episodes when banks were constrained by reserve shortage: see further below.)

Friedman and Schwartz comment exclusively from their own point of view, and can see no force in the opinions of the authorities at the time based on considerations which they dismiss. They quote, for instance, the exchange of views inside the Federal Reserve System in May and June 1930, when most governors felt that there was already 'an abundance of funds in the market' (p. 371); as one remarked, 'We have been putting out credit in a period of depression where it was not wanted and could not be used' (p. 373). Friedman and Schwartz remark 'these views ... seem to us confused and misguided'. To me they seem common sense. Again, in its report for the year 1930 the Reserve Board described its policy as one of 'monetary ease'. This draws from Friedman and Schwartz the comment that: 'this is a striking illustration of the ambiguity of the terms "monetary ease" and "tightness" ... It seems paradoxical to describe as "monetary ease" a policy which permitted the stock of money to decline in fourteen months [by as much as it did], (p. 375). But if one admits that the powers of the authorities are limited, it is not paradoxical at all.

3. Though Friedman and Schwartz rightly devote a good deal of space to the three successive waves of bank failures, these do not take a central place in their argument. At times they speak of their having had a contractional effect on the stock of money.[73] But it becomes clear that what is meant is that the crises drained banks of reserves which depressed the money stock only because (in their view) the authorities did not offset this effect so as to maintain bank reserves. Hence they can say:

the bank failures were important not primarily in their own right but because of their indirect effect. If they had occurred to precisely the same extent without producing a drastic decline in the stock of money, they would have been notable but not crucial. If they had not occurred, but a correspondingly sharp decline had been produced in the stock of money by some other means, the contraction would have been at least equally severe and probably more so. (p. 352; see also p. 357)

I have argued in the main text that the bank failures did indeed have a major effect in accentuating the depression, but quite largely by reducing the amount of bank credit available to business—a question that Friedman and Schwartz do not consider.[74]

---

[73] 'The second banking crisis had far more severe effects on the stock of money than the first' (p. 314; see also p. 648).

[74] Friedman and Schwartz have a curious argument which runs like this. The bank failures provoked a flight from deposits to currency; the former deposits–currency ratio had originally been preferred; hence the flight to cash must have made money less attractive and thus must have reduced the demand for money (that is, deposits and currency). 'Paradoxically, therefore, the bank failures, by their effect on the demand for money, offset some of the harm they did by their effect on the supply of money. That is why we say that if the same reduction in the stock of money had been produced in some other way, it would probably have involved an even larger fall in income than the catastrophic fall that did occur' (p. 353). To be consistent, they should also argue that if bank failures *had* been prevented from causing the money stock to fall (which, as they have already argued, could and should have been done), then the effect would have been to raise income. The paradox in this

4. At the very end of their book there is a passage in which they identify three crucial episodes in US history when the authorities took what is held to be incontrovertibly contractive action. The passage is worth discussing in detail because it is difficult to reconcile with others of their statements, and hence reveals more of their lines of thought; and also because it leads me to qualify what I have said already.

After first commenting that 'it is often impossible and always difficult to identify accurately the effects of the actions of the monetary authorities', they then proceed:

on three occasions the system deliberately took steps of major magnitude which cannot be regarded as necessary or inevitable economic consequences of contemporary changes in money income and prices. The dates are January–June 1920, October 1931, and July 1936–January 1937. These are the three occasions—and the only three—when the Reserve System engaged in acts of commission that were sharply restrictive: in January 1920 by raising the discount rate from 4.75 per cent to 6 per cent and then in June 1920 to 7 per cent, at a time when member banks were borrowing from the Reserve banks more than the total of their reserves balances: in October 1931 by raising the rediscount rate from 1.5 per cent to 3.5 per cent within a two-week period, at a time when a wave of failures was engulfing commercial banks ... and indebtedness was growing; in July 1936 and January 1937, by announcing the doubling of reserve requirements in three stages, the last effective on May 1, 1937, at a time when the Treasury was engaged in gold sterilization, which was the equivalent of a large-scale restrictive open market operation. There is no other occasion in Federal Reserve history when it has taken explicit restrictive measures of comparable magnitude—we cannot even suggest possible parallels. (pp. 688–9)

It seems that the restrictive action by the authorities in 1931 which Friedman and Schwartz have in mind is not high interest rates as such (for the discount rate was low in May 1931), but the authorities acting in a way that put further pressure on the banks at a time when, being already short of reserves, they were particularly vulnerable to pressure. This is perhaps the same point as that made in several passages that discuss bank failures in 1929–33, which blame the authorities for allowing bank reserves to fall (see pp. 318 and 356).

In looking at any particular critical juncture, it must be impossible for a commentator or historian to tell whether (*a*) reserves were adequate because bank lending had fallen first and reduced the need for reserves; or (*b*) reserves were indeed at some stage inadequate, and that had forced banks to curtail their lending and thus to exert a restrictive effect on output. In looking at the whole span of the depression, I have already expressed doubt about whether the banks could have been short of reserves (since, over the whole period, the ratio of reserves to deposits rose). Friedman and Schwartz however are here speaking of a critical period, in which banks were being drained of reserves by the flight to cash. Banks were therefore particularly dependent on action by the authorities to replenish reserves, and it is quite conceivable that the authorities were insensitive to their needs at this juncture. If that is the criticism, I could see some force in it—though it hardly seems to qualify as what Friedman and Schwartz

---

argument springs I think from Friedman's practice of treating velocity as if it represented tastes and propensities, and was an independent force. In my view, velocity changes because the banks adjust lending, and hence the stock of money, to changes in income with a lag of several years: only in the very long term does velocity depend *inter alia* on the demand to hold money.

describe as 'explicit restrictive measures' of a major sort. But (as I argue in the text) it was in any case perhaps chiefly the nature of existing financial institutional arrangements that was to blame.

Having dealt with various particular steps in Friedman and Schwartz's argument, I will in conclusion give two broad general reasons for discounting a monetarist explanation of the Great Depression.

First, Friedman and Schwartz at times admit that there were non-monetary influences at work; but they never explain how these can be integrated into a monetarist interpretation. The point is that one must believe that the great fall in income had a major influence on personal consumption, and the great fall in output a major influence on business investment, and the interaction of the two (once the process started) a dominating influence. At most, then, monetary influences could have initiated the depression, or worsened it when started, but they could not have been the sole dominating influence throughout its course. The parallel fall in the money stock cannot then be taken as evidence of the latter's causal significance.

Second, there is an international dimension which Friedman and Schwartz do not face up to which creates a similar difficulty for their argument. Depression in the United States was so deep that it must, I think, be held to have largely determined the coincident depressions in other countries; and in the transmission process *non-monetary* channels (international trade) must have been important. Now in other countries also there was coincident monetary contraction. Does this mean that in other countries the causation ran from non-money to money (the opposite of what is said to have happened in the USA)? Or is it argued that monetary authorities in all countries coincidentally made identical mistakes?

Appendix A6.2 The Gold Standard as a cause of the Great Depression: A Critique of Eichengreen's *Golden Fetters*

Eichengreen's *Golden Fetters* (1992) is the latest, largest, and most authoritative statement of the view that the Great Depression—in the USA and elsewhere—was caused by the gold standard. Far-fetched to some, to others such a claim will doubtless have great appeal: it thus deserves full critical examination.[75] I will concentrate on this work, not on earlier work by Eichengreen or others,[76] and will also refer to Bernanke's (1993) review of *Golden Fetters*.

This line of thought starts with the perception that the Great Depression was world-wide, and it can be seen as an attempt to find an international cause for an international event.[77] What it fails to notice is that the Depression was very much deeper in the United States than in most other countries. It assumes without discussion that government and central bank policies have strong effects on economies, and that the depression was caused simply and solely by restrictive policies—policies forced on governments by their adherence to the rules of the gold standard.[78] Eichengreen pays little attention to other events that might have precipitated the depression. Transmission of recessionary influences is in his account mainly via financial institutions and financial markets. Other possible channels by which recession might have been transmitted from one country to another—in particular via changes in imports and exports (which I argue must in fact have been crucial)—hardly figure.

In one way, *Golden Fetters* resembles Friedman and Schwartz's *Monetary History*. For the most part it consists not of analysis of how the different parts of a macro-economic system are related, but of a narrative history of financial events—in this case in Europe and the United States, and mostly during the period between the wars.[79]

[75] Bernanke (1993: 253–4) hails it as 'this masterful new book' and continues, '*Golden Fetters* is a *tour de force* that will certainly become a standard reference in monetary economics and in economic history ... an outstanding example of how economic history should be done.'

[76] Eichengreen (1984, 1986, 1988), Eichengreen and Sachs (1985, 1986), Choudhri and Kochin (1980), and Temin (1989).

[77] 'It is not possible to understand the causes of the American slump so long as they continue to be considered in isolation from events in other parts of the world ... the debilitating downturn in 1929–30 was not simply the product of a contractionary shift in US monetary policy but a restrictive shift worldwide' (p. 15). Bernanke (1993: 252) comments: 'the worldwide nature of the economic slump of the 1930s is both a central fact to be explained and a potentially very important clue to the mystery of the Depression's cause'.

[78] 'Policy ... played a pivotal role in the Great Depression' (p. 26). In Bernanke's version it is clear (and in Eichengreen, implicit) that restrictive policy consists of causing or allowing too small an expansion of the money stock, which action (or inaction) he credits with as much potency over output as do Friedman and Schwartz.

[79] As Bernanke (1993: 254) puts it, 'Eichengreen presents a detailed analysis of international monetary and financial arrangements from the beginning of the classical gold standard, in 1870, until the advent of the post-World War II Bretton Woods System.' This requires discussion of 'developments in a wide variety of countries ... from the perspectives of political science and history as well as economics. Eichengreen deals sure-handedly with the complex tangle of events (and the huge associated literature) that made up the interwar period; and like a painter of the Pontillist school, from the building blocks of thousands of small details he is able to construct his remarkably clear and persuasive overarching themes.'

The main thesis of Golden Fetters

A good deal of the discussion is about why the gold standard collapsed. I am not concerned with that, but only with how, while it lasted, it is alleged to have caused the Great Depression. Eichengreen's thesis is conveniently summarized in his first chapter.

Several arguments are adduced in support of the claim that the gold standard caused the depression. The main argument is as follows:

1. World War I left countries other than the USA with weak current account positions. In order to maintain overall balance, they were therefore dependent on continuing capital flows from the USA.
2. If the USA raised interest rates, other countries (having low reserves) had to do likewise in order to preserve fixed exchange rates, as they were constrained to do under the gold standard. (They also felt obliged to tighten fiscal policy.)
3. There was no corresponding obligation on the USA to follow expansive policies in these circumstances: the asymmetry of the system permitted the USA simply to accept growing reserves. The system thus had a contractionary bias.
4. From 1928 the USA began progressively to tighten its policy because it regarded speculative financial markets as inflationary. Tighter monetary policy in the USA, and elsewhere, then produced the Great Depression.

There are four counter-arguments to this case.

1. The reason that countries clung to the gold standard was that they saw it as a bulwark against inflation. Even if they had not been on the gold standard, they would still have resisted downward movements of their exchange rates, and for that reason they would have sought more or less to match US interest rates. That Eichengreen in fact admits. He calls this the 'gold standard ethos' and recognizes that it was this, not the gold standard itself, that was the governing factor.[80]

At a time when the spectacle of hyperinflation in Germany and elsewhere was live and fresh in people's minds, fear of inflation was doubtless stronger than now. But it is still very much the case that governments do not like to see much depreciation of their exchange rates. Contrary to what monetarists have continued to tell them, floating rates do not set governments free from the (allegedly artificial) constraint of a fixed exchange rate.

2. A second counter-observation in the same spirit is that the asymmetry between 'strong' or 'weak' countries was not a product purely of the gold standard, but is a universal fact of life. Borrowers always have to look to their creditworthiness and cannot live too far beyond their incomes, while lenders can (at least for a while) live as much within their means as they like, and not spend more if they choose; bankers can always be smug. That is as true with floating rates as with fixed.

3. Eichengreen speaks as if, had it not been for the gold standard, governments would have followed active policies to prevent depression, and, when depression set in, would have followed actively expansionary policies to counter it.[81] As I have already sought to emphasize [s. 6.1], gold standard or not, that was not how ministers, officials,

---

[80] 'It was not only the gold standard as a set of institutions that posed an obstacle to economic recovery, however, but also the gold standard as an ethos' (p. 21).

[81] For instance, Eichengreen is puzzled 'why governments were so slow to respond as the Depression deepened. If wages failed to fall, officials could have used monetary policy to raise prices. If private spending collapsed, they could have used public spending to offset it' (p. 16). The

central bank governors, or the general public thought at that time (if indeed it is now), and to suppose such activism is unhistorical.

4. Even if none of this were true, it would still have to be shown that the monetary policy that countries followed in 1928 and 1929 was enough to account for the scale of depression that occurred in the next three years. I have already given reason to disbelieve this for the United States; I also argue it was not enough to explain recession in the UK; I would guess the same is true for other countries too. Certainly Eichengreen hardly confronts the question of scale. This is a point to which I will come back.

Eichengreen's second argument

Eichengreen has a second argument, similar but somewhat different, for his case that the gold standard was the cause of the Great Depression. This he states indirectly by his observation that it was the countries that left the gold standard first that recovered first from the depression. He is explicit about the mechanism: these countries depreciated, and depreciation stimulated exports, and hence also growth.[82]

The counter-argument to this is obvious. An exchange rate expresses the value of one currency in terms of another, and what is true of the country at one end of the relation is the opposite of what is true of the country at the other end. An exchange rate change that raises output in one country lowers it in the other. Changes in exchange rates could conceivably explain depression or recovery in half the world, but cannot do so for the world as a whole.

The difficulty of fitting the USA into the argument

There is a third objection to Eichengreen's thesis. An international factor is peculiarly inappropriate to explain depression in the world's most nearly closed major economy, the United States. On the face of it, the gold standard would appear particularly unlikely to have acted as a constraint on US policy; for the United States was the country in the strongest position. As Eichengreen says, in the 1920s it 'became a gigantic sink for the gold reserves of the rest of the world ... accumulating by the end of the decade nearly 40 per cent of global gold reserves ...'. (p. 194). Since the United States was by far the largest economy, and depression was far deeper in the USA than in the rest of the world,[83] the existence of the gold standard seems a most unlikely cause of the 1929–32 depression.

Eichengreen's way of countering this objection (which he never squarely puts) would be to claim that the USA was constrained by the Federal Reserve Act of 1913, in effect

---

answer he proposes to this puzzle is that it must have been the gold standard that prevented countries behaving so. The suggestion that monetary policy could at this juncture have raised prices seems to me to attribute to it a bizarre degree of omnipotence.

[82] 'If the gold standard contributed to the severity of the slump, did its collapse free the World from Depression's thrall? ... Depreciation was the key to economic growth. Almost everywhere it was tried, currency depreciation stimulated economic recovery. ... Output, employment, investment and exports rose more quickly than in countries that clung to their gold parities' (p. 21).

[83] US GNP was about the same as that of Europe, and the percentage fall in output about four times as large; i.e., four-fifths of the fall in output in industrial countries occurred in the USA [s. 6.4 and app. A6.3]. Output also fell in primary-producing countries, but largely as a consequence of depression in the USA and other industrial countries.

to hold gold equivalent to about 50 per cent of the note circulation (p. 194). There are three answers to this:

1. First, that certainly reflects the general mystique that surrounded gold: but it is not part of what most people understand by the gold standard—rather, it was an oddity of US law.
2. Second, it is arguable whether that was in fact the effective constraint on US policy: the Fed certainly thought it was worrying about the Wall Street boom (as Friedman and Schwartz make plain, as well as Eichengreen himself, at pp. 217–20).
3. Third, monetary policy alone is in any case an inadequate explanation for the depth of the US depression (as I have already argued in section 6.3, and argue at greater length in appendix A6.1 above). For similar reasons, I doubt the great efficacy that Eichengreen assumes for monetary policy in other countries.

What Golden Fetters *omits*

These are the main negative arguments as I see them against Eichengreen's thesis. *Golden Fetters* is however open to criticism as much for what it omits as for what it contains. I will concentrate on three of the main ways in which it seems to me defective.

1. The emphasis of the book is very heavily on monetary and financial developments, while the discussion of developments in the real economy—which one would have supposed at least half of the book should be about—is extremely sketchy. It is presumably the fall in output and the growth of unemployment that constitute the depression. But discussion of output is confined to discussion of industrial production, figures of GNP/GDP being I think mentioned only once.[84] No statistics for unemployment are shown. Prices are always measured in terms of 'wholesale' prices, and the estimates quoted are always according to League of Nations, pre-1939, estimates.[85] One consequence of this unrepresentative treatment is that the world depression is usually measured in terms of the industrial production of only four countries: the USA, Germany, France, and the UK. These countries are not typical; and restricting attention to them has the effect of greatly exaggerating the extent of the depression in countries other than the United States.[86]
2. One consequence of the lack of attention to real developments is that there is no analysis of the role in the generation of the depression of possible chains of causation between different parts of the real economy (as for instance in multiplier sequences, or between output and investment). Nor is the possibility considered that it was causal sequences among real factors that predominated, and that drove monetary and financial sequences. One or two passages admit the probability that many causes combined to produce the Great Depression. But in fact the story told is monocausal, running only from money to real events.[87]
3. Another feature of *Golden Fetters* is that the discussion is in a sense parochial. There is practically no reference to previous discussion other than discussion in the

[84] Figure 2.1 of the book shows annual rates of change of British GDP in what appear to be current not constant prices for the period 1859–1911.

[85] Such indices are heavily overweighted with the prices of internationally traded commodities, which fluctuate much more than the GDP deflators of industrial countries.

[86] The extent of depression in different countries is best measured I think by a table such as my table A6.1.

[87] Eichengreen's title does indeed nail him pretty tightly to the monocausal mast.

monetarist tradition (in particular that of Friedman and Schwartz's *Monetary History*). There is no discussion of the relative importance of exogenous and endogenous factors in the causation of the depression, or of the discussion from which that distinction sprang. Everything is attributed to exogenous influences; within them, to policy; and within policy, although fiscal policy gets a mention, it is only a mention: monetary policy is all-powerful.

4. Finally, the Great Depression is discussed as if it were the only event of its sort. In the United States it was much worse than any other recession; but in most other countries it was only *somewhat* worse than other major recessions. Other major recessions were presumably not caused by the gold standard. If not, why was the Great Depression so radically different?

The ideal sort of economic history

Writing economic history is extremely difficult—like making sense of the world. One has enough to do making one's own sense of the story, and piecing together how the different bits fit, without constantly remembering the annoyingly upside-down (and bewilderingly numerous) ways in which other people have told the story and fitted together the bits. What would be ideal would be an account that showed full awareness of all other views and gave, clearly and shortly, convincing grounds for preferring one interpretation. That is too much to hope to achieve. But at least, the task is one for a dispassionate logician stepping delicately over broken stepping stones—not for one who is sure of his own version and thinks he has got everything straightened out into a smooth story of the sort that historians love to tell. Until the broad lines of explanation, and the reasons for them, are truly agreed, it is no use attempting great works of synthesis (as in Eichengreen's aim in *Golden Fetters*); nor does the mass of detail, as treated by 'a painter of the Pontillist school', really help. The real difficulties are theoretical—how to invent a theory that makes true sense of the facts—and the possible theories need to be openly and open-mindedly discussed along with the facts. The theoretical issues cannot be taken as closed: if so, there is no point in writing history. *Golden Fetters* is too full of its own theory, too empty of alternatives. While I am sure that I myself fall far short of the ideal historian, for me—unlike Bernanke—the book is, like Friedman and Schwartz's *Monetary History*, another outstanding example of how economic history should *not* be done.

Bernanke on the underlying logic of Golden Fetters

I will conclude with a comment on Bernanke's review of *Golden Fetters*. Most of the review is taken up not with discussion of points in Eichengreen's book, but with Bernanke's own 'very heuristic explanation' of why adherence to the gold standard 'led to a large inadvertent contraction of world money supplies' (Bernanke 1993: 256). The logic however is probably sufficiently akin to his to throw light on Eichengreen's own procedure.

Having shown to his satisfaction why money supplies contracted, Bernanke feels able to claim that the 'aggregate demand puzzle' has been solved (i.e., he assumes that a contraction of money must cause a contraction of nominal GDP).[88] But that, he says,

---

[88] Bernanke (p. 264) notes that this is: 'a tremendously important step'. Even so, he criticizes Eichengreen for having done only a qualitative job: 'it would be nice to have a sharper sense of the timing and relative importance of the various shocks hitting world money supplies, and of the percentage of output and employment movements accounted for by money supply changes in various countries in various years'. One would, indeed, have thought that was important.

still leaves open 'the aggregate supply puzzle, viz. "Why did declines in nominal income ... lead to such deep and protracted falls in real variables such as output and employment?"'[89] This is a puzzle to Bernanke because, on his version of macroeconomic theory, a fall in money (produced by the authorities) causes a fall in prices, but not (or not for long) a fall in output. If that is so, one would have thought it rather useless to turn to such a theory to explain the Great Depression, which precisely consisted of a fall in real output.

Bernanke's theory, and perhaps also Eichengreen's, is one of a wider group of theories which picture a world in which departures from full employment ought not to happen. Since in fact they obviously do, the reaction is to save the theory by finding good theoretical reasons why, contrary to what this kind of theory first suggests, prices and wages are in fact inflexible. I have already argued [s. 3.1] that the puzzle cannot be solved that way. In any case, it is easier and more satisfactory, to my mind, to give up the starting point of the theory (i.e. that the authorities decide money, and money decides output), admit that money follows output, and look for more or less real causes for occasions when real output declines. These are the questions that *Golden Fetters* raises, and which need to be discussed, but which which the book does not discuss.

---

[89] 'Or [adds Bernanke] to put the question in the jargon of macroeconomics: "what accounts for such a massive and long-lasting non-neutrality of money ... ?"'

Appendix A6.3 A Model of the International Transmission of the US depression

The model here described is intended to illustrate the impact of the Great Depression in the United States on the rest of the world. Though the relevant interactions in the world trading system are fairly complex, the orders of magnitude of the main effects can be illustrated simply by a stylized analysis of the reactions of a three-bloc trading system comprising the United States (US), Europe (EU), and the primary-producing countries (PP), here taken to be countries other than the United States and Europe. Europe is defined as in table 6.17 above. Since the depression lasted three years in countries other than the United States, all changes are measured as between 1929 and 1932. Over that period US GNP declined 28 per cent and GDP in Europe is estimated to have fallen by 7 per cent.

The trade flows between the three blocs in 1929 can be roughly estimated to have been as shown in table A6.1. In the determination of cyclical downswings or upswings, the main line of causation is assumed to run from industrial countries (represented by the USA and Europe) to the primary-producing (PP) countries. Induced changes in PP output or prices will then in turn influence PP imports from the USA and Europe.

As will be seen, half of US exports were to the primary producers and a third of its imports came from them. Despite the small role of trade in the US economy, US imports from the primary producers were significant, constituting over a third of PP exports outside the area. As it happened, the US GDP was almost the same as that of Europe (defined as in table 6.17). Table 6.18 shows the relation to the GDP of either area of the six trade flows relevant to the present analysis. (These figures serve as weights in estimating the contribution of changes in exports or imports to a change in each areas' GDP.)

Table A6.1   The pattern of world trade in 1929

	Trade to:[a]				
	United States (US)	Europe (EU)	Primary producers (pp) ($ bn)	Total	Total excluding intratrade
Trade from:					
US		2.5	2.8	5.3	5.3
EU	1.2	(10.5)	4.2	15.9	5.4
PP	2.8	5.4	(3.2)	11.4	8.2
Total	4.0	18.4	10.2	33.6	
Total excl. intratrade	4.0	7.9	7.2		19.1

[a] The value of the same trade flow is recorded differently by the exporting and importing countries. The differences arise because imports are recorded inclusive of carriage and insurance, which typically adds about 9% to the value; and because of differences of timing and errors and omissions in the recording. Since the differences are not large enough to affect the argument, a simple average of two valuations is drawn.

Source: See app. A6.4.

The model of the world economy quantifies effects along six legs of the transmission process [fig. A6.1]. The model incorporates not only effects transmitted via changes in the *volume* of trade flows, but also effects transmitted via relative price changes. The fall in demand for the output of commodity producers is assumed to have depressed the price of commodities relative to manufactures. That is taken to reduce the demand by primary producers for the exports of the USA and Europe. The same shift in the terms of trade is assumed to have increased purchasing power and demand in the USA and Europe in proportion to their imports of commodities.

The feedback on the United States from one round of this process depends on the assumptions made as to the size of the key parameters, but it is relatively small. (With the illustrative assumptions taken below, it is of the order of one-tenth of the initial change in US GDP after allowing for the offset from the terms-of-trade benefit noted above.) The feedback from a second round of the process will therefore be of the order of a tenth of a tenth of the initial change, and will here be ignored along with other second-round iterations.

On the assumptions chosen, the impact on Europe, after allowing for the partially offsetting effect from the shift in the terms of trade, amounted to only part of the observed change in Europe's GDP (7 per cent). It was assumed that shocks domestically generated in Europe explained the rest of the decline in European output. These will in turn have had some (relatively small) effect on the USA. This second chain of effects can be analysed in terms analogous to those used in the analysis of the effects emanating from the United States. The legs of this second transmission process are similar to those of the first, with Europe and the United States substituted for each other [fig. A6.2].

The illustrative numbers chosen are such that, of the 28 per cent fall in US GNP, 26 per cent is attributed to domestic shocks and somewhat over 1 per cent (net of the

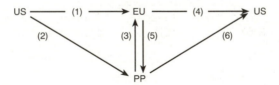

Fig. A6.1   International effects of the US depression: trade links between three main blocs, US, primary producers (PP), and Europe (EU)

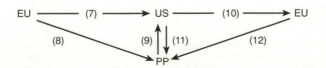

Fig. A6.2   Secondary effects of induced recession in Europe (EU) on US and primary producers (PP), and tertiary effects back on Europe

terms of trade offset) to the feedback from Europe. That part of the fall in European GDP which on these assumptions is attributed to shocks of European domestic origin contributed the remaining 1 per cent of the fall in US GNP (this figure likewise incorporating the partially compensating effect of the shift in the terms of trade).

It is assumed that the level of industrial countries' imports depends on the level of their real income (GDP). The volume of the imports of the two industrial blocs from each other were assumed to fall by 1.5 times the proportionate fall in their output; and the volume of their imports of commodities, in simple proportion to the fall in their output. Since Europe was less depressed than the United States, these assumptions mean that Europe's current balance was unfavourably affected—which somehow Europe managed to finance. In the case of the primary producers, it was assumed that they were not able to finance a deterioration in their current accounts, and therefore had to reduce (by direct balance of payments measures if necessary) imports from Europe and the United States in proportion to the fall in the real value of their combined exports to Europe and the USA.[90]

The working of the model depends on further relationships which (*a*) determine the relative price of world commodities, and (*b*) fix the size of the internal 'multipliers' in the United States and Europe.[91] These are discussed below.

Direct information about the price of the relevant trade flows is not available. The most reliable relevant information that we have are estimates of the price of US and UK manufactured exports, and of US and UK commodity imports. The first, which puts the 1932 price at 0.60 (1929 = 1.0), is taken to be representative of the valuation of third world imports from the USA and Europe; and the second, which puts the 1932 price at 0.44, is taken to represent the price of US and European imports from the third world. Trade between the USA and Europe consisted partly of manufacturing and partly of foodstuffs, and it is assumed that an average of the price indices is appropriate to its valuation.

On the above estimates, the price of commodities relative to that of manufactures (with 1929 = 100) fell to 0.45/0.60 = 0.75, or by 25 per cent. The export earnings of the primary producers expressed in terms of their purchasing power over US/European manufactured exports were thus reduced both by the volume fall, estimated at 14 per cent, and by the terms-of-trade fall of 25 per cent, or in total by about 35 per cent. That is here treated as an effect of the fall in the volume of industrial countries' imports of commodities. On that interpretation, the 14 per cent fall in volume is taken to have reduced primary producers' 'real' export earnings by 35 per cent. The term-of-trade 'gearing factor' is therefore taken to be 35/14 = 2.5.

In an interrelated system, the size of the multiplier relationships inside each industrial area is part of the international transmission process. (The multipliers in Europe affect legs (4)–(6), and those inside the United States affect legs (10)–(12), of figs. A6.1 and A6.2.) The assumptions here are the most uncertain of the assumptions made in the calculation. The combined multipliers[92] for the USA and Europe were assumed to be

---

[90] This seems to be what happened: primary producers' invisible outgoings seem to have fallen in proportion to their earnings on visible exports.

[91] 'Multipliers' here means what in ch. 5.1 were called 'consumption' and 'investment amplifiers'.

[92] The combined multiplier $= 1/(1-c-n)$ where $c =$ the proportion of a change in GDP spent on consumption and $n =$ the proportion spent on investment.

Table A6.2   Assumed value for domestic multipliers in Europe and the USA

	Consumption multiplier $(1/(1-c))$	c	n	Combined multiplier $(1/(1-c-n))$
Europe	1.3	0.23	0.27	2.0
United States	1.6	0.375	0.375	4.0

4.0 and 2.0 respectively [table A6.2]. Given the apparent importance of confidence effects, these values may well be too low.

Estimation of the international transmission of the depression

With these assumptions, the interactions between the three areas may be estimated. The estimation may be thought of as being carried out in three stages:

1. Estimate the effect of the fall in US GDP on the volume of exports of primary producers and their terms of trade, and the volume of exports of Europe, and also the indirect effects of the former on Europe (legs (1)–(3) of transmission process); estimate the additional effect on primary producers from that (leg (4); finally, estimate the feedback from these changes (legs (5) and (6) on the USA.
2. Estimate the partially offsetting effect of the induced change in the terms of trade on Europe and the USA and hence the net impact on the USA and Europe.
3. Only a part of Europe's depression, on these assumptions, is explained in this way. The rest is regarded as domestically induced. The third stage is to estimate the effects of that on the primary producers and the USA (which are similar to but smaller in scale than those of the US depression itself).

These three stages of estimation are set out in parts (*a*), (*b*), and (*c*) of table A6.3 and are summarized in part (*d*) of the table.

In these calculations, what is described as the initial fall in US GDP is taken to be caused by shocks originating in the United States, as magnified by the domestic multipliers operating in the States. The initial value shown is chosen to be such that, minus feedback via international trade, plus the impact on the USA of domestically originated depression in Europe, it equals the actual fall in US GDP of 28 per cent. The value chosen for the initial fall in Europe similarly has to add to the actual fall of about 7 per cent. These values are thus the result of trial and error to satisfy these two constraints.

The values that emerge on the assumptions made about the consumption and investment multipliers carry the implication that almost all the US depression was of domestic origin, and that the US depression accounted for only a fifth of the depression in Europe. The rest has to be attributed to a shock arising independently in Europe at the same time. For that there is independent evidence; for it seems likely that depression in Germany started earlier, and for distinct reasons, and that depression in France was magnified by factors peculiar to France. Table A6.4 shows the effect of doubling the assumed size of the domestic multipliers.

Table A6.3 International transmission of the Great Depression, 1929–1932

(a) Impact of the US depression on Europe and primary producers

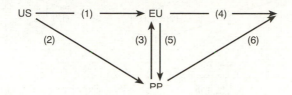

Leg	Direction of impact		% fall in GDP (EE) of area 1[a]	Propensity to import of area 1[b]	Exports to area 1 as fraction of GDP of area 2[c]	Multiplier (*TOT* factor) of area 2[d]	% fall in GDP (EE) of area 2[e]
	Area 1	Area 2					
	(1)		(2)	(3)	(4)	(5)	(6)
1	US on	EU	25.9	1.5	0.012	2	0.93
2	US on	PP	25.9	1	0.33	2.5	21.4
3	PP on	EU	21.4	1	0.044	2	1.88
Total on EU							*2.81*
4	EU on	US	2.81	1.5	0.024	4	0.40
5	EU on	PP	2.81	1	0.67	2.5	4.70
Total on PP							*26.8*
6	PP on	US	26.8	1	0.26	4	2.79
Total on US							*3.20*

[a] GDP of US or EU; export earnings (EE) of PP.
[b] Marginal propensity of area 1 to import from area 2 expressed as proportion of GDP (or EE) of area 1.
[c] Exports of area 2 to area 1 as proportion of GDP (US or EU) or EE (PP) in base year 1929.
[d] For US or EU, consumption *plus* investment multiplier. For PP, terms of trade (*TOT*) factor: TOT factor = % change in price of PP exports ÷ (% change in price of PP imports × change in volume of PP exports).
[e] Product of columns ((2) × (3) × (4) × (5)).

(b) Terms-of-trade effects

Initial fall in GDP(%)	% fall in real EE of PP	*of which, change in TOT*	Stimulus to US[a] (% of GDP)	Stimulus to EU[b] (% of GDP)
From recession in US (table A)				
25.9	26.8	18.0	1.94	1.87
From recession in EU (table B)				
5.40	10.7	6.42	0.69	0.66

[a] *TOT* change × weight of imports from PPs in GDP of US (0.027) × multiplier (4).
[b] *TOT* change × weight of imports from PPs in GDP of EU (0.052) × multiplier (2).

(c) Impact of the depression in Europe on USA and primary producers

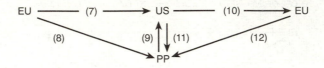

Leg	Direction of impact		% fall in GDP (EE) of area 1[a]	Propensity to import of area 1[b]	Exports to area 1 as fraction of GDP of area 2[c]	Multiplier (*TOT* factor) of area 2[d]	% fall in GDP (EE) of area 2[e]
	Area 1	Area 2					
	(1)		(2)	(3)	(4)	(5)	(6)
7	EU on	US	5.40	1.5	0.024	4	0.76
8	EU on	PP	5.40	1	0.67	(2.5)	9.04
9	PP on	US	(9.04)	1	0.028	4	1.01
Total on US							*1.78*
10	US on	EU	1.78	1.5	0.012	2	0.06
11	US on	PP	1.78	1	0.33	(2.5)	1.47
Total on PP							*10.7*
12	PP on	EU	10.7	1	0.052	2	1.11
Total on US							*1.17*

Notes: as for part (*a*).

(d) Summary of five main influences on USA and Europe, 1929–1932 (% of GDP)

Impact of domestically generated depression				Impact of domestically generated depression in other industrial areas		Total
Initial fall in GDP	Feedback via direct and indirect fall in trade volume	*less* offset via shift in TOT	Total	Effect via fall in trade volume	*less* offset via shift in TOT	
(1)	(2)	(3)	(4)	(5)	(6)	
From: Part (*a*)/part (*b*)				Part (*c*)/part (*b*)		
US 25.9 + 3.2 − 1.9 = 27.2				1.8 − 0.7 = 1.1		28.3
From: Part (*c*)/part (*b*)				Part (*a*)/part (*b*)		
US 5.4 + 1.2 − 0.7 = 5.9				2.8 − 1.9 = 0.9		6.8

Table A6.4 International transmission: effect of doubling the size of the domestic multipliers

	Initial fall in US GDP	Net feedback on USA	Net effect on Europe	Room left for initial fall in Europe (% of GDP)	Net feedback on Europe	Total fall in Europe	Net effect on USA	Total fall in US GDP
First basis[a]	25.9	1.3	0.9	5.4	0.5	6.8	1.1	28.3
Second basis[b]	25.0	2.5	1.7	4.4	0.4	6.5	0.7	28.2

[a] Combined multiplier of 2 in Europe and 4 in USA.
[b] Combined multiplier of 4 in Europe and 8 in USA.

Appendix A6.4 List of Statistical Sources

The main list below gives sources used for GDP and trade of individual countries. Works there referred to by author's name are listed in the References section at the end of the book. Statistical handbooks are listed at the end of this appendix.

Variables

1. Current values of commodity exports and imports from and to other countries
2. Volumes of total commodity exports and imports
3. GDP, current prices
4. GDP, constant prices

Statistical sources by countries

Country	Variable	Source
USA	1,2	*USA* (1960)
	3,4	*US National Income and Product Accounts* (1982)
Europe		
Austria	1	*Statistik des Außenhandels*
	2,3,4	Kausel *et al.* (1965)
Belgium	1	*Annuaire Statistique de Belgique*
	2 (exp.)	*Review of World Trade* (1938)
	2 (imp.)	Estimated with world deflator[a]
	3	1930: Bauduin (1958); rest estimated
	4	Maddison (1989)
Bulgaria	1	*Statisticheski Godishnik*
	3,4	UN (1948)
Czechoslovakia	1	*Annuaire Statistique*
	2 (exp.)	Pryor *et al.* (1971)
	2 (imp.)	*Review of World Trade* (1938)
	3	1929: Pryor *et al.* (1971), linked to UN (1950)
	4	Pryor *et al.* (1971)
Denmark	1	*Statistisk Aarbog*
	2	*Review of World Trade* (1938)
	3,4	Mitchell (1975)
Finland	1	Vattula (1983)
	2,3,4	Hjerppe (1989)
France	1,2	*Annuaire Statistique, Resumé Rétrospectif* (1966)
	3,4	Toutain (1987)
Germany	1	*Statistisches Jahrbuch*
	2	*Review of World Trade* (1938)
	3,4	SB (1972)
Greece	1	*Bulletin Mensuel Statistique*
	3,4	UN (1950)

Country	Variable	Source
Hungary	1	*Statsztikai Havi Közlemenyek*
	2	*Review of World Trade* (1938)
	3,4	Eckstein (1955)
Ireland	1	*Statistical Abstract*
	2	*Review of World Trade* (1938)
	3,4	Flora *et al.* (1987)
Italy	1,2	*Annuario Statistico*
	3	ICS (1976)
	4	Maddison (1991a)
Netherlands	1,2,3,4	CBS (1989)
Norway	1,2	SSB (1969)
	3,4	*National Accounts* (1953)
Poland	1	*Concise Statistical Yearbook*
	3	Estimated, equal to per capita GDP in Greece[b]
	4	Spulber (1966)
Portugal	1	*Annuário Estístico*
	3,4	Nunes *et al.* (1989)
Romania	1	*Annuarul Statistic*
	3	UN (1950)
	4	Spulber (1966)
Soviet Union	1	Sowjetwirtschaft und Außenhandel (1931) no. 4
	2 (exp.)	*Review of World Trade* (1938)
	2 (imp.)	Estimated with world deflator[a]
	3,4	Calculated from Moorsteen and Powell (1966)
Spain	1	*Annuario Estadístico de España*
	2,3,4	Barciela *et al.* (1989)
Sweden	1	*Statistisk Arsbok*
	2	Fridlizius (1963)
	3,4	Mitchell (1975)
Switzerland	1	*Statistique du Commerce*
	2	*Review of World Trade* (1938)
	3,4	Mitchell (1975)
UK	1	*Statistical Abstract for the UK*
	2	Schlote (1952)
	3,4	Feinstein (1972)
Yugoslavia	1	*Statisticheski Godishnak*
	2	*Review of World Trade* (1938)
	3	Estimated, equal to per capita GDP in Greece[b]
	4	Vinski (1961)
Third Countries		
Australia	1	*Official Year-Book of Australia*
	2	*Review of World Trade* (1938)
Canada	1	*Canadian Statistical Review* (1957)
	2	Urquhart and Buckley (1965)

Country	Variable	Source
New Zealand	1	*Official Year-Book of New Zealand*
	2	*Review of World Trade* (1938)
Japan	1	*Historical Statistics of Japan* (1987)
	2	Ohkawa and Rosovsky (1973)
Korea	1	Suh (1978)
	2	Maddison (1985)
China	1,2	Hsiau (1974)
Taiwan	1,2	Ho (1978)
Indonesia	1	CKS (1938)
	2 (exp.)	van Ark (1988: 120)
	3 (imp.)	*Review of World Trade* (1938)
India	1	*Statistical Abstract of British India*
	2	*Review of World Trade* (1938)
Sri Lanka	1	*Statistical Abstract for the British Empire*
	2	Birnberg and Resnick (1975)
Thailand	1	*International Trade Statistics* (1937)
	2	Birnberg and Resnick (1975)
Malaya	1	*Statistical Abstract for the British Empire*
	2 (exp.)	*Review of World Trade* (1938)
	2 (imp.)	Estimated with world deflator[a]
Philippines	1	*Statistical Bulletin of the Philippine Islands and Statistical Handbook of the Philippines*
	2	Birnberg and Resnick (1975)
Iran	1	*International Trade Statistics* (1937)
	2	Estimated with world deflators[a]
Turkey	1	*Istatistik Yilligi*
	2	Estimated with world deflators[a]
Egypt	1	*International Trade Statistics* (1937)
	2	Birnberg and Resnick (1975)
Algeria	1	*International Trade Statistics* (1937)
	2	*Review of World Trade* (1938)
Nigeria	1	*Statistical Abstract for the British Empire*
	2	Birnberg and Resnick (1975)
Zaire	1,2	*Annuaire Statistique de Belgique*
Kenya/Uganda	1	*Statistical Abstract for the British Empire*
	2	Estimated with world deflators[a]
South Africa	1	*Trade and Shipping of South Africa*
	2	*Review of World Trade* (1938)
Brazil	1	*Commercio Exterior de Brasil*
	2	Maddison (1985)
Argentina	1	*Annuario del Commercio Exterior de Argentina*
	2	Maddison (1985)
Uruguay	1	*Annuario Estatístico de Uruguay*
	2 (exp.)	*Review of World Trade* (1938)

Country	Variable	Source
	2 (imp.)	Estimated with world deflator[a]
Chile	1	*Estadística Annual Commercio Exterior de Chile*
	2	Maddison (1985)
Colombia	1	*Annuario de Estatistica General de Colombia*
	2	Maddison (1985)
Peru	1	*Extracto Estatistico del Peru*
	2	Estimated with world deflators[a]
Mexico	1	*Estatistica del Commercio Exterior de Mexico*
	2	Maddison (1985)
Cuba	1	*Commercio Exterior de Cuba*
	2	Maddison (1985)
Jamaica	1	*Statistical Abstract for the British Empire*
	2	Birnberg and Resnick (1975)

[a]The world deflator for exports from European countries and imports into third countries is an unweighted average of the UK and US unit value indices of exported manufactured commodities. The world deflator for imports into European countries and exports from third countries is an unweighted average of the UK and US unit value indices of imported raw materials.
[b]Bilateral exchange rates calculated via the US dollar.

Exchange rates are obtained from *US Statistical Abstract and Statistical Year-Book of the League of Nations.*

Statistical handbooks referred to

CBS = (Netherlands) Central Bureau of Statistics (1989), *Negentig Jaren Statistiek in Tijdreeksen, 1899–1989.*
CKS = (Indonesia) Centraal Kantoor voor Statistiek (1938), 'Handelsstatisttiek Neder-landsch-Indië 1874–1937', *Mededeeling van het Centraal Kantoor voor Statistiek* no. 161.
UN = United Nations (1948), *National Income Statistics of Various Countries 1938–1947.*
UN = United Nations (1950), *National Income Statistics of Various Countries 1938–1948.*
USA = United States of America (1960), *Historical Statistics of the United States: Colonial Times to 1957.*
SSB = Norwegian Statistik Sentralbyra (1969), *Historik Statistikk.*
ICS = (Italy) Instituto Centrale di Statistica (1976), *Sommario di Statistiche Storiche dell', Italia, 1861–1975.*
SB = Statistisches Bundesamt (1972), *Bevölkerung und Wirtschaft 1872–1972.*

7 The Long Interval without Major Recession, 1945–1973

The quarter-century or so after World War II was a period when growth was relatively fast, demand was high, and unemployment was low—and when there were no large fluctuations as defined in this study. The character of this chapter is therefore different from that of the other three historical chapters: it is not a question of detective work as to why large recessions occurred, for there were none. The period—here referred to in shorthand as the *Golden Age*—does however raise some large questions of a sort central to the purpose of this study.

Section 7.1 gives an overview of the period. Section 7.2 then considers the main questions: what caused fast growth and high demand to continue for so long, or prevented small recessions developing (as in other periods) into big ones? Were the conditions that produced the Golden Age simply exceptional in the history of developed economies—something we are unlikely to see again? If so, what did this lucky chance consist of?

While there were no large fluctuations, there was a succession of small ones. It is useful [s. 7.3] to compare these with the larger fluctuations that occurred in other periods, and to look again at the question, once much discussed, of whether they were due to mistaken policy or to something more basic.

Section 7.4 comes back to the larger issues. Did this Golden Age contain within itself the seeds of its own destruction? Were there developments in the period (such as accelerating inflation, or the flagging of investment demand) which would anyhow have brought the long period of fast growth and high demand to an end without an exogenous shock? Finally, section 7.5 draws some general conclusions about the behaviour of the economy.

Relatively few studies have directly addressed the larger issues discussed here, though there have heen a series of studies of parts or aspects of the period.[1] Much of the discussion of the post-1973 period and the continuing general macroeconomic debate also bears on the questions discussed. Many studies, including my earlier book (Dow 1964), have discussed the genesis of the minor fluctuations and will be noted below.

---

[1] The most relevant are Matthews (1968); Matthews *et al*. (1982: esp. 303–16); Matthews and Bowen (1988), and Cairncross and Cairncross (1992). Van der Wee (1986) attempts to combine a review of the running controversy among economists with narrative of events. Of the many studies that have discussed why the Golden Age succumbed to stagflation may be mentioned McCracken *et al*. (1977), Boltho (1982), Emerson (1984), Cornwall (1984), Bruno and Sachs (1985), and Maddison (1991*a*).

7.1. Overview of the period

This section summarizes first the main economic characteristics of the period, and then political events.

7.1.1. Economic features

The main characteristics of the period, in comparison with the interwar period that came before it and the post-1973 period that followed, may be summarized as follows.

1. The rate of growth of output was nearly half as much again as before the war, or than it was to be after 1973 [table 2.2].
2. The pressure of demand was high, and unused capacity (as indicated by unemployment) a fraction of what it was prewar and post-1973 [table 2.2].
3. Demand varied less than before the war or after 1973, so that the variation of rates of growth was much less. Calendar-year on calendar-year, there was barely a year that showed a fall in output.[2]
4. Inflation was, by later standards, moderate [fig. 2.2]. In the interwar period there had been zero or negative inflation (depending on the terminal dates selected); in the 1945–73 period it averaged 3 per cent a year (though approaching 10 per cent on two occasions, the early 1950s and the 1970s). In the twenty years after 1973 inflation was well over twice as high, averaging 8 per cent a year (and was about 20 per cent a year in the few years after OPECs I and II).

Other industrialized countries had much the same experience. Figure 2.2 and table 2.11 show that growth in the five other largest countries was both faster and steadier than before 1940, or after 1973. (The sixteen largest countries, also, had faster growth, though their ranking order in respect of growth rates shifted: see fig. 7.1.) It will be argued that the generality of faster growth was an important reason for growth being fast.

Though output growth was faster in this period than it was prewar and after 1973, the underlying growth of productivity was probably much the same: estimates of the trend rate of growth of output between major recessions adjusted for cyclical fluctuations are broadly similar in all periods (table 2.4, method A).[3] That is an important part of the picture; it may not be true of other countries [s. 7.2 below].

The rate of output growth in the UK was consistently slower than in most other industrial countries. Reasons for differences in inter-country growth rates

---

[2] The nearest was the year 1958, for which the 1996/7 estimates say that GDP at 1990 factor cost fell 0.14%, but at 1990 market prices rose 0.37%.

[3] This statement relates to output per worker. Matthews *et al*. (1982) show—for rather different periods of comparison—faster growth of output per hour in the postwar period than in the interwar period, as hours of work were reduced more rapidly.

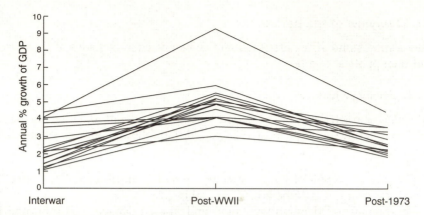

Fig. 7.1   Sixteen countries' growth rates in the three main periods

The countries are: Australia, Austria, Belgium, Canada, Denmark, Finland, France, Germany, Italy, Japan, Netherlands, Norway, Sweden, Switzerland, UK, and USA.

Growth rates are between pairs of terminal dates, viz, 1924 & 1925 to 1928 & 1939; 1950 & 1951 to 1973 & 1974, and 1975 & 1976 to 1988 & 1989.

Source: as for fig. 2.3.

have occasioned a lot of discussion, which inevitably remains somewhat specu-lative [see ch. 4]. But the question is of only tangential interest to what this study is concerned with.

Within the period 1949–73 [fig. 7.2] there were five mini-cycles.[4] Though there were no falls in output, there were alternations of faster or slower growth (six periods of faster growth interspersed by five periods of slow, at times minimal, growth). The dating of these mini-cycles as of other fluctuations is here established by the deviations of level from trend [middle band of fig. 7.2].

Only after 1954 was there a significant correlation between fluctuations in the UK and other industrial countries [fig. 7.3, bottom band]; before that there was little. The dip in UK output growth in 1952, seven years after the ending of hos-tilities, marked the ending of the period of postwar excess demand (Dow 1964: ch. 2)—a longer period than after World War I, when the much more violent 1921 recession came three years after the end of the war. The UK cyclical dip in 1952 coincided with a cyclical peak in the USA, caused by the build-up of Korean War expenditure [fig. 7.4]. Other countries had been more damaged by World War II than the UK, and postwar recovery took longer; unlike the UK, they experienced no comparable dip in 1952. Thus, there was no synchronized slowdown in world demand till 1954, and no large one till 1958. In that sense, the quarter-century of relatively continuous growth in the post-World War II period got off to a good start.

---

[4] Use of the term 'mini-cycle' does not imply that the fluctuations were endogenous.

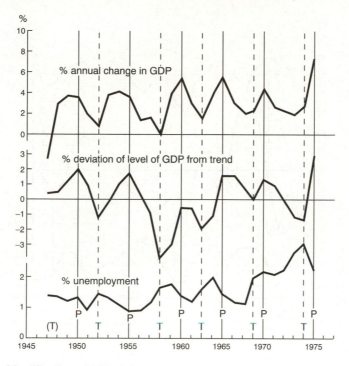

Fig. 7.2 Identification of UK mini-cycles, 1947–1973

The end-years of expansion phases are shown as continuous vertical lines and those of contraction phases as broken lines. P marks peaks and T troughs.

Sources: Feinstein (1972); CSO, *Economic Trends*, 1990.

The Korean War caused a boom in world commodity prices. That sharply worsened the terms of trade of industrial countries, including the UK, [fig. 1.1], and seriously accelerated domestic inflation in all countries [fig. 7.5]. The commodity boom then subsided as rapidly as it came and the industrial countries' terms of trade swung back. For the next twenty years they continued to improve at the expense of the primary producers [fig. 7.6]. (Despite steady growth of demand, the availability of commodities presumably grew even faster.)

That long-continuing improvement in their terms of trade helped to moderate inflation in the industrial countries throughout the middle years of the period. The new world commodity boom of 1972 that preceded OPEC I, and the fourfold rise in oil prices that then followed, led to a second great deterioration, which gave a new spurt to domestic inflation. In the UK there were other factors also affecting inflation, in particular a general level of demand higher than elsewhere, and the devaluations of 1949 (partially followed

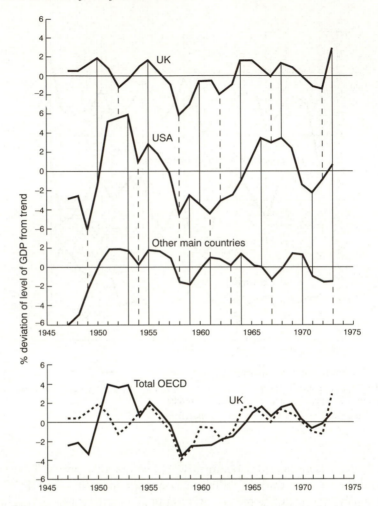

Fig. 7.3   Comparison of cycles in the UK and other OECD countries, 1947–1973

'Other main countries' are: Canada, France, Germany, Italy, and Japan.

'Total OECD' countries are: Australia, Austria, Belgium, Canada, Denmark, Finland, France, Germany, Italy, Japan, Netherlands, Norway, Sweden, Switzerland, and UK.

Cycles for the UK and USA are identified as in figs. 7.3 and 7.5. Cycles for other main OECD countries and total OECD area are identified similarly. The correlation coefficient between GDP variations of the UK and of total OECD (excluding the UK) is 0.176 for 1948–73 and 0.622 for 1954–73.

Sources: Maddison (1989).

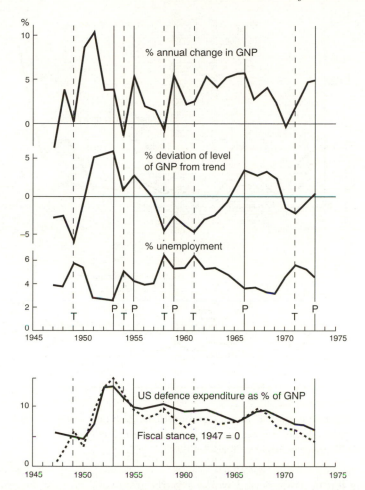

Fig. 7.4 Cycles in the USA, 1947–1973

The end-years of expansion phases are shown as continuous vertical lines and those of contraction phases as dotted lines.

'Fiscal stance' = cumulative total of fiscal impact on annual changes in GNP as shown in table A5.3

Sources: *National Income and Product Accounts of the USA*, 1986.

by most other industrial countries) and 1967 (not followed by others) and the effective depreciation in 1973.[5]

---

[5] In both 1949 and 1967 devaluation was unwisely delayed: these delays in devaluing had previously been a *moderating* influence on inflation. In 1973 the fixed rate was abandoned and sterling floated down. Another factor which became important in 1974 was the disastrous arrangement ('threshold agreements') undertaken as part of 'incomes policy', whereby extra wage increases were tied to retail prices [s. 7.4].

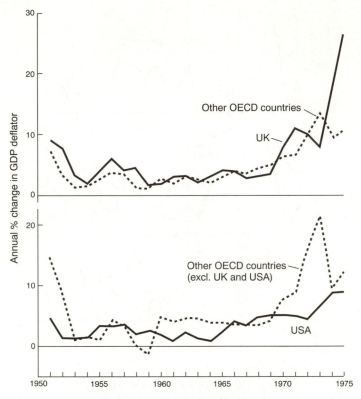

Fig. 7.5   Inflation in the UK and six other OECD countries, 1950–1975
The six other OECD countries are: Canada, France, Germany, Italy, Japan, USA.
Sources: OECD, *National Accounts*; Maddison (1989).

During the postwar period world exports grew very rapidly, in contrast to the years before the war.[6] That partly reflected the fact that the rate of growth of output and demand was generally higher; but national economies were also steadily becoming more open, exporting and importing more in relation to total output. Neither the first factor nor the second can be read (in any direct sense) as explaining faster world growth. (In the first case faster growth of exports was not the cause but the result of faster growth: in the second, the addition to demand growth provided by faster growth of exports by each country was offset by the way that faster growth of imports subtracted from each country's demand growth.)

Nevertheless, trade must have had indirect effects that favoured growth. The increased integration between national economies exposed more sectors to

---

[6] Maddison (1991*a*: table 3.15) estimates that the exports of the industrial countries grew at 8% or 9% a year in 1950–73 compared with 1% in 1913–50.

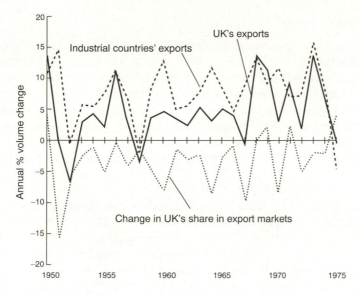

Fig. 7.6 Fluctuations in export growth: UK and industrial countries, 1950–1975

The industrial countries are: Australia, Belgium, Canada, Denmark, Finland, France, Germany, Italy, Japan, Netherlands, Norway, Sweden, UK, USA.

'Change in UK's share in export markets' = percentage increase in UK's exports *less* percentage increase in industrial countries' exports.

international competition, and also facilitated greater worldwide division of labour and concentration on areas of national comparative advantage. Both these developments could have stimulated faster growth of world productivity, and, by this supply-side route, led to a faster growth of world output.

The growth of world exports tended as always to fluctuate more than world GDP growth. That must have resulted in part from short-term fluctuations in the 'world' terms of trade.[7] UK exports tended to fluctuate in sympathy with fluctuations in world exports (and in particular the combined exports of industrial countries). But the UK share of the latter also declined fairly steadily throughout this period [fig. 7.6]. This trend is not accounted for by a corresponding shift in the competitiveness of UK exports as usually measured, but rather must be the consequence of further countries continuing to industrialize [table 4.2]. The erratic fluctuations in export growth played an important role in the generation of domestic fluctuations. (The international transmission of fluctuations is thus one of the factors to be included in the discussion of fluctuations in section 7.3, along with the role of domestic policy.)

---

[7] When primary producers earn more as a result of a change in the terms of trade, they tend to spend what they earn on goods produced in the industrial countries.

7.1.2. Political events[8]

Looking back, the quarter-century after World War II can appear a period of success for the aims of economic policy; but at the time it did not seem like that. Each year seemed to bring its crises and unexpected twists of fate. In twenty-eight years there were thirteen Chancellors of the Exchequer. The policies of this long succession of short-lived ministers were therefore essentially short-term; and short-term failures seemed all the worse because governments then were more inclined than nowadays to get closely involved. Something of this air of inglorious busy-ness remains in political memory to typify the period.

The international political background

The Cold War may be dated from early 1947, when the Soviet representatives walked out of the conference that was to result in Marshall Aid; all countries that followed Mr Molotov's lead then became Soviet satellites. Political uncertainty and the diversion of effort to defence may have put some brake on productivity growth in the United States and Britain; in the Soviet Union the effect must have been much greater, but difficult to distinguish from the inefficiency of a mammoth command economy. On the other hand, the nuclear stalemate also provided a very long period free of total war in the West. Violence erupted in the Korean War (1950–3) and the Vietnam War (especially 1965–75)—episodes that for Europe happened off-stage.

The international economic and financial regime

The international currency regime remained throughout the period one of fixed but adjustable exchange rates, as had been envisaged under the Bretton Woods agreement. (The peg to gold and hence the US dollar was moveable, but between moves rates were fixed within a narrow band.) The first years after the war were marked by 'dollar shortage': most currencies were not freely convertible into the US dollar, and the transfer of dollars to pay for imports from dollar areas required official approval. Until December 1958, therefore, when most countries made their currencies generally convertible into dollars, the world was divided into two: the dollar area and the rest.

The currency regime of the non-dollar world was effectively regulated not by the International Monetary Fund (IMF), but by the European Payments Union (EPU), which was set up in 1950 within the OEEC to supersede a tangle of bilateral trade and payment arrangements between European countries that had grown up since the war. The EPU worked like an IMF in miniature, and behind the barrier constituted by dollar inconvertibility maintained convertibility and fixed (adjustable) rates for the currencies within its area. The adoption of convertibility put an end to the EPU: it was only then that the IMF came into its own.

---

[8] This account partly follows Dow (1964) and Blackaby (1978).

Both the IMF and the EPU were essentially managed systems, and thus in a broad sense Keynesian. Countries were expected to manage internal demand so as to maintain both domestic economic balance and balance on their external accounts, so far as the two were consistent. When they were not consistent—when for instance it seemed that deflation to eliminate an external deficit would cause a level of unemployment that was recognized to be unacceptable—countries were expected to devalue (as the UK did in 1949 and 1967). The most complicated exchange adjustment undertaken was the devaluation of the US dollar, eventually accomplished in the Smithsonian Agreement of December 1971.[9] The Bretton Woods regime effectively came to an end in March 1973, when the major countries agreed to let their currencies float—a move that had been preceded by the UK's unilateral adoption of a floating rate in June 1972.

The postwar period saw two major, rather successful, exercises in tariff cutting, the Dillon Round (1960–2) and the Kennedy Round (1963–7), each requiring years of multinational negotiation. The formation by the original six members of the European Economic Community (EEC) in February 1957, and, as a countermove, that of the European Free Trade Area (EFTA) in November 1959, each involved the abolition of tariffs on trade within these areas. Taken all together, these tariff reductions probably explain most of the disproportionate growth of world trade relative to that of national products;[10] i.e., the result was to re-route trade flows so that more of output crossed national frontiers on its way to the ultimate consumer. Whether the effects went beyond that, and raised output, will be discussed in section 7.2.

The character of UK domestic economic policy

The sort of domestic economic policy that was followed by the UK in the first peacetime years emerged from intensive bipartisan preparatory discussion while the war was still being fought. The 1944 White Paper on *Employment Policy* (published by the wartime coalition government) initiated a somewhat interventionist style of demand management. Reliance was placed mostly on fiscal policy as an instrument, and its stance was changed fairly frequently but mostly in a small way. In time more emphasis reverted to monetary policy, mostly under Conservative governments—by Butler (in 1952), by Thorneycroft (in 1957), and by Barber, who in 1971 stood godfather to the Bank's first exercise in deregulation known as 'Competition and Credit Control'—a phase that ended in late 1973 with a reversion to direct monetary controls. Despite some differences, Conservative and Labour administrations had a largely common attitude to economic policy;[11] that lasted till the 1980s and Mrs Thatcher.

---

[9] Complicated because it required international negotiation: see Dow (1989).

[10] See Batchelor *et al.* (1980) and sources there quoted.

[11] As the term 'Butskellism' signified, both Labour policy (under Gaitskell) and Tory policy (under Butler) followed a similar approach.

Looking back over that divide, many devices of policy, since fallen into disrepute, now look strange. Monetary moves were often accompanied by calls for special deposits (then thought an effective restraint); by appeals to the banks for restraint in lending; and by hire-purchase restrictions. Fiscal policy was given greater flexibility by the (1961) 'Regulator'—under which certain indirect taxes could be varied quickly without prior parliamentary assent. The concern for flexibility arose basically out of the insecurity of the balance of payments. Under the fixed-rate regime, payments deficits led, despite exchange controls, to speculative runs on the reserves, not as later immediate fluctuations in the exchange rate. Until abolished, import controls were often used in the hope of protecting the balance of payments—as were an import surcharge in 1964 and import deposits in 1968. Balance of payments weakness lasted till North Sea oil began to come on-stream after 1973.

To counter this short-termism in policy, moves were made in the early 1960s to establish a longer-term framework for policy. The National Economic Development Council, with representatives of government, employers, and trade unions, was set up in 1962 under a Conservative administration. It was in part an attempt to implant French-style 'indicative planning' as a means of building confidence about continued economic growth and to bring growth in the UK closer to continental standards. A similar hope underlay the Wilson Government's National Economic Plan of 1965. Another contrast with later policy was intermittent resort to incomes policy in the hope of controlling inflation—under Cripps in the late 1940s, under Heathcoat Amory in the early 1960s, under the Wilson Government in the mid-1960s, and under Heath in 1972–3.

Successive chancellors of the Exchequer

There were six years of Labour rule (1945–51) followed by thirteen of Conservative governments (1951–64); then six more of Labour (1964–70) followed by three and a bit Conservative years (1970–74) [table 7.1].

Labour's first postwar chancellor, Hugh Dalton, is most remembered for his flamboyant 'cheap money' policy. There followed Stafford Cripps, memorable for the austerity with which he presided over postwar recovery, and Hugh Gaitskell, who stepped outside his role as finance minister to press for rearmament in support of the United States in Korea, and split with Bevan on the issue.

Butler became chancellor in the returned Churchill Government in 1951, and again under Eden—by which time the economy had recovered from the war and, along with the rest of the world, was in high boom. Butler was followed by Macmillan, who presided over only a year of disinflation. The Suez crisis then ended Eden's tenure at No. 10 and propelled Macmillan into it. His place at the Treasury was taken by Thorneycroft, a monetarist before due time, who resigned a year later in dispute with the rest of the Cabinet. Heathcoat Amory then had two years of middling success with demand management, and left his successor, Selwyn Lloyd, a new balance of payments crisis. Maudling, who

Table 7.1 Key political events, 1945–1973

Complexion of government[a]		UK key policy events	Political and economic events abroad
Prime minister	Chancellor of Exchequer		
1945 Labour gov't (393)			
Atlee	Dalton till Nov. 1947, then Cripps	End of lend-lease	World War II ends IMF set up
1946		Bank of England and coal industry nationalized	
1947		Fuel crisis Sterling crisis	
1948			Marshall Aid agreed: OEEC setup
1949		Devaluation of sterling	NATO set up
1950 Labour gov't (315)			
Atlee	Cripps till Oct. 1950, then Gaitskell	Marshall Aid to UK ends	Korean War (1950–3)
1951 Conservative gov't (344)			
Churchill	Butler		
1955 Conservative gov't (344)			
Eden till Jan. 1957, then Macmillan	Macmillan till Jan. 1957, then Thorneycroft, then Heathcott Amory, then Selwyn Lloyd,		
1956			Anglo-French Suez operation
1957		Convertibility of £	European Economic Community set up

Table 7.1 (Continued)

Complexion of government[a]		UK key policy events	Political and economic events abroad
Prime minister	Chancellor of Exchequer		
1959 Conservative gov't (365)			
Macmillan till Oct. 1963, then Home	Selwyn Lloyd till July 1962, then Maudling		de Gaulle president of France (till 1969). European Free Trade Area agreed
1961		UK applies to join EEC (de Gaulle veto)	
1964 Labour gov't (317)			
Wilson	Callaghan till Nov. 1967, then Jenkins		
1965			Vietnam War intensifies
1967		UK re-applies to join EEC (2nd de Gaulle veto) Devaluation of sterling	
1970 Conservative gov't (330)			
Heath	Barber[b]		
1971		Changeover to decimal currency	Smithsonian agreement $ devalued in general realignment of currencies Major currencies float
1973		UK joins EEC	
1974 Labour gov't (301)			
Wilson	Healey	3-day week for industry (miners' overtime ban)	Middle East War followed by oil price quadrupling (OPEC I)

[a] No. of MPs of government party elected in House of 640 (1945), 625 (1950 and 1951), 630 (1955–70) and 635 (1974).
[b] Macleod died after one month as chancellor.

took his place, proclaimed a 4 per cent 'growth target'—a rate which nothing suggested was to be had for the wishing.

The Wilson Government of 1964, with Callaghan as chancellor, none the less came in with the aim of improving on the Conservatives' growth record. Any hope that it might do so was destroyed by Wilson's refusal until 1967 to devalue. Jenkins, who succeeded Callaghan shortly after devaluation, acquired a sort of halo for the severity of his post-devaluation disinflation.

The Heath Government of 1970 started with aims akin to those of Mrs Thatcher nearly a decade later: less government and more room for free enterprise. By 1972 growing unemployment brought a U-turn, and the chancellor, Barber, ended as chief stoker of what is still one of the two largest postwar booms. The government was brought down by conflict with the miners, and the ignominy of the three-day week.[12]

7.2. Reasons for faster growth and high demand

The most important questions about the quarter-century after World War II are about the period as a whole: why (compared with the interwar years and the years after 1973) was growth fast and demand high? With such broad questions it is not possible to establish that one answer or another is correct, but only to make a case for believing that certain factors were probably important.

The argument to be made here asserts some circularity in causation, which it may be helpful to summarize at the outset. The argument is that:

- *continuous high demand* ensured
- *steady uninterrupted growth*, which caused
- *high investment*, which ensured
- *high demand*.

The argument implies a degree of historical determination (things are what they are in part because they were what they were). The key question to break in on appears to be why demand remained high—though that is almost the same (given that demand started high) as why growth was steady.

Much of what happened in the UK was common to the industrial world as a whole. To avoid giving the argument twice, once for the world and once for the UK, I start below with the world, since the universality of the experience was an important part of its causation; and then add details for the UK.

7.2.1. Growth and demand in the industrial world

In the years 1945–73, output in the seven other largest OECD countries as a group grew by nearly 5 per cent a year [table 2.11], and, as in the UK, there was no year in which GDP fell. A number of reasons can be suggested for

---

[12] The coal strike reduced coal supplies to the power stations, and industry had to be restricted to a three-day working week.

the relatively smooth course of world growth after 1945, compared with the disturbed growth path of the interwar years and of the era after 1973.

It has been argued earlier [ch. 3] that an economy habituated to a continuing process of productivity growth output will tend to continue to expand unless downward demand shocks intervene. If so, the question of why growth was fairly steady and continuous resolves itself into asking why no shocks occurred that were sufficiently large to check the course of growth. One answer might simply be good luck. But one can probe deeper and ask whether and how conditions were different from times when such good luck had not been available.

I suggest four ways in which circumstances were especially favourable:

1. The period started with high demand left over from the war.
2. The habit of fast growth bred confidence that growth would continue; the consequent high investment provided a second support to demand.
3. In many countries unusually favourable supply-side opportunities led to unusually fast growth, which reinforced investment demand.
4. Industrial countries' terms of trade improved steadily—by 15–20 per cent between 1951 and 1971 [fig. 7.7]—perhaps because of steady world expansion.

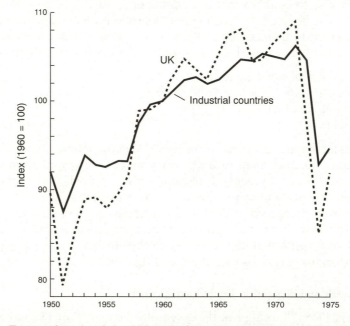

Fig. 7.7 Terms of trade of the UK and of twenty-one industrial countries, 1950–1975 (Price of industrial countries' exports divided by the price of their imports)

The industrial countries are Austria, Australia, Belgium, Canada, Denmark, Finland, France, Germany, Iceland, Ireland, Italy, Japan, Luxembourg, Netherlands, New Zealand, Norway, Spain, Sweden, Switzerland, UK, USA.

Sources: IMF, *International Financial Statistics, Supplement on Trade Statistics*, 1982 and 1988.

5. For most of the time, despite fast growth, inflation remained moderate and did not provoke disruptive counter-measures.

Worldwide high postwar demand

Most countries emerged from World War II with levels of demand in excess of available supplies. In all belligerent countries—which included all the main industrial countries—very large resources had been directed to the war effort. New investment had ceased, maintenance of the existing capital stock had been skimped, and consumer spending on durables had been heavily curtailed. At the end of the war, firms and individuals had stocks of liquid assets they had been unable to spend during the war years. In all countries, therefore, there was more demand than could immediately be met. This overhang from the war took five years or so to work off.

Something of the same had been true after World War I, which however was followed three years later by the sharp recession of 1921 [ch. 6.2]. Then, output rebounded after just one year, and in most countries (not the UK) it rebounded very strongly. Why was there no similar recession after World War II?

1. Arrears of unsatisfied demand were larger. World War II was probably several times as expensive as World War I (measured by the proportion of current GDP devoted to it), and more destructive of property.
2. Both the USA and UK controls were retained longer than after World War I, precisely in order to avoid the sort of speculative boom and recession that followed the first war; and probably in fact helped to do so.
3. The price system had everywhere become much less flexible. At times of scarcity inflexible prices operate as an unofficial rationing system (see Dow 1964: 167, 172). Contrary to one sort of economic orthodoxy, price flexibility may have contributed to real economic instability in 1921, and price inflexibility helped to prevent boom and recession in 1945–50.

After World War II, the overhang of demand from the war provided a good start to growth. In many countries there was a fall in output at the end of the war, as the extraordinary exertions of the war years ceased; because of this, and disorganization and bottlenecks in those countries, postwar expansion was slow to start. But OECD output growth became fairly brisk by 1948 and 1949. It then received another large demand fillip from the Korean War, which in the three years 1951–53 could have added as much as 3 or 4 per cent to total OECD national expenditure [fig. 7.4]. From the point of view of the OECD economies, this addition may have arrived providentially at a time when the stimulus resulting from World War II had begun to flag.

Strong postwar investment demand

A second reason for continued growth was that investment demand became an increasingly strong support to demand in the postwar period. Maddison's estimates (1982: table 5.6) suggest that the stock of non-residential capital in the main countries grew two or three times as fast in the years 1950–73 as in the preceding three-quarters of a century. As the effects of World War II and the Korean War fell away, investment demand took their place; this perpetuated conditions of high demand and fast growth.

The strength of investment can be seen as a consequence of fairly rapid uninterrupted growth—which must have confirmed industry in the habit of expecting each year to bring a continuing expansion of demand. As we have seen, output grew more than twice as fast in the main industrial countries in the period 1950–73 as in the interwar years [table 2.11]. In most of the other seven main countries the acceleration was much faster than in the UK, and especially so in Japan; and the acceleration of investment tended to follow this pattern.

In the UK the acceleration of growth can be explained in demand terms. In the faster-growing economies the acceleration of growth was more dramatic, and one has also to explain the faster growth of supply. Fast growth in these countries implied convergence on higher US income levels, and can be seen as a process whereby converging countries adopted US techniques. In 1945–73 the catching-up must have been especially rapid. Perhaps World War II had interrupted the process and left a backlog of technologies ripe for application. Levels of education also must have been improving. Recipient countries may have reached a stage where new techniques were more readily transmittable; or the techniques themselves may have come to be of a sort that was more readily transmitted. The high growth rates achieved then by some countries were much greater than anything reached in earlier stages of industrialization. This could have been a once-for-all stage for these fast-growers—though something like it has been repeated elsewhere.

Productivity growth tends to be faster in manufacturing than in other industries. One can perhaps conclude that the world was ripe for a burst of growth in the output of manufactures. Technically, the preconditions existed for accelerated growth in this sector. At the same time, final consumers were ready (given the fall in their relative prices made possible by the acceleration in productivity growth) to spend disproportionately more on such goods. The UK (as we shall see) participated in this development; other countries participated even more fully.

The relative quiescence of inflation

The Golden Age was luckier with regard to inflation than the subsequent period. That can be considered a third (negative) reason why growth was relatively fast and demand could continue to remain high.

Both in the UK and in other countries, inflation tended after the war to decelerate up to about 1959 and then gradually to accelerate [fig. 7.5]. It had become a distinctly more serious problem by about 1970; rising world commodity prices, and the quadrupling of oil prices (OPEC I), then gave a further large upward hike to the price level. That prompted restrictive policies in most countries which, while not the main cause of the 1973–5 recession, certainly worsened it [ch. 8.5]. A similar inflationary shock was to lead to restrictive policies in 1979–82.

It may be considered bad luck that these shocks occurred in 1973 and 1979; or good luck for the Golden Age (and for other periods in history and pre-history) that they did not arrive earlier. A similar shock in, say, 1960 might have turned a minor recession into a major one and brought the Golden Age to a premature end.

It is sometimes said that the Golden Age was due to policy having then been directed towards growth and full employment, and that it ended because the aim of policy changed to combating inflation. That is less than half true. In some countries, but not all, governments accepted high employment as an aim. (That was true of the UK, the Netherlands, and the three Scandinavian countries, less true of the USA, and at best only vaguely true of the three major European countries.) But it is not true that governments did much—or had to do much—to achieve this end: it happened without them.[13] It is however true that after each oil shock policy became more restrictive because of faster inflation; and that was part-cause of the recession of 1973–5 [ch. 8.2] which marked the demise of the Golden Age.

The financial environment

There are two other possible (negative) reasons why high demand and uninterrupted growth endured as long as they did. In other periods—both in the interwar period and after 1973—there have been occasions, particularly after phases of continuous growth, when expansion got out of hand, and generated speculative boom conditions, which later went into reverse and led to recession. (Examples are 1919–20 and 1922–9 in the USA and 1972–3 and 1985–8 in the UK.) Continuous expansion in the Golden Age, as we have seen, also led to growing confidence and rising investment. Why did excessive euphoria not develop then?

Two possible reasons may be suggested. The first is the fixed exchange rate system. A fixed rate system does not impinge equally on all countries. But for those countries with relatively weak payments positions—likely by definition to be about half the total—such a system punishes excessive expansion with a crisis caused by lack of reserves. That, or a fear of it happening, is likely to lead governments to react to moderate expansion. (Countries with strong payments positions are likely to have acquired that status because they were cautious by disposition.) The power of a fixed rate system to impose a brake thus goes fairly

---

[13] Boltho (1982: 3), speaking of Europe, makes what seems to me extravagant claims: 'economic policies were important in shaping Europe's post war history ... the use of demand management policies contributed to the dampening of cycles and to the acceleration of economic growth ...' (but see also the more cautious assessment by Bispham and Boltho in the same book, pp. 320–4). Similar claims have been made for the USA by Baily (1978), and for industrial countries generally by Maddison (1991*a*).

wide. It did not impose a comparable restraint on the United States because in that country the foreign sector has been too small for the consequences of ignoring it to worry the authorities. It is perhaps only half an accident that the end of the Golden Age came with the end of the Bretton Woods system.

A second reason for the long continuance of the Golden Age may have been the less competitive nature of national banking systems. Banks play a crucial role in providing interim finance for firms' expansion.[14] The less competitive and more custom-bound banking systems of the 1950s and 1960s will have been less ready to expand lending at expansionary times than they became later. That may have imposed a restraint on the expansion of investment, and hence on the pace of expansion, in the upward phase of fluctuations. Bankers are by profession cautious, and have traditionally been slow in undertaking a process of collective expansion of this sort. Their hesitations were greatly reduced when it became accepted practice for them to go out and borrow on the whole-sale money markets, rather than passively wait for greater deposits to appear. That change—to what was called liability management (see Goodhart 1984: 150–9)—came in the 1970s or later, at different times and to different degrees in different countries [see ch. 9.2]. In the UK it had been prevented by direct lending controls, in force up to 1971.

7.2.2. UK economic performance 1945–73

Fast and fairly steady growth in the world as a whole, and high capacity utilization, must have had a strong influence on individual countries, and tended to make growth fast and steady and demand high in each. If that influence was predominant it would be unnecessary, and misleading, to look for factors peculiar to the UK to explain UK performance. In fact, UK performance was not merely a scaled-down replica of the world average.

Reasons for high demand in the UK

The first question is whether the higher level of UK demand and employment in 1945–73 compared with the interwar period was due to government policy. In the 1944 White Paper on *Employment Policy* the government undertook to maintain a high level of employment, and this intention underlay almost all major changes in fiscal and monetary policy in the years up to 1973. High employment did in fact prevail, and it is not unnatural to attribute that to policy.

---

[14] The essential function of bank intermediation in this process is to ensure that the unplanned addition of saving that arises at numerous unpredictable points within the system in the course of the expansionary process is made available to finance the initial investment. Banks make funds available to lenders simultaneously with the generation of saving in the course of the expansion, but without it being clear in advance who it is that will hold the additional deposits' (Dow and Saville 1988: 198). See also ch. 10 appendix A10.

But high postwar employment cannot be attributed to any very *active* use of fiscal policy (see Matthews 1968); for the public authorities' current account was not in smaller current surplus/larger current deficit after the war than before it (indeed, the contrary). Nor was policy ever strongly tested. No major recessions threatened comparable with earlier and later periods. Adjustments of policy were relatively minor compared with those that would have been needed to contain a recession like that of 1973–5; and had such a recession occurred, the scale of counter-measures required would very likely have exceeded the courage of ministers or officials, or the limits of what financial markets would accept without alarm [see further ch. 12.1]. It is still possible that endorsement of full employment as an aim may have helped to preserve confidence, maintain investment, and keep disturbances small. But other factors were probably more important.

A first suggestion as to the causes can be got from a comparison of the pattern of expenditure in the period 1945–73 compared with that in the interwar years. Table 7.2 (from Matthews *et al.* 1982) compares the pattern of expenditure in the interwar years (1925–37), when unemployment averaged 12 per cent, with that of the quarter-century after World War II (represented by 1952–73), when unemployment was under 2 per cent. The degree of capacity working (defined here as 100 less the percentage unemployed) thus rose from 88 to 98 per cent (10 points). The table highlights changes in two expenditure categories, investment and exports; the effect of changes in other items is subsumed in changes in the propensities to import and to save, also shown.

The table shows (first two columns) that investment and exports, expressed as a share of what GDP would have been at full employment, were in each case higher in the postwar period than interwar. The last column shows estimates of the effect that the change in these expenditure ratios had on the degree of capacity utilization, allowing for multiplier effects (the latter being calculated on the *ceteris paribus* assumption of no change in the propensities to save and to import between the two periods). The changes in the saving and import ratios in the two periods are also shown, as is (column (4)) the effect of such changes on capacity utilization (here estimated on the *ceteris paribus* assumption of no change between the two periods in the levels of investment and exports).

The conclusion is that the rise in fixed investment was the main factor accounting for postwar high employment. Much of the effect that this, on its own, would have had was however offset by the simultaneous rise in the propensity to save; and when looked at closely, much of that can be regarded as having been a consequence of the rise in GDP—and thus, as to the greater part, a consequence at one remove of the rise in investment.[15] But even after

---

[15] Much of the rise in saving consisted e.g. of a disproportionate rise in the undistributed profits of companies (see Matthews *et al.* 1982: 139–51). But that was the result of the rise in output— which is to be attributed mostly to investment. The rest of the rise in saving can be regarded as the induced effect of the rise in exports (as the second main factor). As will be seen, there was no rise (indeed, a slight fall) in the import ratio.

Table 7.2   Change in capacity working across World War II analysed by expenditure categories and propensities[a]

	Interwar 1925–37 (1)	Postwar 1952–73 (2)	Change across World War II (3)	Effect on degree of capacity working (4)
% capacity working	88.3	98.2	9.9	
Categories of expenditure (% of full employment GDP)				
Fixed investment	8.8	17.3	8.5	24.6
Exports	16.2	20.4	4.2	12.1
Income from abroad, adjusted	2.6	0.7	−1.9	−5.5
Total of above	27.6	38.4		31.2
Propensities				
Savings	9.4	18.1	8.7	−23.0
Imports	21.7	21.0	−0.7	1.9
Total	31.1	39.1		−21.1
Total change in level of activity (GDP/F/E GDP) (%)				10.1

[a] The table is based on a transformation of the national income identity $Y = C + I + X - M$, where $Y = $ GDP at annual market prices, $C = $ consumption both private and public, $I = $ investment, $X = $ exports, and $M = $ imports. Defining $A = $ income from abroad, $s = $ ratio to GDP of savings (private plus public) and $m = $ that of imports,

$$Y = \frac{I + X + A(1 - s - m)}{s + m}$$

Full employment GDP ($\bar{Y}$) is defined as $\bar{Y} = Y/(1 - u)$, where $u = \%$ unemployment, and the degree of capacity working as $Y/\bar{Y}$.

   The table shows (in the final columns) the value of these ratios in the interwar and postwar periods and (in column (3)) the change in their values across World War II. The effect of activity (shown in column (4)) represents (i) the multiplied value of the changes in expenditure categories, i.e. the latter, and (ii) the effect of changes in the ratios s and m given constant values for the expenditure categories. The formal identity applies only within a single period, and when applied between periods yields only an approximate result.

Source: Matthews *et al.* (1982: 303–5).

allowing for that, the rise in investment (partly offset by the induced rise in saving) remains the most important reason for postwar full employment.[16] The rise in exports—allowing similarly for some induced effect on saving—appears as the factor second to investment responsible for high employment.

[16] This analysis differs in detail, though not in main thrust, from the conclusion in Matthews *et al.* (1982: 306).

One must go on to ask: why then was investment high? The answer is: it was high because growth was fairly fast, so that demand continued to be high. One is driven then to ask further: why was growth fast?

Reasons for fast growth

Table 7.3 applies a similar scheme of analysis to show what items of expenditure were responsible not, as before, for higher employment, but for faster growth. The analysis is again in terms of two categories of expenditure, investment and exports, which are treated as primary. Again, changes in these expenditure items have not only an initial effect, but indirect multiplier effects of a size depending on the propensities to save and to import.

Table 7.3 first explains in these terms the growth rate *within* each of the two periods, 1920–38 and 1950–73; then (third column) it points to the differences between the two periods. The top part of the table shows the contribution to output growth of each of the two expenditure items, estimated on the assumption that s and m remain unchanged at their average value for each

Table 7.3 Change in rate of output growth across World War II analysed by expenditure categories and propensities

	Contribution to annual % rate of growth in GDP[a]		
	Interwar 1920–38	Postwar 1950–73	Change interwar to postwar
Effect of changes in growth rates of expenditure categories			
Investment	1.9	2.7	0.8
Exports	−0.3	2.4	2.6
Total of above	1.6	5.0	3.4
Effects of changes in propensities			
Savings	−0.2	−1.2	−1.0
Imports	−0.3	−1.3	−1.0
Total	0.4	−2.4	−2.0
Total as estimated above	1.2	2.6	1.4
Residual unexplained	(0.3)	(0.4)	(−0.1)
Actual GDP growth rate	1.7	3.0	1.3

[a] The principles of the calculations are as follows. The first two rows show the changes in total investment and exports through each period expressed as a contribution to the annual % rate of growth of GDP and as 'multiplied', i.e. multiplied by $1(\bar{s}+\bar{m})$, where $\bar{s}$ and $\bar{m}$ are the average values of s and m in each period.

The second pair of rows shows the effect on growth of the change through each period in the fitted trend of the saving and import ratios respectively, i.e. the effect of the resultant change in the value of the multiplier assuming investment and exports are unchanged at their average value. Ratios are similar in concept to table 7.2 but are defined in relation to GDP, not GNP.

period. The lower part of the table shows, on the assumption that investment and exports remain constant at their average value for each period, the contribution made by changes throughout each period in the saving and import propensities.[17] This method of calculation clearly provides only an approximate estimate, so that as with table 7.2, the components do not sum exactly to the actual growth rate of GDP.[18] Growth rates are here calculated as between terminal rates (not as elsewhere from fitted trends) so as to facilitate the calculation of the component factors contributing to growth rates.

What the table claims to show may be summarized as follows.

1. Growth *during the interwar period* was associated largely with investment, while exports fell slightly and were thus a minor drag. Despite the imposition of tariffs in 1931, the import ratio rose—thus retarding demand growth, though much less so than in later periods. The savings ratio also rose slightly through the period (thus also retarding demand growth).
2. The faster growth *during the period after World War II* was associated about equally with faster growth in investment and in exports. About half the effect that this might have had was offset by the concurrent rise in the savings and import propensities.
3. The *acceleration of growth* across World War II (column (3)) is thus shown to have come chiefly from the acceleration in export growth. Investment expenditure did rise after the war, but not much faster than it had risen through the interwar period; whereas the acceleration of exports (from zero through the interwar years) was very marked. Over half the effect this must have had was offset by the faster rise in the savings and import ratios in the course of the period. Probably much of the former, and most of the latter, was an acceleration induced by the faster rise of output. Allowing for that, the faster rise in investment can be regarded as explaining little, and the faster rise in exports as explaining most, of the acceleration of growth.[19]

The rapid growth in demand and output, largely owing to exports, helped to create the higher level of investment, which in turn created (as table 7.2 showed) the high level of output and employment. (Another reason for higher

[17] The contribution of changes in s is here calculated on the assumption that m is unchanged at its *average* value for the period; and similarly for the contribution of changes in m.

[18] The balance of payments implications cannot be read directly from the table. The higher level of exports relative to full-employment GDP will have improved the current balance in real terms, as did the slight fall in the import propensity; but the move to fuller employment will have worsened it.

[19] Again, the balance of payments implications cannot be read directly from the table. Exports rose faster in real terms, but this was offset by the increase in imports resulting from the faster rise in output, assuming a constant import propensity (an effect not shown in the table), and by the increase in the import propensity (shown). In fact, the current account (as a proportion of GDP) deteriorated during both the interwar and the postwar periods, but by more interwar; in that sense there was an improvement in the trend of the current balance.

investment was the shift to higher employment—itself largely produced by the higher investment; i.e., there was a gradual self-reinforcing process.)

Historically, these interconnections unfolded in gradual progression, one supporting another. One way to explain high postwar demand is to say that the economy had become fully employed during the war, and subsequently grew fairly steadily at the capacity rate. This means that other classes of final expenditure quickly took the place of government wartime expenditure. Up to 1950 this was exports, as will be shown by tables 7.4 and 7.5 below; these tables show the alternations of fast and slow growth. In each successive 'fast' period, however, and in each successive 'slow' one, the contribution of investment became progressively greater. Exports, on the other hand, contributed to growth on a progressively decelerating scale—until the late 1960s, when they were given a temporary fillip first by the 1967 devaluation,[20] and then the (unsustainably large) world expansion of 1973. Thus, in the 1950s, investment was as important as exports as a factor supporting growth; but by the 1960s—until 1968[21]—it had become twice as important.

It was suggested earlier that uninterrupted expansion of output tends to lead to a progressive rise in the ratio of investment to GDP [ch. 5]. As figure 7.8 shows, the investment ratio rose rapidly in the postwar period, from 12 per cent in 1948 to 19 per cent in 1968. Excluding investment in dwellings, and looking only at private non-residential investment, the rate of rise of the ratio, at first very rapid, slowed down after about 1960.[22]

These examples indicate some ways in which conditions of fast growth and high levels of demand were perpetuated. They continued fast and high because they had got going that way, and because there had been no major shocks to interrupt the process. Given the openness of the economy, it depended crucially on the growth of exports, and hence on growth worldwide.

7.3. Minor fluctuations of the period

Though growth was fairly continuous, in that output hardly fell, there was a series of minor fluctuations, when the rate of growth varied. They did not cause the same setbacks to productivity growth as major recessions; and the effect on unemployment was proportionately much less and tended to get reversed in the following fast phases. They were thought important at the time; now, in the light of later, worse, recessions, they seem trivial.

---

[20] The 1949 devaluation must have been partly responsible for the rapid growth of exports in 1947–50, though world demand for manufactures was then also rising fast. After the first impact of the devaluations of 1949 and 1967 had worn off, the UK tended to lose the competitive edge temporarily afforded by devaluation, so that the effect of changes in the real exchange rate over the whole period may have been negligible.

[21] Developments after 1968 are discussed in s. 7.5.

[22] The ratios quoted are at constant prices. Investment goods prices rose more than the average, and at current prices the peak occurred not in 1969 but 1974.

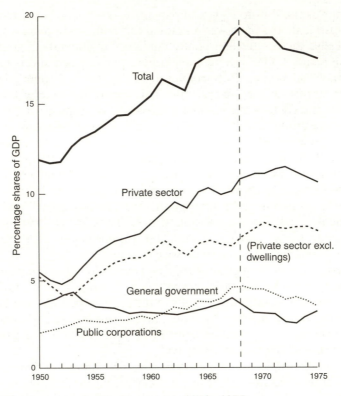

Fig. 7.8   The investment ratio, by sectors, 1950–1975

Sources: Economic Trends for gross fixed capital formation as % of GDP (A) at 1985 prices; for years before 1962, figures for separate sectors are derived from current price series deflated by deflators for investment in dwellings and for other investment as appropriate.

These minor fluctuations are nevertheless worth considering here, for three reasons:

1. This study seeks to explain major recessions in terms of exogenous shocks or other disturbances (confidence fluctuations). Does such a scheme of explanation [s. 7.3.1] apply also to these minor fluctuations?
2. Acts of policy are one sort of shock, and (as will be argued) acts of policy appear to have worsened, not mitigated, these fluctuations. Does experience in handling, or mishandling, minor fluctuations have lesions [s. 7.3.2] for the problem of handling major ones?
3. We must probe further the question why these minor fluctuations did not (as later) turn into major ones [s. 7.3.3].

7.3.1. Causation of the minor fluctuations

Figure 7.3 distinguishes six phases of fast growth and five of slow growth in the period 1947–73. We may leave aside the first and last of these—the first because it represented postwar recovery, the last because it is included among the fast-growth phases already studied separately [s. 5.3]. In the remaining nine phases, annual output growth averaged $4\frac{1}{2}$ per cent in the fast phases and about 2 per cent in the slow phases [tables 7.5–7.7]. There was some coincidence between fluctuations in the UK and elsewhere [fig. 7.3], and rather more coincidence (though still incomplete) between fluctuations in UK exports and the total exports of the industrial countries [fig. 7.6].

These minor fluctuations in the period 1945–73, like the major ones in preceding and succeeding periods, can be partly (but only partly) explained in terms of the shock indicators developed in chapter 5. In some cases these greatly over-predicted [tables 7.6 and 7.7] the extent of fluctuation. The 'accuracy measure' shown in the tables counts over-prediction as an error equally with under-prediction. On that showing, in fast phases the accuracy was rather under 40 per cent, and in slow phases about 60 per cent (irrespective of whether the AA or BB estimates are taken). When cumulated, explanation in terms of exogenous shocks roughly tracks actual fluctuations [fig. 7.9]; but, although calculated effects usually point in the same direction as actual fluctuations, the errors are fairly large.

The numerous deficiencies of the measures of shocks, and of the methods used to test them, have already been emphasized [ch. 5.2].[23] In a context where all evidence is bound to be imperfect, these results suggest that minor fluctuations (like larger ones) were brought about in some part by exogenous demand shocks.

The expenditure composition of successive fast and slow phases is shown in table 7.4 [summarized in table 7.5]. The fast phases tended to be dominated by bursts of investment and exports. As already noted, as the period went on, investment increasingly took the place of exports as the dominant component. Slow phases tended similarly to have slower growth in these components. They also saw slower growth in consumer spending—probably reflecting not only multiplier effects, but also monetary policy. (In this period high interest rates were usually accompanied by hire-purchase restrictions.) Fluctuations in stock-building made the scale of fluctuations in final spending half as much again as they would otherwise have been [table 7.5].[24] But their impact on GDP must

---

[23] Briefly, no *ex post* measures of the degree of unexpectedness of events can be perfect; the measures do not pretend to be complete; and the series to be explained (and in some cases the explanatory series) are detrended by use of trends estimated over what are inevitably very short periods.

[24] Stock changes were destabilizing in the sense of exaggerating changes over fast or slow phases, but not [see s. 5.1] in the sense of making the level of output on average further from its trend value.

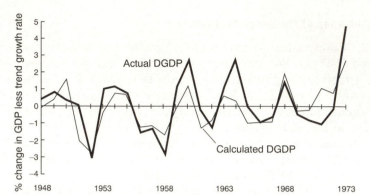

Fig. 7.9   Explanation of UK fluctuations in terms of exogenous shocks, 1948–1973
Shock effects are estimated on method B (see ch. 5.2).

have been considerably dampened by the parallel disproportionate variation in imports (shown only implicitly in tables 7.2 and 7.3 as the difference between TFE and GDP changes). The terms of trade were a dominant influence on two occasions: the slow phase of 1950–2, and then, in reverse, in the fast phase of 1952–5 [tables 7.6 and 7.7].

7.3.2. Demand management in the Golden Age

Governments had accepted responsibility for maintaining high demand, and had varied policy instruments to prevent or mitigate fluctuations in demand. There has been a discussion (stemming I think from Dow 1964) about whether policy intervention did not increase rather than dampen the extent of fluctuations.

Two questions need to be distinguished: (1) whether policy shocks were positively correlated with GDP fluctuations, and thus can be judged to have contributed to fluctuations, and (2) whether policy interventions kept the level of GDP closer to its trend path than if there had been no policy change. My earlier conclusion (Dow 1964: 284), based on this first criterion, was that fluctuations were 'chiefly due to government policy'.[25] Others have confirmed this conclusion for the UK, but not for other countries.[26] Little (1962) and Worswick (1970), however, rightly argued that the first criterion is myopic, and the second more important. But even on this criterion, policy was I believe destabilizing.[27]

[25] This was written in the early 1960s in the light of the limited experience then available (two phases of fast growth and one of slow).
[26] Prest (1968), Musgrave and Musgrave (1968), Bristow (1968), and Hansen (1969). For a general review of this discussion see Llewellyn *et al.* (1985: 19–26).
[27] Policy appears both to cause deviations from trend and (later) to reverse them, and it can be estimated that growth would have been closer to a sustainable trend had it done neither. Snyder (1970) and Boltho (1981) however come to the opposite conclusion; but it is clear that there are some difficult questions of judgement involved.

Table 7.4 Expenditure components of growth: fast and slow phases, 1947–1973

Contribution to % change in TFE[a]

	1947–50	1950–52	1952–55	1955–58	1958–60	1960–62	1962–64	1964–67	1967–68	1968–72	1972–73
	F	S	F	S	F	S	F	S	F	S	F
Consumer expenditure	3.1	-0.7	6.6	2.8	4.3	2.3	4.0	2.9	1.4	6.3	2.6
Government expenditure[b]	0.2	3.9	-0.1	-1.1	0.7	1.3	0.6	2.0	0.1	1.2	0.7
Fixed investment	1.9	0.2	2.7	1.3	2.1	1.4	2.4	2.5	1.0	0.6	1.0
Exports	5.4	-0.4	2.3	0.8	1.3	0.7	1.2	1.5	1.9	3.9	2.1
Total final sales	10.9	3.0	11.6	3.7	8.4	5.6	8.3	8.9	4.3	12.0	6.5
Stock change[c]	-2.6	1.0	0.7	-0.5	1.4	-1.5	1.7	-1.1	0.3	-0.7	1.9
Total final expenditure[d]	9.0	2.7	13.4	3.8	10.2	3.9	10.2	7.6	4.7	11.5	8.6
% change in GDP(A)	10.1	2.8	11.7	3.0	9.6	4.2	9.6	7.0	4.3	8.9	7.6

[a] F = fast; S = slow.
[b] Current expenditure on goods and services.
[c] Includes expenditure adjustment, GDP(A) *less* GDP(E).
[d] GDP(A) *plus* imports.

Source: as for table 2.1.

Table 7.5 Expenditure components of growth: summary, 1950–1973

| | Contribution to % detrended change in TPE in each phase[a] | | | | |
| | Period 1950–72 | | | Period 1950–73 | |
	4 fast phases	5 slow phases	Average F+S	5 fast phases	Average F+S
Consumer spending	1.1	−1.4	−1.3	1.1	1.3
Government[b]	−0.8	−0.1	−0.3	−0.6	−0.2
Fixed investment	1.3	0.1	0.6	1.2	0.5
Exports	6.8	0	0.4	0.9	0.5
Total final sales	2.3	−1.5	1.9	2.6	2.0
Stock change[b]	1.0	−0.6	0.8	1.2	0.9
Total final expenditure (TFE)[b]	3.8	−2.2	3.0	4.2	3.2
% change in GDP(A) relative to own trend	3.0	−2.9	3.0	3.3	3.1

[a] Detrended change is average change in fast and slow phases *less* average of slow and fast phases disregarding sign: phases vary from 1 to 4 years (see table 7.4).
[b] See notes to table 7.4.

Source: from table 7.4.

Table 7.6 Explanation of mini-cycles 1950–1972: fast phases

| | % change during each phase | | | | |
	I 1952–5	II 1958–60	III 1962–4	IV 1967–8	Average
% change in GDP[a]	2.1	3.2	3.2	1.1	2.4
No. of years of fast phase	3	2	2	1	2
% of GDP change explained by separate factors					
Exogenous shocks[b]					
Exports (*EX*)	−1	−7	−8	83	17
Terms of trade (*TOT*)	182	38	11	17	62
Monetary policy (*MP*)	(−43)	(40)	(41)	(20)	(15)
Fiscal policy (*FP*)	99	−37	−12	−8	11
Total	237	36	33	113	105
Measure of accuracy[c]					
Method AA	−37	36	33	87	30
Method BB[d]	55	37	28	30	37

For definitions and methods of estimation see ch. 5.2.
[a] % deviation of GDP(A) over each phase from constant-employment trend.
[b] As estimated on method AA, using theoretical value of parameters [ch. 5.2]
[c] Defined in table 5.7, n. *a*.
[d] Method BB uses values for parameters as estimated in table 5.5.

Table 7.7 Explanation of mini-cycles 1950–1972: slow phases

	% change during each phase					
	I 1950–2	II 1955–8	III 1960–2	IV 1964–7	V 1968–72	Average
% change in GDP[a]	−3.6	−6.6	−2.2	−2.6	−3.9	−3.8
No. of years of slow phase	2	3	2	3	4	2.8
% of GDP change explained by separate factors						
Exogenous shocks[b]						
Exports (*EX*)	45	19	31	25	−21	20
Terms of trade (*TOT*)	129	−14	−16	−34	−9	11
Monetary policy (*MP*)	(2)	(30)	(60)	(75)	(−6)	(33)
Fiscal policy (*FP*)	−17	48	−8	75	69	33
Total	160	82	68	140	34	97
Measure of accuracy[c]						
Method AA[b]	40	82	68	60	34	57
Method BB[d]	86	63	97	88	−33	60

For definitions and methods of estimation see ch. 5.2.
[a] % deviation of GDP(A) over each phase from constant-employment trend.
[b] As estimated on method AA, using the theoretical value of parameters [ch. 5.2]
[c] Defined as in table 5.7, n. *a*.
[d] Method BB uses values for parameters as estimated in table 5.5.

The pursuit of fast growth

I now think that the conclusions drawn from this discussion were based on a misleading analogy. The theory of stabilization policy has been influenced by the engineering concept of an automatic governor which keeps a machine's speed between preset limits: if the governor is badly set (e.g. responds with too long a delay), it may widen, not dampen, fluctuations. My original perception, followed I think by others, was that UK policy had responded too slowly in this sense. That has been claimed in support of the (probably unjustified) generalization that governments always tend to be slow, and therefore should not attempt closely adjusted intervention ('fine-tuning').

The experience of this period—much of it subsequent to my 1964 book—suggests that a mistake of a cruder sort was being committed. Governments, notably in the UK, at different phases caused (or failed to restrain) faster growth than could be sustained, which then had later to be restrained. The mistake was a positive one: it happened not because policy-makers were inefficient in pursuing a sensible aim, but because they pursued a misguided one to the point where its impossibility became obvious. That is, it was 'go–stop', not 'stop–go'.

Thumbnail sketches of successive fast and slow phases will illustrate what was happening (details are in Dow 1964, and Blackaby 1978). From 1952 on, fast phases owed much to policy:

- 1952–5: Butler's fairly deliberate expansion owed much to tax reductions; the reversal of the previous shift in the terms of trade was also important (and probably not fully allowed for). *This was followed by three years (1955–8) of cautious policy under Macmillan and Thorneycroft* [table 7.7].
- 1958–60: Amory intentionally presided over a gradual acceleration of growth—*followed by two years (1960–2) of forced restriction under Selwyn Lloyd.*
- 1962–4: Maudling announced a 4 per cent growth target which was more than attained and ended with a balance of payments crisis. *There were then three years of slow growth (1964–7): the Labour Government's 4 per cent growth target was prevented by repeated payments crises.*
- 1967–8: A year of fast growth was due this time not to policy, but to a world boom and a rapid rise in exports. *The following period of slow growth (1968–72) was caused at first by restrictive policies taken in the wake of the 1967 devaluation (under Jenkins) and then by the austere policy followed at first by the Heath Government.*
- 1972–3: This was a year of extremely rapid growth, fostered both by a world boom and the resultant rise in exports, and by Heath's 'U-turn' and the resultant expansionary policies under Barber [see further ch. 8].

It is sometimes asserted that this go–stop cycle was politically motivated, i.e. that fast phases were caused by politicians creating economic conditions calculated to please the electorate and help the government to get re-elected. That must be partly true: a government likes to be associated with prosperity, and at times electoral considerations were probably influential in shaping macroeconomic policy.[28]

The oscillations of policy were, however, also due partly to a mistaken view about the capabilities of the economy. The 'stop' phases were at the time often seen as tiresome interruptions to growth, inflicting unnecessary damage on industry. Though not all Keynesian economists agreed, the more optimistic persuaded themselves that the way to improve growth performance was to ensure that demand grew rapidly. But the capacity rate of growth proved not to be easily force-fed. On average, it was probably about the same as the rate at which output grew, and the uncertainties of the go–stop cycle may even have reduced it. Without

---

[28] Most of the phases of overfast growth came not under Labour but under Conservative governments. When a Labour government tried it, financial conditions often prevented the attempt from getting started. That is more than accident, for three reasons. First, business tends to be more confident under Conservative administrations and perhaps quicker to invest and expand. Second, Conservative governments tended to act as if the economy is best left to manage itself, and were more active in discarding financial controls (in 1971–3, and later after 1980). Third, financial markets gave Conservative governments the benefit of the doubt: a Conservative government was less likely to provoke a quick financial crisis by what it did than a Labour government.

requiring chancellors to be superhuman, one can imagine them being better advised or having a better comprehension of what they were doing.

The same mistakes were apparently not made in other countries. There is a widespread view that before the mid-1970s British economic policy was too preoccupied with maintaining high demand and too little concerned with avoiding inflation. Governments of both political persuasions, I think, sought to retain a level of unemployment that was undesirably low, and frequently attempted or permitted impracticable rates of expansion. But the fact that there was mismanagement does not necessarily imply that any attempt at managing the economy is misguided; nor that, since policy was misguided, the economy should be left to itself. This period of mini-cycles has some lessons for the harder task of avoiding major recessions [see ch. 12].

7.3.3. How did minor fluctuations get reversed?

It was argued in section 7.3.1 that phases of faster or slower growth were reactions to exogenous shocks. If so, there remains a further question: why did each phase come to an end? Was it accident that an opposite shock arrived soon, or was there an underlying reason? Or is there room for there being also an endogenous mechanism that generated self-reversing fluctuations?

Part of the answer has already been discussed [s. 7.3.2]. The domestic causes of fluctuations were domestic fiscal and monetary policies. In so far as domestic factors were dominant, phases of fast growth were ended by these policy shocks not being repeated (or in some cases being reversed—either because of inflation or, more imperatively, because of balance of payments difficulties). Similarly, phases of slow growth came to an end because the acts of policies that brought them on were not repeated, and often policies were relaxed—as the symptoms they were imposed to deal with eased, and because the policies themselves were onerous and were not retained longer than needed.

For various reasons, the external shocks that impinged on the economy were also of a sort that tended to get reversed within a few years. The external shocks were changes in exports, and changes in the terms of trade originating in large changes in world commodity prices,[29] both of which can ultimately be attributed to fluctuations in the level of activity in the main industrial countries, particularly the United States—and thus to their policies. In general, other countries' acts of policy which caused booms were not repeated or got reversed for the same reasons as brought about reversals in the UK. In this period booms in commodity prices originated in the two Far East wars in which the USA took part;[30] in both wars, periods of high expenditure lasted only a small number of years.

---

[29] Ch. 5 included as another kind of shock changes in stock appreciation (inventory profits), which also originated in changes in world commodity prices.

[30] Assessments of their economic impact are given in Hansen (1969) and McCracken *et al.* (1977).

These are probably the reasons why phases of fast world export growth were short-lived and were followed after a year or two by phases of slow growth; and why phases of rising world commodity prices were soon succeeded by phases of falling prices. (In later periods, this was sometimes only half true: the OPEC oil price rises came to an end, but were not reversed for a long while [ch. 8].)

One other reason should be mentioned for the tendency of the minor fluctuations in this period to be reversed. In small fluctuations, the effect of stock changes (inventory fluctuations) is particularly important [ch. 5.3]. Stock cycles are inherently short-lived: and strong effects on activity in one direction are inevitably followed by opposite effects within a short time span. (Note that, though stock cycles could be said to be an endogenous mechanism, their effect is to amplify fluctuations originating elsewhere, not themselves to generate fluctuations.)

Prima facie, the fairly regular minor fluctuations in this period might appear as promising candidates for explanation in terms of an endogenous self-perpetuating cyclical mechanism. But the factors listed above provide an alternative explanation in terms of shocks, and this seems the most plausible explanation: if accepted, it would rule out endogeneity as an explanation.

7.4. Was the Golden Age doomed anyway?

It will be argued in the next chapter that it was large exogenous shocks that caused the 1973–5 recession, and thus brought the previous quarter-century of fast growth and high demand abruptly to an end. Many people, however, ask whether the transition was not in fact a gradual one. Were there not signs that the earlier phase was coming to an end before the blow struck, and were there not some developments in train that would in any case have undermined its continuance? Two issues are especially relevant: the development of inflation in the 1945–73 period [s. 7.4.1], and the peaking of investment in the late 1960s [s. 7.4.2].

7.4.1. The scale of the inflationary problem

Inflation became a more serious problem during the period: the question is, how crucial was it? Was it enough on its own to undermine the conditions for fast growth and high employment?

In most previous periods of history, prices fell as often as they rose; for example, prices were lower in the UK in 1938 than in 1920. But throughout the 1945–73 period, the UK price level rose every year; in fact, it had risen every year since 1935. Thus, 1945–73 was an inflationary period, although, compared with what came later it was only moderately inflationary.

There was high inflation at the beginning of the period and again at the end [fig. 7.5]. From a rise in the GDP deflator of about 10 per cent in 1947, it declined to 3 per cent in 1949, and, after a smaller peak in 1950, to 2 per cent

Table 7.8 Explanation of inflation, 1950–1973

$\Delta FEDA$=annual change in final expenditure deflator adjusted for stock appreciation (see below).
ΔIP=annual change in deflator of imports (goods and services).
ΔGDP=deviation of GDP from trend.
$\Delta M1$=annual change in M1.
$\Delta M3$=annual change in M3.

The equations as fitted were:

(a) **Monetary variables alone**

Equation		$\bar{R}^2$
(1) $\Delta FEDA=$	$3.45+0.30\ \Delta M1$	0.13
(2)	$3.33+0.36\ \Delta M1_{-1}$	0.20
(3)	$3.15+0.53\ \Delta M1_{-2}$	0.22
(4)	$3.13+0.24\ \Delta M3$	0.20
(5)	$3.14+0.30\ \Delta M3_{-1}$	0.18
(6)	$2.74+0.48\ \Delta M3_{-2}$	0.16

(b) **With other variables also**

Equation	Constant	Trend	ΔIP	ΔGDP_{-1}	$\Delta M1$	$\Delta M3$	$\bar{R}^2$
(7) $\Delta FEDA=$	1.52	0.12	0.33				0.82
(8)	1.47	0.13	0.32	0.34			0.83
(9)	2.01	0.46	0.28	0.65	0.23		0.87
(10)	2.51		0.27	0.70	0.28		0.87
(11)	2.56		0.28	0.54		0.16	0.84

$\Delta FEDA$ is calculated as (the value of final expenditure *plus* stock appreciation) *divided by* (volume of final expenditure). The deflator so defined is related to costs currently incurred, whereas the unadjusted deflator relates to historical costs. Results are shown only where the *t*-ratio is larger than 1.8 except for ΔGDP, where the parameter though not significant at the 5% level is included in the view of evidence from previous studies of this period that pressure of demand was influential. Coefficients on unemployment as an explanatory variable were not significant. The coefficient on $\Delta M1$ or $\Delta M3$ becomes significant only when the time trend is dropped (equations (10) and (11)).

Source of basic data: CSO, *UK National Accounts* and *Economic Trends*.

in 1959; it then remained in low single figures until the 1970s, but accelerated in 1974 and 1975 to postwar record rates of over 20 per cent.

Both peaks of inflation (1950 and 1974–5) were associated with large rises in world commodity prices, which were reflected in UK import prices. Correlation analysis [table 7.8] suggests that two factors provide an adequate explanation of inflation: changes in the average value of imports, and a measure of the degree of unutilized capacity.[31]

[31] Addition of the rate of change of money, narrow or broad, does not improve the explanation. These results are consistent with those that Britton (1991: 272–81) obtained for the post-1970 period [ch. 8.1].

World commodity prices affected internal prices in other industrial countries in a similar way [fig. 7.5]. To a considerable degree, therefore, inflation was a world tendency. (For the period 1950–75, the correlation between inflation rates in the UK and all OECD countries gives $r^2 = 0.88$: between those in the UK and OECD Europe, $r^2 = 0.84$.) For all countries together, commodity prices can be taken to be an endogenous variable, determined by the pressure of demand in all industrial countries as a bloc; but for a single country, the impact is exogenous.

The finding that UK inflation was highest at times of world boom does not however catch the full problem. It was equally important (*a*) that, in contrast to previous eras, inflation was now always positive; (*b*) that inflation in the UK was a third as much again as in the other main OECD countries;[32] and (*c*) that it was tending slowly to accelerate. (Insertion of a term representing time in an equation purporting to explain inflation suggests that, *ceteris paribus*, inflation was tending to accelerate by an eighth of a percentage point a year, or by 3 per cent over the 1950–73 period.)

The phenomenon of continuously rising prices was probably the result of the spread of imperfectly competitive markets, both in the UK and elsewhere.[33] That also meant that inflation was likely to accelerate.[34] Acceleration must have been the greater because of high demand, particularly in the UK. Had UK unemployment averaged not 1.5 per cent but 3 or 4 per cent, inflation might have been no faster in the UK than elsewhere.[35]

Even though inflation was becoming more of a problem as the period progressed, up to 1973 it had by no means reached a point that threatened to interrupt the process of continuous growth and plunge the economy into major recession. After 1973, inflation became different in degree from anything in the preceding years [fig. 7.11]. That suggests that the change arose from a new outside shock, and was not merely a natural extension of the previous twenty-five years. Later discussion [ch. 8] will show that three factors were then to be important: extremely high demand, both in the world and the UK; a wage indexation policy in the UK that was fatally misconceived, and went badly wrong; and a very steep rise in world commodity and oil prices, made all the worse by the depreciation of sterling in 1973. Between 1972 and 1974 import prices rose 75 per cent, which alone must have directly contributed 15 per cent out of the total 23 per cent rise in final prices. These were new factors, not something that sprang from the experience of the previous twenty-five years.

[32] The other six G7 countries, 1950–73: a rough estimate taken from not strictly comparable figures assembled in Maddison (1991).

[33] The reasons for this crucial change in behaviour have, surprisingly, been little discussed; e.g. it is mentioned, but neither discussed nor explained, in Brown (1985).

[34] As many predicted: e.g. Dow (1964), Phelps (1967), and Friedman (1968).

[35] See the illustrative calculation in Dow (1964: 362).

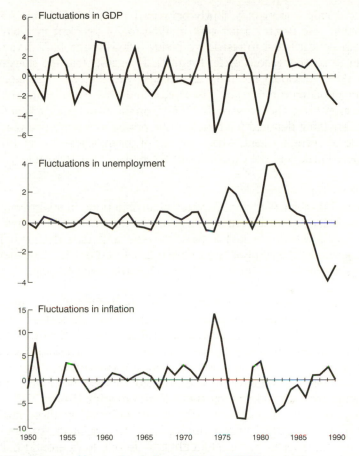

Fig. 7.10 Degree of innovation in fluctuations of GDP, unemployment, and inflation

Innovation in GDP fluctuations is measured as % changes in GDP (A) each year less average of % changes in preceding three years; similarly for fluctuations in unemployment rate and inflation (% changes in TFE deflator)

Source: Basic data as for table 2.1.

7.4.2. Did the long boom have to end?

Several writers see the 1945–73 period as a long boom that was showing signs of coming to an end well before 1973. Matthews and Bowen (1988: 383), for example, say '[t]he years between 1968 and 1973 were a transition phase', and 'it is clear that the boom was running out of steam in almost all OECD countries. The rate of capital accumulation had everywhere passed its peak.' Interpretation of events is inevitably coloured by theoretical presuppositions; and such a view appears to borrow authority from an implicit assumption that the economy moves in long cycles, so that any deceleration is to be read as leading on to actual downturn.

Output did indeed grow only slowly between 1968 and 1972 [table 7.4], and unemployment rose (from 1.5 per cent in 1966 to 2.4 per cent in 1968). That however can be attributed to restrictive policy following the 1967 devaluation, rather than to an endogenous cycle. Figure 7.11 suggests that the slowdown in growth in 1968–72 should not rank as a break with the past (any more than inflationary developments already discussed), and was trivial compared with what came after 1973. The recession of 1973–5, on the other hand, was in distinct contrast to anything that had happened in the preceding twenty-five years. The same is true of unemployment, where the rise of unemployment after 1973 also marks a clear break with the experience of the previous quarter-century.

The behaviour of fixed investment

Matthews and Bowen (1988) also discern a change in trend in investment. They describe the behaviour of investment in terms of the ratio of fixed investment to capital stock, which reached a peak in 1968 and then declined. In the alternative terms of the ratio of fixed investment to GDP [fig. 7.8], there was also a steep rise in the years up to 1969, and then (on constant-price estimates) a decline.[36]

To a large extent, the change in trend chiefly reflected a decline in investment by the public corporations. Such investment was at this date centrally planned, and had been geared to the over-ambitious growth projections of the National Plan. The consequent rapid expansion of the capacity of the nationalized public utilities appeared clearly excessive when output growth slowed down; and cuts in their investment programmes thus constituted a large part of the restrictive measures that had to be taken after the 1967 devaluation (Price 1978).

The ratio to GDP of other investment, not affected by these measures, continued to rise after 1967, but more slowly. The rise in the private-sector component of the investment ratio had already slowed down around 1960, and then from 1970 remained nearly flat for the next four years [fig. 7.8].[37] It was to be expected that the first surge in investment after the war would abate and that the investment ratio would eventually rise more slowly. That would have made it likely that growth would be less rapid. But it would not have made inevitable the abrupt fall in output that occurred after 1973.

The main reason to reject these arguments (drawn from UK experience) is that the 1973–5 recession was international, and has to be explained [as ch. 8 will argue] in terms of international causes—worldwide inflation and the OPEC oil price shocks, OECD-wide counter-inflationary policies, and the demand-side effects in all industrial countries of the worldwide shift in the terms of trade.

---

[36] The constant-price estimates are probably the relevant series here: the current-prices series (as noted) peaked in 1974.

[37] Matthews and Bowen (1988) also point to the decline in profits, which they interpret as a sign that investment had previously been too fast, i.e. in excess of some sort of equilibrium rate.

It may seem rash to assert now, from this distance, that the Golden Age could have continued indefinitely. In historical interpretation there is always a cowardly tendency to 'inevitabilize' history and treat what happened as having been the only course events could have taken—in much the same way as (it is often said) history as written gets written by the victors. When discussing a past reality where one knows little about the relationships at work, it seems bold to assert that a counterfactual alternative was really possible. But to write history like that is to rob it of any usefulness it may have.

The evidence that the recession of 1973–5 was due to large outside shocks is strong; and I will argue [ch. 8] that there is good reason to suppose that that recession did not emerge endogenously from the past, and would not have happened but for these shocks.

7.5. The behaviour of the economy: conclusions from 1945–73 experience

This study is concerned not with history as such, but with what we learn from it about the economy's modes of behaviour. I will now try to summarize the conclusions about the economy which this discussion suggests can be drawn from the period 1945–73.

- Since the period saw no major fluctuations, it may not appear very relevant to this study. But that itself is of great significance. One hypothesis proposed in this study has been that growth proceeds in a straight line unless interrupted by an exogenous shock. In the years 1945–73 growth, admittedly, was not absolutely steady. Some observers, moreover, detect signs that forces integral to a state of high demand and continuing growth—in particular, inflation—were destined to bring it to an end; but that argument seems overdone [s. 7.4]. I would claim that the period provides a rough demonstration of the possibility of an indefinite continuation of steady growth.
- This implies that, in principle, the conditions of 1945–73 could recur. But the experience of high demand and rapid growth depended (it was argued) on three pieces of luck: the good start provided by World War II and the Korean War (good luck from the point of view of growth and employment demand); the fact that high demand and rapid growth were worldwide; and the absence of major, downward, demand shocks. The equivalents of these lucky accidents could reconstitute themselves, but are unlikely to recur frequently or completely, and would be difficult to reassemble by deliberate action.
- The minor fluctuations that occurred form a fairly regular sequence of phases of above-trend and below-trend growth. It might be thought that endogenous cyclical mechanisms had played an important role in causing them. In fact, it seems possible to explain the minor fluctuations—as other

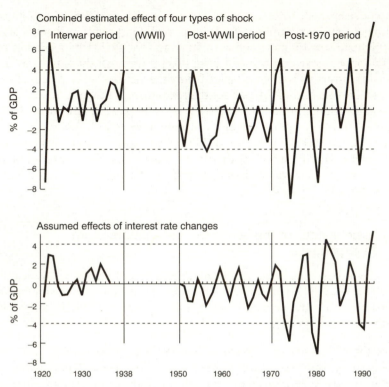

Fig. 7.11   Indicators of the scale of exogenous shocks in three subperiods, 1921–1992

Smoothed series: data shown are two-year sums expressed as % of GDP.

Shock indicators are changes in monetary policy (interest rates), fiscal policy, export volume, and terms of trade; indicators are derived on method AA as in ch. 5.2. Assumed effects of interest rate changes are shown separately.

chapters suggest that major fluctuations can be explained—as a result of exogenous events coming either from the outside world or from changes in UK policy.

• One implication of this finding is that the reversal of each fast or slow phase occurred because positive (expansionary) shocks were soon supplanted by negative ones, which in turn were supplanted by new positive ones. Analysis suggests there were reasons for this, deriving from the nature of the shocks, not from mechanisms built into the economy. Fluctuations remained small because in this period shocks were small and tended to reverse themselves. They became much larger around 1970 [fig. 7.11].

8 The Two OPEC Recessions (1973–5 and 1979–82)

The recession of 1973–5 was the first occasion since the war when total output fell absolutely. The shock was the greater for coming after a quarter-century of relatively steady growth, to be followed six years later by the recession of 1979–82, when output again showed an absolute fall.

The question that this study started out to answer [ch. 1.1] was why 1973 was so crucial a turning point: before that, most people expected employment to stay high and growth to remain fairly rapid; after that, few did. To determine why 1973 was so crucial, one has to look at all the major fluctuations of the economy since 1920. Nevertheless, the recession of 1973–5 and that which followed in 1979–82 retain a central interest.

Each of these two recessions coincided with one of the vast jumps in the world price of oil, known as OPECs I and II. I will argue that these played a large role in their genesis; and though in each case there were other causes also, the two recessions will be referred to here as the OPEC recessions. There are some important differences between them but also important similarities, and they were very different from the major recessions that came before the war or the next one. They are therefore discussed together in this chapter, which takes the story to 1982—the year when the economy can be considered to have emerged from the second of the two recessions.[1]

Table 8.1 shows the two successive phases of recession, each followed by resumed growth, between 1973 and 1989, and the impact on unemployment and productivity. As will be seen, by 1983 GDP was 18 per cent below a projection of the pre-1973 rate of growth.

Figure 8.1 also compares the actual trend of output with what UK output would have been had it continued to grow at the 1950–73 rate. This decline in the rate of output growth took the form [fig. 8.2] partly of a decline in the rate of growth of (labour) productivity, partly of a rise in unemployment, and partly of a fall in the participation rate. (That is, the proportion of people in work fell, without an equivalent increase in those registered as unemployed; the difference is labelled 'concealed unemployment' in fig. 8.2.) By 1982—nine years after 1973—the shortfall of output from past trend was about 20 per cent; almost half of this was reflected in a shortfall of productivity growth, almost a third in unemployment, and about a fifth in concealed unemployment.

---

[1] In this study recessions are considered to end when the trend growth rate is resumed; the previous trend growth path is never regained [see ch. 2.2].

Table 8.1   Four phases of recession and growth, 1973–1987

	1973	1975	1979	1981	1987
Cumulative developments (1973=100)					
Pre-1973 trend of GDP	100	105.9	118.7	125.7	149.2
GDP[a]	100	97.7	107.3	103.1	124.7
% shortfall		−7.7	−9.6	−18.0	−16.4
Changes by sub-periods	Pre-1973	1973	1975	1979	1981
(annual % changes)	trend	−75	−79	−81	−87
GDP[a]	2.9	−1.2	2.4	−2.0	3.2
Output per head[a]	2.5	−1.0	2.0	0.3	2.6
Change in % unemployment		2.4	0.9	4.4	3.6[b]

[a] Excludes North Sea output.
[b] Changes in average unemployment in period 1981–7 adjusted to eliminate the effect of official training schemes. Unemployment follows a change in the course of output with some delay; the table shows the change in unemployment between years one year subsequent to years of peak or trough output.

Source: as for table 2.1.

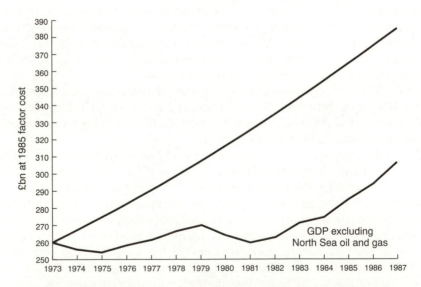

Fig. 8.1   UK output growth 1973–1987 compared with the pre-1973 trend
Pre-1973 trend was obtained by fitting a straight line to logs of GDP over the period 1950–73 and adjusting to pass through the 1973 figure for GDP.
Sources: *Economic Trends*, 1989, and *UK National Accounts*, 1988.

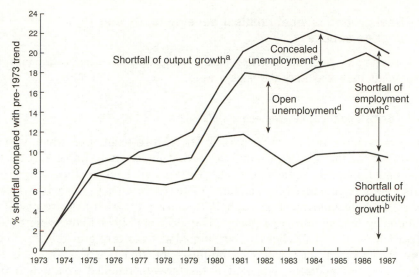

Fig. 8.2 The slowdown in output growth and the associated slowdown in employment and productivity growth, 1973–1987

[a] Pre-1973 trend of GDP *less* GDP (excluding North Sea output).
[b] Pre-1973 trend of output per head *less* GDP (excluding North Sea output) per head.
[c] (*a*) *less* (*b*).
[d] % unemployment as recorded, adjusted to include numbers on official training schemes.
[e] (*c*) *less* (*d*).
Source: as for fig. 8.1.

The questions to be answered are why output failed to grow as fast as before; and why a large part of that shortfall was represented not by a rise in unemployment but by a failure of productivity to rise. That is important, since the latter could in principle be due to supply-side rather than demand-side factors; and it has to be considered how far the rise in the price of oil could (as sometimes alleged) have had such a supply-side effect. The rises in the world price of oil were accompanied on both occasions by a large rise in other commodity prices, and thus by a large deterioration in the UK's terms of trade. Such events are here treated as shocks which reduce total demand [ch. 5.2]; it is thus of interest to describe how these shocks arose (section 8.1). They not only had demand effects, but also caused waves of inflation [discussed in app. A8].

Section 8.2 gets down to the main business of seeking to explain the fluctuations of UK demand and output in the period. Here it is necessary to start before 1973 and examine the boom of 1972, seen as one cause of the recession that followed. Section 8.3 considers the general lessons to be derived from this decade.

8.1. Background issues: political developments and the oil price shocks

This section annotates the British political scene, and the origin of the oil price movements that constitute the background.

8.1.1. British political developments 1972–82

The period starts with the latter part of Mr Heath's reign, after which Labour held office for the middle years of the period under study [table 8.2]. In the remaining third of the decade the Conservatives were back in office—the spring of their long reign under Mrs Thatcher. (The rest belongs to the next chapter.)

Growing unemployment through 1971 caused the Heath Government to abandon its initial restrictive policy. The 1972 and 1973 Budgets were both expansionary: the Chancellor (Barber) aimed at 5 per cent growth—2 per cent more than seemed likely without stimulus—and that rate was attained. The Chancellor also made it plain that if fast growth entailed devaluation that would be accepted: the pound was in fact set free to float down in mid-1972. At this time Conservative governments still talked with unions about incomes policy: these resulted in the disastrous 'threshold' agreements—perhaps the most inflationary act committed by a British government. At the end of 1973 the government was confronted by a miners' strike over pay. Mr Heath appealed to the country in an election on that issue, and lost.

Labour's first months saw the country struggling with the consequences of the miners' strike, electricity shortages, and the three-day week; there were also the longer-term difficulties created by the first oil shock. The combined effect of rising commodity and oil prices, *plus* the 1972 devaluation and the 'threshold' wage agreements, produced a rate of inflation unprecedented in normal times.[2] The Barber boom had already been followed by a flattening of output growth, which was soon to turn into absolute recession.

In all countries governments faced an intractable dilemma: measures to counter unemployment would worsen inflation; measures to counter inflation would worsen unemployment. Neither the old Keynesian recipe nor any other had an answer to this; policy was about as much use as oars in a rowing boat on the Atlantic. Since accelerating inflation had accompanied rapid monetary expansion, Conservative theorists saw that as its cause—while Labour began to retreat from what it had previously advocated towards the monetarism its opponents were beginning to adopt. Successive versions of incomes policy continued to be tried, but from 1976 on the government began to run a policy of monetary targets alongside.

There was a large balance of payments current deficit in 1974 (3.8 per cent of GDP). However, unlike previous occasions, this was now a problem shared by

---

[2] The postwar inflation of 1919–20 was as fast.

Table 8.2 Key political events, 1973–1982

Complexion of government[a]		UK key policy events	Political and economic events abroad
Prime minister	Chancellor of Exchequer		
1974 Labour gov't (319)[b] Wilson till April 1976, then Callaghan	Healey	1975 Mrs Thatcher leader of Conservative Party 1975 Referendum on membership of EC: 67% in favour North Sea oil—first landing 1976: UK asks for IMF standby	
1979 Conservative gov't (339) Mrs Thatcher	Howe	1979 exchange controls abolished	1979 EMS starts (without UK) Direct elections to European Parliament 1979: Volcker chairman US Fed. Reserve Board 1979: Reagan elected president of USA 1981: Mitterand elected president of France
		1982 HP controls abolished	1982: Argentina invades Falklands: UK expedition
		1984 miner's strike (lasts a year)	

[a] Number of MPs of government party elected to House of 635 members.
[b] 301 in February election; 319 in October election.

most of the industrial world: a collective deficit was the unavoidable counterpart of an OPEC surplus—though, by the same token, it was readily financed.[3]

---

[3] Since the demand for oil is highly price-inelastic, elimination of the OPEC surplus would have required manifold contraction of demand and output in industrial countries. As it was, the oil producers acquired funds which they wanted to invest in the West.

Table 8.3   North Sea output and the balance of payments, 1973–1982 (% of GDP)

	Output of North Sea oil and gas	Balance of payments surplus or deficit
1973	—	−1.3
1974	—	−3.8
1975	0	−1.4
1976	0.5	−0.6
1977	1.6	0.0
1978	1.9	0.7
1979	3.3	−0.2
1980	4.4	1.2
1981	5.5	2.6
1982	5.9	1.7

Sources: CSO, *Economic Trends Annual Supplement*, 1992; *Blue Book*, 1986.

The year 1976 saw a payments crisis, confined to the UK, of quite a different sort. There was acute distrust of the pound, a large fall in the exchange rate, panic acts of government, and a loan from the IMF obtained after tense negotiation. But there was in fact little about the state of the economy that justified such alarm.[4] After a large payments deficit in 1974, the trend was improving [table 8.3]; output was starting a modest recovery from the recession of 1973–5; the rise in wages and prices was slowing and, with it, the rate of growth of the stock of money.

What this episode illustrates, in my view, is the vulnerability of a Labour administration to the hostility and distrust it was apt to inspire in financial circles. The City distrusts government spending, especially if it seems profligate. The government was an uneasy balance of moderates and left-wingers, the latter natural spenders. There was conflict, also, between the views of the official Treasury, still Keynesian, and those of the City, increasingly monetarist. The tension was made more dangerous by official Treasury policy being suspected (correctly) of favouring a downward drift of the exchange rate. What was most fatal was that, in a situation which required handling with great finesse, the government was too preoccupied with its internal quarrel to be aware of the dangers of a visible parade of disarray. Intervention by the IMF proved necessary to lance the crisis. This served to resolve the predicament even before the agreement was signed; in fact, the Letter of Agreement called for barely any change in policy.[5]

---

[4] 'If we confine ourselves first to what was going on within the United Kingdom, it is not at all obvious that the situation in 1976 was more critical than at other times in the 1970s' (Burk and Cairncross 1992: 215).

[5] 'Our conclusions are stark and simple. First of all the visit of the IMF was absolutely necessary: governments that wish to borrow money need the confidence of lenders: the British government had lost this confidence, and the Imprimatur of the IMF was required for its return. But secondly the visit of the IMF mission ... made no lasting change ... Since it became clear in

This chapter extends to the first two years or so of Mrs Thatcher's Conservative government that followed the May 1979 election. These years were dominated by the repercussions of OPEC II—much as, five years earlier, Harold Wilson's two first years had been dominated by OPEC I. Policy appeared more single-minded [see further s. 9.3.1], the defeat of inflation having been declared the sole aim. Incomes policies were discontinued, and all hopes were pinned on monetary control, which in the event was not successful in its own terms. But the high interest rates to which it led must have had considerable (unintended) effect in restricting demand, and thus also in slowing inflation, By 1979 the development of North Sea oil production [table 8.3] ensured for this government, in contrast to all its postwar predecessors, freedom from serious worry about the balance of payments.

8.1.2. The nature of the oil-price shocks

Some have argued that general world recession cannot plausibly be attributed to so local an event as a rise—even a massive rise—in the price of oil. It is argued here that the oil shocks (though not the sole causes) *were* one main cause of the recessions. It is useful to indicate the almost accidental way in which they came about and to sketch their international repercussions.

The world price of oil rose fourfold between 1972 and 1974, and more than doubled again between 1978 and 1980 [fig. 8.3]. The price increase on the second occasion was proportionately less, but the initial price was so much higher in 1978 than in 1972 that in absolute terms the rise was as large as the first time. After sagging for some years, in 1986 the price of oil fell to half what it had been at its peak in 1980–2.

How the oil shocks occurred

Though short-run supply and demand conditions at times clearly had strong effects on the price of oil, the huge increases in the world price of oil after 1973 must be seen as chiefly arising from the new strength of OPEC as a producers' cartel.[6] Before that, the producing countries had long struggled to increase their share of oil revenues. They learned only gradually to work together, and only gradually did they discover their power.

1977 that all and more than the IMF asked for was already in train before it arrived, it may appear that the IMF had no more than a walking-on part' (Burk and Cairncross 1992: xix; 225).

[6] How far these two oil price increases were due to market forces and how far to the oil producers' cartel is a question to which no close answer can be given. The long-term equilibrium price is fairly intangible—depending as it does on the future rate of world economic growth and the ability of the world to economize on energy in response to price changes (where neither the future growth rate nor the long-run demand elasticity can be more than guessed at); and on the future rate of discovery of oil reserves, and the ease with which reserves can be tapped or substitute sources exploited (two other semi-unknowns). It is therefore difficult to gauge what the equilibrium price was from which the actions of the cartel caused the actual price to depart.

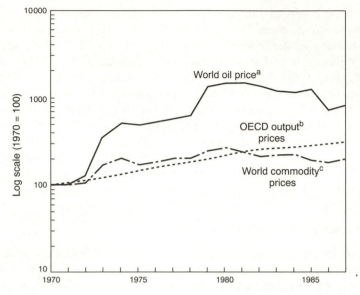

Fig. 8.3   World oil and commodity prices, 1970–1987

[a] Dollar spot market refined product prices (c.i.f.): from OECD, *Economic Outlook*, various issues.
[b] GDP deflator for OECD countries: from OECD, *National Accounts 1960—1986*, vol. I, and *Quarterly National Accounts*, 1987(IV).
[c] Index of world commodity prices: from IMF, *International Financial Statistics.*

The Organization for Petroleum Exporting Countries (OPEC) was founded in 1960.[7] At that time, by far the greater part of the sale value of the petroleum products went either to the oil companies (as costs or profits) or to governments of importing countries (as tax); the share left for governments of exporting countries may have been little more than a twentieth.[8] OPEC's aim was simply to increase that share. The producers' revenues from oil had been declining with the decline in world oil prices throughout the 1960s. That reflected the discovery during the previous decade of numerous giant oil fields, whose exploitation was stimulated by the high profits earned earlier. The existence of excess productive capacity and quickly exploitable reserves limited the gains the producers could at first make, more especially as the member countries of OPEC for long failed to observe production limits agreed between them.

During the 1960s, the position of the oil-producing countries was strengthened by a mixture of market forces and political accidents. There was a gradual shift from world excess capacity to world excess demand. Consumption grew rapidly

---

[7]   By five major oil exporters: Iran, Iraq, Kuwait, Saudi Arabia, and Venezuela.
[8]   Griffen and Teece (1982) quote an estimate of 6% as the exporting government's share of the sales value of petroleum products sold in Europe in 1961.

with strong economic growth in consuming countries; and the United States, with its own production ceasing to expand, began to import. The closure of the Suez Canal after 1967 and the sabotage of the trans-Arabian pipeline resulted in high prices and high tanker rates. This favoured Libyan oil, which required only a short trip to Europe; and enabled Libya, in 1970, to demand higher prices. That example pointed the way to the Teheran Agreement in 1971, when for the first time OPEC negotiated collectively with the oil companies, and for the first time enforced higher prices.

The continuing rise in market prices, together with accelerating inflation in the United States and the devaluations of the dollar, made OPEC think again; by 1973 it had determined to demand a modification of the agreement, originally with only modest aims. The situation was then dramatically changed by the outbreak of the Arab–Israeli War in October. The Arab OPEC members announced a unilateral tax increase, instituted production cutbacks, and placed an embargo on oil to the United States and the Netherlands. Panic buying sent prices rocketing. Saudi Arabia secured the gain to itself by raising tax rates and royalties, and other producers quickly followed, thus effectively setting a lower limit to prices in future. The oil companies' concessions in the Middle East were *de facto* nationalized, the companies becoming in effect merely buyers of crude.

There followed a period of tranquility till 1978. Prices rose in 1975, 1976, and 1977, but by less than world inflation. The OPEC producers may even have been restrained to some extent by fear of the economic consequences of high oil prices.[9] It was, again, political events that triggered the new round of dramatic price increases in 1978–9. Production in Iran was heavily reduced by the revolution in 1978, and further reduced by the subsequent Iran–Iraq War. There was some rise in output elsewhere. But it was shortage of supply that raised world oil prices, rather than a decision of the producers, who in fact failed to agree on prices and on collective decisions concerning output. The origin of this second oil shock was thus considerably different from that of the first.

In the subsequent period market forces shifted progressively against OPEC. In time, the high price of oil led to increasing economy in use by consumers everywhere. The high price also encouraged the development of alternative sources of energy supply, including oil from non-OPEC sources (which rose from under half in the early 1970s to two-thirds of the world total by the mid-1980s). OPEC attempted to continue with its strategy of restricting output but member countries again failed to agree on quotas, the crucial element being that Saudi Arabia was by now unwilling to act as a 'swing producer', i.e. to contract its own output to accommodate over-production by others (Heal and Chichilnisky 1991: 67–9).

---

[9] The Deputy Secretary General of OPEC stated later that to 'a great extent the conservative post-1974 OPEC pricing policies were motivated by concern over the world economy after the initial price shock ... Holding down the oil prices in real terms would, it was thought ... help to achieve sustained growth in the world economy' (Al-Chalabi 1980: 95–6).

Thus, supply and demand conditions limited the producers' bargaining strength in the 1960s, strengthened it in the 1970s, and thereafter reduced it. OPEC, moreover, has not proved a cohesive cartel. By the 1990s the 'real' price of OPEC oil may have been little higher than before the two oil shocks, and the power of the cartel had probably become quite small. But the vastly higher price of oil at its peak than in earlier decades was plainly due to the organized strength of the producers, compared with their previous weakness in face of the international oil companies. Their tardy realization of their power to break the postwar system gave the world economy a momentous jolt which, as will be shown, was to help permanently to alter its course.

International repercussions

The oil shocks affected output and the pattern of trade in all areas. The following paragraphs give a schematic account of the sequence of repercussions between the main blocs making up the world economy.

Consider first a *two-bloc world* in which there are only oil-producing and oil-consuming countries. Assume that the latter are all industrial countries. (The non-oil developing countries also consumed oil and will be brought in later.) The scale of all changes will be measured as a percentage of the combined GDP of OECD countries. The sequence of shock and repercussion is then as follows.

1. The oil shock raises the incomes of producing countries.
2. The rise in the price of oil provokes a rise in factor incomes in consuming countries, at first much less than commensurate. Final prices in the latter (the average of domestic factor and import prices) therefore rise proportionately less than factor income, so that there is a fall in real incomes in consuming countries.
3. Expenditure in consuming countries therefore falls.
4. Producing countries hardly raise their expenditure at first, so that total world expenditure falls. (That slightly reduces the volume of oil consumed compared with what it would have been otherwise, and thus slightly reduces the rise in oil price, but the inelasticity of demand is such that that is a small offset.)

On the assumption that the consequent increase in oil producers' spending is zero, all of their extra real income is saved; i.e., the observed rise in their income equals the increase in these countries' saving—which also equals the increase in consuming countries' current account deficits.

Now consider a *three-bloc world*, consisting of OPEC, non-oil developing countries, and industrial countries. (Oil-consuming countries are now divided into two groups, industrial countries and non-oil developing countries, or NODCs). The latter are less able and/or willing to borrow to finance payments deficits than industrial countries. Hence their reaction to the oil price rise is to cut imports from the industrial countries (either by allowing a downward spiral

Table 8.4 Current balances of OPEC and the developing countries, and OECD exports, 1973–1987

	Developing countries' current balance of payments (% of OECD GDP)			OECD exports (% volume change)		
	OPEC countries	(Cumulative OPEC balance)	Non-oil countries	To non-OECD	Within OECD	Total
1973	0.2	(0.2)	−0.2			
1974	1.5	(1.7)	−0.6	22.5	0.0	7.5
1975	0.6	(2.3)	−0.7	13.0	−9.5	−4.0
1976	0.7	(3.0)	−0.4	5.0	12.5	10.0
1977	0.5	(3.5)	−0.2	6.3	5.0	5.5
1978	0.0	(3.5)	−0.4	7.3	5.5	5.8
1979	0.8	(4.3)	−0.6	3.0	7.5	6.2
1980	1.3	(5.6)	0.8	7.8	2.3	4.0
1981	0.6	(6.2)	−1.0	11.5	−1.3	2.5
1982	−0.1	(6.1)	−0.7	−4.8	−1.0	−1.8
1983	−0.2	(5.9)	−0.4	−2.0	5.8	2.8
1984	−0.1	(5.8)	−0.2	3.0	13.3	10.0
1985	0.0	(5.8)	−0.2	−1.0	6.5	4.0
1986	−0.2	(5.6)	−0.1	−7.0	6.8	2.5
1987	−0.1	(5.5)	0.1	1.8	6.6	5.8

Sources: OECD, *Economic Outlook*, various issues; *National Accounts* 1960–86; and *Quarterly National Accounts*, 1987 (IV).

in real income, or by imposing direct restrictions on imports). This operates as a downward shock to industrial countries in addition to that arising from the effect of the oil price rise. (In fact, as figure 8.3 shows, the price of other commodities rose as well as that of oil, so that NODCs' export receipts were increased, and hence also their ability to sustain imports from industrial countries. But, though an offsetting factor, this was outweighed by the effect, unfavourable to them, of the rise in the oil price. The current accounts of OPEC and NODCs swung in opposite directions [see table 8.4].)

Consider now the reaction of *industrial countries*. In the course of contracting output, they cut imports from each other. Each therefore experiences a fall in demand for its exports from the others, as well as from the NODCs. That amplifies the original shock.

No *ex post* statistics can provide a perfect measure of the size of the *ex ante* exogenous shock. An approximate measure is the increase in the OPEC payments surplus over the first two years after each oil shock. This was about 2 per cent of the combined GDP of OECD countries, or, excluding the USA (which was largely untouched by the oil shocks), nearly 4 per cent of GDP of other industrialized countries. That scale of effect is sometimes dismissed as unimportant,[10] but historically an observed effect of 3 or 4 per cent qualifies as a large—even an extremely large—shock.[11]

The shock arose basically because OPEC's expenditure could not be adjusted quickly to such unprecedented increases in income. Other energy prices rose in parallel, which resulted in a large unspent rise in other energy-producers' incomes—with effects somewhat similar to that of OPEC's unspent balances.[12] The rulers of the OPEC countries were unable to decide quickly how to spend most of the vast increase in their income. In the course of years, they did begin to spend much of their current income; but they continued to add to their financial balances each year until 1982 [table 8.4] and since have reduced them only a little. The fact that the oil price shocks were very incompletely reversed even after many years is one reason why the shock effects were so large and long-lasting.

8.1.3. Did the oil price shocks have supply-side effects?

This section considers how far supply-side factors could have caused the drop in productivity in the two recessions. (Note that this would also explain an equivalent drop in output, income, and hence expenditure; but not the rise in unemployment and the fall in output, income, and expenditure associated with that.) The conclusion will be that supply factors were *not* a major element.

The productivity setbacks that occurred at times of recession in the UK and other main countries have already been shown in chapter 2 [figs. 2.3 and 2.4]; and are summarized in table 8.5. The table shows (a) the pre-1973 growth rate; (b) the scale of the productivity setback as estimated on the charts (expressed both as a percentage of GDP and as the number of years of pre-1973 growth at pre-1973 rates of growth that were lost); and (c) the subsequent rate of growth after OPEC II (expressed as a ratio of the pre-1973 growth rate of productivity).

In absolute terms, the setback appears to have been larger for Germany, France, and Japan, which were the fast growers, than for the USA and the UK. In terms of years of growth lost, almost the opposite was true: the USA and UK (but also Germany) lost five or six years' growth; France and Japan only about two. But these two countries, which were among the fastest growers, then found their growth rate halved after OPEC II compared with before 1973. The USA, the slowest grower, also found its growth rate reduced, but on these estimates by much less, while the UK and Germany were not much affected.

We will first consider the extent to which the vast increase in the relative price of oil—rather than demand effects—could explain the productivity setbacks. Since different sources of energy are close substitutes, the rise in the

---

[10] Heal and Chichilnisky (1991: 78) belittle it as 'significant, but not overwhelming'.

[11] Major recessions showed about a 10 per cent shortfall in demand, most of which can be explained by several shocks each estimated to explain a fraction of the total shortfall [s. 5.2].

[12] Llewellyn *et al*. (1985: 35). The rise in the profits of other energy industries was probably reflected much more quickly in increased spending than the new wealth of OPEC. On the methods adopted in the present study, much of this latter deflationary effect will be picked up as an increase in government revenue from the taxation of profits, and thus counted as contractionary fiscal policy.

Table 8.5 Setback to productivity growth in OPEC recessions in five main countries

	Pre-1973 growth rate (1960–73) % p.a.	Setback to productivity growth[a]				Post-OPEC II growth rate as ratio of pre-1973 rate
		OPEC I		OPEC II		
		% of GDP	(years lost)[b]	% of GDP	(years lost)[b]	
USA	1.8	5.5	(3)	6.3	(3.5)	0.8
UK	2.9	5.4	(3)	6.2	(2)	1.0
Germany	4.4	2.8	(3)	14.6	(3)	1.0
France	6.2	4.0	(0.5)	11.6	(2)	0.5
Japan	11.1	16.5	(1.5)	2.4	(–)	0.5
Average	4.7	6.6	(2)	7.9	(2)	0.8

For comparison: setback in Great Depression[a]

	Pre-1929 growth rate	As % of GDP	Years of productivity growth lost[c]	Post-1934 growth as ratio of pre-1929
USA	2.1	28.4	(13.5)	1.5
UK	1.2	5.5	(4.5)	1.0

[a] Average of the two estimates (*w* and *x*, and *y* and *z*, respectively) shown in figs. 8.5 and 8.6.
[b] At pre-1973 rate of growth.
[c] At pre-1929 rate of growth.
Source: Year-by-year data are shown in figs. 8.5 and 8.6.

price of oil raised the price of other sorts of energy also; and it is convenient to conduct the analysis in terms not just of oil but of energy in general.[13]

There are two ways in which the rise in the price of energy might have reduced full-employment GDP.

1. Some processes and some products were rendered in part unprofitable, so that capital equipment specific to those processes and products was rendered useless. The useful capital stock was thus in effect reduced (for examples see Baily and Chakrabarti 1988).
2. Dearer energy prompted energy saving, which required some input of labour and capital, i.e. substitution for energy of other factors, and a cost, inasmuch as output was diverted from final uses. In the short term, energy

---

[13] Most previous studies have concluded that the supply-side effects of dearer oil were small. The exceptions are (a) Tatom (1981), whose argument is effectively criticized in Denison (1985) and following him Maddison (1987); and (b) Jorgensen (1984a,b, 1988, 1990), whose arguments are effectively controverted in Oulton and O'Mahony (1994). Other studies of the oil price effect are Matthew's (1982) conference volume; Schurr *et al.* (1983); Baily and Chakrabarti's (1988) set of industrial studies; and studies of productivity more generally, e.g. Denison (1979), and Savage and Biswas (1986). The present arguments follow these earlier arguments, but in some respects further minimize the importance of supply-side effects.

Table 8.6   Classification of US energy use

	% of total energy use	Years life of capital stock	Possibility of economizing in energy in short term
Electricity generation and large boilers	32	25	Small
Motor vehicles	18	8	Moderate
Space heating	16	20	Moderate
Others including industrial use	34	10–20	Usually small

Source: Illustrative figures for USA in early 1970s from Nordhaus (1980: table 3).

could be saved by reducing waste without change in the design of basic processes; in the long term, it involved redesign of basic processes to make them more energy efficient.

Induced obsolescence of part of the capital stock

Most energy is consumed in uses where the quantity used per unit of output cannot be varied much in the short term, and where the capital equipment in which it is used is long-lasting, and hence will only slowly be replaced with more energy-efficient equipment [see US figures in table 8.6]. Nevertheless, adjustment of a sort can still take place. If the price of energy rises sufficiently, some of the existing equipment will become uneconomic and will go out of use. This will happen most in industries where existing processes are highly energy-intensive, so that demand switches to processes that are less dependent on energy or with products that have a large energy content from which demand switches to substitute products.

It seems unlikely that this effect was important, though the evidence is incomplete and difficult to interpret. In the first place, it is unclear how far either scrapping of plant or obsolescence increased after 1973.[14] Dearer energy may have caused some scrapping in energy-intensive sectors of industry, or (more subtly) caused less continuous or less intensive use to be made of the least energy-efficient plant. (That would have reduced such plants' value, and its contribution to output.) This could have occurred in sectors such as steel, aluminium, nylon, or air travel.

Second, total factor productivity as measured declined after 1973 because investment was not cut back when output fell, so that capital (which still

---

[14] Baily and Chakrabarti (1988), based on six US industries, think not. Smith (1988) cites evidence for the UK that the capital stock in manufacturing fell rather than rose as it would have done if it had been scrapped after a normal life. But that will have been due to the recession, not dearer oil.

counted as input) was left unemployed. According to Baily and Chakrabarti (1988), this was worst in capital-intensive sectors, such as chemicals and electricity. (One reason why demand fell in these industries was that they were heavy users of energy, for which the relative price rose sharply.)

The clear impression, however, is that these various effects were relatively unimportant. It seems possible to indicate some orders of magnitude. Obsolescence of the capital stock by reason of dearer energy cannot have greatly affected the two-thirds of the capital stock embodied in dwellings and other buildings and works. The annual return on the remaining third might on the normal reckoning be put at around 10 per cent of GDP in total. Suppose the proportion of that third rendered useless by dearer energy was somewhere between 1 and 10 per cent (probably generous limits). The extent to which potential total supply will thereby have been reduced would then be between 0.1 and 1 per cent of GDP. Even the larger figure is only a fraction of the actual total loss of productivity that occurred during OPECs I and II [table 8.5].

Cost of substituting factor output for energy

Reducing energy waste (with essentially unchanged equipment) saved some energy—at a cost of, say, insulation or keeping equipment better tuned. More important was the gradual replacement of old equipment with new equipment which required less energy input.

Even before 1973, consumption of energy was growing less fast than GDP in OECD countries—0.8 per cent a year less fast on average [table 8.7]. After 1973 the differential became much larger—2.5 per cent per annum in the period 1973–84. It is possible that the acceleration was due to dearer oil, in which case it could be said to have prompted a saving of energy between 1973 and 1984 of 1.7 per cent a year.

Table 8.7   Trend to economy in energy consumption, 1913–1984

	Annual % rate of growth of energy consumption less that of GDP				
	1913–50	1950–73	1973–84	Difference: (1950–73) *less* (1913–50)	Difference: (1973–84) *less* (1950–73)
France	−0.66	−0.52	−2.06	0.44	−1.54
Germany	−1.30	−1.22	−2.15	0.08	−0.93
UK	−1.28	−1.32	−3.17	−0.04	−1.85
Japan	−0.26	−0.16	−3.29	0.10	−3.13
USA	−0.91	−0.72	−2.24	0.19	−1.52
Average	−0.89	−0.78	−2.53	0.13	−1.75

Source: Maddison (1987: table 15a).

Impressionistic data in Nordhaus (1980: table 9.2.1) give an idea of how this happened:

1. Some of the energy saving came through elimination of a few extremely high-energy usages (already discussed). Its contribution to aggregate energy saving must however have been small.
2. Elimination of waste without installing new equipment probably also made only a small contribution (e.g. a fraction only of the 1.7 per cent per annum). The possibilities of saving were confined largely to space heating and the operation of motor vehicles, where only a small proportion of energy could easily be saved immediately.
3. The bulk of the saving probably came from the gradual replacement of old motor vehicles by more fuel-efficient models, and of old machines of all sorts; the latter would have taken longer to replace than cars and trucks, but in aggregate was perhaps twice as important in reducing energy usage. Over time, the opportunities of saving energy were greatest here.

The question is, what was the cost, in terms of GDP forgone, of undertaking the adjustments that economized in energy use? One can reason as follows.[15]

1. Taking post-OPEC II relative prices, energy input was worth 9 per cent of the GDP of the average OECD country (less in Europe, somewhat more in the USA) [table 8.8].
2. The energy 'saved' each year was therefore worth $1.75 \times 0.09 = 0.16$ per cent per annum of GDP.
3. The energy saving would not have been undertaken unless it had been worth at least as much as it cost. Therefore the cost must have been *at most* 0.16 per cent of GDP in this period. Allowing for less expensive intra-marginal saving, it was probably considerably less (e.g. 0.1 per cent of GDP).
4. This cost was a diversion of resources from normal ways of spending the national income. But only a part will have been recorded in the national accounts as a deduction from GDP. (Expenditure by business on reducing energy waste will have been treated as an expense, and hence a deduction. But similar expenditure by persons will have been treated as a way of using national product, not a deduction from it; and the same will have been true of investment, whether by persons or firms, in energy-saving plant.) If not recorded as a deduction, this cost is irrelevant to explaining the recorded slowdown in GDP.
5. The effect of expenditure on energy saving on GDP as recorded must then be very small, e.g. well under 0.1 per cent of GDP per annum.

---

[15] Most studies treat such substitution as movement round a production function, the effect of which on labour productivity can be estimated from the assumed form of the function. An objection to that procedure is that the process of substitution is slow, requiring say a quarter-century to complete, so that the scale of elasticities over a few years can be only rough guesswork.

Table 8.8 Energy input as a percentage of GDP, 1973, 1983, and 1987

	1973	1987	1983
France	1.7	5.2	7.3
Germany	2.1	6.3	8.6
UK	2.1	6.1	8.6
Japan	1.6	5.0	6.2
USA	2.8	9.0	11.9
Average	2.2	6.8	9.1

Source: Maddison (1987: table A19). Energy is valued at world price per ton of input. GDP at current factor cost is converted to dollars by use of OECD estimates of purchasing-power parities.

The supply-side effects of the oil price shocks seem then to have been very small. The partial obsolescence of the capital stock seems to have been more important than the diversion of resources to energy saving. But together they seem capable of explaining a shortfall of GNP only of the order of perhaps 1 per cent, whereas the total shortfall to be explained is in the range 10–20 per cent, according to country [table 8.5].

Other possible explanations for negative effects on productivity growth

We may now recapitulate other possible explanations for the sharp setbacks to productivity during each recession.

One possible explanation of the loss of productivity (as recorded) is that firms are slow to cut back employment (the Okun effect). Labour, though still on firms' payrolls, is underemployed (*concealed unemployment* or *labour hoarding*). When demand recovers, slack labour will become fully used again, recorded productivity will recover, and the apparent dip in the path of productivity will then prove to have been temporary. But there are reasons to believe that, when growth was resumed, it was on a path starting from well *below* its old peak [ch. 2.2].

Another explanation is that the break in trend was no more than accident. The rate of growth of productivity has changed from period to period over the past two centuries, for reasons not easy to identify. Against this are the facts that productivity growth was affected in all countries, and that the effect was large and abrupt. The apparent loss of productivity was unlike anything that had happened except in times of recession, and something similar had happened in the previous large recession (1929). This suggests that the effect on productivity resulted from a fall in demand.

The standard explanation of productivity growth is that output per head grows because of the more or less steady advance of technical progress, with some of the technical advance being embodied in successive vintages of ever-improving capital equipment. Unless capital is destroyed on a large scale, which was not the case, this view leaves no room for the process not merely to slow down or stop, but to go into reverse. What then has to be explained is how past gains in productivity can be partially destroyed and not restored automatically when the demand shock has passed.

I earlier proposed [ch. 4.2] an explanation that may be summarized as follows. Technical progress is embodied not only in physical equipment, but also, less tangibly, in the working practices of those who utilize it.[16] In a recession, three kinds of disruption occur:

1. Work-teams are partially or completely disbanded, so that the efficiency of those that remain is impaired.
2. Those disemployed are likely gradually to find their skills as workmen deteriorating, and also to lose their specific value of being part of a team which their work experience has given them.
3. Production is a cooperative process between many firms, supplying or being supplied with specific components or services to/from each other in many specific ways. If a fraction of firms goes bankrupt, a fraction of these interpersonal and interfirm linkages is destroyed and productivity probably impaired. Just as it is a slow, risky, and costly process to set up a new business from scratch, so the working arrangements that get destroyed in a recession are difficult to rebuild: management does not have time. This would explain why, after a recession, the growth of productivity should start not along its pre-recession path, but from the point it has reached at the end of the recession.

In recessions the stock of capital as usually valued typically continues to grow, though more slowly than usual.[17] Most of the setback to productivity therefore may have to be accounted for by organizational disruption of the economy of various sorts. On this view, table 8.5 might suggest that such disruption caused the loss of several years' normal work of organizational improvement.[18]

Conclusions for the larger argument

We may now summarize the place of the rather detailed arguments of this section in the larger argument of this study. One conclusion is that the setback

---

[16] Baily and Chakrabarti (1988: 108) give some support for what Schmookler (1966) argued: that lack of demand discourages innovation. This would be part of the kind of effect here envisaged, but would not explain an absolute setback to productivity.

[17] The perpetual inventory method (PIM) usually used may overstate, and (as already noted) some evidence suggests that in the UK the capital stock, at least in manufacturing, shrank. The same might be true of other countries. Part of the drop in productivity in the OPEC recessions (or in 1929–32) could then be due to that, but, on the standard logic of growth accounting, and given the numbers, probably only a small part.

[18] For the UK and some other countries, the once-for-all setback is all that needs to be explained. For others (Japan, France, and to a lesser extent the USA among the five), there appears to be another equally puzzling phenomenon: namely, that after 25 years of fairly regular and fairly constant growth, post-recession growth was resumed at a markedly slower pace. Some explanations were offered in ch. 4.2.

in productivity growth after 1973 did not originate in an oil-generated supply-side effect.

We could stop at that point, and be content with that negative conclusion. Changes in the pace of productivity growth have long been seen as mysterious. We could treat the coincidence of the major drop in productivity, along with the major fall in demand, as an unexplained accident—which is about where the lengthy inconclusive debate on this question leaves it to date. The alternative is to suppose that the fall in productivity was *due to* the fall in demand with which it coincided.

8.2. A demand-side explanation of the OPEC recessions

Having concluded that a supply-side explanation can by and large be ruled out, I now set out an explanation of the OPEC recessions in terms of demand shocks. One conclusion will be that the recession of 1973–5 was in part a result of the previous boom—which therefore has to be looked at first. The two recessions will then be looked at in sections 8.2.2 and 8.2.3, respectively.

8.2.1. The boom of 1972–3

The boom of 1972–3 was not confined to the UK, but was worldwide. This world boom needs to be seen as the culmination of a series of swings in the policies of the major countries, starting in the late 1960s. The first peak came in 1968–9, with growth in the OECD area rising to an annual rate of about $5\frac{1}{2}$ per cent (even more in continental Europe) [fig. 8.4 and table 8.9]. This followed expansionary policies in both the United States and Europe.

Before that, in the course of the 1960s, inflation in OECD countries had already doubled (to 5 per cent) [table 8.10 and fig. 8.5], with 1968 seeming to mark a new stage in the process. This acceleration of inflation was due in part to the fast rate of expansion; but the response to high demand seems to have been exceptionally large.[19]

The acceleration of inflation led to restrictive measures in many countries, which in turn brought a mild recession in 1971 [table 8.9] and some growth in unemployment—without, however, immediately slowing inflation much. Countries' policies then rather generally swung to being more expansionary. That produced—and not only in the UK—a phase of exceptionally rapid

---

[19] See McCracken *et al.* (1977: 44–66), and Allsopp (1982). Acceleration of inflation may have been due in part to a wave of labour unrest; but if so the reasons are obscure. The 'events' in France in May 1968 always get quoted; but they started with student not worker unrest: trade union involvement and wage demands came only later. There was also a strange abeyance of civil authority (including General de Gaulle's prolonged absence abroad). An additional wage increase (which increased wages by perhaps 6%) was ordained by the government, but almost as a way of bringing the affair to a decent end. This act may have had (non-economic) demonstration effects on wages in other countries.

Table 8.9 OECD growth rates, 1967–1973

	% change in GDP at 1970 prices						
	1967	1968	1969	1970	1971	1972	1973
USA	2.9	0.7	2.7	2.8	2.3	4.7	5.1
Europe (3)[a]	3.1	5.4	7.0	5.4	3.1	3.8	5.5
UK	2.1	4.0	2.2	2.3	1.9	3.6	7.3
OECD	4.0	5.6	5.6	3.7	3.4	5.1	5.9

[a] France, Germany, and Italy: weighted average.

Source: OECD, *National Accounts*, 1995.

Table 8.10 OECD inflation rates, 1967–1973

	% change in GDP deflators						
	1967	1968	1969	1970	1971	1972	1973
USA	2.7	5.2	4.9	5.7	5.4	5.1	6.3
Europe (3)[a]	2.4	2.5	4.7	7.1	7.2	6.1	9.2
UK	2.5	4.8	5.3	8.0	9.5	8.0	6.9
OECD	2.0	4.5	5.0	6.3	6.6	5.9	8.3

[a] France, Germany and Italy: weighted average.

Source: OECD, *National Accounts*, 1995.

growth,[20] which in turn produced a rise in world commodity prices again many times larger than might normally have been expected (see McCracken *et al.* 1977: 59, chart 8). That unusually large response must have been due in part to the rise in demand coinciding with a number of food crop failures and restrictions. In part it also reflected, given the prevailing conditions of monetary ease, inflationary speculation. The large commodity price boom helped to produce a general resurgence of inflation in 1973 and 1974. That in turn prompted a new shift back to restrictive policies—which (as we will see) were to be one main cause of the worldwide recession of 1973–5.

The whole period 1968–75 can then be seen as a case of go–stop misjudgement on a world scale. If the fixed exchange rate system had not begun to crumble from 1971 on, it might have made governments behave more cautiously,

[20] Between the first halves of 1972–3, GNP in the OECD area grew by no less than 7.5%. With all countries growing together (and consequently a low import leakage for the area as a whole), multiplier effects will have been unusually large.

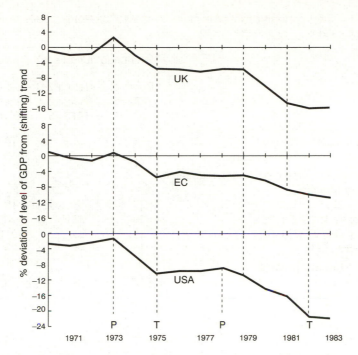

Fig. 8.4 Comparison of cycles in the UK, EC, and USA, 1970–1983

This chart is intended to establish turning points, not to measure absolute deviations from the pre-1973 trend. In the case of the EC, the trend rate of growth as estimated is allowed to decline at each recession, so that the cumulative deviation shown from the trend is less than half the deviation from the pre-1973 trend.

Sources: CSO, *Economic Trends Annual Supplement*, 1992; *National Accounts*, 1960–87.

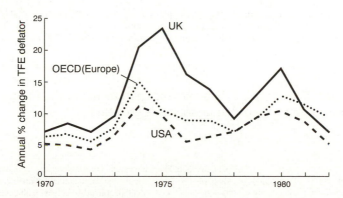

Fig. 8.5 Inflation in the UK, Europe, and the USA, 1970–1982

'OECD (Europe)': calculated as a weighted sum of changes in GDP deflator and import price index.
Sources: OECD, *Historical Statistics* 1960–84; *National Accounts* 1960–87.

Table 8.11   The boom and two recessions of the 1970s–early 1980s in the UK: partial explanations

	% change during each phase		
	Boom of 1972–3	1st OPEC recession 1973–5	2nd OPEC recession 1979–82
% change in GDP[a]	4.7	−8.1	−10.6
No. of years of boom or recession	1	2	3
% change in GDP explained by separate factors			
Exogenous shocks[b]			
Exports (EX)	27	8	18
Terms of trade (TOT)	30	22	−10
Monetary policy (MP)	(0)	(63)	(31)
Fiscal policy (FP)	46	−4	29
Other contributory factors[c]			
Change in saving ratio (SR)	−10	9	−3
Change in non-residential investment (NRI)	5	3	5
Change in investment in stocks (CS)	37	31	9
Total explanation as shown by measure of accuracy[d]			
Total shocks, method AA[b]	96	88	68
Shocks, method BB[e]	63	69	74
Other contributory factors[f]	02	21	21

For definitions and methods of estimation, see ch. 5.2.

[a] % deviation of GDP(A) over each phase from constant-employment trend.
[b] As estimated on method AA, using the 'theoretical' value of parameters (see ch. 5.2).
[c] Defined as in table 5.7, n. *d*.
[d] Counts over-explanation and under-explanation equally as errors: for definition see table 5.7, n. *a*.
[e] Method BB uses values for parameters as estimated in table 5.5.
[f] Net of terms of trade effect (TOT) to avoid double-counting (see table 5.7, n. *d*).

and moderated the excessive 1972 boom: for up to then [ch. 7.2] fixed rates had probably been a factor contributing to stable growth.[21]

[21] This does not mean that I think the Bretton Woods system could have lasted. In my view it foundered not (as is often said) because of the growing international mobility of capital, but because the USA (being a largely closed economy) was never prepared to adjust policy for balance of payments reasons. This became an issue only when dollar shortage turned to dollar glut in the late 1960s. Paul Volcker has given a vivid description of the US lack of commitment at this juncture to maintaining a fixed rate (see Volcker and Gyohten 1992: 62, 104). A fixed-rate system between countries of small or moderate size (as in Europe) is more likely to be possible.

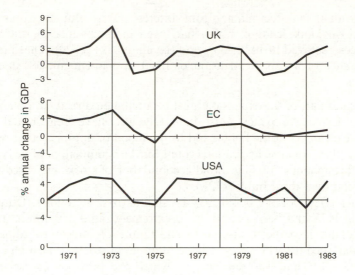

Fig. 8.6 Output fluctuations in the UK, EC, and USA, 1970–1983

Sources: OECD, *National Accounts* 1960–87, vol. I, 1989; *Economic Outlook*, no. 44, December 1988.

The boom in Britain

In the UK the boom of 1972–3, though brief, was among the fastest phases of expansion recorded. Between 1972 and 1973 total final expenditure rose by nearly 9 per cent [table 8.14 below]; between the first halves of 1972 and 1973, it rose almost 10 per cent [fig. 8.6]. There appear to have been four main reasons for the exceptional pace of expansion [table 8.11]:

1. As already noted, the UK boom coincided with the equally exceptional boom abroad. That helps to explain the rapid rise in exports.[22]
2. Paradoxically, the UK was still benefiting from the pre-boom terms of trade, in which import prices were rising less fast than domestic costs, so that (allowing the effect to operate with a lag) the terms-of-trade effect [table 8.11] was still positive.
3. After the U-turn in policy provoked by rising unemployment [s. 8.1.1], fiscal policy became deliberately very expansionary. The 1972 Budget may have directly added 0.8 per cent to GDP, and the 1973 Budget, 1.8 per cent [app. A5].

---

[22] UK export markets expanded, and so did the UK share of export markets [fig. 8.7]. The exchange rate fell 10% in effective terms, when it was set free to float in mid-1972. The effects will have been seen mainly in the following year—in raising export volume compared with what it would have been otherwise; and, along with other factors, reversing the earlier favourable movement in the terms of trade.

4. No stimulative effect came from interest rates. But the quantitative control on bank lending, which had been in force since World War II, had been removed in 1971 (Dow and Saville 1988: 117–20). That facilitated the finance of a rapid expansion of fixed investment and of stocks (see below).

The greater part of the expansion must be attributed directly to policy (3 and 4 above). Expansive policy must indirectly also have contributed to the speculative elements in the boom, and to the mood of optimism that was slow to collapse: that slowness helped to account for the continuation of heavy stock-building throughout 1973. (The rapid accumulation of stocks increased the rate of expansion by a third [table 8.12].)

The later effects of the boom may be summarized as follows. Output and demand in 1972 had been geared up to extremely rapid expansion, at a rate that could not have been sustained. The failure of output to adjust when demand flattened in 1973 caused a huge build-up of stocks, which had later to be worked off. That was one way in which the previous excessive boom contributed to the subsequent recession.

Second, the boom generated various speculative developments.

- Personal indebtedness almost doubled in the two years from mid-1971; this borrowing supported heavy spending on durables and on house purchases. (The counterpart lending by the banks was reflected in a rapid growth of M3, which continued right up to the end of 1973.)
- There was a large speculative element in housing demand: the rapid rise in house prices gave rise to speculative purchases, which in turn raised prices further.

Table 8.12   The 1972–3 boom: expenditure composition

	Contributions to % change in TFE	
	1971–2	1972–3
Consumer expenditure	3.0	2.7
Government current spending	0.8	0.9
Fixed investment	—	1.0
Exports	0.2	1.8
Total final sales	4.0	6.4
Change in stocks	−0.3	2.4
Total final expenditure (TFE)	3.7	8.8
GDP (% change at factor cost)	2.8	7.5

Source: Economic Trends Annual Supplement, 1994.

- There was an equally large speculative element in office building, particularly in London, supported by bank loans, some of which later turned out to be unsound.[23]

Speculative elements in demand inevitably unwind. When the euphoria ceased, these speculative elements went into reverse and added to the recession. The banks shared in this switch of mood: having over-extended credit in the boom, they tightened lending facilities sharply when it broke, which also amplified the downturn (Dow and Saville 1988: 188–90).

8.2.2. The first OPEC recession, 1973–5

The 1973–5 recession was in part (as we have seen) a reaction to the preceding boom. In part it was a reaction to new shocks, in particular the oil price shock and the rapid tightening of monetary policy. The latter has to be seen as reaction to the acceleration of inflation, which itself has to be seen chiefly as the effect of the previous world boom.

Causation was thus complex and interactive. Table 8.11 gives a first rough estimate of the magnitudes of the factors at work: in particular, the effects of the change in the terms of trade, the change in monetary policy, and the change in stockbuilding.[24] These separate causal impulses interacted, and a fuller and more complex assessment will be given at the end of this discussion.

Terms-of-trade effect

First, however, it is necessary to explain the impact of the change in the terms of trade. In the Great Depression of 1929–32, the terms of trade had a favourable effect on the UK: cheaper imports supported demand [s. 6.4]. In the 1973–5 recession, for the first time, a switch in the terms of trade had a strong *unfavourable* effect.[25] That has to be seen as part of the (unusual) concurrence of major recession with major, worldwide inflation; and that in turn as due largely to the exceptional event of the first oil price shock.

The terms-of-trade effect as here defined occurs when import prices (and hence also the total final expenditure deflator, which includes import costs) rise faster than the GDP deflator—the latter here seen as a measure of the home factor income earned on a unit of output.

Import prices rose rapidly in 1973 and 1974, at first because of the depreciation of sterling in 1972, later because of dearer oil and commodities.

---

[23] Speculative euphoria was not however universal. Equities peaked at end-1972 and were declining through most of 1973 (probably reflecting the course of profits, which were no longer expanding much).

[24] As already emphasized [ch. 5.2], the estimates in table 8.11 need to be viewed as rough indications. In this case they over-explain what happened since they leave too little room for confidence effects; they probably overstate the impact of the change in monetary policy.

[25] There had been a similar effect on a smaller scale in the Korean War boom [ch. 7.1].

Table 8.13   Effects of terms of trade on real income, 1972–1975

	% change in average values		
	1972–3	1973–4	1974–5
Analysis of changes in import costs			
Sterling price	23	41	14
of which due to:			
Exchange rate[a]	14	4	9
Foreign currency price	8	36	5
of which[b]			
Oil	1	14	−1
Other commodities	2	5	2
Effects on real domestic purchasing power[c]			
GDP deflator[d]	10	19	25
TFE deflator[e]	14	25	22
Purchasing power of unit factor income[f]	−3	−5	3
Memorandum item:			
Purchasing power of total factor income[g]	5	−6	2

[a] Change in effective rate (from OECD data).
[b] Contribution to change in price of all imports of goods and services.
[c] From *UK National Accounts*, 1993.
[d] Excludes stock appreciation.
[e] Weighted average of import and domestic costs (weights = average 1972–5).
[f] GDP deflator divided by TFE deflator.
[g] Total domestic income divided by TFE deflator.

Source of basic data: CSO, *UK National Accounts* and *Economic Trends*.

Thus, the surge in prices must have taken around six months to affect final prices ('prices in the shops'). Meanwhile dearer stocks had to be financed (i.e. stock appreciation rose), so that the first impact was on firms' finances.[26]

In 1973 import prices rose by a quarter, in 1974 by almost twice as much. Of the first year's rise, more than half was due to the depreciation of sterling [table 8.13]. Of the second year's (even faster) rise, almost a third was due to the rise in the price of oil, about a seventh to that of other commodities. Even though other prices and domestic incomes were now also rising briskly, the rise in import prices was still faster, so that the purchasing power of domestic factor incomes fell in both 1973 and 1974. The oil price accounted for only part of the rise in import prices. But, without that, the latter would not have been so disproportionate, and the terms of trade (on a simple *ceteris paribus* calculation) would not have resulted in any great deterioration in purchasing power in 1974.

The rise in prices subsequently led to an acceleration in the rise in domestic incomes, which in 1975 overtook the rise in final prices, so that, if other things

[26] Profits were also disproportionately affected: see below.

had been unchanged, real domestic purchasing power would have regained some of the loss of the first two years. In the meantime, however, private real incomes were squeezed severely.

The squeeze on consumers was delayed by the predominant practice of cost-plus pricing—which delayed the impact until goods embodying now-more-costly imports had passed through the chain of distribution and come to be sold to final buyers. Because of this delay, the surge in prices must have taken around six months to affect prices in the shops. Cost-plus pricing also meant that the cost of dearer stocks (stock appreciation) was not self-financing. Since selling prices were raised only with delay, and dearer stocks had still to be financed, the first impact was on firms' finances. (Figure 8.7 shows the sharp effect that stock appreciation had in cutting the financial balance of the corporate sector.) When the impact hit final prices, in 1974 and into 1975, that turned the rise in real domestic incomes into a fall, and brought a fall in consumers' real spending. Spending by companies fell much less than proportionately, so that there was a big fall in companies' financial surplus as early as 1973, and in 1974 a switch into deficit.[27]

Other shock effects

The worsening of the terms of trade was heightened by the simultaneous fall in the UK *exchange rate*: it was roughly doubled [see table 8.13]. That must have magnified the acceleration of inflation (and hence the rise in stock appreciation) almost as much. The consequent deflationary effects of depreciation on consumer demand and business spending accompanied the expansionary effect of the fall in the exchange rate on exports and in discouraging imports: the immediate *net* effect of the exchange rate fall on demand may then at first have been quite small.

World trade also fell in 1975. From the viewpoint of a single country, that has to be counted as a third exogenous factor. Its effect on the UK was masked by the fall in the exchange rate, and probably for this reason UK exports fell much less than those of other OECD countries.

Monetary policy was tightened progressively in the course of 1973. The proximate signal to which the authorities reacted was the acceleration in monetary growth (Dow and Saville 1988: ch. 7). But that reflected an unsustainable pace of real expansion, accelerating inflation, and increasingly speculative conditions of demand. Short-term interest rates (banks' base rates) averaged 6 per cent in 1972, 10 per cent in 1973, and 12.5 per cent in 1974.

---

[27] There was a parallel—consequent—swing into deficit in the country's balance of payments. The financial balance of companies swung from +2.1% and 0.3% of GDP in 1972 and 1973 to −2.4% in 1974, a total swing of 4.4% of GDP. This was reflected in the UK's borrowing abroad: the current account balance swung from −0.3% to −1.2% and then to −3.0% of GDP in these years, a total swing of 2.7%. Borrowing diminishes the impact of a cut in income compared with a situation in which borrowing is impossible. But it does not prevent a cut in income having a shock effect on spending, since those whose income has been reduced cannot/do not want to incur indefinite debt.

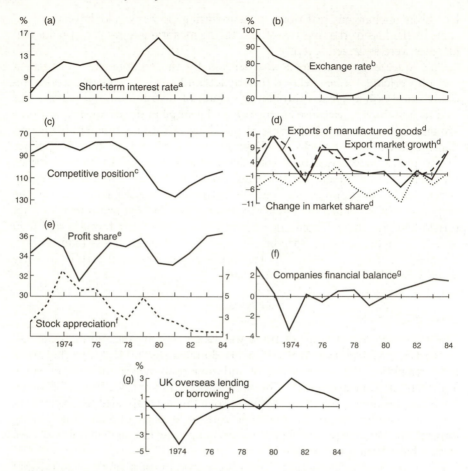

Fig. 8.7   Sundry UK economic indicators, 1972 – 1984

[a] Banks' base rates.
[b] Effective exchange rates, indices 1970(Q1) = 100: from OECD.
[c] IMF Index of normalized relative unit labour costs.
[d] Annual % change
[e] Share of non-employment income in total domestic income
[f] % of total domestic income
[g] Industrial and commercial companies only; expressed as % of GDP at current factor cost.
[h] Current balance of payments as % of GDP at current factor cost.
Sources: CSO, *Economic Trends*; OECD, *Economic Outlook*.

When that appeared insufficient to curb monetary expansion, a form of direct monetary control was reimposed at the end of 1973. The main impact on the economy of monetary tightening was probably felt only in 1974, but more was to come in 1975.

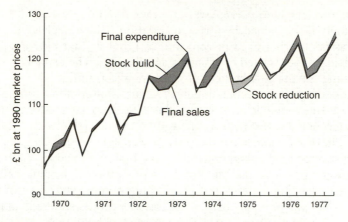

Fig. 8.8 The course of total expenditure by quarters, 1970–1977
Source: as for fig. 8.1.

Delayed reaction of the economy to the 1973 shocks

Though output started to decline only in the fourth quarter of 1973, the turnround in total final sales occurred nine months earlier. (Thus, at 1973(Q1) *output* was up 10 per cent compared with the first quarter in the year before: after that it stayed almost flat.) The turnround of *sales* was then even more dramatic [fig. 8.8]. Consumer expenditure rose 8.5 per cent in the year to 1973(Q1), then fell 3 per cent in the year following; while fixed investment rose 10 per cent in the year to 1973(Q1), then fell 2 per cent. Exports continued to rise, though more slowly, and started to fall only at the end of 1974. As already noted, output failed to adjust to the slowdown in final sales and must have been 1.5 per cent higher than if it had kept pace (i.e. than if there had been no stock-build). The stockbuilding was halted in 1974, but was reversed only in 1975.

The first point to be explained is what caused the original sudden check to the course of consumption. That it was not due to the oil price rise is clear from the dates. Import prices began at the end of 1972 to rise at an accelerated pace, and by 1973(Q2) were 20 per cent above the year before.[28] But that took some time to affect final prices, whose rise started to take off only after mid-1973; only then did the rise in consumers' real incomes (RPDI) start to slow down.

Consumer spending, however, paused much earlier, in 1973(Q1), first for a temporary reason—there was heavy buying in anticipation of the imposition of value added tax in April, and a pause afterwards—and second because,

---

[28] Primary producers' imports from Europe were affected earlier, but UK exports were shielded by the 1972 depreciation of sterling.

underlying this irregularity, there was an upward jump in saving.[29] Such a rise would usually be explained by a rise in inflation (which depletes the value of financial assets bearing fixed or zero interest); but at that date (as just seen) inflation had not yet started on its great acceleration. The explanation may be that consumer saving rose because of growing uncertainties.

Fixed investment, after expanding in 1972, also slowed down during 1973. In part this was due to public investment, where the slowdown reflected long-term factors determining investment by the public utilities [ch. 7.4.2]. Most of the slowdown, however, came from the private sector. Housebuilding began to be restrained by credit rationing imposed by the building societies. (At that time, when market rates rose the building societies rationed lending rather than raising their lending rates.) Industrial and commercial investment also hesitated. That was probably because of the way profits suffered, and because of the diversion of finance to pay for dearer stockholding.[30] After mid-year there was also a progressive rise in interest rates.

The total effects

After 1975, output growth was resumed on a path almost 10 per cent below the pre-1973 trend line. The calculations in this study do not permit a precise allocation of this effect among the contributory causes. Three groups of factors were probably of roughly equal importance:

1. *The after-effects of the 1972–3 boom* Even without additional exogenous shocks, that would have reduced consumer spending, fixed investment, and stocks, and could well have stopped expansion, i.e. produced a 'growth recession'.
2. *External effects* The terms-of-trade effect of rising commodity and oil prices probably (given the lags in passing on costs) fell chiefly on investment and stockholding. There was also a slowing of export growth.
3. *The tightening of monetary policy*, imposed to counter inflation and restrain the boom in demand.

The amplifier effects of these exogenous shocks and of inherited effects were large because both consumer and business confidence were severely shocked.

Comparison with EC countries' experience

The dating of recessions in the EC and USA is established here on the basis of the figures for output and unemployment shown in figure 8.5 and follows the

---

[29] See the contemporary analysis in the *Bank of England Quarterly Bulletin* for this period.

[30] Profits were affected disproportionately because of two features of firms' behaviour which earlier analysis has illustrated. Because firms failed to cut employment in proportion to output, output per head showed a fall, not the usual trend rise. Firms also failed at first to raise their prices enough to compensate for the lower path of output per head [ch. 2.4], so that for a number of years the share of profits remained abnormally low.

principles followed earlier for the UK [ch. 2.2]. In other countries the downturn was broadly similar, but differed in degree.

The loss of output compared with pre-1973 trend was greatest in Japan, and least in the United States. The situation of the other EC countries, exposed to much the same shocks as the UK, was more nearly comparable; and it is useful as a check to compare UK experience with theirs.

In other EC countries, although there was no absolute fall in output, the recession, measured as a shortfall below previous trend (previously considerably faster than in the UK), appears slightly larger than in the UK [table 8.14]. Among explanatory factors, the rise in import prices must have been similar to that of the UK, except that their exchange rates did not fall. The latter also meant that their exports—unlike those of the UK—fell in sympathy with world trade.

8.2.3. The second OPEC recession, 1979–82

I will argue that the recession of 1979–82 was due in part to the second oil shock, just as the 1973–5 recession had been partly due to the first. The two recessions were similar in many ways; but there were also important differences, of which table 8.11 gives a first indication.

Table 8.14   The first OPEC recession: the UK and EC compared

Categories of expenditure	Contribution to % change in final expenditure					
	UK			Other EC 11		
	Annual rate of growth		Shortfall over 2 years[a]	Annual rate of growth		Shortfall over 2 years[a]
	1960 –73 (1)	1973 –75 (2)		1960 –73 (1)	1973 –75 (2)	
Consumer Spending	1.5	−0.4	−3.8	2.6	0.9	−3.4
Fixed investment	0.4	−0.3	−1.4	1.2	−0.9	−4.2
Exports	0.5	0.4	−0.2	1.4	0.4	−2.0
Final sales[b]	2.9	0.3	−5.2	5.7	0.8	−9.8
Investment in stocks	0.0	−1.3	−2.6	0.0	−0.5	−1.0
Total final expenditure	2.9	−1.2	−8.2	5.8	0.1	−11.4
(% change in GDP)	(2.9)	(−1.2)	(−8.2)	(5.1)	(0.6)	(−9.0)

[a] Over the recession period the shortfall is twice $((1)-(2))$.
[b] Includes government consumption (not shown separately).
Source: *OECD National Accounts.*

One important difference was that by now North Sea oil production was rising fast, which put the UK well on the way to being self-sufficient in oil. That did not make the price shock less, since North Sea oil was priced at the world price. But it transformed the balance of payments, underpinned confidence in sterling, and contributed to a large rise in the exchange rate. The second OPEC recession came at the same time as the election victory of Mrs Thatcher; and a second main difference from the first recession was the more restrictive fiscal and monetary policy adopted by the new government. The response of the economy was also somewhat different this time. In particular, disinvestment in stocks was only a small part of the shortfall in expenditure.

The present analysis suggests that the 1979 recession was due to four main exogenous shocks: the loss of exports, fiscal policy, monetary policy, and an underlying rise in import prices.[31] Each seems to have been important, and they interacted as follows.

Fiscal policy

The 1979 budget was deflationary (large reductions in direct taxation were more than offset by large increases in indirect taxation and by some reductions in spending); the budgets of 1980 and 1981 were deflationary, too. The present estimates suggest that the impact was to reduce total demand by somewhat under 1 per cent in both 1980 and 1981, and by over 1 per cent in 1982—in total, a very sizeable effect.[32]

Monetary policy

Minimum Lending Rate was raised progressively from 6.5 per cent in early 1978 to 14 per cent in early 1979, and to 17 per cent by November. As in the first recession, the overt reason was not directly the state of the balance of payments, nor yet the rate of inflation. It was rather to control the rapid growth of broad money, which the new government had made the proximate aim of policy. The attempt to control monetary growth was not successful.[33] But the resulting rise in interest rates probably had a large effect on demand.

From the very beginning of 1980, the combined impact of the fiscal and monetary policy must have been large. The stance of policy had been long premeditated, and the deflationary effect it was going to have might seem

---

[31] i.e. a rise in import prices expressed in terms of foreign currency, whose effect on the economy was masked by the rise in the exchange rate.

[32] To measure the oil price shock, it is best to redefine the UK economy to exclude North Sea output from GDP and treat North Sea output as an import to the UK: that allows inclusion of the effect of dearer oil in the terms-of-trade effect (also appropriately redefined). For consistency, this also requires that receipts of petroleum revenue tax (PRT) (which reflected dearer oil) should not be included in the estimate of the impact of fiscal policy (since they figure in the terms-of-trade effect). Assuming that changes made in April affected total spending in the following calendar year, the fiscal impact (estimated in app. A5) can be adjusted as shown in table 8.15.

[33] The 'Corset' control did not prevent a big rise in bank lending from the beginning of 1980 (Dow and Saville 1988: table 10.1), and was itself removed in mid-1980.

Table 8.15 Fiscal impact of 1979 oil price shock

	1980	1981	1982
		(% changes)	
Total fiscal impact including PRT[a]	1.1	1.5	1.5
PRT	0.4	0.6	0.3
Total impact, excluding PRT[b]	0.7	0.9	1.2

[a] Petroleum revenue tax.
[b] This row roughly concurs with the estimates in Britton (1991: table 14.10).

Sources: as in ch. 5.2 and CSO, *National Accounts*.

obvious. The new government did not think in those terms, however, and probably did not take into account how demand and output would be affected by policy, or how the oil price shock would reinforce that effect.[34]

The exchange rate, oil, the terms of trade and exports

The rise in the exchange rate and in the price of oil interacted in complex ways. The strands need to be set out separately.

The exchange rate   With some bumpiness, the effective exchange rate rose in the course of 1979 by about 13 per cent, and by as much again in the course of 1980. There has been dispute whether this rise was due to (belated) recognition by markets of how North Sea oil would transform the UK's balance of payments, or to the rise in UK interest rates, or was a market reaction to the advent of a Conservative government and the policies it might adopt. It probably reflected all three, and thus can be regarded in a broad sense as a policy effect. Certainly the government took no steps to limit the rise in the exchange rate, seeing it as helpful in reducing the rate of inflation.

The rise in the exchange rate (as always) had opposing effects—practically stopping export growth, but cushioning the rise in import costs and hence its effect on domestic demand (see further below). In the long run, the effect of a fall in the exchange rate is to increase demand; but in the short run its opposing effects probably cancelled out, and had little net effect during the recession years.

The rise in oil prices   Though the United Kingdom was now close to self-sufficiency in oil, the rise in oil prices had much the same effect as in the first recession. The rise in North Sea oil prices (in line with world oil prices) brought a large increase in the profits of North Sea companies, some 85 per cent of which accrued to the UK government as taxes; and, given the kind of fiscal

---

[34] All Budgets since 1948 had been justified in the Budget speech by arguments based on the impact of the Budget on total demand. That practice was discontinued in 1980.

Table 8.16 Effects of terms of trade on real income, 1977–1981

	1977–8	1978–9	1979–80	1980–1	1977–81
			(annual % changes)		
(a) Analysis of changes in input costs[a]					
Foreign currency price of input	2	15	25	13	67
of which, due to:					
Oil prices		6	10	6	24
Commodities prices		—	2	1	3
Other imports[b]		9	13	6	39
Exchange rate[c]	−1	−5	−9	−3	−17
Sterling price of input[d]	1	9	13	10	38
(b) Effects on real domestic purchasing power					
Non-oil GDP deflator[e]	13	13	18	9	63
TFE deflator[f]	10	12	17	10	57
Non-oil domestic real income					
per unit of output[g]	2	1	1	—	4
Memorandum item:					
Purchasing power of total					
non-oil domestic income[g]	3	4	−4	−3	0

[a] Input is defined as imports *plus* output of North Sea oil and gas.
[b] Other goods *plus* services.
[c] OECD estimates of effective rate: Bank of England figures show a bigger fall in year 2 but no fall in year 4.
[d] Index of sterling prices of input = index of foreign commodity price *times* index of effective exchange rate.
[e] Factor cost deflator: this measures non-oil domestic factor income per unit of output.
[f] Weighted average of sterling price of input *plus* domestic costs, weights being 1970–6 average. (This eliminates distortions due to stock fluctuations.)
[g] GDP deflator divided by TFE deflator.

Source of basic data: CSO, *National Accounts* and *Economic Trends*.

policy being followed, this additional revenue was not spent by the government. The effect on the real economy (though not on the reserves) was, then, much the same as if the profits had been received—and held unspent—by OPEC producers.

In percentage terms, the rise in world oil prices in the second oil price shock was less than the first [table 8.16]; but in absolute terms, the starting point being so much higher, it contributed as much to the rise in UK 'input' costs.[35]

[35] Since most of the oil consumed was now home-produced, the rise in the oil import bill (as already noted) fails to measure the impact of dearer oil on the UK price structure. Table 8.16 treats the North Sea as if it were a separate country outside the UK and North Sea output as import; i.e., North Sea output is subtracted from GDP and added to imports. Average value series are then calculated for imports plus North Sea oil output (= 'input'), and for non-oil GDP.

As in 1973–5, that constituted less than half the total rise in the value of imports, but it was a large addition to the price rise.

Combined impact of a higher oil price and a higher exchange rate   This time the rise in the price of oil, instead of being preceded as in the earlier recession by a large fall in the exchange rate, was accompanied by a large exchange rate rise. That protected home demand from the impact of dearer oil, and shifted the restrictive effect to exports. Thus, the rise in the exchange rate almost halved the rise in 'input' prices compared with what they otherwise would have been and greatly dampened the effect of dearer oil; and there was no cut, as on the first occasion (but rather a continued rise), in the purchasing power of unit domestic factor incomes [see table 8.16]: purchasing power fell only because fewer factors were employed.

While the rise in the exchange rate protected domestic purchasing power in this way from a terms-of-trade loss, that advantage had to be paid for. In the first recession, the fall in the exchange rate had largely shielded exports from the effect of the fall in world trade: in the second, the opposite was the case. UK export markets continued to expand, but UK export growth was halted and then reversed. Probably also because of these exchange rate changes, imports declined only a little in the second recession, whereas in the first they had fallen sharply. Thus, exchange rate appreciation both gave a net addition to the deflationary effect of dearer 'input' and at the same time deflected its impact—offsetting the effect on domestic demand that the latter would have had, but worsening the balance of trade.

The response of the economy

This recession, like the previous one, put companies under great financial pressure. They were less affected by the terms of trade, and stock appreciation rose less; but margins had never fully recovered from the first recession, so that companies' financial position had been attenuated during five very lean years,[36] and now again fell. Probably for that reason, firms were much quicker to cut back when demand fell away.

Employment was curbed almost as quickly as output fell. Hence, while productivity again fell to a permanently lower growth path, it fell less; and unemployment rose much more promptly and steeply than in the first recession [table 8.17].[37] Since productivity on the second occasion fell less, profits might have been expected to be less affected. But the rise in the exchange rate bit

---

[36] As already noted, productivity had never recovered to its old growth path; and it was only in 1978 or so that firms' pricing caught up with that [ch. 2.4]. Till then, therefore, profit margins had remained much lower than before 1973.

[37] It was said at the time that the political shift to the right at the national level in 1979 was mirrored by a shift of power and confidence within firms, away from unions and towards management. That could have made firms quicker to sack workers and insist on economy. If there was such a 'Thatcher' effect, it will have worked along with financial pressures.

Table 8.17   Contrasted behaviour in respect of productivity and unemployment growth in the two recessions

	Periods of four years from output peak to recovery of peak		
	Output (1980=100)	Consequent change in:	
		Output per head (1980=100)	Unemployment[b] (% rise)
First recession			
1973	95.3	95.5	2.2 ⎫
1977	98.2	99.3	4.9 ⎬ 2.7
Growth (%)	3.0	3.9	
Potential growth (%)[a]	11.6	10.0	
Potential growth lost (%)	8.6	6.1	
Second recession			
1979	102.3	101.3	6.1 ⎫
1983	102.8	108.8	11.4 ⎬ 5.3
Growth (%)	0.5	7.4	
Potential growth (%)[a]	11.6	10.0	
Potential growth lost (%)	11.1	2.6	

[a] Growth over four years at pre-1973 rate.
[b] Lags output by one year.

Source of basic data: CSO, *National Accounts* and *Economic Trends*.

deep into the profits of industries producing tradeables, and corporate profits fell as much in the second recession as the first. Stocks were cut much more promptly even though on a smaller scale; this time firms had kept stocks low before the recession. Fixed investment was cut back more promptly and more largely than on the first occasion, as if firms were now more ready to revise expectations downward.

The above reactions comprised in large part the secondary reactions to adverse shocks, and thus may be classed as amplifying effects. The cutback in stocks and in fixed investment, however, will also have been due partly to the rise in interest rates. The total effect of the multiplying mechanisms must have been large, as in the first recession.[38]

The general conclusion is that the recession can well be explained as the direct and indirect results of a number of identifiable demand shocks.

---

[38] There was a current account deficit in 1980 and later years up to 1986. This is the more noteworthy in that the balance of payments was now benefiting largely from North Sea oil (for which see *Bank of England Quarterly Bulletin* 64, (1982), table 6).

Table 8.18 The second OPEC recession: the UK and EC compared

Categories of expenditure	Contribution to % change in final expenditure					
	UK			Other EC 11		
	Annual rate of growth		Shortfall over 3 yrs[a]	Annual rate of growth		Shortfall over 3 yrs[a]
	1975 –79 (1)	1979 –81 (2)		1975 –79 (1)	1979 –82 (2)	
Consumer spending	1.2	0.2	−3.0	1.6	0.4	−3.6
Fixed investment	0.4	−0.5	−2.7	0.5	−0.3	−2.4
Exports	0.6	—	−1.8	1.3	0.6	−2.1
Final sales[b]	2.6	−0.1	−8.1	3.8	1.1	−8.1
Investment in stocks	0.0	−0.5	−1.5	0.4	−0.6	−3.0
Total final expenditure	2.6	−0.6	−9.6	4.2	0.8	−10.2
(% change in GDP)	(2.6)	(−1.5)	(−12.3)	(3.5)	(1.0)	(−7.5)

[a] The shortfall is thrice ((1) − (2)).
[b] Includes government consumption (not shown separately).

Source: OECD National Accounts.

Comparison with EC experience

In contrast to the UK, output in the other EC countries showed no fall in the second recession. But if recession is measured as the shortfall below the previous trend rate of growth, it again appears (as in the first OPEC recession) comparable in size to that in the UK [table 8.18]. The start of the recession in the EC has to be placed at 1979, and its ending at 1982, putting its length at three years as for the UK [fig. 8.4].

There were special features in the UK, stemming (as noted) from the severity of policy, and the coming on-stream of North Sea oil. But along with these differences were features common to the UK and other EC countries: the adverse shift in the underlying terms of trade as a result of the rise in the world price of oil and (less important) of other commodities; the inflationary twist this gave to prices; and, in reaction, the deflationary bias this gave to policy.

Elsewhere in the EC, policy did not shift towards deflation so quickly, or so severely, as in the UK.[39] Other EC countries experienced not severe appreci-ation in their exchange rates (+25 per cent change in effective rates), but

[39] The estimates by Price and Muller (1984) probably exaggerate the difference, for part of the appearance of severity is due to the inclusion in UK government revenue of taxation of North Sea profits. Even apart from this, my estimates [app. A5] are considerably lower than Price and Muller's.

moderate depreciation (–5 to –10 per cent). Real incomes were not protected as in the UK, but, as a result, EC countries had the benefit of a generally better export performance.

Essentially, then, the UK and other EC countries were hit by the same external shocks, with broadly similar results. Thus, the kind of account that provides a plausible line of explanation of UK experience seems, with suitable adjustment, also to explain events in other EC countries.

8.2.4. The resumption of growth after the two recessions

Although growth in the UK started up again after each recession (i.e. in 1975 and 1982), it was at only a moderate pace, and for some years there was no true recovery as the term is used in this study [ch. 2.2]. Unemployment had hardly started to fall after the first recession before the next one started. After the second, there were three years of slow or hesitant growth (1982–4), and unemployment did not start to fall until after the boom of 1985–8 was underway [ch. 9]. In neither case would output growth appear to have been due to exogenous shocks. There were, in particular, no strong policy initiatives: on each occasion interest rates retreated only gradually from their high points in the recession, while fiscal policy was inactive rather than expansionary. This tends to support the hypothesis proposed earlier in this study [ch. 3.2] that, in the absence of forces to the contrary, growth tends to resume at about the capacity rate.

8.3. Assessment of the 1970s experience

It is now useful to stand back from proposing detailed explanations to consider in a broader way what happened in the 1970s, and what it shows about the nature of modern economies. This section notes some broad conclusions, compares present results with other studies, and comments on the policy dilemma during this period.

8.3.1. General conclusions

In some previous recessions there seems room for doubt about causation. In the case of the two UK recessions of the 1970s, there seems to me little doubt.

- In 1973–5 three factors were clearly operative, and together could account for most of the recession: the depressive *aftermath of the* 1972–3 *boom*; the fall in domestic expenditure resulting from the deterioration in the *terms of trade*, coupled with the failure of OPEC to offset this by spending its real income gain; and the tightening of *domestic monetary and fiscal policy*, in response to the acceleration of inflation arising largely from the escalation of world commodity and oil prices.

- In 1979–82 two factors were operative: the second, similar, *OPEC shock*; and strongly *restrictive policy*, which was partly counter-inflationary and partly a reflection of the new government's general ideological stance.

The factors at work were thus unusual, and were unlike what had happened in the two previous major recessions. There is reason to believe that in large recessions changes in expectations ('confidence') are especially important [s. 5.1]. Allowing for confidence effects, the two OPEC recessions in the UK seem entirely explicable.

Other European countries experienced similar recessions; and, with some differences, similar factors appear to explain the output shortfalls there also. That increases the credibility of the explanation here offered.

In this study the depth of a recession is measured by the shortfall of output below previous trend; judged in that way, the UK recessions of the 1970s approached the scale of the UK depression of the 1930s. For other industrial countries as a whole, they were probably larger. (The Great Depression affected some countries severely but others little.) Because recessions are not usually depicted this way, it is not often noticed how very large a disaster these two recessions were. (Looked at as the year-by-year change in GDP, the two recessions may seem little different from the minor fluctuations of the postwar epoch of 1945–72.)

After-effects of the recessions

As in other large recessions, the ground lost during these recessions was not made good afterwards: output appears to have started to grow again along a lower growth path than before. That implies a similarly lower growth path for demand. One has therefore to ask what factors on the demand side resulted in the setback not being reversed (a question not usually put in this way). Part of the answer is that the downward displacement of the productivity growth path itself implies (by the national income identities) a lowering of the level of real factor income, and thus of demand, compared with a projection of the old trend.

The other half of the answer is that the downward shocks that caused the recessions were not followed later by comparable upward shocks that reversed their effect. Fiscal and monetary policies ceased to be contractionary, but did not become strongly expansionary. Similarly, OPEC countries, having first underspent their income, did not subsequently vastly overspend [see table 8.4]. (After some years OPEC countries did exceed their annual income a little; but the stock of financial assets built up in each of the recession phases remained largely intact.) Since there were no large upward shocks to reverse the setback, no reverse multiplier processes got activated either.

If demand had recovered in full, it is unlikely that it could have been met: for the supply setback could not have been fully reversed. About half the supply loss took the form of higher unemployment [fig. 8.2], which is (in time) reversible; the other half took the form of the setback to productivity growth—which my earlier theorizing [ch. 4.2] suggests is not reversible, and which certainly shows little sign of being reversed.

8.3.2. Other accounts of the 1970s recessions

The present analysis differs from most other studies in rating the scale of the recessions as larger; in attempting a more quantitative estimate of their causes; and in putting more nearly exclusive influence on shocks to demand as the cause. Much of these differences stem from the fact that other studies define recessions in terms of absolute falls in output, which minimizes what happened, while the present study defines recessions in terms of cumulative shortfalls below previous trend. There appear to have been few attempts to explain head-on why the recessions occurred—in part because some of the discussion has been incidental to other purposes; and in part because attention was not on the cumulative shortfall from trend.

One of the earliest of these recession studies was the OECD McCracken Report of 1977, written before the second OPEC recession (McCracken *et al.* 1977). Like the present study, it saw the recession as caused primarily by demand influences, resulting both from the preceding boom and subsequent steps to control it and from externally generated shocks. A notable contribution to the discussion after OPEC II was Buiter and Miller (1981). Their main purpose was to analyse the 'change in regime' represented by the Thatcher Government; but in doing so they gave a clear account of the second recession, emphasizing (as here) the effects of fiscal and monetary policy, but saying little about shocks originating externally (though these were also important). They failed to recognize the full scale of the recession in Europe.[40]

In the National Institute conference volume devoted to 'slower growth' and edited by Matthews (1982), attention concentrated on the supply side. Though inadequacy of demand was accepted as having been important, the emphasis was not on why demand became inadequate but on why there was a slowdown in productivity growth, which was conceived as a separate question. Looking back at it now, it does not seem that the discussion cast much light on that puzzle.

There have been two different approaches since then to explaining the slowdown in productivity growth. The first, with Lindbeck (1983) as an example, seeks to explain it as the result of long-run economic and social factors. According to Lindbeck, the slowdown reflected trends in Western economies that had been developing for a decade or more, e.g. gradually accelerating inflation, falling profit shares, growing malfunctioning of markets,

---

[40] Buiter and Miller remark e.g. that Germany and France were little affected by the recession—a comment that would not have been made had they been looking at the degree to which output fell below previous trend.

increasing failure to respond to economic incentives, and the 'fading away' of circumstances previously favourable to growth—in short, to a great many 'distortions, disincentives, inflexibilities and uncertainties', which Lindbeck calls, no doubt half seriously, 'an emerging arteriosclerosis of the Western economic systems'. That explanation fits awkwardly with the facts, however—the setbacks were abrupt, occurring about 1973 and again in 1979, and are best described not as a slowing down, but as an absolute fall—and I find it unconvincing.

Bruno and Sachs (1985) attempt an econometric explanation of the performance of the major industrial countries in the period of the two 1970s recessions. They attribute the rise in unemployment in part to high real wages—a view against which there are I think strong counter-arguments [ch. 3.4]—and in part to lack of demand, caused (as in the present analysis) by terms-of-trade loss and restrictive monetary policy. Bruno and Sachs see the fall in productivity growth (as here) as an effect of the fall in output growth.

Britton's (1991) study focuses on UK macroeconomic policy since 1974, less on the vicissitudes of the economy. Estimates are given of the effect of fiscal and monetary policy (in the first case similar to those given here). The two major recessions are not regarded as being on so major a scale as in the present account; a change in attitudes to work is invoked to explain the slowdown in productivity.

Other studies which contain *inter alia* discussion of the 1970s recessions include Boltho's (1982) introduction to the symposium he edited on Europe; Llewellyn, Potter, and Samuelson's (1985) book on economic analysis at the OECD; and the essays on stagflation edited by Emerson (1984). These are generally eclectic and combine Keynesian elements with socioeconomic types of explanation or with the High Real Wage thesis.

Econometrically based explanations

The studies that are closest to the present approach are four econometric exercises by Budd (1981), Worswick (1981), Artis *et al.* (1984), and Saville and Gardiner (1986). This is not an accident, since they were in effect precursors of the present study.[41] Like it, these studies sought to explain the shortfall of output for a projection of its previous trend rate of growth, and follow a similar methodology. All used econometric models developed for short-term analysis and forecasting, and treated as exogenous the sort of explanatory variables usually so treated in such models (world trade, world prices of commodities and oil, indicators of UK fiscal policy, and, to represent monetary policy, UK real interest rates).

The first three studies dealt only with the first OPEC recession. That by Saville and Gardiner (1986) sought to explain the (considerably greater)

---

[41] The studies by Budd (1981) and Worswick (1981) were commissioned by the Bank of England (during my time as a director of the Bank) for discussion in the Bank's Panel of Academic Consultants. The paper by Saville and Gardiner (1986) was undertaken at an earlier stage of work on the present book.

shortfall of output compared with its pre-1973 trend over the course of the two OPEC recessions. All these studies had partial, but only partial, success—explaining something like half of the shortfall of output growth compared with the immediately previous trend. Saville and Gardiner attempted also to explain UK price behaviour in an analogous manner, with less success.

One reason for the partial failure of these studies may be that they underestimated multiplier effects. The present study has suggested that changes in expectations play a larger role in large than in small recessions (on the experience of which short-term models are largely based). The way in which output changes generate changes in expectations is clearly not well modelled in the available models and may indeed defy formalization. The implications are further discussed later [ch. 10.5].

8.3.3. The relative importance of policy

It is not the purpose of this study to pass judgement on the rightness or wrongness of the policies that governments adopted in the 1970s recessions. It is however relevant to discuss some of the difficulties they faced.

The external forces that hit economies like the UK, and created both the recession and the inflation of these years, were very large. They were probably, indeed, too large for any government to counteract, more especially given governments' limited understanding of what was happening, and their limited political readiness to act on any decisively large scale.

The fact that the problem consisted of both recession and inflation at the same time, and that Keynesian demand management—the conventional wisdom for twenty-five years—had no answer to it, has been held to discredit Keynesianism. But no other policy emerged with an answer; and I think none could. In practice, governments in all countries adopted restrictive policies to some degree.

An idealized version of the logic of this course can be stated as follows. The deterioration in the terms of trade inevitably means a loss of real income for countries in the position of the UK.[42] If the factors of production (more particularly, wage-earners) simply accept, speedily and without demur, the fact of their impoverishment, then recession and inflation will be limited to the effect of the initial terms-of-trade deterioration. If they insist on 'compensation' for their loss, this will cause an indefinite perpetuation of inflation, while not reducing at all the inevitable real income loss. The case for a restrictive policy intervention is that it will encourage acceptance of the inevitable, and thus lessen and shorten the scale of inflation.

The disadvantage of such restrictive intervention is that it will inflict additional real loss. By reducing domestic output more than otherwise, the

---

[42] Oil-consuming countries as a bloc inevitably had to borrow so long as OPEC countries had an income higher than they were able or willing to spend; and most of them, like the UK, did run current account deficits.

growth path of productivity is lowered further; and this results (on the arguments of this study) not in a transitory and perhaps brief additional loss of productive capacity, but in a significant permanent impoverishment.

The policy followed may have prevented much larger inflation; but it was not immediately effective in moderating claims; i.e., there was still a lengthy cost–price spiral. It is therefore unclear to me what the best strategy would have been. Even if the 'commonsense' course of going some way towards countering inflation by deflation is accepted, just how far along that path is right? It is common to say that by the time of the second recession governments had learnt the wisdom of countering inflation boldly. I doubt where wisdom lay; and I also doubt whether governments had learnt and did act differently: inflation was less in the second recession, but so probably were the forces making for inflation.[43]

It would be truer to say that in both recessions policy was in fact extremely confused. Governments could not but be aware that what was happening was unusual, but typically they did not fully understand what. In neither recession, I think, did the British government of the day know, when it tightened policy crucially, that a recession was about to happen; certainly it did not know its scale. Nor, while inevitably aware of accelerating inflation, did it understand how much was from abroad, and thus in effect half outside its control. It would be wrong for economists, in hindsight, to suppose that governments at the time took a fully realistic look at the situation, and made a conscious choice among the options.

Recovery, when it occurred, was not in any way a tribute to policy. Inflation did wane—partly because the economy was so depressed, which was partly the (unintended) result of policy; partly because world commodity prices eased (as did the world price of oil, especially after 1985); and partly because, when expansion is resumed, rising productivity gradually attenuates a wage–price spiral. The waning of inflation, furthermore, was not the cause of the reawakening of economic growth. Modern economies do grow, and given half a chance the growth process will start up. But after a severe recession it takes at least a period of years for profits to be restored and confidence to revive.

The dilemma for policy was particularly acute on the occasion of these two recessions because (unusually) each was accompanied by strong inflation. But some element of a dilemma is always present. The relative impotence of

---

[43] It is often said that by the time of the second oil shock policy-makers had become wiser; and had 'learnt the need for caution and the need to maintain discipline to prevent a sustained rise in inflation' (Britton 1991: 129). I doubt this. The *rhetoric* of policy was certainly different; but it is not clear how different policy was. Comparative estimates of fiscal policy impact are difficult and unreliable [app. A5]. But what international data are available suggest that the fiscal stance of the major countries was only a little tighter in 1979 and 1980 than in 1973 and 1974 (see Price and Muller's 1984 estimates, quoted in Llewellyn *et al*. 1985: 32). The tightening of monetary policy in Europe, then, was a reaction not to inflation as such, but to US policy, which under Volcker's inspiration pursued stricter monetary targeting at the end of 1979. Other countries were driven to tighten also, to protect themselves from the exchange rate consequences.

policy at this juncture needs to be remembered when we come at the end of this study to discuss the possibilities of policy more generally [ch. 12]. One broad lesson—both for moderating inflation and for restoring full-capacity working after a recession—will be that the dilemmas of policy can be resolved only over lengthy periods of adjustment.

Appendix A8   The Inflationary Surges of the 1970s

This appendix reports the results of an econometric analysis of the cause of inflation in the UK in the period 1970–82, and a similar analysis for the eleven other members of the European Community (EC) at that time. Both UK recessions of the 1970s were accompanied by a new wave of inflation [fig. 8.5].

On the occasion of the first recession, the rate of inflation in the UK rose from 7 per cent in 1972 to 23 per cent in 1975; on the second occasion, from 10 per cent in 1978 to 17 per cent in 1980. (Inflation is here measured as the rate of change in final prices, chosen as the most comprehensive measure of price.) In 1974–5, prices in the UK accelerated half as much again as in Europe generally, chiefly because of the 10 per cent depreciation of sterling in 1972 and the effect of the 1973 threshold agreements.[44]

At the time of OPEC II, sterling *appreciated* by 13 or 14 per cent. That on its own tended to reduce the price rise in the UK; but the switch from direct to indirect taxation in 1979 worked the other way, so that prices rose about as much in the UK as on the Continent. As might be expected, given the closed nature of the US economy, inflation in the United States accelerated less than in Europe.

Table A8.1 shows the results of an econometric analysis of inflation in the UK in the period 1970–82.[45] Four explanatory variables were tested:

1. the change in final prices lagged one year ($DEFDA-1$ or $DEFD-1$) (this variable was included because previous studies suggested that, as a result of wage–price interaction, inflationary or deflationary shock to prices will iterate on a diminishing scale);
2. the contemporaneous change in import prices (DIP);
3. a variable to represent the pressure of demand, of which the most successful was the percentage deviation of GDP from a simple trend fitted to the period 1970–82, lagged one year ($YDV-1$); other measures tested and rejected were unemployment and a measure based on responses to CBI enquiries about capacity utilization in manufacturing;
4. the lagged percentage growth on M3 and M1 (in view of the widespread belief that the acceleration of inflation was due to monetary expansion).

Approaching the data without strong prior theoretical preconceptions, two possible interpretations emerge from the analysis:

1. The accelerations and subsequent decelerations of inflation were due to variations in the pressure of demand ($YDV-1$) and in import prices (DIP); together these could account for 85 per cent of the variation in the dependent variable.

---

[44] Under these agreements, the government had agreed that if retail price rises exceeded a stated threshold figure, wage increases would be augmented (per cent for per cent) to compensate for the excess. The undertaking was not expected initially to be activated, but world commodity prices rose far more than expected. It is reasonable to believe that the operation of the threshold agreements added 10% to the price level over and above what would otherwise have happened. (It was not possible to test the size of the effect in the econometric analysis presented below.)

[45] The results shown in table A8.1 are similar to those of Britton (1991: 267–81), which are for a somewhat longer period (1970–87). The measure of inflation used in table 8.8 was the annual change in final prices *adjusted to exclude stock appreciation* from the value of expenditure ($DEFDA$). On this definition, changes in prices reflect contemporary cost changes without delay. The alternative is to use unadjusted data and allow for lags. That too was done: the correlations were similar but slightly weaker.

Table A8.1   Correlation analysis of UK inflation, 1970–1982

Dependent variable

$\Delta FEDA$ = annual change in final expenditure deflator adjusted for stock appreciation.

Independent variables

YDV_{-1} = deviation of GDP from trend fitted for 1970–82, lagged one year.

ΔIP = annual change in deflator of imports (goods and services).

$\Delta FEDA_{-1} = \Delta FEDA$ lagged one year.

$\Delta M3_{-2}$ = annual change in M3 (broad money), lagged two years.

(a) *Simple correlation*

	YDV_{-1}	ΔIP	$\Delta FEDA_{-1}$	$\Delta M3_{-2}$
YDV_{-1}		0.59	0.28	0.51
ΔIP			0.20	0.66
$\Delta FEDA_{-1}$				0.58

(b) *Multiple correlation* (dependent variable = $\Delta FEDA$)

Equation	Constant	YDV_{-1}	ΔIP	$\Delta FEDA_{-1}$	$\Delta M3_{-2}$	$\bar{R}^2$
One independent variable						
(1)	12.25	1.79				0.63
(2)	8.08		0.37			0.49
(3)	(5.61)			0.57		0.28
(4)	4.65				0.65	0.65
Two independent variables						
(5)	5.51	1.08	0.19			0.85
(6)	7.57	1.55		0.38		0.26
(7)	(3.04)		0.32	0.44		0.68
Three independent variables						
(8)	5.51	1.08	0.19	0.36		0.85
(9)	5.90	1.21		(0.19)	0.33	0.85
Four independent variables						
(10)	5.21	1.04	(0.12)	0.25	0.21	0.87

Inflation is defined as annual change in final expenditure deflator adjusted to exclude stock appreciation.

Deflator of imports is not adjusted to include North Sea oil.

Source of basic data: CSO, *National Accounts* and *Economic Trends*.

2. Alternatively, the observed behaviour of inflation can be explained as an effect of changes in the rate of growth of broad money lagged two years ($DM3-2$). The results could suggest that broad money on its own explains two-thirds of the variation in the rate of inflation (equation (4)) or 85 per cent when the pressure of demand is also included (equation (10)). On this interpretation, neither past price change nor import price change greatly improved the explanation.

Table A8.2 Correlation analysis of inflation in other EC countries, 1970–1982.
(a) *Simple correlation*

	ΔIP	ΔFED_{-1}	YDV_{-1}
ΔIP		0.07	0.22
ΔFED_{-1}			−0.05

(b) *Multiple correlation* (dependent variable=ΔFED)

Equation	Constant	ΔIP	ΔFED_{-1}	YDV_{-1}	$\bar{R}^2$
One independent variable					
1	6.73	0.28			0.77
2	5.67		0.43		0.15
3	9.53			(0.61)	−0.01
Two independent variables					
4	3.40	0.27	0.37		0.94
5	6.76	0.27		(0.18)	0.75
6	3.38	0.26	0.38	0.24	0.95

Inflation is defined as annual change in final expenditure deflator, other terms defined as in table A8.1.

Source of basic data: CSO, *National Accounts* and *Economic Trends*.

Since the variation in the growth of broad money was fairly strongly correlated with the dependent variable and all the independent variables, these two views could not be distinguished on statistical grounds. But in my view, the monetarist interpretation should be rejected on theoretical grounds, for reasons set out in Dow and Saville (1988), which can be summarized as follows. By far the largest counterpart of the growth of broad money (and thus almost identical with it) is the growth of bank lending. That varies with the rate of growth of the incomes of the persons and firms to which banks lend; and the variations in its growth in this period can mostly be explained as a result of variations in the rate of growth of incomes.[46] Variations in the rate of growth of broad money can therefore be taken to have been caused mostly by variations in the rate of growth of prices or of real output, so that money cannot be used as an independent variable in explaining price change. Thus I opt for interpretation 1 above.

An analysis similar to that in table A8.1 was applied to the data for the eleven other EC countries taken as a group [table A8.2].[47] Variation in the rate of import price

[46] I argue also that the rate of growth of money is not controlled directly by monetary policy, since the means available to the authorities to do so are ineffective—as was demonstrated by the unsuccessful experiment with monetary targets. The rate of growth of broad money is however affected by changes in the willingness of banks to lend at a given level of income. This also influences the rate of growth of income, though it is by no means the sole determinant.

[47] Without the inclusion of money as a possible explanatory variable. Since estimates of stock appreciation in other OECD countries are not readily available, the analysis was in terms of unadjusted final prices.

increase alone accounts for three-quarters of the rate of inflation of final prices (equation (1)); and if *past* price increase is added as an additional explanatory variable (itself reflecting variation in earlier import price inflation), the degree of explanation is brought up to 94 per cent (equation (4)). (Domestic demand pressures are not credited with having a large effect: see equation (6).)

To judge from UK experience [tables 8.13 and 8.16], only part of the variation in import price rise will have been due to the oil price shocks: variation in the rate of change of world commodity prices, and of the prices of other imports from outside the area, seem to have been equally important.

9 The Credit Expansion of the Late 1980s and the Recession of the Early 1990s

This chapter covers the period of accelerating growth experienced by the UK in the late 1980s, particularly the years 1985–8, followed by protracted decline into deep recession. Other industrial countries went through something like the same phases, though with many differences in degree and timing. These developments were everywhere unexpected: each stage came as a surprise, and forecasts were repeatedly wrong. In hindsight, the recession is widely seen to have resulted from the boom, a view with which this survey agrees: boom and recession are therefore discussed here together in one chapter.

This recession once more was very different from its predecessors. Each of the two 1970s recessions seemed due in large part to external shocks; and it seemed possible at the time to gauge something of what was going to happen, and why. On this latest occasion, it now seems clear that the causes of the recession grew out of previous developments in the domestic economy, which at the time lay undetected—as if there had been no compelling reason for recession to happen.

The explanation proposed agrees with the common view that the recession was not due to exogenous shocks of the normal sort, but attributes the boom to over-optimism rather than (as often argued) financial deregulation. Section 9.1 sets out this thesis more fully before going on to describe the evidence that bears on it. Section 9.2 summarizes the parallel fluctuations in other industrial countries, since they are an important part of the background. Section 9.3 then gives the analysis of boom and recession in the UK. Section 9.4 considers what the experience of this decade contributes to our understanding of recessions; and section 9.5 discusses the resumption of growth after the recession.

9.1. Summary of thesis: the interrelation between real and financial disturbances

It is a widespread view (*a*) that 'financial deregulation' led to an increase in borrowing, and that that in turn largely accounted for the strength of the expansion; (*b*) that the pace of expansion was unsustainable, and had to be checked, though not necessarily thrown into reverse, by policy measures; and (*c*) that the private debt build-up during the expansion explains the depth of the recession.

This view is accepted here only with a number of major reformulations. The thesis I propose puts emphasis not on changes in official regulations, but on changes in the degree of optimism in the expectations of consumers and firms about the prospect for future incomes. This thesis is based on a general view about how the system operates, which may be summarized as follows.

1. The expectations of both consumers and business are adaptive, and thus are based on recent past experience of income (or profits or sales) growth. Thus, in a recovery agents become more optimistic: in a downturn, less.

(*a*) More optimistic expectations about future income growth lead *consumers* to wish to rearrange lifetime expenditure and save less in the present than before. Given existing financial plans or commitments, however, consumers may not wish (or be able) to adjust in this way unless they can borrow more largely. Banks or building societies ('lending institutions') are typically the main or only available source of borrowing. Thus, to some large extent greater present spending will be contingent on the ability to borrow more from lending institutions.

(*b*) More optimistic expectations will also lead *firms* to invest more, and to borrow more. For small and medium-sized firms, lending institutions are once again a crucial source of finance.

2. Seen in the context of an expanding economy, deposit-taking institutions enable borrowers to obtain purchasing power without negotiating with those who will be the ultimate lenders, or indeed before anyone knows who will perform the counterpart act of saving.

3. Greater spending by consumers and firms will increase the pace of expansion. That will make expectations yet more optimistic, and will increase spending further. A move in the direction of greater (or less) optimism is thus for a while self-reinforcing and self-justifying.

4. Optimism based on an unsustainable rate of expansion must inevitably be moderated at some point. When it is moderated, that will reduce the growth of spending; and that in turn, by reducing the growth of incomes, will further reduce expectations, and thus will start a self-reinforcing downward process. A check to expansion at the capacity ceiling for instance is thus likely, not merely to put a limit on the speed of expansion, but to convert expansion into recession.

5. Lending institutions are also influenced by the general climate of optimism (or pessimism); they will lend more to borrowers if they rate their income prospects higher (or the reverse). The amount that consumers or firms can borrow, therefore, is limited not only by official controls, but by the changing prudential limits set by lenders.[1] It is argued that in the 1982–8 expansion lenders themselves eased access to credit, and that that was more important than official deregulation.

6. When optimism increases, consumers and firms extend borrowing and spend more; and when it collapses, they repay debt and contract spending.

---

[1] See discussion of credit rationing by banks, and references to the literature, in Dow and Saville (1988: 18).

In this latter case, they contract not because debt is high, but because expectations and attitudes to debt have changed: debt willingly incurred when expectations were optimistic comes to seem excessive when prospects for steady income growth look poorer. Thus, 'debt deflation' is a misleading phrase, since it is not the level of debt that is the operative factor.[2]

The thesis is that the 1989–93 recession was due to expectations having worsened after having been very buoyant in the days of expansion, which started a drawn-out cumulative process in which spending contraction reduced expectations a further notch, which in turn reduced spending and expectations again, and so on. This explanation will be elaborated further in the course of the detailed discussion of the UK recession [s. 9.3].

The distinction between the effects of deregulation and the effects of a change in the climate of expectations may seem unreal. It can be argued that the government intended deregulation to make banks and financial institutions compete more aggressively, and that that was bound to lead, as should have been realized, to relaxations of prudential standards and excessive lending. Two reasons lead me to maintain this distinction.

1. Euphoric conditions followed deregulation only after an interval of several years, and it is not clear that the euphoria was inevitable: tighter monetary policy might have prevented it [see s. 9.4].

2. To put the blame on a single historical act (deregulation) seems to imply that—since that once done cannot be repeated—a new swing to euphoria need not be feared. That would be over-sanguine.

The international studies of debt developments in this last expansion and recession[3] have put the emphasis on financial deregulation and the consequent importance of balance-sheet adjustments, and in my view have given too little weight to the swing first to over-optimistic expectations and later to greater caution. UK discussion of the recession comes closer to my view set out above.[4]

9.2. Boom and recession in other countries

Though there were many differences between economic developments in OECD countries, financial developments were often similar and played an important role. As a prelude to looking in detail at the UK, this section surveys fluctuations in ten countries, selected because developments in financial sectors

---

[2] Debt deflationists use the term 'reconstruction of balance sheets' to describe what firms do in a recession. The phrase is misleading since it suggests that what firms then have to do is merely to rearrange financial assets and liabilities, whereas what they are forced to undertake is a more painful and fundamental rearrangement of their affairs so as to survive after having incurred serious unexpected loss. In particular, they have to save more and invest less.

[3] See IMF, *World Economic Outlook* (May 1992): 47–51; (November 1992): 24–5 and 57–68; OECD, *Economic Outlook* (December 1992): 41–9.

[4] See J. R. Sargent (1991) and M. King (1991); also Allsopp *et al.* (1991), Muellbauer (1991), Lawson (1992): chs. 50–1, and M. King (1994).

played a crucial role. These comprise the seven major countries—the USA, Canada, Japan, and the four major European countries (Germany, France, Italy, and the UK) and three others: Australia, Norway, and Sweden.

Figure 9.1 shows for each of these countries deviations of output growth from estimated capacity growth rate. As an indicator of ease/restraint in the creation of credit, figure 9.2 compares the growth of broad money (the counterpart of bank lending) with growth of nominal GDP in each country.[5] Figures 9.3–9.5 show debt levels and savings ratios; figure 9.6, short-term interest rates; and figure 9.7, share price indices in the ten countries.

A distinction has sometimes been drawn between the financial systems of 'Anglo Saxon' countries, or what are here called the English-speaking countries ('ES countries': the USA, the UK, and Canada) and those of Continental Europe and Japan ('CEJ countries').[6] Four features distinguish CEJ from ES countries: (1) banks are more dominant in corporate finance and securities markets and institutional investors correspondingly less dominant; (2) companies have higher debt, most of it debt to banks; (3) banks have closer relations with client (medium and large) companies and are more ready to rescue them; and (4) banks lend less to the personal sector. In CEJ countries there is also less competition between banks and other financial institutions, less disclosure of information by companies, more industrial cartelization, and greater involvement by the public sector in lending, including ownership of banks.

Countries' financial systems however are in the course of rapid evolution, which will probably make them more competitive and more similar to each other. There is a general shift away from banking to securitized money and capital markets, which has probably gone furthest in the USA, the UK, France, and more recently Japan (Goldstein *et al.* 1992: 2–9). The shift may be said to have resulted essentially from market innovation, and has also depended on deregulation—both the removal of quantitative controls on bank lending, as in the UK, and (elsewhere) more general deregulation, e.g. withdrawal of legal limits on what banks may do.

Countries fall into two groups according to their economic performance [fig. 9.1]; their differing financial institutions may have something to do with this, in particular by affecting how far their banking systems borrowed on wholesale money markets [cf. ch. 7.3]. All four English-speaking countries were alike in having a strong rise in output over most of the period, and in reaching the peak of their boom in 1989. The three major continental countries and Japan had relatively slow growth up to 1987, and only then a pick-up in expansion, which in Germany and Japan lasted until 1991 or 1992.

---

[5] The index is taken as a measure of ease of access to credit on the presumption that, if lending institutions make no change in severity of their lending criteria, their lending will vary proportionately with their customers' incomes (Dow and Saville 1988: ch. 2).

[6] This categorization appears to have originated in OECD monetary studies: the summary here follows Davis (1992: 23–4).

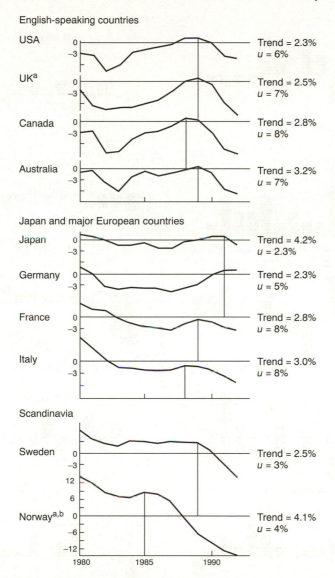

Fig. 9.1 Booms and recessions in ten countries, 1980–1993 (% deviation of GDP from trend of constant-employment GDP)

u is the % unemployment level taken as zero on scale (see text).
[a] Excluding North Sea oil.
[b] Note that vertical scale is smaller than for other countries.
Source: OECD, *Quarterly National Accounts*; *Economic Outlook*, various issues.

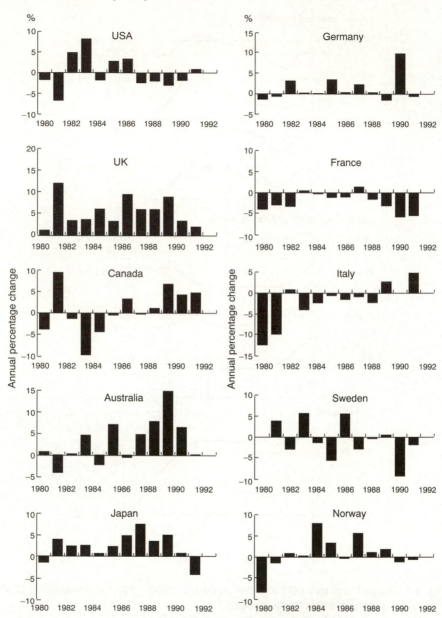

Fig. 9.2   Excess growth of money in ten countries, 1980–1992

Annual % change in broad money less nominal GDP growth rate.
(Broad money is currency plus deposits from IFS; for UK M4 is used.)
Sources: IMF, *International Financial Statistics*; CSO, *Economic Trends*.

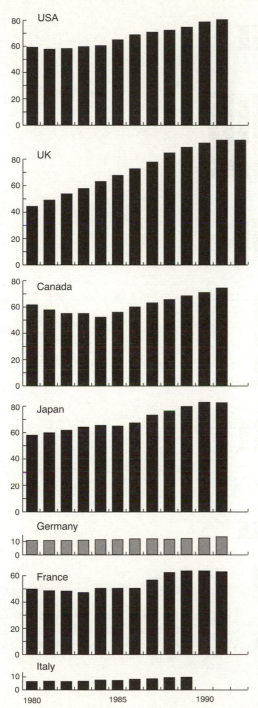

Fig. 9.3 Households' debt in G7 countries, 1980–1992

Data for Germany exclude liabilities associated with the acquisition of real assets.

Source: OECD, *Economic Outlook*.

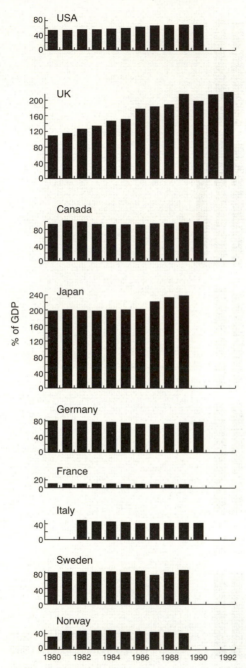

Fig. 9.4 Corporate debt in nine countries, 1980–1992

Source: OECD, *Financial Statistics*, except for the UK which is CSO.

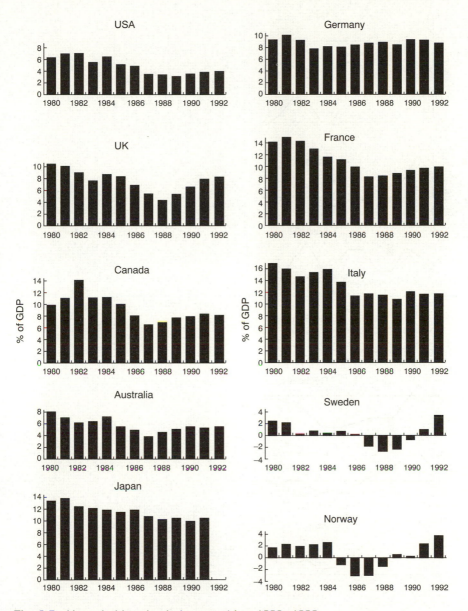

Fig. 9.5 Household saving in ten countries, 1980–1992
Source: OECD, *Quarterly National Accounts*.

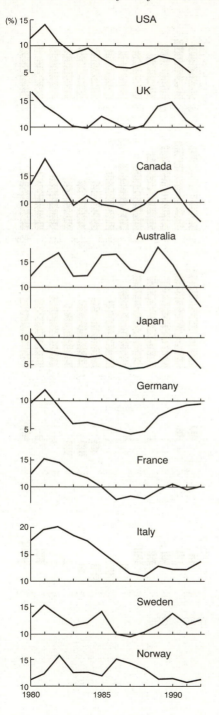

Fig. 9.6 Short-term interest rates in ten countries, 1980–1992

Source: representative short-term rates as shown in OECD, *Economic Outlook*.

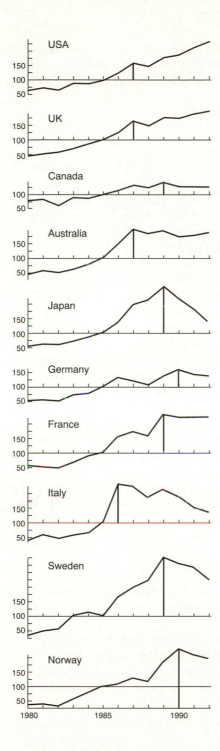

Fig. 9.7 Share price indices in ten countries, 1980–1992

Vertical lines mark peaks.

Source: OECD, Main Economic Indicators.

The Scandinavian countries hardly fit this characterization; their financial institutions are perhaps 'continental', but their economic performance was mixed: Swedish activity stayed high right up to 1989, while Norway's peaked early in 1985–6.

9.2.1. World trends

World expansion in the 1980s was relatively rapid. In the six years 1983–9, OECD GDP grew by 3.5 per cent a year, and OECD exports even faster. This constituted a sustained recovery after the OPEC II recession, though slower than in the long period of growth after World War II. Under the influence of this expansion, unemployment in the area as a whole fell each year (i.e., growth was above the capacity rate throughout the period).

The price of oil fell by half in 1986. This boosted demand, but to a much lesser extent than previous doublings in the price had put a brake on it; the net addition to world demand amounted perhaps to only 0.5 per cent of OECD GDP. The rise in oil prices in the 1970s had reduced *oil-consumers'* real purchasing power and spending, but had led to little immediate rise in the *oil producers'* spending despite the rise in their real income [ch. 8.1]. Now, when oil prices fell, oil-consuming countries' spending power was increased and they spent more; but many of the oil producers had no spare funds and had to cut spending as their earnings fell: the two sides were thus more balanced.

In the Stock Exchange crash of October 1987, equity prices in New York fell about 25 per cent—followed (in decreasing scale) by stock prices in the UK, other European countries and Japan. But, contrary to fears and expectations at the time, this had little effect on activity. Expansion continued to be rapid, and (most clearly in the UK) was above the capacity rate in the later stages of the boom. (In the three years 1986–9 it may have averaged 1 per cent a year faster than the capacity rate.) I will first look briefly at expansion up to 1985, then in more detail at the later years.[7]

9.2.2. First phase of expansion (up to about 1985)

Until about 1985, expansion was concentrated in three main countries—the UK, Canada, and above all the USA—which in 1983–4 accounted for three-quarters of the growth in the OECD area.

Two main factors account for high demand in the *United States*. First was Reagonomics: the build-up in defence spending, and the 'supply'-motivated tax cuts, together probably added on average 1 per cent a year to GNP in each of the three years 1982–4 (EO38: 4), and thus, as on some previous postwar

---

[7] The following account draws on issues of the OECD *Economic Outlook* for these years (referred to by serial number, e.g. EO30).

occasions, provided a significant addition to world demand. Second, Paul Volcker's experiment in 'practical monetarism', which from 1979 on had 'produced over two and a half years of oscillating, but essentially flat, real GNP' (EO32: 69), gave way in 1982 to a fairly rapid credit expansion (5 per cent faster in 1982 and 1983 than the rise in nominal GNP) [fig. 9.2].[8] The accompanying 3 per cent decline in mortgage rates produced a 40 per cent increase the following year in residential investment (a good part of the rise in GNP that year) and a surge in consumer confidence. Expansion in *Canada* followed that in the United States. The *United Kingdom* is discussed in section 9.3.

9.2.3. The years after 1985

After 1985 rapid expansion became much more nearly general. The USA and the UK continued to enjoy growth above the capacity rate, as did Canada and Australia after 1986; and after 1987 they were joined by Japan and the three major continental European countries (Germany, France, and Italy). Fast expansion in the English-speaking countries lasted until about 1989; in Japan and Germany (where it had started later) it went on till 1991; in France and Italy (where it had been less strong) it petered out in 1988 or 1989. In three of these countries (UK, Australia, Japan) easement of lending conditions probably played a role in the expansion, but, on the showing of figure 9.2, not in the USA or elsewhere.

Despite some similarities, the boom clearly had a different basis in different countries. I will concentrate on four: the USA, the UK, Japan, and Germany.

United States

In the United States, the depreciation of the dollar by over 30 per cent in early 1985 was a major cause of the subsequent boom; there was a rapid rise in exports over the next three years, while domestic demand rose only moderately. The rise in credit must have stimulated consumer spending (though it did not rise fast after 1985, nor did the saving ratio fall much). It also facilitated (up to 1986) large residential investment, and considerable speculative investment in city centres. But although the build-up of debt in the USA has been well publicized, it was moderate in comparison with other countries [fig. 9.3–9.5].

United Kingdom

In the UK the acceleration of expansion was much greater; in 1987 GDP grew by nearly 5 per cent, against only 3 per cent in the USA. Growing euphoria could account for most of the rapid acceleration of expansion in the UK [see s. 9.3]. The boom in the other two English-speaking countries was different

---

[8] The change in policy was prompted partly by the Mexican debt crisis and its repercussions on US banks.

again. Both *Australia* and *Canada* had an export boom (running on to 1989 and 1990 respectively), but in their case this was due not to depreciation (as in the USA) but to higher basic demand for their products. In each case rapid credit creation was driven by higher consumer spending; the saving ratio fell.

Japan

Japan and the three European majors joined the boom only later. The reason why Japanese expansion was delayed was probably the appreciation of the yen (35 per cent between 1984 and 1986—the other side of the dollar depreciation that boosted US expansion). That must have depressed Japan's exports, output, profits, and hence investment: business investment revived only in 1988. The swings in world exchange rates, along with the extremely public pressure put on the Japanese by the US authorities, must have been highly disturbing to the Japanese economy in this period. These effects were greatly worsened by the unbalanced development of Japanese financial and property markets. Equity and land prices rose steeply; there was over-investment in property development, and excessive borrowing by both companies and households on the security of real estate; moreover, the banks, in pursuit of balance-sheet growth, lent imprudently on the security of rising asset markets.[9] The downturn came in mid-1993 when the Bank of Japan, recognizing the need to bring asset price inflation under control, raised interest rates progressively. Asset prices fell precipitately, which checked domestic demand (partly because the banks became much more cautious in lending). The yen also strengthened, which checked export growth.

Germany

The strength of the boom in Germany (unlike other countries) was due to a political shock—German reunification. Fast expansion had got going by 1988 on the back of high demand abroad. Reunification in 1990 added three other factors: high spending on West German consumer goods by East Germans out of lavish transfer payments from the West; investment by West German companies in newly acquired subsidiaries in the East; and infrastructure investment in the East financed by the federal authorities.

Many factors contributed to the onset of recession in 1991. The East German consumer boom, for instance, was in part a once-for-all spree; federal taxes and interest rates were raised to curb inflation; furthermore German goods were pricing themselves out of world markets; and world demand for investment goods, Germany's forte, also fell as world recession spread.

Developments were thus very different in these four countries; and previous excessive borrowing was not always part of the picture.

---

[9] There were other hazardous elements. The banks' assets included large holdings of equities, so that when equity prices fell this not only caused losses to the banks but also threatened to take them below the Basle capital–asset ratios; and there was much cross-shareholding between companies, including banks and their customers (see Wood 1992).

Other countries

Remaining countries must be dealt with very briefly. In most, though not all, there is evidence of large swings in confidence.

1. In *France* domestic demand remained consistently weak through most of the 1980s—basically no doubt because of the conservative financial policy required to maintain the 'strong franc'. Weak demand persisted despite a significant build-up in consumer debt between 1984 and 1988 (accompanied as elsewhere by a steady decline in the saving ratio). When the turn came and confidence broke, the rise in the saving ratio reinforced the weakness of demand.

2. Weak growth in *Italy* (which as in France had persisted since the end of OPEC II) gave place in 1988 to a pick-up even more muted than in France. That faded the following year, perhaps because of renewed efforts at a more austere fiscal policy. Household debt in Italy is low, and borrowing hardly played a role.

3. *Sweden* enjoyed remarkably steady growth and high moderate demand right up to 1990. Debt grew rapidly in the second half of the 1980s. In 1990 severe recession set in, probably triggered by falling competitiveness, weak overseas demand, and a rise in interest rates. This seems to have led to a general erosion of confidence: the investment boom collapsed, and consumers made extreme cuts in spending.[10] Recession led in turn to very large losses at financial institutions, forcing government support for two large banks.

4. The boom in *Norway* gave place to recession in 1987 because domestic inflationary pressures forced restrictive measures, and because the fall in the world price of oil halved the value of what was Norway's main export. The effect of restrictive measures was greater than foreseen. Real estate prices fell abruptly; and the banks made large losses on loans. Here too the government had to give heavy support to the banks.[11]

Though the factors at work in different countries differed enormously, one generalization can be drawn from this review. There was some correlation between countries where borrowing increased most (which I interpret as a sign of growing euphoria) and those where expansion was fastest [figs. 9.1 and 9.3] (see M. King 1994) and also between these and countries where recession was deepest and earliest. It was in the UK that debt-financed borrowing was largest, expansion most rapid, and recession deepest.

9.3. Boom and recession in the UK

This section discusses the causation of the UK boom of 1985–8 and the recession of 1989–93. Table 9.1 [based on ch. 5.2] is a first survey of the evidence.

---

[10] Corporate debt as a ratio to GDP had risen 50 percentage points between 1984 and 1990, and total private-sector bank debt by over 140 percentage points. The consumer saving ratio rose from −4.5% of disposable income in 1989 to −1% in 1990, and to +2% in 1991.

[11] Government support for the banks amounted to 2.5% of GNP. Similar government intervention was required in Finland (see *Bank of Finland Bulletin*, May 1992).

Table 9.1   Boom and recession UK 1985–1993: partial explanations

	% change during each phase	
	Boom of 1985–8	Recession of 1989–93
% change in GDP[a]	5.6	−12.4
No. of years of boom or recession	3	4
% change of GDP explained by separate factors		
Exogenous shocks[b]		
Exports (*EX*)	3	3
Terms of trade (*TOT*)	77	−27
Monetary policy (*MP*)	(−1)	(11)
Fiscal policy (*FP*)	6	−13
Total	85	−26
Possible secondary effects[c]		
Change in saving ratio (*SR*)	36	25
Change in non-residential investment (*NRI*)	18	10
Change in investment in stocks (*CS*)	9	6
Shocks plus secondary effects[d]	71	43

See explanation and cautions about these and similar estimates in ch. 5.2. A negative sign indicates that the factor in question, far from helping explanation of the expansion or recession, detracts from it.

[a] % deviation of GDP(A) over each phase from constant-employment trend.
[b] As estimated on method AA, using the 'theoretical' value of parameters (see table 5.8, n. *d*). In this case the values are very close to estimates on method BB which (estimated as in table 5.6) are 80 and −22 respectively.
[c] 'Other explanatory factors' as defined in table 5.8, n. *d*.
[d] Excludes terms-of-trade effect since some will be included in savings effects (see table 5.7, n. *d*).

It suggests that, while the boom can be partially explained in terms of exogenous shocks, the recession owed nothing to them, and that in both phases confidence factors must have been very large. The task then is to explain why, the absence of obvious exogenous factors notwithstanding, the recession occurred. At the time the expansion was not thought to have caused the recession; but by now it is widely accepted that it did.[12]

9.3.1. The political background in the UK

Most of the years dealt with this chapter are within the period covered by Mrs Thatcher's administrations. The government that came to office in 1979 had

[12] The following explanation is broadly accepted by Mr Lawson, who as chancellor presided over the expansion (Lawson 1992: ch. 50–1); and also e.g. by J. R. Sargent (1991); Allsopp *et al.* (1991); Muellbauer (1991); and M. King (1991, 1994).

a distinct approach to economic policy. It was strongly anti-interventionist—more intent on setting free the micro energies of private enterprise than with oversight of the macro results. Thus, what the government did not do in these years is as important as what it did.[13]

Table 9.2 gives an impressionistic calendar of main events. There were four years (upto 1983) with Sir Geoffrey Howe as chancellor; six years and some months (until 1989) with Mr Lawson; then one year with Mr Major; at the end of 1990 Mrs Thatcher was ousted and Mr Major became prime minister. There was then a year and a half with Mr Lamont as chancellor, who was in turn displaced (in mid-1993) by Mr Clarke. Some main macroeconomic numbers are given in table 9.3.

The 'New Conservative' philosophy

The Thatcher government came to power with plans ready-made and with high confidence that its approach would transform the economy. The 'New Conservatism' had two strands: first, monetarism; and second, at the micro level, belief in the free market (see Lawson 1992: annex on 'The New Conservatism').

The prime object of macro policy was to eliminate inflation; control of the size of the stock of money was seen as the sole and sufficient means.[14] Monetary policy was thus the 'centrepiece' of economic policy. Control of the money stock was understood to require not only steps that the Bank of England could take, but also reduction of government borrowing. Being monetarist, the policy was in general anti-Keynesian. In effect (for reasons not fully argued), it appeared to ignore the effect of policy actions, especially fiscal, on demand or output.[15] There seemed an assumption that the economy had the power to get itself back to high employment, and that elimination of inflation sufficed to ensure growth and high employment.

Belief in the free market meant removal of governmental controls, the abolition of privately imposed restraints on trade, and the encouragement of competition. It meant reducing the scale of government, reselling the nationalized industries to the private sector; reducing (direct) taxation to improve economic incentives, and, not least, curbing the power of the trade unions.

[13] Of the many surveys covering some or all of the period, I here draw on Riddell (1983), Walters (1986), Maynard (1988), Keegan (1989), Britton (1991), Johnson (1991), and Nigel Lawson's (1992) own memoirs.

[14] Though the government was confident that it could control money, there was no agreement on how: whether by monetary base control or by discretionary variation of interest rates—an occasion for later disputes (see Dow and Saville 1988).

[15] It was part of the cost of 'conviction politics' that there was little public exposition of official thinking: occasional lectures by Mr Lawson, pamphlets by the Institute of Economic Affairs and, later by Walters—came the nearest. Because the government never rigorously defended its policy, but merely ignored criticism, public discussion of policy issues tended to lapse. The atmosphere of policy-making tended to be anti-intellectual. In internal discussion, questions outside a certain range were not welcome, and a reputation for unorthodoxy could well blight an official's career. It might be only an exaggeration to say that discussion inside the Treasury (not inside the Bank of England) was conducted as though under the supervision of the thought-police.

Table 9.2 Selective calendar of events, 1979–1993

	Political events in UK	Economic events in UK	Political events in other countries
1979	MAY: Conservatives win General Election. Mrs Thatcher becomes PM.	MAY: Sir G. Howe becomes chancellor of Exchequer. JUNE: Budget: switch from direct to indirect taxes.	AUG: Volcker becomes chairman of US Federal Reserve Board.
1980		MARCH: Budget presents medium-term financial strategy (MTFS). JUNE: Corset control on £M3 removed. OCT: exchange controls removed.	NOV: Reagan elected president of USA.
1981	JAN: Breakaway move to set up Social Democratic Party (SDP). MARCH: Letter of protest by 364 economists.		MAY: Mitterand becomes president of France.
1982	APRIL–JUNE: Falklands war.		JUNE: Devaluation of French franc by 10%.
1983	JUNE: Conservatives win General Election. OCT: Mr Kinnock leader of Labour Party.	JUNE: Mr Lawson becomes chancellor of Exchequer. JULY: Mr Leigh Pemberton governor of Bank of England.	
1984	JUNE: Dispute over EC Budget contribution settled.		NOV: President Reagan re-elected.
1985		JUNE: Securities and Investment Board set up.	SEPT: Plaza agreement to depreciate the $.
1986	OCT: Mr Heseltine resigns over Westland affair.	MARCH: Target for £M3 abandoned. OCT: 'Big Bang': lifting of restrictions on stock exchange.	MARCH: Chirac becomes PM of France.

Year			
1987	JUNE: Conservatives win General Election.	OCT: 'Black Monday': NY stock market crash.	FEB: Louvre accord to stabilize currencies. JUNE: Greenspan becomes chairman of US Federal Reserve Board. JULY: France and UK sponsor Channel Tunnel.
1988			NOV: Bush elected president of USA.
1989		OCT: Mr Lawson resigns: Mr Major becomes chancellor of Exchequer, Mr Hurd foreign secretary.	NOV: Berlin Wall dismantled.
1990	NOV: Sir G. Howe resigns from Cabinet. Mrs Thatcher resigns; Mr Major becomes PM.	APRIL: Poll tax starts. OCT: sterling joins ERM in 6% band. NOV: Mr Lamont becomes chancellor of Exchequer.	JUNE: Russia declares its independence. OCT: East and West Germany are reunited.
1991		JULY: Bank of Credit and Commerce International (BCCI) shut down by Bank of England.	JAN–FEB: Gulf War hostilities. JUNE: Yeltsin elected president of Russia. AUG: Schlesinger replaces Pohl as president of Bundesbank; attempted coup in USSR against Gorbachev. DEC: Gorbachev resigns.
1992	APRIL: Conservatives narrowly win General Election. AUG: Mr Smith leader of Labour Party.	MARCH: Hong Kong/Shanghai Bank takes over Midland. SEPT 16 (Black Wednesday): sterling forced out of ERM and floats down.	JUNE: Russia becomes a member of IMF. NOV: Clinton elected president of USA.
1993		JUNE: Mr Clarke replaces Mr Lamont as chancellor of Exchequer. JULY: Mr George becomes governor of Bank of England.	

Table 9.3 Chief economic indicators: UK, 1980–1993

	Change in prices[a] (% GDP deflator) (1)	Change in output[a] (% GDP) (2)	Unemployment[b] (%) (3)	External current balance (% of GDP) (4)	Effective exchange rate (1985=100) (5)	Growth of broad money (% M4) (6)	Interest rates[b] (banks' base rates) (7)
1980	19.4	−2.0	6.0	1.2	117.7	17.3	16.3
1981	11.5	−1.0	9.4	2.5	119.0	20.8	13.3
1982	10.8	1.8	10.9	1.7	113.7	12.4	11.9
1983	5.3	3.7	10.8	1.2	105.3	13.3	9.8
1984	4.5	3.2[c]	11.0	0.4	100.6	13.5	9.7
1985	5.3	2.8[c]	11.2	0.6	100.0	13.0	12.1
1986	3.3	4.0	11.2	−0.2	91.5	16.0	10.8
1987	5.2	4.6	10.2	−1.1	90.1	16.0	9.8
1988	6.0	5.0	8.2	−3.5	95.5	17.3	10.1
1989	7.1	2.2	6.4	−4.4	92.6	18.8	13.8
1990	6.4	0.6	5.8	−3.5	91.3	12.1	14.8
1991	6.5	−2.1	7.8	1.4	91.7	6.0	11.5
1992	4.6	−0.5	9.7	−1.6	88.4	3.5	9.4
1993	3.2	2.2	10.4	−1.8	80.2	5.8	5.9

[a] % change between annual averages.

[b] Annual average.

[c] Adjusted for effect of miners' strike (as estimated in Britton 1991: 69). Unadjusted numbers are: 1984, 2.0%; 1985, 4.0%.

Sources: Figures in columns (1), (2), and (4) are from *Economic Trends*, 1996/97, and OECD, *Economic Outlook*, 1996, and are different from estimates made near the time.

Macroeconomic developments and macroeconomic policies

The Conservatives' period in office opened as the world price of oil was again rising steeply. It was largely because of that, and the associated rise in world commodity prices, that domestic prices rose so rapidly in 1980. Unemployment rose in the recession; and inflation later slowly subsided (in the UK and elsewhere) as these shocks got absorbed. The exchange rate rose steeply—probably because the UK was now a producer of oil and because of overseas confidence in a strong Conservative government.

Oil exports led to a large external surplus—and thus to a freedom from anxiety about the balance of payments not paralleled under any previous government since the war. The rise in the price of oil was, too, part-cause of the deep recession [ch. 8.2]; the seeds of recession were thus already sown as incoming ministers, settling at their new desks, took out the programmes they had prepared before taking office. Meanwhile, the rapid rise in prices and nominal incomes, notwithstanding intentions to the contrary, also provoked a continued rapid rise in the money stock.

Monetary targets (which had been started in 1976) were continued. Minimum Lending Rate was raised to 14 per cent in June 1979 and to 17 per cent by November. The main presentational innovation came with the publication in 1980 of a 'medium-term financial strategy' (MTFS: three-year projections for the growth of M3 and government spending, revenue and borrowing). This was intended to provide a 'stable framework for private decisions' and to signify that monetary restraint and curbs on spending would be persisted with; that inflation would not be 'accommodated'; and—to spending ministers—that they faced a constraint which, if ignored, would force tax increases. As Nigel Lawson (1992: 72) says, the numbers in the MTFS were 'not fulfilled in any literal sense', but they may have affected events.

Exchange controls were removed in October 1979, and direct monetary control (the Corset) in June 1980. The former probably made little immediate difference: for exchange control had prevented neither huge short-term flows nor runs on sterling. Removal of domestic monetary controls opened the way to, even if it did not cause, the high lending of later years [s. 9.3.2].

The 1979 Budget reduced direct taxes and raised indirect taxes. The object was to improve incentives, but it must also have raised prices significantly.[16] The Budget was also considerably contractionary in its impact on total demand [table 8.10][17]—as was the equally controversial 1981 Budget.[18]

---

[16] Perhaps by 3.5% (Britton 1991: 44): in Conservative thinking, prices were supposed to be controlled by keeping a grip on the growth of money.

[17] The aim was to cut borrowing. The Budget came before the onset of major recession was evident; oil prices had by then risen only a fraction of what they were to do later.

[18] This was the occasion of the letter by the 364 economists to *The Times* in protest at the budget. As Lawson (1992: 98) notes, economic growth in fact resumed the following year. He does not note that not for two more years was growth fast enough to stop unemployment continuing to rise.

Privatization served both to reduce the scope of the public sector and to reduce government borrowing. Sales of public-sector assets were concentrated in the four years 1986–9, with BP and British Gas amounting to nearly half. By 1990 receipts totalled nearly £30 billion (7 per cent of a year's GDP). Partly because of this, and partly because of taxes on North Sea profits, public-sector borrowing was temporarily eliminated by 1987. The aim of reducing tax rates was realized: as a percentage of GDP, total taxation fell from 35 per cent in 1988 to about 32 per cent in 1994.

The Government must be judged unsuccessful with monetary policy. Rises in interest rates failed to restrain bank lending; and monetary targets, though regularly subject to upward 'base slippage', were exceeded as often as met (Dow and Saville 1988). In October 1986 broad money targets were abandoned; the target of policy gradually shifted towards the exchange rate, and by 1984–5 'monetary policy ... had many of the characteristics of an explicit exchange rate policy ...' (Lawson 1992: 483). That policy was the subject of constant battle between the Chancellor and a Prime Minister reluctant ever to sanction a rise in interest rates. In October 1990 Mrs Thatcher at length agreed to let sterling adhere to the EMS exchange rate system. It was forced out two years later, on Black Wednesday in September 1992; but by then both Mrs Thatcher and Mr Lawson were gone from office, and it was on their successors, Mr Major and Mr Lamont, that the shame of that fiasco rebounded.

Another major plank in Conservative policy was diminution of union powers. That included change in trade union law, but also direct confrontation. The coal industry had been identified, even while the Conservatives were still in opposition, as the likely battleground. The coming showdown with the National Union of Mineworkers was made the subject, as one observer noted, of thorough 'quasi-military style of advance planning' (Johnson 1991: 154, 219).[19] To that was owed the defeat of the miners' strike in 1984. The strike probably reduced national product by over 1 per cent that year (Britton 1991: 69). But union power was decisively weakened by the combination of that victory together with legislative changes.

The wider aim was to bring down inflation, and the rate of inflation did decline dramatically (from a rise in the GDP deflator of 14.5 per cent in 1979 and 19.5 per cent in 1980 to one of just 2 per cent in 1994). Part of the deceleration was due to the effect on wage increases of recession and unemployment; but most must have been due to worldwide causes (including the decline in world oil and commodity prices) which reduced inflation in all countries (see Britton 1991: 270–81).

The Government's *laissez-faire* philosophy made it for some years distance itself from responsibility for the level of output. But when productivity started

---

[19] The proposals (later carried out) included the building up of coal stocks, 'recruitment of non-union lorry drivers by haulage companies', and provision of 'a large mobile squad of police equipped and prepared to uphold the law against violent picketing'.

to grow rapidly, that became an achievement for which the Government claimed the credit.[20] The fall in output in the recession of 1979–82 had, as in earlier major recessions, been accompanied by a setback to productivity. Then, in the seven or eight years after the second OPEC recession, productivity growth was faster even than in the pre-1973 'Golden Age'. Different studies have produced different answers as to why productivity growth accelerated, and the question seems impossible to settle on the basis of a relatively small number of years. But, however caused, good UK performance was short-lived: when demand fell in 1989, productivity growth again went into reverse.

9.3.2. Expansion 1982–8

The questions now to be considered are: why was expansion in the period 1982–8 as fast as it was, and in that context what was the role of borrowing and of financial deregulation?

After a year of recovery (1982), there were three years of *average* growth preceding the three of *rapid* growth. In the first phase (1982–5), when normal growth was resumed,[21] the crucial factor was the acceleration of exports [table 9.4, col. (5)]: world growth picked up as other economies emerged from their recessions, and the UK exchange rate was now 15 per cent below its 1981 peak. Private-sector investment also recovered, and consumer expenditure resumed its normal role in an expanding economy. (From 1983 on, real personal disposable income started to grow again; the saving ratio also fell a bit further.)

It was in the second phase (1985–8) that expansion turned into boom. By 1988 the annual rate of increase of final expenditure reached over 6 per cent [table 9.5]. A major underlying factor, not usually noticed then or later, was the steady improvement in the terms of trade;[22] this moderated the rise in import costs, and hence in final prices and increased factor purchasing power, enough (by 0.8 per cent a year on the calculations of table 9.1) to account for nearly half of the divergence of growth from trend.

It is remarkable how much of the acceleration took the form of consumer spending: table 9.6 suggests that three-quarters of 'above-normal' spending in the years 1985–9 consisted of consumer expenditure. (Consumers' real incomes grew unusually fast, which accounts for over half the acceleration of consumer spending; the rest was due to a further marked fall in the savings ratio—now associated, as it had not been before, with a surge in borrowing.)

---

[20] The claim is implicit in the title of Alan Walters's (1986) *Britain's Economic Renaissance*.

[21] On this occasion, as on previous ones, recovery consisted of a *resumption of growth from the low point of the recession*, not a return to a projection of the pre-recession growth path.

[22] The terms of trade on the standard definition worsened somewhat. But the terms-of-trade effect as defined in this study was positive: UK domestic costs (GDP deflator) grew moderately (4% a year) between 1985 and 1988; while, despite the fall in the exchange rate, import costs fell.

Table 9.4 Expenditure composition of expansion and recession: summary, UK, 1982–1993

	Contributions to % change in TFE in each phase			Normal' annual Contribution[a]	Excess or deficiency in each phase over normal contribution[b]		
	Expansion		Recession		1st 'go' phase 1982–5	2nd 'go' phase 1985–9	Recession 1989–93
	1st phase 1982–5	2nd phase 1985–9	1989–93				
	(1)	(2)	(3)	(4)	(5)	(6)	(7)
Consumer expenditure	5.0	11.0	0.6	1.4	0.7	5.4	−5.1
of which, due to							
Real income[c]	5.1	9.6	3.2	1.5	0.5	3.4	−3.0
Change in savings[d]	−0.2	1.4	−2.5	−0.1	0.2	1.9	−2.1
Government consumption	0.5	0.7	0.8	0.5	−0.9	−1.2	−1.0
Fixed investment	2.2	4.5	−1.9	0.4	1.1	3.0	−3.4
of which							
Private non-residential	1.9	3.9	−1.4	0.2	1.2	3.0	−2.3
Exports	3.1	3.1	2.1	0.6	1.2	0.6	−0.4
Final sales	10.8	19.4	1.7	2.9	2.1	7.8	−9.9

Total final						
expenditure	11.4	19.8	1.3	2.9	2.7	8.2	−10.3
of which						
Imports	3.9	7.7	1.5	0.6	2.0	5.2	−1.0
GDP	7.7	12.0	−0.3	2.3	0.9	3.0	−9.3
% change in GDP						
Total	9.7	15.5	−0.4	2.9	1.0	3.9	−12.0
Non oil	9.2	17.3	−1.0	2.9	0.5	5.7	−12.6

[a] Assumes TFE and its components grow at the same rate as capacity GDP as estimated in table 2.4.
[b] Difference between actual contributions to % change in TFE and the 'normal' contributions in column (4).
[c] Real personal disposable income.
[d] Calculated as the difference between the contributions of consumer expenditure and of real income.

Source: from table 9.5

Table 9.5 Composition of changes in total final expenditure: UK, 1980–1993[a]

% contributions to annual change in TFE

	1980	1981	1982	1983	1984	1985	1986	1987	1988	1989	1990	1991	1992	1993
Consumer expenditure	0.0	0.0	0.5	2.2	0.9	1.8	3.1	2.7	3.6	1.6	0.3	−1.0	0.1	1.2
of which, due to														
Real income	0.9	−0.4	−0.3	1.4	1.9	1.8	2.2	1.9	3.2	2.4	1.3	−0.3	1.3	0.9
Change in savings	−0.8	0.5	0.8	0.7	−0.9	0.0	0.9	0.8	0.5	−0.7	−1.0	−0.8	−1.2	0.4
Fixed investment	−0.7	−1.3	0.7	0.6	1.1	0.5	0.3	1.2	1.9	1.0	−0.5	−1.4	−0.1	0.1
Exports	0.0	−0.2	0.2	0.4	1.4	1.3	1.1	1.3	0.0	0.8	1.0	0.1	0.4	0.6
Final sales[a]	−0.5	−1.3	1.5	3.6	3.6	3.6	4.7	5.4	5.6	3.6	1.4	−2.0	0.5	1.9
Stock change	−1.6	0.0	0.5	0.6	−0.1	−0.1	0.0	0.1	0.6	−0.3	−0.7	−0.4	0.4	0.3
Total final expenditure	−2.3	−1.4	2.0	4.3	3.5	3.6	4.7	5.5	6.2	3.4	0.7	2.4	0.9	2.2
% change in GDP														
Total	−2.1	−1.3	1.7	3.7	2.3	3.8	4.1	4.8	4.4	2.1	0.5	−2.2	−0.6	1.9
Non oil	−2.9	−1.9	1.3	3.1	2.8	3.4	3.7	4.9	5.4	3.2	0.7	−2.7	−0.8	1.8

[a] Government consumption is not itemized in the table: it increased each year but on a considerable scale only in 1990. It is included in final sales and final expenditure items. Imports also are not shown. They rose massively in 1984, as a result of the coal strike; and in 1987–9 (especially in 1988) as a result of excess pressure of demand.

Sources: CSO, *National Accounts* and *Economic Trends*.

Table 9.6 Persons' borrowing, saving, and acquisition of assets: UK, 1982–1992 (% of GDP)

	Borrowing[a] *plus* Saving[b]		*equals:*		
			Investment in real assets[c]	Acquisition of financial assets[d]	Residual[e]
1982	7.7	9.8	5.8	13.5	−1.7
1983	7.5	8.5	6.1	13.0	−3.1
1984	7.3	9.8	6.0	11.6	−0.5
1985	7.9	9.1	5.8	12.0	−0.7
1986	9.5	7.5	6.3	12.2	−1.5
1987	10.5	6.0	6.9	12.2	−2.6
1988	13.1	5.0	8.3	11.7	−2.0
1989	10.4	5.9	7.4	9.9	−1.0
1990	8.1	7.3	6.4	10.7	−1.8
1991	5.2	8.8	5.3	9.9	−1.1
1992	3.1	11.4	4.9	9.7	−0.2
			equals:		
	Increase in *plus* borrowing[f]	Fall in saving ratio	Increase in investment in real assets	Increase in acquisition of financial assets	Residual
1982–5	0.4	0.6	0.0	−1.5	1.0
1985–8	5.2	−4.1	2.5	−0.3	−1.3
1988–92	−10.0	6.4	−3.4	−2.0	1.8

References are to the National Accounts item codes.
[a] Total transactions in financial liabilities (*CJKU*).
[b] Includes capital transfers (*CFBT*).
[c] Fixed investment, increase in stocks, taxes on capital and capital transfers to public corporations (*CFBT − AABH*).
[d] Total transactions in financial assets (*CJKV*).
[e] Balancing item (*AAQB*).
[f] Change between terminal years of phases shown.

Source: *UK National Accounts, 1993*, tables 4.2 and 4.3.

Investment also accelerated, adding 0.75 per cent to the annual rate of growth over the four-year period. Some investment was in dwellings (though much less than the surge in mortgage borrowing). Little was on behalf of manufacturing; most was on behalf of financial and other services. There was a surge of new office building—in the City of London and the new area of the

London Docklands, and elsewhere in southern England.[23] The latter was due in part to the euphoria created by Big Bang, generated by the takeover of brokerage houses by banks and other institutions after the Stock Exchange's restrictive rules were lifted in October 1986; in part it was due simply to over-optimistic expectations and an uncoordinated rush to increase supply, often precariously financed, much of it by foreign banks. In 1988 and 1989 rents were rising by around 20 per cent a year; and the new construction underway was enough almost to double the office space available to City firms. Unlet space, and the rise in interest rates (culminating in the rise to 15 per cent in October 1989), brought the property boom to an end.

The role of borrowing

Throughout the period of expansion households were adding rapidly to their debt [table 9.6].

In the first phase (1982–5) personal debt had increased by 15–20 per cent a year, against a rise in nominal incomes of something not much more than half that rate. As well as borrowing, consumers saved. Table 9.6 suggests (note the considerable statistical residual) that, of total saving *plus* borrowing, a third went on purchasing real assets (half of it dwellings), and two-thirds on acquiring financial assets (half of it being contractual saving through life insurance and pension funds; half, deposits with banks, building societies, and 'national savings' instruments).

In the second phase (1985–8) consumers further increased their rate of borrowing [table 9.6]. Most of the increase was matched by less saving, i.e. was reflected in current spending; a third of the increase went to purchase real assets (mostly dwellings). One can say that the greater optimism associated with the greater borrowing led to an increase in spending equivalent each year to about 2 per cent of GDP, either as current spending or as investment in dwellings—enough to explain the larger part of the acceleration of total final spending.

Borrowing by industrial and commercial companies increased absolutely by about as much as borrowing by persons [table 9.7: note the considerable residual in this table too]; but the direct effect on spending seems to have been less. Over half of the increase in borrowing was used to buy shares in other companies—evidence of the spate of takeovers—or to acquire other financial assets. (The effect here was not to add to companies' demand for real assets, but to leave companies as a group more highly geared.) Retained profits fell, and part of the higher borrowing in effect offset that. The remaining 40 per cent went to finance fixed investment and a rise in stocks. Here too one can say that greater optimism led to both greater borrowing and greater investment.

---

[23] A detailed account is in Goobey (1992).

Table 9.7 Companies' borrowing, saving, and acquisition of assets UK 1982–1992 (% of GDP)[a]

	Borrowing[b]	Undistributed profits[c]	*equals:* Acquisition of financial assets		Investment in real assets		Residual[h]
		plus	Company securities[d]	other[e]	Fixed assets, etc[f]	Stocks[g]	
1982	3.8	9.4	0.8	2.4	7.4	0.8	1.9
1983	3.1	10.5	0.8	3.4	6.9	1.7	0.8
1984	1.6	11.5	2.2	1.6	8.1	1.9	-0.6
1985	5.3	11.1	2.1	2.5	9.4	0.8	1.5
1986	7.3	10.5	2.5	4.6	9.2	0.8	0.6
1987	10.1	11.9	3.4	4.7	10.2	1.6	2.1
1988	12.8	11.6	5.3	3.3	11.1	2.5	2.3
1989	14.8	9.1	6.0	4.0	12.1	2.1	-0.2
1990	10.2	8.3	1.9	2.5	11.6	0.8	1.7
1991	6.1	7.4	1.9	1.3	10.2	-0.6	0.7
1992	2.3	8.1	1.1	-1.4	9.4	0.0	1.3

	Increase in borrowing[b]	Fall in undistributed profits	*equals:* Acquisition of financial assets		Investment in real assets		Residual
		plus	Company securities	Other	Fixed assets, etc.	Stocks	
1982–5	1.5	1.7	1.3	0.1	2.0	0.0	-0.4
1985–8	9.5	-2.0	3.9	1.5	2.7	1.3	1.7
1988–92	-12.5	-1.0	-4.9	-2.6	-2.7	-2.1	1.5

References are to the National Accounts item codes.
[a] Industrial and commercial companies. [b] Debt *plus* equities, i.e. total transactions in financial liabilities (*CIIO*). [c] Includes capital transfers (*FMCI*). [d] Investment in UK company securities plus overseas securities (*AICC+AANU*). [e] Total transactions in financial assets less investment in securities (*CIIR−AICC−AANU*). [f] Fixed investment, taxes on capital, and capital transfers (*AAAS+FMCL+CISB*). [g] Increase in stocks (*AAAT*). [h] Balancing item (*AAOB*). [i] Change between terminal dates of phase shown.

Source: UK National Accounts, 1993, tables 5.4 and 5.5.

Financial deregulation in the early 1980s

The great expansion of borrowing is often attributed to financial deregulation. But that is probably to credit to identifiable acts of decontrol change that in fact was due to a more anonymous evolution of behaviour. Financial innovation is another phrase describing part of what happened. But the essential was not so much the exploitation of new techniques as the more aggressive spirit with which financial institutions conducted business, and also a relaxation of former standards of prudence: both of these made it easier for borrowers to borrow.

Financial deregulation, as Nigel Lawson remarks, is not a precise term. In a discussion of other countries' experience, it usually means (as already noted) the liberalization of legal restrictions on the classes of business that banks were allowed to undertake. In the UK it usually means removal of more detailed controls that previously restrained banks from being highly competitive in their lending and led them to ration their lending. There had been an earlier phase of deregulation in the UK in 1971–3 [ch. 8.1.1].

In the 1980s, three steps were important.[24]

1. the removal of exchange controls (October 1979);
2. the removal of the 'Corset' control over bank lending (June 1980);
3. the gradual erosion of the self-imposed restraints that the building societies had observed in their lending, which finally (October 1983) led to the Building Societies Association ceasing to make 'recommendations' as to its members' lending rates.

The first of these was of indirect importance only, since it did not itself directly affect the ease of borrowing. It is often said to have necessitated the removal of control on bank lending eight months later.[25] But controls over domestic credit would most probably have been removed anyhow. Nor did the end of exchange control transform the foreign exchange market, for control had never been completely effective. It did however make British financial markets more open to competition from abroad, and signalled, at the outset of the new government's reign, its free-market intentions.

---

[24] The following analysis takes minor issue with the accounts given in J. R. Sargent (1991) and Lawson (1992). An account rather fuller on some points was given in Dow and Saville (1988: 192–5). The lifting of a number of other restrictions, though often included under the rubric of deregulation, are here judged unimportant or irrelevant in the present context. The ending of certain stock exchange restrictive practices in the so-called 'Big Bang' of October 1986, for instance, came late in the day, and did not affect the scale of lending in any direct way. The abolition of remaining controls on hire-purchase transactions in July 1982 was also unimportant because they had been so ineffective

[25] Removal of exchange controls would have made the control of bank lending to large firms less effective. But in my view direct control on lending to persons and small firms probably could still have been an effective restraint, despite the absence of exchange control [ch. 12].

Though framed to allow some flexibility, the Corset control of bank lending had in effect frozen each bank's lending at its level on a prescribed date (see Dow and Saville 1988: ch. 10.1). First imposed in December 1973 as a remedy for the credit boom of that era, it was twice removed and twice reimposed in the next four-and-a-half years, and in that time was in abeyance for almost as long as it was operative. Previous occasions when the control had been lifted, however, had not led to new bursts of lending. This time it did, probably because this time it was clearly a final removal. It had become decreasingly effective in limiting the borrowing of large firms, who were able to bypass the control by borrowing via the issuance of bills or longer-term paper in their own name; but for small borrowers it remained an effective restraint.

Previously there had been an informal understanding that the banks would not compete with the building societies in the mortgage market. That lapsed when the Corset was removed, and within a year the banks were providing a quarter of all new housing loans. Their competition forced the building societies to be more commercial.

Building societies had never been subject to any formal government control, so there was not a question of such control being removed. Being 'friendly societies' (savings cooperatives), their practice had been to keep their lending rates stable in face of fluctuating market rates. Thus, when market rates rose, they were unable to borrow as much as before and rationed how much they lent (also at unchanged rates). This system was gradually eroded by market pressures, stemming in part from government derestriction of the banks. But beyond that, the government stood back and watched.[26]

Reasons for the explosion of lending

The great expansion of borrowing is often attributed to financial deregulation. In my view that is mistaken. This expansion could not have happened without deregulation, but it was probably not inevitable. One reason to insist on the distinction is that there was a gap of five years between the removal of lending controls and the time when credit creation started to accelerate. It could be argued that the financial system is ineluctably unstable and that at some point lending if left uncontrolled was bound to get excessive. But that is not the whole answer, for a properly timed, appropriately restrictive stance of policy might have avoided a credit boom despite decontrol.

Deregulation is likely to have two effects, which need to be distinguished. Deregulation removes a barrier to flows previously frustrated; and thus will be followed by an increase in borrowing by those whose borrowing was curtailed in the regulated regime. Their motives for borrowing more may be either to

[26] Because of the unpopularity of higher interest rates, the government found it politically advantageous for mortgage rates *not* to rise when it put short-term interest rates up, and so did not hasten to make the system disintegrate. That process is sometimes referred to as 'the collapse of the building societies' cartel'. But the Building Societies Association did not operate a cartel in any normal sense, and if anything kept lending rates low, not high.

anticipate future income and increase current consumption, or to increase holdings of assets, real or financial. The second can be called a balance-sheet adjustment and would result in a temporary increase in borrowing, after which debt would cease to expand so rapidly. The increase in borrowing in the 1980s was for a time thought to be of this sort, but it became increasingly clear that that was not all that was happening.

In the second stage of expansion there were in addition two other, more 'dynamic', developments: (1) growth of a pervasive optimism about future prospects; and (2) an erosion of prudential standards. The years 1982–8 were a longer period of relatively fast growth than any since 1973, and led to greater optimism about future growth. Such a shift in expectations will lead consumers (to the extent that financial constraints allow) to anticipate higher future income growth than before and to increase present consumption; it will also cause a rise in investment.[27] Greater optimism is likely to be shared by lenders and to make them on their side more willing to lend. An increase in optimism was a powerful influence in the 1985–8 boom.

The mood of optimism went along with a lowering of lenders' prudential standards. Where lending was subject to quantitative rules, as in mortgage lending, the rules were relaxed; where the rules were more informal, as in lending to business, traditional caution was laid aside. These influences inter-twined. In practice, there is little difference between taking a more easygoing approach to a customer's borrowing and underrating the likelihood of his failure. The expansion of lending and borrowing, many observers agree, was driven by a form of collective, manic euphoria, to which there have been many, though probably less extreme, parallels in the past. In my view this was much more important than a relaxation of official restraints, necessary condition though that was. The rise in both household and corporate debt in the period from 1982 to 1988 or 1989 was faster, and went further, in the UK than in any other country [figs. 9.4 and 9.5].

Expansion accompanied a steady rise in asset prices. House prices [fig. 9.8] and property prices rose increasingly steeply up to 1989; equity prices rose fairly steadily [fig. 9.7], with a dip at end-1987 (to be commented on later). The New York Stock Exchange crash of October 1987 was widely expected to bring the world boom to an end. In fact it failed to do so; nor (except in Australia) did it for long interrupt the upward march of equity prices. One may—tautologically—conclude that expectations had not then yet reached a vulnerable stage.

9.3.3. The recession of 1989–93

I come now to the recession of 1989–93, and the reasons why I believe that it grew out of the boom already described.

---

[27] M. King (1991) regards this as an expectation by agents of 'a shock to the rate of growth of technical progress'. He notes that the effects 'look very similar to those of an unsustainable short-term demand expansion'.

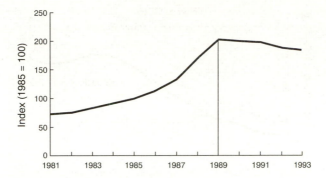

Fig. 9.8 House prices in the UK, 1981–1993
DoE index of house prices, all dwellings.

Output (measured against trend) peaked in 1990 but its growth began to slow in the course of 1988; in 1989 the rate of growth fell below trend (or capacity rate, estimated in table 2.4 above at 2.9 per cent a year). On the principles set out earlier [ch. 2.2], 1989 is therefore identified as the start of the recession [fig. 9.1]. Output ceased to fall in the course of 1992; in 1993 it started to grow, and regained the assumed capacity growth rate. Therefore 1993 is taken as the end of the recession. The recession as here reckoned thus extended over four years—longer than any previous recession. Figure 9.9 shows the shortfall of output relative to previous trend, the smaller shortfall of productivity, and the effect on unemployment.

Table 9.1 provides a first indication of the causation of the recession. On this showing, very little was due to a fall in exports; and the recession occurred despite some positive stimulus from the terms of trade.[28] Thus, the recession seems to have been entirely (or more than entirely) home grown. It would not seem to have been due to governmental policy; for, while interest rates rose up to 1990 [tables 9.1 and 9.3], this was accompanied by fiscal policy changes that went in the other direction [tables A5.2 and 9.1].

My conclusion is that this recession, unlike all the previous four, was not due to exogenous shocks, but was entirely due to a reversal of the over-confidence that had been built up in the preceding boom years.[29] The following paragraphs illustrate in detail the way this confidence switch took effect.

Table 9.4 shows the expenditure composition of the recession. Most of the downward deviation from trend was due to shortfalls in consumer spending

---

[28] The rise in import prices was relatively restrained in these four years, so that home factor costs (the GDP deflator) rose more than final prices and home purchasing power again showed a rise, as it had in the boom. As here calculated, the GDP deflator is adjusted to exclude North Sea oil from GDP, but that makes little difference in this period.

[29] Most observers, I think, broadly agree with this conclusion. One study is Catào and Ramaswamy (1996).

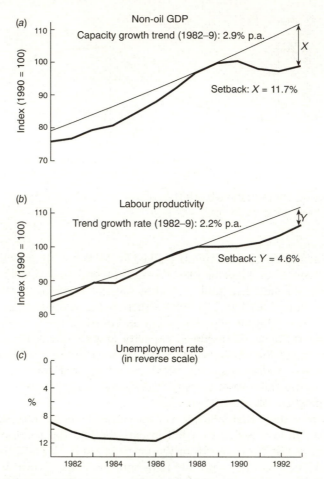

Fig. 9.9 Setback to output and productivity in the UK, 1989–1993 recession
(a) Non-oil GDP
(b) Labour productivity
(c) Unemployment rate (in reverse scale)

Source: *UK National Accounts*.

and fixed investment (column (7)). Remarkably little was due to running down of stocks (compare the rates of decline of final sales and final expenditure), just as the previous expansion had owed little to stock-building. Very little (as already noted) was owed to exports—this too (in reverse) had been the case in the boom.

The year-by-year course of expenditure is also revealing [table 9.5]. In the first year of the recession (1989), the check to growth reflected a check to both the growth of consumer spending and (rather less important) fixed investment, mostly for private industry.[30] The pause in consumer spending was not due to a pause in the growth of consumer incomes—which, for one more year, grew as rapidly as before: rather, it was because the saving ratio, instead of continuing to fall as it had for some years, now rose quite abruptly. The change in savings behaviour in 1989 thus marks a crucial break in trend, which was to be carried further as the recession gathered force. Why that happened must be a crucial element in the explanation of the recession.

Changes in the personal savings ratio have been interpreted in this study as an (imperfect) indication of changes in confidence [ch. 5.2]. It was argued above that the decline in the propensity to save (increase in the propensity to spend) during the boom reflected an upward shift in consumers' expectations of the growth of future income. The collective effect of the increase in spending in turn increased income growth, which must have further bolstered expectations, so that the process will have become cumulative. In like manner, favourable current experience must have bolstered firms' expectations of future sales and profits, and had similar cumulative effects via firms' investment. A cumulative process of this sort is however fragile. Any check (even a check to the *rate* of acceleration of output and income growth) may be capable of putting the causal sequence into reverse.

The expansion contained various unsustainable elements. Output was rising above the capacity rate, and the rise was accelerating. Domestic and commercial property prices were rising, in part because demand for property was being enhanced by speculative purchases made in anticipation of a continued rise in property prices at a rate that could not continue for long. Demand pressures were beginning to cause an acceleration of price inflation [table 9.3], and market operators must have been aware that at some stage counter-inflationary policy was likely. Expectations must then have been fragile.

By 1988 the authorities were becoming concerned at the course of the economy. As early as February 1988, after fears had subsided about the impact of the New York Stock Exchange crash, UK short-term interest rates were raised 0.5 per cent because the economy appeared so buoyant (*Bank of England Quarterly Bulletin* 1988: 8). Though rates were then lowered again for a while (to 7.5 per cent in May), they were raised progressively from June on, in a rise that carried them to 12 per cent in August.[31]

That rise in interest rates would have been enough to act as a trigger, given the probable fragility of the expectations on which continued expansion depended. Given the background, it was probably also inevitable, though

---

[30] Table 9.5 shows also a pause in export growth in 1988. But that was due not to a flagging of demand but to supply difficulties in the North Sea, which interrupted both output and exports of oil. World demand continued to rise, since few countries at first were hit by recession, and UK non-oil exports continued to expand as before.

[31] Rates were raised so as to 'exert downward pressure on inflation and the growth of demand' (*BEQB* 1989: 305). After August, interest rates were to continue their rise—to 15% by October 1989, where they remained for 12 months.

almost totally unexpected at the time, that the rise in rates would not just lightly moderate the pace of growth but would lead on to a long and deep recession. For a confidence cycle is asymmetric: as has long been observed, a rapid break in confidence is followed by protracted recovery [see ch. 5.1].

The role of debt

It is frequently said that the recession was a case of debt deflation, i.e. was due to the level of debt having become excessive.[32]

In a phase of expansion, debt is accumulated as part of a plan that each agent then thinks optimal. When the situation changes and expectations are lowered, the capital in which the debt has been invested no longer appears so profitable. Consequently debt service obligations, though in the first place willingly assumed, come to seem excessive ('a burden'). But they seem so only because expectations have changed; if optimism returned, they would no longer seem burdensome. An agent who had bought the same capital out of accumulated profits i.e. without incurring debt, would be in a similar position as a result of a change in expectations. It is incorrect therefore to say that debt is the cause of recession—or even, as it is sometimes expressed, 'an exasperator'.

Changes in debt can however be used as an indicator of the changes in the expectations underlying debt changes. During the expansion of 1982–9, household debt grew by 35 per cent of GDP [fig. 9.10]. This was matched mostly by the fall in personal saving, which (in a sense) it financed; but some went to finance greater personal investment in housing and other real assets [table 9.6].

When considering company financing, it is best to look at changes in debt *plus* equity, not just debt-proper. Traditionally firms reduced dividends when profits fell, but in recent years they have become reluctant to cut dividends; equities have thus acquired some of the character of debt. Figure 9.10 for that reason shows the stock of debt *plus* equities. (In some of the following discussion, 'debt' is also used loosely in this broad sense.) In the years 1982–9, company debt *plus* equities (companies' accumulated financial deficit) grew from 125 to 215 per cent of GDP— considerably more than household debt [fig. 9.10]. Unlike households, that went (until 1989) with only a small rise in corporate saving (undistributed profits). Over half of what companies saved and borrowed went to acquisition of real assets [see table 9.7]. But in this expansion phase, a large part also went to acquisition of financial assets. Some of the latter, particularly in the early years, will have represented a balance-sheet adjustment following the removal of financial controls; but most of the borrowing, even in the early years, will have been for greater investment under the influence of more optimistic expectations. After confidence collapsed, borrowing declined steeply.

---

[32] The clssic general citation concerning debt deflation is Fisher (1933). Two authors writing on the 1989–93 UK recession who also adhere to this view are M. King (1991) and Young (1993), for whom see other references.

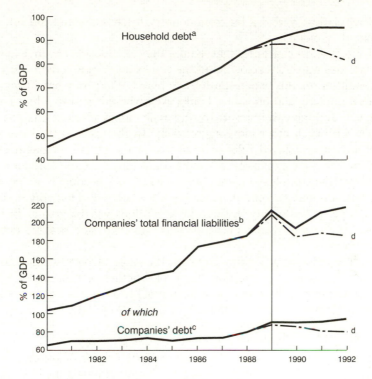

Fig. 9.10   Debt-GDP ratios in the UK, 1980–1992

References are to National Accounts codes.
[a] Personal sector total financial liabilities (*AXDY*).
[b] Industrial and commercial companies' total financial liabilities (*AXCX*)
[c] Total financial liabilities *less* issues of UK company securities (*AXCX–RICJ*).
[d] Dotted line shows actual debt as a ratio of what GDP would have been if it had continued to increase in 1980–92 as fast as in 1985–8.
Source: *UK National Accounts*, 1993, tables 12.2 and 12.3.

The UK's recession seems to have been deeper than that of any other major country [fig. 9.1]; among the smaller countries shown, only Norway's appears deeper. The swing to optimism during the preceding expansion may have been larger in the UK than in other countries; thus, both household and corporate debt [figs. 9.3 and 9.4] seem to have risen much more in the UK than elsewhere.

The worldwide nature of boom and recession

Why did severe recessions develop in almost all the main industrial countries at about this time (though not quite simultaneously)? As often remarked, recession struck first in the English-speaking countries (the USA, the UK, Canada, and Australia). One explanation is that the movement towards deregulation went further in these countries than elsewhere. But what got called 'deregulation' varied a lot from country to country, and did not in all cases amount to much.

It has already been argued that banks play a crucial role in expansion [ch. 7.2; see also app. A10 below]; and the provision of bank credit must have been a condition for this expansion to take place. What may have been more important than deregulation is that banks everywhere began to adopt liability management, and increasing resort to wholesale money markets enabled them to compete with each other more aggressively. In the process, banks in many countries may have relaxed rules of prudence in the pursuit of balance-sheet growth. The excessive expansion of credit could have spread from country to country under the stimulus of competition—which has become more potent as banking business has become increasingly international. That might suggest that the danger of instability in financial conditions will be greater in future that it was in the past—unless central banks on their side become better at controlling booms.

Without the removal of lending controls, the surge of borrowing would not have occurred. There is a question, then, of whether restoration of lending controls, or arrangements to reimpose them quickly in case of need, would not be a practicable possibility. I come back to the question later [ch. 12.3].

Policy in the 1985–93 boom and recession

If the above analysis is correct, one must seek the origins of the recession in the years before 1988 when the boom was still building up. Thus, 1982 marked the resumption of growth after the recession, and 1983–5 were years of what must be judged relatively restrained growth (annual output growth averaged 3.2 per cent—which did not however bring a fall in unemployment) [table 9.3]. The boom then hotted up: 1985 saw growth at what is now estimated at 4 per cent and the next two years, at 4.5 and 5 per cent. It is not easy to say exactly when the boom would have had to have been moderated if excessive expansion was to be avoided: perhaps in the course of 1987, certainly by the beginning of 1988. Note however that unemployment was then still about 10 per cent—hardly down from its recession peak. The economy did not evolve smoothly, and the message of contemporary statistical indicators was, as always, not clear-cut. There was an apparent pause in expansion in late 1986, and in October 1987 came the New York Stock Exchange crash, which revived memories of 1929 and led central banks everywhere to relax policy. No one, I think, inside or outside officialdom, foresaw the full scale of the boom and its inevitable recessionary aftermath.[33] To have reined in the boom at the halfway stage would have required not only clear sight but a very firm hand; restrictive action then, unless very persuasively presented, could have appeared perversely over-cautious.

The boom is often attributed to over-lax policy. If one judges by actions rather than results, that may seem unjust. On my estimates, the Budgets of 1985, 1986,

[33] I include myself here.

and 1987, and indeed that of 1988 [table 9.1], were not expansionist, but rather the reverse.[34] Interest rates were indeed reduced in the period 1985–8, but not greatly [table 9.3].[35] I would characterize policy as being fairly neutral. But questions regarding the technical stance of policy are not very relevant here. Policy clearly was not such as to put a brake on the boom, nor was it intended to be.

The basic reason why no action was taken to moderate the boom was that that the government did not consider that kind of action to be part of the responsibilities of government. Ministers trusted in the self-directing powers of unrestricted free enterprise (as well as having a more justified distrust of the ability of governments to do better). Optimism on the part of business was seen as valuable, and as far as possible ministers encouraged it.[36] The objects of policy were first to defeat inflation and second to set the economy free: given success with inflation, a governing hand on the economy was not believed to be necessary. If economic cycles resulted, cycles were held to be inevitable. Intervention was therefore not required—neither (for instance) with excessive office development,[37] nor even with the activities of the banks.[38]

In judging the government's record, two points need to be remembered. First, the forecasts available at the time did not, until 1988, indicate that the pace of growth was going to be especially high.[39] Second, even in 1987 unemployment remained high: it did not start to fall much till 1988 [table 9.3]. Growth at something above the trend rate, or above a rate that could be sustained, must have seemed then positively desirable. Signs of danger were thus not obvious.

It would require a fuller and more detailed analysis to venture a confident judgement. Nevertheless, looking back, my tentative judgement now is that the excessive pace of expansion ought to have been recognized by mid-1987. The forecasts ought not to have been fully believed—not so much because of the

[34] This is contrary to a common belief. For instance, Allsopp *et al.* (1991) say that the first of these Budgets in particular 'was widely regarded as a tax-cutting budget', which 'fuelled expenditure'.

[35] After February 1987 UK monetary policy was locked to the policy of shadowing the Deutschmark; that prevented interest rates being raised in 1988, as by then was beginning to be recognized was desirable. Lawson (1992: 800) quotes with approval a conclusion that 'the shadowing of the Deutschmark had no bearing whatever on our underestimating the strength of the boom.' But it did prevent an adjustment of policy once the underestimate was recognized.

[36] Nigel Lawson (1992: 632) notes that he regarded 'the creation of a climate of confidence as a major objective of policy', and strove to promote it in his speeches.

[37] It was obvious from an early stage that the scale of office development was being overdone and would lead later to depression in the construction industry.

[38] Nigel Lawson, while admitting that higher interest rates were what might have been needed, admits it in a tone that implies that 'to have raised interest rates sooner and even more sharply than I did' would hardly have been a practical possibility. 'Was the Government', he asks rhetorically, 'responsible for the banks taking leave of their senses?' (Lawson 1992: 630). That seems a strange question for a finance minister to ask—especially one who was more or less a monetarist. The answer must surely be that the authorities cannot disown responsibility for controlling what banks do.

[39] The Treasury forecasts are given in table 9.8. One reason for the under-forecasts may have been that contemporary estimates of outturns understated growth.

Table 9.8 Forecasts and outturns, 1986–1988 (% rise in GDP over previous calendar year)

	1986	1987	1988
Forecasts in March *Budget Report*	3	3	5
Subsequent estimate of out-turn:			
in following *Budget Report*	2.5	4	4.5
in 1996/7 *Economic Trends*	4.0	4.6	5.0

acceleration of inflation (which was not great) or of equity prices (which fell in 1988), but more because of other evidence: the rapid rise in both corporate and household debt and broad money [figs. 9.2–9.4], from about 1986 the rate of rise of house prices [fig. 9.7], and from 1987 the continued fall in the personal saving ratio [table 9.4].

9.4. What the 1989 recession contributes to our ideas about the behaviour of the economy

We can now step back from close inspection of this last recession, and consider what it contributes to our ideas about the behaviour of the economy.

The 1989 recession, in contrast to previous major recessions, appeared to owe nothing to exogenous shocks, and to be due entirely to a change in mood by consumers and business. This makes it clear (which had not been clear before) that recessions can occur without any exogenous shock and entirely because of a change in confidence or expectations. (The recession occurred, however, in reaction to over-optimism in the preceding boom; and that seems to have owed something to an exogenous happening, in particular to the terms-of-trade change.)

The 1989 recession forced me to reconsider the forces at work on previous occasions,[40] and to give more weight to downward shifts in confidence in response to exogenous shocks in earlier major recessions: such shifts probably played a large role in amplifying them (1920–1, 1929–32, and 1973–5; less clearly, 1979–82).

If the 1985–8 boom is seen not as due to deregulation, but as expectations-led, there is no guarantee that boom and recession cannot recur: indeed, the contrary is more likely.[41]

The above modification of my earlier view that fluctuations take place entirely in reaction to exogenous shocks does not imply reinstatement of the idea of a self-perpetuating cyclical mechanism, or of the idea that the cycles

---

[40] It occurred after work on this study was well advanced.

[41] Nigel Lawson (1992: 631) has said the opposite: 'the third conclusion, and the most reassuring, is that what Britain went through in the late 1980s was to a considerable extent a once-for-all occurrence: the change from a financially regulated to a deregulated economy'.

have to be of fairly regular periodicity; but it leaves open the possibility that expectational factors are inherently unstable (Minsky 1977, etc.).

I have argued that steady continued expansion is likely to produce an increase in consumer and business confidence, i.e. a rise in the propensity to consume and invest at any given income—hence a gradual reduction in unemployment. The expansion of 1985–8, though unfortunately at a pace that soon proved unsustainable, provides good evidence of such an effect.

Forecasters typically failed to predict either the acceleration of expansion, or the onset of recession and its subsequent depth. This suggests that standard forecasting procedures did not fully allow for the way in which changes in expectations both amplified the boom and later brought on the recession. The predictability of major recessions will be considered later [ch. 10.5].

9.5. Postscript: the resumption of growth, 1992–5

The recession of 1989–92 was followed by a period of resumed growth and falling unemployment. Discussion of this phase is placed in a postscript because it has little relevance to the question discussed in the rest of the chapter of why the 1989–92 recession occurred, and also because trends in this phase are difficult to interpret.

The average rate of growth in the three years 1992–5 was 2.8 per cent (in the four years 1992–6, 2.7 per cent). On the basis of earlier analysis, relatively moderate growth of this sort could, on my calculations [ch. 2.2], be expected to produce little or no fall in unemployment. In fact, unemployment on the usual definition fell nearly 3 percentage points—less, but not so much less, than the 4 per cent fall during the three years 1986–9 at the height of the Lawson boom.

There are reasons to suspect that in this phase unemployment was being reduced by special factors, unrelated to the state of demand:

1. The rise in employment after 1993 was largely confined to the service industries where productivity rises less than in manufacturing after a recession. Moreover, these industries recruited mostly women; and, probably as a result, working hours fell, and part-time working increased. These factors made the rise in employment (and fall in unemployment) unusually large in relation to the output change.
2. Firms appear to have become more ruthless in discharging workers (particularly older workers) to improve efficiency; some of those made redundant, having lost hope of finding work, will have retired from the labour force.
3. Claimant unemployment (the usual definition) was reduced by increasingly strict administration of the benefit provisions, a process carried further by the introduction of the job-seekers' allowance in 1996 which made some ineligible who were previously eligible for benefit.

Table 9.9 Estimated effect of exogenous shocks, 1992–1995

| | Estimated contributions to % rate of growth over three-year period | |
	Method AA	Method BB
Exports[a]	1.1	2.2
Terms of trade[b]	−2.9	−2.5
Monetary policy[c]	2.6	2.6
Fiscal policy[d]	3.3	2.7
Total	4.1	5.0

[a] Contribution of actual export growth *less* trend export growth.
[b] Estimated as % change in GDP deflator *less* % change in TFE deflator.
[c] Change in base rates × 0.4, lagged one year.
[d] Estimated from OECD estimate of change in structural balance of general government (OECD, *Economic Outlook*, 60, table A31), lagged one year.

Sources: The effects shown above are estimated by methods roughly comparable with those used in ch. 5.2. For explanations and cautions see that chapter.

For such reasons, some commentators discount about half the rise in unemployment as a measure of the state of demand; even more could be discounted.[42]

Earlier analysis suggested that in previous periods the trend rate of growth (i.e. the rate at which, in the absence of special factors, unemployment could be expected to remain constant) was 2.5–3 per cent a year. Despite the fall in unemployment in the recent phase, that could remain the case: there is as yet too little experience to be able to judge.

On this interpretation [see fig. 2.1] the years 1992–6 would be seen as years in which growth was resumed, not years of recovery as that term has been used here (i.e. not years of above-trend growth in which unemployed capacity was reduced). Additional evidence supporting this view is the absence of some usual coincidental signs of rapid growth. Thus, the ratio of fixed investment to GDP failed to rise after the 1989–92 recession (indeed, it fell slightly); and the personal saving ratio, which usually recedes in a growth period, remained close to its recession peak. That suggests that following the recession consumer and business confidence both remained weak.

---

[42] See Sheldon and Young (1997: 21), who prefer to rely on the inactivity rate (proportion of the population of working age of those without work) rather than the unemployment rate as a measure of demand. But the inactivity rate, as well as the unemployment rate, will probably have been affected by factors 1 and 2 above.

One piece of evidence against this view is that exogenous shocks, as measured in the study, appear to have been significantly positive. Table 9.9 suggests that shocks may have added 4–5 per cent in the years 1992–5 (i.e. 1–1.5 per cent a year).[43] A possible way to reconcile this evidence with the interpretation that growth remained little above trend is to suppose that confidence was so weak at this juncture that without the expansionary policies growth would have been even slower (e.g. 1–1.5 per cent a year).

Further years of experience will be needed to answer these questions. In view of these uncertainties, the years 1992–5 are not included among the fast-growth phases [see tables 2.5 and 11.2 below].

[43] Short-term interest rates were reduced from 11.7% on average in 1991 by 5.5 percentage points in the next two years; and fiscal policy was expansionary in 1992, though not thereafter. These stimuli were partly offset by the unfavourable shift in the terms of trade.

Part III

Conclusions

10 The Theoretical Model: The Economy's Behaviour in Major Fluctuations

The discussion of previous chapters results in a view of the economy which appears novel in a number of ways. This view has emerged piece by piece; and by way of summarizing the discussion, this chapter aims to put the elements together, and to draw out some implications of the theoretical model that results.

Chapter 11 will summarize the empirical results of the study (which have implications for how the economy works). This chapter and the next are therefore designed to be self-contained, and briefly repeat key facts and arguments (but not detailed references) from earlier chapters. They are intended to be read together, and to provide a background for the later discussion of policy in chapter 12.

Some elements of the model here presented are more firmly grounded than others. The whole picture represents my view; but not all the elements will commend themselves equally to all readers, and the different elements do not all stand or fall together as a bloc.

The arrangement of the chapter, which starts with the most general points, is as follows. Compared with many existing models of the economy, the model presented here lacks some elements of self-adjustment: this is described in section 10.1. Section 10.2 describes how it is supposed that major recessions originate, and how the view here taken differs from that of other models. Section 10.3 notes how the shape taken by major recessions as here conceived differs from what is usually assumed, and goes on to set out the implications for the role of changes in expectations or confidence in determining major recessions. The Appendix sets out intersectoral relationships more formally and in particular illustrates the financial implications of fluctuations and the key role of the banking system.

10.1. A picture of an economy lacking some elements of self-adjustment

In order to analyse how the economy responds to shocks, it was necessary first to give an account of how a growing economy behaves if left unshocked. This account is built primarily on theoretical reasoning and a critique of existing theory. (The empirical parts of this study, however will claim to show that an interpretation of events in these terms provides a plausible story.)

The resulting model of the economy lacks important powers of self-adjustment which much orthodox macroeconomic theory assumes that economies possess. In section 10.1.1, I summarize the arguments that justify the present picture of the economy; then in section 10.1.2, I note the general implications. The model applies only to major recessions, not to smaller fluctuations.

10.1.1. The basic mechanisms

How the economy behaves in the absence of shocks is held to depend on three basic mechanisms. The first two mechanisms explain

1. the forces that produce steady growth in the absence of shocks (mechanism A);
2. how, in the absence of shocks, steady growth persists even when the economy is underemployed, i.e. why underemployment persists (mechanism B).

The process of steady growth

It was argued [ch. 3.2] that steady output growth requires steady growth of both real supply and real demand. Steady growth of demand is assumed to be limited by the technical possibilities of improving productivity; but it is not automatic, and requires positive efforts by firms to utilize technical possibilities. In conditions of imperfect competition (here assumed), such efforts will not be forthcoming unless firms have come to expect a fairly steady growth of total demand.

Abstracting from shocks, steady growth of demand requires firms collectively to raise unit prices of output by less than the increase in income paid by firms per unit of factor production. Maintenance of this requisite relation depends on the expectations of firms: it is argued that firms will maintain the gap only if they expect productivity to increase and increased output to be sold.

Realized productivity growth and realized growth in factor incomes thus both depend on firms' expectations about the continuation of real growth. Both are influenced by past experience, and therefore tend to be conservative, i.e. to replicate the past. This tends to produce consistency between supply and demand augmentation, and to make growth in the absence of shocks a steady process.

The hypothesis of a complex mechanism of this sort provides a rationale for treating growth at some average past rate of growth as a norm (i.e. a rate of growth that does not call for special explanation), and for treating departures from the norm as the *explicanda*, which do have to be explained (i.e. by the intervention of demand shocks).

The stability of underemployment

The above argument implies that in the absence of shocks output will grow at the rate of growth of capacity. It implies further [ch. 3.3] that this is so irrespective of whether capacity is fully or less than fully employed.

This contention contradicts the widespread view that low employment will result in lower wages, and that lower wages will result in higher employment. (That would imply that in conditions of underemployment output growth tends to be *faster* than the capacity rate of growth.) Even on this view, it is usually admitted that the process is slow, because it is said that wages are sticky.

In opposition to that view, I argue that any such presumed process of self-adjustment to high employment is blocked by what is here termed 'sectoral interdependence'. Thus, the level of activity is determined by a sort of simultaneous circular process: firms do not employ more workers because demand is inadequate; demand remains inadequate because more workers are not employed.

This view implies a rejection of the view that persistent unemployment is due to sticky wages. One piece of evidence for my view is that capital as well as labour gets unemployed; i.e., unemployment is not due to a defect of the labour market as such.

Recession effects on productivity

A third mechanism of a rather different sort (mechanism C) explains how a downward shock to employment resulting from a shortfall in demand causes a deterioration of physical and intangible capital stocks; that is, it results in a downward displacement of the growth path of supply (i.e. of 'potential' or 'capacity' output).

The argument rests in part on empirical evidence [ch. 2.2, summarized in ch. 11.1]. A theoretical rationale is also given: I argue [ch. 4.2] that in a major recession underemployment results in the deterioration and premature scrapping of physical equipment, and that disbandment or underemployment of a firm's workforce similarly results in the partial destruction of working practices and working relations. The latter constitute the intangible capital of a firm, the value of which is an important fraction of its market value as a going concern. The capital stock, physical and intangible, takes time to build up, and its destruction cannot be made good rapidly; in effect, therefore, the destruction is quasi-permanent.

In this way demand shocks impact on supply. A major recession causes a downward displacement of the growth path of productivity (or potential or capacity output); after the recession, the 'stable growth' mechanism described by the first mechanism will in the absence of further shocks start to operate again; i.e., normal growth will be resumed from the low point of the recession.

10.1.2. General implications

The first two mechanisms imply that the economy lacks the ability to adjust itself towards full employment. It may get to full employment by lucky exogenous shocks; but these cannot be relied on, and exogenous shocks may equally well take the economy further from full employment, as the empirical results of the study [summarized in ch. 11] claim to show. The results also suggest that continuation of growth at about trend rate will generate increasing confidence and hence a rise in demand from a low point. When that happens, it may overshoot.

The result is to provide a possible case for demand management of a medium-term sort, provided that other necessary conditions are met—in particular, that the authorities possess effective instruments, have sufficient understanding, and have a sufficiently strong political base to act on it [ch. 12]. This conclusion departs from most neoclassical theory which assumes that the economy has the ability to self-adjust to full employment. (A more connected rebuttal of the neoclassical arguments of policy ineffectiveness will be given later [ch. 12.1.1].

The third mechanism has another important implication. If major recessions deflect downwards the capacity growth path, this means that the future equilibrium path of the economy is not given independent of lapses from full employment, but is influenced by the present and is path-dependent.[1]

Neoclassical theorists argue that action to counter inflation entails no permanent output loss. This third mechanism contradicts that view. It is often also assumed that, if inflation is avoided, that by itself is enough to ensure adequate growth and/or high employment: the first mechanism propounded above denies that contention.

The above three mechanisms together define the path the economy will follow. In the absence of major shocks, output and real demand will grow along the capacity growth path or a path parallel to it. Departures from this path (growth above or below the capacity rate) are therefore what shocks cause. Methodologically, then, these assumptions give definition to what it is assumed that shocks have to explain. The downward displacement of the growth path described above does not figure in standard macroeconomic analysis. In other respects, the picture described above resembles the assumptions of many econometric forecasting models.

10.2. The nature of major recessions

I turn next to the nature of major recessions as conceived in this study, and contrast the view here presented with the different accounts formerly or presently current.

10.2.1. Demand versus supply explanations

The present account sees short-term output fluctuations as driven by demand not supply disturbances, and in this sense is Keynesian.

Since the 1970s, the chief opposition to neo-Keynesian models has come from New Classical (NC) macroeconomics, and its successor Real Business Cycle (RBC) theory. Both NC and RBC theories have sought to show how business cycles could happen, even in perfectly competitive economies, in which (it is argued) a general shortage of demand thus does not arise. New Classical theory explains cycles in terms of imperfect information and monetary misconceptions; while RBC theory[2] explains cycles in terms of random changes in technology or

---

[1] The empirical results of this study provide some evidence that major recessions cause downward displacement of the growth path.

[2] See Stadler (1994); Barro (1981; 1989b). Stadler (1994: 1751) writes: 'RBC theory views cycles as arising in frictionless, perfectly competitive economies with generally complete markets subject

productivity. Theorists of these schools chose to start from the idea of a perfectly competitive economy because that conformed with what economic theory appeared to say is the 'essential' nature of actual economies, and because this assumption therefore (it was held) provided proper micro foundations for macro theory.

Real Business Cycle theory is rejected in the present study for three reasons [ch. 4.3]:

1. There is no direct evidence for the occurrence of shocks of the required type. Large recessions would require large supply-side causes to explain them, of a sort that would be very evident (e.g. big plagues, droughts, or strikes) and widely remarked on. These have not happened at the relevant times on the scale required to explain almost simultaneous severe contractions in all major economies.[3]
2. The assumption of a perfectly operating economy, far from being a useful initial assumption, is a perverse starting point. When in a recession firms cut output, or workers fail to find a job, lack of demand seems to them a harsh reality; and their perception of events has some claim to be respected as evidence.
3. The present study claims to demonstrate that major recessions can, alternatively, be well explained in terms of the rapid emergence of inadequacy of demand.

RBC theorists claim it as a virtue that RBC theory explains fluctuations in growth in the same terms (fluctuations in productivity) as it explains growth (the Solow residual = growth of total factor productivity). That however is a formal and empty symmetry. I see major recessions not as of the same stuff as steady growth, but as occasions that interrupt it. Apart from major recessions, the rate of growth of capacity can and does vary for supply-side reasons—but, except in rare catastrophies, only on a small scale from year to year [ch. 4].

For my purposes, I only need elements of a theory of growth in order to explain what it is that recessions interrupt; and do not need a fully developed theory of a sort that would explain the causes of varying growth rates everywhere over the centuries. (For some observations on these topics however, see chapter 4.) I need only explain the fairly steady sort of growth that mostly

---

to real shocks. RBC models demonstrate that, even in such environments, cycles can arise through the reactions of optimizing agents to real disturbances such as random changes in technology or productivity. Furthermore such models are capable of mimicking the most important empirical regularities displayed by business cycles. Thus RBC theory makes the notable contribution of showing that fluctuations in economic activity are consonant with competitive general equilibrium environments in which all agents are rational maximizers. Coordination failures, price stickiness, waves of optimism or pessimism, monetary policy, or government policy generally are not needed to account for business cycles.' These factors may not be 'needed' to explain fluctuations; but, I argue, they in fact provide the explanation.

[3] The only events that RBC theorists usually point to are the two OPEC price shocks. I claim [ch. 8.1] that these events must have had powerful demand effects, whereas their supply-side effects were minimal.

seems to occur in the intervals between major recessions. (Section 10.1 above sketched elements of such a theory of steady but interruptable growth.)

A special sort of supply-side view is that unemployment is due to excessive real wages. There are, to me, compelling theoretical arguments and statistical evidence against the real-wage hypothesis [app. A3.2]. That view tends to be popular at times when unemployment has risen, and evidently it then appeals as plausible. But it is much less plausible to suppose that the big *falls* in unemployment (as at World War I, and before and into World War II) occur because the excessiveness of wage levels then somehow melts.

10.2.2. Demand-side explanations of fluctuations

Most work on cycles up to the 1970s explained fluctuations in output (as the present model does) as a product of fluctuations in demand. Since the present model is designed to explain big recessions, occurring perhaps rarely at apparently random intervals, it differs from many previous accounts, which discuss fluctuations, irrespective of size, that appear to occur with some regularity and so justify description as (trade or business) cycles.

There have been several variants within this general approach. The Keynesian models of the 1940s and 1950s (e.g. Samuelson 1939; Kalecki 1937b; Kaldor 1940; J.R. Hicks 1950) were variants on the idea of endogenous self-generating, self-perpetuating cycles. The present model rejects this conception. It makes some use of the propagation mechanisms contained in these models, but gives a big role to shifts in confidence. Though such shifts are admitted to be at times partly endogenous in origin, the view here taken differs from Minsky's view (e.g. Minsky 1977) that cyclical swings in confidence are inevitable.

Later Keynesian models have accepted the idea that fluctuations in output result from demand shocks that are exogenous in origin.[4] Though fluctuations have been short-lasting, recurrent, and (very roughly) regular in periodicity, they have not (as we know) been regular in depth. Theoretical neo-Keynesian models explain periodicity as a result of ceilings and floors and the nature of the propagation mechanisms. Economic forecasting models, which are basic-ally Keynesian in inspiration, are not wedded to the idea of regular periodicity, and explain events as a product of irregularly occurring exogenous shocks, as does the present model.

It has more recently been argued that erratic fluctuations are the result of nonlinear (unchanging) response functions. On the view here espoused, non-linearity is accepted, but any long-run result stemming from nonlinearity is seen as being dwarfed by the short-run changes in the scale of relationships

---

[4] Frisch (1933) and Slutsky (1937) demonstrated that random exogenous shocks could, in combination with some types of propagation mechanism, produce regular cycles similar to those that could be produced by a model of self-generating, self-perpetuating, endogenous cycles. The present analysis accepts some but not all that picture: what I need to explain is a sequence of very *irregular* fluctuations.

that can occur as a result of shifts in confidence during the course of a single fluctuation.

The measurement of shocks

Shocks are by definition unexpected events. It is sometimes argued that agents' foresight is so good that important events are anticipated. The best answer to that is that the course of output in fact undergoes erratic fluctuations, and the best explanation is that unexpected events occur.

This study has sought to measure four types of demand shock, two of which consist of changes in government policy (monetary policy and fiscal policy), and two that originate largely outside the UK (terms-of-trade changes and deviations of exports from trend). It is assumed that these four types of event are unforeseen (or, if partly foreseen, that the degree of foresight is constant). The shock indicators here used are evidently imperfect; the results nevertheless seem to show that they have considerable explanatory power [ch. 5.2, summarized in ch. 11].

One type of event here treated as a shock is changes in fiscal policy (tax rates or government spending). Many theoretical arguments, including the argument of Ricardian equivalence, have been advanced for supposing that changes in fiscal policy have no permanent or long-term impact on private spending. This contention is hardly possible to test statistically (for how long is long?); but on the plane of theory there are counter-arguments to each [ch. 5, esp. app. A5]. The present empirical results [ch. 11], moreover, appear to show that the fiscal policy indicator helps to explain major recessions and other types of fluctuation, i.e. that, in the short term at least, fiscal policy affects spending.

Changes in expectations (confidence effects)

It is here argued that shocks, in addition to affecting spending directly, affect it indirectly by changing expectations (or confidence). The induced change in expectations (confidence) thus magnifies the direct effect of shocks on spending. This indirect effect does not depend on a sequence of rounds in which change in spending → change in income → change in spending, and so on (as in the classical exposition of the multiplier mechanism). Rather, it operates instantaneously, and can rapidly become self-amplifying and thus very large [ch. 5.1]. To denote these large, unstable effects, the term *consumption amplifier* is used. I argue that there is an analogous *investment amplifier* which operates in the short term. The classical accelerator mechanism remains important as a long-term argument.

Agents' conceptions of their future income are not precise but very vague. (Most people do not even know their actuarial life probability.) For this reason the vaguer term *confidence* has been preferred to the term *expectations* (which suggests quantifiability: the distinction is analogous to the distinction in Knight (1930) between risk and uncertainty).

There is evidence that big swings in confidence have occurred that have not been provoked directly by shocks, which, even in the absence of exogenous shocks, can (as in 1989–93) [ch. 9] cause a major recession.

The interrelation between different elements in the system in the course of a major fluctuation are set out more precisely in the appendix to this chapter. Three points demonstrated there are: (1) how a fall in the price and wage level in a recession (if that occurred) would be likely to leave unchanged the balance between total demand and available supply, and thus would do nothing to remedy unemployment; (2) how the sector that, from a position of steady growth, initiates an upward movement of the economy must draw on cash reserves or borrowing facilities; and (3) how the banking system thus plays a crucial role in providing the condition for an expansionary sequence.

10.3. The shape of major recessions and the role of expectations (or confidence)

10.3.1. The shape of major recessions

As here conceived, major recessions have an abrupt downward phase which is not followed by any automatic recovery phase. This proposition is based largely on theoretical reasoning, but appears to provide a satisfactory basis for empirical explanation.

The asymmetric shape of a major recession is held to result from two mechanisms. First, it is easier to shatter confidence than to restore it. A break in confidence results in a sharp contraction of spending and output. When the contraction is over, it is held that output resumes at the normal or trend rate (mechanism A) [s. 10.1]. A protracted period of steady expansion at or about the trend rate will however result in a gradual recovery of confidence.[5] Though that occurs only slowly and gradually, it is of great importance, particularly for policy [see ch. 12]. This is held [ch. 3.2] to be the only mechanism by which the economy returns to high employment.

Second, a major recession of demand is held [ch. 2.2] to result in a downward displacement of the path of capacity growth (mechanism C) [s. 10.1]; i.e., the path of full employment (when, if ever, regained) is on a lower level—though on a path that may be parallel to a projection of the previous capacity growth path; i.e., some economic capacity is permanently lost.

This picture of the shape of a major recession contrasts with the traditional picture of fluctuations, in which the downward phase is followed by a positive upward phase which brings output back to, or above, the previous trend. The contrast between this traditional picture and the present one is depicted in figure 10.1. In the present picture there is no automatic positive upward phase; i.e., unless new shocks occur, growth at the trend rate is simply resumed from the low point of the recession.

---

[5] There is little exact knowledge of what causes a revival of confidence (or of whether there are regular laws of behaviour). The assumption that after a disturbance output growth resumes at (no more than) the trend rate is adopted as an approximate statement of the first reaction.

In view of this asymmetry, the term *recession* here comprises only a downward phase. That has determined the principle on which recessions (and other fluctuations) are dated [ch. 2.2]. A recession is deemed to start when the rate of growth clearly starts to fall short of the trend rate, and to end when it regains the trend rate. (Methods used to estimate trends are summarized in ch. 11.1.) Similarly, a period of above-trend growth is deemed to start when output growth exceeds trend, and to end when it falls back to trend. This methodology places the start of a recession earlier, and its end later, than when, as is usual, recessions are dated according to the absolute change in output.

A major recession is seen as an interruption to the process of normal growth, and when the shock causing the interruption ceases, normal growth is resumed along a lower growth path. To that extent, the picture corresponds to the view that shocks have permanent rather than transient effects. But for fast-growth periods, and for small fluctuations, it is here assumed that the growth rate of

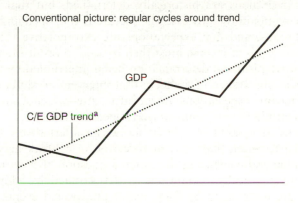

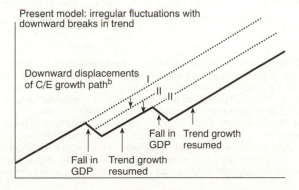

Fig. 10.1 Conventional model of cycles compared with the present model of two major recessions

[a] Trend growth of constant-employment GDP.
[b] Path displaced from I to II to III.

capacity is left unaffected. The present picture therefore agrees in part only with the contention (see Nelson and Plosser 1982, and other writers) that shocks have permanent effects on output [ch. 2.2].[6]

10.3.2. The nature of changes in expectations or confidence

It may be helpful to clarify the nature of changes in expectations or confidence that is implied by this account.

One basic theoretical insight advanced in this study is the explanation proposed for stable underemployment (mechanisms A and B, summarized in section 10.1 above). This may be not novel—it seems to me the essence of Keynes, and is implicit in most econometric forecasting models—but it is not now commonly stated, and it has wide implications for our understanding of what happens to the economy during fluctuations.

The mechanisms proposed to explain the stability of unemployment imply that income expectations are historically determined, but that shocks may produce break-points in the process. The picture is that spending depends on income expectations, and that expectations are extrapolative. The transition from high to low levels of income must then be seen to result from the normal process of iterative historical determination being interrupted by the intervention from outside the system of a shock: that intervention shifts income (and therefore also income expectations) downward—after which a smooth process of historical determination is resumed [see appendix A10.2].

What happens as a result of a large shock can alternatively be seen as a break in confidence: seen that way, the occasion of a break may seem more readily acceptable and convincing. It is then a question of how, in a world in which the future is basically unknowable, patterns of activity adopted in times of tranquility are interrupted by some major unexpected event, and of how accustomed patterns are after an interval resumed.[7] Put that way, the question appears not one of knowledge, but of how courage gets broken and restored.[8]

---

[6] I concur with this thesis only in the case of large, downward shocks, but not in other cases. In cases between major recessions therefore I see it as legitimate to estimate trends. Another difference is that here I am talking not about output, but about output adjusted to a constant-employment basis (which I argue falls permanently in a major recession), while that part of a fall in output associated with a fall in employment is temporary and reversible.

[7] Marshall and Marshall (1879: 52–5) describes the 19th-c. trade cycle entirely in psychological terms: 'when distrust has taken the place of confidence, failure and panic breed panic and failure. [W]hen it is over there is a calm, but a dull heavy calm. Those who have saved themselves are in no mood to venture again ... the chief cause of the evil is want of confidence ... the revival of industry comes about through the gradual and often simultaneous growth of confidence among various trades ....'

[8] Compare Keynes (1936: 161–2): 'Even apart from the instability due to speculation, there is the instability due to the characteristic of human nature that a large proportion of our positive activities depend on spontaneous optimism rather than on a mathematical expectation ... Most, probably, of our decisions to do something positive, the full consequences of which will be drawn out over many days to come, can only be taken as a result of animal spirits ... not as the outcome

The idea of break-points at which there is a transition from one state of expectation or confidence to another has implications for the predictability of major recessions, to be discussed later [ch. 11.5].

of a weighted average of quantitative benefits multiplied by quantitative probabilities ... Thus if the animal spirits are dimmed and the spontaneous optimism falters, leaving us to depend on nothing but a mathematical expectation, enterprise will fade and die ... individual initiative will only be adequate when reasonable calculation is supplemented and supported by animal spirits, so that the thought of ultimate loss ... is put aside as a healthy man puts aside the expectation of death.'

Appendix A10   A formal account of interactions during fluctuations

Macroeconomic fluctuations involve interaction between one part of the economy and another, and to understand the behaviour of the system one needs a model describing the main interactions between separate parts. This appendix sets out, more formally than in the text, a system of interrelations between sectors which appears necessary and sufficient to explain the economy's reaction to shocks. It starts with interreactions between two sectors, and the mechanisms A, B, and C as set out in section 10.1 above. Among other points, it demonstrates the financial counterpart to fluctuations, and the key role of the banking system. The propositions, set out below, at first are of minimal simplicity and later are amplified to allow the real world to be more easily recognized.

A10.1. *Indefinite stable reiteration*

Stable states of underemployment [as argued in s. 10.2] depend on the fact that in a developed economy individual agents are interdependent. Interdependence is symbolized most dramatically (though it is not essential to the argument) by assuming two or more interacting sectors. Let us start with an extremely simple model of two sectors: persons and firms. The function of a firm here is simply to employ persons to produce consumer goods (which are the whole of output), all of which firms sell to persons. The whole of persons' incomes comes from the sale of their labour, all of which is sold to firms.

Let C = persons' spending and firms' income and E = firms' spending and persons' income. Let persons' spending in one period be a function of their income in the previous one, and similarly for firms, so that

$$C_2 = c(E_1) \qquad \text{and} \qquad E_2 = e(C_1).$$

Now let $e = c = 1$ and $E_0 = C_0$. The system must then reiterate indefinitely at whatever level of income ($E_0 = C_0$) it starts with.

The counter-argument to this account of stable reiteration at under-full employment (already noted) is that reiteration at under-full employment cannot persist because (*a*) at under-full employment wages will fall, and (*b*) lower wages will produce fuller employment. The present simple model allows it to be shown very clearly that this argument is wrong—not only in this simple case, but generally. The counter-counter-argument is as follows.

The second premiss (*b*) fails because, though lower wages would promote higher employment if persons' incomes out of which the products of labour are to be bought *remained unchanged*, here, as a result of the circularity of the system, persons' income are reduced in equal proportion to the fall in firms' wage payments (to which they are here identical). Hence real demand (hence also unemployment) is unaffected.

Another objection (empirically based, so less universal) is that the first premiss (*a*) fails because prices in industrial countries no longer (since the 1930s) fall absolutely in conditions of underemployment.[9]

---

[9] A further counter-argument (the Real Balance effect)—in my view also untenable—is usually deployed against stable reiteration at under-full employment. This is (*a*) that (as before) in under-employment prices will fall; (*b*) that persons own money (or other financial assets bearing fixed or zero interest) which, when prices fall, rise in real value; and (*c*) that with greater wealth persons spend more, so that employment rises. What is wrong with this argument is its asymmetric assumptions about the behaviour of different parts of the economy. Thus, (*a*) financial assets are

Table 10.1 Shock caused by a once-only rise in persons' spending

Period	c	C		E	Change in money holding or credit position of:	
					Persons	Firms
1		100	→	100		
2	1.0	100	→	100		
3	1.0	100	→	100		
4	1.1	100	→	100	−10	+10
5	1.0	110	→	110		
6	1.0	110	→	110		

A10.2. *Demand shocks and their impact*

In a closed system (e.g. of the sort represented in the model), a demand shock can be depicted only by supposing a break in the closed system.[10] In table 10.1, a shock is depicted by a once-only change in one or other of the income–expenditure relationships (C or E). Assume, for instance, that the system at the start is running at 100 (as in periods 1–3). Then let C rise for one period to 1.1 and then revert to unity. Since persons spend more (= firms sell more), firms employ more (= persons' incomes rise)—which is what leads persons to continue spending at the new higher level. Thus, by being 'extravagant', consumers produce the higher income which 'justifies' the extravagance. The system thereafter reiterates indefinitely with income and spending at the new higher level of 110. A similar result follows from a once-only rise in E; and inverse effects follow from a once-only fall in either parameter.

On these assumptions, a once-for-all shock has permanent effect on the level of activity, and moves the economy to a new stable position of fuller or less full employment.

A10.3. *The financial counterpart to economic fluctuations*

Transitions from one level of employment of capacity to another necessitate the transfer of financial assets between agents.

debts to persons but wealth to banks or government, and the latter are assumed *not* to spend less in the mirror of the situation in which persons spend more; and (b) fixed interest rates are a form of price-stickiness, and are assumed not to crumble in circumstances when for current goods and services price-stickiness is supposed to dissolve. Asymmetric assumptions of this sort do not provide an adequate basis for a general statement about the working of the macroeconomy. The assumed behaviour on the part of governments could indeed be regarded as a case of expansive fiscal policy (maintenance of spending despite depletion of wealth). That perhaps is the best way to state the kernel of truth in the real balance effect.

[10] With a model with more sectors, we will later be able to represent a shock coming from outside the present two (private) sectors, which are all the model as yet contains.

Assume that agents all start with holdings of money, or alternatively that persons are able to borrow from firms, or firms from persons; and that the size of money holdings or credit availability is adequate to finance the transactions to be described.

If the economy is running at an unchanged level of activity and employment, persons and firms are each for their part spending their income; thus, neither sector draws on, or adds to, financial balances. Now suppose there is a positive shock (which leads as before to a rise in employment): suppose, for instance, that there is as before [table 10.1, period 4] a rise in consumer spending. That means that persons buy more from firms, and as a result their financial balances fall and those of firms rise.

Note that the shock could not occur in the first place if persons had no money holdings and could not borrow. A similar result follows if the shock had been initiated by firms deciding to employ more persons: they would similarly have to expend money balances or borrow. The conclusion is that shocks are limited by finance. This result is true not just for the present two-sector model, but generally.

A10.4. *Introduction of banks*

Banks intermediate regarding financial transactions between sectors, but they do more than intermediate. When banks lend, they give persons or firms the means to spend: they put at the disposal of their borrowing clients power to spend deposits placed with them by lenders. Banks act in advance of having found permanent finance for the rights to spend that they authorize; i.e., they do not have to do what nonbanks would have had to do had they arranged finance not through banks but through financial markets. As the spending so allowed takes place, income and activity rise (provided that the economy is not already at full employment); additional savings are made and are held either as bank deposits or in alternative financial securities issued by the banks. By the end of the process, the banks' action in financing additional consumption or investment is thus validated.

Banks thereby play a major role in providing finance *in advance of agreements to lend by the ultimate final lenders*. By so doing, they remove a financial constraint that would otherwise tend to prevent any expansionary sequences.[11] Without borrowing, agents would be constrained unless they owned sufficiently large cash balances which they could run down.

A10.5. *Introduction of expectations: the amplification of shocks*

Suppose that spending is a function not directly of income but of expectations about income, and that the propensity to spend out of income depends at least in part on expected income.

How far shocks are amplified depends on how shocks affect expectations about future income—in other words, on how they affect 'confidence'. Suppose that persons' spending depends not directly on their income (E) but on the lifetime income they expect (E^e), and that their expected income depends on consumer confidence (cc), itself part-dependent in some complex way on their actual income in recent years (n years before the present):

$$C_2 = c(E_1^e), \qquad E_1^e = cc(E_{1-n}).$$

Similarly, suppose that firms' spending on labour depends on their expected income (C^e); and that that depends on business confidence (bc), itself a complex function of

---

[11] Banks need to increase their own reserves when they lend more. Normally they do so by depositing a small portion of the growth of their own deposits with the central bank. The central bank can act to offset this, and keep the banks short of reserves, but normally (as is evident) it does not.

firms' past income:

$$E_2 = c(C_1^e), \qquad C_1^e = bc(C_{1-n}).$$

From this it follows that the scale of the secondary effects of a shock depend on how far the initial change in income affects expectations of future income.

At this stage, consider only the personal sector. Suppose that a shock comes from elsewhere. (In the present simple model, it has to come from the business sector employing more, or fewer, people.) If the shock strongly affects what persons expect their lifetime income to be, it will (if financial constraints allow) affect spending a lot: if persons' expectations are unchanged, it will leave spending also unchanged.

Three applications of this line of thought are important [see ch. 5.1]:

1. If (as above) shocks change persons' expectations and changes in them then change consumer spending, this is a mechanism that enlarges the effect of a shock. This effect, which could be regarded as the multiplier, is here called the *consumption amplifier* (see below).
2. Small shocks, as in small recessions, seem to leave expectations little affected; and big shocks seem to have significant effects on them.
3. When the size of the propensity to consume varies in this way, it takes effect immediately, not gradually. The multiplier as usually conceived works through successive rounds, which take time. In big fluctuations, when confidence factors become important, the consumer amplifier thus outclasses the multiplier as usually conceived. (The same is true of its analogue, the investment amplifier relative to the accelerator: see below.)

A10.6. *Introduction of investment and business confidence*

Now introduce a second factor of production, *capital*; and make firms (as in real life) play a dual role: not only hiring labour and taking short-term production decisions, but also owning capital and undertaking investment. In practice, firms' expectations of sales and profits (business confidence) cause fluctuations not only in what firms spend on employment (as we have hitherto assumed), but also in what they spend on investment. There is thus an *investment amplifier*,[12] analogous to the consumption multiplier already discussed.

Expectations of future income are clearly influenced by present income, but if they are a function of income it is not a simple linear function. This makes it difficult to define the relationship between change in income and change in expected income (if indeed an ultimate stable relationship exists). That is probably why econometric explanations of past big recessions, and predictions of future ones, have both been poor [ch. 11.5].

A10.7. *Government and the rest of the world*

Now introduce two additional sectors: government, and 'abroad' (or 'the rest of the world'). Both sectors may originate shocks, i.e. change their own spending independently of a change in their income (whose nature and behaviour I do not pause to define). The spending both of government and of the rest of the world, ultimately limited by financial constraints, is usually not closely limited. These sectors thus can be (and have been) major sources of shocks impinging on the two domestic private sectors.

---

[12] In an expansion, firms' profit and sales forecasts strengthen, so that both the desire to invest and the finance for investment increase when GDP rises. The investment amplifier is a (short-term) relation between investment and the *level* of GDP, in contrast to the accelerator, which is a (long-term) relation between investment and the *rate of growth* of GDP.

A10.8. *Floors and ceilings to fluctuations*

Fluctuations do not explode to infinitely high demand, nor do they implode to zero levels of activity. Even in the Great Depression of 1929–33, activity in the USA fell only to about 45 per cent below full employment [ch. 6.3]; in the UK the all-time low has been 12 or 13 per cent below [table 11.1].

One reason for a floor is that gross investment cannot be reduced below zero: that would create a lower limit perhaps 20 or 25 per cent below full employment (depending on the share of gross investment in GDP before the recession). Consumer spending also falls, but not without limit: that may in part be because, even in a big recession, agents nevertheless retain a degree of confidence, and so believe that output, having sunk a certain distance, will start to rise again at a date not many years ahead.

The upper limit to a boom is defined by the physical upper limit to output. But near-approach to that limit causes inflation, and gives rise to the expectation that the government will seek to counter inflation. Every economy has a government on its back, potentially interventionist even if presently inactive; and, except in conditions of social chaos, market expectations incorporate that fact.

The floor and the ceiling are wide apart, but it must make a great difference to the economy's performance that they should be there. Also important for the general picture—if these explanations are correct—is that expectations play an important role in *shaping* the future; i.e., it is here not a question of whether expectations rationally assess a future that is independently determined, but rather that expectations shape what the future is to be.

A10.9. *Speculative price effects* (*bubble effects*)

Above-trend expansion raises expectations about future spending [ss. A10.5 and A10.6] and hence increases spending. That in turn will raise expectations further; and so it goes on. In markets for goods or assets with flexible prices, a more speculative sequence may then occur. A general increase in demand will raise flexible prices particularly; expectations that this will continue further raise demand for flexibly priced goods/assets; and that will then further raise total demand (e.g., consumers spend more when house prices or stock market prices rise); and so on.

In such a sequence, the relative price of flexi-priced goods/assets is raised above its equilibrium value, and is supported in that position only so long as expectations of continuing price rises persist. It is inevitable that at some point such expectations will cease; the sequence will then reverse.

Shifts in confidence and speculative price sequences may interact and be mutually reinforcing.

A10.10. *Two possible origins of major recession*

History points to two possible sources of major recession [see summary of chs. 5–9 given in ch. 11.3 below]. First, it may occur as a result of a downward demand shock: that will depress confidence and bring downward speculative price effects, each of which will amplify the effect of the shock. Alternatively, recession may occur without exogenous shock as a result of an autonomous collapse of confidence and/or a break in speculative price sequences. Historically, this has happened only as a reaction to an usually large boom.

11   The Causation of Major Recessions: Summary and Discussion of Empirical Findings

The empirical findings of this study rest on two sorts of evidence: first, a set of detailed case studies of the five major UK recessions since 1920; and second, a statistical analysis which seeks to explain these and other fluctuations in terms of indicators of four types of exogenous demand shock. This chapter summarizes this evidence and its underlying rationale. It needs to be read along with chapter 10. Like chapter 10, it aims to be self-contained, and thus briefly repeats findings given earlier. Some parts may prove more acceptable than others; the picture does not have to be accepted or rejected as a bloc.

The arrangement of the chapter is as follows.

The *explicanda* of the study are taken to be not absolute falls in output during a recession, but deviations of output from previous trend rates of constant-employment growth. Section 11.1 summarizes how such trends are estimated; this, incidentally, provides a rough estimate of the output loss resulting from major recessions.

Section 11.2 summarizes the statistical analysis of the causation of major recessions and other fluctuations, and recapitulates the methods used to estimate the scale of shocks and their effect on output.

Section 11.3 provides a summary of the case studies [chs. 6–9] of the five major UK recessions, along with a digression on the Great Depression in the USA, 1929–33.

The long period from World War II to 1973 saw fairly steady growth without major recessions [ch. 7]: section 11.4 summarizes possible reasons.

Section 11.5 concludes with notes on, first, the effect of the three major recessions since 1973 on the stock of public debt; and, second, whether major recessions are predictable.

11.1. Estimation of constant-employment growth rates: the loss resulting from major recessions

The procedure in this study has been to try to explain why output grew more or less fast than what its trend would have been if the economy had remained at constant levels of unemployment. This section summarizes how such trend rates were calculated. The calculations suggest that major recessions resulted in a downward displacement of a semi-permanent sort in the path of productivity growth.

11.1.1. Methods of estimation

To estimate trend output, GDP was first adjusted to a constant-employment basis. The associated annual change in percentage unemployment was used to estimate what the annual change in output would have been if unemployment had remained unchanged. Log-linear trends were then fitted to the adjusted series.

Two estimates were made. The first (method A) assumed that in the course of a major recession the movement to a lower level of output raises percentage unemployment in proportion to the fall in output (i.e., constant-employment GDP = GDP $(1+u-u^*)$, where u is actual rate of unemployment and u^* is an arbitrary rate of unemployment taken as a standard of comparison). The second estimate (method B) employed the relation (Okun's Law) between year-to-year changes in output and unemployment, taking big and small fluctuations together. Correlation of such annual changes indicates that the percentage change in unemployment is typically only a fraction (e.g. 0.3) of the change in output.

Estimates of the trend of constant-employment output as estimated on method A show a downward break at each major recession, with more or less constant trend growth rates between major recessions. The second method results in estimates of trend which show (on UK data) no significant breaks. The estimate of the increase in unused (and presumably usable) capacity as a result of a major recession is, on method A, proportional to the increase in percentage unemployment; on method B it is several times as large.

Of the two procedures, method A was here preferred, for three reasons:

1. Big recessions cause bigger changes in unemployment relative to output than small ones [table 11.2]—as method A assumes.[1]
2. Method B results in implausibly large estimates of unutilized capacity.
3. There are general theoretical reasons [ch. 4.2, summarized ch. 10.1] to expect the sort of destruction of economic capacity implied by method A.

Though the choice of method affects the height of the estimated trend growth path, it leaves the slope of the estimated trend little affected [table 2.4], and thus has little effect on estimated divergences of growth from trend during a recession period, which constitute the *explicanda* in this study. But since there is an element of doubt, results on both methods are shown in many tables.

11.1.2. Estimates of downward displacement of growth path

The estimates of trend suggest that output in the 1990s was well below what it would have been had there been no major recessions since World War II.

---

[1] The estimates of table 5.9 show an effect on unemployment in major recessions of 0.5 times the proportionate change in output; the estimates are rough, and more refined ones would probably show a larger coefficient.

A projection forward for twenty years of a past trend is clearly at best only a crude indication; but since in the UK the rate of growth of capacity (constant-employment output) appears to have been fairly constant, the procedure can claim some rough plausibility. Figure 11.1 suggests that in 1993 output was of the order of 25 per cent below a projection of the 1952–72 trend. This does not imply that the economy was in deep recession—at least, not a deeper recession than that implied by the 10.3 per cent level of unemployment—but rather that in the course of three recessions (1973, 1979, 1989) productive capacity got destroyed, but for which economic capacity by the end of the period would have been some 15 per cent higher than it was.[2]

Figure 11.1 provides circumstantial evidence in favour of two broader propositions:

1. It supports the view that shocks come from the side of demand, not supply. Thus, unemployed capacity was at a minimum in each world war: wars are times when governments spend without restraint and when demand is obviously high; so fluctuations in total demand seem to explain the high-capacity working in wartime, and thus by inference the lower levels of capacity employment at other times.
2. The figure also gives support to the view that the economy has little innate capability of regaining high employment once it is lost. If the economy had extreme self-adjusting powers, unemployment would not occur; the facts not only belie any such extreme view, but suggest that any such powers are weak and slow-acting. Unemployment was very low in World War I, and again in World War II and the twenty-five years following. After these phases, in two periods of twenty years, unemployment tended (though with important ups and downs) to grow, not disappear. When recoveries happened, one can for the most part trace some special reason, such as rearmament in the 1930s [ch. 5.3]. Prolonged periods of steady growth tended to rebuild confidence [see s. 11.4].

11.2. Explanation of major recessions in terms of exogenous demand shocks

Figure 11.2 shows the course of the five major UK recessions, each depicted as shortfall below previous trend.

11.2.1. Methods of estimating shocks and testing their effect on output

For the statistical analysis, measures were constructed of the scale of five types of shock, of which one was discarded [ch. 5.2].

---

[2] The calculations appear to suggest that the scale on which capacity got destroyed varied as between recessions, but they are not accurate enough to establish any such conclusion.

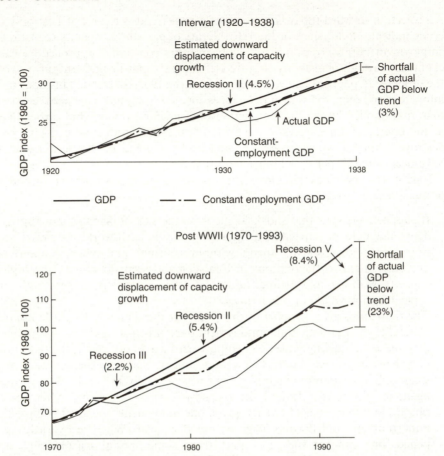

Fig. 11.1   Estimates of downward displacement of path of capacity growth at major UK recessions

Constant employment GDP = GDP $(1 + (u - u^*))$, where u^* is an arbitrary level of unemployment taken as a standard of comparison. Trends are fitted to constant-employment GDP.

This chart is essentially an enlargement of fig. 2.4, designed to show more clearly divergences from trend. As in that chart, trends are fitted to constant-employment GDP, estimated by method A (summarized in the text). The slope of the line depends on the fitted trend, while its absolute level is arbitrarily chosen. Here the line for the interwar period corresponds to a level of unemployment of 9.8% (the actual average for the period). For the 1970–93 period the line corresponds to a level of unemployment at the start of the period (1.8%). That is to be considered a relatively low point, i.e., high level of demand.

Source: as for fig. 2.4.

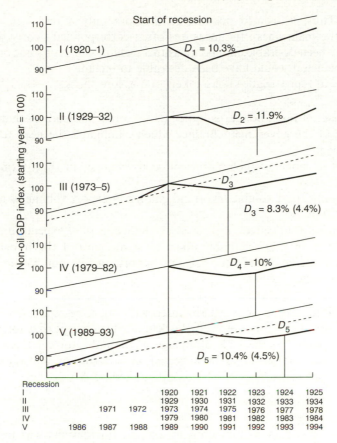

Fig. 11.2 Stylized picture: the five major UK recessions

Trend as estimated in table 2.3 on method B; D = depth of recession = shortfall from pre-recession trend as shown in table 2.5, method B (bracketed figure = shortfall reckoned from start of previous boom).

There are two sorts of difficulty in constructing such measures. The first is general and basic. A shock is by definition an unexpected event. But there is no way of knowing what portion of events on any occasion is expected and what unexpected. Output would not fluctuate abruptly if the factors causing it to do so were perfectly foreseen. Big fluctuations are thus themselves evidence (if evidence for that is needed) that agents' foresight is partial. The fact that events treated as shocks proved to be correlated with output fluctuations is evidence that the events were not fully foreseen, and also that the degree of foresight showed some stability.

The second reason why measurement of shocks must be imperfect is the practical difficulty of devising statistical measures of what one would like to measure. Thus, it seemed possible to measure only a few sorts of shock (possibly the main ones); the measures often corresponded poorly with what would have been desirable; and no measures seem possible for some other types of shock, which it would have been desirable to include.[3]

Changes in four variables were taken to measure shocks:

1. the impact of fiscal policy, as indicated by a new measure of change in the balance of the government Budget which eliminated the need for cyclical adjustment;[4]
2. changes in monetary policy (measured as changes in short-term nominal interest rates);
3. changes in export volume *less* trend change in export volume as a percentage of GDP;
4. the terms-of-trade effect, measured as change in final expenditure deflator *less* change in GDP deflator, taken as a measure of the impact of disproportionate changes in the price of imports on the purchasing power of domestic factor incomes.

Other shock indicators were experimented with but were rejected.

The statistical definition of each shock indicator (except that for monetary policy) was such that the scale of change in the indicator corresponded with the percentage change in GDP expected as a result of that shock. (This correspondence is the basis of what is called method AA.)

Tests of the effect of shocks on output

The ability of shocks so measured to explain fluctuations was tested by a two-stage process:

1. Annual changes in the shock indicators were related to annual changes in GDP. No single indicator provided a significant explanation of output changes. But taken together, the shock indicators (though claiming to be neither accurate nor complete) explained almost two-thirds of the annual variation in GDP ($R^2 = 0.60$). (The empirically derived estimates of the parameters for the effect of each shock indicator provided the basis for what is here called method BB.)

---

[3] The effect of exchange rate changes e.g. was poorly modelled. Also, the effect of *real* interest changes could not be modelled, since that would have required knowledge we do not possess about how far changes in inflation rates were expected: different plausible assumptions gave very different results [ch. 5.2].

[4] The measure treated fiscal drag as an effective increase in tax rates. In detail, the measure was: changes in public authorities' expenditure on goods and services *less* changes in tax receipts net of transfers in excess of changes in tax base, expressed as a % of GDP, all components being weighted according to estimated impact on private spending [see app. A5 for a detailed discussion of methods used, and of theoretical objections to such measures].

2. Estimates were then derived for the effect of each type of shock on output over the period of each fluctuation, using both the theoretically expected values (method AA) and the empirically derived values (method BB). The results of the methods varied somewhat, but each appeared capable of explaining much of most major recessions [see table 11.1], and also much of other types of fluctuation [table 11.2].

The procedure was rough in two further respects. First, shocks were related to output without detailed modelling of transmission mechanisms; i.e., the implicit assumption was that the transmission process could be modelled as a constant, or by additional variables representing consumer or business confidence. Second, the treatment of lags, given the limitations of the data, had to be highly simplified.

The procedure is not basically novel; though a fully specified econometric model was not used, the procedure is in logic similar to that used in econometric explanation.

11.2.2. Results of the analysis of causation of recessions

The method of analysis described above appears able to explain much of three of the major recessions (recessions I, III, and IV) [see summary table 11.1], but not the other two. But detailed year-by-year scrutiny of what happened [s. 11.3] makes it evident that recession II for much of its course was driven by loss of exports (an indirect effect of the US depression).

Detailed scrutiny also makes it clear that recession V was driven not by exogenous shocks but by a downward shift in business and consumer confidence, in reaction to the previous speculative boom. Such confidence effects must also have been important in other cases, particularly recessions I and III which also followed large booms.[5]

The estimates of the effect of these four types of shock can by no means be taken to be exact. Nevertheless, as the detailed narrative in section 11.3 helps to confirm, they may correctly indicate the size and rough magnitude of the effects of four sorts of shock.

Table 11.2 can therefore be taken to show how various were the origins of these five recessions. Recession I (1920–1) seems to have been due mostly to fiscal policy (and probably confidence effects), *plus* the collapse of world trade [ch. 6.2]. Recession II (1929–32) owed more than the table shows to the fall in exports: the recession would have been much worse if world commodity prices had not plunged. The first OPEC recession (recession III: 1973–5) seems to have been due partly to the unfavourable shift in the terms of trade and partly

---

[5] That makes it likely that the estimates in table 11.2 overstate the effect of shocks in these two recessions, since they seem to leave little room for confidence effects.

Table 11.1 Summary: estimated causation of five major UK recessions 1920–1993 (together with US Great Depression)

	Interwar			Post 1973			Average of five major UK recessions
	I 1920–1	(US 1929–33)	II 1929–32	III 1973–5	IV 1979–82	V 1989–93	
No. of years of recession	1	(4)	3	2	3	4	2.6
% change in GDP[a]	–10.6	(46)	–12.6	–8.1	–10.6	–12.4	–10.9
% reflected in unemployment[b]	88	(47)	66	11	49	32	49
% of GDP change explained by exogenous shocks[c]							
Total	89	(8)	12	104	76	–23	52
Exports	29	(5)	41	8	18	3	20
Terms of trade	4	(–2)	–33	22	–10	–27	–9
Monetary policy[d]	(12)	(3)	(–2)	(63)	(31)	(11)	(23)
Fiscal policy	40	(2)	7	–4	29	–13	12
Accuracy measure[e]	86	8	13	88	68	–26	46

[a] % deviation of GDP(A) over each phase from constant-employment trend.
[b] The change in % unemployment as % of % deviation of GDP from trend.
[c] As estimated on method AA, using theoretical value of parameters (see table 5.7, nn. b and c). Method BB explains a larger proportion of recession II: in other cases the results are less different.
[d] Rough estimate (see ch. 5.2).
[e] Counts over-explanation as an error equally with under-explanation.

Source: as in ch. 5.2.

Table 11.2 Summary: estimated causation of four types of fluctuation, 1920–1993

	Mini-cycles (1950–72)		Maxi-fluctuations (1920–38 and 1972–93)	
	4 fast phases	5 slow phases	4 fast phases	5 major recessions
Average duration of phase (years)	2.0	2.8	2.8	2.6
Height/depth of boom or recession (%)[a]	2.4	−3.8	5.6	−10.9
% reflected in unemployment[b]	13	16	55	49
% of GDP change explained by exogenous shocks[c]				
Total	2	−3.8	4	
of which:				
Exports	0.1	−0.7	1.4	−2.2
Terms of trade	1.4	−0.4	1.0	1.2
Total external shocks	1.5	1.1	2.4	−1.0
Monetary policy[d]	(0.4)	(−1.3)	(0.7)	(−2.5)
Fiscal policy	0.1	−1.4	0.9	−1.3
Total policy changes	0.5	−2.7	1.6	−3.8
Accuracy measure[e]	30	57	65	46

Averages for each type of fluctuation: for more detail see tables 5.6, 5.11, 7.6, and 7.7.

[a] % deviation of GDP from constant-employment trend.
[b] The change in % unemployment during each phase as % of % deviation of GDP from trend during that phase.
[c] Contribution to % change in GDP.
[d] Rough estimate, (see ch. 5.2).
[e] Counts over-explanation as an error equally with under-explanation.

Source: as in ch. 5.2.

to monetary policy (even if less than the table suggests). Recession IV again owed much to fiscal and monetary policy—and to the appreciation of the exchange rate (not shown in the table, but reflected in the fall in exports).

The shape of the five major recessions is depicted in figure 11.2. A similar analysis of other types of fluctuation is summarized in table 11.2. The evidence shown in table 11.1 helps to support the propositions that these five recessions originated in demand not supply factors, and were activated largely by exogenous shocks (though amplified by, and in one case solely caused by, confidence factors); thus, they did not stem from an endogenously driven trade cycle.

11.3. Case studies of the major recessions: summary

This section summarizes the preferred interpretation proposed in the light of the detailed case studies [chs. 6–9] of each of the five major recessions in the UK and the Great Depression in the USA. The case studies repeatedly emphasize the uncertainty attaching to interpretation of cause and effect; for example, on some big questions I have changed my mind several times. In order to keep this summary brief, however, I will omit qualifications and write as if I knew.

11.3.1. Recession I: 1920–1 [ch. 6.2]

The recession of 1921 came in a highly abnormal interval between wartime and settled peace. For supply-side reasons output had fallen steeply in each of the past two years, as millions were discharged from the forces and war factories. But it was nevertheless a time of excess demand; and both in the UK and worldwide, the fairly rapid price inflation of the war years continued up to 1920. Then output in the UK fell abruptly, by perhaps 8 per cent in one year—still a record today—while unemployment grew even more steeply, by 9 percentage points in one year (another record). After their rapid rise prices, too, fell abruptly (by 17 per cent—again a record). All this is very different from present conditions, when the general price level hardly ever falls.

The recession was not simply due to the ebbing of an immediate postwar phase of abnormal demand; for after one year's recession, in the UK and elsewhere, output rebounded rapidly. I attribute the depth of the recession to three causes:

1. First was the extremely large deflationary impact of *fiscal policy*. Government spending on goods and services was reduced in 1920 by the equivalent of 11 per cent of GDP, while taxes and other spending were left unchanged. The political and financial establishment was strongly motivated by a desire to get back to prewar standards of financial rectitude. In the relatively unsophisticated state of public discussion at the time, no one, it seems, gave thought to the severe impact this policy would have.
2. Second, there had been an excessive boom, and an extreme speculative buying of commodities and property. The subsequent reaction, as in other instances before and after, was excessive contraction.
3. Third, Bank rate was raised progressively to 7 per cent in April 1920 (a record in peacetime), which could have been the immediate trigger that collapsed the boom. Given London's then position as the world's financial centre, it could have broken boom psychology worldwide. Once prices began to fall, the rise in interest rates must have become greatly more onerous.[6]

---

[6] The *real* impact of monetary policy will have been greater than allowed for in table 11.2, which takes account only of changes in nominal rates (for reasons already indicated).

I argue that the general flexibility of prices at that time must have exacerbated both the previous boom and the recession that followed.

11.3.2. The US Great Depression 1929–33 [ch. 6.3]

The Great Depression affected most countries, but very unevenly. Output fell 30 per cent in the United States, but only 7 per cent in Europe. Within Europe it fell 16 per cent in Germany (where recession started before that of the USA) and about as much in France (where recession lagged recessions elsewhere), but only 5 per cent in the UK (where it was contemporaneous with that in the USA). Measured as a shortfall below trend, output in the USA itself must have fallen little short of 50 per cent.

This makes it plausible to seek the cause of the Great Depression primarily in the United States. Depression was spread worldwide, I argue, by trade links [app. A6.3]. That is, it reduced US imports, including imports from the primary-producing countries. That caused a large fall in world commodity prices. The resulting fall in incomes of primary-producing countries reduced their ability to buy the exports of Europe, as well as those of the USA, and so reduced European output—which in turn reduced Europe's imports; which further reduced commodity prices; and so on.

Two factors, which must have interacted and progressively amplified it, could account for the extreme size of the US depression.[7]

1. the collapse of confidence after the boom years (by as early as 1930 GDP had fallen 9 per cent without much evidence of large specific exogenous shocks);
2. the wave of bank failures from 1930 on.

The seven years preceding the Depression had in the USA (unlike the UK) been years of rapid growth (averaging 5.5 per cent per annum), with unemployment dropping from 11 per cent in 1921 and 7 per cent in 1922 to a low of 3.5 per cent. Rapid expansion had been due partly to the development of new products (motor vehicles, and the urban transformation they brought; also electric power, other utilities, and telephones). There had been speculation in city development, and a housing boom, which gradually tailed off. There was a mood of over-confidence that the good times were for ever. Stock exchange prices had doubled between 1926 and 1929, as had profits.

By 1929 the investment boom had eased; exports also seemed to be growing more slowly. Industrial output peaked before the stock exchange crash of October 1929; but the crash may have tipped the scales more decisively. The crash on Wall Street could in turn have been precipitated by the rise in the

---

[7] None of these factors would figure largely in a straightforward account of expenditure changes in terms of past real variables, as in an econometric model. For this study, shock indicators were calculated for the USA similar to those for the UK [table 5.9], but they explained practically none of the US depression. Indeed, they explain less than the table seems to indicate: more than half of the small effect shown is attributed to the fall in US exports, but that itself reflected the effect on other countries of recession in the USA.

discount rate in August. The Fed had been known for months to be anxious about the boom; that must have increased the effect when at length it raised interest rates. But from these factors alone one could have expected a large—not an enormously large—recession.

The fall in US farm prices was the domestic counterpart to the fall in world commodity prices. In real terms, farmers' incomes fell about 10 per cent a year in the three years 1929–32. That was a transfer from farm to town. Since the farm population comprised about a third of the total population, the urban population must have benefited to the tune of about 3 per cent a year. But the impact must have been asymmetric: the fall in urban living standards was mitigated, but many farmers were reduced to penury. Output also fell heavily in the 'Rust Belt' in which the older, now depressed, industries were concentrated.

The steep fall in incomes and output in the first year of recession must have led to the train of massive bank failures, which were concentrated in the depressed rural and urban areas. Over the four years of the depression, bank suspensions reduced the number of banks by 40 per cent; banks' balance sheets (in 1929 about 70 per cent of GNP) fell by 29 per cent. Bank failures must have been catastrophic for banks' customers: deposits were frozen for long periods; existing loans were called in, compelling forced sales of the borrowers' assets; and accustomed sources of credit were blocked, at a time when alternative sources were practically unobtainable. Bank failures must have caused bankruptcies among non-banks, and these, in turn, more failures of banks. Under such a severe strain, the banking system was revealed as chronically insecure. The collapse of a third of it must have worked as an amplifier of unparalleled potency. But the introduction of deposit insurance in 1934 stopped runs on the banks and brought massive bank failures to an end.

Two factors made the US banking system vulnerable. First, most banks were small and local, so that those in hard-hit areas could not spread the losses. Second, these small banks had no access to lending of last resort. The Fed had not at that time heeded Bagehot, or seen the need for last resort lending. It was also remote from small banks, unable either to assess their need for support or to act. Nor were the big New York banks at all inclined to act as a channel.

This explanation for the US depression, though giving a large role to the banks, differs radically from Milton Friedman's monetarist explanation [see ch. 6.3 and app. A6.1].[8]

The causation of the Great Depression is sometimes traced to Germany. Thus, it is often said that what triggered the German collapse was a 'cessation' of US lending. I argue [ch. 6.3] that that is incorrect. My interpretation is that, when US interest rates began to rise in 1928, Germany's reserves came under pressure. Given the history of hyperinflation, the German authorities dared not countenance devaluation. They therefore raised interest rates in

---

[8] It also differs from Eichengreen (1992), who attributes the worldwide depression to the existence of the gold standard [see app. A6.2].

Germany (as well as tax rates); and investment therefore fell. Recession in Germany will have had some effect on demand in the USA—but not much, for direct trade flows were small.

11.3.3. The Great Depression in the UK: recession II (1929–32) [ch. 6.4]

The 1929–32 UK recession is not fully explained by my shock indicators [table 11.1]; yet on a closer look the story seems fairly clear. In the first year (1930) exports fell nearly 40 per cent, and accounted for almost all the fall in GDP, and in the second year accounted for most of it [table 6.20]. By the third year investment and consumer spending also were falling heavily, and by then they contributed most of the fall in output. That can be seen as being due to failing business confidence, which in turn can be seen as an indirect consequence of the fall in exports.

The older UK industries (especially coal and textiles) had been depressed ever since the war, as countries to whom Britain traditionally exported progressively developed their own industries. These older industries, heavily reliant on exports, had been hit also by the high exchange rate fixed when the UK returned to gold in 1925. They were concentrated in the north and west, which had gone into depression even before 1929.

Once recession started, confidence must have been further weakened by the falling trend of prices, and by the disastrous news coming from the United States. Later in the recession the confidence of lending institutions also must have been weakened by the major bank crashes in Austria and Germany in 1931, and by the run on sterling that brought the devaluation of the pound in September. Till that date monetary policy was not especially restrictive, and fiscal policy was only moderately so. The recession thus seems not to have been due in any large part to UK policy; it was (to a unique extent) export-driven, and must have been strongly amplified by confidence effects.

Recession in the UK, despite the UK's dependence on world trade, was much less severe than in the USA or Germany. One reason is that the UK was highly dependent on world markets, not only as a destination for exports, but also as a source for food and materials. The collapse in the price of world commodities greatly benefited the UK's terms of trade and supported consumers' incomes. Thus, real consumer spending, though it ceased to rise, showed no fall through the recession: without that, the recession would have been much more severe.

11.3.4. The first OPEC recession: recession III (1973–5) [ch. 8.2]

Recession III followed recession II after an interval of forty years. The 1973 recession in the UK was due to the coincidence of three causes:

1. There had been a world boom in 1972–3, which then went into reverse.
2. The UK superimposed its own boom by the expansionary fiscal measures of 1972 [table 5.11].

3. The rise in world commodity prices (a result of the world boom) and in world oil prices (following OPEC's discovery of its monopoly power) caused a steep rise in import prices. That had two effects on the UK:

   (*a*) a sharp acceleration of inflation, which after mid-1973 brought increasingly restrictive monetary policy;

   (*b*) a sharp worsening in the terms of trade (hence in real UK purchasing power), which contracted spending. The fall in the exchange rate, following the decision the year before to let sterling float, also worsened the terms of trade.

These two deflationary consequences of world inflation—the one direct, the other indirect—broke the UK boom. Other countries had similar experiences. It was probably the advent of the OPEC oil price increases that turned a small world recession into a big one. Though the causation was more complex than that, the recession thus deserves to be called the first OPEC recession.

This was the first major recession for forty years, and it caught UK industry unawares. For two years there had been hectic expansion, permitted by the abolition of lending controls in 1971. All through 1973, firms failed to notice that demand had turned; stocks built up on a very large scale, and subsequent correction of this mistake served to exaggerate the recession. To halt the boom (more precisely, to halt the rise in the money stock that went with it), interest rates were raised steeply (from under 8 per cent at mid-1973 to 13 per cent in November), and at end-year a new lending control was imposed. The banks, which had previously lent as rashly as their customers had borrowed, now turned strict, especially to personal customers. Table 11.1 suggests that two exogenous effects were especially important: monetary policy, and the worsening of the terms of trade; as important must have been the collapse of confidence.[9]

11.3.5. The second OPEC recession: recession IV (1979–82) [ch. 8.3]

The second OPEC recession resembled the first in some but not all ways. Recession in the UK was accompanied by recession in other industrialized countries—again, partly as a result of a new large rise in the world oil price, whose effect on consuming countries' purchasing power was about equal to the first. But the way it affected the UK was more complex.

By 1979 the UK was close to self-sufficiency in oil, and could have insulated itself from the change in the world price. But in fact North Sea oil was priced at the world price. Its rise created large profits for the oil companies, the bulk of which was taxed away by the UK government, and the revenue (it can be said) not spent. While the effect of the first oil shock is often *likened*

---

[9] The recession must have been due in considerable part to a collapse in confidence in reaction to the over-confidence during the previous boom. The estimates in table 11.1 leave no room for this; the table probably overstates the effect of monetary policy.

to that of an (unspent) indirect tax, that of the second was, for the UK, precisely that.

There were political factors also. The second oil price shock coincided with the election of the Thatcher Government. Probably because of that, and because North Sea oil now gave the prospect of payments surpluses for years to come, the exchange rate appreciated (by 25 per cent during 1979 and 1980). The terms of trade as here measured, in contrast to the first OPEC recession, therefore actually improved. But the high exchange rate made exports less competitive, so that exports fell. That was one main impulse to recession.

The new government's policy provided the second main impulse. Interest rates were raised steeply (from 8 per cent in 1978(Q2) to 15 per cent in October 1979). (Inflation had accelerated as a result of rising world commodity and oil prices; and with faster inflation the growth of the money stock—the trigger to monetary policy—had again accelerated.) Taxes also were raised sharply in 1979, and again in each of the next two budgets. These policy changes would seem not to have been intended to depress demand;[10] but because of them, recession in the UK came a year earlier than in Europe, and went deeper.

11.3.6. The 'debt recession' of 1989–93: recession V [ch. 9.3]

Unlike its predecessors, the recession of 1989–93 appears to have owed nothing to exogenous shocks. Recession followed three years of over-rapid expansion; and it now seems clear that the recession was basically a reaction to the excess of confidence built up in the previous boom.

The surge in demand during 1985–8 had owed much to the favourable turn in the terms of trade, a factor not usually cited [table 5.6]. For the rest, it was (I think) due essentially to growing confidence, which fed on, and in turn fed, continuing rapid growth. This strengthened both consumer and investment demand. (The saving ratio fell, and business and residential investment alike rose strongly [fig. 11.5].)

Waves of confidence are inherently fragile. When the boom broke, confidence collapsed; and the excesses of the boom went into reverse. The saving ratio rose steeply, consumer spending fell, and housebuilding and business investment contracted.[11] The rise in interest rates in autumn 1989 (from 8 per cent in early 1988 to 12 per cent in August 1989 and 15 per cent in October) could have helped to trigger the turn-round. Neither exports nor inventory changes played much role.

---

[10] On the government's monetarist philosophy, monetary policy would correct inflation without depressing activity; nor was account taken of the effects here attributed to Budget policy. The tax measures were motivated by other considerations: the switch from direct to indirect taxes was intended to foster incentives, and the net increase in taxes was undertaken to reduce government borrowing.

[11] The terms of trade continued to improve [table 11.2]: without that, the recession would have been even deeper.

This recession is sometimes called a 'debt recession'; but that is to focus on symptoms. Debt certainly built up during the boom, on a scale that later seemed excessive: at that stage prospects seemed bright, and investment and the borrowing required to finance it were preferred options. When prospects later worsened investors wished they had not borrowed or invested. But what changed was expectations: those who had invested out of their own financial resources, and had not increased debt, were in much the same situation—though less strapped for cash.

The boom (and hence also the subsequent recession) is sometimes said to have been due to financial deregularization. Financial decontrol can have three kinds of effect:

1. It can permit a rearrangement of financial assets, without any change in real spending.
2. It can release an existing desire, hitherto blocked, to borrow in order to spend.
3. It can give rein to a later desire to borrow and spend more, e.g. resulting from a subsequent increase in confidence.

Bank lending was decontrolled in mid-1980. That led to greater competition among banks and between banks and building societies, and to a large growth of lending by both.[12] Part of the rise in borrowing in 1981–4 must have represented processes 1 and 2: these must however have been largely completed by 1985. What happened later is best attributed to later euphoria, not to the decontrol of five years earlier. Though permitted by decontrol, it was not really due to that once-for-all event. That is important—for (contrary to some claims) it could recur.

11.4. The long period without major recessions (1945–73): possible lessons

The central question for the future is how we are to avoid or mitigate further major recessions. It is therefore useful to recapitulate the negative evidence of the Golden Age [discussed at length in ch. 7]. This section summarizes possible reasons as to why demand remained high for so long [s. 11.4.1]; why growth did not get out of hand, as it often has in other periods [s. 11.4.2]; and why the break in 1973 was as disruptive as it seems to have been [s. 11.4.3].

11.4.1. How did demand remain high for such an extended period?

In this long quarter-century, there were minor fluctuations in the rate of growth of output, but no major recession. This is here taken to imply that

---

[12] Lending rose half as fast again as money GDP in the four years 1981, 1982, 1983, and 1984 (Dow and Saville 1988: fig. 11.6).

demand grew fairly steadily throughout the period. Why did this happen then, unlike other periods?

Government policy was somewhat Keynesian in many countries. In the English-speaking countries, Scandinavia, the Netherlands, and perhaps Japan—but less wholeheartedly in the major countries of continental Europe—governments had accepted responsibility for maintaining a high level of demand and employment. But governments were never called on to do much to achieve this aim. Had a large downturn occurred, governments, even if they allowed the automatic stabilizers to operate fully, might have been reluctant to take large stimulatory measures. The continuation of high employment cannot therefore be attributed directly to government policy, but perhaps to a mixture of good luck and mildly good government—in the negative sense that, if policy had been much more restrictive than it then was (e.g. as it had been after World War I), that might have destroyed the balance of forces that combined to produce continuous high demand and steady growth.

The hangover of excess demand inherited from the war was probably much larger than after World War I, and proved sufficient to keep economies operating full out for about six years. The Korean War came as the impetus of World War II was beginning to fade. It may have added 1 per cent to world GDP in each of the years 1951, 1952, and 1953 [fig. 7.4].

Once established on an expansionary path, the UK economy generated forces that supported expansion. Confidence led to high investment, which between 1950 and 1973 contributed one-third of the total growth of output of 3 per cent a year, twice its absolute share of GDP [table 2.3]. This is the clearest example in our period of the tendency of a long spell of sustained growth to foster confidence and create demand.

There was probably another side-effect. The terms of trade, both for the UK and for other industrial countries, improved greatly through the period 1952–72 [fig. 7.7]; this contributed to the continuing growth of demand in the industrial countries. That may have been because faster world growth stimulated productivity growth in primary-producing countries: steady world expansion must have provided more attractive markets for primary producers than the switchback conditions of the interwar years. This suggests that one main reason for the persistence of fast growth was that it was worldwide; i.e., it provided favourable conditions which fostered producers' confidence in all countries.

11.4.2. Why did growth not get out of hand?

In other (shorter) periods of relatively fast growth, the pace of growth has tended to accelerate and become too fast; i.e., inflation has accelerated, and/or economy-wide euphoria has developed. Why, in a period of over twenty-five years of barely broken expansion, did such excess not build up, and force a correction which would interrupt the process? I suggest [ch. 7.4] two possible reasons.

First, under the Bretton Woods system, the UK, along with many industrial countries, operated fixed (adjustable) exchange rates throughout the period 1945–72. That system put a brake on governments. Overfast expansion tended to bring a loss of reserves, which persuaded governments to take restrictive measures and slow expansion.[13]

A second factor that may have put a brake on over-expansion is that direct controls over bank lending remained in operation until 1971. I have argued [app. A10] that a movement from one level of capacity working to a higher level requires that the sector activating this transition should have access to additional bank finance. Up to 1971, the scale on which such access was available was strictly limited by the simple and rigid monetary control in operation.[14]

However, the world as a whole—which did not have the British system of financial controls—also avoided major recession for a quarter-century. Perhaps the explanation is that banks everywhere were not, in a general sense, highly competitive. As in the UK at this date, they tended not to lend beyond what their usual customers chose to deposit with them. Only later did they adopt what has been called liability management; i.e., only later did they begin going out into wholesale markets and borrowing anonymous funds. That change in manner of operation transformed the role of the banks; in the UK such a change was prevented until 1971 by direct lending controls.

It was once much debated whether the mini-fluctuations of this period were due simply to inept policy. I still believe[15] that this interpretation is partially correct. Policy contributed to all fast phases of all the mini-cycles of this period; but it was not their main cause [table 7.6]. It would be an exaggeration to say that this series of fluctuations was caused by periodic fits of over-expansionary policy, but true to say that governments tended to tolerate over-fast growth, since prosperity appeared politically advantageous, and corrective action always tends to be unpopular.

It was Conservative governments that presided over the most spectacular 'dashes for growth'—in 1952–5, in 1962–4, in 1972–3, and again later in 1985–8. That was perhaps because financial markets did not allow the necessary leeway to Labour governments, whose periods of office were punctuated

[13] When the UK adopted a floating rate in 1972, it did so precisely so as to make room for what proved to be one of the most expansionary excesses on record; and the brakes had to be put on a year later. If fixed rates had been retained, the 1972 boom, and therefore the 1973–5 recession also, would have been less severe. (The same might have been true if the UK had been on fixed rate in 1985–8.) I am here attributing importance to the monetary regime in which economies operate. But I am almost reversing one view, recently fashionable, that the gold standard caused the Great Depression [see app. A6.2 on Eichengreen 1992].

[14] This argument provides a justification for monetary targets. To be effective, monetary targets need to be enforced either by direct controls, or by interest rates high enough to slow economic growth. In Dow and Saville (1988), I criticized the use of monetary targets. But this was on the grounds that, not being stringently enforced, the targets were ineffective; and that the hope of controlling inflation without stringent restrictive measures was illusory (see the additional 1990 preface to Dow and Saville 1988).

[15] As I claimed in Dow (1964), which seems to have started this debate.

by foreign exchange crises. At the time, these crises were often regarded as a factor that helped to cause economic fluctuations. With hindsight, however, the fact that markets imposed limits on what governments did is perhaps better seen as one reason why fluctuations were moderate in this period, and why relatively steady growth was maintained. Without fixed exchange rates, the exchange rate sags when confidence in the currency wanes. That, too, is some deterrent to governments to avoid excessive expansion—but, it seems, less of a deterrent.

11.4.3. Why 1973 was critically disruptive

The recession of 1973–5 broke the process of fairly stable expansion that had continued for twenty-eight years. How is it that it was so disruptive? That matters to us now because we need to know how irretrievable the effects are.

The effect of the 1973 recession was large and abrupt. It caused a sudden loss of business confidence, and a major fall in fixed investment. From that shock the recovery was to be very gradual.[16] The shock was the greater because it coincided with a steep rise in import prices, and an abrupt acceleration of inflation (to 25 per cent in one year), with long-lasting effects on price expectations [fig. 2.2]. Restoration of full employment might require the ratio of investment to GDP to be raised back nearer the level it then was.

The relatively balanced growth of the Golden Age occurred because it started that way, because it was worldwide, and because (until 1973) nothing happened to stop it.[17] Once interrupted, it must be difficult, though not necessarily impossible, to reassemble by deliberate action the conditions necessary for a new period of this sort. That is a summary of what we lost when the high demand and steady growth of the Golden Age got destroyed.

11.5. Concluding remarks on public debt, and on the predictability of major recessions

At the conclusion of the empirical part of this study, it is convenient to end with remarks on two questions relevant to policy, which is to be discussed in the next chapter: first, the consequences that major recessions have had on the stock of public debt; and second, whether major recessions are predictable.

11.5.1. The effect of major recessions on public debt

In the period since World War II, the ratio of public debt to GDP fell fairly steadily up to about 1975: since then it has been level or rising [fig. 11.3].

---

[16] The ratio of fixed investment to GDP (1990 prices) was 11.3% in 1948 and had risen to 26.6% by 1970. After the 1973–5 recession it was by 1979 reduced to 17.5%. The boom of 1985–8 brought it back to 21.0%—still well below 1970. After the 1989–93 recession it was by 1995 back down to 17.0%. Figure 11.5 shows these swings in business investment and residential investment.

[17] See ch. 7, which discussed why the Golden Age came to an end, and whether the conditions that supported it could have continued.

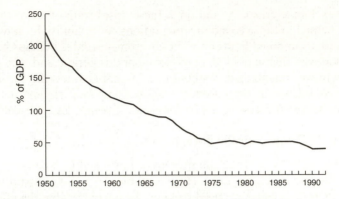

Fig. 11.3   National debt-GDP ratio in the UK, 1950–1992

Sources: Mitchell and Jones (1971); CSO, *Economic Trends: Blue Book*, and *Financial Statistics*, various issues.

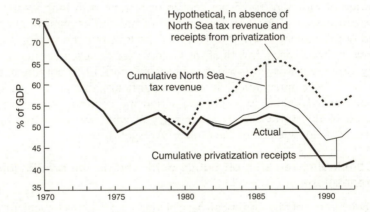

Fig. 11.4   National debt-GDP ratio in the UK, 1970–1992

Sources: as for fig. 11.3.

The change in trend after 1975 occurred despite two exceptional sources of revenue: the taxation of the profits of North Sea oil production, and the proceeds of the privatization of public corporations. Without these, the ratio would have shown a rising trend [fig. 11.4].

The worsening of the budgetary position, and the tendency of the debt ratio to start rising again, is often ascribed simply to the profligacy of governments; but the origin of the situation was more complex. A recession must always reduce government revenues. In a small recession where output quickly returns to trend, this does not greatly matter. In a large recession, however, the downward displacement of the growth path is, I have argued [ch. 2.2], semi-permanent.

On the other side, parallel adjustments to government expenditure are clearly not automatic. In a growing economy, government expenditure normally takes a share of the growth, i.e., is on a rising trend. When a recession comes, the public is reluctant to accept curtailment.

The three major recessions since 1973, taken together, could well have reduced output by 25 per cent below what it otherwise would have been [see fig. 11.1], and thus could have reduced government tax revenue in real terms, as compared with the previous trend, on at least this scale. Government spending was also reduced compared with the pre-1973 trend, but not by so much. While many other factors have affected it, the higher level of government borrowing is to be explained primarily in terms of the large loss of tax revenue induced by the series of three large recessions.

The national expenditure counterparts to the fall in national product during major recessions comprised in large part falls in private investment and in private consumption: the latter was largely a multiplier effect, but in some major recessions it reflected also a fall in the personal saving ratio, indicating a reduced propensity to spend. (Companies also saved less, but chiefly because profits fell.) Figure 11.5 shows the course of private investment and private saving since 1920.

One way to demonstrate the importance of the fall-off in investment demand is to look at its effect on the pattern of sectoral financial balances. The three recessions after 1973, by reducing private investment, greatly increased the financial surplus of the private sector; by the same token, they greatly increased the deficit of the public sector.[18]

One can say that in a recession the private sector chooses to expend a smaller part of its income on purchases of goods and services, and a larger part on the acquisition of financial assets (which in practice are largely the liabilities of the public sector). As a result of its reduced income, the public sector, on its side, borrows more, i.e., issues liabilities (which in practice are largely bought by the domestic private sector). Thus, in a recession the private sector opts on an exception scale for financial assets rather than goods and services. If and when confidence revives, the preferences of the private sector will change: it will demand more goods and services and fewer savings instruments. Thus, the situation in the first decade or so after one or more major recession is not likely to be the average situation to be expected from that point on.

There is, then a two-way relation between the public and the private sectors, and causation may flow in either direction. In the three major recessions of the 1970s and 1980s, causality was largely from private to public sector; i.e., abrupt falls in private demand increased public borrowing. The relative failure of

---

[18] There is by definition an inverse relation between the changes in the financial balance of the public sector and of other sectors of the economy. The causation of changes may start from either side. The changes since 1973 originated primarily from weak private demand. The resultant enlargement of the public-sector deficit powerfully affected the subsequent course of public debt [see app. A11].

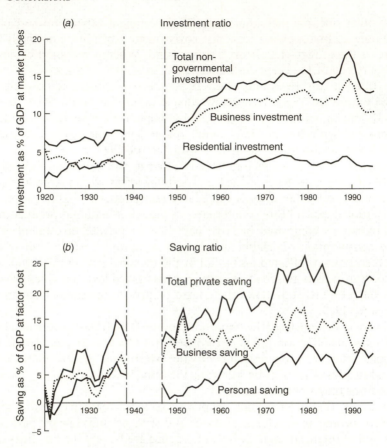

Figure 11.5   Investment and saving ratios, 1920–1995

Sources: For investment ratio, years 1920–48 are from Feinstein (1972): business investment as here defined excludes residential investment, and consists of private sector *plus* public corporations *less* investment in dwellings (i.e., assumes public-sector investment in dwellings is nil). Years 1948–95 are from *Economic Trends*: business investment here equals total investment *less* public sector non-residential investment *less* investment in dwellings. For both periods it thus excludes investment by unincorporated enterprises. The total shown equals investment by private sector *plus* public corporations (and thus includes business and residential investment as shown on chart *plus* investment by unincorporated enterprise).

For savings ratio, years 1920–63 are from Feinstein (1972): business saving is defined as savings of companies and public corporations *plus* corporate additions to tax, dividends, and interest reserves: personal savings include additions to tax reserves. Years 1963–95 are from *Economic Trends*: business saving is saving of industrial and commercial companies, of financial companies, and of public corporations. Total private saving is the sum of business and personal saving as thus defined.

the government to cut spending commensurately constituted the automatic stabilizer effect, without which the three recessions would have been very much deeper. Attempts to rectify the position of the public finances at a later date amount to *ex post* reversal of the automatic stabilizer effects from which the economy benefited earlier; and, unless accompanied by countervailing forces or policies, must tend to lower demand and output.

The problem for policy is discussed in chapter 12. A detailed analysis of factors affecting the public debt–GDP ratio is given in appendix A11.

11.5.2. The predictability of major recessions

Major recessions, if forecast at all, have been poorly forecast. This section considers that failure, and the more general question of whether major recessions are essentially unpredictable. The discussion is concerned with the predictability of *major* fluctuations: forecasting minor fluctuations has been more successful. We are here talking about the possibility of econometrically based forecasting: econometric modelling has aspired to explain macroeconomic experience, with ability to forecast seen as the crucial test.

Explaining history and forecasting major recessions

Forecasting models attempt to predict future events in terms of shocks to the economy and of the transmission mechanisms that model the economy's response to such shocks. The method of the present study has been similar; it seeks to explain fluctuations in terms of exogenous shocks, conceived in a similar way, and has differed from such models only in that transmission mechanisms were not modelled in detail. As already indicated, the present study has only partially explained shortfalls of growth during large recessions, or the fast growth of fast-growth periods [table 11.2]. It is probable that, as suggested earlier, some or all of the unexplained residual is accounted for by unexplained swings in confidence. A number of earlier attempts to explain post-1973 UK recessions, based on a similar approach, have also had only partial success.[19]

Box 11.1 summarizes the OECD forecasting experience in the three major recessions since 1970.[20] The results suggest that, when recessions were in some large part caused by import cost shocks (as in 1973–5 and 1979–82) the effect could be predicted, or partly predicted, a little way ahead, because the transmission mechanisms took some time to transmit the full effect. Even so, the full scale of the events treated as shocks (i.e., events that the forecasts made no attempt to predict) was not known much in advance of the event. On the other hand, when recessions were caused primarily by shifts in confidence

---

[19] One of the most extensive of these previous studies was that by Saville and Gardiner (1986), which was made as part of the research undertaken for the present book. Earlier studies were Artis *et al*. (1984) [see ch. 7.3.2].

[20] OECD forecasts were chosen because they cover all major countries throughout the period since 1970, and because OECD was probably better placed than forecasters elsewhere to diagnose the first OPEC recession. In the next two major recessions its forecasts were fairly typical of macroeconomic forecasting. Britton and Pain (1992) give a detailed post mortem on forecasts of the 1989–93 UK recession.

Box 11.1   OECD's record in forecasting major recessions

1973–5 recession: poor forecasting performance

- The world oil price began to rise steeply in late 1973, but how large it would be was not known till mid-1974.
- In 1974, because of that and other factors, UK output fell, G7 growth halted. This was first 'forecast' only in mid-1974.
- In 1975 UK output fell, G7 output fell slightly. Forecasts for 1975, first made at end-1974, wrongly predicted a *rise* for the UK, but came close to predicting the G7 result.

The 1979–82 recession: forecasts broadly correct

- The main factors (oil price rise, world inflation, countries' policies) were known only at end-1979.
- In 1980 UK output fell, G7 growth slowed. 'Forecasts' for 1980 were first made at end-1979, i.e., late in the day; they were broadly correct on both counts.
- In 1981 UK output again fell, while G7 output now rose; forecasts, first made in mid-1980, were again broadly correct.

The 1989–93 recession: forecasting failure

- Both in the UK and elsewhere, the recession seems to have been due not to identifiable shocks but to a sudden shift in confidence.
- UK output fell in 1991 and again in 1992, while G7 growth slowed only in 1991. None of these developments was predicted.

Source: from OECD, *Economic Outlook*, various issues. Forecasts were made half-yearly, at mid-year and end-year. G7 denotes the seven major OECD countries as a group (USA, Japan, Germany, France, Italy, UK, and Canada).

(as in 1989–93), the scale of the recession was not foreseen, presumably because confidence was volatile, and shifts in confidence had rapid effect.[21]

The possibilities of improving prediction seem then to rest (*a*) on the possibility of predicting confidence and bubble effects; and (*b*) on possibility of endogenizing events now treated as exogenous.

Prediction of confidence and price bubble effects

If private agents were able to predict major recessions, private fortunes would be made by use of this information. The fact that this has not happened

---

[21] Before World War II there was nothing like the regular forecasts by established forecasting teams which is now normal. Had there been, I am sure that neither the 1920–1 nor the 1929–32 recession, both heavily amplified by confidence shifts, would have been well predicted.

suggests that it is difficult for anyone—including macroeconomic forecasting groups and government economic advisers—to predict major recessions. Some events can be predicted in general terms, for example that a boom cannot last and will reach its peak some time. But to be practically useful (either to businessmen in search of profits, or to governments wanting to take countermeasures) relatively precise predictions are needed, particularly as to the time when events will occur.

Lack of success in forecasting major recessions has been due not only to the fact that shocks occur at short notice, but also to the fact that when confidence collapses the effect is transmitted quickly, and that the scale of the reaction of business and consumer confidence has not proved predictable.

The difficulty of predicting confidence effects arises because there is a threshold effect, i.e., a rapid transition from one type of behaviour to another, at the point when confidence crumbles. Analytically the case may be somewhat like an experiment to test the strength of an iron bar in which the bar is tested to destruction. If one knew enough about the individual bar, it might be possible to predict when it would snap. But without very detailed knowledge of the individual bar, it is only possible to say that a bar of this size, composition, and shape is likely to break when the pressure on it is between X and Y, i.e., limits too broad to be of use for a close forecast. In the present case we lack detailed knowledge of the circumstances of individual operators, and of the way that individuals will react to each other.[22]

Similar difficulties arise in predicting the duration of *speculative bubbles* in markets where prices are flexible. Here, extrapolative expectations on the part of short-term operators drive prices up (or down) more than otherwise to some break-point or threshold at which the process goes into reverse. Though there are limits to the scale of bubbles, the limits can be established only by crude inference, and the point when the threshold will be reached seems incapable of close prediction. If there were market operators who could forecast market behaviour accurately, not only would they stand to make large gains, but *their activity would tend to smooth out price bubbles*. Thus, the fact that bubbles occur is itself evidence that behaviour is in practice unpredictable.

The difficulty in forecasting major recessions probably reflects the fact that fluctuations in financial markets, which are themselves difficult or impossible to explain or predict, play a large role in the generation of major economic

---

[22] The question has not been much studied, and the results of deeper study might well be interesting. This is a case where it might, e.g. be possible to conduct experiments as a means to quantify reactions. Animals too live in an imperfectly knowable world, and (since we are dealing with animal spirits) it is possible that experiments with animal behaviour might also be enlightening. But more knowledge might at best suffice only to fix narrower limits to break-points. Britton and Pain (1992) suggest that forecasting might be improved by greater use of surveys of business opinion. In my view, greater use of opinion surveys would give prompt information about the current situation (i.e., what has already happened), but not information on what is going to happen, e.g. how confidence will change.

fluctuations.[23] World commodity markets—though among the most perfectly competitive of markets—also display much the same behaviour characteristics as financial markets. Thus, 'unpredictable' fluctuations in world commodity prices make it impossible to foresee terms-of-trade shocks to consumer countries or to predict swings in inflation which may provoke the authorities to impose monetary counteraction (which also affects demand and output). Again, 'unpredictable' swings in equity or house prices affect business and consumer expectations and confidence, and hence total output. Swings in confidence and bubble phenomena are difficult to foresee partly because they are crowd phenomena (where the action of all affects that of each, and vice versa); and the behaviour of crowds appears impossible to predict closely.

Prediction of events now treated as exogenous

To its practitioners forecasting may appear a bold game, but the kind of forecasts usually made are in some respects notably unambitious. For example, they do not attempt to forecast the large variables treated as exogenous shocks. These can be taken account of only a short time before they start to have their effects; thus it is only the response to the shocks that the forecasts attempt to predict. In practice, also, macroeconomic forecasts do not usually extend much beyond the calendar year following the date at which the forecasts are made.

It might seem that it would be a big improvement if events now treated as *exogenous shocks* could themselves be forecast. In formal terms this would simply be extending the area of the model, so that events now treated as exogenous would become endogenous. The kind of events that would have to be included are (*a*) changes in the domestic macroeconomic policy of the country in question and (*b*) such events as changes in the rate of growth of world trade and of world commodity prices. Some reflect natural events (such as droughts or bumper harvests) which, like the weather, are impossible to predict closely. But most are man-made, either directly or at some remove. To some extent, changes in policy are responses by governments to circumstances, and could possibly be predicted in such terms. For example, monetary policy could be treated as a reaction to domestic inflation, which could be treated as a reaction to world commodity price fluctuations, which could be treated as a reaction to the pace of world growth, which in turn could be treated in part as a consequence of the policy of the dominant countries at an earlier stage.

---

[23] Attempts to explain the behaviour of financial markets in terms of rational expectations have been notoriously unsuccessful: see Frankel and Foot (1987), Dornbusch and Frankel (1987) and Ito (1990) for the foreign exchange market; and Schiller (1988) for the stock market. Goldberg and Frydman (1996) seek to explain foreign exchange market behaviour in terms of imperfect knowledge, which on their presentation results in large breaks in the pattern of behaviour at crucial points of time. See also the discussion of bounded indeterminacy as regards exchange rates, and also short-term interest rates, in Dow and Saville (1988: chs. 3 and 5).

Commodity price fluctuations also dominate terms-of-trade changes (treated in this study as an exogenous variable). Such trains of causation, however, are long drawn-out and are not likely to be well behaved or well forecast.

Even granting some success in creating an integrated world model with the exogenous elements reduced to a minimum, two intractable elements would remain.

First, though some elements of government policy may be semi-predictable responses to events, many are not—for example, decisions to go to war, how to finance a war, to change social policy in a big way, or (in the case of OPEC governments) to exploit newly discovered monopoly power. Such decisions are made by very small groups of people. (Governments are themselves relatively small, but here it is a case of small groups within a government.) Decisions by individuals or very small groups are unlikely to be more predictable than are crowd reactions.

Second, several of the factors usually treated as 'exogenous' depend on the behaviour of international commodity prices. Commodity prices are flexible prices, the behaviour of which is likely to remain impossible to predict closely, because these are subject to speculative influences, as already discussed.

Models of the world economy endogenize some events that are treated as exogenous in models of a national economy, but they stop well short of altogether eliminating shocks. For the reasons stated, I doubt the possibility of close prediction of all events now treated as shocks.

Conclusion

It may be premature to conclude that major recessions are inherently unpredictable. But there are probably good and ineluctable reasons why major recessions have not been forecast, or not at all completely, or much in advance of the event. That restricts the possibilities of economic policy. But, as the next chapter will try to show, there is still scope for precautionary action, and for policy to react to the current (if not the future) situation.

Appendix A11   The National Debt since World War II

This appendix analyses the factors affecting the public debt ratio, i.e., the ratio of national debt to GDP. As noted in the text, the ratio fell fairly steadily up to 1975, and since then has been relatively level [fig. 11.3].

Figure A11.1 relates to the first part of the period (1950–75) and decomposes annual changes in the debt ratio into three components: the effect on the ratio of

1. the change in nominal debt (real GDP and prices assumed constant);
2. real growth (nominal debt and prices constant);
3. change in prices (nominal debt and output constant).

This shows that the reason why the debt ratio fell up to 1975 was not that debt was repaid: indeed, debt increased in most of those years. But the effect of real output growth (by about 3 per cent a year) was to reduce the ratio in most years—on average by enough to offset the effect of rising debt. Inflation also reduced the debt ratio (twice as large an effect as that of real output growth); this effect was greatest at the beginning (Korean boom) and the end (Barber boom and OPEC I inflation).[24]

Figure A11.2 gives a similar analysis for the later part of the period after 1975, in which the ratio fell much more slowly. Figure 11.4 has shown that this was despite two exceptional sources of revenue: taxes on the profits of North Sea oil production, and the privatization of public corporations. The debt ratio fell from 48 per cent in 1975 to 41 per cent in 1992: without these exceptional receipts, it would have risen to 57 per cent.

Comparison of figures A11.1 and A11.2 indicates why the debt ratio ceased to fall as rapidly after 1975 as it had before. The main reason was that, chiefly because of the big recessions, nominal debt now started to rise considerably more rapidly.

After 1975 real growth and inflation had only a small effect on the ratio, partly because by then the debt ratio had been reduced to under a quarter of what it had been in 1950. The effect of growth and inflation on any *given* level of debt of course continued to depend on the rates of growth, and of inflation. In the period 1975–92 the first was less, the second greater, than it had been in the period 1950–75, while the combined effect was not greatly changed.

---

[24] The effect on the debt ratio of interest payments is here included in the effect of the increase in nominal debt, and is not separately distinguished. The effect of payment of interest was partly offset, or more than offset, by the effect of rising prices and output; i.e., real interest rates in this period were low and less than the rate of output growth.

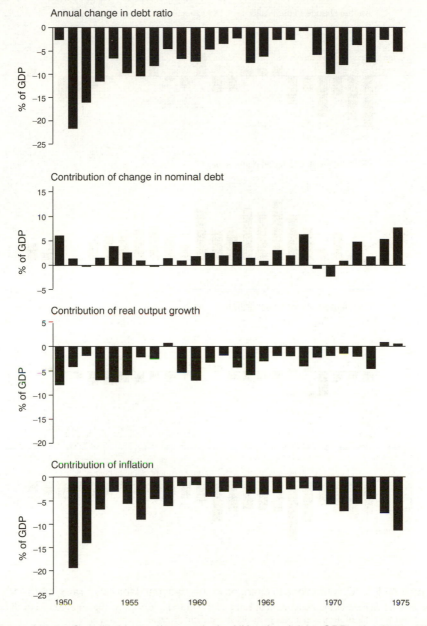

Figure A11.1 Contributions to changes in the UK national debt–GDP ratio, 1950–1975

Source: as for fig. 11.3.

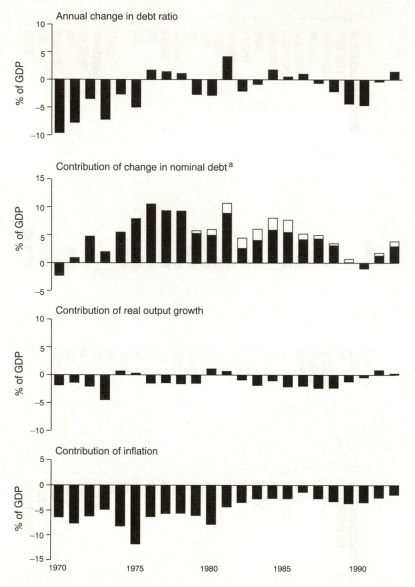

Figure A11.2   Contributions to changes in the national debt–GDP ratio, 1970–1992

[a] Additional change in the nominal debt ratio as it would have been in the absence of North Sea taxes and privatization receipts is shown by the unshaded area.

Source: as for fig. 11.3.

Table A11.1 Factors responsible for changes in national debt ratio, 1950–1992

	1950	1975	1992
National debt/GDP (%)	223.8	48.5	41.3
	% change 1950–75		% change 1975–85

	in period	per year	in period	per year
Total % change in debt ratio	−78.3	−5.9	−15.0	0.9
of which, due to changes in				
Nominal debt		2.4		9.4
Real output		−2.6 ⎱ −8.3		−1.8 ⎱ −9.6
Price level		−5.7 ⎰		−7.8 ⎰

Principle of calculation of the table: Where the ratio of debt (D) to GDP (Y) in year 1 is D_1/Y_1, the change in debt ratio between two years (Q_{1-2}) is calculated in ratio form as $(D_2/Y_2)(Y_1/D_1)$, so that values above unity denote a rise in the debt ratio, and values below, a fall. The change in debt ratio over a period of years (Q_{1-n}) is then $(Q_{1-2})(Q_{2-3}) \ldots (Q_{(n-1)-n})$. The calculation shows the contributions to the change in the debt ratio between two years of each of the three factors, change in nominal debt (N_{1-2}), in real GDP(V_{1-2}), and in prices (P_{1-2}). These contributions are calculated on the assumption that the other two factors are unchanged between the two years. They too are calculated in ratio form so that (Q_{1-2}) can be obtained as the product $(N_{1-2})(V_{1-2})(P_{1-2})$.

12 Are Recurrent Major Recessions Inevitable?

Previous chapters of this book have sought to explain why the major recessions of the twentieth century occurred. The purpose of seeking an answer to this question was the thought that, if we knew what had gone wrong, we would be better placed to avoid it in future. This chapter tries to answer the question whether recurrent major recessions are inevitable, or whether there are steps that governments (or central banks) can take to avoid or mitigate them.

Whereas positive analysis (as in earlier chapters) can aspire to objectivity, normative discussion (as here) can hardly do so. There are usually many solutions, or solutions of a sort, to a practical problem, and everyone is likely to have different ideas. My own conclusions may nevertheless be worth setting out and perhaps will help others to formulate their own.

The questions involved here extend beyond those the earlier chapters dealt with, and raise not only the disputable issues of economic theory but many new ones, including broadly political questions. In this chapter I take the lines of thought developed in earlier chapters and try to see what conclusions they lead to. Full answers would require another book; what follows is a semi-reasoned statement of belief, or a series of essays intended to give an idea of the considerations that led to my conclusions.

The arrangement of the chapter is as follows. Section 12.1 deals with background issues. I first attribute a degree of effectiveness to policy, and recapitulate this and other respects in which my view differs from a neoclassical view [s. 12.1.1]; I then discuss the general limits to state action [s. 12.1.2]; finally, I set out a view about inflation—since, although this book has not been about inflation, policy has to be concerned with it [s. 12.1.3].

Section 12.2 deals with general questions about the instruments of economic policy. Despite the waves of deconstruction that are generally taken to have destroyed the intellectual foundations for a Keynesian fiscal policy, I see a theoretical case for it; but I also see severe practical limits, stemming from the reactions of financial markets to government borrowing [s. 12.2.1]. I then go on to discuss the effect and role of monetary policy [s. 12.2.2].

Section 12.3 turns to practical possibilities, and considers the kind of action that, despite the above constraints, ought to be possible. Section 12.4 then assesses the likelihood that governments will in fact avoid or minimize major recessions in future.

The chapter is concerned with combating major recessions, not minor ones, nor with stabilization policy as a whole. But I will argue that that involves action before, during, and after a major recession, i.e. most of the time. It is thus one aspect of macroeconomic policy, which must have other aims also—in particular, reasonably full employment and avoidance of severe inflation, separate objectives the pursuit of which should as far as possible be integrated. The focus of concern here, as in the rest of this book, is the UK, but the problem for a larger country (e.g. the USA) or for the European Monetary Union (also a large area) is noted.

There is every reason to treat seriously the questions discussed. Major recessions are very costly. On the estimates given earlier [table 11.2], a typical major recession reduced output by 10 per cent below its previous trend growth path; some of this was recoverable later, but about half (I argue) was a more or less permanent loss. Also, each recession is likely, for a considerable time afterwards, to rob 5 per cent of the working population of the assurance of having a job and being part of the working community—thus making it difficult, as we know, for school-leavers to get jobs, and for those thrown out of work to regain entry to paid employment.

The fact that recessions cause widespread loss does not however mean that society is capable of finding a way to avoid them. Assurance of peace between nations, or the establishment of a minimum standard of good government (including for instance freedom from arbitrary arrest and from the official use of torture) would do more for human welfare than would the avoidance of economic recession; but either will be difficult to the point of impossibility to secure, and is not likely to be achieved in the lifetime of anyone now living.

12.1. Background issues: theory; politics; inflation

12.1.1. Theoretical premisses

The view one has of the economy has a close bearing on the role one sees for policy. The implications for policy of the model of the economy that emerges from this study [ch. 10] appear most clearly when contrasted with those contained in the New Classical model.[1]

In New Classicism, the economy either is always on its competitive equilibrium path (CEP) or, if not, is subject to strong forces that produce an early return to it. Consequently there is nothing much to be gained from policy: policy efforts intended to improve on the outcome that natural equilibrating forces will produce are at best otiose, at worst counter-productive. The CEP itself is determined by technological factors (as, on some versions, are temporary fluctuations); and the path is not altered by temporary fluctuations

---

[1] My reasons for disagreement with the New Classical model are similar to those of Hahn and Solow (1996), though the alternative view summarized here and in ch. 10 is I think somewhat different. Hahn and Solow describe the line of thought they are criticizing 'as roughly the line of thought that runs from Lucas's famous price-misperception model of 1974 to the "real, business cycle theory" of Prescott, Kydland, and others'.

from it. Consequently the CEP as it stretches ahead is foreseeable—and will be foreseen by rational agents; and their rational expectations are among the forces that produce an early return to the CEP in the face of any tendencies to depart temporarily from it.

Such expectations also mean that any attempt to improve on the ordained CEP will be ineffective, since rational agents will see through them and will expect such efforts to be futile; and their actions will counteract the effect that policy would otherwise have, and ensure that policy is indeed ineffective. Economic agents will be wise to the folly of intervention and will not be fooled, or not for long.

By contrast, on the view set out in this study, the CEP is not a useful concept. The economy does not operate under conditions of perfect competition. Even if it did, demand may fall short of, and remain below, what would be required for the full employment of technologically given availability. Forces producing a return to full employment are weak or non-existent, so that lapses from full employment may be long-lasting and semi-permanent. Full employment thus is not an equilibrium position. Increases in labour unemployment *of the sort that occurs in major recessions, and persists in their aftermath* reflect lack of demand—not, for instance, a sudden increase in the desire for leisure, or maldistribution between the supply of and demand for different types of labour, or high real (product) wages.

The strength of demand (i.e. the degree of full employment) affects the pace of inflation. The concept of a level of unemployment at which inflation would be zero (or, alternatively, non-accelerating) therefore does not appear to me unreasonable. But I see no reason to believe that there are forces that will tend to keep demand at this point; nor do I see evidence that it has done so; i.e., I do not believe that the 'natural' rate of unemployment 'attracts' the actual rate. It is not variations in inflationary pressures that have caused the big fluctuations in unemployment that have occurred in the course of major recessions (except in so far as governments have adopted policies to counter inflation which had this effect).

The path of full-employment output—the nearest I get to the concept of the CEP—is not, on my view, completely predetermined by technological factors. A major recession will (*a*) cause a permanent lowering of that path (alternatively to be called the capacity growth path); and (*b*) reduce the degree to which capacity is employed, in a way that in principle is reversible but in practice may take a long time to reverse, and is not automatic. Assertion (*a*) means that the future path of optimum output is not independent of the course followed by actual output.

Major recessions seem to be largely unpredictable [ch. 11.5]. Thus it is not possible for economists to give a close prediction of a country's real output (actual or potential) in ten or twenty (still less fifty or a hundred) years' time. Moreover, individual agents' prospects are not closely geared to the national average, and are still less predictable. Therefore for an individual agent, future income is largely unknowable; individual consumers or firms have only a vague idea of what it is going to be. States of confidence are, thus, akin more to animal spirits than to mathematically formulatable expectations. The state of expectations (or confidence) is one factor that determines what the course of the economy is going to be; i.e., there is no preordained future which it is rational to expect, but rather an unformed future which expectations help to produce. Expectations are (actively) effective, not (passively) rational.

The fact that the future is only vaguely foreseeable is in my view one of the reasons why, contrary to classical doctrine, policy is effective. As already argued, it is not true that the path of the economy is so tightly determined by equilibrium-tending forces that it is immune to influence by the government or central bank. The fact that individuals can only vaguely foresee their own income is one factor that undermines the doctrine of Ricardian equivalence [see s. 12.2.1]. Again, because the future rate of return on real assets is only vaguely foreseeable, the central bank can fix the rate of interest on (at least short-term) financial assets [see s. 12.2.2]. This study has treated changes in fiscal and monetary policy as one source of the shocks that have brought major recessions about. Accordingly, changes in fiscal and monetary policy are also treated as one way in which the shortfalls of demand that have caused major recessions can, at least in part, be reversed.

Since I do not see macro-equilibrating forces acting forcefully and rapidly, or the economy as operating in an ideal way, there is, in principle, scope for policy action designed to produce a socially preferable position. That view diverges most from the kind of classicism represented by the real business cycle approach—the attempt to explain business cycles in an economy that is nevertheless constantly in a position of competitive equilibrium. On such a view, the optimal policy is restricted to the task of ensuring that, in the face of fluctuations generated by fluctuations in technical productivity, the government finances itself with a minimum loss of welfare arising from distortions caused by changes in tax rates.

In my case, by contrast, where fluctuations in output are due to fluctuations in demand, one main task of policy is to minimize fluctuations in demand; and the gain to welfare through reducing fluctuations in real income is held to far outweigh the welfare cost of varying tax rates.

There are a large number of arguments that have been used to justify the view that policy actions are ineffective. It is convenient at this point to redefine, in the light of the preceding discussion, the objections to what has come to be called Ricardian equivalence, i.e. that debt-financed government expenditure has the same effect as expenditure met by taxes. There are three main legs to that doctrine: (1) that government debt will have at some time to be repaid, i.e. out of an increase in taxes; (2) that consumers know this; and (3) that rational consumers will provide for this repayment now, i.e. by not spending any present decrease in taxes that results in government borrowing.

For me, the telling counter-arguments are as follows:

1. There is no certainty (or even probability) that public debt will be repaid. In a growing economy, debt can increase a certain amount without increasing the ratio of tax to GDP. Even apart from that, past debt has probably tended *not* to get repaid.[2]
2. Even if it were predictable that taxes would rise, it would not be predictable what kind of taxes, and therefore which taxpayers, would be involved.
3. As argued above, anyone's income ten or twenty years ahead is largely unknowable: one more uncertainty will therefore make little difference.[3]

The theory of the natural rate of unemployment should, according to the letter of the doctrine, be held to invalidate policy action to counter inflation—since, given the forces 'attracting' unemployment to the 'natural' rate, it could be argued that additional policy action would be unnecessary and harmful. That however is not what most classical economists argue. No more do I: in my view, demand management is needed to counter inflation; and countering inflation, along with stabilizing output, has to be a main aim of policy.

New Classicists are able to claim, since in their view the future path of output is predetermined, that policy action to control inflation, which may depress output temporarily, involves no permanent loss, i.e. that there is no 'trade-off', or graduated choice, between pursuing price stability and output stability: output will be what it has to be, but price stability has to be earned. In my view, achieving price stability does have a cost in terms of output (perhaps permanently) forgone; and that means that policy has to compromise. I admit that the skill of governments and central banks, and the instruments available to them, are both imperfect, and that that limits what is achievable and what should be attempted.

For the sake of clarity, I have stressed how the view adopted here differs from New Classicism, which in its various forms must be counted the dominant orthodoxy at present, particularly in the United States. However, economists are (perhaps especially at present) very divided in their views. Many academic economists remain sceptical of New Classicism (and some will agree with much of this chapter). Looking beyond the profession, governments and central banks, politicians and political commentators have all been much influenced by New Classicism. In practice, nevertheless, all governments and central banks attempt in some degree to steer demand, and most pay attention not only to price stability, but also to output stability—and commentators and

---

[2] See app. A11 for UK experience since World War II. Debt has often been reduced by unexpected inflation.

[3] For fuller discussion of Ricardian equivalence, see Buiter and Tobin (1979), and Buiter (1985); also Dow and Saville (1988: 102–3). App. A5 discussed various other arguments claiming to show the ineffectiveness of fiscal policy.

public opinion expect them to do so. I am therefore unsure where current orthodoxy lies and how unorthodox my views are: I do not claim to be alone or original.

12.1.2. The political limits to state action

Before discussing fiscal and monetary policy, and their limitations, it is useful to look more generally at the factors that limit all sorts of state action. The bias of this chapter is towards a degree of management of the economy. But, as has to be admitted, a government, whether a democratically elected one or a non-elected dictatorship—is not ideally constituted to perform the role of managing a complex entity like the economy of an industrial country.[4] Moreover, there are limits to how much a government can persuade its citizens to accept—limits that vary with circumstances, so that there are no obvious fixed rules.

Even if one confines one's attention to parliamentary democracies in industrial countries, the extent of the government's role varies greatly. Governments in wartime do much more than they do, or could do, in times of peace; and in peacetime governments are able to act more boldly in some circumstances than in others.[5] Managing an economy is a complex political task: under what circumstances is it likely to be possible?

The modus operandi *of state power*

It is a central conundrum that the power of a government should be so large— in many cases enormous—while the number of people who decide policy consists of a very small group. If one includes only ministers, their supporters in Parliament, and their senior advisors, it might be at most a thousand or two.[6] The effectiveness of law must rely on a habit of obeying law and on broad consent to particular laws. Even the least active of modern governments interfere a lot. It must then be clear that societies are much more cohesive than is allowed for by an atomistic picture of a collectivity of millions of unrelated individuals.

---

[4] Economists who recommend an active economic policy do not usually pause to consider the limitations of the institutions to which they propose to entrust its implementation. By pointing out that governments have grave imperfections, I do not imply that anything better is available: in particular, central banks also have limitations [s. 12.2.2].

[5] The question of what determines the (changing) limits of the economic powers of the state appears not to have been much studied. This may be because regularities are hard to discern, but also because the question as here posed is of interest chiefly to one (Keynesian) type of macroeconomist rather than to social scientists in general. It also seems that political science has been more concerned with description than with seeking explanations: see e.g. such compilations as Marsh and Stoker (1995), or Goodin and Klingemann (1996). Finer's *History of Government* (1997) does not (and does not seek to) answer the particular questions here at issue; but his comparative method could help to do so.

[6] If one included all who administer and enforce laws and official regulations, those in government would be many times greater. But it cannot be said that it is these people who are imposing their will on the rest of society.

In the academic study of politics there are two chief ways of conceiving the role of governments. One sees them as mere agents of the voters who elect them. If politicians show great concern to be re-elected, that would (on this view) not be a demeaning failure, but only what is proper for an agent competing with others to be selected to carry out the wishes of his constituents.

The alternative and more traditional view of the role of government is that it is there to provide leadership. Good government can be held to require more than the representation of the sum of a majority of individual voters' will. One argument is that voters can make intelligent choices only if they are presented with packages in which individual issues are combined in cohesive bundles, and if someone on behalf of voters surveys the future as well as the immediate present. It can also be argued that voters want a degree of moral leadership: they want to be led by someone whose character they can respect towards purposes they think good.

In practice, governments have to fulfil both roles. Great leaders need first to get themselves elected, and politicians who are power-seekers may not get elected unless they persuade voters that they have some claim to leadership and vision. At some periods it seems to be the duller sort of governments that gain power. At other times the electorate seems to long to be led, and perhaps inspired with a grand cause: at such times governments are likely to be allowed more power to act.

Leadership is clearly at a premium in times of war, and governments then have most power. They can conscript, tax, spend, and borrow as they like, and (while the war goes well) have the upper hand over financial markets. But there are also many occasions in peacetime when a government has played an unusually dominant role. Roosevelt exerted strong leadership, and intervened extensively—whatever the effectiveness of New Deal economic policies [ch. 6.3].[7] The postwar Labour government in the UK played a leadership role in postwar social and economic reconstruction; de Gaulle had dominance in France; and the reunification of Germany in 1990, carried out in a fit of nationalistic compulsion, sparked large-scale spending much as a war would have done.

Why a country should sometimes be in one mood and at other times in another seems a question of circumstances. Looking back over the last century, it would seem to depend on the character of contemporary politicians; on the situation of the different countries (whether, for instance, there was a readiness to support a large effort of national reconstruction, or whether—that perhaps having been done—there was a general desire to relax); and on the hundred

---

[7] President Roosevelt's charismatic appeal was evident from the start of his presidency. Schlesinger (1960:1) notes the response to the new president's inaugural address: 'People said "It was the finest thing this side of heaven"; and "Your human feeling for all of us in your address is just wonderful"; and "It seemed to give the people, as well as myself, a new hold upon life" …'.

accidents that affect politics, ranging from the state of readiness of this or that political party as a fighting machine to the changing health of political leaders. This does not go far to establish general political laws, though it may suggest a vaguely defined rhythmical pattern.

The state and macroeconomic policy

In the UK, the state made tentative steps towards having an economic policy, in the sense that we now know it, in the 1930s. Only at the end of World War II did the government, under the influence of Keynesian ideas, adopt responsibility for the behaviour of the economy and set up the requisite bureaucracy.[8] Since then UK governments have sought to distance themselves from full responsibility; but they continue to claim credit when things go well, and to be blamed when they do not. Sometimes a little later, and sometimes less explicitly, much the same has happened in other industrial countries.

The apparatus of government on which these cares have been imposed, on top of many other immense responsibilities, is not ideally constructed to deal with economic policy. The most obvious discrepancy is that the response of the economy to a change in policy may take a half or a whole decade—damping down inflation, or recovering from major recession are slow processes—whereas the life of a parliament is usually four or five years, that of a government less and that of a minister of finance (chancellor of the Exchequer) usually less again. Equally crucial is the nature of political life. Politicians are inevitably busy, without time to devote to finer issues. The tenure both of governments and of their individual members is always insecure, and all have to spend much time maintaining contacts with numerous groups merely to stay in power. In addition, most governments are not strong and cohesive entities but impermanent alliances of ambitious personalities, and weak coalitions of competing interest groups. In these circumstances, politicians inevitably concentrate on immediate issues, and longer-term issues are crowded out.

The political process nevertheless plays an essential positive role. The broad direction of economic policy needs to have the support of substantial sections of the electorate; and the dependence of governments on parliament goes some way to making them attend to public opinion.

The bias of policy towards disinflation rather than expansion

In practice, policy has repeatedly been rigorous in the negative direction (i.e. to counter inflation), most dramatically so after the OPEC price shocks. In peacetime it has hardly ever been used strongly and consistently in a positive direction, e.g. to promote a recovery after a recession. For this there may be two reasons. First, inflation hurts (or may appear to hurt) most of the

---

[8] In the UK the key event was the White Paper on Employment Policy (1944); the bureaucracy centred on the Economic Section at first in the Cabinet Office, later in the Treasury (Cairncross and Watts 1989). In the USA the Council of Economic Advisers had similar symbolic and practical significance.

population, while recession acutely disadvantages only some. Second, recovery is a much longer process; it is easy and quick to destroy business confidence and slow and hard to recreate it. Politically, these factors reinforce each other.

In this book the high employment of the Golden Age (1945–73) has often been contrasted with the high unemployment of subsequent decades. Compared with the mere maintenance of employment at a high level, it is a task altogether more difficult to recreate high employment once lost. To illustrate the political problem, it is worth listing the difficulties involved in such a process of re-creation.

1. A majority of the electorate would probably vote for low rather than high unemployment if given the option, but it is never given a clear option. Hence many, it may be supposed, do not give it first priority among the things they vote for—more especially if social security protects the unemployed from visible acute deprivation.
2. A programme of curing unemployment would be a gradual process, so that its effect would take years to appear, which reduces its political appeal. Equally important, long-drawn-out processes have to be well managed, and thus involve many possibilities of mistakes and error; for instance, economic forecasts are fallible, and large-scale public administration is frequently inefficient. Well-meant programmes of expansion could even turn out to have perverse economic or political effects.
3. The deterrent effects of uncertainty are cumulative. Financial markets distrust innovative and ambitious government plans. Economists are divided and give contradictory advice. Warnings by economists, and the groundswell of unease in the City, interact; both cool voters' hopefulness. That too strengthens City caution and undercuts politicians' enthusiasm.
4. All these groups feel intuitively (as is correct) that for a country the size of the UK to act alone increases the risk. Expansion on the back of expanding exports as a result of other countries expanding would be more comfortable all round.

The result is that politicians do not persuasively put forward the programmes that, if put to the voters, might mobilize their support. The explanation proposed in this study for the existence of unemployment as a stable state [chs. 3.2 and 10.2] was that it arose from interlocking obstacles of the kind where A prevents B and B prevents A. (Thus, consumers do not spend because, being unemployed, they lack the income to demand firms' products; firms do not re-employ those unemployed because there is no demand for greater output while unemployment persists.) The explanation given here of the difficulties in the way of getting different sections of economic society to support deliberate political action against unemployment is, not by accident, similar.

But if, by luck, there were high employment to start with, voters would vote to keep it; politicians would not propose a programme to end it—or, if they did, voters' disapprobation would be not protracted but immediate. Neither the electorate, nor politicians, nor economists, nor financial markets would perceive high employment as an impossible state of affairs, or maintain that it was a risky and untried aim: it would be the *status quo*. The difficulty is in the transition, and in the multiple complexities of orchestrating an expansion of different elements that have to be kept in step.

Despite the formidable difficulties, it is argued here that a programme of expansion is not impossible, and that some circumstances, and some sorts of action, are less difficult than others.

12.1.3. Aspects of inflation

The nature of inflation has varied in the three-quarters of a century covered by this study. This is true even if one omits as exceptional the cases of hyperinflation that occurred in some European countries after the great wars, and in Latin America, but not in the UK and the USA. In all industrial countries prices have become much less flexible since the 1930s, and therefore less freely responsive to demand pressures. That undoubtedly reflects the growing predominance of imperfect competition, and of administered pricing. This has made the price level in industrial countries open to cost pressures. The cost pressures have originated in two sectors of the world price system that have remained demand-sensitive. World commodity prices have for the most part remained completely flexible and thus highly demand-sensitive both upwards and downwards; and the pressure exerted by the resultant fluctuations in world commodity prices has dominated movements of the level of final prices in industrial countries.[9] Wage levels have also remained sensitive (though in a far less flexible manner) to demand pressures in national labour markets; and the final price level has remained open (at least in the upward direction) to cost pressures originating there.

The result has been that the world price level, which before the mid-1930s was as likely to fall as to rise, has since then tended only to rise, either slowly or more rapidly. This has created strongly based expectations about future inflation—looking ahead, there is now good reason to think that prices are more likely to rise than to fall—and that has made expectations a much more important factor. Waves of particularly fast inflation have been fairly slow to recede, so that inflationary expectations also have been slow to moderate. Economic theory needs to take account of such institutionally determined facts about the working of inflation.

Economists' ideas about inflation, too, have gone through various phases in the last half-century. One landmark was the formulation of the Phillips curve (Phillips 1958): before that there was little quantitative theorizing, afterwards perhaps too much. That relationship made it natural to envisage a neutral

---

[9] In earlier chapters this dominance has been illustrated in terms of the relationship between UK import prices and final expenditure prices [see fig. 2.3 and tables 7.8, 8A.1, and 8A.2].

point at which inflation would remain at zero, or (as a deduction from a more elaborate form of the relationship) a point at which inflation would not accelerate. But the empirical basis for such theorizing remained questionable. It is noteworthy that the original Phillips curve explained not the rate of change of prices, but that of wages, in terms of the level of unemployment; and it was based on a century's experience, going back to the mid-nineteenth century, i.e. to a time when prices were much more flexible. The work by Dicks-Mireaux and myself at this same time was based on more recent history, and took account of the differences between inflation in commodity and industrial product markets (Dicks-Mireaux and Dow 1959; Dicks-Mireaux 1961). The exact scale of the relationship between the pace of inflation and the pressure of demand (as proxied by unemployment) has always seemed to me an observation of a sociological sort, reflecting many aspects of group behaviour, such as trade union organization and wage-bargaining procedures; it may therefore easily change—and change *inter alia* as a result of experience of inflation.[10] That is, it does not reflect (or does not only reflect) any deep economic law based on optimizing behaviour at the micro level, such as economic theorists search for.

Earlier belief in the NAIRU, or its cousin the Natural Rate of Unemployment, seems now to have waned.[11] The main reason was that estimates of what the natural rate was appeared so unstable. As actual unemployment rose (particularly in Europe after the OPEC shocks), estimates of the natural rate followed actual inflation upward. That probably reflected the fact that, with higher inflation, expectations of inflation also rose. More recently (i.e. since about 1992) there seems to have been a tendency for forecasting equations to over-predict—perhaps now reflecting a gradual fall in inflationary expectations.

Monetarists see the rate of inflation as uniquely related to the rate of growth of the money stock; consequently they see monetary policy as uniquely concerned with the control of inflation, and not at all with growth or unemployment. This assignment of monetary policy derives from two prior assumptions: (1) that the rate of growth of supply (potential output) is independent of the rate of growth of demand; and (2) that the economy, if diverted from the full employment of potential output, will rapidly return to it. Granted these assumptions, the argument goes, a policy of monetary restraint, initiated (let us suppose) to reduce the rate of inflation, will have no permanent effect on the level of output, and the only important effect will be to reduce the rate of inflation. I have already stated reasons to dispute these assumptions [s. 12.1.1].

---

[10] See discussion in preface to the 1990 paperback edition of Dow and Saville (1988).

[11] See the essays in Cross (1995). The 'natural rate' hypothesis comprises two parts: (1) the idea of a rate of unemployment at which inflation is non-accelerating (discussed above), and (2) the idea that actual unemployment tends to this rate, as to an equilibrium point.

This view of the relationship between monetary growth and inflation rests also on two views as to causality, both of which I think are mistaken: (1) that inflation is determined by the rate of growth of the money stock; and (2) that the growth of the money stock (hence also inflation) is easily controlled by the authorities. As to the first proposition, the reverse in my view is true: monetary growth is largely determined by the rate of growth of the price and volume of output, which factors are largely otherwise determined.

As to the second proposition, the growth of the money stock in my view cannot be directly controlled by the monetary authorities: to exercise control over it, the authorities must cause output to grow more (or less) rapidly, and by so doing they will also control the rate of change in the price of output—both of which factors in turn determine monetary growth.[12]

Dependence of inflation on monetary expansion is given some apparent credibility by experience of hyperinflation in some countries in the aftermath of World Wars I and II. Money creation, though it played a role, was not I think the basic cause of the inflation: that was rather the general breakdown of a stable social system, as a consequence of which governments lost their power to collect tax revenue. Since they continued to spend, that created extreme excess demand. It is true that they could continue to spend only because they could issue increasingly worthless paper money, and because the banks lent to them. But the first step to stop the process was effective tax collection to restore fiscal order (as is true, now, in the similar situation in the aftermath of communism in the ex-Soviet countries).

Experience of hyperinflation still colours folk memories, but hyperinflation is not a near-danger in more normal times. It remains true nevertheless that, if neglected, inflation can easily get out of control. Experience of inflation affects expectations of inflation; and, once established, it is a slow and difficult process to eradicate expectations of faster inflation. The fact that inflation among industrial countries has, since World War II, been relatively well contained can probably be attributed to the rather cautious policies followed for most of the time by the majority of industrial countries.

Implications for policy

Policy in my view must have two aims, not just one: not only to keep inflation reasonably low, but also to maintain reasonably fast growth and reasonably high employment. Since the level of demand affects both the rate of inflation and the rate of growth of output (i.e. one instrument for two policy variables), there is a potential conflict between these two objects of policy; i.e., compromise is inevitable.

It may be argued that when the objectives conflict moderation of inflation should have priority over maintaining growth, on the grounds that, if high

---

[12] For a fuller version of this second argument see Dow and Saville (1988); and for a fuller version of the first, see 1990 preface to that work.

Table 12.1   Coincidence of major recessions with periods of high inflation, 1920–1993

Major recession	Pace of inflation[a]	Contribution of domestic policy to the recession[b]
I 1920–21	−17	50
II 1929–32	−4	5
III 1973–75	20	60
IV 1979–82	11	60
V 1989–93	5	0

[a] % compound rate of change in total final expenditure deflator in period of each recession.
[b] Estimated contribution of policy to deviation of output from previous trend: from table 11.1 (rounded).

inflation is not tackled now it will (because expectations will be affected) get consolidated, and will be more costly to tackle later.[13] But if neglect of inflation has long-run costs, it is true too, as this study has exemplified, that neglect of recessionary conditions also has costly long-run consequences. That suggests that neither objective should be given overriding priority.

For individual countries (as already noted), the origins of inflation have been mostly international. International shocks of this sort, even if less sharp than in the last part of the twentieth century, will no doubt continue, and at times will undo the effects of the best judged domestic policy. However, most of the situations that provoke peaks of world demand, and hence accelerations of world inflation, after a few years either cease or (more usually) get reversed. Wars do not go on for ever; peaks of world demand arising for other reasons either reverse themselves or tend to get reversed by the actions of foreign monetary authorities; and commodity price booms, if not reversed by such corrections on the demand side, are reversed by the supply-side response to high commodity prices.

Conflict between the aims of price stability and output stability does not always arise. There is no conflict when growth and inflation are both excessive: both criteria then call for policy restraint.[14] The conflict is most acute when recession coincides with fast inflation, as happened most clearly in the OPEC recessions: the criteria then point in opposite directions. But that conjunction has been uncommon [table 12.1], and is perhaps unlikely in future. Most situations are situations of only moderate conflict.

---

[13] For this reason I think it would have been better if the UK economy in the postwar years (1945–73) had been run at a lower pressure of demand, i.e. with higher unemployment. As I argued at the time (Dow 1964: 403–5), properly managed, the cost to output and growth could have been quite small.
[14] Before the 1930s there would seem to have been no conflict: prices, being more flexible, rose at time of boom, and fell at times of recession.

The moral I draw is that, while excess demand conditions at home must always be dealt with, temporary outbursts of inflation originating abroad should not be given too much importance. Even if action to control inflation at the cost of slowing growth is pressed some way, it has to be accepted that in an incompletely stable world complete success in stabilizing domestic inflation is not possible.

The control of inflation is a more awkward problem for someone like myself than it is for a monetarist. In my view, both fiscal and monetary policy help to determine the strength of demand; and that in part determines inflation, so that both have to be formulated with inflation in mind. The awkwardness is that action to affect the strength of demand changes not only prices but also unemployment; i.e., control of inflation can be purchased only at the cost of creating unemployment.

To this dilemma, what used to be called incomes policy promised a way out. In practice, this amounted to voluntary restraint on the part of wage-earners (or trade unions representing them) in the vigour with which they pressed their periodic claims for higher wages. Incomes policy is now out of fashion, but that may be a symptom of the times. The case for an incomes policy is that to put people out of work in order to moderate the rate of rise of prices is a clumsy and perhaps cruel way to curb inflation. The case against it is that it is likely to break down because it requires people not to act in the way their individual interests point.[15] It was always a weak instrument; i.e., it did not provide an effective barrier against demand pressures, or allow governments to pursue high employment regardless of inflationary consequences. But there is some evidence that in earlier postwar years, when social bonds were probably stronger than they became later, incomes policies had some effect. If we had a government with a strong intention of intervening in the economy in order to improve social conditions, and one that was strongly supported in this ambition by the electorate, it might be in a position to operate such a policy.

My own views about the control of inflation may now be shared by many people. Inflation can be controlled only indirectly, by manipulating the strength of demand. For several reasons, however, that still provides only an uncertain, and slow, degree of control. For it is *expectations* of inflation even more than present inflation that governments must seek to control, and these are difficult to manipulate or foresee.

12.2. The traditional tools of macroeconomic policy

In face of the many arguments to the contrary, I restate the case for regarding fiscal and monetary policy as means by which the economy can be managed. But for both kinds of policy I emphasize practical constraints, different from

---

[15] I do not mean that wage-earners as a whole are better off if they break a policy of restraint than if they adhere to it. But those who first break the restraint do better for themselves than those who for a time continue to obey it.

those usually urged, which severely limit their use. The arguments here are general; section 12.3 attempts to map out what can be done in practice to counter major recessions.

12.2.1. Fiscal policy

In a highly uncertain world, the creditworthiness of governments, as of any kind of borrower, is finite. That limits the extent to which governments can borrow, and thus limits also how far fiscal policy can be used as an instrument of demand management. The fact that the world is uncertain makes it impossible to put exact limits to creditworthiness; and I shall probe various ways into this question.

Truisms about limits to debt

Agent A will lend B money if it seems probable that B will be willing and able to repay the capital and to pay the interest meanwhile. A will also lend, even if B may not wish to repay the capital, if it seems probable that others will remain willing to lend to B. B will then be able to repay to A on demand even if his assets are illiquid. But others will not be willing to lend to B if he is able to pay interest only out of additional borrowing; for then it will appear that B may be driven to incur ever-increasing debt. Since that will be evident to all, B's creditworthiness will be eroded. There will then be an evident risk that B will be unable to repay the debt when due; i.e., he may be driven to repudiate his debt.

The same is true of a government as a borrower, with the addition that a government can increase its income by raising tax rates. But there is a limit to how far a government can raise tax rates without provoking evasion, or rebellion of some sort; and a lower limit beyond which a sensible and responsible government would not wish to go, since that would destroy the incentive to work or drive good citizens to other countries. Since there is such a limit, indefinite borrowing by a government would at some point make it evident that the government was on a course where it might opt to repudiate its debt.

In a well ordered and prosperous country, that sort of risk may seem remote. Nevertheless, it is in the background (and even in relatively 'safe' countries not far in the background). To lenders the risks appear greater because the character and composition of a government, like any institution, can change radically in the course of a relatively few years, so that it can never be certain what sort of government will be in power in any country in five or ten years' time. One indication of the emergence of distrust is when the government of one country can borrow only at a differentially high interest rate.

The prescription of rules for public deficits and debt ratios

One reaction to the danger of excessive government borrowing is to try to devise rules that if observed would prevent public debt becoming excessive.

Table 12.2 Public debt ratios in OECD countries, 1980–1995

	General government gross financial liabilities as % of nominal GDP			
	1980	1985	1990	1995
USA	37.0	49.5	55.5	63.4
Japan	51.2	67.0	65.1	80.6
Germany	31.1	42.8	45.5	62.2
France	30.9	38.6	40.2	60.7
Italy	58.1	82.3	104.5	124.7
UK	54.0	58.9	39.3	60.0
Canada	44.0	64.1	72.5	100.5
Total of above 7 countries	41.6	54.9	58.3	72.0
14 smaller OECD countries	32.8	51.9	50.8	63.3

Source: OECD *Economic Outlook*, no. 61, table A34. Definitions differ in detail from UK figures in app. A10.

The ratio of debt to GDP has usually risen in times of war, and fallen in peacetime—either because debt has been repaid, or because the value of debt has been reduced by inflation. Recent history has been unusual. Three major recessions within a couple of decades drastically worsened the state of public finances in almost all countries. In most OECD countries public debt as a ratio to nominal GDP rose a lot in the twenty years after 1973. (Table 12.2 shows the rise since 1980.)

During each recession, the automatic stabilizers were either allowed to work, or not overridden much, so that budget deficits rose. The subsequent recovery of national output and income was incomplete, so that there was an incomplete recovery of government revenue compared with the previous trend. Though government spending was trimmed in the years after each recession, enlarged public deficits thus continued. That process was repeated three times in the period, and public deficits tended to be made larger each time. Many special factors also affected the position in individual countries. In the UK, public debt as a ratio to GDP fell for the first thirty years after World War II, stayed about flat for the next fifteen years (1975–90), then (about 1990) started, as in other countries, to rise steeply [app. A11].

This rising trend has bred fears that levels of debt were in danger of getting out of control, and has led many governments to make it an aim of policy to cut spending and raise tax rates so as to limit the growth of debt and stabilize or reduce its level in relation to GDP. On this way of thinking, a deficit that remains in constant proportion to GDP is taken to remain financeable. Debt can thus be allowed to increase in so far as GDP is on an upward trend, and also to increase temporarily if GDP is temporarily depressed for 'cyclical reasons, as in a recession:[16] deficits above these limits are treated as unsustainable. Though there is some logic in such precautionary rules (e.g. as in the Maastricht Treaty) they represent little more than a codification of the behaviour of the best-behaved governments at the time. They ignore some probabilities (discussed below) of what happens after major recessions, and should not be held to rule out stimulative fiscal measures during recessions.

The case for deficit financing after major recessions

The argument that follows for a stimulative fiscal policy in the aftermath of a major recession accepts the view that debt cannot be increased without limit, and rests on the argument that private demand is likely to revive, so making it unnecessary for stimulative action to continue indefinitely; the increase in debt as a result of such action will thus be limited, or even temporary.

After a major recession output is typically likely to be 10 per cent below its previous trend, and unemployment, say, 5 percentage points above its level before the recession [ch. 11.1]. Assuming that before the recession demand was at a reasonably high level, demand would have to rise by 5 per cent above its recession low point in order to restore high employment.

After a major recession, private demand is likely, for two reasons, to revive, and thus after some time to displace the need for continued stimulus. The first reason works even in the absence of a stimulus; the second happens as a result of confidence effects which amplify the effect of the stimulus.

Natural revival of confidence A major recession is accompanied by, and partly caused by, a collapse of consumer and business confidence. Continued steady growth, even at a low level of employment, is likely [ch. 11.2] to cause confidence gradually to recover; i.e., the saving ratio will fall to a more normal level, and investment will rise.[17]

Induced increase in confidence as a result of stimulative measures Stimulative measures will accelerate the return of confidence; i.e., the direct effect of the measures will be amplified by the effect they have on confidence [ch. 11.2]. This confidence effect appears considerable; for example, it might increase the direct effect of stimulative measures by 50–100 per cent.

---

[16] In practice it is not easy to measure what part of a change in the government deficit is 'cyclical' and what is not. Reasons against the concept of a 'cycle' are summarized in ch. 10.1.

[17] It could be argued that there is a separate, third reason why private spending will rise. The counterpart to debt-financed government spending is additional private holdings of debt; and if Ricardian equivalence is rejected, to the holders these represent wealth. The increase in wealth will increase the propensity to consume; i.e., consumers will gradually cease to want to add to their wealth at an abnormal rate, so that the saving rate will revert to normal. This however seems a complicated way of saying that after a major recession consumer's confidence is weak (and saving is high); and later recovers (and saving falls). It is not clear therefore that this wealth effect is additional to that of the general revival of confidence described above. If it is separable, it is clearly closely allied to the first reason, and adds to the drift of the present argument.

The aftermath of a major recession is by definition a time when confidence is unusually low, and the private propensity to consume and invest thus correspondingly low.[18] A period of five to ten years in which, perhaps because of stimulative measures, growth is consistently somewhat above the normal rate would be likely to restore confidence sufficiently for private demand to support full employment without the need for continued stimulative measures— and might even produce a situation in which *contractionary* measures are required to restrain demand, which (if fiscal) will then involve repayment of debt.

These considerations help to provide some indication of the scale of policy stimulation that would be appropriate. The two effects above supplement those of any stimulative measures, i.e. reduce the scale of measures required to restore high employment. The evidence does not provide a basis for precise estimation. But as a rough indication, stimulatory measures equivalent to between 1 and 3 per cent of GDP per year for a period of years, continued on a diminishing scale for a number of years, might (in conjunction with the revival of private demand) be enough to reduce unemployment by the 5 percentage points likely to be required to restore high employment. Because of the danger of provoking inflationary pressures, recovery from a major recession needs to be kept slow and gradual; for example, output growth should not be more than 0.5–1 per cent above the trend rate. If so, restoration of high employment would take from five to ten years. Assuming that all the stimulative action came from fiscal (not monetary) policy, and was needed on a diminishing scale for up to 10 years, then the increase in public debt required over the whole period would seem likely to be of the order of up to 10 per cent of GDP.

That would be a significant, but not a particularly large, increase; and if logic ruled, ought not to be considered particularly alarming—especially in cases where public debt was not already particularly high by international standards. Debt levels have in fact varied greatly without noticeable effects on the performance of the economy. For instance, the UK national debt in relation to GDP, already high before the Napoleonic War, rose to about 290 per cent by 1815, then fell continuously to about 30 per cent by 1914.[19] World War I took it back to 200 per cent; in the interwar period it fell back only moderately (to 150 per cent); then World War II again nearly doubled the ratio, taking it back to over 270 per cent. In the postwar years, as already noted, partly because of rapid growth, more because of inflation, the ratio again fell steadily [fig. 11.3]. In the face of such variety, fixed rules about the permissible level of government debt can have little absolute validity.

---

[18] Between 1972 and 1996 the ratio of personal saving to RPDI was mostly above 10 %; between 1950 and 1972 it was mostly below that ratio. Investment too was obviously low after each of the last three major recessions.

[19] See Buiter (1985); chart reproduced in Dow and Saville (1988: fig. 6.1).

The true constraints on fiscal policy, however, arise not from the sort of considerations discussed so far, but from more primitive considerations relating to the behaviour of financial markets, now to be discussed.

Constraints imposed by the reaction of financial markets to government borrowing

Government borrowing—or unusually large government borrowing—is likely to cause financial markets to take alarm. I will argue that this arises because good information about the future is scarce, so that agents' expectations are poorly based and weakly held. I will also argue that for this same reason financial markets are often willing to take a lead from the authorities; so that the degree of constraint that the potential fickleness of financial markets imposes on government policy varies according to circumstances.

Borrowing by a government from the market is possible only if those in the market trust the government to honour its promise to service and repay its debt. This trust can be undermined by what to the market appears imprudent behaviour on the government's part. Large-scale borrowing is one sort of behaviour that is likely to appear imprudent.

The reason for the exaggerated reactions of financial markets is that, the future being to a large extent unknowable, operators have to judge the situation on the basis of very incomplete signs and symbols. Financial markets are far from being perfectly informed or perfectly self-confident; and expectations, being weakly held, often vary quickly for little good reason.

One reason why governments are not fully trusted by financial markets is that governments change. An existing government may look as respectable a body as any that has dealings in financial markets. But the composition of governments alters from year to year, and the ruling political party may be swept away in an election, so that the character of a government a few years hence could be very different from now.

Financial markets tend in any case to be suspicious of government spending, and to believe that the political pressures to which governments are subject make them prone to overspend. It is always difficult for the Treasury or Finance Ministry to maintain control over government spending in face of departmental and political pressures; and an expansionary fiscal policy is likely to undermine that discipline—a good reason for financial markets to distrust such a policy.

The consequences of ignoring the susceptibilities of financial markets is to raise the interest cost of public borrowing, perhaps making long-term borrowing impossible, and—in a country much of whose public debt is held by non-residents—to lower the exchange rate. Alarm in the markets, once aroused, is likely to cumulate, until a credible reversal of the policy that caused the alarm has been demonstrated.[20] The danger of provoking such reactions is likely to

---

[20] The UK crisis of 1976 [ch. 9.1] is an example of how, in a situation not basically alarming, financial markets can take alarm. It was ended only with the intervention of the IMF.

dissuade most governments, most of the time, from embarking on a debt-financed expansionary policy.

The same factors, however, that make financial markets unstable also make them susceptible to influence by the authorities. To other operators in financial markets [see further s. 12.2.2], governments appear big and in some ways privileged operators, with access to more information than private agents, and even capable of determining the future.

Thus, it is not the case that governments are always at the markets' beck and call. There is a two-way possibility of dominance between financial markets as lenders and governments as big-borrowers. The position of the government in relation to financial markets is strongest in times of war, and in war governments have been able to borrow on a scale they never could in peace time. That is probably largely because in war governments command overwhelming popular support and authority, whereas in peacetime a government's political position is likely to be less solid. Even so there are differences of degree. Some governments are able to command more popular assent for an active policy than others [s. 12.1.1], and to convince markets that they have sound reasons for borrowing. What governments are in a position to do in this respect depends on how impressive they appear to financial markets.

Conclusions about the use of fiscal policy

I now give my conclusions, based not on fundamental economic theory but on practical judgement, about how far it ought to be practical to use fiscal policy to counter major recessions.

1. Countries with debt–GDP ratios much above the average are, I think, bound to take steps to limit any further rise in the ratio, and probably to reduce it. Conversely, countries not in this position need to take care not to get into it, but otherwise need not be so actively concerned about the ratio.

2. Governments ought to be able to resist pressures to override the automatic stabilizers during a major recession. They ought also to be able to resist pressures to reverse the effects the automatic stabilizers had during a recession too soon after it, i.e. at times when consumer and business confidence is low, and unemployment high—unless the effects can be offset by low interest rates (not always possible: see section 12.2.3).

3. A strong government that was prepared to defend its policy and appeared competent and businesslike might be in a position to adopt a more positive and explicit policy of expansion that involved enlarged deficits for a period of years. Weaker governments are likely to find that impractical. Various schemes of public/private investment, which would raise demand without involving public borrowing (see further section 12.3.2), should however always be possible.

12.2.2. Monetary policy

Before discussing how monetary policy needs to be used, I first consider how it works.

The modus operandi *of monetary policy*

My view of how monetary policy has its effect on the real economy (Dow and Saville 1988: chs. 3 and 4) starts from the observation that the actions of the central bank by which it seeks to deploy its influence are typically extremely small-scale compared with the widespread influence they evidently have on interest rates throughout the financial system and, through that, on private-sector expenditure. The authorities' influence cannot be explained in terms of official action impinging on a system where the linkages between returns on financial assets and real assets respectively are tightly determined; and the classical theory that the rate of interest equilibrates the supply of savings with the demand for savings—i.e. the demand from those who use borrowed savings to invest in investment goods—can be of no assistance in explaining their influence.

The central bank's influence is possible only because, contrary to what is implied by the concept of rational expectations, the interest rate expectations of operators in financial markets are poorly based and not sharply determined. That in my view reflects the great uncertainty about the future course of events, and in particular the future return on real investment. Compared with most private operators in financial markets, the monetary authorities are, potentially at least, large-scale operators; and compared with them they appear better informed about the future. The authorities can therefore exercise a leadership role in markets, and—provided always that they do not press their influence beyond the range of the credible—can have large influence on private operators' interest rate expectations.

The central bank is thus able, within broad limits, to put the nominal interest rate (and thus also the real interest rate) on short-term financial assets where it likes. The limits are determined by reference to the long-run real equilibrium rate of interest at which the desire on the part of savers to hold wealth and the desire on the part of investors to employ capital would be in equality. There are no forces in the economy that drive the actual rate to this equilibrium point. But actual rates cannot diverge by more than a margin from this point, as envisaged by market operators; for if they did, transactions would take place that would drive market rates back within the limits. Beyond that point, the creditability of the central bank's power and its ability to fix rates would be eroded.

Short-term market rates may thus be said to be indeterminate within a range centred on the market's idea of the fundamental equilibrium rate of interest; i.e., the central bank has power within that range to fix the rate on short-term assets. Since the long term is a succession of short terms, and given that there are no forces that cause market rates to approach equilibrium rates in the long term, the central bank retains this power in the indefinite long term.

The interest rate on long-term assets is related both to the short-term rate and to the market's idea of the fundamental equilibrium rate; i.e., long-term financial assets are closer substitutes for real assets. Thus, the rate on long-term assets is determined in the same way as the rate on short-term assets, except that the bounds to its indeterminacy are narrower and perhaps much narrower.[21] Accordingly, the central bank has less power to determine real interest rates (and thus also nominal rates) on long-term financial assets, in either the short term or the long.

Monetary policy by these routes appears to exert a powerful influence over the level of demand [chs. 5.2, 11.2]; and thus also (along with fiscal policy and other instruments) a significant influence over the rate of inflation. On my view, this influence comes from official manipulation of interest rates, not directly from official control of the rate of monetary expansion—which is indeed barely controllable except as a by-product of the effects of interest rates and fiscal policy on the real economy.

The role of monetary policy

The role allotted to monetary policy in the UK has varied greatly: in other countries it has perhaps varied much less. Between about 1950 and 1973, it was generally held that the rate of growth of demand should be controlled so as both to keep output expanding at a satisfactory rate and to keep moderate the rate of increase of prices; and that interest rates should be varied as one means, along with fiscal policy, of achieving these twin objectives.[22] Since 1973 officials have for most of the time emphasized the control of inflation as the sole aim of monetary policy. Between 1976 and 1986 monetary policy aimed to control the rate of growth of broad money, because this was thought to determine inflation; and quantitative targets were set for the rate of growth of the broad money stock. This policy was abandoned basically because control of the growth of the money stock proved impossible (see Dow and Saville 1988). The aim of monetary policy then (1987–92) came to be control of the exchange rate. Since 1994, the monetarist bias was revived in the practice of stating the aims of monetary policy in terms of inflation targets, i.e. rates of inflation that are supposed to be achieved by the use of monetary policy.

It is in my view not satisfactory to define the role of monetary policy solely in terms of countering inflation; by itself, even if successful in its own terms, that will not be enough to ensure a reasonably fast growth of demand and output, or reasonably full employment. These latter objectives therefore also have to be given weight in the control of demand, and monetary policy can have a large impact on the level of demand. Hence, as a general rule, monetary policy along with fiscal policy has to be used to influence demand, with the twin objectives of achieving stability of output and stability of prices. Since the use of fiscal policy to influence demand is liable to be greatly constrained [s. 12.2.1], the total dedication of monetary policy to the control of inflation

---

[21] It is suggestive that market expectations of the real rate of interest on long-term financial assets, while not constant, appear to have varied relatively little, even at times of considerable volatility in short rates; see e.g. Barr and Campbell's (1997) study of UK nominal and index-linked bond prices.

[22] For this period and the period before 1950, see Dow (1964: ch. IX).

would deprive the authorities of a valuable and flexible means of stabilizing output.

There are however limitations also to the use of monetary policy for stabilizing output and prices. Changes in interest rates relative to those in other countries cause changes in exchange rates. Under- or over-valuation of exchange rates will cause shifts in the balance of payments which, over a period of, say five to ten years, will cause the initial mis-valuation to be reversed. Unsustainable exchange rates thus cause severe over- or under-expansion of a country's export industries (and the reverse in the foreign-trade sectors of countries that are its trading partners). Such reversals of the trading conditions faced by these sectors causes major disruption. The need to ensure a sustainable exchange rate ought therefore to be taken account of along with the more general objectives of securing stability of growth and of prices.[23] Given several objectives for the single instrument (interest rates), compromise between objectives is inevitable. Movement of exchange rates may be impossible to avoid entirely; but in a country like the UK, utilization of interest rate policy for demand management is bound to be constrained by these considerations.

For a large country such as the USA, exchange rate stability matters less because its tradeable goods sector is relatively small; and it will determine its monetary policy without great regard to such considerations. For a small country, however, such stability may be paramount; and if it is a close neighbour to a large country (as Canada is to the USA) it will be compelled to follow its large neighbour's policy fairly closely. The central banks of continental Europe have increasingly followed the Bundesbank's interest rate policy, and thus acted as a bloc; and being a large area, the policy of the bloc (like the USA) is determined more by its internal situation than by exchange rate considerations. The UK as a small neighbour to this large bloc has thus lost some of its freedom to follow an independent monetary policy; and this constraint is likely to increase as time goes on, and as trading relations with Europe grow closer; the formation of a European Monetary Union—even if the UK remained outside—will reduce its independence further. This seems likely to drive the UK and other countries similarly placed at some date to join a European monetary union, when they will again have some say in determining what monetary policy is. For Europe, monetary policy will continue to be an instrument that can be used to manage demand in the area as a whole.[24]

---

[23] The argument is set out more fully in Wren-Lewis (1997).

[24] For a number of decades ahead, the USA and the new Europe are likely to be the dominant economic blocs in the world; and how demand is managed in these large areas will determine how stable international commodity prices are. That will be as important as the state of domestic demand in each area, or perhaps more so, for the stability of prices in the dominant blocs. This consideration should therefore be given a large weight in the formulation of US and EU policies. With only two blocs, it may be easier to agree a joint approach.

The independence of central banks

The case for an independent central bank rests primarily on the proposition that the directorates of central banks are likely to be more competent and more responsible at directing monetary policy than political ministers of finance. The counter-arguments are that control of inflation is not a sufficient aim for policy; that central banks are likely to be over-biased towards control of inflation at the expense of growth and employment; that, even if inflation were the only aim, fiscal and monetary policy have both to be used, and coordination between them is likely to be more difficult if the central bank is independent; and, finally, that economic policy requires popular assent and support, which is better ensured if decided by ministers more directly responsible to an elected parliament.

For me, the counter-arguments seem persuasive, so I am somewhat opposed to central banks being independent of political control. Nevertheless, I believe that that arrangement can work fairly well.

Granting independence to a central bank is bound to change its character, and to make it more likely than for a dependent one that it will pursue a balanced rather than an extreme policy. If it is the central bank rather than the minister of finance that decides interest rates, that does not protect the central bank from political pressures but directly exposes it to pressures from which it was previously protected. This will force it to behave like a political institution, i.e. a centre of power that will develop relations with other centres of power; and it will aim to preserve its own position of power in the face of the political pressures that might destroy it. Officials of the bank, even if their own tenure of office is secure for a number of years, may want to be reappointed; and will want the institutional independence of their bank to continue. To do this, they will have to deliver an outcome that is satisfactory to parliament and the electorate. That includes avoidance not only of inflation, but of high unemployment and pronounced economic stagnation.

In practice, whatever their counter-inflationary rhetoric, the Federal Reserve System and the Bundesbank—the two major independent central banks—have not neglected other considerations. It may be also that the more detached position of a central bank, as compared with a ministry of finance, is calculated to allow it to pursue a more consistent long-term policy. In my view, it would nevertheless be advantageous if the mandate given to independent central banks instructed them to pursue stability of output growth as well as stability of prices, and to report regularly to a parliamentary committee—as the Fed does and the (newly independent) Bank of England, but not (as yet envisaged) the European Central Bank.

12.3. Possible policies to counter major recessions

This section turns to consider more concretely what instruments the authorities can use to counter a major recession [s. 12.3.1], and, as a check, how much past major recessions might have been mitigated [s. 12.3.2]. I do look not at past attempts—since there hardly were any—but at whether attempts to counter past recessions would have been possible.

12.3.1. Counteractive measures

There seem [chs. 11.2, 11.3] two main causes of major recession: downward exogenous shocks, and reaction to phases of excessive boom. There is need, then, for the authorities to be able at certain times to expand demand to counter the threat of recession and its aftermath, and at other times (before recession has started) to moderate demand to avoid excessive boom. Major recessions appear unlikely to be forecastable much in advance of their becoming manifest in a downturn of output [ch. 11.5]. In general therefore counteraction is confined to the following lines of action:

1. general precautionary action to reduce the probability of a future recession, or its scale, in particular by avoiding the build-up of boom situations;
2. action during the course of a recession to moderate its scale; this merges into
3. action after a recession has touched bottom to speed recovery.

At each stage success is likely to be incomplete, leaving more to be attempted at the next stage.

Without policy action, growth is likely to revive at about the trend rate.[25] That is likely in time to bring a gradual revival of consumer and business confidence, which will bring a gradual acceleration of growth and thus a slow recovery. More rapid recovery is likely to require a policy stimulus. It has already been suggested [s. 12.2.1] that after a typical major recession the stimulus might ideally need to be of the order of 1–3 per cent of GDP a year, on a decreasing scale, extending over five to ten years.

Measures against excessive boom

Either fiscal or monetary policy could be used to impose restraint. But the most suitable way may be to raise interest rates, since this can be done quickly and sufficiently sharply for it to be effective even when used alone.

It will however always be difficult to adopt a firm policy of restraint at a sufficiently early stage of a boom. Only when it has already become excessive will it be quite clear that restraint is called for; before that, the signs are likely to be ambiguous and action politically unpopular. It would therefore be safer not to rely entirely on prompt discretionary action, but also to have built-in safeguards in place.

---

[25] In past cases early recovery, i.e. resumption of above-trend growth, happened either because of the actions of the UK government (by fiscal and monetary policy, or by having depreciated the exchange rate); or because the rest of the world was expanding also; or by other sorts of exogenous shock—i.e. by lucky accidents which cannot however be counted on.

Over long periods in the past, direct monetary controls appear to have provided a safeguard against excessive boom of the sort that is needed.[26] A return to monetary controls now would be dead against the fashion, and many say that in modern conditions a direct control of lending could not be made effective. My judgement is that lending control would be able to restrain most personal and small business borrowing. It would be inequitable between big and small borrowers, but might still have been valuable. I doubt whether financial institutions' behaviour will prove so stable that the authorities can afford to dispense with whatever safeguards are possible.[27]

Measures against recession

It is convenient to take together measures to be used in a recession and measures to speed subsequent recovery. I start with relatively conventional measures.

First must be listed *reductions in interest rates*. Doubts have always been expressed as to the efficacy of lower interest rates at a time when business confidence has been seriously shaken. But the evidence presented earlier [ch. 5.2, summarized in ch. 11.2] suggests that this effect has been important in the past. (That may be partly due to the effect of lower interest rates in lowering the exchange rate—which may at times be disadvantageous in that it produces an unsustainable exchange rate.) The need to counter inflation is less likely to be a constraint, since demand will by definition then be very low.

Second are *conventional fiscal measures* comprising either increased expenditure or reduction of tax rates—in addition to the effect of the automatic stabilizers, which are assumed already to have increased government borrowing. The difficulties of such action have already been discussed [s. 12.2.1], but that does not mean that some steps in this direction could not be taken.[28]

A third measure I describe under the heading of *public/private investment schemes* (i.e. investment under a degree of government control, but financed by private bodies). Since this possibility has not been much discussed, I consider it at greater length.

---

[26] Excessive booms did not occur [chs. 7 and 9] when monetary controls were in operation (1945–71, and end-1973–80); and did occur when monetary controls were removed (1971–3 and 1985–8). App. A10 explains why bank credit is crucial in financing excessive expansions.

[27] A degree of permanent protection might also be provided under the aegis of banking supervision; but probably not enough. The argument for seeking to use an essentially micro control for a macroeconomic purpose, and for wanting bank supervisors to look not only at individual banks but at the state of the banking system in total, is that excessive expansion by banks collectively weakens the balance sheets of individual banks. But the main beneficiary would be not the individual banks but the general good; and the difficulty in any attempt to impose prudence on individuals (which has a cost to them) on the grounds that it would serve the general good is that it would undermine the banks' willingness to accept the irksomeness of supervision.

[28] A further possibility (Britton 1986*b*) is to *change the structure of taxation*, i.e. by reducing taxes with a large effect on spending and raising those that had a small expenditure effect, thus leaving the balance of the budget unchanged. In view of the distributional effects, this approach could not be pursued far.

1. One option is for the government, rather than undertake public investment itself, to arrange for private-sector bodies to build what the government requires, and then lease the plant or construction so provided.[29]

2. A bolder version of the same approach would be *public/private infrastructure programmes.* The execution of certain infrastructure projects would be carried out on a joint public/private basis;[30] the planning and timing of projects would be public decisions, while private firms would finance and carry out the investment and also operate the facility. The construction of motorways or high-speed rail tracks might be organized on these lines.

3. An extension of the same principle would be to make the scale and timing of utility investment vary in the light of demand considerations. Thus, the timing of investment by private utilities to improve town drainage or water supplies could be advanced by requiring compliance with higher environmental standards, the timing to be determined by the government.

On these last two schemes, the cost of investment would be paid for out of (state-regulated) tolls or other charges paid by the public, and their economic impact would be similar to an indirect tax; thus (on the analogy of the balanced budget theorem), the net effect would be stimulatory. Such schemes would provide a stimulus to demand by means that did not weaken the government's fiscal position.

There would be two sorts of difficulty, however, both serious. First, the timing of projects would have to take account of many factors other than the state of the economy (e.g. users' needs, environmental consequences), which would limit the degree to which it was practical to vary timing. Second, such programmes would have to be prepared in advance; for many would require extensive prior public discussion of land use and negotiation of land purchase. Once started, the timing could be altered only at additional cost.

Despite these disadvantages, control of public/private investment may be a better way to attempt macroeconomic management than varying government expenditure and tax rates. As already pointed out, it would have the important advantage of not undermining the normal discipline of public expenditure control.[31]

Conclusion: the instruments crude but useful

The means of control proposed above may appear a collection of very crude instruments. It is crude to be able to stabilize prices only (as I see it) by

---

[29] This is the principle of the British government's (1992) 'private finance initiative'—which however was not conceived as a variable device to be activated according to whether there was a shortage of demand.

[30] The general principle of mixed public/private investment projects has not been common in the UK but has long featured in other countries, e.g. motorway construction in France, though not specifically as a counter-recessionary device.

[31] It is noteworthy that Keynes in the *General Theory* proposed public works (which are somewhat akin to what is recommended here) but never advocated deficit spending on the ordinary Budget. His work in the Treasury may have made him appreciate why ministries of finance are likely to distrust playing around with the ordinary Budget.

Box 12.1   Could past major recessions have been avoided?

Recession I (1919–20) and partial recovery (1920–9)   [ch. 6.2]

The preceding boom could have been far better controlled. Wartime controls should have been retained for several years (as after World War II). If monetary policy had been tightened earlier, that also would have reduced the boom and thus the recession. I attribute the depth of the recession to massive fiscal retrenchment—which should be easy not to repeat. (However, the slow growth in some European countries in recent years resulting from pursuit of the Maastricht fiscal criteria is similar.)

After a first partial recovery, further recovery was slow because of tight monetary policy and the resulting high exchange rate—also easy not to repeat. (Again, however, France's pursuit of the *franc fort*, and the near stagnation that that produced, is similar.)

Recession II (1929–32) and the subsequent recovery   [chs. 6.3 and 6.5]

I attribute the depth of the US recession to massive bank failures, and thus to a faulty supervisory infrastructure—not now likely to recur. In the UK laxer fiscal and monetary policy might have shortened the resulting recession. Recovery after the recession (1932–8) was adequately rapid. Reasons for it in the first phase were the lower exchange rate, the imposition of tariffs, the easing of monetary policy, and the housing boom; in the second phase, debt-financed rearmament. That illustrates what can be done.

Recession III (1973–5) followed by non-recovery (1975–9)   [ch. 8.2]

The preceding boom (part of a world boom) was exaggerated by UK fiscal policy, and by the removal of lending controls. More cautious policies would have reduced the boom—and thereby the recession.

The recession was due, also, to the worldwide deflationary effects of the OPEC oil price rises; and to the tightening of UK monetary policy in response to the (worldwide) acceleration of inflation. Given inflation, UK policy could not I think have been much less restrictive, either in the recession or in the subsequent phase. (The conjunction of high inflation and major recession—repeated in the next recession—seems unlikely to recur.)

Recession IV (1979–82) and first stage of recovery (1982–5)   [ch. 8.2]

This recession was due partly to OPEC II, and partly to the tightening of UK monetary and fiscal policy, which went much further than called for by the rise of inflation. A less extreme policy might have halved the recession. It is more difficult to judge how much better a laxer monetary policy *after* the recession would have been, given the boom that was soon to follow.

Recession V (1989–93) and the subsequent phase   [ch. 9.3]

This recession was due not to policy or other shocks, but to the rebound from the previous boom psychology. If lending controls had not been removed in

---

Box 12.1 (*Continued*)

1980, the boom might have been prevented; alternatively, it could have been moderated by an early tightening of policy [but see ch. 9.4]. The ensuing recession would then have been moderated. An *easier* policy in the course of the recession would also have speeded recovery—at the cost of a less rapid slowing down of inflation. (The recovery after 1993 is as yet difficult to assess: see ch. 9.5.)

---

destabilizing output. It is crude, too, that each method of controlling demand and output has serious adverse side-effects—for instance by varying tax rates in ways otherwise undesirable; or varying government spending, always difficult to control and now made more so; or varying interest rates, liable to cause unsustainable exchange rates and thereby seriously to disrupt the pattern of output.

Control by such means is certainly a much rougher process than is represented in earlier Keynesian texts, and cruder too than Classical theorists advocate, who (if they admit the need at all) see it being done by a painless sort of monetary policy. It is medieval compared with the controls that engineers fix to machines. But fate has not given us a perfect economic system. Any attempt to exercise control over the behaviour of people is bound to be imperfect. That is true not only of economic policy but of many other spheres. Success in business for instance is fairly problematical; firms merge and demerge, rise and fall and fail. Nor do armies on the battlefield operate smoothly as if by clockwork. Crude though they are, the instruments listed above are I think potentially powerful.

12.3.2. How far could previous recessions have been avoided?

As a check on how effective one might hope action could be in future, it is useful to reassess the past. Box 12.1 takes a final look at the five major recessions to ask how, in each case, policy might have been better.

This analysis of past experience seems to suggest that, if similar recessions were to occur in future, it would be possible to reduce their depth considerably—in many cases by up to half. That would particularly be the case if (as seems quite likely) recessions did not in future coincide, as in recessions III and IV, with severe inflation, and if (as seems possible) booms were kept more moderate.

This means that, using the means already at their disposal, governments and central banks should be able not to eradicate major recessions, but to reduce very considerably the effects on output that major recessions have had in the past. Whether they are likely to use the opportunity is discussed in the next section.

12.4. The chances of avoiding major recessions in future

This final section evaluates the chances of success in dealing with major recessions in future, taking account not only of the technical economic possibilities discussed above but also of the practical limitations of governments and central banks.

The question stated

In the interwar period it was widely claimed, as it has been again in the years since 1973, that some or even most of the unemployment was either due to high wages, or was 'structural'. But on those occasions when demand strongly revived, employment rose as if these alleged obstacles had melted away. The rapid absorption of unemployment in the late 1930s and the early years of World War II is the most striking case.

It is true that what is required to absorb unemployment may be not only sufficient demand but also a retraining of the unemployed, especially those long-unemployed. In 1939–43 retraining was generally provided for those entering both the armed forces and civilian war work. In the crude sort of way one expects of wartime, it was a well organized and forceful example of curing unemployment. That must show that there is no absolute economic obstacle to achieving high employment: I do not doubt that if a war like World War II recurred we would again have very low unemployment.

This study asserts that in this sense high employment is feasible. Nevertheless, high unemployment has persisted over most of the past twenty years of our period (1975–95). What should one think about that? Governments have (in a cagey way) accepted responsibility for managing their economies. Because of that, governments being governments, they are loathe to admit or publicize failures. High persistent unemployment has thus somehow got marginalized and kept out of the centre of public attention. But if one tears aside this veil, is the persistence of high unemployment to be seen as some sort of scandal? I think not, for four reasons.

First, three major recessions in twenty years have dealt hard blows to both consumer and, even more, business confidence. Without a revival of confidence, there can be no full recovery of the economy. Government action cannot replace it; and though governments can nurse confidence, they are far from having any direct handle over it.

Second, even if governments had ample means to stimulate demand, there are strict limits to the speed with which recovery can be allowed to take place, since very rapid expansion is likely to cause a reaction and consequent recession, and also inflation.

Third, the authorities thus have the task of managing expansion so that it is neither too slow nor too fast, which must always be difficult. Clumsiness may provoke setbacks (witness 1989–93), and a degree of ineptitude and error has to be accepted as inevitable.

Fourth, politically it is now far harder to reconstitute the conditions of prosperous certainty and high employment, such as existed worldwide in the Golden Age of 1945–73, than it was for politicians of those days to preserve such conditions. Then, it was a matter of going on roughly as before; now, it would have to be a most complicated endeavour in which a host of things would have to be made to go just right.

These constraints are basic and powerful. Because of them, I think that protracted periods of high unemployment after major recessions are inevitable, and are part of the cost of having major recessions.

The likelihood of downward shocks

One can think of reasons why shocks and swings in confidence may be less serious in future [s. 12.1]—inflation for instance might be less, and so might occasion less severe deflationary counter-measures (which worsened some past recessions). But novel sources of disturbance are likely to occur, as in the past, and these cannot be foreseen; for instance, as banks become more international, credit creation may prove less stable and less easy to control. One cannot predict that disturbances will become less serious.

Once a major recession has started, much of the damage is done: counter-action later can only moderate it. That is especially the case if, as this study contends, it is correct that major recessions cause a downward displacement in the growth path of potential output [ch. 2.2, summarized in ch. 11.1].[32]

Advance action to be taken against recession

Possible advance action to be taken against recession is largely confined to avoiding or moderating phases of boom. The early recognition of boom-like situations presents difficulties almost as great as the advance spotting of recessions.[33] I have already suggested that these considerations constitute a case for having permanent constraints such as a system of lending controls in place (or ready to be put in place) to prevent a runaway boom. But it is unlikely that any government will impose such controls, or any Bank governor press for them—at least not before the next major boom, after which it might be seen that they would have been useful.

Hopes then rest on discretionary action. An independent central bank may in this respect perform better than a government; and in any case the authorities, whether government or central bank, ought to be able to improve on the

---

[32] That contention is disputable, and readers may need to be reminded that the proportion of capacity lost appears to have differed, for reasons not clear, in different recessions [table 2.2; fig. 11.1]. That might suggest that behaviour in other countries could differ from that of the UK.

[33] There has been little discussion of the methodology of monitoring incipient booms (when e.g. is fast monetary growth, or a rise in equity prices, innocuous, and when a danger signal?). The problem is increased by the fact that, after a major recession, the economy needs to be allowed to grow at somewhat above its trend rate; and the occurrence of recession may have made it uncertain what the trend rate now is. A periodic report on the adequacy of capacity utilization might be as worth while as a quarterly *Inflation Report*.

worst mistakes in the past, such as the Barber and Lawson booms. But if asked whether the authorities will succeed in producing a quarter-century as free of speculative booms as was the quarter-century after World War II, I would say that the chance is at best 50/50.

Action to be taken after a recession has started

One favourable likelihood [s. 12.1] is that a future major recession seems unlikely to occur at a time of high inflation, so that it should be possible to reduce interest rates to low levels early in the recession. Though it must always take time to recognize that a major recession is happening, monetary policy should be able to reduce its depth.

In view of the 'financial market' constraints to government borrowing, overtly expansionary fiscal policy may not be feasible [s. 12.2.1]. Even so, provided the groundwork had been prepared, schemes to increase public/private investment [s. 12.3.2] could play a role in reducing a recession and accelerating recovery. One has to add that governments frequently do not act quickly and are frequently not well prepared; the test is whether one can observe that preparatory steps are being taken before recession occurs. At the time of writing, they are not.

Qualitative aspects of the economy

In this study, macroeconomic behaviour has been assumed to depend on quantitative factors, which vary in the short term. It is possible however that the behaviour of an economy in major fluctuations depends also on more qualitative characteristics. For example, the degree to which economic capacity is damaged in the course of a recession, or the ability of an economy to recover from recession, could depend on the flexibility with which factors of production respond to changes in conditions, or on the general level of training and education, or on how far the population is endowed with enterprise and self-help. It is beyond the power of governments fully to determine such social characteristics, but they can influence them. Although they have been outside the scope of this study, I am inclined to think they are important.

The chances of a strong effective government

The chance of avoiding a major recession depends not only on the technical economic possibilities, but, at least as importantly, on the kind of government that is in power at the time. The task of avoiding booms can possibly be delegated to central banks. But central banks are less likely to be good at stimulating demand in the face of a large and unexpected recession: vigorous action, if it comes at all, has probably to come from governments. I have argued that, given a strong and decisive government, big recessions could be made into much smaller ones. What are the chances of there being such a government?

Effective economic policy has to rest on the general acceptance of a suitable theory of economic policy; i.e., there has to be a general consensus that policy action is possible and useful. Theoretical neoclassicism, the academic ortho-doxy of the 1980s, tends to deny both the possibility and the desirability of discretionary action and of the management of demand. Governments strongly influenced by this negative regard for action are unlikely to be effective in the task of moderating recessions. Neoclassical views remain influential, and may continue to be so. That must surely reduce the chances of avoiding major recessions.[34]

Leaving ideology aside, a government's political ability to undertake the ambitious task of managing the economy effectively enough to mitigate recessions will differ according to how strong its political position is, and how far it aspires to lead. For example, a determined government that had established general respect for its leadership, and created a constituency for a programme of social action and high employment, and had thus a relatively firm hold on power and was in a position to be patient, could do a lot; a short-lived and insecure government, plainly, could do much less.

Strong and wise governments unfortunately are likely to be rare. There is a painting by Lorinzetti in the City Hall of Siena entitled 'The Effects of Good Government'. A painting with that title carries two implications: that what governments do matters; and that a country is lucky if it has a good one.[35] But it is also true that half-good governments can do half-good things, i.e. more than nothing.

The importance of priorities

Prosperity requires both the avoidance of rapid inflation and the avoidance of major recessions. I would say that, on a very broad view, the authorities both in the UK and in the other main industrial countries have been relatively successful with the first, and unsuccessful with the second.

My own view is that finding ways to avoid major recessions without losing control over inflation ought to be the major challenge for economic policy in the twenty-first century. The prevention of recessions should get as much attention as is now properly given to the prevention of inflation. Widespread perception of the need for such a shift in macroeconomic purpose would do more than anything else to increase the chances of finding ways to deal with major recessions.

---

[34] Fashions in economics are as difficult to predict as anything else. The passage of time and the fickleness of fashion may work to reduce the neoclassical influence, as might the evidence for a contrary view, which I think is strong. But what I see as over-idealization of the economy is a strand deeply ingrained in economic thinking.

[35] At one time I hoped that the dust jacket of this book might be based on a version of that painting (or a version of it by R. B. Kitaj).

References

Al-Chalabi, F. J. (1980), *OPEC and the International Oil Industry*, Oxford, Oxford University Press.

Aldcroft, D. H. (1970), 'Economic growth in Britain in the interwar years: a reassessment', *Economic History Review*.

Allsopp, C. (1982), 'Inflation', in Boltho (1982).

——Jenkinson, T. J. and Morris, D. J. (1991), 'The assessment: macroeconomic policy in the 1980s', *Oxford Review of Economic Policy*.

Anderson, T. M., and Moene, K. O. (1993), *Endogenous Growth*, Oxford and Cambridge, Mass., Blackwell.

Arndt, H. W. (1944), *The Economic Lessons of the Nineteen Thirties*, London, Oxford University Press.

Artis, M. J., Bladen-Hovell, R., Karakitsos, E., and Divalatsky, B. (1984), 'The effects of economic policy, 1979–82', *National Institute Economic Review*.

Baily, M. N. (1978), 'Stabilization polity and private economic behaviour', *Brookings Papers on Economic Activity*.

——and Chakrabarti, A. K. (1988), *Innovation and the Productivity Crisis*, Washington, Brookings Institution.

Bank of England (1981), *Factors Underlying the Recent Recession* (Bank of England Panel of Academic Consultants, paper 15), London, Bank of England.

Barciela *et al.* (1989), *Estadísticas Historicas de España: Siglos XIX–XX*, Madrid, Fundación Banco Exterior.

Barr, D. G., and Campbell, J. Y. (1997), 'Inflation, real interest rates and the bond market: a study of UK nominal and index-linked government bond prices', *Journal of Monetary Economics*.

Barrell, R., and Sefton, J. (1995), 'Output gaps: some evidence from the UK, France and Germany', *National Institute Economic Review*.

Barro, R. J. (1974), 'Are government bonds net wealth?' *Journal of Political Economy*.

——(1978), 'Unanticipated money, output and the price level in the United States', *Journal of Political Economy*.

——(1981), 'The equilibrium approach to business cycles', in R. J. Barro, *Money, Expectations and Business Cycles*, New York, Academic Press.

——(ed.) (1989a), *Modern Business Cycle Theory*, Cambridge, Mass., Harvard University Press.

——(ed.) (1989b), *Real Business Cycle Theory*, Oxford, Blackwell.

——and Grossman, H. I. (1971), 'A general equilibrium model of income and employment', *American Economic Review*.

——(1976), *Money, Employment and Inflation*, Cambridge, Cambridge University Press.

Batchelor, R. A., Major, R. L., and Morgan, A. D. (1980), *Industrialisation and the Basis for Trade*, Cambridge, Cambridge University Press.

Bauduin, F. (1958), 'Prix, consommation, balance et revenus en 1957', *Bulletin de l'Institut de Recherches Economique et Sociales*.

Baumol, W. J. J., Blackman, S. A. B., and Wolff, E. N. (1989), *Productivity and American Leadership*, Cambridge, Mass., MIT Press.

Bayoumi, T. (1993), 'Financial deregulation and household saving', *Economic Journal*.

Beaudry, P., and Koop, G. (1993), 'Do recessions permanently change output?' *Journal of Monetary Economics*.

Beenstock, M., Capie, F. C., and Griffiths, B. (1984), *Economic Recovery in the United Kingdom in the 1930s* (Bank of England Panel of Academic Consultants), London, Bank of England.

Bellman, H. (1938), 'The building trades', in *Britain in Recovery* (British Association Report), London, Pitman.

Bernanke, B. (1983), 'Non-monetary effects of the financial crisis in the interpretation of the Great Depression', *American Economic Review*.

——(1993), 'The world on a cross of gold: a review of *Golden Fetters*', *Journal of Monetary Economics*.

—— and James, H. (1991), 'The gold standard, deflation, and financial crisis in the Great Depression: an international comparison', in R. Glen Hubbard (ed.), *Financial Markets and Financial Crises*, Chicago, University of Chicago Press for NBER.

Beveridge, W. H. (1944), *Full Employment in a Free Society*, London, Allen & Unwin.

Birnberg, T. B., and Resnick, S. A. (1975), *Colonial Development*, New Haven, Yale University Press.

Bispham, J., and Boltho, A. (1982), 'Demand management', in Boltho (1982).

Biswas, R., Johns, C., and Savage, D. (1985), 'The measurement of fiscal stance', *National Institute Economic Review*.

Blackaby, F. T. (ed.) (1978), *British Economic Policy 1960–74*, Cambridge, Cambridge University Press.

Blanchard, O. J. (1990), 'Suggestions for a new set of fiscal indicators', Paris, Organisation for Economic Cooperation and Development.

—— and Fischer, S. (1989), *Lectures on Macroeconomics*, Cambridge Mass., MIT Press.

—— and Quah, D. (1989), 'The dynamic effects of aggregate supply and demand disturbance', *American Economic Review*.

Bohn-Bawerk, X. (1889), *The Positive Theory of Capital*, trans. G. D. Huncke and H. F. Sennholz, Amsterdam, North Holland, 1959.

Boltho, A. (1981), 'British fiscal policy 1955–71: stabilising or destabilising?' *Oxford Bulletin of Economics and Statistics*.

——(ed.) (1982), *The European Economy: Growth and Crisis*, Oxford, Oxford University Press.

Boserup, E. (1981), *Population and Technological Change: A Study of Long-Term Trends*, Chicago, University of Chicago Press.

Bowley, M. (1947), *Housing and the State 1919–1944*, London, Allen & Unwin.

Bristow, J. A. (1968), 'Taxation and income stabilization', *Economic Journal*.

Britton, A. (1986*a*), *The Trade Cycle in Britain 1958–1982*, Cambridge, Cambridge University press.

——(1986*b*), 'Can fiscal expansion cut unemployment?' *National Institute Economic Review*.

——(1991), *Macroeconomic Policy in Britain 1974–87*, Cambridge, Cambridge University Press; reprinted in paperback 1994.

—— and Pain, N. (1992), *Economic Forecasting in Britain* (National Institute of Economic and Social Research Report no. 4), London, National Institute of Economic and Social Research.

Broadberry, S. N. (1984), 'Fiscal policy in Britain during the 1930s', *Economic History Review*.

——(1986), *The British Economy between the Wars*, Oxford, Basil Blackwell.

Brown, A. J. (1985), *World Inflation since 1950: An International Comparative Study*, Cambridge, Cambridge University Press.

Brunner, K. (ed.) (1981), *The Great Depression Revisited*, Boston, Martinus Nijhoff.

Bruno, M., and Sachs, J. D. (1985), *Economics of Worldwide Stagflation*, Oxford, Basil Blackwell.

Budd, A. (1981), 'Factors underlying the recent recession' (Bank of England Panel of Academic Consultants), London, Bank of England.

Buiter, W. H. (1985), 'Government deficits reinterpreted', *Economic Policy*.

——and Miller, M. H. (1981), 'The Thatcher experiment: the first two years', *Brookings Papers on Economic Activity*, no. 2, Washington, Brookings Institution.

——and Tobin, J. (1979), 'Debt neutrality: a brief review of doctrine and evidence', in G. M. von Furstenberg (ed.), *Social Security versus Private Savings*, Cambridge, Mass., Ballinger.

Burk, K. and Cairncross, A. (1992), *Goodbye, Great Britain: The 1976 IMF Crisis*, New Haven, Yale University Press.

Burns, A., and Mitchell, W. C. (1946), *Measuring Business Cycles*, New York, National Bureau of Economic Research.

Cairncross, A. (ed.) (1971), *Britain's Economic Prospects Reconsidered*, Washington, Brookings Institution.

——and Watts, N. (1989), *The Economic Section 1939–1961: A Study in Economic Advising*, London, Routledge.

Cairncross, F., and Cairncross, A. (eds.) (1992), *The Legacy of the Golden Age: The 1960s and their Economic Consequences*, London, Routledge.

Calomiris, C. W., and Garton, G. (1991), 'The origins of banking panics: models, facts, and bank regulation', in R. G. Hubbard (ed.), *Financial Markets and Financial Crises*, Chicago, University of Chicago Press.

Capelle, H. (1938), 'Le volume de commerce extérieure de la Belgique, 1830–1913', *Bulletin de l'Institut de Recherches Économiques Louvain*.

Carbonnelle, A. (1959), 'Recherches sur l'évolution de la production en Belgique de 1900 à 1957', *Cahiers Économiques de Bruxelles*.

Carré, J. J., Dubois, P., and Malinvaud, E. (1972), *French Economic Growth* (trans. 1976), Stanford, Stanford University Press.

Catão, L., and Ramaswamy, R. (1996), 'Recession and recovery in the United Kingdom in the 1990s: identifying the shocks', *National Institute Economic Review*.

Caves, R. E. (ed.) (1968), *Britain's Economic Progress*, London, Allen and Unwin.

Chand, S. K. (1977), 'Summary indicators of fiscal influence', *IMF Staff Papers*.

Chick, V. (1978), 'The nature of the Keynesian revolution: a reassessment', *Australian Economic Papers*.

Choudhri, E. U., and Kochin, L. A. (1980), 'The exchange rate and international transmission of business cycle disturbances: some evidence from the Great Depression', *Journal of Money, Credit, and Banking*.

Chouraqui, J. C., Hagermann, R. P., and Sartor, N. (1990), 'Indicators of fiscal policy: a re-examination' (OECD Working Paper 70), Paris, OECD.

Cipolla, C. M., revised by Woodall, C. (1993), *Before the Industrial Revolution: European Society and Economy 1000–1700*, London, Routledge.

Clarke, P. (1988), *The Keynesian Revolution in the Making 1924–1936*, Oxford Clarendon Press.

Clarke, S. V. O. (1967), *Central Bank Cooperation 1924–31*, New York, Federal Reserve Bank of New York.

Clower, R. (1965), 'The Keynesian counter revolution: a theoretical appraisal', in Hahn and Brechling (1965).

——(1969), *Monetary Theory*, Harmondsworth, Penguin.

Cohen, W. M., and Levinthal, D. A. (1989), 'Innovation and learning: the two faces of R & D', *Economic Journal*.

Cornwall, J. (ed.) (1984), *After Stagflation: Alternatives to Economic Decline*, Oxford, Basil Blackwell.

Crafts, N. C. R., and Lee, R. D. (1981), 'British economic growth 1688–1959', in R. Floud and D. McCloskey (eds.), *The Economic History of Britain since 1700*, Cambridge, Cambridge University Press.

Cross, R. (ed.) (1995), *The Natural Rate of Unemployment*, Cambridge, Cambridge University Press.

Darby, M. R. (1976), 'Three-and-a-half million US employees have been mislaid: or, an explanation of unemployment, 1934–1941', *Journal of Political Economy*.

David, P., and Reder, M. (eds.) (1973), *Nations and Households in Economic Growth: Essays in Honor of Moses Abramovitz*, New York, Academic Press.

Davis, E. P. (1992), *Debt Financial Fragility and Systemic Risk*, Oxford, Oxford University Press.

De Long, J. B. (1988), 'Productivity growth, convergence and welfare: comment', *American Economic Review*.

——and Summers, L. H. (1986), 'Are business cycles symmetrical?' in R. J. Gordon (ed.), *The American Business Cycle: Continuity and Change*, Chicago, Chicago University Press.

Denison, E. F. (1962), *The Sources of Economic Growth in the United States and the Alternatives before Us*, New York, Committee for Economic Development.

——(1967), *Why Growth Rates Differ: Postwar Experience in Nine Western Countries*, Washington, Brookings Institution.

——(1974), *Accounting for United States Economic Growth*, Washington, Brookings Institution.

——(1979), *Accounting for Slower Growth*, Washington, Brookings Institution.

——(1985), *Trends in American Economic Growth 1929–82*, Washington, Brookings Institution.

Dimsdale, N. H. (1981), 'British monetary policy and the exchange rate 1920–38', in Eltis and Sinclair (1981).

——(1984), 'Employment and real wages in the interwar period', *National Institute Economic Review*.

Dicks-Mireaux, L. A. (1961), 'The interrelationship between cost and price changes 1946–59', *Oxford Economic Papers*.

——and Dow, J. C. R. (1959), 'The determinants of wage inflation United Kingdom 1945–56', *Journal of the Royal Statistical Society*.

Dornbusch, R. (1989), 'The dollar in the 1990s: competitiveness and the challenges of new economic blocs', *Symposium on Monetary Policy Issues in the 1990s*, Federal Reserve Bank of Kansas City, August.

——and Frankel, J. (1987), 'The flexible exchange rate system: experience and alternatives', paper presented at conference in Basel, Switzerland, October.

Dow, J. C. R. (1956), 'Analysis of the generation of price inflation', *Oxford Economic Papers*.

——(1964), *The Management of the British Economy, 1945–1960*, Cambridge, Cambridge University Press.

——(1986), 'Trade unions and inflation', *Lloyds Bank Review*.

——(1989), 'The Organization for Economic Cooperation and Development', in Pechman (1989).

——(1990*a*), 'How can real wages ever get excessive?' (NIESR Discussion paper no. 196), London, National Institute of Economic and Social Research.

——(1990*b*), 'The high-wage theory of unemployment: theory and British experience, 1970–89' (British Academy Keynes Lecture 1990), in *Proceedings of the British Academy: 1990 Lectures and Memoirs*, Oxford, Oxford University Press.

——and Saville, I. D. (1988), *A Critique of Monetary Policy*, Oxford, Clarendon Press; paperback (1990) with additional preface. First published 1984.

Dowrick, S., and Nguyen, D.-T. (1989), 'OECD comparative economic growth 1950–85: catch-up and convergence', *American Economic Review*.

Duesenberry, J. S. (1958), *Business Cycles and Economic Growth*, New York, McGraw-Hill.

Eckstein, A. (1955), 'National income and capital formation in Hungary, 1900–1950', in S. Kuznets (ed.), *Income and Wealth*, v, London, Bowes and Bowes.

Eichenbaum, B., and Wyplosz, C. (1986), 'The economic consequences of the Franc Poincaré' (CEPR Discussion Paper no. 136), London, Centre for Economic Policy Research.

Eichengreen, B. J. (1979), 'Tariffs and flexible exchange rates: the case of the British general tariff of 1932', Ph.D. thesis, Yale University; quoted in Broadberry (1986).

——(1984), 'Central bank cooperation under the interwar gold standard', *Explorations in Economic History*.

——(1986), 'The Bank of France and the sterilization of gold, 1926–1932', *Explorations in Economic History*.

——(1988), 'Did international economic forces cause the Great Depression?' *Contemporary Policy Issues*.

——(1992), *Golden Fetters: The Gold Standard and the Great Depression 1919–1939*, New York and Oxford, Oxford University Press.

——and Sachs, J. (1985), 'Exchange rates and economic recovery in the 1930s', *Journal of Economic History*.

——(1986), 'Competitive devaluation and the Great Depression: a theoretical reassessment', *Economic Letters*.

Eltis, W. A. and Sinclair, P. J. N. (eds.) (1981), 'The money supply and the exchange rate', *Oxford Economic Papers*.

——(1988), *Keynes and Economic Policy*, London, Macmillan and NEDO.

Emerson, M. (ed.) (1984), *Europe's Stagflation*, Oxford, Clarendon Press.

Emminger, O. (1979), 'The exchange rate as an instrument of policy', *Lloyds Bank Review*.

Ercolani (1969), 'Documentazione di Base', in G. Fuà (ed.), *Lo Sviluppo Economico in Italia: Storia dell Economica Italiana Negli Ultimo Cento Anni*, Milan, Angeli.

Evans, G., and Reichlin, L. (1994), 'Information, forecasts and measurement of the business cycle', *Journal of Monetary Economy*.

Falkus, M. E. (1975), 'The German business cycle in the 1920s', *Economic History Review*.

Feinstein, C. H. (1972), *National Income Expenditure and Output of the United Kingdom 1855–1965*, Cambridge, Cambridge University Press.

Feivel, G. R. (1975), *The Intellectual Capital of Michael Kalecki*, Knoxville, University of Tennessee press.

Finer, S. E. (1997), *The History of Government from the Earliest Times*, Oxford, Oxford University Press.

Fisher, I. (1932), *Booms and Depressions*, New York, Adelphi.

—— (1933), 'The debt–deflation theory of Great Depressions', *Econometrica*.

Fleming, J. M. (1962), *Domestic Financial Plans under Fixed and Floating Rates*, Washington International Monetary Fund.

Flora, P., Kraus, F., and Pfennig, W. (1987), *State, Economy and Society in Western Europe 1815–1975: A Data Handbook in Two Volumes*, London, Macmillan.

Floud, R., and McClosky, D. N. (eds.) (1981), *The Economic History of Britain since 1760*, vol. 2:1, *1860 to 1970s*, Cambridge, Cambridge University Press.

Foreman-Peck, J. S. (1980), The British tariff and industrial protection in the 1930s: an alternative model', *Economic History Review*.

Freeman, C. (1974), *The Economics of Industrial Innovation*, Harmondsworth, Penguin Books.

Frankel, J. A. and Foot, K. A. (1987), 'Using survey data to test standard propositions regarding exchange-rate expectations', *American Economic Review*.

Fridlizius, G. (1963), 'Sweden's exports 1800–1960: a study in perspective', *Economy and History*.

Friedman, M. (1962), *Capitalism and Freedom*, Phoenix, Ariz., Phoenix Books.

—— (1968), 'The role of monetary policy', *American Economic Review*.

—— and Schwartz, A. (1963), *A Monetary History of the United States, 1867–1960*, Princeton, Princeton University Press.

Frisch, R. (1933), 'Propagation and impulse problems in dynamic economies', *Economic Essays in Honour of Gustav Cassel*, London, Allen & Unwin.

Galbraith, J. K. (1952), *A Theory of Price Control*, Cambridge, Mass., Harvard University Press.

—— (1955), *The Great Crash*, London, Hamish Hamilton.

Goldberg, M. D. and Frydman, F. (1996), 'Imperfect knowledge and behaviour in the foreign exchange market', *Economic Journal*.

Goldstein, M., Folkerts-Landau, D., El-Erian, M., Fries, S., and Rojas-Suarez, L. (1992), *International Capital Markets: Developments, Prospects and Policy Issues*, Washington: International Monetary Fund.

Gollop, F. M., and Jorgenson, D. W. (1980), *US Productivity Growth by Industry 1947–1973*, in J. W. Kendrick and B. N. Vaccara (eds.), *New Developments in Productivity Measurement and Analysis*, Chicago, University of Chicago Press.

Goobey, A. R. (1992), *Bricks and Mortals*, London, Century Business.

Goodhart, C. A. E. (1984), *Monetary Theory and Practice: The UK Experience*, London, Macmillan.

Goodin, R. E. and Klingemann, H.-D. (1996) (eds.), *A New Handbook of Political Science*, New York, Oxford University Press.

Gooding, D., Pinch, T., and Schaffer, S. (eds.) (1989), *The Uses of Experiment: Studies in the Natural Sciences*, Cambridge, Cambridge University Press.

Gordon, R. A. (1951), 'Cyclical experience in the interwar period: the investment boom of the twenties', in Universities/National Bureau Committee for Economic Research, *Conferences on Business Cycles*, New York, National Bureau of Economic Research.

——(1974), *Economic Instability and Growth: The American Record*, New York, Harper & Row.

Gordon, R. J. (ed.) (1986), *The American Business Cycle: Continuity and Change*, Chicago, Chicago University Press.

——and Wilcox, J. A. (1981), 'Monetarist interpretations of the Great Depression: an evaluation and critique', in Brunner (1981).

Gramlich, E. M. (1990), 'Fiscal indicators' (OECD Department of Economics and Statistics Working Paper no. 80), Paris, OECD.

Gregory, D., and Oxley, L. (1996), 'Discontinuities in competitiveness: the impact of the First World War on British industry', *Economic History Review*.

Griffen, J. M., and Teece, D. J. (1982), *OPEC Behaviour and World Oil Prices*, London, Allen and Unwin.

Habakkuk, H. J., and Deane, P. (1963), in W. W. Rostow, *The Economics of Takeoff into Sustained Growth*, London/New York, Macmillan.

Hahn, F. H. (1984), *Equilibrium and Macroeconomics*, Oxford, Blackwell.

——and Solow, R. (1996), *A Critical Essay on Modern Macroeconomic Theory*, Cambridge, Mass., and London, MIT Press.

——and Brechling, F. (eds.) (1965), *The Theory of Interest Rates*, International Economic Association Series, London, Macmillan.

Hamilton, J. (1987), 'Monetary factors in the Great Depression', *Journal of Monetary Economics*.

——(1988), 'The role of the international gold standard in propagating the Great Depression', *Contemporary Policy Issues*.

Hansen, B. (1969), *Fiscal Policy in Seven Countries, 1935 and 1965*, Paris, Organisation for Economic Cooperation and Development.

Harvey, A. C., and Jaeger, A. (1993), 'Detrending, stylised facts and the business cycle', *Journal of Applied Econometrics*.

Hatcher, J. (1993), *The History of the British Coal Industry*, i, *Before 1700*, Oxford, Clarendon Press.

Hawtrey, R. G. (1933), *The Gold Standard in Theory and Practice*, London, Longmans Green.

——(1950), *Currency and Credit*, London, Longmans & Green.

Heal, G., and Chichilnisky, G. (1991), *Oil and the International Economy*, Oxford, Clarendon Press.

Hickman, B. G. (1973), 'What became of the business cycle?' in David and Reder (1973).

——(1992), *International Productivity and Competitiveness*, New York/Oxford, Oxford University Press.

Hicks, J. R. (1932), *The Theory of Wages*, London, Macmillan.

——(1950), *A Contribution to the Theory of the Trade Cycle*, Oxford, Oxford University Press.

——(1989), *A Market Theory of Money*, Oxford, Clarendon Press.

Hicks, U. K. (1938), *The Finance of British Government 1920–1936*, Oxford, Oxford University Press.

——(1951), *British Public Finances: Their Structure and Development*, Oxford, Oxford University Press.

Hilgerdt, F. (1945), *Industrialization and Foreign Trade*, Geneva, League of Nations.

Hjerppe, R. (1989), *The Finnish Economy 1860–1985: Growth and Structural Change*, Helsinki, Bank of Finland.

Ho, S. P. S. (1978), *Economic Development of Taiwan 1860–1970*, New Haven, Conn., Yale University Press.

Hoffmann, W. G. (1965), *Das Wachstum der Deutschen Wirtschaft seit der Mitte des 19. Jahrhunderts*, Berlin, Springer.

Hopkin, B., and Reddaway, B. (1994), 'The meaning and treatment of an unsustainable budget deficit', *Banco Nazionale del Lavoro Quarterly Review*.

Howson, S. (1975), *Domestic Monetary Management in Britain 1919–38*, Cambridge, Cambridge University Press.

Hsiau, Liang-li (1974), *China's Foreign Trade Statistics 1864–1949* (Harvard East Asian Monograph no. 56), Cambridge, Mass., Harvard University Press.

Ito, T. (1990), 'Foreign exchange rate expectations: micro survey data', *American Economic Review*.

Johnson, C. (1991), *The Economy under Mrs Thatcher 1979–1990*, Harmondsworth, Penguin Books.

Jones, E. L. (1988), *Growth Recurring: Economic Change in World History*, Oxford, Oxford University Press.

Jorgensen, D. W. (1984*a*), 'The role of energy in productivity growth', *American Economic Review*.

——(1984*b*), 'The role of energy in productivity growth', in J. W. Kendrick (ed.), *International Comparisons of Productivity and Causes of Slowdown*, Cambridge, Mass., American Enterprise Institute and Ballinger Press.

——(1988), 'Productivity and postwar US economic growth', *Journal of Economic Perspectives*.

——(1990), 'Productivity and economic growth', in E. R. Berndt and J. E. Triplett (eds.) *Fifty Years of Economic Measurement: The Jubilee of the Conference on Income and Wealth*, Chicago, University of Chicago Press.

——Gollop, F. M., and Fraumeni, B. (1989), *Productivity and US Economic Growth*, Amsterdam, North-Holland.

Joshi, V., and Little, I. M. D. (1994), *India: Macroeconomics and Political Economy, 1964–1991*, Washington, World Bank.

Kaldor, N. (1940), 'A model of the trade cycle', *Economic Journal*.

——(1986), *The Scourge of Monetarism* (2nd edn.), Oxford, Oxford University Press.

Kalecki, M. (1937*a*), 'The principle of increasing risk', *Economica*; reprinted in M. Kalecki, *Essays on the Theory of Economic Fluctuations*, London, Allen & Unwin, 1939.

——(1937*b*), 'A theory of the business cycle', *Review of Economic Studies*; reprinted in M. Kalecki, *Essays on the Theory of Economic Fluctuations*, London, Allen & Unwin, 1939.

——(1944), 'Prof. Pigou on "The Classical Stationary State": A Comment', *Economic Journal*.

——(1954), *The Theory of Economic Dynamics: An Essay on Cyclical and Long-Run Changes in Capitalist Economy*, London, Allen and Unwin.

Kausel, A., Németh, N., and Seidel, H. (1965), 'Österreichs Volkseinkommen 1913 bis 1963', *Monatsberichte des Österreichischen Instituts für Wirtschaftsforchung, 14. Sonderheft*, Vienna, Österreichischen Instituts für Wirtschaftsforchung.

Keegan, W. (1984), *Mrs Thatcher's Economic Experiment*, London, Allen Lane.

——(1989), *Mr Lawson's Gamble*, London, Hodder & Stoughton.

Keese, D. (1967), 'Die volkswirtschaften Gesamtgrössen für das deutsche Reich in de Jahren 1925–1936', in W. Conze and H. Raupach (eds.), *Die Staats- und Wirtschaftskrise des Deutsches Reiches*.

Kendrick, J. W. (1961), *Productivity Trends in the United States*, Princeton, Princeton University Press.

——(1973), *Postwar Productivity Trends in the United States, 1948–1969*, New York, NBER and Columbia University Press.

Keynes, J. M. (1936), *The General Theory of Employment Interest and Money*, London, Macmillan.

Kindleberger, C. P. (1973), *The World in Depression 1929–1939*, London, Allen Lane.

King, M. (1991), 'On policies toward saving' (address to SUERF Colloquium), London, Bank of England.

——(1994), 'Debt of deflation: theory and evidence', *European Economic Review*.

King, R. G., and Rebelo, S. (1989), 'Low frequency filtering and the real business cycle', *Journal of Economic Dynamics and Control*.

——Plosser, C. I., Stock, J., and Watson, M. (1991), 'Stochastic trends and economic fluctuations', *American Economic Review*.

Knight, F. H. (1930), *Risk, Uncertainty and Profit*, Boston, Houghton Mifflin; reprinted London School of Economics, 1933.

Landes, D. S. (1969), *The Unbound Prometheus: Technological Changes and Industrial Development in Western Europe from 1950 to the Present*, Cambridge, Cambridge University Press.

Lawson, N. (1992), *The View from No. 11: Memoirs of a Tory Radical*, London, Bantam Press.

League of Nations (1931), *The Course and Phases of the World Economic Depression*, Geneva, League of Nations.

Leijonhufvud, A. (1968), *On Keynesian Economics and the Economics of Keynes*, Oxford, Oxford University Press.

——(1981), *Information and Coordination*, New York/Oxford: Oxford University Press.

Leland, H. E. (1968), 'Saving and uncertainty: the precautionary demand for saving', *Quartely Journal of Economics*.

Lewis, W. A. (1949), *Economic Survey 1919–39*, London, Allen & Unwin.

——(1952), 'World production, prices and trade 1870–1960', *Manchester School of Economic and Social Studies*.

Lindbeck, A. (1983), 'The recent slowdown of productivity growth', *Economic Journal*.

Lipsey, D. E. (1963), *Price and Quantity Trends in the Foreign Trade of the United States*, Princeton, Princeton University Press.

Little, I. M. D. (1962), 'Fiscal policy', in Worswick and Ady (1962).

——Mazumdor, D., Corden, W. M., and Rajapatirana, S. (1993), *Boom, Crisis and Adjustment: The Macroeconomic Experience of Developing Countries*, Oxford, Oxford University Press.

Llewellyn, J. Potter, S., and Samuelson, L. (1985), *Economic Forecasting and Policy: The International Dimension*, London, Routledge & Kegan Paul.

Lucas, R. E. (1972), 'Expectations and the neutrality of money', *Journal of Economic Theory*.

—— (1978), 'Unemployment policy', *American Economic Review*.

—— (1988), 'On the mechanics of economic development', *Journal of Monetary Economics*.

MacDougall, G. D. A. (1938), 'General Survey 1929–1937', in *Britain in Recovery* (British Association Report), London, Pitman.

Mackenzie, G. A. (1988), 'Are all summary indicators of the stance of fiscal policy misleading?' (IMF Working Paper WP/88/112), Washington, International Monetary Fund.

Maddison, A. (1962), 'Growth and fluctuations in the world economy, 1870–1960', *Banca Nazionale del Lavoro Quarterly Review*.

—— (1964), *Economic Growth in the West*, London, Allen & Unwin.

—— (1982), *Phases in Capitalist Development*, Oxford, Oxford University Press.

—— (1985), *Two Crises: Latin America and Asia 1929–1938 and 1973–1983*, Paris, OECD.

—— (1987), 'Growth and slowdown in advanced capitalist economies: techniques of quantitative assessment', *Journal of Economic Literature*.

—— (1989), *The World Economy in the 20th Century*, Paris, OECD.

—— (1991*a*), *Dynamic Forces in Capitalist Development*, Oxford, Oxford University Press.

—— (1991*b*), 'A revised estimate of Italian economic growth, 1861–1989', *Banca Nazionale del Lavoro Quarterly Review*.

Maizels, A. (1963), *Industrial Growth and World Trade: An Empirical Study in Production, Consumption and Trade in Manufactures from 1899–1959*, Cambridge, Cambridge University Press.

Malinvaud, E. (1977), *The Theory of Unemployment Reconsidered* (Yrjö Jahnsson Lectures), Oxford, Basil Blackwell.

—— (1980), 'Macroeconomic rationing and employment', in E. Malinvaud, and J. P. Fitoussi (eds.), *Unemployment in Western Countries*, London, Macmillan.

—— (1984), *Mass Unemployment*, Oxford, Blackwell.

Marsh, D. and Stoker, G. (eds.) (1995), *Theory and Methods in Political Science*, Basingstoke and London, Macmillan.

Marshall, A., and Marshall, M. P. (1879), *The Economics of Industry*, London, Macmillan.

Matthews, R. C. O. (1959), *The Trade Cycle*, Cambridge, Nisbet and Cambridge University Press.

—— (1968), 'Why has Britain had full employment since the war?' *Economic Journal*.

—— (ed.) (1982), *Slower Growth in the Western World*, London, Heinemann.

—— and Bowen, A. (1988), 'Keynesian and other explanations of postwar macroeconomic trends', in W. Eltis and P. Sinclair (eds.), *Keynes and Economic Policy*, London, Macmillan and NEDO.

—— Feinstein, C. H., and Odling Smee, J. C. (1982), *British Economic Growth 1856–1973*, Oxford, Clarendon Press.

Matthias, P. (1963), *The First Industrial Nation*, London, Routledge; rev. edn. 1983.

Maynard, G. (1988), *The Economy under Mrs Thatcher*, Oxford, Basil Blackwell.

McCallum, B. T. (1989), 'Real business cycle models', in Barro (1989b).

McCracken, P. *et al.* (1977), *Towards Full Employment and Price Stability*, Paris, OECD.

Metzler, A. H. (1976), 'Monetary and other explanations for the start of the Great Depression', *Journal of Monetary Economics*.

——(1981), 'Comments on 'Monetarist interpretations of the Great Depression', in Brunner (1981).

Middleton, R. (1981), 'The constant employment budget balance and British budgetary policy, 1929–39', *Economic History Review*.

Miles, D. (1992), 'Housing markets, consumption and financial deliberalization in the major economies', *European Economic Review*.

Minford, P. (1983), *Unemployment: Cause and Cure*, Oxford, Oxford University Press.

Minsky, H. P. (1977), 'A theory of systemic fragility', in E. I. Altman and A. Sametz (eds.), Financial Crises, New York, John Wiley.

——(1982a), 'Debt deflation processes in today's institutional environment', *Banca Nationale del Lavoro Quarterly Review*.

——(1982b), *Inflation, Recession and Economic Policy*, Brighton, Harvester Wheatsheaf.

——(1986), *Stabilizing an Unstable Economy*, New Haven, Yale University Press.

Mishkin, F. S. (1978), 'The household balance sheet and the Great Depression', *Journal of Economic History*.

Mitchell, B. R. (1975), *European Historical Statistics 1750–1970*, London, Macmillan.

——(1983), *International Historical Statistics: The Americas and Australasia*, London, Macmillan.

——(1988), *British Historical Statistics*, Cambridge, Cambridge University Press.

——and Jones, H. G. (1971), *Second Abstract of British Historical Statistics*, Cambridge, Cambridge University Press.

Moggridge, D. E. (1972), *British Monetary Policy, 1924–1931: The Norman Conquest of $4.86*, Cambridge, Cambridge University Press.

Moorsteen, R., and Powell, R. P. (1966), *The Soviet Capital Stock 1928–62*, Homewood, Ill., Irwin.

Morris-Suzuki, T. (1994), *The Technological Transformation of Japan in the Seventeenth to the Twenty-First Century*, Cambridge, Cambridge University Press.

Muellbauer, J. (1991), 'Productivity and competitiveness', *Oxford Review of Economic Policy*.

Mullineaux, A., Dickinson, D. G., and Peng, W. (1993), *Business Cycles*, Oxford and Cambridge, Mass., Blackwell.

Mundell, R. A. (1963), 'Capital mobility and stabilization policy under fixed and flexible exchange rates', *Canadian Journal of Economic and Political Science*.

Musgrave, R. A., and Musgrave, P. B. (1968), 'Fiscal policy', in R. Caves (ed.), *Britain's Economic Prospects*, Washington, Brookings Institution.

Nelson, C. R. and Plosser, C. I. (1982), 'Trends and random walks in macroeconomic time series', *Journal of Monetary Economics*.

Nelson, R. R. (1994), 'What has been the matter with neo-classical growth theory?' in Silverberg and Soete (1994).

Nevin, E. (1953), 'The origins of cheap money, 1931–2, *Economica*.

Nickell, S. (1985), 'The government's policy for jobs: an analysis', *Oxford Review of Economic Policy*.

Nordhaus, W. D. (1980), 'Oil and economic performance in industrial countries', *Brookings Papers on Economic Activity*.

North, C. D. and Thomas, R. P. (1973), *The Rise of the Western World*, Cambridge, Cambridge University Press.

Nunes, A. B., Mata, E., and Valério, N. (1989), 'Portuguese Economic Growth 1833–1985', *Journal of European Econmomic History*.

Ohkawa, K., and Rosovsky, H. (1973), *Japanese Economic Growth: Trend Accleration in the Twentieth Century*, Stanford, Calif., Stanford University Press.

Okun, A. M. (1962), 'Potential GNP: its measurement and significance', in J. M. Pechman (ed.), *Economics for Policymaking*, Cambridge, Mass., MIT Press, 1983.

——(1975), 'Inflation and its mechanisms and welfare costs', *Brookings Papers on Economic Activity*.

——(1981), *Prices and Quantities*, Washington, Brookings Institution.

Olson, M. (1982), *The Rise and Decline of Nations: Economic Growth Stagflation and Social Rigidities*, New Haven, Yale University Press.

Oulton, N. (1990), 'Labour productivity in UK manufacturing in the 1970s and in the 1980s', *National Institute Economic Review*.

——and O'Mahony, M. (1994), *Productivity and Growth: A Study of British Industry 1954–1956*, Cambridge, Cambridge University Press.

Patinkin, D. (1948), 'Price flexibility and full employment', *American Economic Review*.

——(1965), *Money, Interest and Prices*, 2nd ed., New York, Harper & Row.

Pechman, J. A. (ed.) (1989), *The Role of the Economist in Government: An International Perspective*, Hemel Hempstead, Harvester Wheatsheaf.

Persson, K. G. (1988), *Preindustrial Economic Growth: Social Organisation and Technological Progress in Europe*, Oxford, Basil Blackwell.

Petri, P. A. (1984), *Modelling Japanese–American Trade: A Study in Asymmetric Interdependence*, Cambridge, Mass., Harvard University Press.

Phelps, E. S. (1967), 'Phillips curves, expectations of inflation and optimal unemployment over time', *Economica*.

Phillips, A. W. (1958), 'The relation between unemployment and the rate of change of money wage rates in the United Kingdom 1861–1957', *Economica*.

Pigou, A. C. (1947), *Aspects of British Economic History 1918–1925*, London, Macmillan.

Pippard, B. (1989), 'Stumbling towards consensus', review of Gooding *et al.* (1989), *Times Literary Supplement*, 28 September.

Pollard, S. (1962), *The Development of the British Economy 1914–1950*, London, Edward Arnold.

Prest, A. R. (1968), 'Sense and nonsense in budgetary policy' *Economic Journal*.

Price, R. W. R. (1978), 'Budgetary policy', in F. T. Blackaby (ed.), *British Economic Policy 1960–74*, Cambridge, Cambridge University Press.

——and Muller, P. (1984), *Structural Budget Indicators and the Interpretation of Fiscal Policy Stance in OECD Economies*' (OECD Economic Studies no. 3), Paris, OECD.

Pryor, F. L. *et al.* (1971), 'Czechoslovak aggregate production in the interwar period', *Review of Income and Wealth*.

Quah, D. (1993), 'Galton's fallacy and tests of the convergence hypothesis', in Anderson and Moene (1993).

Redmond, J. (1980), 'An indicator of the effective exchange rate of the pound in the nineteen thirties', *Economic History Review*.

Rees, G. (1970), *The Great Slump: Capitalism in Crisis, 1929–33*, London,

Richardson, H. W. (1962), 'The basis of economic recovery in the 1930s: a review and a new interpretation', *Economic History Review*.

——(1967), *Economic Recovery in Britain 1932–39*, London, Weidenfeld & Nicolson.

Riddell, P. (1983), *The Thatcher Government*, London, Martin Robertson.

Robbins, L. (1934), *The Great Depression*, London, Macmillan.

Romer, P. M. (1986), 'Increasing returns and long-run growth', *Journal of Political Economy*.

Rostow, W. W. (1960), *The Stages of Economic Growth*, Cambridge, Cambridge University Press.

Samuelson, P. A. (1939), 'Interactions between the multiplier analysis and the principle of acceleration', *Review of Economic Statistics*.

Sandmo, A. (1970), 'The effect of uncertainty on saving decisions', *Review of Economic Studies*.

Sargent, J. R. (1991), 'Regulation, debt and downturn in the UK economy', *National Institute Economic Review*.

Sargent, T. J., and Wallace, N. (1975), 'Rational expectations, the optimal monetary instrument and the optimal money supply rule', *Journal of Political Economy*.

Savage, D. (1982), 'Fiscal policy, 1974/5–1980/1: description and measurement', *National Institute Economic Review*.

——and Biswas, R. (1986), 'An analysis of postwar growth rates', *National Institute Economic Review*.

Saville, I. D., and Gardiner, K. (1986), 'Stagflation in the United Kingdom since 1970: a model-based explanation', *National Institute Economic Review*.

Sayers, R. S. (1956), *Financial Policy 1939–45*, London, HMSO and Longmans.

——(1976), *The Bank of England, 1891–1944*, Cambridge, Cambridge University Press.

Schiller, R. (1988), 'Portfolio insurance and other investor fashions as factors in the 1987 stock market crash', *NBER Macroeconomic Annual*.

Schlesinger, A. M. (1960), *The Coming of the New Deal*, London/Melbourne/Toronto, Heinemann.

Schlote, W. (1952), *British Overseas Trade from 1700 to the 1930s*, Oxford, Basil Blackwell.

Schmookler, J. (1966), *Invention and Economic Growth*, Cambridge, Mass., Harvard University Press.

Schumpeter, L. (1912/1934), *Theory of Economic Development*, Cambridge, Mass., Harvard University Press; UK edn. 1955.

Schurr, S. H., Sonenblum, S., and Wood, D. O. (1983), *Energy, Productivity and Economic Growth*, Cambridge, Mass.,

Schwartz, A. J. (1981), 'Understanding 1929–1933' in Brunner (1981).

Scott, M. F. (1989), *A New View of Economic Growth*, Oxford, Clarendon Press.

Sedgwick, P. N. (1984), 'Economic recovery in the 1930s' (Bank of England Panel of Academic Consultants), London, Bank of England.

Sefton, J., and Weale, M. (1995), *Reconciliation of National Income and Expenditure*, Cambridge, Cambridge University Press.

Sheldon, M., and Young, G. (1997) 'The UK economy,' *National Institute Economic Review*.

Shinohara, M. (1970), *Structural Changes in Japan's Economic Development*, Tokyo, Kinokuniya Bookstore.

—— (1972), *Long-Term Economic Statistics of Japan since 1868*, x, *Mining and Manufacturing*, Tokyo, Keizai Shiposha.

Silverberg, G., and Soete, L. (eds.) (1994), *The Economics of Growth and Technical Change: Technology, Nations, Agents*, Elgar.

Skidelsky, R. (1967), *Politicians and the Slump: The Labour Government of 1929–33*, London, Macmillan.

Slutsky, E. (1937), 'The summation of random causes as the source of cyclic processes', *Econometrica*.

Smith, A. (1776), *An Inquiry into the Nature and Causes of the Wealth of Nations*, London.

Smith, A. D. (1987), 'A current cost accounting measure of Britain's stock of equipment', *National Institute Economic Review*.

—— (1988), 'Changes in output, employment and the stock of equipment during the 1980s: the experience of fifty companies' (NIESR Discussion paper no. 144), London, National Institute of Economic and Social Research.

Snyder, W. W. (1970), 'Measuring economic stabilization: 1955–65', *American Economic Review*.

Solow, R. M. (1957), 'Technical change and the aggregate production function', *Review of Economics and Statistics*.

—— (1962), 'Technical progress, capital formation and economic growth', *American Economic Review*.

Spulber, N. (1966), *The State and Economic Development in Eastern Europe*, New York, Random House.

Stadler, G. W. (1994), 'Real business cycles', *Journal of Economic Literature*.

Storry, R. (1960), *A History of Modern Japan*, Harmondsworth, Penguin.

Suh, Sang-Chul (1978), *Growth and Structural Changes in the Korean Economy, 1910–1940* (Harvard East Asian Monograph no. 83), Cambridge, Mass., Harvard University Press.

Summers, R., and Heston, A. (1984), 'Improved international comparisons of real product and its composition, 1950–1980', *Review of Income and Wealth*.

Tatom, J. A. (1981), 'Energy prices and short-run economic performance', *Federal Reserve Bank of St Louis Review*.

Taylor, A. J. P. (1965), *Oxford History of England 1914–1945*, Oxford, Oxford University Press.

Temin, P. (1976), *Did Monetary Forces Cause the Great Depression?* New York, W. W. Norton.

—— (1989), *Lessons from the Great Depression*, Cambridge, Mass., MIT Press.

Thirsk, J. (1978), *Economic Policy and Projects: The Development of a Consumer Society in Early Modern England*, Oxford, Clarendon Press.

Thomas, T. J. (1981), 'Aggregate demand in the United Kingdom 1918–45', in Floud and McClosky (1981).

Tobin, J. (1980), *Asset Accumulation and Economic Activity*, Oxford, Basil Blackwell.

—— (1992), 'Price flexibility–output stability: an old Keynesian view' (Cowles Commission Discussion Paper no. 994R), New Haven, Yale University.

Torres, R., and Martin, J. P. (1990), 'Measuring potential output in seven major OECD countries' *OECD Economic Studies*.

Toutain, J. C. (1987), 'Le produit intérieur brut de la France de 1789–1982', *Économies et Sociétés* (Cahiers de l'ISMEA, Série Histoire Quantitative de l'Economie Française no. 15), Grenoble: Presses Universitaires de Grenoble.

Universities/National Bureau Committee for Economic Research (1951), *Conference on Business Cycles*, New York, NBER.

Urquhart, M. C., and Buckley, K. A. H. (1965), *Historical Statistics of Canada*, Cambridge, Cambridge University Press.

van Ark, B. (1988), 'The volume and price of Indonesian exports, 1823 to 1940: the long-term trend and its measurement', *Bulletin of Indonesian Economic Studies*.

van der Eng, P. (1992), 'Measuring fiscal stance for the UK 1920–90' (Australian National University Working Papers in Economic History, no. 171), Canberra, Australian National University.

van der Wee, H. (1986), *Prosperity and Upheaval: The World Economy 1945–1980*, Harmondsworth, Penguin/Viking.

Vattula, K. (ed.) (1983), *Suomen Taloushistoria*, iii, *Historiallinen Tilasto*, Helsinki, Kustannusosakeyhtiö Tammi.

Verspagen, B. (1993), *Uneven Growth between Interdependent Economies: An Evolutionary View on Technology Gaps, Trade and Growth*, Aldershot, Avebury.

Vinski, I. (1961), 'National product and fixed assets in the territory of Yugoslavia 1909–59' in P. Deane (ed.) *Studies in Social and Financial Accounting, Income and Wealth*, ix. London, Bowes & Bowes.

Volcker, P. A., and Gyohten, T. (1992), *Changing Fortunes: The World's Money and the Threat to American Leadership*, New York, Times Books.

Wadhwani, S., and Wall, M. (1986), 'The UK capital stock: new estimates of premature scrapping', *Oxford Review of Economic Policy*.

Wallis, K. F., Andrews, M. J., Bell, D. N. F., Fisher, P. G., and Whitley, J. D. (1984), *Models of the UK Economy*, Oxford, Oxford University Press.

Walters, A. (1986), *Britain's Economic Renaissance: Mrs Thatcher's Reforms 1979–1984*, Oxford, Oxford University Press.

Ward, T. S., and Neild, R. R. (1978), *The Measurement and Reform of Budgetary Policy*, London, Heinemann.

Wicker, E. (1996), *The Banking Panics of the Great Depression*, Cambridge, Cambridge University Press.

Williamson, P. (1992), *National Crisis and National Government: British Politics, the Economy and Empire 1926–32*, Cambridge, Cambridge University Press.

Wilson, T. (1942), *Fluctuations in Income and Employment*, London, Pitman.

Worswick, G. D. N. (1970), 'Fiscal policy and stabilisation in Britian', in A. Cairncross (ed.) *Britain's Economic Prospects Reconsidered*, London, Allen & Unwin.

——(1981), 'Factors underlying the recent recession' (Papers Presented to the Bank of England Panel of Academic Consultants, no. 15), London, Bank of England.

——(1984a), 'The recovery in Britain in the 1930s' (Bank of England Panel of Academic Consultants), London, Bank of England.

——(1984b), 'The sources of recovery in the UK in the 1930s', *National Institute Economic Review*.

——and Ady, P. H. (1962), *The British Economy in the Nineteen Fifties*, Oxford, Oxford University Press.

Wren-Lewis, S. (1997), 'The choice of exchange-rate regime', *Economic Journal*.

Young, G. (1992), 'Corporate debt', *National Institute Economic Review*.

——(1993), 'Debt deflation and the company sector: the economic effects of balance-sheet adjustment', *National Institute Economic Review*.

——(1996), *The Influence of Financial Intermediaries on the Behaviour of the UK Economy* (NIESR Occasional Paper no. 50), London, National Institute of Economic and Social Research.

Youngson, A. J. (1960), *The British Economy, 1920–1957*, London, Allen & Unwin.

General Index

accelerator, relation to investment
    amplifier 96, 381
aggregate supply/demand diagram rejected 45
amplification:
    defined 90
    dependent on expectations 89–90, 380
amplifiers, consumption and investment 90,
    92–5, 99, 373
animals and animal spirits 407n
'Arteriosclerosis' in 1970s 313
asymmetries in fluctuations 3, 374–5
Auctioneer, the Great 51
availability of finance in recessions 95

bank failures, see Great Depression in US
bank financing in fluctuations 251, 298, 302,
    322, 358, 374, 379–80
Barber, A., Chancellor of Exchequer 244, 276
booms:
    of 1920s in US 161–2, 167
    of 1972–3 in UK 295–7
    of 1985–8 in UK 335–52
    effect of financial deregulation 321–2, 350–1
    role of borrowing 343–59
    scope for policy 358–60
    see also recovery
Bretton Woods system: 242
    macro effect of 251, 400
    why it ended 294n
    see also fixed exchange rates
Building Societies' cartel 351
Butler, R., Chancellor of Exchequer 244, 264
'Butskellism' 244

Callaghan, J., Chancellor of Exchequer 247
case studies, method of 4
'catching up' 59, 61; see also economic growth;
    growth rates
causal structure of economy 38–40
central banks:
    influence of 434
    pros and cons of 'independence' 437
Clarke, K., Chancellor of the Exchequer 337
Cold War (1947) 247
combined amplifier 99, 380–1
'Competition and Credit Control' (1971) 243
confidence, role of 91, 95, 105, 373; see also
    expectations changes
constant-employment growth rates 25, 383–4
constant-employment output defined 21–4

consumption amplifier defined 90, 373, 381
controls on bank lending, see lending controls
'Corset' control of bank lending 300, 341, 350,
    351
counter-recessionary policy 437–46
    action against booms 438–9, 444–5
    action to raise demand 439–45
    and banking supervision 439
    political and practical limits to 443–4
    possible effectiveness of 441–3
    public/private investment schemes 439–40
    role of lending controls 438–9
    uncertainty of good government 446
    see also economic policy; fiscal policy;
        monetary policy
Cripps, S., Chancellor of the Exchequer 244
Cunliffe Committee (1919) 153–4

Dalton, H., Chancellor of the Exchequer 244
'dashes for growth' under Conservative
    governments 262–5, 400
dating of recessions and fluctuations 25–6, 375
debt deflation, idea rejected 91, 97–9, 323–4,
    356–7, 398
demand shocks as causes of fluctuations 101–11,
    388–9
demand management:
    case for 428–33
    financial market constraints 443–4
    in Golden Age (1945–73) 260–5
    in OPEC recessions 276, 314–5
    see also economic policy; counter-recessionary
        policy; fiscal policy; monetary policy
demand pressure defined 57
demand versus supply explanation of
    recessions 57–80
deposit insurance in US (1933) 178, 181
depth of recessions, how measured 26
devaluation of sterling:
    in 1931 247
    in 1949 200, 257n
    see also exchange rate depreciation
Dillon round (tariff cutting) 243
dollar shortage 242
downward shift in growth path 21–4, 384–5

economic capacity (or potential) defined 18
economic growth:
    before and after World War II 254–7
    effect on of major recessions 14, 21–6, 369

and factorial purchasing power 41–2, 368
process not automatic 72–3
relation to export growth 7, 63
summary of known facts 57–70
supply versus demand influences 57–80
see also growth rates
economic policy:
in Golden Age 243–4, 252, 260–5
in interwar years 139–46
in the OPEC recessions 276, 314–6
under Mrs Thatcher 9/14–17, 304, 336–43, 359, 397
Eichengreen's *Golden Fetters* criticised 217–22
Employment Policy White Paper (1944) 243, 252
English-speaking countries' financial system 324, 357
equities now similar to debt 356
European Economic Community (1957) 243
European Monetary System (EMS), UK membership (1990–92) 342
European Monetary Union (EMU) and UK 436
European Payments Union (1950–8) 242
exchange controls removed (1979) 341
exchange crisis of 1976 278
exchange rate:
appreciation in 1980 305, 341
depreciation in 1972 2, 97
and monetary policy 436
see also devaluation
expansion phases:
in 1972–3 291–7
in 1982–8 332, 343–52
in 1992–5 361–3
see also boom
expectations changes during fluctuations 7, 89–90, 94–6, 117, 292–7, 302, 322, 360–1, 373, 376–7; *see also* confidence
experimentation, role of in science 6

fast growth phases:
compared 391
defined 25–6
explained 113–7
financial counterpart to fluctuations, *see* bank financing in fluctuations
financial deregulation, effect of 321–2, 351–2, 398
first OPEC recession, *see* Recession III
fiscal policy:
case for deficit financing 428–73
conclusions about 433
constraints set by financial markets 432–3
deficits and debt ratios 402–5, 428–32
indicators of impact 103, 118–29, 388
fixed exchange rates, macro effects 251, 400; *see also* Bretton Woods system

floors and ceilings to fluctuations 100, 382
fluctuations, types compared 112
Friedman, Milton, *see* Great Depression in US
full employment, difficult to reconstruct 421–3

Gaitskell, H., Chancellor of the Exchequer 244
Germany 168–70, 334, 394; *see also* industrial countries
gold standard:
and the Great Depression 184, 217–22
UK goes back to gold (1925) 144–5
UK leaves gold (1931) 145–6
Golden Age (1945–73) 234–72
demand management's role 252, 260–5
end of 266–71
summary 271–2, 398–401
see also mini-cycles
go-stop cycles 260–5, 292–3
see also dashes for growth
government, agent vs leadership role 420
not good at economic management 421
good governments rare 446
role in war 420
Great Depression:
model of world trade in 185–9, 223–33
in primary producing countries 170–1
scale in different countries 158–9, 186
in UK, *see* Recession II
Great Depression in US (1929–33) 157–83
antecedents 160
banks' balance sheets 174–5
bank failures 175–8, 394
deposit insurance 178, 181
events in Germany 168–70
farm prices 180
gold standard not the cause 184, 217–22
monetarist explanations 172–4, 211–16
recovery after 181–3
summary 393–5
growth accounting methodology queried 81–3
growth rates:
convergence/divergence among nations 59–62, 76–7
explanations of variations 70–77
and export performance 63–7, 76–7
at the firm level 75
limits to 78
negative growth 78–9
pre-industrial 58
in other countries 33
since 1800 58
see also economic growth; industrial revolution

Hawley-Smoot tariff 179
Heath government, the 264, 247, 276

Heathcoat Amory, Chancellor of the
    Exchequer 244
High Wage Theory of unemployment
    rejected 45, 53–6, 372
housing boom:
    of 1930s 203–5
    of 1970s 296
    of 1980s 348
Howe, G., Chancellor of the Exchequer 337
human capital 73
    destroyed in major recessions 74–5, 289–90
hyperinflation 425

import controls 244
incomes policy 244, 427
industrial countries:
    in 1929–32 (Great Depression) 136–8, 158,
        185–6
    in 1947–73 237–8, 247–9
    in 1972–82 (OPEC recessions) 285–9, 293
    in 1982–93 323–45
    convergence between 54–61
    growth in since 1920 15–16, 33, 69, 236
    productivity growth in 67–8, 82–3, 285
    shares in world output since 1870 64–5
    shares in exports of manufactures 63–5
    sources of growth in 67–8
    terms of trade 256
    see also Japan; Germany; United States
industrial revolution:
    in Britain 61–3
    in Japan 63
    worldwide spread 64–7
inflation:
    changing ideas about 423–7
    changing nature of 423–4
    in interwar period 139, 147–8
    in 1920–2 138–9
    in 1929–32 191
    in 1950–75 235, 240–1, 250, 2657–9, 293
    in 1970s 291–2, 305–7, 317–20
    inflation shocks get reverted 426
    relation to money 404, 425–5
    relative success of policy towards 425
    in whole period (1900–95) 16–17
inflation targets 435
innovation, requires effort 72–3
inventory investment, *see* stock investment
investment amplifier, relation to the
    accelerator 96, 373, 381

Japan 63, 76, 334; *see also* industrial countries
Jenkins, R., Chancellor of the Exchequer 247,
    264

Kennedy round (tariff cutting) 243
Keynes and public works 440n
Korean War (1950–53) 237, 242, 249

Lawson, N., Chancellor of the
    Exchequer 336n, 337, 341n 342, 350, 359n,
        360n
lending controls, effect of 251, 358, 400, 439

Macmillan Committee (1931) 145
Macmillan, H., Chancellor of the
    Exchequer 244, 264
Major, J., Chancellor of the Exchequer 337
major recessions:
    absent before 1900 31–2
    asymmetric shape 3, 27, 374–5
    compared with small recessions 111–13
    dating of 25–6, 375
    defined 2
    effect on growth rates 27–8, 374
    effect on prices 36–7
    explained by demand shocks 110–11, 389–91
    five recessions compared 111–13, 390
    historical changes affecting recessions 100–1
    output loss resulting 21, 36, 74–5, 79, 370,
        374, 384–5, 415
    predictability of 405–9
Marshall Aid 242
Maudling, R., Chancellor of the
    Exchequer 244, 264
May 1968 'events' (in France) 291n
'medium-term financial strategy' 341
Mexican debt crisis (1982) 333n
miners' strike (1973–4) 342
mini-cycles in 1947–73 112, 236, 400
    dating of 237
    demand policy in 250, 260–5
mismatch of labour supply and demand 48–9
monetary policy:
    general role 435–7
    modus operandi 434
    in 1920s 155
    in 1930s recovery 204
    post 1945 cheap money 244
    in 1971–3 296, 299–300, 302
    in 1978–9 304–5
    in 1979–88 342
    in 1989–93 355–6, 359
    in US Great Depression 164–5, 171, 172–8,
        191, 193
    see also monetary targets; central banks
monetary targets 341–2
money, place in system 9, 40, 424–5
Montague Norman before Macmillan
    Committee 13n
multiplier, relation to consumption
    amplifier 88–90

NAIRU 423–4; *see also* natural rate of
    unemployment
National Economic Development Council
    (NEDO) (1962)244

natural rate of unemployment 416; *see also*
  NAIRU
'New Classical' view of economy 415–6, 446
  contrasted with this study 416–9
  see also Real Business Cycle Theory
'New Conservatism' of 1980s 337
New Deal (1930s in US) 182
nineteenth century fluctuations 31–2
non-linearity 5, 24, 100, 102, 372
North Sea oil 244, 279, 304, 305–6

oil price shocks 266, 279–89, 396–7
  effect on UK tax revenue 304n
  international repercussions 283–4
  reversed 332
  stimulates energy saving 287–9
  see also Recessions III & IV (OPEC
    recessions)
Okun's law 21, 354
OPEC recessions, *see* Recessions III & IV
Organisation for Petroleum Exporting
  Countries (OPEC) 280

Pepys, Samuel 62n
permanent versus transitory shock effects
  18–24, 375
Phillips Curve 423–4; *see also* NAIRU; natural
  rate of unemployment
'practical monetarism' (Volcker's experiment)
  (1979–82) 332
predictability of major recessions 405–9
'private finance initiative' 440n
profits share in recessions 34–6
public debt, effect of recessions on 401–5
  ratio to GDP 401–2, 410–13
public/private investment schemes 439–40

Reaganomics: effect on demand 332
real balance effect rejected 47–8, 378n
Real Business Cycle Theory (RBC) rejected
  79–80, 370–1; *see also* New Classical view
real interest rate changes, effect not
  measurable 103
real wages 34–6
Recession I (1920–1) 146–56
  summary 392–3
Recession II (1929–32) in UK 189–95
  Change in terms of trade 190
  industrial incidence 194
  recovery from 195–210
  summary 395
  see also Great Depression in US
Recession III (1973–5) (first OPEC
  recession) 297–303
  summary 395–6
Recession IV (1979–82) (second OPEC
  recession) 303–10
  causes of 304–7

effect of rise in exchange rate 305
Europe and UK compared 309–10
resumption of growth 1992–5 310
summary 396–7
Recession V (1989–93) 322, 352–60
  effect of financial deregulation 323, 350–2
  policy in 341–3, 358–9
  the role of 'debt' 356–7
  summary 360–1, 397–8
  see also major recessions
recovery in 1930s 197–209
  causation of 26–7
  depressed areas 208
  housing boom 203–5
  role of defence expenditure 206
recovery by UK, 1982–8 343–53
'Regulator', the (1961) 244
residual in growth accounting 83–4
Ricardian equivalence rejected 417–8

savings ratio and consumer confidence 105,
  110–11, 355
'sectoral interdependence' as cause of
  under-employment 42–4, 369, 378
Selwyn Lloyd, Chancellor of the
  Exchequer 264
severed trends 18
shocks:
  effects on output 88–99, 111–13
  explanatory power of 105–11, 389–91
  measurement of 101–5, 373, 385–8
Smithsonian agreement (1971) 243
Snowden, P., Chancellor of the
  Exchequer 192–3, 202n
special deposits 244
speculative price effects 382
state power, limits to 419–23
steady growth process, the 41, 71–2, 368, 378–9
sticky wages, not cause of unemployment
  45–8, 369
stock appreciation, impact of changes in
  102–3, 299–300
stock exchange crash:
  of 1929 165–7, 391
  of 1987 332, 358
stock investment, destabilising 96–7
stop-go, *see* go-stop
Suez crisis (1956) 244
supply and demand explanations of
  recession 77–80, 391
supply falls, major examples 78–9

tariffs imposed 1931–2 202
terms of trade:
  effect defined 11, 102–3
  UK shock 1929–32 190; 1932–5 202–3;
    1935–8 206
  world shock 138

Thatcher's administrations 336–343
  New Conservative philosophy 337–343
  and the trade unions 342
  fiscal policy 341–2
  monetary policy 341
Thorneycroft, P., Chancellor of the
    Exchequer 244, 264
three-day week (1972–3) 247
'threshold agreements' (1973–4) 239n, 276, 317
total factor productivity:
  alternative estimates 30, 81–2
  course of since 1955 30
'Treasury view' on budgetary policy 145
trends and fluctuations, estimation of 18–25,
    384

unemployment, causes discussed 367–9
  in other countries 34

High Real Wage theory rejected 378
  persistence explained 42–4, 368–9
  ultimate conditions for 51–2
United States:
  in Great Depression 139, 391–4
  in 1920–1 recessions 151–2, 157–83
  in 1947–73 239
  in 1982–88 332–3
  see also industrial countries
unpredictability of major recessions 405–9

Vietnam war (1950–64) 242

wage inflexibility and unemployment 45;
    see also High Real Wage theory
wars and unemployment 208–9, 385
working practices as human capital 73, 369
World War II, macro effect of 249, 253

Author Index

Al-Chalabi, F. I. 281n
Aldcroft, D. H. 199n
Allsopp, C. 291n, 323n, 336n, 359n
Andersen, T. M. 71n
Arndt, H. W. 168
Artis, M. J. 313, 405n

Baily, M. N. 250n, 285, 286n, 287, 290n
Barr, D. G. 435n
Barrell, R. 18n, 23n
Barro, R. J. 44, 118, 174n, 370n
Batchelor, R. A. 76n, 243n
Baumol, W. J. J. 59, 60
Beaudry, P. 23n
Beenstock, M. 199n
Bellman, H. 203n
Bernanke, B. 169, 173, 174, 178n, 217, 221–2
Bispham, J. 250n
Biswas, R. 120n, 285n
Blackaby, F. T. 242n, 264
Blackman, S. A. B. 59, 60
Bladen-Hovell, R. 313 405n
Blanchard, O. J. 1n, 5n, 18n, 39n, 45n, 88n, 96, 118n, 119n
Böhm-Bawerk, X. 81
Boltho, A. 234n, 250n, 262n, 313
Boserup, E. 62n
Bowen, A. 234n, 269–70
Bowley, M. 203n, 205n
Bristow, J. A. 262n
Britton, A. 88n, 267n, 313, 315n, 317n, 337n, 341n, 342, 405n, 407n, 439n
Broadberry, S. N. 192n, 195n, 199, 201, 202n
Brown, A. J. 268n
Brunner, K. 173
Bruno, M. 56, 234n, 313
Buck, K. 278n
Budd, A. 313
Buiter, W. H. 118n, 312, 418n, 431n
Burns, A. 3n, 5n, 356

Cairncross, A. 234n, 278n, 421n.
Cairncross, F. 234n
Calomiris, C. W. 177n
Campbell, J. Y. 435n
Capelle, 85
Capie, F. C. 199n
Carbonelle, 85
Carré, J. J. 83n
Catao, L. 353n

Chakrabarti, A. K. 285, 286n, 287, 290n
Chichilnisky, G. 281, 284n
Chick, V. 44n
Choudhri, E. V. 217n
Chouraqui, J. C. 18n
Cipolla, C. M. 58
Clarke, P. 144n
Clarke, S. V. O. 193n
Clower, R. W. 44
Cohen, W. M. 73n
Corden, W. M. 80n
Cornwall, J. 234n
Cross, R. 424n

Davis, E. P. 324n
Deane, P. 58n
De Long, J. B. 23n, 59
Denison, E. F. 81, 83n, 84n, 285n
Dicks-Mireaux, L. A. 424
Dimsdale, N. H. 199n, 200n
Divalatsky, B. 313, 405n
Dornbusch, R. 408n
Dow, J. C. R. 9, 35n, 52, 40, 53n, 56, 118n, 120n, 213n, 234, 236, 242n, 243n, 248, 251n, 260, 262, 264, 268n, 296, 297, 299, 304n, 319, 322n, 324n, 337n, 342, 350n, 351, 398n, 400n, 407n, 418n, 424, 425n, 426n, 431n, 434, 435
Dowrick, S. 61
Dubois, P. 83n

Eichengreen, B. J. 133, 202n, 217–22, 394n, 400n
El-Erian, M. 324
Emerson, M. 234n, 313
Evans, G. 18n

Falkus, M. E. 169
Feinstein, C. H. 81n, 83n, 85, 135, 148, 150n, 152, 153, 204, 208n, 234n, 235n, 252, 254n
Fischer, S. 1n, 5n, 39n, 45n, 88n, 96
Fisher, I. 97, 356n
Fleming, J. M. 118
Folkerts-Landau, D. 324
Foot, K. A. 408n
Foreman-Peck, J. S. 208n
Frankel, J. A. 408n
Fraumeni, B. 84n
Freeman, C. 73n

Friedman, M. 4n, 118, 133, 151, 155, 157n, 164, 165, 171, 172, 173, 174, 175, 177, 211–16, 217, 220, 221, 268n, 394
Frisch, R. 3n, 88n, 372n
Frydman, F. 408n

Galbraith, J. K. 165n
Gardiner, K. 313, 405n
Garton, G. 177n
Goldberg, M. D. 408n
Goldstein, M., 324
Gollop, F. M. 83n, 84n
Goobey, A. R. 348n
Goodhart, C. A. E. 251
Goodin, R. E. 419n
Gooding, D. 6n
Gordon, R. J. 168
Gramlich, E. M. 118
Gregory, D. 155, 156n
Griffen, J. M. 280n
Griffiths, B. 199n
Grossman, H. I. 44
Gyohten, T. 294n

Habakkuk, H. J. 58n
Hagermann, R. P. 18n
Hahn, F. 42, 415n
Hansen, B. 120n, 262n, 266n
Harvey, A. C. 18n
Hawtrey, R. 155
Heal, G. 281, 284n
Heston, A. 59
Hickman, B. G. 18n, 168
Hicks, J. R. 40n, 56, 88n, 372
Hicks, U. K. 192
Hilgerdt, F. 85, 86
Hoffmann, W. G. 85
Howson, S. 144n, 145n, 154, 155, 193n, 203n, 204n

Ito, I. 408n

Jaegar, A. 18n
James, H. 169
Jenkinson, T. J. 323n, 336n, 359n
Johnson, C. 337n, 342
Jones, E. L. 62n
Jorgensen, D. W. 18n, 83n, 84n, 285n
Joshi, V. 80n

Kaldor, N. 40n, 76n, 88n, 372
Kalecki, M. 46, 76n, 95n, 372
Karakitsos, E. 313, 405n
Keegan, W. 337n
Kendrick, J. W. 23n, 83n, 152
Keynes, J. M. 51, 100, 144, 145n, 376, 440n
Kindleberger, C. P. 165

King, M. 323n, 335, 336n, 352n, 356n
King, R. G. 18n
Klingemann, H.-D. 419n
Knight, K. H. 373
Kochin, L. A. 217n
Koop, G. 23n

Landes, D. S. 61n
Lawson, N. 323n, 336n, 337, 341, 342, 350, 359n, 360n
Leijonhufvud, A. 51
Levinthal, D. A. 73n
Lindbeck, A. 312–13
Little, I. M. D. 80n, 262
Llewellyn, J. 262n, 284n, 313, 315n
Lucas, R. E. 42n, 71n, 118, 174n

MacDougall, G. D. A. 203n
Maddison, A. 58, 59, 61n, 67n, 83, 85, 152, 234n, 240n, 249, 250n, 267n, 285n
Major, R. L. 76n, 243n
Malinvaud, E. 56, 83n
Marsh, D. 419n
Marshall, A. 3n, 356, 376n
Marshall, M. P. 3n, 356, 376n
Matthews, R. C. O. 32n, 81n, 83n, 100, 204, 234n, 235n, 252, 254n, 269–70, 285n, 312
Matthias, P. 58n, 61n
Maynard, G. 337n
Mazumdor, D. 80n
McCallum, B. T. 80n
McCracken, P. 234n, 266n, 291n, 292, 312
Metzler, A. H. 168, 179
Miller, M. H. 312
Minford, P. 199n
Minsky, H. P. 97, 360, 372
Mishkin, F. S. 168
Mitchell, B. R. 85, 86
Mitchell, W. C. 3n, 5n, 356
Moene, K. O. 71n
Moggridge, D. E. 144n, 145n, 201n
Morgan, A. D. 76n, 243n
Morris, D. J. 323n, 336n, 359n
Morris-Suzuki, T. 63n
Muellbauer, J. 323n, 336n
Muller, P. 120n, 309n, 315n
Mullineux, A. 4n, 80n
Mundell, R. A. 118
Musgrave, P. B. 120n, 262n
Musgrave, R. A. 120n, 262n

Neild, R. R. 120n
Nelson, C. R. 6n, 23n, 376
Nevin, E. 203n
Nguyen, D.-T. 61
Nickell, S. 46
Nordhaus, W. D. 288
North, C. D. 62n

O'Mahony, M. 285n
Odling-Smee, J. C. 81n, 83n, 204, 234n, 235n, 252, 254n
Ohkawa, K. 83n, 85
Okun, A. M. 22n, 39n
Olson, M. 71, 81, 84
Oulton, N. 285n
Oxley, L. 155, 156n

Pain, N. 405n, 407n
Patinkin, D. 44
Persson, K. G. 58
Petri, P. A. 76
Phelps, E. S. 268n
Phillips, A. W. 423
Pigou, A. C. 147n, 148n, 150, 152, 154, 155
Pinch, T. 6n
Pippard, B. 6n
Plosser, C. I. 18n, 23n, 376
Pollard, S. 144n, 145n, 154n, 192
Potter, S. 262n, 284n, 313, 315n
Prest, A. R. 262n
Price, R. 120n, 309n, 315n
Price, R. W. R. 120n, 270

Quah, D. 18n, 61n

Rajapatirana, S. 80n
Ramaswamy, R. 353n
Rebelo, S. 18n
Redmond, J. 200n
Rees, G. 146n
Reichlin, L. 18n
Richardson, H. W. 199, 203n
Riddell, P. 337n
Robbins, L. 56, 199n
Rojas-Suarez, L. 324
Romer, P. D. 59, 71n
Rosovsky, H. 83n, 85

Sachs, J. D. 56, 217n, 243n, 313
Samuelson, L. 262n, 284n, 313, 315n
Samuelson, P. A. 88n, 372
Sargent, J. R. 323n, 336n, 350n
Sargent, T. J. 118
Sartor, N. 18n
Savage, D. 120n, 285n
Saville, I. D. 9, 52, 40, 118n, 213n, 251n, 296, 297, 299, 304n, 313, 319, 322n, 324n, 337n, 342, 350n, 351, 398n, 400n, 405n, 407n, 418n, 424n, 425n, 431n, 434, 435
Sayers, R. S. 144n, 193n
Schaffer, S. 6n
Schiller, R. 408n
Schlesinger, A. M. 182n, 420n
Schlote, W. 85

Schmookler, J. 290n
Schumpeter, L. 63, 72, 81
Schurr, S. H. 285n
Schwartz, A. 4n, 133, 151, 155, 164, 165, 172, 173, 174, 175, 177, 211–16, 217
Scott, M. F. 71, 81, 84
Sedgwick, P. N. 195n, 203n, 205n
Sefton, J. 18n, 23n
Sheldon, M. 362n
Shinohara, M. 63n, 85
Skidelsky, R. 144n, 145n
Slutsky, E. 3n, 88n, 372n
Smith, A. 62
Smith, A. D. 83n, 286n
Snyder, W. W. 120n, 262n
Solow, R. M. 72, 81, 415n
Sonenblum, S. 285n
Stadler, G. W. 370n
Stock, J. 18n
Stocker, G. 419n
Storry, R. 63n
Summers, L. H. 23n
Summers, R. 59

Tatom, J. A. 285n
Taylor, A. J. P. 146n
Teece, D. J. 280n
Temin, P. 178n, 217n
Thomas, R. P. 62n
Tobin, J. 48n, 118n, 418n
Toutain, J. C. 85

van der Eng, P. 85, 119n
van der Wee, H. 234n
Verspagen, B. 71
Volcker, P. A. 294n, 333

Wadhwani, S. 83n
Wall, M. 83n
Wallace, N. 118
Walters, A. 337n, 343n
Ward, T. S. 120n
Watson, M. 18n
Watts, N. 421n
Wilcox, J. A. 168
Williamson, P. 144n
Wilson, T. 155, 165
Wolf, E. N. 59, 60
Wood, C. 334n
Wood, D. O. 285n
Worswick, G. D. N. 195n, 199, 203n, 204n, 262, 313
Wren-Lewis, S. 436n

Young, G. 356n, 362n
Youngson, A. J. 144n